Contemporary Authors®
Autobiography Series

ISSN 0748-0636

Contemporary

Authors

Autobiography Series

Shelly Andrews
Editor

volume **26**

GALE

DETROIT · NEW YORK · TORONTO · LONDON

EDITORIAL STAFF

Shelly Andrews, *Editor and Desktop Publisher*
Linda Andres, Alan Hedblad, and Tom McMahon, *Contributing Editors and Desktop Publishers*
Motoko Fujishiro Huthwaite and Sheryl Ciccarelli, *Associate Editors*
Marilyn O'Connell Allen, *Assistant Editor and Graphics Manager*
Cindy Buck, Laurie C. Hillstrom, Charity Anne Dorgan, Mary Gillis, Heidi Hagen, Carolyn C. March,
Sara Pendergast, Adele Sarkissian, Kathleen Witman, and Lauri Wulf, *Contributing Copyeditors*

Victoria B. Cariappa, *Research Manager*
Corporate Research Information Service

Hal May, *Publisher*
Joyce Nakamura, *Managing Editor, Children's and Young Adult Literature*

Mary Beth Trimper, *Production Director*
Deborah Milliken, *Production Assistant*

Barbara Yarrow, *Graphic Services Manager*
C. J. Jonik, *Desktop Publisher (book cover)*
Randy A. Bassett, *Imaging Supervisor*
Robert Duncan, *Imaging Specialist*

Theresa Rocklin, *Manager, Technical Support Services*

Copyright © 1997 by Gale Research
and by individual authors whose essays appear in this volume.

Gale Research
835 Penobscot Building
645 Griswold Street
Detroit, MI 48226-4094

Library of Congress Catalog Card Number 86-641293
ISBN 0-7876-0116-0
ISSN 0748-0636

Printed in the United States of America

10 9 8 7 6 5 4 3 2 1

Contents

Special Thanks   vi
Preface   vii
A Brief Sampler   ix
Acknowledgments   xi

Michael Bishop 1945- 1

David Mansfield Bromige 1933- 21

Dorothy Bryant 1930- 47

Victor di Suvero 1927- 65

Carl Djerassi 1923- 85

Edward (Halsey) Foster 1942- 109

Richard Harteis 1946- 131

Marvin R. Hiemstra 1939- 147

Leza Lowitz 1962- 163

David Meltzer 1937- 185

Sarah Menefee 1946- 199

Sheila E. Murphy 1951- 215

Stephen Schwartz 1948- 231

Thomas Lowe Taylor 1938- 249

Nanos Valaoritis 1921- 263

Julia Vinograd 1943- 293

C. K. Williams 1936- 311

Cumulative Author List   333
Cumulative Index   339

Special Thanks

We wish to acknowledge our special gratitude to each of the authors in this volume. They all have been most kind and cooperative in contributing not only their talents but their enthusiasm and encouragement to this project.

We also would like to thank past, current, and future contributors and other individuals who have taken the time to provide feedback and make recommendations for this series.

Bob Arnold

Dorothy Bryant

Cid Corman

Ruth Daigon

Vincent Ferrini

Jack Foley

Marvin R. Hiemstra

Edwin Honig

Jim Leftwich

Nanos Valaoritis

Lisa Zeidner

We encourage our readers to explore the whole *CAAS* series. Please write and tell us if we can make *CAAS* more helpful to you. Direct your comments and suggestions to the editor:

MAIL: Shelly Andrews, *Contemporary Authors Autobiography Series*
Gale Research
835 Penobscot Bldg.
645 Griswold St.
Detroit, MI 48226-4094

TELEPHONE: (800) 347-GALE

FAX: (313) 961-6599

E-MAIL: sandrews@Gale.com@GALESMTP

Preface

A Unique Collection of Essays

Each volume in the *Contemporary Authors Autobiography Series (CAAS)* presents an original collection of autobiographical essays written especially for the series by noted writers.

CA Autobiography Series is designed to be a meeting place for writers and readers—a place where writers can present themselves, on their own terms, to their audience; and a place where general readers, students of contemporary literature, teachers and librarians, even aspiring writers can become better acquainted with familiar authors and meet others for the first time.

This is an opportunity for writers who may never write a full-length autobiography to let their readers know how they see themselves and their work, what brought them to this time and place.

Even for those authors who have already published full-length autobiographies, there is the opportunity in *CAAS* to bring their readers "up to date" or perhaps to take a different approach in the essay format. In some instances, previously published material may be reprinted or expanded upon; this fact is always noted at the end of such an essay. Individually, the essays in this series can enhance the reader's understanding of a writer's work; collectively, they are lessons in the creative process and in the discovery of its roots.

CAAS makes no attempt to give a comprehensive overview of authors and their works. That outlook is already well represented in biographies, reviews, and critiques published in a wide variety of sources. Instead, *CAAS* complements that perspective and presents what no other ongoing reference source does: the view of contemporary writers that is shaped by their own choice of materials and their own manner of storytelling.

Who Is Covered?

Like its parent series, *Contemporary Authors,* the *CA Autobiography Series* sets out to meet the needs and interests of a wide range of readers. Each volume includes essays by writers in all genres whose work is being read today. We consider it extraordinary that so many busy authors from throughout the world are able to interrupt their existing writing, teaching, speaking, traveling, and other schedules to converge on a given deadline for any one volume. So it is not always possible that all genres can be equally and uniformly represented from volume to volume, although we strive to include writers working in a variety of categories, including fiction, nonfiction, and poetry. As only a few writers specialize in a single area, the breadth of writings by authors in this volume also encompasses drama, translation, and criticism as well as work for movies, television, radio, newspapers, and journals.

What Each Essay Includes

Authors who contribute to *CAAS* are invited to write a "mini-autobiography" of approximately 10,000 words. In order to give the writer's imagination free rein, we suggest no guidelines or pattern for the essay.

We only ask that each writer tell his or her story in the manner and to the extent that feels most natural and appropriate. In addition, writers are asked to supply a selection of personal photographs showing themselves at various ages, as well as important people and special moments in their lives. Our contributors have responded generously, sharing with us some of their most treasured mementoes. The result is a special blend of text and photographs that will attract even the casual browser. Other features include:

Bibliography at the end of each essay, listing book-length works in chronological order of publication. Each bibliography in this volume was compiled by members of the *CAAS* editorial staff and submitted to the author for review.

Cumulative index in each volume, which cites all the essayists in the series as well as the subjects presented in the essays: personal names, titles of works, geographical names, schools of writing, etc. To ensure ease of use for these cumulating references, the name of the essayist is given before the volume and page number(s) for every reference that appears in more than one essay. In the following example, the entry in the index allows the user to identify the essay writers by name:

> Auden, W.H.
>   Allen **6:**18, 24
>   Ashby **6:**36, 39
>   Bowles **1:**86
>   etc.

For references that appear in only one essay, the volume and page number(s) are given but the name of the essayist is omitted. For example:

> Stieglitz, Alfred **1:**104, 109, 110

CAAS is something more than the sum of its individual essays. At many points the essays touch common ground, and from these intersections emerge new patterns of information and impressions. The index is an important guide to these interconnections.

For Additional Information

For detailed information on awards won, adaptations of works, critical reviews of works, and more, readers are encouraged to consult Gale's *Contemporary Authors* cumulative index for authors' listings in other Gale sources. These include, among others, *Contemporary Authors, Contemporary Authors New Revision Series, Dictionary of Literary Biography,* and *Contemporary Literary Criticism.* For autobiographical entries written by children and young adult authors see *Something about the Author Autobiography Series.*

A Brief Sampler

Each essay in the series has a special character and point of view that sets it apart from its companions. A small sampler of anecdotes and musings from the essays in this volume hint at the unique perspective of these life stories.

Michael Bishop: "My earliest memory finds me awakening in a rented house in Southern Pines, North Carolina, where we had moved so my father could attend paratrooper training at Fort Bragg. I clamber from bed and wander through breeze-kindled rooms in search of my parents. Walls tower on ferocious slants, but the house yields only musty furniture and a screen door filtering through its mesh a humid green morning. I bang outside. A patchy yard shows me shrubbery, maybe hydrangeas. Beyond the yard, a strip of tarry asphalt meanders who-knows-where. No people. People have fled to realms lost or privileged. Panic flails in my chest and throat. Cries for rescue issue from me as imploring bleats. I have no words—hardly even a mental glimmer—with which to frame the sensation, but I am surely the orphan of a bizarre disaster: an overnight plague that dissolves the molecules of adults, a secret outbreak of parentnapping, the deployment of a ray that leaves property unscathed but obliterates people. Only I have escaped this catastrophe, suffering in my moot good luck a cruel abandonment. Eventually, and probably quickly, my mother rescued me, but the memory of this orphan lostness endured through an otherwise happy childhood whose sole major disappointment lay in my parents' divorce. I begin with it not because it traumatized me forever, but because I can recall nothing earlier and because the search for belonging and place surely marks every human life."

Dorothy Bryant: "My grandfathers were typical patriarchs of the time, given to dictatorial tantrums, probably worsened by the humiliations they suffered as powerless, despised immigrants whose health had been ruined. But my mother's father was pathological. He beat my mother regularly and severely for trivial reasons. He kept a lock on the food pantry—minimal single helpings were doled out at mealtimes. He worked rarely, sending each of his three daughters out at age ten to support the family as live-in maids. They also picked fruit in harvest season. (My father's father drew the line at field labor for his daughter.) Everyone in the region, including all children, worked in the canneries in summer and fall. My maternal grandmother remained apparently indifferent as her children were starved and beaten. Perhaps she feared the violence might turn toward her. Whatever the reason, my mother never forgave her. Nor could I ever warm up to the old lady who moved near to my parents after her husband died in the 1950s."

Carl Djerassi: "To wit: I am told that I still have residues of an accent, colored by my mother tongue (German, with Viennese nuances) and by the fact that I learned English from a mix of British and American instructors among a sea of Slavic accents of my fellow classmates at The American College in Sofia. It is only when I listen to my voice on the radio or on a tape do I realize that I speak no language accentless—not even my mother tongue—and most certainly not others such as Spanish, which I acquired in the 1950s during my five-year sojourn in Mexico City. But until I met Diane Middlebrook, I suffered under the delusion that my English was grammatically impeccable. After all, it is the only language in which I dream—to me the ultimate criterion of idiomaticity."

David Meltzer: "Whatever I'd imagined Hollywood to be was challenged by the mediocre facts before me. Listening to the radio in Brooklyn, Lux Radio Theater, the Academy Awards; watching movie stars in movies about Hollywood at the Rugby Theater on Utica Avenue; the star-studded preview presences filing into Grauman's Chinese in the *Movietone News;* reading movie magazines at the local candy store, looking through the thick, green-covered annual movie issue of *Variety* my father brought home—all added to my colossal dream of Hollywood. . . . I wasn't prepared for a few flat blocks of gift and souvenir shops, hamburger joints, department stores, two ornate movie palaces (Grauman's Chinese and Pantage's Egyptian) plus a handful of ordinary neighborhood movie theaters, a couple of bookstores, and everything closed down around ten o'clock at night. . . . Hollywood Boulevard was the main stem of a lazy burg low to the ground in the shadows of towering alien palm trees. Coming from the nonstop energy of New York, skyscrapers, all-night movies, music, museums, galleries, bookstores, cafeterias to sit in and rethink the world, Hollywood might as well have been a silo in the middle of an Iowa wheat field. Beneath radiant postcard-blue skies I felt like a skulking teenage vampire. The place seemed populated by either incredibly beautiful young tanned men and women looking like movie stars or movie extras, or ancient men and women sitting on bus stop benches decorated with advertising for mortuaries and grocery stores."

Julia Vinograd: "As well as being a local poet, I'm known as the Bubblelady. And that got started as part of People's Park. There was going to be a riot the next day, but I was a pacifist and didn't want to throw stones and besides I'd probably miss. At the same time I was angry and wanted to throw something. I decided I'd blow soap bubbles all night in the park, and if they wanted to arrest me for it, fine. I bought two large bags full of bottles. There were two rookie cops in the park, and I marched up to them and announced my intentions. They pretty much shrugged. I started making bubbles and after a while one of the rookies asked if they could try. I told myself this wasn't happening, didn't say anything out loud, and handed them each a bottle. They started a contest. 'Mine's bigger than yours.' 'Yeah, but look at mine go, it's the motion that counts.' I quote. After about twenty minutes of this, a cop car with a real cop in it turned the corner, saw us all blowing bubbles, and screeched to a halt. (I think he thought I'd dosed his rookies. This was the sixties when everyone, including the cops, believed some morning we'd all wake up with the water supply dosed and everyone stoned.) Anyway, he ran up to us, checked out the rookies, and damned if one of them didn't try to hand him a bottle. He said he didn't play childish games and stalked off, while the other rookie commented, 'He's just scared 'cause his would be too small to see.' Again I quote."

These brief examples only suggest what lies ahead in this volume. The essays will speak differently to different readers; but they are certain to speak best, and most eloquently, for themselves.

Acknowledgments

Grateful acknowledgment is made to those publishers, photographers, and artists whose works appear with these authors' essays.

Photographs/Art

Michael Bishop: p. 18, Yvonne Navarro.

David Mansfield Bromige: p. 21, B. J. Fundano; p. 23, Michael Collins; p. 24, Mary Bufkin; p. 27, Susan Bee Bernstein; pp. 28, 36, David Bromige; pp. 30, 40, Margaret Bromige; p. 34, Judy deBarros; p. 44, Harold Bromige.

Dorothy Bryant: p. 47, Robert Bryant.

Victor di Suvero: p. 67, *San Francisco Call Bulletin*.

Marvin R. Hiemstra: p. 147, Todd Ostling; pp. 159, 160, Rick Bradford.

Leza Lowitz: p. 163, © Louis Templado; p. 176, Leslie Stanford; pp. 179, 181, © Ralph Koch.

Sarah Menefee: pp. 199, 211, Sarah Menefee; p. 208, Fran Furey; p. 212, Maria Letzia Gabriele.

Stephen Schwartz: pp. 231, 236, Diane Church; p. 238, © Claude Beagarie/*San Francisco Chronicle;* p. 241, Ivo Ravnik; p. 243, V. Vale; p. 244, Cristina Pagès; p. 245, Bartomeu Obrador; p. 246, Maria Bidegain.

Thomas Lowe Taylor: p. 249, Carola; p. 259, Marjorie Kalins.

Julia Vinograd: p. 293, Alice G. Patterson; p. 306, Richard Gibson; p. 309, Howard Munson.

Illustrations/Art

David Mansfield Bromige: From the "kin" section of the cover *Ten Years in the Making* by David Bromige and Robert Duncan. Vancouver Community Press, 1973. Reprinted with permission of the author.

Text

David Mansfield Bromige: Excerpts from The Difficulties (the David Bromige issue), written by Stephen Ratcliffe, Tom Sharp, and Ron Silliman. The Difficulties, 1987. Reprinted with permission of Tom Beckett/The Difficulties.\ Excerpts from poems "Num-

Contemporary Authors®
Autobiography Series

Michael Bishop

1945-

MILITARY BRAT: A MEMOIR

My earliest memory finds me awakening in a rented house in Southern Pines, North Carolina, where we had moved so my father could attend paratrooper training at Fort Bragg. I clamber from bed and wander through breeze-kindled rooms in search of my parents. Walls tower on ferocious slants, but the house yields only musty furniture and a screen door filtering through its mesh a humid green morning.

I bang outside. A patchy yard shows me shrubbery, maybe hydrangeas. Beyond the yard, a strip of tarry asphalt meanders who-knows-where. No people. People have fled to realms lost or privileged. Panic flails in my chest and throat. Cries for rescue issue from me as imploring bleats.

I have no words—hardly even a mental glimmer—with which to frame the sensation, but I am surely the orphan of a bizarre disaster: an overnight plague that dissolves the molecules of adults, a secret outbreak of parentnapping, the deployment of a ray that leaves property unscathed but obliterates people. Only I have escaped this catastrophe, suffering in my moot good luck a cruel abandonment.

Eventually, and probably quickly, my mother rescued me, but the memory of this orphan lostness endured through an otherwise happy childhood whose sole major disappointment lay in my parents' divorce. I begin with it not because it traumatized me forever, but because I can recall nothing earlier and because the search for belonging and place surely marks every human life.

My parents, a happy-go-lucky country grasshopper and a tenacious city-of-the-plains worker ant, collided in Lincoln, Nebraska, in 1942, when the farm boy came north as part of his military service and caught the pretty Nebraskan's eye as one of thousands of invading servicemen. With her girlfriend Doody Leacock, my

"Dad's mother, Zelma, at the grave site of my grandfather Lawson Payton Bishop (1898–1936) near Lepanto, Arkansas, June 1995. Three months later she celebrated her ninety-seventh birthday."

mother soon thereafter escaped to California for a vacation that turned into an extended stay when she and Doody got jobs in Los Angeles, Mom as a receptionist and PBX operator in the law offices of Stephens, Jones, Inch, & LeFever. Dad hunted her up there late in '42, talked Mom into marrying him, and, to avoid California's waiting period, took her on a packed train to Yuma, Arizona, where a Methodist pastor married them on January 9, 1943.

But let me backtrack:

Maxine Elaine Matison, the youngest of three children, was born in Ashland, Nebraska, on August 3, 1920, the daughter of a barber, Herman Matison, and a taciturn seamstress and housewife, the former Ida Mae Hoffmaster. Maxine had a brother, Robert, six years older, who married well and became an oil-business executive, and a sister, Lorraine, three years older, whose move to Wichita after marrying an army captain from California would one day prompt Mac to seek work in that city. (Friends and family usually called Lorraine "Larry" and Maxine "Mac.")

Leotis Bishop (no middle name), the oldest of three kids, was born in Frye's Mill, Arkansas, on December 26, 1920, the son of a logger, Lawson Payton Bishop, and a feisty transplant from Maypearl, Texas, the former Zelma Maxwell. Leotis had a younger brother, Frank, who died in his forties (Lawson had died fairly young, in 1936), and a younger sister, Geraldine, better known as Tootsie. Leotis, who later styled himself Lee Otis, and his two siblings grew up on a farm near Lepanto, Arkansas. Friends called him Sonny or Sonny-Man. When Zelma bought another farm near Harrisburg in 1937, none of her three children wanted to move there, regarding it as "the end of the world." Sometime before the war, Zelma married a cousin of Lawson's from Mississippi, William Cody Philyaw, whom I always knew as Grandpa Cody. Cody, in turn, always called me either Punkin or Knothead.

In the 1920s and '30s, Maxine grew up the youngest Matison in a household that acknowledged the value of books. She read greedily, plundering Ashland's Carnegie library and devouring everything from *The Bastible Children* to such hefty adult tomes as Hervey Allen's hot-selling *Anthony Adverse*. On the Nebraska plains, particularly in summer, what better way to pass the time? Herman, staggering under the Depression's impact, moved into a room in his Norfolk barbershop; his family, to reduce expenses, lived in their unsold house in Ashland. During this separation, the marriage came apart. When Herman and Ida Mae, called May, divorced, he married a widow, Mrs. Whitaker. (I got my ears from Herman, but have no memory at all of the man himself.)

In 1935, May Matison and her girls moved to Lincoln, where May supported her daughters doing seamstress work for a men's clothing store. Maxine took an English class at Lin-

"Wedding announcement in Lincoln newspaper on February 12, 1943: 'Mrs. Lee Bishop was Miss Maxine Matison prior to her January wedding.'"

coln High from Willa Cather's sister, Elsie, and published a story in the school literary magazine. Another teacher, a man, grilled her about an original writing, giving her the impression that he suspected plagiarism. She took heart from her own suspicion that Elsie Cather thought she had talent. After graduation, she wanted to write, but necessity led her to take a job as a telephone operator, at a time when operators manually patched through every call. In December, 1940, she financed her own train trip to Pasadena to see Nebraska play Stanford in the Rose Bowl. Even Nebraska's one-touchdown defeat on New Year's Day failed to daunt her: she relished the whole trip, viewing it as an exhilarating adventure.

In Lepanto, Lee Bishop likewise relished life, even though he hated his farm chores. Chopping cotton was a dull, sweaty task that inevitably led to the equally dull and sweaty task of picking it. He preferred fishing, hunting, and playing six-man high-school football as the scrawniest, meanest, most tenacious lineman on the Lepanto squad. His energy and good looks made him popular. He served as both captain of the football team and president of his senior class. He attended Arkansas State University in Jonesboro, some thirty miles away, and hitchhiked home nearly every weekend. Zelma recalls that once he toted a dog home in a suitcase into which he had cut a large airhole: "He ruined a brand-new suitcase. I was never so disgusted with him as I was that day."

Because, at age six, Lee had laid his younger brother on a wood stove, burning Frank's head so that he never after had any hair on that spot, the degree of my grandmother's disgust may seem disproportionate, but the hole in the suitcase occurred with premeditation, whereas the bald spot on Frank's head had resulted only from tenderness and inattention, and Zelma blamed herself for not being present to intervene. She later treated the burn by pouring ink on it.

Lt. Lee Bishop, Section "K," Lowry Field, Colorado, near Denver, 1945

Soon after Japan's attack on Pearl Harbor, Lee enlisted in the army—less out of patriotism than the desire to outpoint Frank, who had already volunteered, and a heady conviction that military service would prove more interesting than life on the farm. As a private, he wound up in Lincoln, Nebraska. Here, in the summer of 1942, he and Mac met. Their attraction had a lot of physicality in it. The Lepanto kid thought Mac looked like a movie star, while she noted that, in uniform or bathing trunks, he was "cute." Temperamentally and intellectually, they existed on different planes, but Lee's persistence, along with the war and the mobilization at home, initially disguised this truth.

After their Yuma wedding, fresh duty assignments pushed Lee all over the states: Wichita Falls, Texas, for glider training; Miami, Florida, for Officer Candidate School (OCS), from which he emerged a commissioned "ninety-day wonder"; Denver's Lowry Field, where as an earnest young lieutenant he posed for the camera before a ramshackle barracks building; and later, after my birth, Grand Island, Nebraska; Seattle, Washington; and Fort Bragg, North Carolina, among other places.

In Denver, Mac walked face-on into disturbing clues as to Lee's flaky spontaneity and potential unreliability, but chose to ignore them. Once, for instance, driving a car whose fuel line often failed to feed gas to the carburetor, Lee asked a mechanic buddy to help him solve the glitch. A Newtonian with great faith in gravity, this buddy suggested mounting the gas tank on the Ford's roof. They did. The car looked funny, but it ran. Mac, privately mortified, rode in this monstrosity. Returning from a movie one night, it burst into flame. Mac got out, stumbled to a curb. Fire trucks and police cars arrived. Knees together, chin in hands, Mac sat on the curb praying for invisibility.

I was born in Lincoln on November 12, 1945, three months after the end of the Pacific conflict. Mac had returned to her hometown to deliver me while Lee fulfilled a duty assignment on Saipan. The two had agreed on the name Michael for a boy. Mac claimed she had chosen it because of an Italian-American actor on the radio named Michael Raffetto, who played Paul Barbour on *One Man's Family*. Lee claimed that Uncle Mike Maxwell, Zelma's youngest brother, had provided its inspiration. Grandma May disapproved because everyone would call me Mike and to her this meant a roughneck stevedore type. (Uncle Mike jockeyed heavy yellow machinery on road-building crews in the Rockies.) Mac said that she would call me Michael, never Mike, but first took me up with the self-indicting cry, *"Oh, Mike!"*

Although an eight-pounder at birth, as a toddler I suffered devastating asthma attacks. More than once my symptoms nearly strangled me. Mac drove me to army doctors who stuck me with hypodermics, shot after shot to the (literal) point that at the outset of these trips I howled for mercy. But what could Mac do? Without the shots, my chest would deform, constricting my breathing permanently. Luckily, by age three or so, I began to outgrow the asthma, and but for the fact that my own son and daughter have fought periodic respiratory bouts, my escape from the condition has been total.

The war concluded without Lee's ever having seen combat. He drilled, took glider training, even earned a paratrooper's insignia. None of this work put him into battle. Later he survived duty in Korea, where he helped establish a military post office in Seoul, and soldiered, with paltry distinction, stateside and abroad, during the Cold War. He lacked the zeal and the respect (or at least the tolerance) for authority of the gung-ho lifer; and his womanizing, cockiness, indolence, and farm-boy sarcasms often sabotaged his hopes for advancement in his mostly accidental "career."

In 1954 or so, Lee got *riffed*—caught in an Eisenhower Era *R*eduction *in* *F*orce—and, after more than a decade in uniform, separated from the Air Force. He struggled to retrain himself, using the GI Bill to take courses in television broadcasting at the University of Denver and Syracuse University, but found job pickings slim and rejoined the Air Force to finish out his twenty years and obtain a pension. Although he could rejoin only as an enlisted man (a tech sergeant or four-striper), he would retire with a pension based on the salary of his highest Air Force Reserves rank, major. Soon after he had rejoined, an officer took his (unwise) request for permission to remove his shoes at his desk as insubordination and had him busted to airman first class. This lost stripe embittered Lee, who used his court-martial as an excuse to goldbrick. He felt he owed the military nothing. Ike was a sniveling Republican stooge, and most officers, in Lee's aggrieved view,

couldn't tell their rear ends from a parachute pack.

But before the RIF, before the divorce, Lee wore his own officer bars with zest and pride; he must have seen his future as an immense, buffable pearl. Early in 1950, however, while stationed in Tokyo, he discovered that Mac, who had taken an apartment with her mother and me in Wichita, had no plans to rejoin him, ever. He secured an emergency leave through the Red Cross and flew home to convince Mac that she still loved him, that the three of us belonged together. He swore to his mother-in-law that he would improve as a husband. Mac, full of doubts, capitulated.

The Bishops traveled to San Francisco and set sail from there to Japan. Our ship, the U.S.S. *Darby,* embarked in full California sunshine and docked however many days later in the paperweight opalescence of a Yokohama snowfall. The journey itself took place in a pregnant silver-grey dream. Our ship ploughed the swells like a floating hotel. The cabin in which we huddled at night seemed more broom closet than bedroom, an anonymous cranny in the pitching superstructure. High seas. Chairs gliding past bolted-down salon tables. Trays toppling. Silverware racketing. Seasickness. Lifeboat drills during which people in inflatable vests lined up before the gunwales to stare in stoic agony over shifting saltwater crags. What we ate, who we talked to, how we passed the voyage's terror-pocked monotony—all are blanks to me now.

In Tokyo, we lived in an officers' enclave, a fake little America called Washington Heights, where dependent kids could play at cowboys year-round (even the Japanese-American kids among us boasting six-guns and yoke-necked shirts) and, on Halloween, cadge for goodies in improvised costumes. I attended Yoyogi Elementary School, "where the cherry blossoms bloom." My bespectacled kindergarten teacher bore the surname Fish, cheerfully. At home, we had help: a part-time houseboy, Yasuda, and two maids, one of whom I don't recall and the other the delightful Chieko, whom earlier employers had nicknamed Peanuts.

Family tradition, memory snips, and an old photo all attest that Peanuts loved me. Part of her regard undoubtedly stemmed from the Japanese cultural imperative of tot worship, but maybe she also found it hard to resist the wrangler-

"My mother's caption: 'This was our maid, Chieko, whom we called Peanuts. This was at our house in Tokyo—should be about 1950.' In fact, it was."

esque figure I cut in my cowboy outfit. She let me visit her paper-walled house, scrambled up eggs for me, and, in our own quarters, interceded when some mischief of mine prodded Mommy or Daddy, if not both, to the brink of corporal punishment. At such times, Peanuts edged between my parents and me and, chirping in stereotypical pidgen, *"Washy hands, washy hands,"* shoved me to the bathroom to await the passing of their wrath. I have no idea whether, in our hire, she ever suffered the indignity of one of my dad's propositions.

Maybe not. But through much of his adult life, Lee motored along on libido and redneck charm. The idea of his refraining to put the moves on a pretty young woman in his own household strikes me as naive. Lee always claimed to have loved no woman the way he loved Mac, but he still played her false (as he did his second wife, Scottie). By this time in our Tokyo stay, the union was unraveling again, and one of my parents' verbal bouts left me bawling in my pajamas at a bedroom door.

"He wants me," cries one parent, snatching me up.

"No, he wants me," from the other, who snatches me away. I dangle between the odors of lipstick and Old Spice, gingham and gabar-

dine, until one adult—Mac, no doubt—sees the imbecility of this tug-of-war and restores me to bed.

I don't remember that bed. I don't recall the gist of my bedside pacification. But this midnight set-to seared into my heart the knowledge that the single flesh of one's mother and father could rip like a decaying rag. Our family would return stateside unmendably riven.

Happier memories of Japan ease the sting. On the Ginza, Tokyo's Broadway, I sometimes visited a department store whose top floor had a bumper-car rink. These visits stayed with me so vividly that in 1980, when my British friend Ian Watson and I collaborated on a novel, *Under Heaven's Bridge,* with a Japanese protagonist, I used the experience to describe one of Keiko Takihashi's memories: "Electricity crackled under the roof of the pavilion as adults and children charged their squat vehicles around the concrete floor, banging the cars together or whirling them in noisy holding patterns. . . ." Keiko screams when a fleet of such cars converges on her own, but I always chauffeured myself with the élan of a pint-sized Richard Petty. (Right.)

Another adventure, pleasanter in the recollection than in the doing, involved an illicit journey from Washington Heights to the city center. (Maybe we didn't get *that* far.) Butch, a Japanese-American pal, and his brother led me—I lacked their navigational savvy—via a maze of sewage ditches, alongside their stinking khaki rainbow surfaces, into a canyon of gaudy pennants and groaning carts. (Trucks called honey wagons hauled human waste from residential areas to treatment sites; their chance run-ins with other traffic sometimes produced aromatic Laurel-and-Hardy happenings.) What we did in this distant place I forget, but we arrived home at bruising lavender sunset. Peanuts, even if she hadn't already left for the day, could have done nothing to delay the tail-blistering I earned.

In the spring of 1951, Mac and I returned aboard a United Airlines charter to the United States. Despite her many other travels, Mac had never flown before. Over the Pacific, she plotted crazy stratagems for saving me if our plane went down. Fortunately, we landed on both Hawaii and the mainland without incident. In Wichita, where her sister Larry now lived with their mother and Larry's husband, Matt Palacio,

Mac drove the '47 Plymouth that Matt had secured for her to a Civil Service examination for clerk-typists. Her 93.5 score certified her at the top of the Office of Personnel Administration's employment list, and she soon had a job. We moved into a small apartment, where, as Mac ironed clothes or washed dishes, we listened to radio programs like Art Linkletter's *House Party, Gangbusters,* and *The Lone Ranger.*

The Pentagon had just chosen Wichita as the site of a new Strategic Air Command facility, McConnell Air Force Base, and Mac transferred from OPA to this post's temporary venue in the old Kittredge Building downtown. A cadre of people from Vance Air Force Base in Enid, Oklahoma, arrived to help McConnell get up and running. Millie Reddick, payroll chief from that cadre, became friends with Mac in the civilian personnel office and at length convinced her to move from Wichita to Mulvane, a hybrid bedroom-and-farming community about ten miles south. Millie, her husband Ernie, an aircraft-maintenance foreman, and their young son Greg, only four days my senior, had already settled in Mulvane, which Millie extolled as a Norman Rockwellesque Elysium where decent, down-home parents could raise their kids into upright, hot-dog-gobbling, all-American citizens. Mom bought the argument because in Mulvane she could afford to rent a small house, not just a small apartment, and the commute to McConnell over the aptly named Rock Road did not unduly fatigue anyone traveling it.

Mulvane put an indelible stamp on my boyhood. I left the town every June to visit my military dad for the whole summer, but because I lived there seven years, the place exists for me then, now, and always as my hometown. It crops up in a novel, *No Enemy but Time* (1982), and in the novella "Blue Kansas Sky" (1997), under the quasi-anagram of Van Luna. In Mulvane, I first watched television, including Elizabeth II's coronation parade, her coach very like the transformed pumpkin in Walt Disney's *Cinderella.* I made friends: Greg Reddick, Dennis Ward, Craig Selley, Steve DeVore. (I pined over a girl named Billie Jean Dye, who preferred my flattopped pal Steve, a grade-school Robert Cummings.) I became scholar, athlete, and Crayola artist. I imagined myself going on from triumph to triumph: Brooklyn Dodgers shortstop, undisputed Picasso of the Plains, president of the United States. I played one-boy acorn hockey on the street outside our

first rental house (we lived in five different houses in Mulvane), heard Santa Claus and his reindeer on our roof one Christmas Eve (see the story "Icicle Music" from *At the City Limits of Fate* for an odd take on this memory), and cut out and colored models of the planets, laying them out in vast, floor-consuming facsimiles of the solar system. I also cut out planet-hopping rockets. Later, in another house on another street, I indulged in after-school vidfests in front of creaky Buster Crabbe *Flash Gordon* serials.

These serials enthralled me. Mom had bought a big Zenith TV set after seeing cartoons, of all things, on the Reddicks's set. Our model stood on four tall legs, weighed as much as a Nash Metropolitan, and glared out at us from its ugly Cyclops eye. I immersed myself in the Crabbe episodes, specifically a batch of shows through which the lumpen proletariat clay-people of a hostile Mars crept like stealthy moles. These wretches interfaced effortlessly with their world's clayey soil, moving from air to packed earth and back again like clumsy humanoid amphibians. I loved and feared the clay-people, and pulled for Flash and Dale to quash Queen Azura and the duplicitous Emperor Ming with the clay-people's creepy help. One afternoon, at a crucial narrative point, the Zenith flashed and sizzled; its picture shrank to a dot; a stream of acrid sawdust drained from its belly. Guilt overcame me. What had I done to trigger this cathode-ray-tube crash?

"Never mind," Mom said when she saw and smelled the results of the TV's treason. "Cheap set, cheaply made." (Years later, the clay-people turned up, little changed, in a story of mine, "A Gift from the GrayLanders," which appears in *Close Encounters with the Deity.*)

For a period, before allowing the TV to baby-sit me in the afternoons, Mom gave me into the care of a kindly woman, Mrs. Whited, who kept me before school and welcomed me back to her house after. I watched TV there, too, a tiny, droning set toward which I glanced occasionally during the Army-McCarthy hearings. I paid closer attention during *The Howdy Doody Show,* but even as I worked jigsaw puzzles or painted a German shepherd from a paint-by-numbers kit, the scowling pomposity of Tail-gunner Joe troubled me. Or have I worked backward from attitudes that I acquired later to make my kiddy self appear uncommonly intuitive? (Joseph Brodsky notes that trying to recall the past is like a baby's efforts to seize

a basketball: "one's palms keep sliding off.")
But I do remember that set's ceaseless pointillistic
flicker and my sense that Mrs. Whited would
protect me from the ugly senator and his ilk
by giving me daily access to her home.

In 1952 or '53, Mom married an Air Force
lieutenant from McConnell named Howard
Miller. Miller had flaccid blond good looks, a
formal demeanor, and a kind of exasperated
aloofness. He loved neither me nor the idea
of me. When he and my mother quarreled and
their relationship seemed shattered, Mom drove
me to his apartment in Wichita, left me in
the Plymouth, and went inside to make amends.
Her pride-swallowing, maybe legitimate, perhaps
sincere, worked (at least short-term), and soon
I had a stepfather, the first of two.

Today, Howard Miller's fleeting presence in
my life seems dreamlike, unreal. My table manners, which lacked elegance, dismayed him. He
insisted that I sit up and wield my knife, fork,
and spoon either one at a time or in deco-
rous harmony. We acquired a shaggy mongrel
dog while Miller presided over our reconsti-
tuted family, and his naming of this animal
activates my only truly pleasant memory of his
stay. Even this naming has its sardonic aspect,
though, for Miller called the puppy Seagull.
Its tendency to drop messes about the house,
and its shrill cries, inspired the name. Seagull,
with his black mask and tan caterpillarlike eyebrows, nonetheless became my romp-around pal
until a car ran over him. Miller disappeared
in a similarly hackneyed fashion, neglecting to
return to us after a duty posting to Hawaii.

We moved to another small house, and my
grandmother came to live with us. This house
had a storm cellar in the backyard, a berm
with a rusty tin-plated door. As in *The Wizard
of Oz,* tornadoes plagued our part of the Kansas plains, and one night we scrambled down
into this cellar with a portable radio to escape
the storm. The banging of trashcans, the crashing
of tree limbs, and the radio's staticky litany of
twister warnings so upset me that I threw up.
On another night (May 25, 1955), the town of
Udall, six miles away, suffered a slam-on hit,

"My mother's caption: 'You & 3 of your cowboy friends at Washington Heights where we lived.
(Two were Japanese-American boys.)' I am on the right."

many injuries and deaths, and such vivid wreckage that *Life* magazine ran a grim photo feature on the disaster.

I dreaded storm season, but loved the town. Earlier this year, it amazed me to read that Mom had not felt about Mulvane as I had. In a letter she told me that it "didn't amount to much, but did have the essentials," namely, bank, post office, supermarket, churches, and so forth. I, on the other hand, always saw the place as Camelot, albeit a twister-menaced Camelot.

Miller may have left, but I always knew I had a dad. Mom, as a policy matter, refused to enumerate Lee Bishop's various sins. She admitted to me that he made a better father than he had ever made a husband; his betrayals, however, escaped not only detailing but mention, as if the son deserved a courtesy that the father had forfeited but for the son's ungainsayable presence. Further, Mom never kept me from visiting Dad when that was possible, and my summers with him, away from Mulvane, and later from Tulsa, focused my every year from the second through the eleventh grades. I spent time with him at Francis E. Warren AFB in Cheyenne, Wyoming; in Denver, Colorado; at Scott AFB in East St. Louis, Illinois; in Memphis, Tennessee; at the Air Force Academy near Colorado Springs; in Lincoln, Nebraska; in Seville, Spain, where his final tour of duty, at a SAC base near Morón de la Frontera, qualified him for his long-sought pension; and, after he had retired, in Walsenburg, Colorado, a coal-depleted town in the foothills of the northern Sangre de Cristos.

From about 1953 on, whenever I visited Dad, I also visited the handsome black Labrador retriever that he had acquired in Wyoming and, with the aid of a book, trained rather skillfully himself. Always a hunter, Dad wanted a good field dog, and in this alert young retriever he got not only that but also an oddly intuitive companion. Dad named him Black Prince Michael and called him Mike; in contrast to Mom's practice, Dad now invariably called me Michael, to distinguish between me and his AKC-certified Lab.

Mike seemed to me the smartest canine this side of a TV screen, easily as smart as Lassie or Rin Tin Tin. Each June, when I showed up after a long winter's absence, he barked and ran in ever-widening welcoming circles. He could shake hands, roll over, speak on com-

mand, catch cookies or Lifesavers out of the air, gulp down or daintily lick an ice cream cone depending on Dad's signals, retrieve fallen waterfowl, and swim like a burly otter. Summers, he loomed almost as large in my boyhood as did Dad himself or my devotion to baseball.

Maybe Dad saw something of himself in Mike. If a female came into estrus, for example, Mike ignored all restraints to answer her pheromonal summons. Neither ropes nor locked doors nor metal fences could deter him. Sometimes he stayed gone for days. More than once, Dad had to ransom him from the animal shelter in Colorado Springs. Eventually, when Mike was six or seven, a woman with a female poodle grew so incensed at his idiot ardor that she tied him to a clothesline and dumped a pan of boiling water on him, leaving him with a silken gray saddle of scar tissue and ruining him for the show circuit. This cruel act outraged me, but also taught me something vivid about mutability.

"My father, the hunter, with his Labrador retriever Mike," Idaho, 1953

*"Two Mikes (I'm the one with the canteen),
Scottie sits on a blanket to the left,"
Colorado, about 1955*

Mike inspired my story "Dogs' Lives," which appeared in *The Missouri Review* and later in *Best American Short Stories 1985;* he also figures prominently in all three episodes of the story "Three Dreams in the Wake of a Death," from the July 1996 issue of *Fantasy & Science Fiction.* He no doubt also had much to do with my moving on from *The Call of the Wild* and *White Fang* to collect Grosset & Dunlap dog stories by Eric Knight, James Oliver Curwood, Albert Payson Terhune, Marshall Saunders, Jim Kjelgaard, and others. When Dad went to Spain in 1962, Mike died of heart worms and heartbreak, and Scottie, by herself in Nebraska, saw angrily to his burial.

In 1955, Mom married another military man, Charles Edwin Willis, a bomber pilot who, during World War II, had won the Distinguished Flying Cross for nursing a B-17 back to England after it took heavy fire in a raid over Germany. (An article in *Popular Mechanics,* with photographs, profiled Captain Willis and detailed

this heroic feat.) Charles had two teenage kids from an earlier marriage—suddenly I had a stepbrother and a stepsister!—and an infectious enthusiasm about almost every undertaking. He won Mom with the same methodical cheerfulness with which he built a house or drew up a flight plan: she would say yes if only he declared his goal and stayed on task. (He did, and she did.) And, in fact, Charles proved both a good husband and a caring stepfather, who once had base authorities in Tulsa prepare my dependent ID card with the name *Michael Willis,* a touching but illegal gesture.

Charles's less endearing character traits included that old male bugaboo, hypercompetitiveness, along with perfectionism, an intolerance of dissenting approaches to problem-solving, a tendency to gloat over minor triumphs (games of Ping-Pong, pool, Putt-Putt), and, occasionally, a transparent currying of praise, as if his own delight in an achievement would wither if others did not extol him too. He also liked to press-gang me and my friends into his projects, whether sweeping the garage or relocating five hundred bricks via wheelbarrow. (Buddies began asking me to come over to *their* houses to play.) He took up golf after turning forty and soon earned certification as a teaching pro. Once, visiting his daughter in the hospital, he introduced himself to a nurse as "Chuck Willis" and with false self-effacement allowed her to assume him a minor celebrity on the professional golfers' tour.

Charles had another peculiarity, one I found at once nifty and unsettling. He liked scary, off-center stuff. He believed in UFOs, purchased pulp magazines like *Sexology* and *Fantastic Universe,* and doted on sci-fi and horror films. He toppled like a chump for Hollywood's radiation-spawned giant mutant insects (ants, tarantulas, grasshoppers), and he loved such gimmicky come-ons as theremin soundtracks and 3-D glasses. In Wichita once, shopping, he asked me if I wanted to see a really spooky movie with him and Mom, *House of Wax.* In the abstract, this idea had enormous appeal; besides, Charles really wanted to see it. I said yes, with a promise not to chicken out, but discovered in the dark that despite the amusing 3-D effects—a red paddleball bursting repeatedly through the plane of the screen—the tossing of human beings, especially comely nude females, into vats of hot molten wax induced in me a cringing terror. I got through the film, but barely, and insisted on a night-light for many nights after.

As for Charles's sci-fi pulps, many of them had covers showing youthful human women in body-hugging spacesuits or in lovely dishabille in the arms or tentacles of ugly aliens. I read a few of the stories, most of which excited me less than did the covers. But I stumbled upon one tale—by Lloyd Biggle, Jr.?—about a dumpy humanoid alien who carries a major-league ball club to a pennant through his power to *think* the bloopers off his bat into loopy home runs. This story totally seized me; in fact, it may have keyed a scene or two in my Southern gothic World War II baseball novel, *Brittle Innings* (1994). Even if it did not, those magazines, lying on counters, stuffed into drawers, wedged into a lounger's pockets, attuned me, early on, to a bizarre but enticing realm on the border of the orthodox and the acceptable.

Mom and Charles never attended church. Away from Zelma and the farm, neither did Dad (who had a submerged God-hunger that eventually, after a debilitating illness and a botched surgery, would claim him utterly). I did not miss sitting every Sunday morning in a gloomy or even a radiant sanctuary to listen to a lot of earnest prattle about salvation. Sunday mornings were for sleeping in, scoffing scrambled eggs, and lazily perusing the full-color funnies, paying special heed to "Li'l Abner," "Pogo," "Dennis the Menace," and "Prince Valiant," although in this last case more for the elaborate art than for the clotted accompanying text.

In Mulvane, however, I fell in with a group undergoing confirmation training at the Methodist church. The pastor took questions on a walk in front of the building. How do we know God exists? one child asked. The pastor nodded at a nearby tree. God spoke to us daily, he said, through birdsong, leaf rustlings, even tangles of sky among the branches. I bought this idea as a helpful mystical profundity—not old-fashioned heterodox pantheism, but received revelation, fanciful and ambiguous: God as ventriloquist, the material world as his multivoiced dummy. This concept made me shiver. With no parental input at all, I arranged my tardy baptism and joined the church. As for my promises to honor my membership with "my prayers, my presence, my gifts, and my service," I neglected them all, without premeditation or guilt.

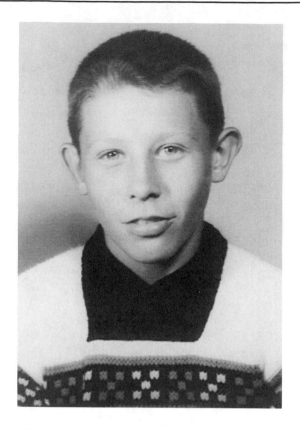

"My Mulvane Elementary School photo for the 1957–58 school year. I was not quite twelve."

Every summer that Dad, his second wife Scottie (a British war bride whose first marriage had come undone), and I visited the farm in Arkansas, I did pray. I prayed we would arrive after or leave before Sunday morning services at Valley View Baptist, a cinder-block building near some hazy cottonfields. Zelma lived her Christianity, reading daily from her spavined King James Bible and doing as much for others as she could find time for—cooking, visiting, giving away her fresh or canned garden products. My step-grandfather Cody, however, practiced less a Christian walk than a go-along/get-along Christian slouch. On Sundays, he perched in his stained khakis on a back pew, cleaning his fingernails with a pocketknife and intermittently dozing off. I knew this for bad behavior, but also saw in his inattention a weaselly sort of heroism.

One summer after my baptism in Mulvane, Zelma took me into a hotbox where she taught a group of young teenagers Sunday school. At length, she stopped to ask me if I was "saved." I began to sweat, literally and philosophically.

If I said Yes, I would appear to foreknow my private spiritual fate or to boast before God. If I said No, I earned the label "unsaved." The freckled kids in Zelma's room would assume me a potential murderer, an autosodomite, a closet Pinky Lee fan. Hopelessly, I said, *"I don't know."* Zelma began to cry, silently. Her students looked at me as if I had carried a sack of mildewed potatoes into their midst. Although Zelma went on to finish her lesson, I rode home that day in a funk of bemused disgrace, a victim of vast theological ignorance.

Thus, in 1958, when Charles received orders to report to the Air Force Modification & Acceptance Program at Douglas Aircraft in Tulsa, and we left Mulvane in the winter of my seventh-grade year, I had no religion but a hash of inert Christian metaphors and imagery. Nonetheless, I was happy, alert, and decidedly tenderhearted toward others in my Christ-haunted heathenism. Looking back, I have trouble seeing that state as either wicked or perilous.

Leaving Mulvane proved gut-wrenching. In my last year and a half there, I earned a Tenderfoot badge in Boy Scouts; took part in a happily humiliating snipe hunt; examined stacks of a friend's dad's *Playboys*, one of which included Ray Bradbury's "In a Season of Calm Weather" (as if I cared); watched Leonard Bernstein's "Young People's Concerts" for extra credit in a music class; and played guard on our junior-high basketball team, earning a green-and-white letter jacket for my efforts. How could Mom and Charles uproot me from this Eden? How would I adjust to a big impersonal city like Tulsa?

At first I didn't. Woodrow Wilson Junior High School, miles from our ticky-tacky bungalow at 7608 East 22nd Place on Tulsa's south side, resembled—at least to me—a Soviet-style penitentiary. It had three stories and, in case of fire, a segmented metal tube from the upper floor as an exit ramp. Chain-link fences. A dingy sprawling auditorium. Boys wore a virtual uniform (think *Grease*): white T-shirts, crisp new blue jeans, white socks, shiny black loafers (tassleless). In any other getup, a guy risked mockery, ostracism, fisticuffs. Mom drove me to this hell; my stomach kinked; I slunk inside, more krill for the whale's maw.

Awkwardly, then more surefootedly, I sought my place. I met some fellows from my own neighborhood—Lynn Bevill, Sammy Tyree, Bryan Mangram, Don Hendricks—and my peers at Wilson took pity on me because I (a) showed initiative, (b) worked well with others, and (c) followed directions, although not to the point of brownnosing. During the year's final grading period, my classmates elected me president, not of the whole seventh grade but of our homeroom. This honor came to me as hard-won validation. Most military brats had to wage that battle more often than I; however, they usually transferred into schools with many other service dependents who helped them assimilate—no option in Tulsa, where Charles's test-pilot unit consisted of only a few officers and their families.

In Tulsa, the joys of reading seized me as never before. I got a library card at a branch on Harvard Avenue. I visited bookstores downtown and in Utica Square. For wheels I had to rely on Mom, who worked for the Tulsa District Army Corps of Engineers; or on an older pal with a driver's license (Lynn Bevill, who had a classic black '54 Ford); or on Charles, who now scooted about in a snazzy white Thunderbird.

When Charles carried me to the library, he often wore his neon-orange flightsuit, with so many tabs, patches, and zippers that he looked assembled rather than dressed. He discomfited me in this suit, not so much because he favored a circus clown as because he strutted in it, even wearing it when he had had time to change into civvies. On the evening I made a startling find at the branch library, he fluoresced amidst the stacks, an upright lightning bug with no off switch.

My find? While thumbing through several skinny volumes by the greatest of all writers in English, I realized that William Shakespeare had written *Hamlet, A Midsummer Night's Dream,* and thirty-odd other titles not in prose but in dueling stanzas of mostly unrhymed *poetry!* Using verse to fill up a book struck me as cheating, not honest storytelling. I refused to check out a single book, and not until a tenth-grade study of *Macbeth* did I encounter the resonating splendor of what I had snubbed, or truly understand that Shakespeare had written five-act plays rather than stingy little novels.

On the bus going to Wilson, a friend showed me a comic book that grabbed me hard. This comic did not detail the doings of Donald Duck, Little Lulu, or any of the usual superheroes.

"Dad, Scottie, and Mike (look closely) probably at Martin Lake near Walsenburg, Colorado," late summer 1958

It was Classics Illustrated, no. 80, an adaptation of *White Fang* by Jack London, the reading of which sent me to the novel, even though most of my peers used such comics purely as book-report fodder. I searched for other Classics Illustrated titles, read many of the books they were based on, and began a collection of my own, from no. 1, Alexandre Dumas's *The Three Musketeers,* to no. 161, *Cleopatra* by H. Rider Haggard. Many issues stayed out of print forever and left tantalizing gaps to fill.

In a real way, I educated, or miseducated, myself reading these comics and their end-page author profiles. I sent away for the binders advertised inside ("$1.00"; "HANDSOME, durable, permanent—made to last a lifetime of handling": a lie, but who knew?). Using rubber bands and the binders' metal hooks, I mounted twelve issues in each binder, then placed them on my shelves as if showing off the leatherbound works of Charles Dickens. The binders have long since vanished into landfill, but I still have the comics, which had as much to do with my choosing to write as any teacher (of whom I had several good ones) or as any author—although Swift, Poe, London, H. G. Wells, Somerset Maugham, and Hemingway, Faulkner, and Steinbeck all got their licks in.

As an eighth grader trying out for a community football team, the Southeast Bears, I suffered a groin injury that led to a blood clot and sent me to the hospital, where one of the first Charles Schulz *Peanuts* comic-strip volumes kept me sane. Recuperating in bed at home, I read Swift's *Gulliver's Travels* and London's *The Sea Wolf.* Later, I wrote in pencil a long horror story, "Of a Dying God"; two gritty urban fragments, one about a fry cook, another about a would-be jumper approaching a bridge; and some bad poetry, including odes to the ocean and to beer (not then a favorite beverage of mine). I also outlined two novels about wolf-dogs, à la *White Fang,* which I lacked the stick-to-it-iveness to write.

Meanwhile, television fed me such goodies as Rod Serling's *The Twilight Zone,* Sterling Silliphant's *Route 66,* and Max Shulman's *The Many Loves of Dobie Gillis.* Charles liked *The Twilight Zone,* too, and soon I had paperback collections of story adaptations from the series. No doubt I watched too much TV, including late showings of old movies long after Mom and Charles had gone to bed: Charles Laughton in *The Hunchback of Notre Dame,* Henry Fonda in *The Grapes of Wrath,* Errol Flynn in *Captain Blood.* Dozens of others. I often reeled to school the next morning grogged out on ad-infested old films.

In the ninth grade, blessedly, I no longer had to make a long bus commute every day. Nathan Hale High School, still new in the early 1960s, lay only a few blocks from my home. Here I had three good English teachers: Joyce Slagle (ninth), who got a kick out of my George Goble-inspired prose sketches of some of my classmates, but who nixed my desire to do a book report on an Edgar Rice Burroughs Tarzan novel; Judith Burton (tenth), in whose class I first read Shakespeare and on whom I had a mild crush; and James Petty (eleventh), who looked like Ichabod Crane in tweeds.

My friend Sam Tyree, who had a gold front tooth, worked as a part-time janitor in a dance studio. One Friday or Saturday evening Lynn Bevill, Chris Wheaton, and I picked Sam up there and went cruising in Lynn's '54 Ford. Cruising, we sipped from a milkshake cup of vodka-spiked grape soda and spun out jokes, stories, and lies. Someone in the car—Chris Wheaton?—told a story about a trip to Mars and the astronauts' confinement in a nuthouse there. The Martians had assumed that the human astronauts were simply three-dimensional hallucinations of some of their own institution-alized citizens.

This story, the grape-flavored vodka, and our aimless cruising had my head abuzz. "That story comes from a neat book called *The Martian Chronicles,*" said Chris. Somehow we all got home safely, and the title stayed with me until I located a Bantam paperback copy of Bradbury's masterpiece for thirty-five cents. I read it with excitement and wonder. Later, for the same price, I found his collection *A Medicine for Melancholy* (with "In a Season of Calm Weather," "A Scent of Sarsparilla," and "Dark They Were, and Golden-eyed," among other hauntingly titled pieces) and feasted on the stories for days.

During my junior year, I took a journalism class from Janet Elson, a striking woman with white hair and dark eyebrows who wrung good work from her students with her lofty expectations, frugal praise, and temperate scorn for repeating oneself or backsliding into old errors. I saw Mrs. Elson as taskmaster and mentor. When I earned an editorial-writing award from *School Life,* a weekly publication of all seven of Tulsa's senior high schools, for a humorous Socratic dialogue, she noted that I had exhausted the form and urged me to move on. My impatience with sequels, prequels, and series probably stems from her emphasis on literary risk-taking.

Never much of a joiner or socialite, I took my friend David Davenport's dare to try out for our junior-class play, *Flight into Danger,* winning the part of Captain Treleaven, an airline pilot who talks a businessman to a safe landing from a control tower after food poisoning fells most of those on his flight. I had no lines until the second act, but, once on, spieled complex technological explanations for minutes on end. I got through the second performance of our two-night run, but then anxiety slammed me (as it had years before in a storm cellar in Mulvane), and I lost my dinner. I also missed the party that I had foreseen as a good place to hang out with cast members Bee Britten and Sharon Kelly.

In either 1961 or '62, Lee Bishop received orders to report to a SAC base in Andalusia, Spain, thirty miles from Seville. I had taken a year or two of Spanish at Nathan Hale, and Lee asked Mom and Charles to allow me to spend my senior year at a dependent school in Santa Clara, the USAF housing enclave south of Seville. When they agreed, I accepted Dad's invitation to join him and Scottie in Spain. This acceptance effectively cut my last tie to Tulsa, for, during my absence, Charles applied for a hardship assignment to Turner AFB in Albany, Georgia, to be near his arthritic mother.

I flew to Spain early in the summer of 1962, going from Tulsa to LaGuardia Airport in New York and from LaGuardia to Lisbon, Portugal. In Lisbon, I sat in an unfinished-feeling airport for several hours, then boarded a dilapidated two-prop aircraft along with a pair of nuns, some business people, and a few others. My acne had flared owing to lost sleep, untimely meals, and trip-related distress. Also, my Iberian Airlines buzz bomb from Lisbon hit dozens of air pockets on its way to Spain. (*Flight into Danger?* I was on it.) A copilot—he did not look like a steward—exited the cockpit soon after takeoff, disappeared into the restroom, and stayed there until we landed at the airfield at San Pablo, the support center for American military personnel near Seville.

Spain, when I staggered down the movable stairs from the aircraft, opened out into a dusty plain dotted with orange trees or sinuous olive trees. Driving into Seville, where Dad and Scottie had a second-story apartment at 15 Leoncillos, I saw more trees, a Cruz del Campo brewery, and the tower of the city's cathedral, La Giralda. My bedroom had a balcony facing a bar, or bodega; the bar's security grate clattered up or down at openings and closings. A blind man with a white-tipped cane stood out front hawking lottery tickets: "*Lotería! Lotería para hoy!*" Carts, motor scooters, and buses putted or rumbled past, and radio-toting young men roved the cobblestones singing "*Besame Mucho*" or "Speedy Gonzales." How would I ever get any sleep here or feel anything other than an interloper?

I had known Scottie, Dad's second wife, since meeting her one summer in 1953 or '54 in Cheyenne, Wyoming. Her real name was Elizabeth, or Betty, but most people called her Scottie because she hailed from Scotland and spoke with an engaging burr. She had dark hair, fair skin, and a square jaw that tightened when she perceived an affront. Once, I reminded her that she should wear a scarf into church for the christening of the infant of some Spanish friends. Scottie lit into me for patronizing her and refused to go. "Solomon and son," she called Dad and me, an epithet that she meant as a slur even though I had a vague sense that Solomon connoted wisdom. Scottie, however, warped that expression into a withering curse.

Clearly, Scottie faced an untenable situation. She could not speak Spanish and had no interest in learning more than a few words: *please, thank you, hello,* and *goodbye.* Living on the local economy, she had no one to talk to while Dad worked at the base and I attended school. Our young Spanish maid did work that might otherwise have kept her busy and reminded her of how poorly she handled the language. Bored, she read and smoked, imagining new betrayals and watering resentments rather than relationships. Dad simply exasperated her. Although she nursed me through an early bout of gastroenteritis, I must have seemed to her another clueless male and so an enemy.

One evening, Scottie prepared sausages by boiling them as the directions on their packaging dictated. On our plates, however, they resisted cutting. Stupidly, I noted that her failure to remove them from their plastic casings accounted for their uncuttability. Sausages flew, crockery bounced, china struck the walls and shattered. This outburst over, Scottie barricaded herself in her and Dad's room.

I left the building and angled through the back-alley mazes of Seville until I reached la Calle de Sierpes (the Street of the Serpents). I hiked this street toward the Hotel Cristina, the bullring, and the Guadalquivir River, then crossed a bridge into an area where many new highrises clustered. Eventually, on an isolated arc of road around this complex, heading back to the bridge, I came upon a big parked truck. As I passed it, a door above me opened and the driver shouted something at me. I panicked and broke into a run along the embankment. Behind me, the man laughed and cursed. He had wanted only a light for his cigarette. Shame scalded me, but I continued to run. I hoped, inanely, that the darkness had kept him from identifying me as an American.

Not until late did I get back to 15 Leoncillos. Dad lay dozing in a chair. I crawled into bed but could not sleep. The sausage-casing incident and my craven behavior beyond the Guadalquivir recurred again and again in my head. Then I heard footsteps and a creaking of hinges. Feigning sleep, I saw that Scottie

had come to check on me, to reassure herself that I had returned from my walkabout. She resented anyone's taking her for stupid, for she had a sharper intelligence than Dad and a pessimistic sensibility that nonetheless longed for brightness and passion.

When I read Hemingway's *The Sun Also Rises,* Scottie read it too (a break from Shell Scott, Hercule Poirot, and Nero Wolfe) and railed against its pointlessness and nihilism. She loathed the characters' footloose lack of commitment or direction, no matter what the damn First World War had done to them. If you liked bleak books, she said, try William Styron's *Lie Down in Darkness,* a tragedy in which real people struggled to connect. And such beautiful writing, especially about women. Hemingway knew nothing about women except what his balls told him.

My father had that in common with Papa. He made unilateral loans of money and of his '57 Chevy to other airmen, intuited little of Scottie's loneliness, and assumed that the situation would miraculously improve. When Scottie overdosed on aspirin one night, he rushed her to the infirmary in San Pablo. She did improve thereafter, I think, but no doubt because she got counseling as well as medical attention; moreover, Dad made at least a short-term effort to reform himself.

But the Cuban missile crisis occurred in October of 1962, and most SAC bases worldwide went on red alert, their highest level of preparedness. Dad spent days on end, incommunicado, at the base at Morón de la Frontera, to the point that he once faked blindness as an ostensible symptom of a stress-induced crackup so he could get some rest in the infirmary. (Dad told me this story years later, with a bizarre commingling of pride in his resourcefulness, shame for his deceit, and chagrin at his belated candor.) That he did not face a court-martial and a dishonorable discharge strikes me now as a minor miracle or an index of how thoroughly the crisis flummoxed everyone. People feared that mushroom clouds would waltz and fallout sift down in slow-motion torrents.

In that year overseas, I ceased to see the world as a boy. I did not cease to behave as a boy, for first love often made a fool of me and I had no more sophistication than a puppy. But I began to feel the complexity of existence, from life as well as from books, and to forge a variety of relationships—son, stepson, teammate, protégé, sweetheart—with a self-reliance once beyond me. I saw members of the Guardia Civil walking the sidewalks with machine guns, teenagers soured on legally bought alcohol; penitents stumbling under cumbersome roods; condoms for sale despite the power of the Church; the flimflammery and bustle of trade and carousal in the streets.

The teachers at Santa Clara, many of them itinerants with a yen for world travel, had less impact on me than did my peers, but Mary MacDonald, who taught senior English, and the Chases, a married couple with a tony apartment in Seville, linger in memory. Patricia Chase, a social studies teacher, designated Fridays for free reading and set before us a table of colorful paperbacks. You had five minutes to select a book and could exchange it once for another; thereafter you had to live with your choice. I found *Seven Pillars of Wisdom* by T. E. Lawrence one Friday and reserved it for our next session. That option always stood, but I seldom used it because rummaging for a book gave me such an adrenalin rush.

Mrs. Chase and her husband, who taught sophomore English, encouraged my writing. They once invited me to their apartment to discuss a story I had shown them about a feral child in a rubble-strewn tenement. This story undoubtedly displayed less promise than the Chases let on, but they loved good writing and had eclectic tastes. (My yearbook, *Taurus '63*, depicts the elven-looking Raymond reading enthusiastically from a copy of *The Martian Chronicles*.) They also had an astonishing record collection, featuring not only classical music but the voices of well-known writers reading their own work. They played for me a Caedmon recording of Dylan Thomas reciting, in tones like silken thunder, his poem "Lament." This experience galvanized me. I have loved Thomas's poetry ever since.

The Chases also played music for me, classical music, but I could not say if Mozart, Beethoven, Bartok, or Spike Jones had composed it. They asked if I liked any music other than rock 'n' roll. I cited a cast recording of Meredith Wilson's *The Music Man* and an album of movie themes by the pianists Ferrante and Teichner which Mom and I had enjoyed in Tulsa. Later, much later, I understood how revealing of my ignorance this response had been and how graciously the Chases had moved our talk on to other topics.

I wrote in Spain but seldom brought anything but classroom assignments to completion. Too much to see and do: teen-center parties, movie dates, the beckoning labyrinth of Seville. Toward the end of the school year, however, I edited, typed, mimeographed, and collated our literary magazine, *El Toreador*, which contained a dreary existentialist suicide tale of my own. I also supervised the writing of the senior class will. My classmates knew of my writerly ambitions, and one, long since lost to me, scrawled in my annual a request for a signed copy of my first book.

Flying home from Spain was less taxing than my flight over, but I left my first real girlfriend behind and felt exiled from a landscape of belonging unlike any I had known since Mulvane. But I had with me a paperback of Joseph Heller's *Catch-22*, and this laugh-out-loud-funny war satire kept me occupied most of the trip home. I finally landed in Albany, Georgia, where Mom and Charles had moved during my absence, and the homesickness I now experienced focused not on Tulsa or Mulvane but instead on Spain and my still feverish memories of it.

In the fall, I went off to the University of Georgia in Athens and took up residence in Payne Hall, a freshman dorm. ("Where do you live, Bishop?" "In Payne, sir, in Payne.") John F. Kennedy was assassinated that autumn, news that I got from my roommate in our cramped lodgings. About a month later, in the same place, I heard the Beatles's "I Saw Her Standing There" pour through the radio like a raucous wake-up call. I majored in English literature, took as many creative writing classes as I could (including story writing in the school of journalism and playwrighting in the drama department), and, on a blind date in February of my junior year, met Jeri Ellis Whitaker of Columbus, Georgia.

Lee Ellis, a nonpareil Southern character with whom I later wrote an sf story ("The Last Child into the Mountain," *Omni*, 1983), introduced me to Jeri, his first cousin, after touting me to her as a "Renaissance man." Despite this lie, we clicked and dated through Jeri's senior year of high school and her high-octane career at Auburn University, where she took a degree in sociology in three years—to save her parents money and to permit us to marry a year earlier than we might have otherwise. Courting her, I drove to her Columbus home, watched "George of the Jungle" and "Superchicken" cartoons with her younger brother Greg on Saturday mornings, and basked in the unconditional goodwill of her family, as well as in Jeri's own quirky sunshine.

Jeri had dark hair, a healer's smile, and (forgive the cheap-detective-speak) racehorse gams. My attraction to her had a lot of physicality in it. And so does my continuing and permanent infatuation. (How could I have turned out anything other than my father's son?) But in Jeri, luckily, I had also found a person of laughter and integrity, whom my friend David Zindell once described as an "all-out winner." Did she have a fault? Well, if anyone hurt her or her own, she could frame a monster grudge. From the start, though, she supported my writing, listened patiently to my gripes, and refused to let me despair when editors bounced stories I had assumed absolute locks for acceptance. For almost twenty-eight years (we wed on June 7, 1969), Jeri has stayed the course, raising a son and a daughter with me and then resolutely building her own career as an elementary-school counselor.

Even as a college student, I remained a military brat. My father had another year in Spain to serve until retirement, and Charles had a hardship assignment at Albany's Turner AFB, where Mom worked in personnel. Charles, however, suffered racking migraines, and these, along with the medication he took, bumped him from flying status. Eventually, he failed to attain the rank of major within the allotted time frame, and the Air Force moved to muster him out. *Déjà vu,* all over again. As Dad had done, Charles rejoined as an enlisted man. He needed only two more years to secure a pension at his highest Air Force Reserve rank. Re-upping entailed his reassignment to Homestead AFB near Miami and a protracted separation from Mom, who stayed on both to keep her job and to maintain the sprawling cinderblock house that Charles had built among the oleanders and pines of Radium Springs, south of Albany.

"My wife, Jeri, on an observation tower overlooking Chesser Prairie in the Okefenokee Swamp, Georgia," June 23, 1996

Meanwhile, the war in Vietnam intensified, and my parents (all three of them) forcefully advised me to go into advanced Air Force ROTC; upon graduation, I would receive a commission as a second lieutenant and presumably avoid a combat posting to Southeast Asia. (Army ROTC grads and Air Force pilot trainees were less likely to enjoy such a reprieve.) Despite having better than 20/20 vision, and despite the remonstrances of a medic at Eglin AFB, Florida, where I attended summer camp in 1967, I declined to point myself toward pilot training. I did so not to escape going to Vietnam, but to avoid incurring an additional year of service beyond the four to which my ROTC scholarships obligated me. This decision had nothing to do with the war, which even I had begun to regard as foolish, although I would not then have thought to protest it, and everything to do with my desire to write and my mistrust of the Air Force, which had rewarded the service of both my father and Charles with a kick in the teeth and summary expulsion. I would grant no institution, military or civilian, such unappealable control over my life. Writing would perhaps command me, but the skull-crushing juggernaut of a bureaucracy, never.

Or, so I told myself, at least not for long.

A nervous, khaki-clad twenty-two-year-old, I reported to the United States Air Force Academy Preparatory School in the summer of 1968. I had my master's degree in English (with a thesis on the poetry of Dylan Thomas) and one professional publication to my credit, a three-stanza poem owing obvious debts to John Keats and Alan Tate, which my creative-writing instructor Marion Montgomery had pushed on James Colvert, then editor of *The Georgia Review*. I had received an oxymoronically encouraging rejection letter from *The Virginia Quarterly* for a grim tale of murder, "The Birthday Weapon," and I hoped that my teaching duties at the Prep School would leave me a little time to write. Certainly, I needed to sell a story or two before I separated from the Air Force.

Dad was glad to have me in Colorado. He had retired to Walsenburg, where he taught P.E. and science at the elementary school. His marriage to Scottie had ended, and no one knew where she had gone. Although he had dated several women since the split, he now had his eye on a widow, Nora Hobeika, who ran a liquor store next to the local Safeway.

"Our daughter Stephanie (then twenty-one), our son Jamie (then twenty-three), at Stephanie's graduation from the University of Georgia," June 1995

Dad's reputation as a roué had not endeared him to her family, though, and a former girl-friend telephoned Nora periodically to decry his character and to hint at ongoing liaisons. But Dad loved Nora, a woman whose bangly earrings and loud necklaces and bracelets belied her simple goodness, and in time convinced her of this fact and of the more dubious proposition that he had changed.

For an office mate at the Prep School, I had the good luck to draw Captain Klaus Krause, who had come to this country from Germany at age ten and who had master's degrees in both physics and English. Klaus, noting my lack of success at such markets as *Esquire* and *Harper's,* suggested that I write some science fiction—he knew I liked Bradbury and admired Wells—and submit it to *Galaxy* or *Fantasy & Science Fiction*. He introduced me to two classics, Arthur C. Clarke's *Childhood's End* and Theodore Sturgeon's *More Than Human,* and, after Jeri and I had married, took us both to a meeting of a Denver science fiction club at which, pre-

"Jeri and I at the World Fantasy Convention in Baltimore, October 19, 1995. (Jeri suffered from laryngitis but greeted everyone with a lovely smile.)"

dictably late, fantasist Harlan Ellison showed up as guest. Ellison passed around a cover proof of his collection *The Beast That Shouted Love at the Heart of the World* and read aloud his story "One Life, Furnished in Early Poverty," which Damon Knight had purchased for his prestigious series of *Orbit* anthologies. Afterward, I had Ellison sign my copy of *Paingod and Other Delusions* and committed the *faux pas* of asking him if he'd ever written a novel. (He had published at least three.) Ellison's energy, commitment, and suffer-no-fools attitude sent me away from that basement room in a Denver bank semiconvinced that I could make a career too.

Around this time, I wrote a story about three Chicano brothers who find a winged creature in the snow in southeastern Colorado while gathering piñon nuts. I had no title for this piece until Klaus suggested "Piñon Fall," which had at least two apposite connotations and gave me the impetus to send it out to market. Edward L. Ferman at *Fantasy & Science Fiction,* or one of his assistants, slingshot the story back to me within two weeks, such a sudden turn-

around that I felt sure no one had read it. On to *Galaxy,* where "Piñon Fall" remained for so long that I figured it had gone astray in the mails. An inquiry, with a return postcard, vanished down a gravity sink. Writers without at least one calling-card sale had no identity, and the extent of my facelessness was galactic.

As a result, one night I dreamed that I journeyed to the editorial offices of *F&SF* in New York City (even though my conscious self knew that Ferman lived and worked in Cornwall, Connecticut) to argue the merits of my fiction and to protest its recent arbitrary rejections. Ferman's dream office occupied a skyscraper's topmost floor, whose corridor I reached only after an interminable elevator ride. When I stepped into this corridor, though, I saw that I had come in vain. Helmeted men bearing machine guns stood sentinel outside the editor's door and let no clamorous tyros pass. . . .

One afternoon in my third-story Prep School office, I got a telephone call from Jeri. Ejler Jakobsson, editor of *Galaxy,* had just telephoned praising a story titled "Piñon Fall."

"What did you tell him?"

"That you were at work," Jeri said. "Just wanted to warn you that he might call you there. 'Bye."

Shortly after Jeri rang off, Jakobsson did call. "I have a beautiful story here by one Michael Bishop. I'd like to secure it for *Galaxy.* Would a hundred dollars be all right?"

Briefly, I floated above the valley outside my window.

Later I recounted Jakobsson's words to a colleague in the English department, Michael Brown. "A hundred dollars?" Mike said. "You should have asked him if you could pay it off in installments."

With the check we received, Jeri suggested buying something commemorative of the sale. We settled on a painting by Richard Schlect—actually, a reproduction—of a rocking chair at either sunrise or sunset on the porch of an old Southern farmhouse (we chose to see it as Southern), and we hung the reproduction in our fourplex apartment on Westmoreland Avenue. Today, it hangs behind our kitchen table here in Pine Mountain; you can see it on the wall behind me in Patti Perret's photographic study, *The Faces of Science Fiction* (Bluejay Books, 1984).

This first fiction sale foretold the direction of most of what I would write over the next quarter century. It confirmed me in my conviction that although I would always struggle to command my materials, to sidestep the derivative, and sometimes even to get the work done at all, I was in fact a writer, an heir of Homer, Dante, and Shakespeare, a virtual contemporary of Cather, Kafka, and Faulkner, an upstart colleague of Aldiss, Bradbury, and Le Guin. I list these names not to imply that my work rivals that of any of these models, but to underscore my reckless sense of kinship with all who revere the word and who wield it regardfully. I would rather fall short of my aims, as I have often done, than to lapse into a wary but unimpeachable silence.

BIBLIOGRAPHY

Novels:

A Funeral for the Eyes of Fire, Ballantine, 1975 (revised edition published as *Eyes of Fire,* Pocket Books, 1980).

And Strange at Ecbatan the Trees, Harper & Row, 1976 (paperback published as *Under the Shattered Moons,* DAW Books, 1977; published with James Tiptree, Jr.'s "The Color of Neanderthal Eyes," Tor, 1990).

Stolen Faces, Harper & Row, 1977.

A Little Knowledge, Berkley/Putnam, 1977.

Transfigurations (includes the novella "Death and Designation among the Asadi"), Berkley Putnam, 1979.

(With Ian Watson) *Under Heaven's Bridge,* Ace, 1982.

No Enemy but Time, Simon & Schuster, 1982.

Who Made Stevie Crye, Arkham House, 1984.

Ancient of Days, Arbor House, 1985.

The Secret Ascension; or, Philip K. Dick Is Dead, Alas, Tor, 1987.

Unicorn Mountain, William Morrow/Arbor House, 1988.

Apartheid, Superstrings, and Mordecai Thubana, Axolotl Press, 1989.

Count Geiger's Blues, Tor, 1992.

Brittle Innings, Bantam/Spectra, 1994.

Short-story collections:

Catacomb Years, Berkley Putnam, 1979.

Blooded on Arachne, Arkham House, 1982.

One Winter in Eden (includes the novelette "The Quickening"), Arkham House, 1984.

Close Encounters with the Deity, Peachtree Publishers, 1986.

Emphatically Not SF, Almost, Pulphouse Publishing, 1990.

At the City Limits of Fate, Edgewood Press, 1996.

Editor:

(With Ian Watson) *Changes,* Ace, 1982.

Light Years and Dark, Berkley, 1984.

Nebula Awards 23, Harcourt Brace Jovanovich, 1989.

Nebula Awards 24, Harcourt Brace Jovanovich, 1990.

Nebula Awards 25, Harcourt Brace Jovanovich, 1991.

Other:

Windows and Mirrors (poetry chapbook), Moravian Press, 1977.

Short fiction, poetry, and essays have appeared in such periodicals as *Alfred Hitchcock's Mystery Magazine, Amazing, Analog, Chattahoochee Review, Cosmos, Ellery Queen's Mystery Magazine, Fantasy and Science Fiction, Galaxy, Georgia Review, If, Interzone, Isaac Asimov's, Missouri Review, Omni, Playboy, Pulphouse,* and *Shayol,* as well as the following anthology series: Terry Carr's *Universe,* Damon Knight's *Orbit,* Robert Silverberg's *New Dimensions,* Charles Grant's *Shadows,* Bantam's *Full Spectrum,* and others.

Short fiction has been chosen for best-of-the-year collections, including *The Annual World's Best SF,* edited by Donald Wollheim; *The Best Science Fiction of the Year* and *Fantasy Annual,* both edited by Terry Carr; *The Year's Best Science Fiction,* edited by Gardner Dozois; *The Year's Best Horror Stories,* edited by Gerald W. Page; *The Year's Best Fantasy Stories,* edited by Arthur W. Saha; *The Year's Best Fantasy and Horror,* edited by Ellen Datlow and Terri Windling; and the annual Nebula award volumes. The story "Dogs' Lives" appeared in *Missouri Review,* was chosen for *Best American Short Stories 1985,* edited by Gail Godwin and Shannon Ravenel, and for *The Literary Dog,* edited by Jeanne Schinto, as well as in other collections.

Nonfiction reviews, criticism, and essays have appeared in the *New York Times, Washington Post Book World, Foundation, Libertarian Review, New York Review of Science Fiction, Atlanta Journal-Constitution, Mother Earth News, Chattahooche Review, Science Fiction Age,* and *Locus.* Author of "Pitching Pennies against the Starboard Bulkhead," a column for *Quantum* (originally *Thrust*). Poetry has appeared in *The Anthology of Speculative Poetry (TASP)* and *Burning with a Vision,* both edited by Robert Frazier, and in the periodicals *F&SF, Twilight Zone, Star*Line,* and *Isaac Asimov's.*

David Mansfield Bromige

1933-

David Bromige, 1993

a comma. Compelled to make a change, I scanned every line with renewed attention. A lot got cut, some words were added; not better, maybe, but newer. The fetish of the rule modified the fetish of the text.

Desire would appear to be it, that one can't stay put, silent, in the teeth of all that's been done. What keeps us looking, to see what still needs doing. Editing, I sought the poems that best testified to this condition. And to the ways in which desiring constitutes itself through language, and earns its regulation there. The jury, chaired by Bob Hass, summed up as follows:

> Very few poets have watched their own poems unfold with such mordant and skeptical intelligence. *Desire* is nervy and bracing work, not easy to enter, and deeply suspicious of easy entry, but it is that suspicion, impatient, ironic, amused, that gives the book its originality and edge.

This book sold 3,000 copies, and the hardback is still in print. It brought my poetry to a wider public (I was asked to far-flung venues) but at the same time it somewhat misrepresents my work, for the more radical aspects of it have seldom been what John Martin wanted to see between any covers of his, and I hope one day someone will do an "Alternate Selected."

There was an earlier Selected, poems—prose and verse, songs, stories, 1961–1970, done by New Star Press of Vancouver in 1973 and called *Ten Years in the Making.* This was thanks to Stan Persky, whom I'd met in his San Francisco years. It has a cover I put together myself, the cutout letters filled with parts of snapshots of people I'd been close to during those ten years—among them the women I'd married: Ann Livingston, Sherril Jaffe, and Joan Peacock, Christopher's mother (he's there, too). And on the back cover, a photo taken by Dad, of Mum with me and my sister, above a poem about the picture.

DESIRE is the name of a selection of my poetry, spanning the years 1963–1987, which Black Sparrow Press published in 1988. It won the Western States Arts Federation Book Award for Poetry. The award was given, on the strength of the typescript, ahead of publication; because in part it consisted of $5,000 toward the cost of production and advance publicity, John Martin could now make it a bigger book. I went through files to see were there poems I'd not gathered into any of my previous twenty books that would fit? In order to make myself read carefully these and the other, all-too-familiar, items, I made it a rule to alter each poem in *Desire* by at least

"The 'KIN' section of the cover of Ten Years in the Making,*"*
the author and Robert Duncan, 1970

A CAST OF TENS, which would provide a number of pages for an "Alternate Selected," was published by Avec Books in 1994, thanks to my friend Cydney Chadwick, whose press that is, and who has done so much for exploratory writing in the past decade through her journal *Avec*. The title is a joke—this is *not* a cast of thousands—and a truth—written for a couple handfuls of friends, plus new readers, one at a time—but also describes the method followed: every stanza consists of ten lines, although these are clustered variously—3 3 3 1; 3 2 2 3; 2 3 2 2 1, etc.—in a discipline that provides a counter-thrust for the creative swoon to wake up and dodge. And "cast" carries the sense of hazard (as in "Un Coup de dés"). Not that the lines in this book were chosen through such means, but that I did let in phrasings from all over to interrupt (or shut up) each other, and that, since I could not always determine the association or connection, it had for me an appearance of chance.

Writing in the *Washington Review*, Mark Wallace noted, "Long one of the most stubbornly unique voices in contemporary poetry, David Bromige displays in *A Cast of Tens* that

he is also one of the hardest to pin down." He continues, "The poems show how easy it is for human attention to become enthralled by all sorts of languages designed to sell us out, and how we can ignore even the most blatant necessities of living in a time 'when truth and justice / leave the dictionary / sanitized.'" He concludes this thought by noting that "what these poems are finally about . . . is the very nature of attention itself. They call on us to notice what we . . . bring into our attention or ignore, choose to make significant or pretend does not affect us." I am glad for his accuracy, which would apply as well, I think, to

"VULNERABLE BUNDLES," I call them, this suite of poems I've been writing since fall 1994. There isn't a book of this title yet, though. A limited edition—thirty copies—issued in January 1995, I called *From the First Century*. It was sixty-four pages that were thirty-three lines or fewer (dictated by the publisher's format), selected from the first hundred VBs.

In this sequence, I wanted to move quickly enough to keep ahead of the conceptual function. After I read them aloud, Etel Adnan observed, Simone Fattal nodding agreement, "poems like waterfalls"—picking up on the lines from number 30, "We are a waterfall / Gods are the rocks," which are a steal from Hölderlin. This poem goes on:

> Where seizure was divine
> Memory is pathetic
> In its bell-bottom trousers
> Light on boredom for example
> The collapsing abdomen
> Smooth beneath the moon
> The commands and edicts
> Sixth sign of the zodiac

I used a number of books—for example, *The Tantric Way, Man and His Symbols, A Dictionary of Symbols*—loosely, opening anywhere and taking a hit off phrase or picture, everydaying the sacred. This poem collapses into calm at the end, a quiet pool:

> Faces of lust or distrust
> Here is an empty room
> Gray light on the floorboards
> A vase with two flowers

—which reverses and reflects the desolate opening, the two lines that precede "We are a

"Dazzling sun on the Russian River,"
with son Chris, 1972

waterfall," namely "Where the moonlight had shone / Gray light of day" (the sky?). At best, these poems wrote themselves, and many of their endings surprised me—they sound so sure of themselves and of the poem they're in. Number 69, for instance, although in its case the provenance of the final line is known to me, Robert Duncan's "Achilles":

> Being students of bathos
> We had expected this
> First he murdered his mother
> Later he was rude to strangers
> Another pronoun had sex
> Harnessing comic energy
> When you open a book
> (Quand on . . .) you look
> See the radiant line
> Rising from groin to skull
> From skull to ceiling
> Of a person one may yet meet
> Were the world circle-like
> And it is we look up or down
> The island continents' zones
> Energy fields & atmosphere
> A shimmering sun at center
> Stands in for a shimmering sign
> Who must have the perfect now
> Figure who walked splat into wall
> Leaving a face-sized circle of red
> All the coins fit in one small chest
> If one side matched the other
> You would be hideous, handsome
> These arcs would lead back home
> And soon you too would be alone (,)

I wonder at the pleasure I derive from this apparent nonsense (see below for my comments on sense and nonsense), which was derived in turn from the collision of many meanings beginning to disintegrate. I do recall Victor Coleman showing me a doctored picture in which a human face had been rendered completely symmetrical through making one side of the face into the mirror image of the other: it was scary. And Steve Benson remarking, in our colloquy called "Voices Seeking You" (published in a magazine titled *Interruptions*), "I guess the banal is the ultimate framing job" or words to that effect; "banal" and "bathos" meet in "trite," while I've found Ashbery's use of what each term indicates as devices attractive for my own work. Certainly, though, I wouldn't want to provide some ultimate frame for this or any poem I might be supposed to be the first and last authority on. It's essential to keep the discipline that the artist is agency not authority before one always, whether one is reader or creator ("administrative assistant," to borrow Lisa Robertson's phrase for a term, to creation). Or it is for me; all those years of teaching college students how to read texts were rife with tempting shortcuts, "I'll tell you what it can't ever in one thousand years mean, dummkopf" being a sentence I more than once had to strangle on the point of utterance. But throttle the impulse I did, since the picture of a teacher trumpeting "The meaning of this poem is" I find completely repellent. Meanings, when I am listening to the mystery voices of poetry, snarl at my heels like a pack of hounds to be outfoxed. Late night plus meds is one creek to run through; there are many ways of hiding one's scent, for instance the programmatic, as in

"INDICTABLE SUBORNERS," a work which has never been published in toto, only in a reviewer's excerpts. These were in the David Bromige issue of *The Difficulties* (1987), edited by and, as of 1996, still available from Tom Beckett.[1] The reviewer—the poet Stephen Ratcliffe—had heard me read this text and had asked to see the typescript.

It started out "And hands comb some one annual rainfall in the silence after laughter in Brandenburg." Each sentence had to end with the sound that began it, the last word had to be a place name, the first letter of the sentence and the first letter of the last word had to maintain an alphabetical sequence. Finding this too limiting, I inserted between each of the original sentences other sentences unbound by place names, and optional as to the other rules, but somehow generated by the originals. Ratcliffe notes that

> We find two conflicting structural principles operating at once: the alphabetical matrix, which creates order within each whole section, and the local events of each sentence, whose randomness creates an equally urgent disorder of the parts within that whole.

A sentence released from geographical rule is "H was the key broken on her machine when she wrote that letter ("I've been c atting about

[1]Tom Beckett, 131 N. Pearl St., Kent, Ohio 44240.

The author with Robert Grenier, Santa Rosa, 1981

the roug ed-in in t inking wis ing i weren't so ampered by t ese tig ts on my t ig s) I found quite intriguing," and one bound by alphabet and place name is "Finally (finally [finally]), continuity at last (at last [ditto]) found (located [discovered]) asylum (refuge [shelter]) in ([no] wiser for its arrival) Geyserville," where the sound makes a stability of the narrative wish.

To hark back a moment to Mark Wallace's review, "At turns lyrical, moving, philosophical, ironic and capable of great humor, his poetry seems influenced by many theoretical developments in 70s and 80s poetry without ever becoming merely a display of these developments. While always concerned with the many ideas about the value of poetry constantly being contested in exploratory writing, [his] work is never a presentation of such ideas, but always a challenge *to* them." This is the place to observe that

DECONSTRUCTIONISM in my work is solely an -ism thanks to its being an attribute. "I always thought, you know, you were a homegrown deconstructionist, or not even that really, just that whatever was offered you would hand back with a question so that the formulator of the original had to consider your reframe job as it applied to his original," my friend, Bob Grenier told me, more or less. His perspicacity, patience, and impatience have all been equally valuable to me through these nearly thirty years of friendship, and so has the support, advice, and encouragement of others who have been there for me since the sixties and seventies: poet friends Tony Friedson and the late Earle Birney (University of British Columbia teachers), Ken Irby, Kathleen Fraser, Charles Simic, Elizabeth Herron, Barry Gifford, Ron Loewinsohn, Michael Davidson, Michael Palmer, Clayton Eshleman, Ron Silliman, Bob Perelman, Anselm Hollo, Lyn Hejinian, Bruce Andrews, Charles Bernstein, Nick Piombino, Steve Benson; and scholar friends Peter Quartermain, Steve Fredman, Stan Dragland, and the late Toby Oldfield. Novelist, neighbor, colleague and lifesaver, Gerald Rosen. And crucial through those decades, friend and mentor Robert Duncan. (Denise Levertov, early, although as my work developed, it lost its appeal for her.) Some undoubtedly preferred the deconstructive aspects, others, the homegrown; but each has helped me "Bromige around" (as Joan Retallack put it) in the world of poetry. Each has helped me stand up to The Censor.

I speak of The Censor—interior because exterior—who condemns us only to repeat. How to circumvent this ingrained set of prohibitions? As I said in *Le Monde,* "Depuis le premier jour, ma poesie s'est attachee a deconstruire la voix patriarcale qui etait si forte a l'epoque ou j'ai commence a entendre de la poesie." Many ways of circumventing said Censor—of attempting to, in any case—constitute my poetry. I have found it useful to focus on a technique, be it those I have described above in "Indictable Suborners" or *A Cast of Tens* or "Vulnerable Bundles," or others, such as homophonic "translation" or even a regular rime scheme, so that my attention is diverted from what the words are saying at the time of composition. That's when the true intention manifests. Otherwise it's "I know what I'm going to say" and tedious for all, myself foremost.

However, all manner of information needs to be intermittently inserted, grist-into-flour, and Wallace is correct, I *am* concerned with the value of poetry and the debates its unpinnability occasions. In a lifetime, I've read copiously, if not methodically in any conventional sense of the word "method." I'm not going to attempt a list—there were the usual giants—but I'll simply mention a couple of favorites. Somewhat less obviously today, Maurice Merleau-Ponty and Michael Polanyi were of particular use in the sixties. Theodor Adorno's writing I loved from the day I found it—late, I suppose, 1975 or thereabouts. "The given as something indepen-

dent of the spontaneity of consciousness, can be characterized only by turns of speech out of the thing world."[2] Some of my friends don't think he's funny enough, but in *The Jargon of Authenticity* or *Minima Moralia*, every sentence exudes an élan that owes its all to the power of the negative. I know these helped me write

MY POETRY, published early in 1980 by The Figures Press of Berkeley. This triggered—or coincided with—a series of "My" titles, one of them, *My Pleasures,* by Laura Chester, the wife of Geoff Young of The Figures, and another, and surely the best-known by now, *My Life,* by Lyn Hejinian, who was to be the publisher of my next book, *P-E-A-C-E.* Not surprising, really, since we had arrived at the end of what had become known as the "me" decade; I know that's why I picked my title. I was playing with it, and meant it in an anti-"me" sense—meant to say "my *kind* of poetry, no matter by whom." The book is full of appropriations from other writers—is built up out of such. The second word of the title is also asking to be upset, for a quick riffle shows the pages to contain mostly prose. Besides challenging received notions of authorship, I had my eye on genre.

In his introduction to the reprint of *My Poetry* due in 1997 from Sun & Moon Press, Ron Silliman says that "few books change the world. For at least that world which is poetry, this one certainly did." In his view, its being crowded with voices, its being among the first works to display "a free multiplicity of form," its unabashed preference for cross-pollination over purity, and its ability to see in "pollution" the integrity of each element, opened up possibilities for a new generation of poets. "*My Poetry* stood so-called language writing on its head, right side up," he concludes, "[it] is a book that, once begun, initiates a reading that can never end."

The title piece is a poem-essay, made up of phrases and sentences I excerpted from all the reviews I'd had to that date (sometime in 1977). I did it to be a kind of long shrug, "What are the standards for reviewers? Can there be *any* agreement?" but its texture makes it say more than that. Wanting it to have the tone of a for-real essay, I composed poems which

---

[2]*Against Epistemology,* translated by Willis Domingo.

I then "cited." When I moved with Cecelia to The Haight in 1979, a stack of manuscripts was being passed (slowly) around among some dozen of us, and when the draft of "My Poetry" came back to me, it had a lot of marginalia, some of which I incorporated into the final version.

The section called "Six of One, Half a Dozen of the Other," wherein I "review" earlier of my poems by anecdote, each one spoofing a different critical approach, was written in January and February of 1976 following a week-long New Year's party *chez nous* where one of the guests, a Limey named Jon Webb, entertained us for hours with anecdotes. It was catching.

There felt like more on their way—but then I got the news that my father had died, and nothing was worth writing for months. So much shifted; when I wrote again, that particular entrance was bricked up.

The final section, "Hieratics," was an attempt to do a triptych in words—"0" and "4" are the decorative backs of the wing panels, while parts "1-3" make the front wings and the centerpiece. I had read that a triptych was originally a portable altar for use while traveling, and that was just what I needed, because I had left Sherril and my home in Sebastopol to live in San Francisco with Cecelia, and this step restored awareness of the world as a contingent and instable experience. It was difficult to mourn properly while elated and despairing with a new love. So the scenes I (brokenly) depict are of three sacred passages in my previous life, as I now had to acknowledge it was.

The gorgeous—and prescient—cover is by Francie Shaw: Francie and Bob (Perelman) were close friends throughout that time; Bob's encouragement led me to dedicate *My Poetry* to him. The author picture at the end, by Cecelia, taken on a trip to the Long Island town where she went to high school, shows me squatting as though begging for alms in front of a sign that reads WE ARE MAKING ALTERATIONS / SO THAT WE MAY SERVE YOU BETTER . . . BANK OF BABYLON. The eighties came, and we did get served better, eh?

Well, I *did* get a National Endowment for the Arts award just as this book was coming out. I got divorced, we honeymooned on Maui, I had a nervous breakdown, and a year later, settled in Santa Rosa, married.

"ANN AND DAN GOT MARRIED" is the title of a story in *Men, Women & Vehicles: Prose Works.* At its end, Dan, dwelling on the breakup of his marriage to Ann, reflects:

> Her fault, his fault . . . it was the fault of a society that didn't know what it wanted marriage to be: romantic imbroglio, business deal, kindergarten, buddy-system, duel to the death? Dan had learned that the one chance for a marriage to survive was if both parties abandoned every hope they had had of it, save that it persist.

Dan has learned this from his subsequent marriage to Penelope, the woman for love of whom he left Ann. When Dan says this, at least on Tuesdays, Thursdays, and Saturdays, he speaks my mind. As of this date, I have been married for forty years, albeit not to one but to a series of wives.

Ann (not the model for "Ann") Livingston was living in Vancouver when I met her, an immigrant from England, as myself, and just one day younger; we were twenty-three. She'd recently divorced and was headed back to England to study acting at the London Academy of Music and Dramatic Art (LAMDA). It was a bad time to fall in love. After excruciating indecision, I went back and lived in my parents' house with her and worked as a substitute grade-school teacher while she studied. I'd acted in a couple of plays at University of British Columbia and now joined the Tavistock Theatre, appearing in *Anna Christie, The Country Wife,* and *A Winter's Tale.* I wrote on a play, evenings while Ann was at rehearsals: LAMDA students gave a reading of it. Theaters "papering the house" sent free tickets to LAMDA, so we saw many excellent productions.

Ann and I had interests in common and worked to build with them, but I had no experience of living with an intimate stranger, and I venture to say that Ann's youth and background caused us problems also. When the draft—still in force in the UK—caught up with me, found me A-1 but not officer material (not enough years of college)—which meant Ann and I would be apart for my two years (officers' wives only could live on base) and meant I would be in the military, which I had always intended to avoid!—we decided to return to Canada, where no such imposition was found necessary.

But that proved a weary mistake, on Ann's part: the provinciality of Vancouver, as she experienced it, after the thrill and opportunity of London (she was from Birmingham), meant that she was forever trying to tug me back where (for more reasons than the draft, which in any case was soon rescinded) I had now resolved never to go. We split up and didn't keep in touch, except to get a divorce through the mail. . . . An irony given that our courtship had been largely by mail, an exchange of numerous love letters superseding our three weeks as physical intimates, for she had returned to England in May, and I didn't decide to return until September. I feel keenly the pain of our breakup still. We were so vulnerable to one another, so overwhelmed by our young lives, made so desperate and cruel by conflicting demands. I don't know what became of her. Back in England in the sixties, my father told me, she was favorably noted as a singer in Holst's *The Planets* by a reviewer in the *London Times* and later was in pantomime in Nottingham; I haven't seen her name in the theater pages of the occasional English newspaper I buy, nor, when I was in England to give readings, had my friends who follow theater heard of her. I'm sad she didn't get the breaks anybody needs in that business: she moved me very much as Olga in *Three Sisters* and as Cordelia in the LAMDA productions; and she shone as the lead in *The Matchmaker* with Vancouver Little Theater.

Fred Hill, a local character with a genius for publicity and props (he was acting in *The Matchmaker*, too), and a good friend of mine, was also a good friend of Joan Peacock, whom he'd known since their days at University of British Columbia; and he fancied himself as a matchmaker, too. Joan was on the rebound, and so was I: Fred arranged a meeting, we dated, enjoyed one another's company, were attracted, became lovers, I moved in with her, and we embarked on a relationship that brought us both, I believe, much pleasure, comfort, stability and peace. I wouldn't say we were swept away. Having recently been through the failure of relationships begun in that way, this quieter beginning felt better.

With Nick Piombino and Charles Bernstein, New York City, 1989

And it proved to be better. We got along like, this time, the house would be inflammable. Joan, two years my senior, had a precocity that landed her in university at sixteen, so most of her friends were graduating when I, a late entrant, was a freshman; spanning two four-year "generations" made for a large circle of acquaintance, which we both enjoyed very much. Boy, did we party! To save money, we made home brew and saki—potent stuff.

Joan helped me so much. She coached me through college, she introduced me to polite society, she fit in splendidly with my, more bohemian, friends, and she put up with, and even supported, my workaholic conduct—I was taking a three-quarter load of courses, working as a desk clerk at a motel at night, as a substitute teacher during many days, as a paid reviewer of plays, movies, and books for CBC radio, and meanwhile editing University of British Columbia's litmag, *Raven,* and writing articles for a weekly center page spread called "The Critics' Page" in the *Ubyssey,* the campus paper. . . . And we partied every weekend on top of all this and Joan's demanding job as an insurance adjustor. We drank a lot and sometimes tempers flared—she broke a toe kicking me for refusing to return a bottle of hooch to another alcoholic—we hit each other, though not on a monthly basis, had words at parties—after the style of those times—we made love plenty, and used our little spare time to hang out on Trafalgar Beach, one minute from our basement suite.

I wish I could have done without the codependency hangovers and quarrels, but mostly I was having a great time, being with lots of stimulating people, having a lot of laughs, getting straight A's and winning prizes. We kept the present crowded. I didn't look far ahead. But now it was my last year and I was being urged by my mentors to apply for a Woodrow Wilson Fellowship. I did, and I got one. Now what? It could be taken up at any graduate school other than the University of British Columbia's. I hadn't dreamed of leaving town. No more had Joan. Friends had preceded us at the University of California at Berkeley; we visited and found the town, though unpleasantly crowded, interesting; what tipped the scales, though, was poetry—I had begun to write it in earnest, and the Bay Area was then so active with poets that it made sense to be there.

Joan Peacock with Christopher, Berkeley, 1966

I had little sense of Berkeley's distinguished reputation. Not for the first time in my life, I walked into surprise like the hero of a picaresque novel. The amount of (excruciating, hairsplitting) work demanded of me was one shock. The reduction in our social life bothered us both. After I got the master of arts degree in 1964, we took six months off work and school and rented a house in Deep Cove. Joan was pregnant and wanted our child born in Canada. More specifically, too, in Lions Gate Hospital in North Vancouver, where her father and stepmother were both doctors. It was in this period that I developed insulin-dependent diabetes, going into that hospital just before Joan went in to have our son, Chris.

This was a double-whammy of some proportion. The carefree couple of just two years before were now parents; one was chronically impaired; money and time were tight; I was due back in Berkeley to work on my doctorate. And I had stopped drinking, which altered our relationship drastically.

Back in California, our marriage darkened, despite the joy Chris brought. I must have felt displaced: Joan slept with Chris; I slept on a cot in an adjoining room. She wanted me to get my studies over with so that we could go back to Canada. She was working in an office in Oakland, but I was enjoying my job as a teaching assistant, and my poetry was being published. I was giving readings and talking with many, many poets: in no hurry to leave. I kept putting off my Latin exam, my German exam, my doctor's orals, my dissertation. Joan understandably felt obliged to remind me of these. I felt badgered, displaced, and unappreciated. Exaggeration's idiot. A young woman in graduate school caught the scent of my dissatisfaction, made sure I became aware of it. There are angels and devils aplenty, at such times.

After we separated, Joan and I kept a more-than-less amicable relationship going, impelled to do so because we had a child, but out of long friendship and love, as well. We shared the care of Chris, although in these years especially, she was stuck with the lion's share—the lioness's, that should be!

Eventually, she did go back to Vancouver, and when it was time for high school, Chris joined her and her new husband there. But for years, our living apart meant that, like it or not, we had to stay within an hour's drive of one another if we were to go on sharing Chris. It meant that I wasn't going to look for a job outside of the Bay Area. What luck, then, that I secured the post at Sonoma State, as it was then, College.

Backing up, I must say that I was glad to be living on my own. My illegal apartment was tiny, but I spent a lot of time on campus. I learned to like being alone. I was reading and writing constantly. Then, as time went by, I dated—though that's not quite the word for how the sexes related in Berkeley in the late sixties—see my story "David's Rod" in *Men, Women & Vehicles*.

Sherril Jaffe was one of these dates, and as we got to know one another, she became the only one. We moved in together, then, when I got the job in the country, married, so that her parents wouldn't disapprove of her cohabiting with me. I really didn't want to marry again. But I wanted to go on sharing life with Sherril. What a great companion, and a considerate stepmother, too. And she wrote, wonderfully as I felt, and for the second time in my life, I began to feel a full world building around me, around us. It lasted—a spell.

Hindsight needs to be reminded of the obvious: when you're *in* the marriage, you don't see it as an arrangement that's going to end. You hope it's forever—except on those nights when you wish it were over. It's a flower, you tend it. It secures a mutual hope of further happiness.

Plenty of people know that this one, too, went belly-up and know plenty of the details of that capsize. I haven't the heart to retell them—read my stories to see why! Blame me if you want. It's hard for any one of us to fit into the common rules, but plenty manage it. I couldn't accept definitions that felt deadly. I'd have to go crazy before I could learn how to act sane. At this stage in my life, I hadn't suffered enough. I was a white, educated, employed young male.

The closer one approaches the present, the more difficult autobiography becomes. That's when it becomes time, again, to turn and look at the poems. But first, let me say of Cecelia Belle, psychotherapist and executive director, my wife since 1980, stepmother to our grown son Christopher, and mother of our teenage daughter Margaret; of Cecelia, whose great beauty, charm, wit, ear, poetry, competence, vulnerability, love, and Irish volatility—along the lines of Pegeen Mike—swept me off my feet two decades since: There are no words to measure what she has done for me—not the least of her gift being, what she has shown me about myself. I admire her endurance. It can't be easy, living with a language mechanic. They always want to take a wrench to your nuncupation. Other poets want to talk and talk to them over a shared phone. They hug too long when they meet. Given Civilization, they have to embody the Discontents.

What was possible under the dispensations of people in my generation of serial monogamists forms much of the matter in *Men, Women & Vehicles*. Even where the author's eye is on other targets (as in, say, "Down from the Mountain"), the coupled relationship provides plenty of ink. Yaël Katz, in her paper "In Your Face: Stasis of Movement in David Bromige's 'Unwinding the Wound' and 'Ann and Dan Got Married,'" writes:

> [This] narrative . . . achieves perpetual deferral of expectation. And so expectation is spared both aggravation and fulfillment, for it is never realized. It merely stops. Narra-

With Cecelia, Venice, 1993

tive prevents the wait by pretending that there is nothing to wait for. There is nothing to wait for, and nothing does wearily arrive.

Ann in "Ann and Dan Got Married" never learns this, never decodes (what Yaël Katz decodes) the title as "Ann and Ann Got Married." Wedded to her projections, like any one of us, but—as a literary character—more purely, more purely doomed.

I only mention this story, though, because it makes me laugh.

NONSENSE is the truth of sense. "I am making sense of your poetry" announces the reader threatened with being overwhelmed. Fortunately, nonsense can withstand all manner of assault. It is the core of human existence. It is what makes the world go round, for who knows why that should happen? Romantic love, too, is nonsensical. Take someone who's in love! Preach common sense to him! Or *any* kind of sense! He has stumbled upon the secret of the universe, and it is nonsense.

Nonsense kicks our brainwaves higher even than surprise. I would not, however—or therefore—write pure nonsense, even if I could. I plump for figure and ground, the dark-cloud-silver-lining effect. When Maurice Merleau-Ponty's translators, Hubert and Patricia Dreyfuss, in their introduction to *Sense and Non-Sense,* illustrate their author's thought with reference to the plays of Harold Pinter: "At the end of a Pinter play a member of the audience has 'understood' when he has given up expecting an explanation," I welcome the clarity, as also when they remark that "the onlookers are forced to participate in the generation of sense from nonsense." And they can back up their parallel with Merleau-Ponty's "we are condemned to meaning" and "existence is the very process whereby the hitherto meaningless takes on meaning." But I find this only half of the process, as I believe Merleau-Ponty himself meant to be understood; for half the time, we are liberated from meaning, noting how the hitherto meaningful has become without meaning. (A scholar named Marnie Parsons has sound things to say on the topic of poetry and nonsense.)

The book of mine that comes closest to pure nonsense is my collaboration with my friend Opal Louis Nations. *You See* was done by e.g. Press, San Francisco, in 1985. I made the final draft: a poem of fifteen-line sentences in fourteen-line stanzas. (The experience of collaborating was one of never being quite in synch; hence the form to say so.) The poet and teacher Steve Tills writes in the DB issue of *The Difficulties*

> The length and complexity of the sentence units help to deter me from the compulsion towards overall meaning. . . . This writing allows (and encourages) the reader to stay attracted to the individual pleasures and truths discoverable in the local units, the minims of attention. One resists, to withstand the tug of the sentence's headlong rush. This too is a pleasure, almost a kind of kinesthetic sensation, like prolonging the precious moments before an orgasm.

I gladden to learn the kinesthesia comes through. It's certainly here at source, and I've long held that writing, poetry anyway, is an athletic event. I stop, sense myself, so many muscles engaged! Back of this writing practice stand the misery of school desks and the fixed position required, but also the elation of physical release, the soccer games and tennis matches, the all-day cricket, the track and the cross-country runs, the week-long bike tours, the ten-mile hikes, that were the brighter passages of adolescence. The orgasms, too. What do you say to one of those? All great nonsense! And then there's the use of language in other rituals of a spiritual nature, for instance,

Spells & BLESSINGS, also the title of a volume of thirty pages that Talonbooks of Vancouver published in 1975. To draw on Barbara Weber's annotated bibliography (at the back of the David Bromige issue of *The Difficulties*),

> A common thread is the attraction of the unknown, embodied here in myth, the Tarot, sexual desire, and (as Bromige notes in his Foreword) "the face of a question that writing . . . raises: I trust this is so for others." Again, attention lights on language as the mediating agency, itself the primordial mystery: "Your nipples dark / behind *your shirt.*"

In the foreword, I tell of running into an acquaintance on Telegraph Avenue in Berkeley in 1967 or 1968 who was carrying a book by T. Manley Hall that contains a Saxon legend about the light elves and how they have to lure the dark elves up from underground—to be instantly petrified by the light, their evil thus negated. So "how, ever, to know a live dark elf?" Language's cognitive domain being the burden of my songs, I felt an immediate attraction here and wrote the poem called "A Spell" as a result; over time, it drew the other poems of this book around itself.

Unesco defines a book as something at least forty-eight pages long. I believe this would exclude the first editions of either *Lyrical Ballads* or *The Duino Elegies.* The poetic impulse, that repeats itself in a variety of approaches to what, were poetry science, we might call "a problem," then flags, the (non)problem having now been (un)solved. To me this has happened a number of times: *Spells & Blessings* is just one instance.

Others include the 1969 work *The Quivering Roadway,* which was inspired by a Nordic legend and informed by the Vietnam transgression, or the three twelve-page pamphlets issued by Black Sparrow in the 1970s: *Three Stories, Out of My Hands,* and *Credences of Winter.* The first of these consists of three rites-of-passage stories: "Finders Keepers," where the boy realizes he has to assume his power, that his parents are not omnipotent; "Sex-skat-chew'n," where a young man's sexual initiation is "scatted"; and "He Was," with its disguised pun on "heroes" (like a child lisping, that must learn to talk like an adult), where the protagonist thinks his way through many baffles and traps to confront himself. *Out of My Hands* likewise is tripartite, made up of accounts, also chiefly autobiographical, of some shimmer where sureness imbricates uncertainty. The sentence—found in Michael Polanyi's essay "Tacit Knowing"—"But in the language of Azande it is self-contradictory to doubt the efficacy of oracles, and this only proves that Zande language cannot be trusted in respect of oracles," prompted recall of these three occasions. The booklet was written in a week—I was learning to write with a point of view while it was present; they don't hang around me for long.

Credences of Winter paces Stevens's "Credences of Summer" somewhat, not that its eight poems are matched with eight of the ten segments of Stevens's poem, but by the negative, that the mind, rather than "lay[ing] by its trouble," takes it up; rather than being in "a land too ripe for enigmas," we are too ripe with them. But much that is in the "Summer" poem can be found in the *Winter* ones as well. The first lines of the first poem, "An Excrescence," say so:

> Though I am barely human
> The logic of this tree
> Grows clear to me, no matter
> I know it in the summer,
>
> I know the winter in it too.

And continue:

> Light forces it. As boughs
> So forced up & out, so roots
> Are driven into earth, a balance
>
> Even I can find.
> Admittedly with spring
> Excrescences occur—& fall.
> Love among us humans
>
> Never can be otherwise.
> The will of those that love
> Drives into thought concerning what
> Thus drives them
>
> —Into poems even—
> Never can be more.
> For I am barely human
> While speaking with this tree.

Writing in the David Bromige issue of *The Difficulties*, Tom Sharp says of this suite of poems, "each is an enviable example of a poem; it is also a definition of what a poem *can* be, a test of poetry, an exploration of a poetic. A poetic includes more than prosody; it includes an epistemology." A little later he remarks, "The overall effect of a poem with integrity does not depend on what the reader must previously experience and bring to the poem; it must present the grounds of its own being— integrated, from the experience that defined them, during the act of composition, into a whole including its form and its content. . . . What is a poem? A poem is, for example, an excrescence."

Zeroing in on the poem of that name, Sharp continues, "An excrescence is an outgrowth, proof of a relation between an object and the thing from which it grows. This poem presents a growth of understanding, the speaker's experience with

a tree, with love, and with poems." I very much enjoy the logical way in which Tom displays the workings of my poetry here. I worry over that use of "whole" in a general application to poetry, or even my poetry, but it fits with these poems just fine. (Answer: A blossom.)

The suite is prefaced with a sentence from Octavio Paz's essay "Rhythm" in *The Bow and the Lyre:* "In every society there are two calendars."

Then in 1981 there was *P-E-A-C-E,* an eighteen-page chapbook, built around a single impulse, in Barbara Weber's words:

> Peace in pieces. Framed as a history (primarily literary) of the 1990s, told in the year 2020. The clarity of the narrator's vision struggles with the deteriorated language of a collapsed culture. . . . The craftily disordered syntax and vocabulary (Bromige worked from a Swedish text which he "translated" according to its aural cues) make one continually stop and question what is being said.

In an interview with Weber, in *Jimmy and Lucy's House of K,* number 6, I observed, "The Reagan landslide had swept away some final vestiges, I felt, of a great hope." And I continued,

> It's like there are two people, one of whom is very angry and the other watching finds that person's anger comic. . . . The esthetic problem was to write . . . the anger and at the same time contain it, frame it. A fake translation was one way to do it. You appoint a text to be master over you; a lot like *The Inferno,* where Dante's imagination of Virgil prevents him from stopping to gloat or relish his anger. . . . It was some Swedish memoir of lonely childhood and how certain poems found at that time were consolation. . . . [the poems embedded] are previous fake-translations, from the Spanish and the Portuguese.

This was probably the most tactless book I ever published. A number of persons felt themselves targeted—the framing wasn't sufficient. It was hard on the more exclusive kind of ego. *P-E-A-C-E,* nevertheless, proved quite prescient. Probably because its germ—implanted by my office mate, Bob Perelman—was a Dark Ages document examined in Auerbach's *Mimesis.*

Let me end this tour of my little-book museum with a consideration of *Romantic Traceries,* put out by Abacus in 1993. These twelve poems were made by taking the rime-words from a dozen poems by Keats and Shelley, and then writing lines that would end in those words, while preserving the same rime-scheme as the originals. For instance, here's the start of "A Bit of Blancmange'll Be Enough for Me," which is based on "Mont Blanc":

> These years we're just so many things
> Deposited on the present by those waves
> We call the past & this causes gloom
> Even in those who've heard Rilke on springs
> And persuaded themselves that what brings
> True happiness is supernumerary existence, not
>   what we own
> So much as what we own to (.)

To knock up constantly against the words "sleep," "eternity," "fantasy," "wings," "poesy," "breast," "sky," "serene," "deeps," "steeps," "wind," "brook," "moon," "star," "ecstasy," "forlorn," "elf" . . . and so forth, really made things chime. These were the poets I cut my teeth on in adolescence, and their diction *drew forth* much that I owed to them. One of these poems appeared as a booklet from Last Straw Press, Weymouth, UK, under its title "It's the Same Only Different / The Melancholy Owed Categories."

"FINDERS KEEPERS" draws on my experience of the London Blitz. Published first in my first book, *The Gathering*, "Finders Keepers" is a story about itself, for it is an assemblage of impressions from that time, one among which concerns the antiaircraft shell fragments—shrapnel— that we boys delighted in finding in the streets on our ways to school mornings following an air raid. The last paragraph reads

> He still searched for the jagged metals, but now his father had told him where these came from, he treasured particularly those pieces molded like a screw. He saved them up, hoping he would one day have all the pieces, & be able to put them together, like a jigsaw puzzle & build a shell of his own. Would it be mine? he asked the father, Or the Guvinmint's? His father told him, His, if he kept it hidden. So there was that to think about, he could go out looking in the gutters, when the sounds came, late at night.

The "sounds" alluded to are those of an air raid—planes rumbling, antiaircraft guns fir-

ing, then the whistle and crump! of falling bombs.

The whole notion of reassembling fragments to find a coherence contains an esthetics that argues for the good health of art. The story is told from the six-year-old's point of view, so this esthetic needs to be distinguished from elements of fantasy and ignorance if it's to be appreciated, but the fractured time line and the employment of extra-syntactical commas to further fragment the surface (a device, this, learned from Creeley's prose) embody the argument: Let things testify as they lie; refuse to cram them into an unnatural coherence; assemble them with the least degree of force possible. Only in this way will one be able to replicate experience in its actual partiality. The child in this story, whose life heretofore had been lived in peacetime, in the same apartment, where all family members cohabited, now experiences the dispersal of those members, removal to several places out of the target zone, a return to that zone at just the moment when the Blitz begins, and then the destruction of homes and the dismemberment of neighbors by high explosive, always with the threat of his own death or the death of his parents hanging—literally—over his head. War is an experience, whatever other horrors and miseries, of violent disjunction. But it may also be an experience of resistance that realizes (what was so exciting to meet again in the work of Charles Olson) the will to cohere—not generally felt in peacetime, when our governors splinter us to keep their power secure.

Even before the Blitz began, the boy had a frightening experience of innate hostility, when an older boy involved him in a battle with rival teenage gangs. During the Blitz, he senses his parents' terror at their loss of control. And he becomes aware of "Guvinmints"—no matter of which nation—as a general threat to personal coherence. These lessons in limits establish lasting values in his mind.

If experience is the best teacher, I guess Hung-Chow isn't the worst—

IN THE UNEVEN STEPS OF HUNG-CHOW, issued by Little Dinosaur Press of Berkeley in 1982 as one in a series of chapbooks (the other authors: Michael Davidson, Bobbie Louise Hawkins, and Michael Palmer), consists of three tales concerning a Chinese sage as told by his

Paul deBarros, the author, Cecelia Belle, and Barry Gifford at the deBarros home in Seattle, 1994

humorless and gullible disciple. In the words of Barbara Weber, "each tale deals with an aspect of representation. The narrator's lack of humor makes the telling that much funnier." Hung-Chow is an utterly unreliable rogue, who is conning his California disciples out of their discretionary income while basking in their regard and getting to talk about his life—or what he alleges to have been his life. No doubt my decades of experience as a teacher informed these little fables, wherein I descry myself swollen to a grotesquerie. Hung-Chow's disciples, too, in their refusal to see any rip in his armor, are parodies of the adoring student.

I suppose Hung-Chow came out of occidental folklore and is as politically incorrect as most such. He might as well be from India, which I let him be, when I reprinted one of these stories in *Men, Women & Vehicles*. He is to be considered one of those gurus from Asia who have so swayed Americans and Europeans down the centuries. He is the Return of the Repressed, *au fond*, a man making a virtue of his vices— but because he is up-front about these, and,

eventually, speaks openly of his contradictions, hard to dislike. Or so I must hope.

One day in 1982, the tales written, the publisher lined up, I was house-sitting for my friends Bob Grenier and Kathleen Frumkin in the place they shared with poet Larry Eigner in Berkeley. I was going to cut up some magazines I had brought with me, to make a collage cover, and, looking for a pair of scissors, I opened a drawer. Hung-Chow was looking up at me. It turned out to be a sketch Kathleen had done as a teenager. It was uncanny! He was just as his disciple had already described him. And so that became the cover. The acceptance of such "informing accidents" suffuses

Ends OF THE EARTH, THE, my third book, which appeared in 1968 with Black Sparrow. "Benjamin's *nunc stans* had been receiving attention from both theorists and practitioners— from the Beats forward, and there was a lot of slop about it. I was interested in retrieving its clarity and rescuing 'carpe diem' from simple-mindedness. At the same time, I meant to bring the idealism of the times to some earth. Here I began while working within the Projectivist mode stylistically to question its assumptions." How clear indeed it appears to have been to me one day in the mid-eighties when Barbara Weber was interviewing me!

Ends covers the waterfront, all right. From Minimalism—that movement where all the *i*'s sound alike—to Baroque. Some of the short lyric-anti-lyric poems are worth keeping. Like "Why Not":

> What if these clothes
> which so uneasily we sit in
> were to be thrown like reflection
> to the winds that make your hands shake so—
>
> & at dawn, under your window,
> water to the very rooftops, the sky there
> gray, & gray,
> looking up, into a ferocious sun.

Rereading the book for this essay, I found the long, spaced-out narratives pretty strange. Somebody should do a piece on those. I'm thinking of "It's Not My Trip #2" or "Forgets Five." These are visionary poems, that owe something to Clayton Eshleman, with whom I was in conversation at that time, but have a quality now vanished from my palette, nor present, to my knowledge, in anyone else's. "A Final Mission" is visionary also, but the attack is more direct and recognizable.

This was the last book in which I used idiosyncratic spelling, where I let both the sound of the word, and its immediate context, dictate how it was to be lettered: for example, *tangld*, which enhances the feeling of entanglement.

My next book from Black Sparrow, *Threads*, while published after I had moved to Sebastopol, owed a lot, like *Ends*, to being in Berkeley in the late sixties. The intensities of those times, the continual pressure from the illegal war on Vietnam—a war that would distract attention from the battle for civil rights at home—the near-revolution we were caught up in, hoping for and against, the taste of liberty and the feel of community—which informed each and every thought and deed, all our interactions—all of this, however mediated, makes both books testament to their times.

L IVING IN ADVANCE is both a book and the song which names it. Barry Gifford and I

were sitting in his mother-in-law's apartment on Parnassus in San Francisco one afternoon, and he was describing to me his cut of a projected book he was going to write about the lawyer Charles Garry. "I'm gonna get 48 percent royalties," Barry said. "Holy cow!" I exclaimed. "That's a *lot*." "Well," Barry added, "that's 48 percent of what the law firm gets." "And what percentage do they get?" I prompted. "Okay, they get 15 percent of the gross, or 7½ percent of the net, whichever is less [or did he say "more"?], but that's before taxes . . ." I was growing fuzzy trying to figure out how much actual cash would find its way into my friend's pocket. I went over to the piano, sat down, and said, "so, you're living in advance of your advance?" We wrote the song in an hour.

We had written other songs together, as part of a group effort off and on through the decade 1965–1975, other contributors including Paul deBarros, Ray Neinstein, Sherril Jaffe, Judy Smith, Mary-Lou Nelson, and Gordon (then Norman) Pilkington. Paul, Barry, and I wrote most of them. In 1975, Paul transcribed thirty-two of them, fake-book style; his wife Judy typed out ten more whose lyrics are set to familiar tunes; I designed and drew the cover and title page, wrote an introduction, and, the following year, with a small grant from the NEA, published three hundred copies under the "Open Books" title, in lieu of issue number 7 of the magazine I then edited, *Open Reading*.

I continue to compose songs, either with Barry or with Paul, and "Pretty Perdita," written to be the title song of Barry's upcoming movie, will—we hope—be used in it. But mostly, these numbers were part of the timeless squander of song, put together at day- (or two-day-) long parties, and never, never based on a lot of people we all knew.

D ISSOCIATION OF PERSONALITY: Six years old, one night during the Blitz, I was in such terror of maiming and death that I made what I felt at the time was a vow to God. If he would spare me, I would become someone else. Actually, it was more the thought that the situation made it necessary that I become some person obviously *not* destined for bomb damage. Some other. At six, God looked to have agreed to the deal.

Back of that vow and its ideation, which is as novel to the child as it is common to humanity, back of this magical thinking, sat the isolation hospital where I spent the minutes between nineteen and twenty-two months of age. Whatever illness I had, and that isn't—and wasn't—clear, I'd tested TB-positive. My family wasn't permitted to visit the sanatorium. Anna Freud thinks I'd have remembered them for at most five days (five long days). When released (neither better nor worse, physically), I disconcerted my family by being unable to recognize them. Them and their assumptions.

I no doubt was mourning my nurses. This took place at an age when I was coming into language, so that if, as Dante posits, we imbibe our language with our mother's milk (and in his day a child wasn't weaned prior to teething), I suckled on a lot of different tits, so to speak. If Motherer = Muse, maybe the variousness of impulse in my writing owes something to these disturbances, if only that I tended to repeat this imprinting in later life.

If Anna Freud is correct about a two-year-old's memory span, I was born into my family not once but twice—and I like to think Marx is applicable here: the first time as tragedy, the second, farce.

The tragedy is that of the species, that our braincases would be too big to get down the birth canal could we but stay in the womb until ready, so we are born prematurely and never quite get over a sense of helplessness and dependence. The farce: well, I started out writing plays (five or six, none too good; though some won prizes, none was produced), among them a one-act piece that goes as follows: The Apple of Their Eye (I made him a few years older) returns from a trip with a new self-reliance—good, but bad: he recognizes none of his extensive family. Who meanwhile continue their hearty welcomes, but, as Eye-Apple fails to reciprocate, become downright irritable. They had always known he had a Worm in him! Shouting, they beat him to death. They're sorry, afterwards, until suppertime.

That Somebody Else in the cellar? Is who I've made with my writing?

BIRDS OF THE WEST consists of three sections, the first of these a gathering of single poems, the second a serial poem named "Pond," and the third a serial poem called "White-Tail Kite." These are the longest poems I've written, "Pond" being twenty-three pages, the other, twenty-seven. "Pond" is mainly prose, "White-Tail Kite" almost exclusively verse. The entire book uses for its material the landscape and inhabitants of western Sonoma County as I found them, fresh and startling, when I moved from the intersection of Arch and Cedar in Berkeley to a hillside country lane with a view of the ocean, eight miles southwest of Sebastopol, near the Marin County border, in the spring of 1970. The book also contains a nine-page postscript, "Proofs," which relates this material to current issues poetic, philosophical, and political. In it, I write that "I took attention, in various of its modes, as the matter, that is I found these modes subjected me to the mystery of their existence."

Of intensest interest to me was a small bird, a harrier, known as a white-tail kite, which hunted in the meadow next to the house. This bird can stay in place for minutes at a time, its wings spread and held aloft in a rapid but subtle fluttering. Its gaze is toward the ground, anticipating food chain motion in the grass. I found it compellingly beautiful.

*Daughter Margaret Belle Bromige
at Naropa, 1995*

The both of us

so *in*
in this
perusal
of potential

Filled with
the possibility
of the instant
next to this

Wings raising must
contain implicitly
the movement
consequent

. . . .

One never shall
discover him self
here & now

unless an
elsewhere have
declared its

whereabouts
demanding one
attend, & here

takes care
now of itself,
attended from (.)

Edited by Victor Coleman, the book is a stunning production, not least thanks to the cover by David Hlynsky.

Birds speaks to me of that Lincoln-log cabin on the windswept hillside, where Chris and friend Nathan often visited from Berkeley, where often I felt elation, and where I got so much writing done—*Birds* ended after *Tight Corners* was begun. I wrote on these two books without any significant break for two years. Saluté, English Hill. May your violators be exculpated.

Red HATS is a nonsensical title I derived, anagrammatically, from the title of an earlier book, *Threads.* I had decided to work my way through *Threads,* now fifteen years had passed, to see what that had all been about, to see if there were things left to do. "He rooted in his belief. I'm your puppet" was the first pair of phrasings this gave me, and from there, things took on a life of their own. While the earlier book continued to supply sentences—"translations" or "improvements" of its lines—so did a lot of other sources. Having accumulated some sixty pages of prose, I had the notion of organizing it into seven sections, each one titled with a letter of the general title. Sifting through my sentences, I assembled a number of "key" words that began with *R:* rooted, reality, rules, repression, revolution, romanticism, reification, reflection, rationality, representation, and so forth, and then took the sentences that contained those words and jiggled them around until the puzzle was complete, inserting further sentences where this process generated them:

Reality becomes relative, a repression of revolution via tolerance, romanticism its reified reflection, rationality's reduction becomes representation. Her garment glimmered in the gloaming: a tight white sweater to make her boobs look big.

As to whether any given sentence leads to the next, or simply precedes it, the reader herself must decide. I think sometimes yes sometimes no, depending which day it is. (I shall have a little more to say about *interruption* as a move at once esthetic and philosophic, below.) I repeated this process with each of the title letters.

Red Hats was published by Tonsure Press in Ohio in 1986. The publisher found it rough sledding, and the book had some distribution problems. It had one, perspicacious, review, by Aldon Nielsen, which appeared in the David Bromige issue of *The Difficulties.* He found it a good read.

In one other obvious instance an older book generated a newer one. *Tight Corners & What's around Them* has, as its title sequence, a series of brief prose poems, a fusion of short, declarative sentences with a flatness of tone that provided relief from the poetry of stylized emotivity (what I call "folk-poetry") that was the lingua franca of those years. "His rhetoric was rich. The cake was richly crammed with raisins, only nobody eats much Christmas cake these days, & that's their loss. The hilt of the sword was richly studded with jewels. The attic was richly cluttered with junk."

Finding them akin to Kafka's parables, which "juxtapose events, sentences and assertions not to create gestalt epiphanies which suggest a larger (if hidden) order in the universe, but quite the opposite," Ron Silliman, writing in the David

Bromige issue of *The Difficulties*, then distinguishes "Tight Corners" from Kafka's parables (with their "rich strangeness"):

"Tight Corners" seems startlingly straightforward and consciously flat:

'The truck had nearly struck their car. He had screamed. She had asked him not to.'

At first, this seems not to be a parable at all, but rather a miniature narrative whose small instant of humor hinges on the female requesting the male to suppress a reaction which is instinctual and thus involuntary. Yet . . . the effect it creates is radically different from the one it depicts. Rather than being intimately intertwined, each of these three sentences is composed so as to convey a maximum of distance from the others.

   . . . What this narrative points to is not its "tale," but to the chasm that opens between sentences, that ungrounded moment in and through which distinct statements are organized by the writing mind into larger structures of implied continuity. And, not co-incidentally, to that other chasm between presence and representation. The flatness which characterizes "Tight Corners" is, in this sense, much like that of a painter who presents the surface of her canvas as a two-dimensional plane.

Shrewd observations indeed, and to the point, very much, for consideration of everything I've done since the early seventies—of all my mature work, then.

But I was going to say how one book of mine sponsored another. Fifteen years later, having attended one too many more of such readings, and with the extra-Virgilian presence of Anselm Hollo perched on my bust, I began writing what became the volume Brick Books of Ontario issued in 1991 (second printing 1993), *Tiny Courts*, the mirroring of whose title would recall *Tight Corners* and its tonal flatness. Here's one:

> *Manana from heaven*
>
>   I just want a couple acres
>   in beautiful country
>   where I can put two-three chevys
>   up on cinder blocks
>   and abandon a stack
>   of automobile tires (.)

Thinking of that title the poet Douglas Powell, writing in *Witz*, observes, "In the audible world of Bromige, puns and slips of speech substitute for statement—they are more interesting . . . because they only allude to what is being said; they do not evoke by denotation. If there is reference . . . , it seems to happen by accident; . . . the reader assumes responsibility for its decoding."

The sequence "Lines" in my 1993 Sun & Moon book, *The Harbormaster of Hong Kong*, employs a similar technique:

> life is brief
> ——————
> it says here
>
>   dark night of the soul
>   ——————————
>   currently unemployable
>
> famous last words
> ——————
>   i must be immortal

—the top line is momentarily rendered pompous, emptied out by the undercutting qualification, but not in any final way; the initial line reasserts its claim, and a shimmer occurs back and forth. As with the "corners" and the "courts," echoes foreground language. I think it started out with my father saying such phrases as "Well, you're right and I'm wrong, as you usually are." Shimmers enhance cognitive duration. They slow a read.

There's more to *Harbormaster* than "Lines"; it's to my mind a book that addresses the change in relationships among us, as the economics of the world alter. In her excellent piece in *American Book Review*, Rochelle Owens writes, "He has won an international reputation with his irresistibly funny style. . . . He reconstitutes the personal, social and political with the sophistication of a congenial terrorist equipped with a smart bomb. . . . Enlightenment comes in the form of a kick in the pants. . . . He succeeds in penetrating the design of chaos. We perceive our connection to the code in the whacky magnitude of our lives. We let ourselves participate in this crux of meanings." Which was about what I did when composing

"ONE SPRING," a prose piece that appears in *My Poetry*. Barry Watten had published it in his magazine *This*, where the Pushcart editors saw it and awarded it a prize. It's a sunshine sketch of a little town that opens with a hailstorm. It's the little town where I live today and have done, off and on, since the early seventies. Sebastopol, population now seven thousand, then thirty-eight hundred, was Appletown USA when we back-to-the-country hippies and college freaks started settling in and around it at the end of the sixties. Now we're the majority—western Sonoma County, of which it is the hub, has a liberal-radical voting record topped only by Berkeley. Margaret, the daughter of David, a radical Berkeley poet, is acting in the high school play *(Quilt)* with Daniel, son of the Berkeley radical activist, Mario. Mind you, within actual city limits, the political balance can tip either way. Money keeps on yattering.

We have boutiques now and crystal rock shops and cappuccino bars, but it's still the funky place I first found, with its small, wooden homes, its delectable gardens, and weeds sprouting through the hardtop. Main Street, which is part of state highway 116, is choked every rush hour these years, as is the other state highway, 12, whose intersection with 116 makes the middle of our town. But the wetlands to the east hold off Santa Rosa, and the hills like giant nudes that roll up to the west and out to the ocean are still relatively uncluttered with ranchettes, still producing the Gravenstein apple, most delicious of all fresh off the tree at dawn. And the climate, seven months of the year, is superb: it never rains between April and October, the temperature hovers around a non-humid eighty-five to ninety-five degrees during the day, then at night, when the ocean fog comes all or part of the way in, drops into the forties.

I'm telling it in my own words now, but in "One Spring" I used the words of what then was our weekly paper, the *Sebastopol Times*. I composed the piece in 1977, but I used the files of the *Times* from spring 1970, wanting to find out what had been going on just before I moved into the neighborhood. I yanked the real names and inserted the names of my friends. I played around with the paragraphing—newspaper paragraphs aren't real anyway. And I put in a passage from Conrad and another from Turgenev. Ron Silliman in "Modes of Autobiography," *Soup* number 2, 1981, called it "a pastoral composed largely by appropriations from the local newspapers. The irony here is that

daily life in the country (even the modern, strife-filled country) is supposedly the epitome of the Organic, to which the poem's form is diametrically opposed. The piece succeeds . . . because of Bromige's meticulous attention to the ordering of his materials." Yes, that's always the fun part, especially on a computer. It's even harder to stop.

Men, WOMEN & VEHICLES is my one full-length collection of prose. Black Sparrow published it in 1990. The years spanned are 1959 to 1989, and this book includes about one-third of my prose from those decades. There are journal entries, letters, dream-notes, and prose-poems in among more conventional stories (whose modes range between expressionism and realism). A trio of male personae, Dan, Brian, and Sven, and their mates Ann, Vera, and Kathy, pass through some contemporary dilemmas, slowly then quickly. A generation that started remarking (and remaking) the orders of American society early in the 1960s may find portions of its story here.

In recent years, I have attempted lengthier forms in prose. The August 1986 issue of *Writing* contained "Jackfish City Days," a chapter of an unpublished novel called *Robbing Peter*: this chapter tells what life was like on the Canadian prairies in the mid-1950s. Another novel of Canadian life, *Piccolo Mondo,* written in collaboration with friends-since-college Mike Matthews and George and Angela Bowering, and set in 1961, when we *were* at University of British Columbia, is currently being read by a publisher. In 1992, I published a detective novella, *They Ate,* which plays with the pace of its narrative—very fast then very slow. Set in Georgian England, it includes a peasant rebellion nipped in the disgraceful bud by World War I, prefaced by the lynching of a judge and a roomful of lawyers.[3]

Interruptions being some evidence of the existence of other minds, they make for a so-

---

[3]Note to George Bowering: he swiped so many of my ideas over the years, I decided to return the favor and swipe part of his idea for how to write this autobiography. But where he built his on a straightforward A-through-Z template, I have employed the initials of my name—and told it through my works. Thanks anyway, George. And for thirty-five years of elective affinity.

"The Vancouver restaurant is Piccolo Mondo, after which my collaborative novel with the Bowerings is named"—the author with Chris Bromige, George and Angela Bowering, and Cecelia Belle

ciable esthetic. The first Interruptionist Convention was held in our Santa Rosa home the day after New Year's, 1980. It was also the last. We began to issue a manifesto, but continued by eating breakfast.

Present were Tom Sharp, Cliff Schwartz, Bill Vartnaw, Jim and Nancy Jacobs, and Chris Bromige. Tom, Cliff, and Jim had been three of my most gifted students, and I'd like to interrupt myself now to name a few more, who kept me going through the long, crowded semesters at Sonoma State—each of whom went on to public note and (some) fame and/or fortune: Robin Beaman, Kate Braverman, Suzanne Bria, Cydney Chadwick, Trane DeVore, Swift Dickison, Steve Farmer, Carolyn Fleg, Steve Fredman, Nancy Frye, Michael Gallagher, Jim Garrahan, Elizabeth Garrett, David Gilbert, Marty Goldstein, Karen Gordon, Ginger Grant, Leslie Hall, Patricia Hartnett, Sara Howard, Maureen Hurley, Tom Kelly, Bob Klose, Luis Kong, Steve LaVoie, Carol Lundberg, Mary Magagna, Michael McCaffry, Doug McCasland, Andrew McGuire, Jim McCrary, Stella Monday, Jim Montrose, Susanna Napierala, Pat Nolan, Gerrye Payne, Ann Peterson, Sara Peyton, Doug Powell, Angelo Querin, Victoria Rathbun, Chris Reiner, Chris Riseley, Lyn Lilith Rogers, Norma Smith, Colleen Snook, Meredith Stricker, Cole Swensen, Judith Tannenbaum, Steve Tills, Marianne Ware, Lynn Watson, Barbara Weber, Gabrielle Welford, Kimberly Williams, and Patrick Woodworth, writers all, if not always primarily, and forgive me, others, if I've misplaced your name; professors are supposed to be absentminded. But did you ever think that other professionals with three degrees would each have a secretary, whereas we professors had one-sixteenth of a secretary each—a mere one-sixteenth of a mnemonist?

Patient in mien, many times they sat through this and other truthoids. I was the guy who got them a space where they might learn from one another. They suffered me. Their interaction kept me alive while I earned a living.

Gathering, THE, my first published book, came about through the agency of Fred Wah, a member of the Tish group and a fellow student of mine at University of British Columbia, and Robert Duncan. Fred had gone, grace of Robert Creeley, to do graduate work at the University of New Mexico, where he then started his magazine, *Sum*. On a visit there to read, Duncan encouraged Fred to do a series of books and offered one of his own to get the series off to a notable beginning. He spoke well of the writing I, now at Berkeley, was doing, and Fred asked me to be the second author. As it was to turn out, I was also the last; when Creeley moved to State University of New York at Buffalo, Fred followed, and his duties there took up the time and energy he needed to continue the projected series. (In fact, the production was completed in Buffalo, with Fred and the Toronto editor and poet Victor Coleman pasting up the cover.) Only forty pages (thirty-two poems plus "Finders Keepers") and 350 copies, but Ah!, the difference to me.

Existence makes the law an ass. "Justice" as a social function means totally different things to a millionaire and a pauper, no matter the emotions that cause us to thirst for it are identical. The communicative, as distinct from the expressive, function of any word receives heavy negation at source, under any class system—as feminists know. Being not of the ruling class, I bent my verbal skills towards the expressive function; meanwhile, as a kind of clerk, I made my living imparting communicative know-how to would-be middle-classers, in exchange for being permitted to slide no further than their lower fringe. Such salary as I received bought space in which to create expressive forms, a vocation that entails a certain declasse mobility.

That these works should exist at all is highly unlikely. It took Free Trade with its falling farm prices—in response to the unionization of agricultural workers in Britain—to move one third of the village population into the cities, where my mother was born, youngest of ten, in 1899, to a couple from Beaford, North Devon, resettled in Kilburn, London. William Cann and Mary Balkwill—nice match of surnames—might well have stopped with number nine.

Hard times in the English countryside had also moved my father's mother's people into London. The Mansfields came from Lincolnshire, where my great-grandfather had been a baker at Burleigh House, until the night of his murder. Poachers hunted in armed bands back then, so the Burleigh Baker, as he was dubbed thereabouts, had accompanied the gamekeepers to give them armed support. He died during an exchange of fire—fighting for the wrong side, as I felt upon hearing this tale. The Widow Mansfield and her children moved to Marylebone, London, where, when grown up, my grandmother Margaret met Charlie Bromige. Of his origins, I know nothing. According to my father, he was a bit of a rogue. He worked days repairing coaches, but he moonlighted as a set-builder in various music halls. His children were often snuck in to shows, and my father's childlike enjoyment of such spectacles proved lifelong.

My father, the fourth of eight children, quit school at thirteen to work—and three years later he was a delivery boy for a butcher. It was in this role that, delivering a side of beef to a shop in the High Road, Kilburn, he was granted a vision of delight: my mother, aged fifteen, pushing her bike up the High Road, ethereal in white. *That* didn't have to happen, either. Harold and Ada.

Turning eighteen in 1916, World War I raging, my father was ripe for other forms of butchery. He was shot in the knee (two feet higher and we wouldn't have to be deciding whether to go on reading this) and, a year later, mustard-gassed; reported as dead, in fact, the notice arriving at his mother's house on Christmas Eve, 1917.

The war over, my father worked as a newsreel cameraman for Gaumont-British News. Harold and Ada wed in 1922 and had a daughter, Dora (Dad loved Dickens), two years later; try as they might, however (and I was assured they did), they were granted no further issue until October 22, 1933, when I interrupted them at the tennis club. (She'd only gone there that morning to watch Dad, but when not nine months with child, my mother could belt balls back with the best of them; her swim-champion shoulders packed a wallop, as the emerging baby was to find out.) But for now, it was enough to be delivered by one Mrs. New in a taxi, with the pock! of ball on racket and the rattle of a London cab my twin imprints of outside forevermore.

By then, my father was news editor, and he went on to be assistant director (he did all the work, he claimed) on a number of documentaries, among them *A Queen Is Crowned*. He had many friends among the Wardour- and Fleet-Street journalists, and in show biz also; and at least one mistress. My mother was not one to get dressed up and dine out, nor entertain at that level. I guess the mistress was. He certainly worked late at the office.

From what my mother said, she admired my father for his cleverness and stick-to-it-iveness, enjoyed his verbal skills (he was an ace anecdotalist), but deplored his short fuse (which she blamed on the war: "shell shock") and his fumbling insistencies around sex. A Sunday school teacher in her youth, she retained traits prim if not downright repressive, as when she slapped my five-year-old hand away from my million-year-old willy. There were men she admired, mostly movie stars: Lew Ayres, Ronald Coleman, Walter Pidgeon. Gentle, strong monsters of integrity. She admired for a spell a lanky, white-haired Virginian and asked her son (then eight), in this confederate's presence, if he would like to live in America with her suitor and herself.

"But what about Dad?" ruined those plans. There may have been others.

When the order of the two words of her name (she had no middle name: her parents, she joked, had run out of names by the time she was born) is reversed, they almost spell "Canada," so isn't it odd that both her children emigrated there? Well, yes, but she had invited this, tracing cousins who, enlisted in the Canadian armed forces, found themselves in England. Throughout World War II she was hostess to a number of these lively youngsters plus their buddies, some American. The Bromiges had a big house by then because it was dirt cheap because it might be bomb damage before morning, and there were spare rooms where these could stay on furlough. Mum liked them, Dad less so—because they were young, zesty, handsome, and about to die, no doubt—but she *said* because they put on no "side." They all played guitar, and the house was filled with blues and country-western music. Among these musicians was one Matt Meredith, who married my sister and took her back to North

David with his parents, Harold and Ada, early 1940s

Battleford, Saskatchewan. Where I joined them in 1953; after Mum and I summered there in 1949, I always longed to return. I loved what I perceived as the absence of hierarchy—which was shortsighted of me, I now know, but not an entirely inaccurate reading. Also, I, from Austerity Britain, was seduced by the air of easy prosperity. But even better, I, a teenager, was now five thousand miles from my parents!

This hadn't been allowed without a trial run: I lived for a year on a farm in Bjuv, Sweden. Surviving this, I showed my father I could make it on my own. Little did he know what-all I survived. The farmer was a bachelor, a ladies' man, whose dinner parties roared on past midnight, sometimes past dawn. Egon wanted me there so that he might learn English, but I was half his age and we soon talked in Swedish instead. I spent a month in Denmark, going home, where I made some fast friends, and I didn't worry my folks with this blip, either. As Mrs. Murphy more or less said, "You can do things behind their backs right under their very noses and as long as your lips stay sealed, their eyes will stay shut. Get down on your knees and pray you don't put your foot in your mouth, though; without God's ear no tongue can make a lie stand up. And may He forgive you, for I won't."

For nigh on a decade, my mother had a woman to help with the housework, with teenage Dora, and with young Davey—Mary Murphy from Cork, without the music of whose voice in my childhood and the gift of whose gab, I doubt I should have made either poetry or song. For hours they'd sit over a pot of tea, my mother chain-smoking, in a conversation that went on long after Mrs. Murphy's employment with us stopped. Her daughter, Pat, so beautiful, also became a war bride and went off to Newfoundland, where Mrs. Murphy joined her, though decades later. Her son, Johnny, eight years my senior, was forever leading me into mischief—praise be—fatherless, charming, gifted Johnny, whom I loved, my big brother, who sang in the West End and over the BBC, and who destabilized and vanished, the trail gone cold when I returned from Canada. All of those people from my English childhood and adolescence, save Sir Samuel Brittan, and my sister's schoolfriend, the actress Barbara (New) Barrington, have vanished. Extravagant me! I kept moving on. I kept forgetting. Writing became realer than people. Ouch!

So, unlikely as I may find the eventuality, I *was* born and did survive to make these works, whatever their merit. I could have been killed during the Blitz—people all around us were. I should have died on the prairies before my real age caught up with my fake ID, in a DUI crash or a barroom brawl.

However, since I did survive, how obvious from this sketch that I should have made the poetry I did! My father's newsreels and documentaries show his terms were twenty-four frames per second; he lived by editing public perception of reality. Yes, he grew cynical, wanting to show the people what really happens while being required to fit it into a tight and self-censoring format; but he was a very amusing cynic. Good gossip! Chaplin, Olivier, the Duke of Windsor: can't repeat it here. He was loud and excitable, strict and demanding, and too easily disappointed; self-pitying, volatile, likeable, hateful, sweet—but throughout, vivid. He took me on shoots. I got in free to Cup Finals at Wembley and Center Court at Wimbledon. Met Lil' Mo. Once the famous playwright turned ninety, Gaumont-British News always shot George Bernard Shaw on his birthday, and thus I met the Master—Mum's idol. Dad's world excited me.

Meanwhile, my homebody mother kept coming back to the fact of my existence from her preoccupied self, and for two long spells, was as all mine as her personality could allow. In the first year of the war, when she and I were billeted in Bedford by governmental fiat, while my sister was sent to another town and Dad stayed in London to work, Mum and I, like many evacuees—funny new word to be—found our billet intolerable—the resentment!—and moved into a studio flat; and then there were the two years, 1949–1951, when my father was living with another woman. My mother talked to me then, by the hour, day in-day out. She talked to me as though I were an adult not a fifteen-year-old, about feelings, relationships, "life," the need to be true to oneself: *Pilgrim's Progress* was a favorite of hers. So was George Bernard Shaw. But so was Mazo de la Roche. How *not* write for a way to reconcile all this?

When my father moved back in, how mixed my feelings must have been—but among them was a vast relief: I was free to go! I remember discussing my plans with Alan Geller, who wanted to emigrate to Argentina. He was already an emigre, coming with his mother and sister from Poland in the nick of time. There were many

"Cheese, dammit!" David and sister Dora, Stanmore, 1942

Jews lately arrived—though not as recently as us—in Cricklewood and Willesden Green, many of them assimilated for generations to Middle-European culture, persons more cultivated than the British and Irish around them. I got to know their children at school. Walking home with David Swerling or with our doctor's son, Sammy Brittan, or with Alan, I had my first conversations where ideas took on a crucial existence.

And I did emigrate, twice: and met so many and such vivid imprinters in Canada and the USA that I have not dwelt much on these early years—save here—the "formative" years, we're told, but I've remained impressionable. When I go to England, now, I'm taken for an American. I enjoy the mobility this gives me with their still class-bound structure. As a Yank or a Canuck, I don't really count. So an Englishman can reveal more of himself in my presence. Of course, Guv'nor, now you've read this . . .

Alan, I think, did not emigrate again: his mother and sister wouldn't or couldn't go, and he had no father, and he wanted to be their

support. David Swerling, I heard, moved to Israel. Sammy, of course, stayed put and made for himself an eminently successful career in economics and journalism.

These were children who did not perish in Auschwitz or Belsen or Dachau.

After Beckett, we took the "a" out of waiting and inserted an "r." When you play the blues, you no longer have the blues. I just drove home, and I don't know how I did it, on automatic, I was seeing again what I'd seen this morning in the garden, one honeybee, large, grazing on a big, red dahlia—rapt. I suppose the pollen is dropping somewhere as I write.

Some of this is stuff you'll be hearing for the first time, Bromige children, concerning your origins. I hope you remember it's just a version, highly edited. I love your versions of us as somebody new. I hope you find my version of Dad as somebody old, lovable, too.

BIBLIOGRAPHY

Poetry:

The Gathering, Sumbooks (Buffalo), 1965.

Please, Like Me, Black Sparrow (Los Angeles), 1968.

The Ends of the Earth, Black Sparrow (Los Angeles), 1968.

The Quivering Roadway, Archangel (Berkeley), 1969.

In His Image (broadside), Twybyl, 1970.

Threads, Black Sparrow (Los Angeles), 1970.

(Contributor) *The Fact So of Itself,* Black Sparrow (Los Angeles), 1971.

They Are Eyes (broadside), Panjandrum, 1972.

Ten Years in the Making: Selected Poems, Songs, and Stories, 1961–1970, New Star (Vancouver), 1973.

Birds of the West, Coachhouse (Toronto), 1974.

Spells & Blessings, Talonbooks (Vancouver), 1974.

Tight Corners & What's around Them, Black Sparrow (Santa Barbara), 1974.

Credences of Winter, Black Sparrow, 1976.

(Contributor) *Living in Advance,* Open Reading Books, 1976.

My Poetry, Figures (Berkeley), 1980.

P-E-A-C-E, Tuumba (Berkeley), 1981.

In the Uneven Steps of Hung-Chow, Little Dinosaur (Berkeley), 1982.

(With Opal Louis Nations) *You See,* e.g. (San Francisco), 1985.

Red Hats, Tonsure (Ohio), 1986.

Broadside (broadside), imprimerie dromadaire (Toronto), 1987.

Desire, Black Sparrow (Santa Rosa), 1988.

Tiny Courts, Brick (Ontario), 1991.

The Harbormaster of Hong Kong, Sun & Moon (Los Angeles), 1993.

Romantic Traceries, Abacus (Elmwood, Connecticut), 1993.

The Mad Career (broadside), Grey Spider (Seattle), 1994.

A Cast of Tens, Avec (Penngrove, California), 1994.

From the First Century (limited edition), Cricket Press/Potes & Poets Press, 1995.

The Art of Capitalism (broadside), Anchor & Acorn (Petaluma), 1995.

Fiction:

Three Stories, Black Sparrow, 1973.

Out of My Hands, Black Sparrow, 1974.

Men, Women & Vehicles: Prose Works, Black Sparrow, 1990.

They Ate, X-Press Productions (Sebastopol, California), 1992.

Illustrator:

Sherril Jaffe, *Scars Make Your Body More Interesting,* Black Sparrow (Santa Barbara), 1975.

Other:

Also author of *Six of One, Half a Dozen of the Other* (poetry), 1977. Author of plays *Palace of Laments,* 1957, *The Medals,* 1959, *The Cobalt Poet,* 1960, and *Save What You Can,* 1961. Editor of *Raven,* 1960–1962, *R*C* Lion,* 1966–1967, and *Open Reading,* 1972–1976; poetry editor, *Northwest Review,* 1963–1964. Contributor of articles, stories, and poetry to literary magazines.

Dorothy Bryant

1930-

In "How to Talk to a Writer," an article spoofing the writer's life, I wrote: "Do not ask a writer if her novel is autobiographical. First of all, the question implies that the book was created by the material, not by the skill and sweat of the writer. Secondly, the question says that books mean less to you than gossip. Thirdly, it's none of your business."

But you didn't look me up out of idle curiosity. You need to know—perhaps to write—something about me and my writing. And, if you must write about me, I want you to get it right. So I'll relate some personal history that, up to now, I have kept mostly to myself—if I think it's the source of a subject or theme or view of life expressed by my fiction. Other events and relationships remain private, "none of your business."

My parents, grandparents, and great-grandparents were all born in Balangero, a village about thirty miles northwest of Turin, Italy. According to my father, the French border was a day's walk from the village. Until the unification of Italy (1860) Turin was the capital of the Kingdom of Piemonte (Piedmont-foothills), an old monarchy including parts of present-day France and Switzerland. Its spoken language was Piemontese, which sounds rather like abbreviated Italian words mixed with French. These Alpine foothills have occasional snow, therefore strong rivers, therefore water power, which made this the first industrialized region of Italy. (It is still the industrial center, home of Fiat.)

When my father was born in 1901, everyone—both male and female—over the age of ten worked in the textile or the paper mill in Balangero. Old people cared for infants and the infirm. Once out of diapers, children were in full day care with some schooling provided by the mill, until they went to work with their parents. My grandparents were minimally literate in Italian (quite different from Piemontese), an unusual accomplishment in the peasant working-class. Work hours were all daylight hours, six days a week. Staple food was polenta. On

Dorothy Bryant, 1996

Sundays people worked patches of land in the rugged hills, because the total income earned by an entire family working in the factory was not enough to feed it. The men did manage somehow to cultivate grapes and make wine, a comfort and a serious problem, according to my father. A partial view of this hard life might be gained from a 1950s Italian movie starring Marcello Mastroianni, titled *The Organizer* in English, *I Compagni* in Italian. (I learned only a few years ago that the interior factory scenes were shot inside the abandoned factory building where my grandparents had actually worked.) When I first saw the film I told my parents that they must see it because I believed it was a depiction of their childhood. They answered

Bryant's father, Joseph Calvetti, with his parents and his younger sister, about 1918

that if it depicted their childhood, they had no desire to see it.

The Piemontese do not fit the stereotypical American image of the Italian, based on exaggerated traits of southern Italians. "You don't look Italian," the statement which has followed me all my life, is as annoying as "You don't act Italian," by which other Americans mean I do not display my feelings with broad gestures, shouts, and tears. I don't look or act like Anna Magnani in *Open City*. Many Italians, north or south, don't fit this stereotype (any more than all Swedes are gloomy). Yet there are strong regional differences. In Italy the Piemontese are still seen, and often resented, by their southern countrymen as overly prudent and reserved, inhibited workaholics. This hostility is returned by some Northern Italians who say their industries support the whole peninsula. A recent separatist movement fed on these old hostilities. Yet in 1992 one of my Balangero cousins married a Sicilian and moved to Catania. If anything is "typically" Italian, it is a contradiction like that.

My father's maternal grandparents—named Cardone—were highly respected workers, occasional forepersons in the factory, known for their orderly life. My great-grandmother was able to space her eight children two years apart by breast-feeding each infant at least fifteen months. All eight survived to adulthood, a rare accomplishment, partly due, no doubt, to her cultivation of vegetables and fruits to vary the diet of plain polenta that less resourceful families subsisted on. This branch of the family staunchly maintained contact with the American branch after their Rosina married restless young Francesco Calvetti, who eventually took his reluctant wife to America.

My father's family looked down on my mother's parents. Her father had been abandoned (after a halfhearted attempt at infanticide by his mother) and had grown up on the streets. When he went into the army (which he loved because as a soldier he never went hungry), he left my grandmother pregnant but married her during his first leave in time for my mother's birth. (I was fifty years old before my mother told me this fact, so ashamed was she still of the gossip that had crossed the ocean with the immigrants from Balangero.) Despite breast-feeding, my mother's mother became pregnant again soon after my mother's birth and handed her over to be nursed by a neighbor who had just miscarried. Three years later, she had to be forced to take her daughter back.

Both my grandfathers set off for America, separately and alone, each leaving behind his wife and first child (my parents), each seeking a way out of poverty. (Between 1880 and 1910 one third of the population of Italy emigrated.) What both found—each in his separate path— was work on railroads and then in coal and copper mines, the dirtiest and most dangerous work, but highly paid compared to any other work open to immigrants. I'm told both were musical, had fine singing voices, and earned a bit more by singing in saloons at night. My impression from other stories is that, unfortunately, they took too much of their musical performance pay in drinks. Their paths remained parallel, each saving the fare to bring his family over by about 1910, when my father was almost ten, my mother four. For about ten years the families moved from mine to mine: Pennsylvania, Illinois, Utah, Montana. Their wages, between layoffs and debts to the company store, were not enough to feed a family. When my father's sister was born, he, an incredibly innocent ten-year-old, came home from school, saw the baby and burst into tears. "We don't have enough to eat, and you go out and buy a baby!" My grandmothers took in washing and boarders, men whose families were still in Italy. My grandfathers' health had already begun to fail—silicosis. My mother once told me that as a child in Butte, Montana, she could identify each man by his cough as she heard him walk past her parents' cabin.

My father went into the mines at fourteen, but fortunately his mechanical skills won him a topside job. I'm not sure how my mother's family (by then with five children, two of whom later died) finally managed to move on to California. My father's family came because my grandmother was offered a job as cook for ranch hands in Gilroy, her husband by that time being unable to do much manual labor. In any case, both families ended up south of San Francisco, in the then agricultural Santa Clara Val-

ley (now called Silicon Valley for its computer industry).

My grandfathers were typical patriarchs of the time, given to dictatorial tantrums, probably worsened by the humiliations they suffered as powerless, despised immigrants whose health had been ruined. But my mother's father was pathological. He beat my mother regularly and severely for trivial reasons. He kept a lock on the food pantry—minimal single helpings were doled out at mealtimes. He worked rarely, sending each of his three daughters out at age ten to support the family as live-in maids. They also picked fruit in harvest season. (My father's father drew the line at field labor for his daughter.) Everyone in the region, including all children, worked in the canneries in summer and fall. My maternal grandmother remained apparently indifferent as her children were starved and beaten. Perhaps she feared the violence might turn toward her. Whatever the reason, my mother never forgave her. Nor could I ever warm up to the old lady who moved near to my parents after her husband died in the 1950s.

My mother's two younger sisters, like all their friends, left school at fourteen. My mother struggled to continue her education. By age sixteen she had a full-time office job, all her salary claimed by her father. She continued studying at night, going to her teachers' homes (there was no adult night school) so that she could graduate with her high school class of 1925. She was the only one of her generation among family, friends, and acquaintances from Italy to earn a high school diploma.

At this point my father, now working as an auto mechanic in San Francisco, began calling on her at home or arranging to encounter her at the carefully chaperoned Italian family dances which were the only social outlet allowed her. His parents were appalled; they would be shamed—on both sides of the Atlantic—if he married into THAT family. My mother's father was determined not to lose his meal ticket. It was during a beating intended to underline this point that my mother, for the first time, turned and ran. My father took her to his parents. Two weeks later they were married.

Bryant's mother, Giuditta (Judy) Chiarle, in her high school graduation photo, 1925

My father was in love. My mother was in flight from a home that had wounded her for life. Self-supporting or not, for a girl of her class and background to leave home unmarried was inconceivable (as it still was, to a considerable degree, when I reached that age).

My father, at twenty-four, had had a bit of the free bachelor's life, money in his pocket, freedom to travel. He was known as a good dancer. He and some friends had even driven a Model T to Hollywood, hoping to "get into pictures." He once told me he had actually worked as an extra in a couple of films, and I always wondered if one day I'd see an old silent film and recognize him in a crowd (I never did). But that was his bachelor life. When he married my mother, he, like the best of working-class Italian men, put all that behind him and settled down. My mother later complained that when she was finally free of her father, ready to dance, my father refused to take her anywhere. As expected, to save money, they lived with his family, who looked down on her. She continued working full-time until my sister was born, ten months after the wedding. I was born three years later, in 1930, along with the Great Depression.

By then my parents had managed to save enough for a down payment on a house in San Francisco's Mission District, a working-class area of factories and little houses occupied by a mixture of European immigrants arriving in overlapping waves: Scandinavian, German, Irish, Slavic, French, Italian—some of them Jewish, no doubt, but no one cared enough to ask. Families moved from the Mission as they prospered and began to look down on their newer immigrant neighbors, like the Hispanics and "Okies" who were starting to arrive in the thirties. Asians and African Americans lived in districts bordering the Mission, and a sprinkling of them attended schools with us.

San Francisco, while never the liberal free-for-all portrayed in the media, had a long tradition of tolerance, if not true assimilation. The first Jewish, Irish, and Italian mayors (in that order) in the United States were mayors of San Francisco. There were no warring ethnic turfs like those in the East. In the Mission we children were not much aware of our ethnic differences. Yes, racism was alive and well. Yet, a Chinese American was a close friend of my older sister, and when she entered Mission High School in 1941, the student-body president was African American.

My father managed a gas station downtown, fixing cars on the side. He was there from early morning until after my bedtime, and I

With older sister, Rose, about 1933

rarely saw him, except on occasional Sunday afternoons when we drove south to visit *paesani* in the prune orchards. When I started school, my mother found full-time work as a bookkeeper (a double miracle for a woman and a mother during the Depression), earning money to buy my father his own business. I stayed with my grandparents after school until my mother came home from work. They lived on the next block. A haunting memory of my childhood is my unfounded fear of my paternal grandfather—gasping, coughing, furiously shaking his fist at God as his lung disease progressed and then finally killed him when I was fifteen.

My mother worked a full-time job, kept an immaculate house, planted and cultivated a garden that produced vegetables and flowers, cooked a huge meal for the extended family on most Sundays. She kept the books for my father's business (later, she managed their auto-parts shop), wrote all letters in two languages, kept household accounts, balanced bank statements, analyzed and explained contracts and deeds, filled out tax forms—as she had done for her barely literate parents. It was not unusual for immigrant daughters to become the scribes of the household. Probably it goes back to the peasant attitude that literary, schooling, brainwork was effeminate (mainly seen only in the village priest, not in real men who worked with their hands).

My sister and I shared a small bedroom we were not allowed to occupy during the day, lest we disturb the made-up beds which offered the only place to sit. Nor could we enter the dining room or living room, kept clean and ready, hardwood floors highly polished, for company events. (An exception was made when I started piano lessons and entered the living room each day to practice.) Fortunately, San Francisco climate allows outside play most of the year, and the sidewalks and parks were safe, auto traffic minimal. When we were indoors, we sat at the table in our tiny kitchen for eating, homework, reading, whatever. My mother's daily cleaning (after working in an office all day, shopping, and cooking dinner) was more thorough than what I now do weekly, and the weekly cleaning by all three of us was ferocious. In between cleanings, my sister and I lived on tiptoe, afraid to precipitate one of my mother's infuriated, long, crushing lectures.

I have heard similar stories from my contemporaries in immigrant families from Italy, France, Switzerland. Many Italian families in San Francisco covered their furniture and rugs in sheets (later plastic), built a room in the basement of their homes, furnished it with castoffs and a stove, cooked and ate and lived there, creeping upstairs only at night to sleep. Like my parents they had lived on the dirt floors of cramped, crumbling remains of medieval walled villages. As girls the mothers had worked as servants in the homes of middle-class people, polishing wooden floors, dusting fine furniture. Their dream was to own such a home, and their dream came true. But they could not enjoy their trophies of success. They remained servants to their own homes, and their families were, to some extent, intruders who might mar the prize.

My father was the opposite of my grandfathers. He was passive (as my dominated grandmothers had been), indifferent to all but his own simple comforts. Twelve hours a day he sat at his gas station, worrying about his slow Depression business, puttering with an occasional car repair, mostly listening to his radio (I never saw him read a book.) It never occurred to him to take over the management of his business and do the bookkeeping while he sat waiting for customers, or to help with any chore when he was at home. His indifference to my sister and me was benign, compared to the brutal men of the previous generation, and not unusual for his.

My father's passivity might have been a refusal to be a tyrant like his father, but it was also an abdication of responsibility. He remained absent, even when at home, letting my mother take on all responsibility, worry, blame, and self-blame. A neighbor's joking description was true: my mother was the brains of our family, the mother of all—an exhausted perfectionist whose chronic anger at her lost, wounded childhood seethed barely beneath the surface. Thus did my traumatized parents' psyches fit together in a pattern that commonly existed and still exists in various forms in all classes throughout America—the "nice guy" with the unaccountably irritated wife.

This is not an indictment of my parents' marriage, simply a partial description of it. Given their starting point, their accomplishments as a loving, unified, honorable team are extraordinary.

Astonishingly, my dreamily passive father took one stand that deeply influenced my life. He refused to allow his daughters to be baptized Catholic. (His rebellion probably came from a combination of two things: a tradition of northern Italian anticlericalism, and a childhood experience of being asked shocking questions during confession by an Irish-American priest. A case of verbal sexual abuse, we would call it today.) The Mission District was largely Catholic at the time (still is), but Italian Catholicism is rather loose. Grandmothers attended church regularly, mothers and children occasionally, men hardly at all. Prohibitions against contraception were ignored, as were others seen as unreasonable. Confession was a comfort, communion a right. Everyone was baptized, married, and buried by the church—what one did in between those events was no priest's business. To rebel against this social and private comfort was unnecessary—even risky, in case those uptight Irish priests turned out to be right about hell and damnation. Why deny these simple ceremonies to your children? My grandmother was dismayed, my mother uneasy.

The outward effect on my sister and me was minimal. No one shunned us. We were allowed to attend mass with friends when we wanted to, and except for a couple of zealous nuns who followed us about for a while, everyone forgot that we "had no religion." Inwardly, the effect was deeper. With no assigned place in a faith, I had no dogma to take for granted, nor to rebel against later. I believe I went through childhood and into adult life secretly thinking about that probably nonexistent God more than even my grandmother would have wanted me to.

School was an easygoing place in comparison to the strict rules at home. I had excellent teachers in elementary school, the traditional "old maids" who kept order and distance but knew much more about how children learn than we now give them credit for. Inspired by them I told my parents—after a few days in kindergarten—that I would become a teacher. My third-grade teacher, for instance, was a puppeteer who had constructed a theater in the back of her classroom. We made our own marionettes, memorized our roles in a fairy tale, performed for other classes—and, yes, progressed at the normal rate in reading, writing, arithmetic. It has become fashionable in recent years for students to blame the unkindness of some stereotypical "mean old teacher" for their sloppy reading and writing. The facts of my life don't include such stereotypes. My early love of school and my respect for the art of teaching are central to *Miss Giardino* and *Ella Price's Journal,* and an affectionately drawn old woman teacher turns up regularly in other books, like *The Garden of Eros* and *Confessions of Madame Psyche.*

The public library was my only source of books, which were unaffordably hardbound and, in any case, were found in stores that existed nowhere near the Mission District. I can't remember learning to read. I can't remember not reading. It seems as though my conscious life began with reading. It is a pity that I have never kept a journal of my omnivorous, constant reading—what I read, why I read it, how it affected me. Such a journal would make a truer biography of me than this recital of events. I know some people would call this dominance of books a pretty thin sort of life. Possibly, if compared to lives of adventurous exploration. But such lives are rare, and my impression is that in a society like ours most non-readers live a kind of slavery—like Samson, blinded and chained to a treadmill. As a child I read for fun, of course, but I never saw reading as an escape from "real" life. It was and is a heightening of life, a deeper experience than most people and events would, in themselves, reveal to me. The vital thing missing in those days was the completion of the act of reading: the casual but challenging conversation or passionate argument about it with a friend or older relative.

Living and growing through reading permeates *Ella Price's Journal, Prisoners, Miss Giardino.* A section of *Miss Giardino* describes Anna's discovery of my childhood library, which she describes as "this quiet hall, with its sacred smell of old book bindings and glue." That library was my church, and the authors of these wise or dull or beautiful or shocking or dry or exciting books were its saints. It may have occurred to me to wish I were one of them, but to seriously consider, let alone announce, such an ambition would have been blasphemy. I had never met an Author, nor anyone else who had met one. Clearly, such people were something more than mere mortals like me.

Entertainment, aside from frequent family gatherings, was the movies, three double features a week at the neighborhood movie house, plus a Saturday matinee for the children. No concerts, no theater, no literary or political discussions at the dinner table. No guests with as much education as my mother had, and, at the end of the day, she was usually too tired to read or to talk, unless we needed to be scolded. It has become politically incorrect to describe such a childhood as "culturally deprived," yet it was. The harsh alpine poverty of my ancestors cut them off from the rich artistic heritage of both Italy and France. Industrialism had long since stifled their folk culture but for a few songs and feasts. They had thrown off the superstition and oppression of their church, but also its ritual and music. In the prewar, working-class Mission District we were as distant economically and psychically from the larger life of San Francisco as our ancestors had been socially and geographically from the glories of Paris, Milan, or Rome.

Today the Mission District is less monolithically working class, a rich mixture of poor immigrants and bohemian artists, with bookstores all over the place. The movie house where we watched three double features a week has become the Brava Center, an alternative theater.

With best friend Shirley (left) and beloved sixth-grade teachers Miss McCullough and Miss Lyons, 1941

Yet I doubt there is much real contact between the artists who rent lofts in the old factory building where my grandmother worked and the daughters of poor Asian or Hispanic immigrants. I hope I'm wrong.

This heritage is the source of elements in several of my books. *Miss Giardino* uses my mother's childhood, making Anna's father a composite of my two grandfathers. Anna Giardino's mother is like my father's mother, a gentle creature. The nature of the Mission District and Mission High School as an example of a modern inner-city school are detailed in this book. The later Mission District also appears in *A Day in San Francisco,* in *Prisoners,* and in *Killing Wonder.* The agricultural valley south of San Francisco, before it became Silicon Valley, appears as it did in my childhood in *Confessions of Madame Psyche,* as do the lives of immigrant families, as does my parents' birthplace Balangero.

What readers call the feminism in my books also comes partly from this heritage. It is not the feminism of a previously contented middle-class wife and mother who suddenly realizes that she is overprotected, infantilized. Not Nora in Ibsen's *Doll House.* My feminism comes out of the lives of the majority of women on the planet, women who have always worked both inside and outside their homes, servants and factory workers and farm workers, supporting their children and sick or idle husbands, who were their superiors by law, a law that—to this day—rarely holds a man accountable for terrorizing or deserting his family. These women count themselves lucky if their men do neither. Ironically, when they hope for more, it is usually the hope that their daughters will become someone like Nora, the middle-class wife they've served and envied, blind to Nora's more comfortable form of slavery.

I didn't feel poor or deprived in the midst of the Great Depression. Poor? Compared to what? With a home, necessary clothing and food, and medical care when needed, I was infinitely advanced from my parents' hard childhood and more secure than many of my classmates. Frequent gatherings of the extended family for holidays and birthdays were exciting, opening up the forbidden spaces in our house. As a child I was oblivious to the subtle strains between my mother and her in-laws, though I did notice the all-consuming and exhausting, proud yet bitter role women played in creating and supporting this picture of order, security, and conviviality. Yet even this had its positive side: I unconsciously absorbed the conviction that, contrary to what many people, books, and movies told us, women were strong, capable,

Bryant's high school graduation photo, 1947

intelligent. I loved school. I had greater day-time freedom than today's children, to roam alone through safe city streets in what was, even then, considered the roughest part of town.

But then came adolescence, along with World War II, which seems like the right objective correlative for telling about that perilous stage of life. I'm always surprised when people tell me they actually enjoyed their adolescent years. Maybe only writers experience them as total hell. You've read some of those novels that portray the thinly disguised, agonized adolescence of the male author, who eventually triumphs, finding and proving himself in recognized accomplishments. My favorite of these is Butler's classic *The Way of All Flesh.* The slow, timid, embarrassing, stumbling, self-defeating, ridiculous missteps of Ernest (oh, so earnest) remind me of mine—despite my being of another country, class, sex, and century.

In recent years, psychologists have begun to concern themselves with the particular adolescent crisis of girls—the dramatic drop in achievement, the rise in eating disorders and other obsessions related to prescribed female roles. When I entered my teens, this destructive shift was considered normal and healthy, especially among working-class people, who expected girls to marry after high school. At Mission High School, with some shining exceptions (Isabel Becker, who shaped an unruly mob into a choir that performed sacred choruses and Gilbert and Sullivan operettas; Dean of Girls Lena O'Neil, who took a real and perceptive interest in girls, recognized my misery and gave me good advice I did not follow; fearsome Miss McGloin, whose rigorous senior English was the only class that came close to true college prep) most teachers seemed to have given up on us. I don't really blame them, as I tried to show in *Miss Giardino.* How could they (any more than today's teachers) counter the avalanche of mass media-driven peer pressure that drove students, especially girls, to self-inflicted brain death? My parents, with the best of intentions, issued a double message: I must study, go to college, and train for a profession whose function was "something to fall back on in case your husband gets sick." Commitment, meaning, lay solely in being a good wife and mother.

My response was the coward's despairing, dishonest, and doomed attempt to satisfy everyone. I tried to please my mother and my teachers with straight A report cards (all too easy to get at Mission High). I tried to make up for this to my peers by dancing a fair jitterbug and playing a mean boogie-woogie at the piano. At sixteen, I tried to please both my peers and my family by taking as my steady boyfriend an amiable Italian-American boy whose father had long known mine, indeed the only boy whose arrival at the door did not throw my mother into a panic. (Dean O'Neil met him and murmured, "A nice boy, but all wrong for you." I knew she was right.) And when my older sister dropped out of the University of California, married, and left the state, setting off a year of infuriated lectures by my mother about wasted money and betrayed sacrifices, I tried to "make it up" to her by staying at home and attending San Francisco State, which would cost my family nothing. Please note my strange, almost self-destructive timidity, my talent for cutting off any opportunity for escape—if only to a dormitory in Berkeley—from a world arranged to undermine the person I was becoming.

In 1947 I started San Francisco State College, at that time a conglomeration of classes meeting mostly in the shabby basements of crumbling churches on the edge of what had become a Black ghetto. But it was an exciting place of high hope, high morale, indifference to athletics and fraternities, a wide and friendly racial mix including mature family men on the GI Bill. Here were my kind of people, at last, people who read voraciously and argued passionately about what we were reading.

I was shocked at discovering how many junk books I had read, how many junk pieces my dear but inadequate piano teacher had taught me. Could I ever catch up? (Not in music. Name a really good performer-teacher of classical music who grew up in a home with no musicians, no record player, no concertgoers.) Children from immigrant and/or bookless homes like mine start school lacking that vital base of "culture" and usually lose ground steadily (ask any teacher). Those who resist the pressure to dumb-down, surpass their inner-city classmates, and make it to college often drop out in shock at discovering how far behind they still are. And those who stick it out to finish college spend their lives "catching up" and wondering if, when they least expect it, someone will see through them to their abysmal ignorance. My new piano teacher, Jean Leduc (part of a distinguished European musical family that settled briefly in San Francisco), saw the depth of my ignorance and was duly appalled. Yet, not too appalled to invite me into the "family" of students congregating at the austere mansion his wife's family occupied on the other side of town. He and I agreed that I'd never make much of a performer but had a feel for teaching. He and this family were the first people I'd ever known who lived a life devoted to art. From them I learned that most true artists work in relative obscurity. That the reward is in the art. And I learned how to really listen to music so that, even today, when my playing is desultory, listening to music is a great joy.

I was happy, energized, liberated at SF State. Besides being a place where reading and studying were okay, it was a haven of comparatively free discussion as Cold War McCarthyism settled over the land. It was, indeed, the only place where I heard that "anti-communism" might be more dangerous to my freedom than "communism, subversion, crazy ideas," the labels put on most questions and many facts, by the media and by the world I went home to after classes.

Needless to say, my family and I began to get on each other's nerves—especially during those frequent, now obligatory family gatherings. I remained totally acceptable only to that nice Italian boy, by now a construction worker and more a part of my family than I was. I was nineteen when we married. As Butler wrote about the doomed marriage of earnest Ernest in *The Way of All Flesh,* "I think the devil must have chuckled and made tolerably sure of his game this time."

I think the marriage would have ended in a year or two, my having made this acceptable exit from home, finished college, and become self-supporting, but in those pre-Pill days, contraceptive failure left me pregnant in the third month of my marriage. There was now absolutely no question of my doing anything other than staying in this marriage for the rest of my life. But I insisted I would stay in school too. Students and professors stared or dropped embarrassed eyes as I grew visibly pregnant—I was a first—then they shrugged and laughed. (One fellow music student commented on my senior recital: "You were fine at everything except taking your bows.") I had my baby in 1950 during finals week, typing my last term paper between contractions. My bachelor's degree came in the mail, and my family celebrated by giving me presents for the baby.

After a few months of passive wonder at my overwhelming surge of love for my son, I completed my teaching credentials (working my class schedule around hours here and there when my mother and mother-in-law could keep my son) and then had a baby girl. I began teaching high school music and English when she was a year old. All this seems fairly routine now, but in 1953 a teaching mother was more than frowned upon, her job not a necessity like my mother's and grandmother's, but a "career," a sure sign of her rejection of womanhood, motherhood. This view had been stated even more eloquently and more harshly by my psychology professors than by my family. I remained defiant, yet filled with guilt, fearing that no matter what I did, what I *was* would damage my children.

Some of these fears were muted by my luck in finding a saint (I use that term advisedly) named Dorothy Claus, who for the next eight years came on school days to care for my children. She gradually, voluntarily took over the cleaning as well, mothering us all with the patient, unconditional love we hear and read about but rarely see. The money I paid her seemed all to go to presents for her son and grandchildren, who lived about a two hours' drive into the Central Valley. I never spoke to those grandchildren until a few years ago, when she was dying, and they told me their father had drunk himself to death ("heart trouble" she had told me when he died). She had never revealed this pain she lived with during all the time I knew her. Was she ashamed? Did she blame herself? Perhaps if she could have told me, we would both have found some comfort in the fact that, contrary to the mother-bashing Freudianism that permeated all levels of society, here was a perfect mother who'd simply had bad luck.

As a teacher I was less traditional than my Miss Giardino, but just as dedicated to my work, demanding of my students, and critical of the institution. And, like her, I believe that teaching is one of the greatest, if least valued, of the arts. I made lifelong friends among my colleagues during my years (1953–1976) in the classroom, especially among those who were part of the new postwar wave of immigrants—intellectuals from Points East. Bits of these dear, abrasive, challenging friends appear in Dan, the professor in *Ella Price's Journal,* Arno, in *Miss Giardino,* Arthur, in *A Day in San Francisco.*

Yet, from 1950 to 1960, my frantic juggling as wife, mother, graduate student, teacher helped to blur the obvious truth: I had become my mother. I enjoyed my children more and cleaned my house less. Otherwise, I was, like her, the "overeducated," overworked juggler of jobs and responsibilities, the brains of the family whose children included her nice husband.

Then, at about age thirty, I cracked. The crack-up took the form of weariness, depression, dissatisfaction with teaching, and, even more, with my marriage. Inextricably tied up with these "neurotic" symptoms was another—I had begun to write. Like my reading, I can't seem to remember how or why I started. Something just welled up. And with that upwelling came the certainty that I could not go on writing if I went on in my life as it was. Shouts and whispers of two extended Italian-American families and my own conscience were drowned out by an inner voice that grabbed and shook me as it screamed—enraged, threatening. How can I describe it? Again, check out *The Way of All Flesh,* where young Ernest first senses the gap

Bryant's children, son John and daughter Lorri, about 1955

between his outer, conforming self and his buried, inner self, which is trying to tell him, "Obey me, your true self, and things will go tolerably well with you, but only listen to that outward and visible husk of yours . . . and I will rend you in pieces."

My divorce in 1963 inflicted pain on people I cared for, whose suffering I regret. I'm happy to say their suffering didn't last long. My regret—a diffuse sense of failure and guilt—remained (I am, after all, an Italian daughter). Like the ache of an old wound in damp weather, it comes back on me during periods of stress. I wrote *The Test* midway through a prolonged period of stress—from the death of my mother in 1981 to the death of my son in 1994. *The Test* opens this old wound, one of the broken places where, according to Hemingway, we get strong. Others must judge whether, in my case, he was right—whether the retarded, tortuous path toward writing that I have described adds dimension to my work, whether I, admittedly and now gratefully still my mother's daughter, have produced work enriched by our agonized affinity for one another. For, the more time passes, the more deeply I know that my struggle (much as it hurt and frightened my mother) was, in truth, only a continuation of her own.

During my 1960–63 "crack-up" I continued teaching and completed a master's degree in creative writing at SF State. Not that I thought writers were created in a classroom, but if I could get an M.A. and a college job, I might have more time to write. Also, when people asked me what I was doing, it was easier to tell them I was working on an M.A. than to say I had begun my real work, writing.

My creative writing professors were conscientious, good teachers mostly, and all men, as was usual in those days. But something strange happened. The introductory class was more than half women students. In the next semester, when I entered the short story writing class, I found I was the only woman in it. What had happened to the others? What unspoken message had been heeded? I was encouraged by Walter Van Tilburg Clark (who unfortunately left during my second year) and by James Schevill (who is still my friend) but not by anyone else. Throughout the sixties terms like "soap opera" and "effeminacy" were the kiss of death applied to female subjects. (Even as late as 1970, publishers were rejecting my first novel with comments like, "Of course, we all know women like Ella Price, but they are not of sufficient interest to sustain a novel.") My teachers at SF State meant no harm, but in order to find my voice I needed encouragement to explore stories they had unconsciously prejudged not worth telling.

On the other hand, no writer, male or female, should expect anything but resistance to a story that badly needs telling.

In 1964 I got my M.A. and a job teaching at a community college. I was the first woman to be hired in that English department since the one "token" installed twenty years before, when the college was founded.

The disapproval of my relatives was matched by that of most of my colleagues and students when I seemingly turned toward left-wing politics and people. I say "seemingly" because, although the fifties were over, it is amazing how little one needed to do in the sixties to be labeled "left-wing, socialist, communist, sub-versive," and so forth. I signed a few petitions, joined a few anti-Vietnam War demonstrations (described in *Ella Price's Journal*), made some friends among old socialists and liberals—and that was about it. My affection for liberal activists finds its way into many of my novels and plays, but real political involvement is beyond me. It requires sitting through meetings.

My first published novel, *Ella Price's Journal,* was inspired by the older women who began appearing in my classes, diffidently, alone, ignored. Yet another one was sitting in my office in 1966 (when the only "important" topics were hippies and the Vietnam War), weeping as she told me her college attendance was wrecking her marriage. I thought, here's a story no writer would bother to tell, no publisher would print, no reader would think important enough to read. But (and I think this attitude is the sign of a person who truly wants to write, as opposed to one who wants merely to "be a Writer") I decided it would be an interesting story to explore anyway. I wasn't consciously writing a "woman's" story or a "feminist" novel. I was just putting a new twist on the old *bildungsroman,* the novel of initiation and education. Instead of the traditional middle-class, adolescent male, the protagonist would be an older working-class mother—an entirely new phenomenon in higher education. I'm told that *Ella Price's Journal* remains the only novel with an older working-class protagonist who attends a two-year college.

Ella Price's Journal ends without showing how Ella copes after leaving her husband (as my real-life re-entry students so often did). I was still struggling to cope with similar problems when I began the first draft of the novel. People born after the sixties romanticize the period— flower children, exciting protests, bell-bottom pants. But everyone lives his own life; everyone lived her own sixties. My 1960s were those of a single mother trying to write and teach and support and live with two angry teenagers, with no moral support from either family or the general community, quite the opposite. Some of the complaints of Ella's friend Laura draw on my experience of isolated struggle in those pre-feminist days. I was listening to my inner self, but I wasn't out of the woods yet.

In 1967, at an especially low point, came an experience that was the definitive turning point—perhaps the turning point of my life.

But sometimes the big events of our lives are the ones we find hardest to describe.

For thirty-odd years I had trudged through T. S. Eliot's "Waste Land." Suddenly I stumbled into the world of his *Four Quartets,* where "the end of all our exploring / Will be to arrive where we started / And know the place for the first time." I'm referring to an experience of wholeness like what I tried to describe at the end of *The Kin of Ata Are Waiting for You* and midway through *Confessions of Madame Psyche.* This experience revealed to me that I did, after all, have even greater love and acceptance than what I had vainly craved from others. It revealed to me that we are all much more than the experiences I have related in this autobiography. It gave me energy and a little more backbone. It did not cure my faults. It did not stop me from making mistakes. It did not make me a better writer, but it gave me the confidence—that is, the relaxed humility— to work more determinedly at becoming one. It did not lift me above the trials of the hu-

man condition; it grounded me, and it helps me to live them through.

Better attempts at description and analysis than I can offer are contained in a vast literature I never heard about in college. Looking for guidance and understanding, I found this literature (of course!) waiting for me on library shelves. These old, classic writers provide a solid standard against which to measure current outpourings and New Age mush. For an introduction to them—from the *Dhammapada* to Evelyn Underhill—I recommend *The Perennial Philosophy* by Aldous Huxley, published in 1945, long before he experimented with LSD. It was on this literature, and not on my dreams (as some readers like to imagine), that I based my allegorical *The Kin of Ata.* It is this literature that I turn to, for a few minutes a day, no matter what else I am absorbed in reading. You don't have to be a writer or a mystic to find such time well spent.

Some good and wise people, like the man I married in 1968, are put off by talk of mys-

The author with friend and colleague Al Youn in an anti-Vietnam War demonstration, San Francisco, 1966

The author, with husband Robert Bryant, on top of the Duomo of Milan, Italy, 1985

tical experience. So am I. So please don't write to me about your own religious experience. And be careful where you turn for advice on how to hold on to your new consciousness. There are a lot of madmen, charlatans, and fools out there, eager to make you one of them. Here's the advice of a beginner, like you: read the old masters of the perennial philosophy; reinforce them with the rituals and meditative practices of one or more of the mainstream, liberalized religious traditions; express your new insights in your daily actions, not in words. And if you agree to speak up for a specific occasion, like this one, do it briefly and carefully, as I hope I have, admitting that I don't understand the meaning of what I'm telling.

Some readers have said that all my books are about education, about learning. Other, less friendly critics, have labeled one or another of my books "didactic," a pejorative term people use, along with "literature with a message," when they don't like the message, since all stories, in one way or another, directly or indirectly convey a message. I've written two books I would call both autobiographical and didactic, by which

I mean that I started writing with a particular message in mind (not solely an incident or a character, as I usually do).

One of these is *Writing a Novel,* an attempt to share mundane details of my writing process and to gently encourage timid beginners, like the one I was. In a way this book is a much deeper autobiography than anything I've written here. Deeper than the most intimate details of acts and relationships. The essential three parts of me—the reader, the teacher, the writer unite in this book to lead you as far as I can into the core of my life, the hours when I'm writing or thinking about writing.

The second is a protest novel. *A Day in San Francisco* exploded out of my concern when at thirty my gay son briefly embraced the Castro Gay Liberation style of 1980, refusing to listen to my dismayed objections. (His homosexuality was not at issue; he had made me his first confidant when he was sixteen.) I am writing, at length, a separate piece about this book, its inception and reception, to be published elsewhere. This piece will detail the impulse, the research, the publication, the attacks on me in the gay press, the silence of gays who agreed with me, the hate mail, the boycotts of my work—all of which continued throughout the years during which AIDS emerged and claimed hundreds of thousands, including my son, who had long since repudiated the lifestyle I criticized. *A Day in San Francisco* was recently cited in a critical study as "the first AIDS novel," but it is not. It was near completion when the first AIDS cases were reported. It began as an agonized mother's warning to my son. By the time the manuscript was done, he had come to agree with me, and the book became a challenge to the blindness of my kind of people, liberals gay and straight who, in 1980, kept silence or told lies or smiled and averted their eyes from a movement that was self-destructing, devouring its own, in the name of freedom. Nowadays, young gay men cast longing eyes back on what they imagine to have been a beautifully free and loving celebration of sexuality they missed. No doubt most will prefer the recent books that feed this romantic myth, rather than the fact-based, darker side presented in my novel.

In 1968 I settled with my husband in the south Berkeley flatlands, an area very like the working-class neighborhood where I grew up. It differs in having more trees, a darker racial mix, and an overabundance of bookish liberals. Some of our friends and neighbors are the idealists of the doomed commune in *Confessions of Madame Psyche.* More can be glimpsed in three of my books using Berkeley as a setting: *Prisoners, The Garden of Eros,* and *Killing Wonder,* and in my play, *The Panel.*

Prisoners was inspired by the experience of an activist friend I love and admire, the former publisher of *Freedom News,* one of the alternative monthlies that broke the news blackout of the sixties. The reviews and articles I wrote for *Freedom News* from 1969 to 1972 gave me the experience, exposure, courage, and confidence I needed in those years before my first novel was published.

Alternative media in the sixties, like *Freedom News,* probably influenced my decision in 1978 to self-publish my books. I have told the beginning of this complex story in "My Publisher/Myself," printed in several alternative magazines and later in the anthology *Myths to Lie By.* Since my self-publishing may have had an indirect effect on my writing (I have never written to "assignment" nor altered anything for commercial reasons, nor put off writing the next book while waiting for publication) I will try to summarize the story and update it.

It had taken four years and a raging feminist movement to get my first novel, *Ella Price's Journal,* published and five years for the second, *The Kin of Ata.* In 1978 my third novel, *Miss Giardino,* had been bouncing around New York publishers for six years. Two more manuscripts were near completion. At forty-eight I began to wonder if I'd live long enough to see them published. I'd broken the publishing barrier twice. What was wrong? Simply the realities of corporate publishing: I am a mid-list writer, no best seller; my books are all different, making it hard to target and build an audience; serious fiction sales lag behind non-fiction and self-help—it takes years, if ever, to get into print but only months to fall out of print again. And so on. Most writers live with these frustrations of commercial publishing. You read only about the exceptions whose huge advances and sales make the daily papers.

My aim in self-publishing was to get a body of work into print and keep it in print, selling well enough to stay in the black and provide some income, if not a living. This I managed to do. From 1978 to 1992 I published nine books. I also reprinted *Ella Price's Journal* when it went out of print. The disadvantages of self-publishing are the lack of corporate promotion-distribution and the refusal of most critics and scholars to read self-published books. The advantage is that my books remain in print, spreading by word-of-mouth. For a long time, this advantage seemed to outweigh the disadvantages.

But by 1990 self-publishing wasn't fun anymore. I want to devote the final years of my life solely to writing. Posthumous publication sounds fine. The only question for me is whether to keep existing books in print. This question was answered in 1995, when I was approached by The Feminist Press, publisher of new books and neglected classics by women. The Feminist Press keeps books in print "forever" (according to the founder) and markets mainly to college literature courses, where mid-list novels like mine are kept alive. The director proposed a takeover of many, possibly all of my books, beginning with *Miss Giardino* and *Ella Price's Journal* in 1997. Who publishes future ones, and when, doesn't much concern me now.

Since the mid-1980s I have worked mostly on historical fiction and plays. *Confessions of Madame Psyche* is a retelling of the myth of Eros and Psyche set in the Bay Area. This book recreates the Bay Area as it was during my childhood and earlier. It is a mystical picaresque novel, if such a term can apply—Psyche (soul) as an unschooled, poor, half-breed heroine making her spiritual journey toward the god of love among the marginal people on the underside of Bay Area history. The central figures of my four plays and of my most recent novel, *Anita, Anita,* are real women, possibly not very different in their struggles from my fictional protagonists.

Confessions of Madame Psyche also contains a sequence set in Italy, partly in my parents' hometown. Except for my parents' brief visit in 1960, contact with relatives in Balangero had been limited to my mother's Christmas cards and her infrequent letters, laboriously written in Italian. Shortly before her death in 1981, three cousins had surprised us by coming to

visit my parents for two weeks and urging us to come to Italy to visit them. I nodded and smiled, unable to speak a word of Italian, except to stammer, *"è la voce della mia nonna,"* stunned by the reincarnation of my grandmother's voice speaking the old Piemontese dialect out of her niece's mouth. (This niece makes a cameo appearance as Garibaldi's mother in *Anita, Anita.*)

In 1985 I audited a course in beginning Italian at the university, reviving more of the language than I knew I possessed, enough for simple communication. My husband and I went to Italy for a month, ten days of which we spent in Balangero.

No one lived on dirt floors anymore; the miserable cubicles in the old walled city that wraps around the big church had been remodeled into tiny jewel-like apartments. A cousin of my mother's lived in one of these. Thirty of my father's cousins lived outside the old town, in larger, newer houses. Three of the young cousins, university students fluent in

Bryant with cousins in Balangero, Italy, 1989. "The tallest man pictured here is my son John" (d. 1994).

Robert and Dorothy Bryant on Sentinel Dome, Yosemite National Park, 1996

English, were a great help when my limited Italian faltered.

These descendants of my paternal grandmother's seven siblings joyfully greeted us—clearly, we are forever part of this family, no matter what distance might separate us. My son and daughter went to them next, and were similarly embraced. Young cousins have visited our home, enjoying jazz clubs and shopping with my daughter and step-daughter, sightseeing and long talks with my husband and me. They read my books. I have taken my mother's place as correspondent in Italian. The ties we have formed are closer than anything my grandmother gave up hoping for, because we are able to exchange visits and phone calls and faxes with a frequency impossible until recently.

G. B. Shaw said all autobiographies are lies, but I think you'll agree with me that no one would bother to invent such excruciatingly ordinary events. Still, this is my "1996 version" of my life. To my own surprise, it emphasizes class, gender, and especially ethnic issues which, while I was living them, didn't seem worthy of much attention. Do I see dominant influences and experiences more clearly now? Or am I only following political trends of the nineties, like "ethnic identity," which has been promoted into confusion, if not fantasy. A few years from now I might emphasize something else or interpret some events quite differently. By then, perhaps, the "genetic" view will be trendy, and I will tell this story in terms of the newly discovered gene for Writing, sub-type B—bookish timidity and over-conscientious anxiety, often opposed by coexisting genes for messy rebellion, stiff-necked pride, and didactic generalization.

Finally, some of the people I've mentioned here might give a different version of some incidents, or describe others I've forgotten. If I've left big holes in this story, you can, according to Henry James, fill them in yourself, since "the artist is present in every page of every book from which he sought so assiduously to eliminate himself." That means you might learn more about me if you stick to reading my fiction, even more than I know.

But what you learn about my life doesn't really matter. What matters in reading fiction is what you learn about your own.

BIBLIOGRAPHY

Novels:

The Comforter, privately printed, 1971, published as *The Kin of Ata Are Waiting for You,* Random House, 1976.

Ella Price's Journal, Lippincott, 1972.

Miss Giardino, Ata Books, 1978.

The Garden of Eros, Ata Books, 1979.

Prisoners, Ata Books, 1980.

Killing Wonder, Ata Books, 1981.

A Day in San Francisco, Ata Books, 1983.

Confessions of Madame Psyche, Ata Books, 1986.

The Test, Ata Books, 1991.

Anita, Anita, Ata Books, 1993.

Collection:

Myths to Lie By—Short Fiction and Essays, Ata Books, 1984.

Contributor:

The Dream Book: Writing by Italian American Women, edited by Helen Barolini, Schocken, 1985.

Unholy Alliances, edited by Louise Rafkin, Cleis Press, 1988.

The New Family, edited by Scott Walker, Graywolf Annual 8, 1991.

The Voices We Carry: Recent Italian/American Women's Fiction, edited by Mary Jo Bona, Guernica, 1994.

Side Show: Contemporary Fiction, edited by Shelley Anderson, Marjorie K. Jacobs and Kathe Stolz, Somersault Press, 1993.

Where Coyotes Howl and the Wind Blows Free, edited by G. and A. Haslam, University of Nevada Press, 1995.

Nonfiction:

Writing a Novel, Ata Books, 1979.

Plays:

Dear Master, first produced in Berkeley, California, at Aurora Theatre, 1991.

Tea with Mrs. Hardy, first produced in Lafayette, California, at Dramateurs, 1992.

The Panel, first produced in Berkeley, California, at Aurora Theatre, 1996.

Other:

Author of short stories in numerous periodicals, including *Berkeley Monthly, Berkeley Poets Cooperative, Four Quarters,* and *San Francisco Focus;* essays and criticism in *Freedom News, Frontiers, The Nation, Plexus, San Francisco Bay Guardian, San Francisco Chronicle, San Francisco Examiner,* and *San Francisco Review of Books.*

Victor di Suvero

1927-

Victor di Suvero on the Accademia Bridge in Venice, with "my father's family palazzo in the immediate background," 1989

Going to and Arriving in America (1941)

At that moment time changed. My father had been alerted that Thursday afternoon that orders had come to ship us back to Italy and to turn the three smaller children over to the Japanese. We had three days to pack up and get out, out of our lives into new ones if we could. I was thirteen years old, curious, trying very hard to be grown up, and quite excited when my parents had asked me whether I would like to finish school in the United States. That's how they broke the news that our life in the Italian Concession, in Tientsin in China, was over and that we would have a new life in America.

My parents had been expecting something of the sort for some time. The racial laws had been passed in 1938. No Jews were to be allowed to hold any government position from then on. A lot of other provisions having to do with property, pensions, and passports were included. The laws, however, were not enforced as rigorously as one could have thought, and my father's position as secretary of the Italian Concession had not been attacked until May of 1940 when Italy's "stab in the back" of France triggered his decision not to participate any longer in the Fascist rejection of the French,

English, and American friends and the civilized world.

In June they had started to pave the way with the help of contacts at the Vatican in Rome and friends like Mr. and Mrs. Kenneth Yearns in the U.S. State Department. This made it possible for visas to be obtained in one day and for black-market passage on the S.S. *President Cleveland* leaving Shanghai for San Francisco to be negotiated. There was a rush of packing, and on Sunday afternoon six of us crowded into the big official sedan as if we had been going out to the country club; Da Ning, our chauffeur, drove us down to the docks where we boarded the *Jardine Star,* a coastal freighter, and headed down the Pei Ho River to Taku and then down the coast to Shanghai.

With good fortune still smiling we were met by my mother's uncle, Commander Gennaro Pagano di Melito, affectionately known as "Il Pirata" for his many adventures and his outlaw view of the world, who had been appointed Italian consul general in Shanghai. He took us in and sheltered us until the *President Cleveland* was due to sail in a few days. Later, in 1943 when Mussolini abandoned Rome and fled north, he opted for the king, was put under house arrest and was charged with many political crimes, including that of having sheltered us, and ended up being killed on the Tientsin Railroad Station platform as he was being taken up to the concentration camp that had been built to hold foreigners in the Western Hills, west of Peking.

Going aboard the *President Cleveland* was our entry into America. The ship flew the American flag, and my parents heaved that huge sigh of relief that comes when one realizes that an immense danger has passed one by. I was not fully aware of all that meant at the time, and the festivities surrounding the departure with blaring band music, confetti, and all that electricity in the air caught us all up in a promise of delights.

After stopping in Yokohama and Honolulu the ship arrived on the morning of February 27, 1941, outside the Golden Gate, where the pilot came aboard to bring us in to Pier 42 in San Francisco. Father Seeliger, father provincial of the Jesuit Province of California, had come to meet us, and Father Flaherty, representing the archbishop of San Francisco, also came and helped us through the immigration and customs procedures. My mother's family

in Rome had really helped, and there we were, safe, installed at the Colonial Hotel on Bush Street, and time did change.

New Beginnings and the War (1941–1943)

It was before the war, before Pearl Harbor, before news of the Holocaust had filtered out. We learned quickly, almost as if we were relearning something we had forgotten, each in our own way. Mami learned how to cook; Papa learned how to look for a job; I learned to go to school in a new way, with no papers, nothing to prove I had ever been anywhere let alone matriculated for Cambridge the year before. St. Ignatius High School, then San Francisco Junior College, a newspaper route, the *Call-Bulletin,* the same Hearst paper that had our picture on the front page when we arrived, and then the president on the radio with "the day that will live in infamy."

Papa did not get the job at Kaiser Shipyards that had been offered to him because we were, suddenly, "enemy aliens" and that was not very good, but he did get a job as a shipfitter at Marinship in Sausalito. The first manual labor in his life, and he shrank a full two inches that first year.

Mami became a translator for the Immigration and Naturalization Service, and I went on to the University of California at Berkeley while my sister and brothers were still at the Madams of the Sacred Heart on Broadway.

I had joined the California State Guard, and instead of doing anything useful I found myself with evenings of marching down at the Armory on Mission Street with a few old men and a few kids, learning how to present arms with a World War I Springfield. None of that made much sense, and I soon tired of answering questions about "Japs" because I was the only one who had even seen "them." Wanting to do something *real* about the *real war* I went down to Pier 1½ near the Ferry Building and signed on as an ordinary seaman aboard the S.S. *Invader,* an old three-masted schooner run by the Sailors' Union of the Pacific as a school ship, that bore no relationship whatsoever to the work we would be doing or the life we would be living out at sea on the merchant ships we would be sailing on to "support the war effort." I had grown up overnight, I thought,

(Clockwise from top left) Mary Louise, Victor, Henry, and Marco Polo upon their arrival in America, from the San Francisco Call-Bulletin, *1941*

with echoes of Jack London bouncing around in my head, with the fear of running into a Captain Ahab, and with that poem of Masefield's I had learned about wanting "a tall ship and a star to steer her by" that Mami asked me to say again to her on her deathbed forty years later.

Cigarette hanging out of the corner of my mouth, with my new pea coat and my sea bag on my shoulder, I had suddenly become "a sailor" and not a student any longer. Papa had given me Kropotkin to read. I knew Conrad and Gauguin's Noa Noa and that's where I was headed, dangerous grown-up sexy waters, and I would be helping the country that had saved our lives. Even though I was not old enough to be in the navy and never mind a commission, I was with the workers; I had my probationary union card and my seaman's papers in my pocket, and look at what all my father's gold braid had brought us. John Dos Passos had told it like it was, and I would learn my own way and so much for that. The

Celestial was my first ship, a new C-2 on its way to the Russell Islands just north of Guadalcanal where there had been one hell of a battle we heard—and only later understood how much of a turning point it had been. But we did understand quickly that an ordinary seaman's life on the 4-to-12 watch was not romantic and not amusing but a bag full of running and fetching and scraping and painting even though the ship was brand new and I had more to learn than I had ever imagined, but I did get to stand my wheel watches and my turns as lookout with the safety of the ship and the crew in my own hands and in my eyes even though it was only for an hour and twenty minutes at a time.

I learned about how one deals with the bos'n, with the mates, with strangers who had become closer than anyone I had grown up with. How to deal with the officers and how and when to keep my mouth shut, and those lessons stayed with me when the calculus and properties of matter courses of the previous semester had flown out of my head never to return. I began to see the stars instead. I found comfort with the Seven Sisters and the Pleiades became my friends. I saw the Big Dipper sink over one horizon and the Southern Cross come up from another. I got dumped into Neptune's scum bag and ran a gauntlet with the other tyros when we crossed the equator, learned what loneliness could be even when crowded day and night by other bodies, other men.

And after having pulled into the roads off North Island we unloaded part of our cargo, including the four B-25 de-winged fuselages on deck, into the lighters and LSTs that had pulled alongside and then went on to Noumea where we got ashore for one night and then headed back to San Francisco in a hurry. No convoy— just us with no lights at night, not even the running lights, only the stars and the new moon that sliced its way across the sky from where we were going to where we had been.

More War and Then Peace (1944–1947)

The next trip was a long one, aboard the S.S. *Mary Walker,* a liberty ship named after a woman who had been a surgeon in the Civil War, brave, strange, and by just being aboard a ship named after her I began to dig into Walt Whitman's *Leaves of Grass.* Had they known each other? All these questions while we sailed from San Francisco and headed down to New Guinea. Port Moresby, Finschafen, Lae, Hollandia, all names that spelled out who had been in charge of that particular fraction of the island before this war, the British, the Germans, the Dutch, and now the Americans with the incredible quantity of supplies all painted that gray green that was the color of jungle shadows.

There was no news, just that things were going our way, no TV then, no CNN to let us know what had happened the night before. We had heard that inland there were still head-hunters, and the Papuans who came aboard to work the cargo were neat, efficient, eager for cigarettes, smiling, and not talkative enough to share anything at all beyond the time and the work.

The invasion fleet's staging area for the landings at Leyte Gulf was Hollandia, and we were part of that, in that great bay, waiting, but suddenly orders came and we headed for Biak, an island west up the coast that had just been taken by our marines. We picked up a regiment, and as the men came aboard I saw my first lei of ears. It was not a happy bunch, but they were glad to be aboard. They had their own mess kitchen on deck and stayed very much to themselves. They had been through something rough, and we were just civilians, and there was nothing we could talk about together. So, back to Hollandia and then north immediately.

We had a battalion aboard in holds 2 and 3. One of the duties I drew was to go through the holds with a flashlight on fire watch. The bunks were stacked four high, and there wasn't much air even though we had stretched tar-paulins to catch the breeze and shunt it down. One night in the dark with groaning ship noises and mutterings in the heavy air I heard a flute playing. I followed its sound and asked what it was, so clean, so clear I've never forgotten it. "On Hearing the First Cuckoo of Spring" was what he told me.

When we got to Leyte the landings and the main engagements were taking place, but we were on general alarm for three days run-ning, and the Zeros and the Japanese fighter bombers were consistent in their stabs at all of us anchored as we were in a huge arc that seemed to enclose the bay. Our passengers had

landed and we stood down finally, about mid-night on the third day, and then at dawn the general alarm again, after about four hours of sleep. We stumbled on deck looking up, and we heard a cheer in the cool morning quiet, almost as if we had been in a movie, the last stars in a corner of the sky, the striped cirrus catching the pink light. And the cheers went up again across the water—yes—the planes were there all right—only this time they were ours—no mistaking the twin fuselages of the P-38s. And we shouted and banged empty ammuni-tion canisters and pounded on the booms and were as relieved as anyone can imagine.

After Leyte it was back to Hollandia, then back up to the Philippines for the landings at Lingayen Gulf, then home again and a month ashore. I was all of seventeen, but hanging out with all the older men I had sailed with gave me all the assurance I needed to hang out in the bars of North Beach when I finally got back, as if I belonged. One Thursday night at the Iron Pot on Montgomery Street I stopped in when Henri Lenoir was in the middle of running a raffle, usually a drawing or a paint-ing, but this night it was a book that was the prize. It was the only raffle I have ever won. The book was *The Phoenix and the Tortoise* by Kenneth Rexroth, who was there with his wide-

Victor in Shanghai, with the Victory Ship S.S. Ferdinand Silcox *in the background, 1946*

brimmed Stetson and his black cape and walking stick, and with him was James Laughlin, the awesome, eastern publisher of New Directions. When Kenneth asked me, as he signed his book for me, what I did, something caught in my throat and I stammered that I was a poet. He looked at me with a glint in his eye as he asked me, "Are you sure you want to be one? It certainly does not pay," and we went on from there and became friends.

By then my parents had bought a house out on Forty-third Avenue; my sister and brothers were all at Lincoln High School on Taraval Street and I went back out to sea until the war was over in 1945. I still stayed out though I had a chance to go back to China and shipped out on the S.S. *Ferdinand Silcox*. I did have more than a lot of curiosity about the way things had changed, and I thought it an absolute opportunity.

Seeing Shanghai, Tsingtao, Shanhaikwan, Peitaiho, and Tientsin, no longer as a child but as a young man, no longer one of the take-it-for-granted privileged bunch but as an American working stiff made me begin to realize how many realities there are.

And then I found myself in the army hospital in Shanghai not knowing how I had gotten there, with a bad case of infectious hepatitis—thirty days of IV—my weight down to ninety-three pounds—before I was shipped back to San Francisco to the Public Health Hospital there at Fourteenth and Lake to be discharged and let out to go to Inverness, where my parents had been through the war, to recover on my own and to begin to write seriously, I thought.

After the escape from China and the fates that awaited us had my parents not been so thoughtful, so anticipatory, and so effective—after settling into a life that had none of the safety nets and comforts our old one had—after the confrontations of the workplace for my father, for my mother, and for myself—after the tensions of the war felt perhaps more keenly by us than by our neighbors because of the way the Germans and the Japanese had truly become the enemy—and after the relief and exhilaration of both VE- and VJ-days—it seemed appropriate to draw that huge breath that said that we were finally safe and grateful in a new land—and we did—without ever looking back. I found it strange that though my parents had many friends there were none among them that were of Italian origin. I would ask and then be dismissed with a wave of the hand while being told, "It's really that they've made their lives, and it's up to us to make ours." It was only later, much later, that it became quite clear that so many of the Italian Americans in North Beach had strong sympathies for Il Duce, and my parents just preferred to build their new lives without using any old bricks and mortar. This attitude did not mean to cut off old friends and some of the relatives who were still in Italy, but it did teach me to understand why many of the Scandinavian immigrants who settled in the northern plains were adamant about only speaking English with their children.

"We were given eyes in the front of our heads," my father would say, "so that we can look ahead, not back." And so we continued to build our lives from scratch, de novo, without the sustenance and support that other immigrants often had, perhaps a reason for our all having evolved as loners of one kind or another, and so we continued the process of assimilation and Americanization.

Beginning Once Again (1948–1955)

In Seattle, after one of the trips that had brought me coastwise up north before that last trip to China, I had been given Dylan Thomas's *The World I Breathe*. It became an epiphany, a true epiphany for me in the Joycean sense; it opened language in a way that made Swinburne and Eliot and Pound all disappear in a tumble. It made Blake move into today, and I began to sense how it might be to really touch that chord and make that music happen for its own sake. I still have that copy, and I turn its pages when I need to be reminded how it was that afternoon when I opened it for the first time. And I felt admitted to the confraternity because it had been published by New Directions and because I had met Laughlin the year before with Rexroth. I had no way of knowing that I would then be fortunate and would meet Thomas himself at Ruth Witt Diamant's in 1953 after a reading at San Francisco State College just before he left that last time for New York to die—after he had that bet with a stranger that made him drink twenty straight shots at a bar down on University Place before staggering out into the street to fall down and hit his head on the curb, which was the reason and prelude to his last trip down to the hospital to die with unfinished scraps of poems in his hand.

And the next night at Kenneth Rexroth's with Philip Lamantia, there were just the three of us when the phone rang and it was a reporter from the *San Francisco Chronicle* wanting to know if Mr. Rexroth had anything to say about Dylan Thomas's dying. "Why, the greatest poet writing in the English language . . . under forty!" Kenneth said, and we sat down to say how great he had been and what a compulsive drunk and not many like him and if only, if only. . . . And that's where I began to sense that if one did not understand anything at all in time it could easily disappear and that I had missed the chance of catching his spirit on the wing, and that was one of the contacts made with that other world, the one I felt was really mine.

In that interval, between Inverness and the death of Dylan Thomas, I went back to Berkeley, shifted my major to political science, became the editor of the *Occident* (the university's literary magazine), won the Ina Coolbrith Prize for poetry before graduating, graduated, and came to know Robert Duncan and Jess and Bill Everson and Mary Fabilli and Jack Spicer. I took courses from Mark Schorer and Josephine Miles, fell in love with and married Jeanne Hunneyman, with whom I worked a summer as a forest fire lookout on the Hat Creek district of the Shasta National Forest while supervising a gang of San Quentin trustees, fighting fires with them, then back to Sausalito where I had bought the Contemporary Gallery, giving Wayne Thiebaud his first show. Jeanne and I found it had been a mistake to begin with, so we split, going each our separate ways with my going back to sea. I sailed on deck again, now on Standard Oil tankers out of Richmond up the coast to Alaska and Hawaii until I pulled myself together once again. I moved to San Francisco on Glover Street on Russian Hill to begin another time of looking for a way of being that would tie the making of a living with the living of a life.

And so it began. Knowing I could not spend my life at sea, I found myself helping friends with some painting, inside, outside their houses with the know-how I had picked up at sea. Painting led to choosing colors, making suggestions, changing this verandah into a room, and suddenly turning myself into a designer.

With no training except that which my eyes had given me while growing up, I found clients and worked out of the General Paint and W. P. Fuller stores in San Francisco until I started my own shop and called it Design & Color Service. This turned into a business that established design criteria for tract builders in San Francisco and on the peninsula. Model homes and subdivisions, Conway & Culligan, and Joe Eichler—all part of the post-war boom and expansion in the Bay Area. Learning as I went along, and at the same time continuing to write.

The Bay Area had become the place at the end of the continent where everyone came. Refugees from Europe came to New York; refugees from America came to San Francisco. Marin County was bucolic and unspoiled. The sheds and outbuildings of the former shipyard in Sausalito had become a haven for artists looking for studios and living space in an unstructured environment. Jean Varda, teacher, collagist, muralist, raconteur, and bon vivant, had moved up from Monterey to take over the wreck of the S.S. *Vallejo*, a turn-of-the-century ferry boat that had been declared surplus by the navy. He established a salon along with his studio, attracting friends from all over the world, and they came because he was the Prince of Color and because conversations and friendships and futures and possibilities all danced around him. And he made people believe that certain values could not and would not be marketed by IBM and the establishment, and, once he became a naturalized citizen, he declared that as an American he was entitled to pursue happiness but that as an artist he had always been entitled to achieve it.

Varda's magic worked because, once under his spell, all became possible. A war surplus lifeboat bought for $75 was suddenly transformed into a brightly colored hull with magical eyes in its prow and an orange, yellow, and red lateen sail that made its very own statement among the bright white sails of all the other boats on the Bay and Saturday and Sunday sails with Matta and June Deguan, with Chester Arthur and Frances Ney all becoming a tapestry of possibilities.

Pageants were invented and music came out of the air. Roger Somers and his alto sax danced through evenings filled with smoke and laughter. Ancient Greece and the Renaissance all came to life at Varda's court.

Victor (second from right, seated) and staff of The Occident
at the University of California at Berkeley, 1949

Trying my hand in one form and then another, I wrote a two-act play based on the Icarus myth, which was performed at the Marin Art and Garden Center in February of 1951. George Hitchcock played Icarus and Mel Fowler did the costumes. All friends, all involved in the Sausalito–North Beach axis, and all interested in finding ways to say that we were alive and well.

I met Jack Stauffacher, master printer, along with his brother Frank, visionary of the film world, as well as James Broughton, whose wit and wisdom danced about North Beach and Sausalito like St. Elmo's fire. They were just three of the crowd that ran into the place that shaped itself into the Bohemian predecessor to the Beat scene to come. Jack Stauffacher's Greenwood Press had been doing small editions of interesting work, and when Jack and I found time to get together he helped to shape some of the work I had done and published my first book, *Salt and the Heart's Horizons,* in 1952.

Peter Martin also had come west from New York. The son of Carlo Tresca, assassinated by the Communists on the sidewalk in Greenwich Village, Peter walked with a wry sense of immediacy into the scene. He liked it and after a few months of looking around established the City Lights Pocket Book Shop, the first paperback bookstore in America, in North Beach. He later brought Lawrence Ferlinghetti into it as a partner and then sold his interest in it to him. The pot was boiling.

Kenneth Rexroth's apartment over Jack's Record Cellar at Scott and Page was the third point of the Sausalito–North Beach triangle. Rexroth loved jazz and had lived in Italy. His "saloon of a salon" was where everyone went in the city. Phil Whalen, later to become a Zen Buddhist monk, was there and Bill Everson, who later became Brother Antonnius in the Dominican order, also was there. Different sides of the same coin since everyone was looking for the same value, the same spiritual aspect of the world, and then Ginsberg arrived from New York via Mexico and Los Angeles and I first met him there. He had just enrolled at UC and had found a room at the Hotel Marconi in North Beach. The discussions raced around the Hasidim and the Catholic Worker Movement, opera as yellow journalism with music, how America had been betrayed by big business, and how one could not get a decent job without giving up one's soul. *The Ark,* our overt and dedicated anarchist publication, was a magazine that became the precursor of so much of what ended up being called the Beat. It was part of the world photographed by Jerry Stoll, by Gene Anthony, and filmed by Jordan Belson and Frank Stauffacher.

All this flew around in my head while I talked to clients, established a business, maintained a weekly visit schedule with my parents and their lives, and worked on finding out who I was and what I was about in the poetry I still wrote. I did not and could not buy into the total abandon that fueled Kerouac, McClure, and Ginsberg, the one that jettisoned all the prior relations and commitments that we all had, in the same way that Michael Bowen did, and I put all those feelings into a long poem, "Ticket to Ride," that I read at the Six Gallery on Fillmore Street with Peter Farakis, a good friend and a wonderful sculptor who backed me up with a brilliant performance on bongos that night. The reading at the converted commercial garage turned into a gallery came a week after Ginsberg had lit up the sky with *HOWL.* Jim Spencer and Ronnie Bladen and I did have our audience but found ourselves as "also rans" given the impact of the previous readings, proving again that timing has to do with other things than human plans.

Jerry Stoll's photos of the time still show the cast of Beat characters that invaded North Beach from the East without beards. There is a picture of Bob Coulon (Kerouac's Rob Donnelly), Neal Cassady, Allen Ginsberg, Robert La Vigne, and Lawrence Ferlinghetti in front of City Lights in 1955 without a single beard between them, but it was not long after that time that face hair became an advertisement for those who had rejected the prevailing idiom of that time in America and who realized they had come to that fork in the road and chose to take the less traveled one that eventually led to the Summer of Love, to the protests against the war in Vietnam, to the trial of the Chicago Seven, and to the heritage of confrontation we still live with today.

Lenore Kandel also appeared on the scene at the time, and—like the immortal Soraya shin-

ing her open sexuality in beautiful poems that used all "those" words as openly as we say "love" and say "music" and say "together"—she began to weave the net that would end up catching all the feelings that all of us were inventing then.

In my own life, in my own way, I tried to keep a foot in each of the worlds I lived in. I had opened an office on Montgomery Street and was doing my business thing while taking long weekends to sail with Varda or to go down the coast to discover Cannery Row in Monterey and the magic of the Coast Range all the way to Big Sur, with its echoes of Tamar and Cawdor. Robinson Jeffers country with its cliffs and sea spray and its hawks—all new to me. And then one day—when an old family friend of my mother's, Valentino Bompiani, the Italian publisher, showed up in San Francisco with one of his authors, Alberto Moravia, I was asked whether I knew Henry Miller because Moravia wanted to meet him. I had only met Miller once, on a sail with Varda and Anaïs Nin, but a telephone call paved the way and the next day took us down the coast to Partington Ridge overlooking Nepenthe and the Pacific Ocean where Miller lived. To introduce the two strongest writers of their own genre to each other and to listen to their talking about, not sex, not politics, not the social issues nor their craft, but about getting older and grandchildren growing up served as a parable for me as the sun set out in an orange sky over the Pacific—and then taking Moravia and the group away from the light, heading inland for a late dinner with Niven Busch at Tres Pinos before getting back to San Francisco early the next morning—all of that waiting to be described the next day as "a typical day in the life of a writer in California" by Bompiani.

New Life (1955-1977)

Then, on the occasion of the opening of a show of Varda's collages in Los Angeles, a festive caravan was organized to bring a lot of us to celebrate the event in the Southland. There were parties in Los Angeles, in Beverly Hills, and in Malibu, and there I met Henrietta Ledebur and fell in love, seriously for the first time, all else having been prologue. Not long after I managed to convince her to move to San Francisco with her then six-year-old son Marius and to take a flat on Telegraph Hill.

Henrietta, Romana, Alexander, and Victor, Venice, 1967

Four years later we were married at Jo and Walter Landor's place in Kenwood in the Valley of the Moon in an environment that had been designed and built by Varda full of color and light. Varda had built a throne for the bride, and flowers and friends and food all joined in an event typifying the joy and openness in the air at the time. Joel Andrews composed a piece, "Variations on Come Ye Sons of Art by Purcell," that he played on his harp with Roger Somers accompanying him on sax and drums. The then-Reverend Pierre Delattre, the Episcopal minister who had started the Bread and Wine Mission to minister to the Beats in North Beach, officiated and a new life really began for me, moving off Russian Hill into a serious "married" flat in Cow Hollow with a magnificent view of the Bay and the Golden Gate Bridge to the north.

Married, with a business on Montgomery Street in San Francisco that led from real es-

tate sales and marketing to real estate development and financing, while maintaining my curiosity and contacts I came to know Alan Watts, great teacher and carrier of Zen from the western shore of the Pacific to the coast of California and to the Western World. Alan had taken over the landward half of the S.S. *Vallejo* when Onslow-Ford had stopped using it as a studio. Alan's presence, both wise and mischievous at the same time, began to color and enhance the lives of all those around him. Serious discussions about aesthetics, art, and its practitioners would dissolve in gales of laughter evoked by an anecdote or a metaphor invoked by Alan or Varda. The creative fervor was fueled by the laughter, and George Hitchcock and I collaborated on more than one masque presented in honor of Varda and the court he and Alan had gathered.

Our daughter Romana was born in 1963, and Alexander our son was born in 1965 when we bought a house in Sausalito with a wonderful view of the Bay and of San Francisco, and when we moved to Marin County, our lives took an almost suburban coloring with less and less time spent in San Francisco where the Beats were coming into their own. Huncke and Kerouac had started using "Beat" as the label for what was in the air, and Herb Caen coined "Beatnik" after that. Ginsberg and Corso and McClure along with Kerouac had joined with all the "invaders" to make their own scene, which is now remembered in many versions. Bill Graham, who had started out as a waiter after the war in New York, having survived the Holocaust at Bergen Belsen, also came to San Francisco and worked for a while at Enrico Banducci's Hungry I before becoming the impresario of the 1960s, the inventor of the Fillmore, sponsor of some of the greatest rock bands and entertainers of the period, and a legend even before his fiery and untimely death in a helicopter crash in the early 1990s as he and his lady Melissa Gold were charred when the pilot took their craft into the power lines above the Concord Pavilion one stormy night. Bill's driving energy managed to infuse the musicians and the music, making money happen for the outcasts, the ones not of the society but its exotics and its howlers. He presented Michael McClure's first major play, *The Beard*—about Billy the Kid and Jean Harlow in heaven—to standing ovations. Graham's sense of timing and of the heartbeat of the time was impeccable. On the fringes of all this with friends and associates in the straight world, the world of bankers and brokers, I had another life running at the same time, the life of Sausalito and sitting with Alan on Saturday afternoons, sailing with Varda on Sundays, and learning to be a daddy in between poems and parties.

Real estate, as a business, had all the negative connotations that were rife at the time. Suede shoes and fast bucks were labels for one side of the equation. But clear challenges and opportunities did present themselves. Many could be turned into solutions that were interesting in terms of design and functional criteria as well as financial ones. Learning to take disparate elements and fuse them into a reality that served people was analogous to the way I had learned to build a poem. I found myself working with people who had their own valid visions of post-war America: Joseph Eichler, builder of houses beautifully designed by Anshen and Allen, incorporating the aesthetic that had shaped Le Corbusier and the Bauhaus and then translated into visions of affordable order that helped people live well; Jim San Jule, labor activist and left-wing philosopher who found himself by teaming up with Eichler before going to Washington to head up a section of the National Association of Home Builders; Rollin Meyer, developer of the Carolands down the peninsula, who built the upscale houses manifesting the post-war dreams for those who could afford them; and John Archer at Conway & Culligan, whose houses were designed to serve what has now become the "traditional past" invoked by the Disney Corporation. These builders, among others, taught me that it was possible to do well in America, in business, without pandering or cheating—to work with a lot of people representing a variety of interests in order to achieve consensus, whether in the look of a model home or in the sight lines of a subdivision's streets. This realization on my part made it difficult for me to jump on the totally negative bandwagon rolling around the streets of the Haight-Ashbury—denying any value at all to the work still being done in the larger society—and I found myself an outsider once again.

However, there were some situations that permitted me to utilize my newly honed skills to help people achieve dreams that were other than mainstream and exciting because of the scope of their visions. Among these were Alan and Jessica Meyerson, who arrived in San Fran-

cisco from Chicago as graduates of Mike Nichols and Elaine May's Second City looking for financing and a place to house their improvisational theater company The Committee. Jack Berman, lawyer and old friend from Berkeley, called me in to help and we raised the money to start the company and turned the old boccie ball court on Broadway around the corner from City Lights into The Committee, whose wit and presence made manifest so much of the rage that was building up against our involvement in Vietnam.

Another challenge and opportunity came when the Pattersons, another out-of-town couple with vision and a great sense of theatre, were looking for a place to present their concept—a Renaissance pleasure faire—which would recreate an Elizabethan country fair, complete with costumes, singers, food sellers, jugglers, players, dancers, bawds, and bowmen, in a meadow. We did find an oak-dotted hillside meadow in Marin and thanks to my involvement with Jerry Draper, a friend and associate as well as a notable real estate developer, we were able to find the venue, overcome the parking, zoning, and other realty problems to establish the first pleasure faire that has continued for more than twenty-five years, cloning itself into Southern California and spawning other versions of itself such as the Dickens Christmas Fair and the California 49er Gold Mining Extravaganza.

There were other opportunities as well. I brought my father to show him the crest of Russian Hill one day to show him a piece of property I had just optioned. His reaction to the site was immediate and the sketch he made on the back of an envelope became the basis for the design of the Eichler Summit by Neill Smith, another friend and architect with whom the most elegant high-rise building in San Francisco was built. At the time, my father had been working with Jaroslaw Polivka, the noted structural engineer whose association with Frank Lloyd Wright made it possible for them to work together on the V. C. Morris store in San Francisco, the Guggenheim Museum in New York, and the Southern Bay Crossing across the Bay of San Francisco.

"Never build anything you would not be proud to show your children" was a rule my father laid down at the time, and I kept on learning.

Marina Vista was a development of condominiums we built in Sausalito on the site of the old dormitories that had been put up to house the shipyard workers for Marinship. Overlooking Richardson Bay, these units also looked out over Varda's Landing and the *Vallejo* where Alan Watts and Varda and the friends would gather, rounding out my world in an antiphonal but coherent way for me and also for Doug Murdock, who had become an associate and a working partner as well as a weekend celebrant of the festivals and mysteries that took place out at Waldo Point.

With Doug we moved offices to the forty-eighth floor of the Bank of America Building in San Francisco overlooking the Bay and set up a company to mine coal in Tennessee, another one to reopen the Yogo Sapphire Mine in Montana, and yet another to mine jade in the Sierra Foothills—jade that we shipped to China for processing and cutting and that disappeared into thin air between the ship and the dock! All this while working with the developers of Princeville on Kauai and the Four Seasons Resort at Lake Tahoe.

And the way I had chosen kept my nose to the grindstone. I had wanted to meet Christopher Logue because some of the poetry he had written seemed to flow with the spirit and ease I had been working to achieve, and then I heard that he was going to be part of the International Poetry Reading scheduled for a date in June 1965 and that Ferlinghetti and Corso and Yevtushenko and Ginsberg were going to read. I wanted to be there, but it was one of those things I ended up not being able to do because of where I had come to in my own life. A wonderful event and one that should have been memorialized in a much more effective way than it was.

So our tea-for-two family kept on growing in Marin as the world's rumbles began to be noticed again. Henrietta and the children and I marched up Market Street with Dave and Edith Jenkins and Jessica Mitford and Bob Truehaft to join in the Vietnam protests after the Kent State massacre. Again with Vernon Alley and a lot of other friends when Martin Luther King, Jr., was shot and killed. When Jack Kennedy was shot it was as if we had lost a friend, and when his brother Robert followed him I was in New York and cried on the telephone while talking with Henrietta, realizing once again that tomorrow is not promised to anyone at all.

We were friends with Enrico and Sue Bauducci, whose great sense of showmanship

At the Yogo Sapphire Mine, 1976

and unerring ear had given us Mort Sahl and Barbra Streisand and Maya Angelou and the Kingston Trio at the Hungry I and later at Enrico's on Broadway. It was a time of exciting ferment not only in terms of the poetry: Bruce Conner was building his pieces; Ron Boise had his Kama Sutra sculptures, exhibited and then arrested; John Bryan and Joan Barr published *Notes from Underground; Beatitude* came out on the scene; Bob Kaufman was writing about God and Chaplin; and John Webb and Gypsy Lou Webb came in from New Orleans to get stuff for their *Outsider* magazine, collecting Miriam and Kenneth Patchen's work along with Gary Snyder's, Harold Norse's, and Diane Wakoski's—with Larry Eigner and Bukowski and Henry Miller all in the same grab bag. George Hitchcock left the directorship of the California Labor School, having been too "red" to stay, and turned into the editor and publisher of *kayak*, and Andrew Sinclair, biographer of Dylan Thomas, showed up and stayed with us because we had mutual friends in London. The kaleidoscope whirled and kept on whirling with the suburban Bohemian Sausalito life merging with the one out at Stinson Beach while maintaining and reestablishing contacts with the cousins in Italy, running a downtown business, and sitting at the feet of Alan Watts on Saturday afternoon to learn about being centered.

My parents were still ensconced in Inverness, which made for trips up the Marin Peninsula on weekends with the children a welcome change from all the activities in town and around. I had gone back to Italy for the first time after the war in 1951 in order to reestablish contact with relatives. My grandfather's brother on my father's side, Ugo Levi, and his wife Olga had survived the war hidden in the basement of one of the peasant houses on one of the "terra ferma" lands he owned and had been successful in reclaiming the family palazzo on the Grand Canal across from the Accademia. That trip back to Italy had made me understand in a new way how fortunate we had been in our escape to the United States in 1941. Yes, things had changed, and suddenly all the millions of Fascists had disappeared and the Christian democrats had taken their places.

Varda died in January of 1971; my father died in 1972, and Alan Watts died in 1973, leaving me with a lot of mourning and no teachers left to push me on my way. But at Alan's funeral I met John and Tony Lilly once again and found a welcome connection that propelled me into the work that John had been doing with dolphins. Burgess Meredith and I, working with John and Tony, established the Human Dolphin Foundation that sponsored some significant linguistic experiments with our similars on this planet. Early work by John Lilly involved attempts at the teaching of English to the dolphins. This grew into the creation of a metalanguage that served as a bridge between our two modes of communication. The work of the Foundation as well as the expanded requirements of the business meant more trips to Italy, Spain, Switzerland, and Hawaii for business as well as for family reasons.

Our life in Sausalito turned itself into a multifaceted experience. The business pressures continued to increase as the work gained momentum. Henrietta and I spent less time together as Romana and Alexander were growing into their school years. Weekends were crowded and a pattern of busyness established itself. The suburbanite involvements with house maintenance and the families of friends of the children all surfaced, and more energy was devoted to reacting to things than actually planning a conscious course that would have perhaps maintained the marriage. We had become too involved in too many things to protect and nurture the familial center and were not even conscious of the erosion that was taking place.

In 1977 Henrietta gathered all the friends who had worked on the masques for Varda over the years and organized a surprise fiftieth birthday party for me in a nightclub—the Mabuhay—on Broadway in San Francisco's North Beach. Working for weeks she had devised a very complicated strategy bringing friends from Europe and the East Coast to join in a musical review of my life. Friends and relations, some three hundred in all, had conspired to create an event that was truly memorable. It was her way of saying good-bye to me, to the house, and to the life we had been leading, which had become too hectic, too impersonal, and too insecure. I moved back to San Francisco to a flat on Hyde Street near Fisherman's Wharf to begin another chapter in this life of mine.

Beginning Once Again (1977–)

To begin again at the age of fifty served me in a number of ways. The continuing review of the past, the evaluation of the various business transactions and involvements and how they had impinged on the personal life and on my commitment to my writing all made me realize that, fifteen years later than Dante, I had "lost my way in a dark wood." I took another look at the various things I had done and not done in a life that I felt I had wasted. In 1968, Jeff Berner's Stolen Paper Press had published my second book, *Sight Poems,* but I had not been really responsible in my writing and so began a long trek that finally led me back into the world of poetry.

Henry and Olga Carlisle had moved back to San Francisco after many years in France and on Nantucket, and their affectionate and supportive kindness as I began to rebuild my life made things a lot easier for me. Olga, the granddaughter of Leonid Andreyev, had edited the seminal anthology *Poets on Street Corners* and had, by doing so, managed to bring into focus for the American public the work of the two generations of Russian poets that had participated in the building of Communism as well

"Gathering of the clan": Mark, Marie Louise, Victor, and Henry di Suvero,
Stinson Beach, California, 1982

as in the reaction against it. Henry's own work as a novelist and as an editor for years for Scribner's in New York was a model of wit, charm, and craft, and we spent time together both in San Francisco and at Stinson Beach where I still had the house. Thanks to Olga's urging and her editorial help I turned the pile of unpublished material I had built up into two books, *The San Francisco Poems* and *The Net and Other Poems,* that were published in 1987 by Pennywhistle. *The San Francisco Poems* dealt with the events of the city and its public life while *The Net* collected the familial and personal poems. Olga's friendship and interest served to put me back on track.

I began to see many of the old friends, in both San Francisco and Los Angeles. The Beat world was out there, and there seemed to be just enough time to catch up. John Lilly had his crew and the world beyond our normal boundaries beckoned. So many friends were busy reinventing the world not only in terms of spiritual or drug-induced discoveries but out of an appetite for discovery. There were many, and

principal among them was Michael Bowen, who has never really received the credit that should be his for having marshaled and directed the creative energies of so many of the artists in the area. Arriving in San Francisco from Nepal with his lady Serena, he stirred the pot and created a brew of vision that sang loudly and with great heart, along with his own transcendental work that did the same. Michael organized the San Francisco Armory show in February of 1982. The show was meant to be outrageous and it was! From Nanette Baltzell's *Nuns in Leopard Skin* (and high heels) to the drawings of Vicky Chaet—from Azul's work to that of Wolfgang Hersch—sex, drugs, and the visual rock and roll that had all come from the same place that Mouse's posters for the Grateful Dead had come. And a nod of the head and a smile was the only passport required to enter into the world of the initiates, the blessed, the ones who had gone beyond. Azul's manifesto—"Symbolic Visionary Art; or, an End to Meaningless Art"—is valid today and has been the unacknowledged engine driving so much

*"Earth-shaking events do go together"—Victor at City Lights Bookstore, on the day
of the first presentation of Pennywhistle Chapbooks, about one hour after the
San Francisco earthquake, 1989*

of what has gone on to become the visual language of today—taking its cues "from archetypal sources, from the transpersonal realm, from the unknown."

A parallel to my father's new beginnings in his new country in his early fifties struck me hard at that time, and I managed to understand the depths of the depression he would suffer from time to time in new ways. I managed to keep both the real estate and the mining businesses going but drew back to working from the flat, giving up the fancy offices in the Bank of America tower, the membership in the Bankers' Club, and the rest of the panoply that had been seductive and of service in the days and years before.

Memory does not always serve when called upon and little wonder that certain ancient renderings of Memnosyne show the goddess veiled. The next five years flew by on automatic pilot, and then in 1983 I ran into Barbara Windom once again. Barbara had been married to Bill Windom when Henrietta and I would drop down to Malibu from time to time, and we had known and liked each other as one couple will like and get along with another when tastes and attitudes and interests are shared. But now Barbara and I found each other unencumbered, with children grown and lives more or less in order, free to recognize how attracted we had been to each other when we had first met seventeen years before, and so we began a new life together that started with reciprocal commuting between Malibu and San Francisco, progressing to the decision we made in 1987 to pack up and move to Santa Fe in New Mexico.

Before that, in 1986, I had been asked to help establish a poetry festival in Los Angeles and ended up as a catalyst working with Paul Vangelisti, Suzanne Lummis, and Dennis Phillips at Beyond Baroque, presenting poetry as a principal element of the Fringe Festival that had grown out of the art and theatre productions allied with the Olympics of two years before. All this work turned into the beginning of the

Empty Words

And they say we use empty words
They say "Your words are empty,
They do not hold a thing. It's only
Living flesh that counts—the unique person
Standing there in front of you." And yet

All of us are interchangeable,
Queen Isabella's skull and Montezuma's
Look mightily the same today
And all the world's magnificence
Fades into gray as we go on.

It is not bone and muscle that remain,
Not tongue, not brain, but words alone
That sing and come back again with
Tears and joy and pride and tenderness
To shine and shape our days.

We are blessed with voices; let us then
Praise it all, even the pain, the bad choices
And the falling rain; praising fish
And birds and children out at play
Knowing that our empty words are still
The only keepers of our dreams and hopes!

Los Angeles Poetry Festival, still directed by Suzanne Lummis. Charles Bukowski came to the Barnsdale Park auditorium to read, and Michelle Clinton and Michael Lally were among the more than one hundred poets who participated.

The following year Herman Berlandt, the founder and then director of the National Poetry Association, invited me to join the board of directors of his organization and asked me to assume the responsibility of staging the National Poetry Week Festival in San Francisco in 1988. This ten-day event in October featured poets as diverse as the colors of the rainbow and included Francisco Alarcón, James Broughton, Andrei Codrescu, Marilyn Chin, Diane di Prima, Joyce Jenkins, Etheridge Knight, Ishmael Reed, Jerome Rothenberg, Anne Waldman, and David Whyte, among some eighty others. It was then that we created awards for Distinguished Service to Poetry—not the Nobels or Pulitzers—and not for the worth of the work produced, but rather recognition for the work done to promote the art itself. The first three recipients were Maya Angelou, Carl Rakosi, and Tom Parkinson. Working as events coordinator for the festival, I learned once again how difficult the task of presenting poetry properly can be.

The momentum of that festival, joined by the work done by the Geraldine R. Dodge Foundation in New York, the TV series presented by Bill Moyers under the rubric of *The Language of Life*, and the widening circle of acceptance of poetry in the everyday world of America all conspired to evolve into the first National Poetry Month celebrated in the spring of 1996.

Barbara and I started Pennywhistle Press in 1986 in San Francisco (moved to Santa Fe in 1988). Since its inception the Press has published some twenty-four titles featuring the poetry of poets as varied as Joyce Jenkins, Wai-Lim Yip, and Dennis Brutus as well as the first in a series of so-called "crossover" anthologies, including *¡Saludos! The Poems of New Mexico*, the first bilingual (English and Spanish) anthology of the poetry of the area.

And so we moved, books and baggage, to the high desert of New Mexico and built an adobe house to live in. It seemed that after all the traveling, after all the running from and running to, after all the excitements and diversions we finally had come to a place far from all the involvements to which we had been parties in order to create an environment where we could collect our pasts and make it safe enough and gentle and good for all the children as well as all the friends we had. Barbara had grown up with a passion for horses. Through friends we discovered the Peruvian Paso and

With Alexander and Romana at Casa Alegre in Tesuque, New Mexico, "at the adobe house built by Barbara Windom and me," 1989

Our Poems

They converse with the sun,
Take the moon out dancing
And establish correspondence with the stars.

Our poems destroy boundaries,
Include even the exclusive
And permit enemies to share
Our aspirations as well as our doubts.

Our poems have holes in their socks
As well as wings at their heels;
They bear discomfort and splendor
And curiosity on their shoulders.

They acknowledge the lineage of Neruda and
     Whitman
And embrace all others from Adam to Zulu.

Our poems are as concerned about the cry of a
     child
As they are about the turn of a phrase.

Our poems renounce fratricide whatever its color
     or reason.
They are shared as the food that we share,
And the wine and the drink that we share,
And are increased and enlarged by that sharing.

Our poems travel the road of the painful,
Delve into despair, know death and disasters
Without drowning or sinking.

Our poems are survivors, on disks, on paper,
In minds tuned to the future.
Our poems do not diminish.

Our poems honor the fallen, the weak,
The crazies and wanderers,
Those with no home in our houses.

Our poems turn away from the needs of the greedy.
They joy in the dance and the music
And do not submit to the rules of those without
     humor.

They converse with the sun,
Take the moon out dancing
And establish their correspondence
With the stars of the sky.

found its disposition and gentle even gait to
be a marvel. Two new horses soon became four
and soon after many more. Barbara's absolute
ability to research and find out all the details
of any task she sets her mind to brought us
to Peru to learn about the breed in its original environment. We learned that this horse,
as the descendant of the horses that Pizarro
brought down to do in the Inca, in 1532, had
lived in a closed gene pool for 450 years and
had maintained the medieval traveling gait,
making it an ideal horse for the trails and
mountainsides of our new home.

We met a number of experienced and knowledgeable persons in the breed when we went
to the Concurso Nacional in Lima for the first
time in 1991, just after the election of Alberto
Fujimori as president, and were fortunate enough
to begin relationships that have been both generous and supportive in terms of Barbara's declared goal to become a responsible and successful breeder of these horses. I had ridden
as a child in China and then in Marin County
in California with the children as they were
growing up, but nothing had prepared me for
the extent of the involvement with the horses

*Riding Celestina, "one of the Peruvian Paso
horses bred and reared by Barbara and me,"
Santa Fe, New Mexico, 1990*

that evolved. Consequently a new way of looking at the world shaped itself for me.

In the meantime, in 1990, when National Poetry Week was about to come into its own, Herman Berlandt, its founder and chairman of the National Poetry Association, asked me to put a program together in Santa Fe since I had no intention of going back to San Francisco then. With the help of a number of new friends, the fourth annual Poetry Week events we were able to shape at the College of Santa Fe brought more than eighty poets together in a sequence of events that lasted ten days. Jimmy Santiago Baca, Joy Harjo, Nora Naranjo Morse, Francisco Alarcón, Mary McGinnis, Keith Wilson, and Suzanne Lummis headlined a ten-day marathon that reached out and involved over one hundred children presenting haikus written by them as well as Native American poets from the Pueblos, cowboy poets, and poets writing in other traditional forms.

Subsequently, given the organizational experience I had developed, I was asked to help in the formation of PEN–New Mexico and, working with Rudolfo Anaya, was instrumental in launching a successful and growing chapter of the international organization. This was followed by an opportunity to work with a team of interested persons appointed by Governor Bruce King of New Mexico to present the state as the Invitado de Honor at the VIII International Feria del Libro in Guadalajara in 1994. Concurrently I acted as one of the founding directors of the New Mexico Book Association and also established the Poetry Center of New Mexico, which later enlarged its mandate to become the New Mexico Literary Arts Organization.

And the high desert of New Mexico was beautiful in every way—the landscapes that, if one squinted one eye at sunset, could turn into seascapes—restating that this land had been the sea at one time—the clouds that created their own phantasms in broad daylight—the seasons in their constantly changing profusion of color—the people who seemed as if they really inhabited another time as well as this corner of the round world. And so it did become home after all the wandering—and to bring the circle round I had found my old friend Pierre Delattre living up the road in Dixon, a hamlet halfway up to Taos, no longer the pastor to the Beats, having found a new life for himself, but now a painter as well as an art critic, novelist, and poet who had found his new life with Nancy

Victor and Barbara in Peru on their way to Macchu Pichu, 1992

Ortenstone, also a fine painter, in the high Truchas Mountains. We talked of all the things that we had done and undone, about his officiating at my marriage to Henrietta back then in the Valley of the Moon, and I showed him some of the new poems I had been working on. He liked them well enough to write an introduction to them, and that's how *Tesuque Poems* came about in 1993, a slim chapbook but full of my takes on this new life of mine.

Reconsideration

I came to poetry because I was moved by it and thought that it would be good if I could learn to be one of its acolytes and perhaps learn to make my own so as to move others as I had been moved. The lessons I learned from Alan Watts had to do with acceptance and with service. The practice has been intermittent. I've never been very good as a distance runner. At St. Louis College in Tientsin I had made the track team but only for the

Victor di Suvero with Fran Ringold, founder and editor of Nimrod; *William Kistler, founder of Poet's House in New York; and Joyce Jenkins, founder and editor of* Poetry Flash; *Santa Fe, 1995*

50- and 100-yard dashes. The variety of things that I've done and been involved with did not ever give me the extended spaces in time that would have permitted me to embark on a long narrative in a responsible fashion. The poem became a discipline, a way of dealing with the various parts of my life that were all out there, moving in their different ways, each with its own logic and responsibilities. More than once I've turned with a smattering of envy to look at the lives of friends who went from the university out into the world and then to teach at colleges and other universities. The well-ordered and structured lives that have been lived within the strictures of the academic world have made it possible for a quantity of good work to be produced in the latter half of this century, and there are and have been very few poets who have been able to earn a living with their art and craft outside the walls of academe. I chose to try to do it on my own, thinking that the freedom I would enjoy by being out in the world would give me a greater reach.

At this point I am not sure whether the choice I made, or the one circumstances made for me, was the most appropriate one. The time I've made to write has not always been the right time, nor has it been possible for me to clear the air at a certain time to say "this is the time" and to command the muse. I do believe that I have a few years left to sort things out now and trust that much of that which I have learned will serve to make more poetry before I'm done—and—reviewing what I've written here I'm certain that another summary report on the life I've lived could manifest a completely different reality, much as one sees a different side of a piece of sculpture when one takes a walk around it. While finishing this essay I found myself turning to and rereading the memoirs written by both my father and my mother and have been struck once again, how the lineal exposition of a life does not render more than a fraction of its essence. The sounds and smells, the rumble of a crowd or of a cannon in the distance, the cold cutting into one's backbone on a midnight watch or while waiting outside a friend's house in winter in the Village in New York, the utter despair when love comes crashing into pieces, and the total disbelief when one sees one's own newborn children die all become contributors to the fabric of our lives as much as the recollection of all the laughter and the filaments of joy that we are fortunate enough to weave into a pattern while picking up one thread and then one more to complete the story in a manner that we think would be intelligible to another. Yes, Joyce; yes, Proust; yes, Colette and Anaïs Nin; yes, Dante; and yes, all those others whose stories have shaped mine. Yes to all of them knowing how impossible it is to reconstruct a time and all its increments in ways that are absolutely true.

Looking back there is little doubt that the presence of poetry in the land has been growing. Given the media's willingness to get involved with poetry in the presentation of such events as Bill Moyers's *Language of Life* series and Bob Holman's *United States of Poetry*, one can deduce that there is a new opening for the art in the public consciousness. And though it may be true that rap and street poetry and the often misunderstood and underappreciated cowboy poetry do not offer the most demanding intellectual challenges, the awareness of poetry in the public of today is much stronger than it was fifty years ago thanks to the work of poets such as Maya Angelou, Lawrence Ferlinghetti, Gary Snyder, and Allen Ginsberg, who have been indefatigable in their continuing efforts to bring poetry to an ever-widening circle of audiences.

For me poetry is always the wild child. It is the art that always sees things over the edge of the horizon. Poetry is always the one that can draw tears from the eyes of a stolid person because, suddenly, there will be the magic of one word that unexpectedly touches the heart.

Poetry, like the blade of grass that springs out of a concrete sidewalk, will always survive, no matter how tough the suppression, no matter how tough the censorship, academic, financial, or political. Poetry is about the integration of heart, mind, body, and spirit. Acts speak louder than words, and poems speak louder than acts.

John Graham, a poet and friend here in Santa Fe, remarked the other day that in a recent interview in *American Poetry Review*, Donald Justice said the only regret he had about his

Time Is All We Have

Time is all we have, to give, to use,
To share with the beloved, time is all
We have—given to us as long
As body's strength permits us life—
All else does not belong to us—
Stewards of one kind or another,
Caretakers or wastrels, good ones,
Bad ones and some in between,
Solitary, gregarious, committed
To a cause or to acquisitions
We share this passage we call time
While doing all the other things we do.

We sleep, sing, dance and work, bring
Children into the world while killing
Enemies as well as animals and birds.
With each and every act of ours we take
Pieces of our capital without remorse.
Every single thing takes time—sleep
Takes time, stupidity as well—the one
Argument for the good life is economy
Achieved by not wasting time on guilts,
Regrets or even penances.

Time's faces,
The dark one and the light, are the faces
Of our lives—sad and somber,
Serious and wondrous, bright and full
Of laughter from one moment to another
When we notice them reflected
In the mirrors of our time
As we move along our voyages
In the concourse of the stars.

---

writing career was the "Poetry Wars." "If we forget our differences and give each other a pat on the back perhaps poetry and art will once again be recognized as vital elements in our lives," was Graham's comment.

I trust that if we continue to believe that words have their worth and that we can learn how to use them to connect to each other and to the great truths of the universe we will all be better as humans as well as poets!

Coda

We arrived in San Francisco as a family of six in 1941. My father died in 1972 and my mother in 1982. My sister Marie Louise and her husband Mauro Martignoni retired from careers at Oregon State University, where he was a professor of entomology and she was adjunct professor and lecturer in the classics department. Their eldest son, Enrico Martignoni, manages his uncle (my brother) Mark's studio and Socrates Sculpture Park in New York while his younger brother Matteo manages Mark's studio and operation in Petaluma while discharging his responsibilities as vice president of the World Wide Human Powered Vehicle Association. Mark has become one of the most important sculptors of his generation whose work has been featured in major exhibitions around the world. He and his wife Kate and daughter Very are based in New York. My brother Henry, after Harvard Law School and a brilliant career with the ACLU and ECLC, removed himself from the practice of law in California and emigrated to Australia where he is happily married and in private practice. My daughter Romana is married, living in London with her husband, Nicholas Roeg, and their daughter Ava. Romana is a landscape architect, and she and her husband operate a landscaping service paralleling her design business. My son Alexander lives in Hong Kong where he has been based for more than six years working as a photojournalist. Barbara's daughters are Maggie Clare, who is a fashion designer based in New York; Debora Clare, who is a glass artist with her studio in La Villita, New Mexico; and Rachel Windom, who is a graphic designer with Brøderbund in California.

Gathering together from time to time the scattered family members keep up their appetites for exploration, for far horizons, and for adventure. My sense of good fortune and my appreciation for all the happy times that have been our lot has grown, and I am eager to see what this next increment of time left to me will bring.

It is said that on his deathbed Marco Polo, when confronted by a well-meaning priest who urged him to confess that all his stories had been lies, rose to his full height shouting, "I have not even told you the half of it," and then dropped and died.

Consequently, that which I've given you, dear reader, is a summary account told in terms that I believe would serve your curiosity about a life led on the outskirts of the literary city inhabited by all those famous and celebrated authors who have been asked to tell their stories for your information. We all have had a variety of lives within the nominal one we've written about. To see what this life of mine has meant to me, all I can really do is refer you to the books that have been published and the ones still to come with the hope that in them you will find other takes, treatments, and renditions of many of the facts I've mentioned here.

BIBLIOGRAPHY

Poetry:

Salt and the Heart's Horizons, Greenwood Press, 1952.

Sight Poems, Stolen Paper Press, 1968.

The San Francisco Poems, Pennywhistle Press, 1987.

The Net and Other Poems, Pennywhistle Press, 1987.

Tesuque Poems, Pennywhistle Press, 1993.

Naked Heart, Pennywhistle Press, 1996.

The Running River, Pennywhistle Press, 1997.

Contributor of poems and articles to numerous periodicals, including *City Lights Review, Crosswinds, Folio 87, kayak, Nimrod, The Occident,* and *ONTHEBUS.*

Editor:

(With Jeanie C. Williams) *¡Saludos! The Poems of New Mexico,* Pennywhistle Press, 1994.

Sextet/One—Six Powerful American Voices, Pennywhistle Press, 1996.

Also editor of the Pennywhistle Chapbook Series, 1986–1995, covering Jorge H. Aigla, Francisco X. Alarcón, Grace Bauer, Sarah Blake, Dennis Brutus, Judyth Hill, Edith A. Jenkins, Joyce Jenkins, Kerry Shawn Keys, Joan Logghe, Suzanne Lummis, Jack Marshal, Jerome Rothenberg, Richard Silberg, Phyllis Stowell, Viola Weinberg, and Wai-Lim Yip.

Carl Djerassi

(http://www.djerassi.com)

1923-

FROM THE PILL TO THE PEN

For nearly half a century, I led the life of a professional bigamist, working concurrently in both academia and industry. Like most bigamous relations, my professional one was full of potential pitfalls but also spiked with ever provocative stimulation. Still, all of it was acted out on carefully defined turf—namely, science, or more specifically, chemistry. When I am asked for a biographical sketch in connection with some scientific lecture or visiting professorship invitation, I invariably dispatch this. It is also what is always expected.

Carl Djerassi was born on October 29, 1923, in Vienna, Austria, and received his education at Kenyon College (A.B. summa cum laude, 1942) and the University of Wisconsin (Ph.D., 1945). After five years (1942–1943; 1945–1949) as research chemist with CIBA Pharmaceutical Co. in Summit, NJ, he joined Syntex, S.A., in Mexico City in 1949 as associate director of chemical research. In 1952 he accepted a professorship at Wayne State University, and in 1959 his current position as Professor of Chemistry at Stanford University.

Concurrently with his academic positions, he also held various posts at Syntex (in Mexico City and later in Palo Alto, CA) during the period 1957–1972, including that of President of Syntex Research (1968–1972). In 1968, he helped found Zoecon Corporation, a company dedicated to developing novel approaches to insect control, serving as its chief executive officer until 1983. He continued until 1988 as chairman of the board of Zoecon (now a subsidiary of Sandoz, Ltd.).

Professor Djerassi has published over twelve hundred articles and six books dealing with the chemistry of natural products (steroids, alkaloids, antibiotics, lipids, and terpenoids), and with applications of physical measurements (notably optical rotatory dispersion, magnetic circular dichroism, and mass spec-

As a twelve-year-old Boy Scout in pre-Nazi Vienna, 1935

trometry) and computer artificial intelligence techniques to organic chemical problems. In medicinal chemistry he was associated with the initial developments in the fields of oral contraceptives (Norethindrone), antihistamines (Pyribenzamine) and topical corticosteroids (Synalar).

For the first synthesis (1951) of a steroid oral contraceptive, Professor Djerassi received

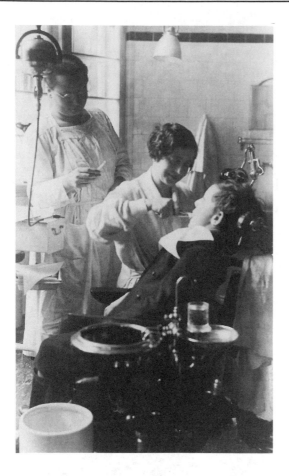

"My mother, Dr. Alice Djerassi, in a pose that explains why I still possess all of my wisdom teeth," Vienna, about 1932

the National Medal of Science (1973), the first Wolf Prize in Chemistry (1978), and was inducted into the National Inventors Hall of Fame (1978). He received the National Medal of Technology for his contributions in the insect control field (1991). The American Chemical Society honored him with its Award in Pure Chemistry (1958), Baekeland Medal (1959), Fritzsche Award (1960), Award for Creative Invention (1973), Award in the Chemistry of Contemporary Technological Problems (1983), and the Priestley (1992) and Gibbs (1997) medals. Other recognitions include the Bard Award in Medicine and Science (1983), the Roussel Prize (Paris) (1988), the Discoverer's Award of the Pharmaceutical Manufacturers Association (1988), the Gustavus John Esselen Award for Chemistry in the Public Interest (1989), the first Award for the Industrial Application of Science (1990) from the National Academy of Sciences, the Nevada Medal

(1992), the Thomson Gold Medal of the International Mass Spectrometry Society (1994), the Prince Mahidol Award (Thailand) in Medicine (1995), and the Sovereign Fund Award (1996). The Society for Chemical Industry presented him with the Perkin Medal (1975), and the American Institute of Chemists with the Freedman Foundation Patent Award (1970) and the Chemical Pioneer Award (1973).

Professor Djerassi is a member of the U.S. National Academy of Sciences and of its Institute of Medicine, as well as a member of the American Academy of Arts and Sciences, the Royal Swedish Academy of Sciences, the Royal Swedish Academy of Engineering Sciences, the German Academy of Natural Scientists (Leopoldina), and the Mexican, Brazilian, and Bulgarian Academies of Sciences. The Royal Society of Chemistry (London) and the American Academy of Pharmaceutical Sciences elected him to honorary membership in 1968. He is the recipient of fifteen honorary doctorates: National University of Mexico (1953); Kenyon College (1958); Federal University of Rio de Janeiro (1969); Worcester Polytechnic Institute (1972); Wayne State University (1974); Columbia University (1975); University of Uppsala (1977); Coe College (1978); University of Geneva (1978); University of Ghent (1985); University of Manitoba (1985); Adelphi University (1993); University of South Carolina (1995); University of Wisconsin (1995); and Swiss Fed. Inst. Technol.—ETH (1995).

But what does that tell the reader about Carl Djerassi, the person, other than providing an inventory of kudos for a successful scientific career? Since he lists so many, he presumably values them. But why? And why quantify the appalling volume of his scientific publications?

Any honest research scientist can answer the first question; many can also rationalize the second. Yet no reader of these dry lines, scientist or layperson, would realize that Carl Djerassi left Nazi Vienna as a Jewish refugee after the *Anschluss* in 1938; that he went first to Bulgaria, where he learned English in The American College in Sofia before arriving penniless (actually with $20, which were promptly lifted by an unscrupulous taxi driver) in New York at age sixteen; that he was married three times—the first time before the age of twenty, an event he hid for nearly forty years. Even the entry "National Medal of Science (1973)" embodied an undisclosed nugget of relevant information: President Nixon presented personally the medals to the awardees, only one of whom—Carl Djerassi—shared the extra distinction of also having been listed that same week on the White House Enemies List of Watergate notoriety.

More recent versions of his CV end with an additional paragraph:

> Under the auspices of the Djerassi Resident Artists Program, he founded an artists colony near Woodside, California, which provides residencies and studio space for approximately seventy artists per year in the visual arts, literature, choreography, and music. Over nine hundred artists have passed through that program since its inception (1979).

Though not dealing with science, these two sentences again disclose little about Djerassi's persona, other than that he seems to have a streak of generosity as well as the means of

With his father, Dr. Samuel Djerassi, a dermatologist and specialist in venereal diseases, Sofia, Bulgaria, 1938

As a recently arrived sixteen-year-old immigrant who has just learned touch typing, Newark, New Jersey, 1940

exercising it. It does not tell about his two children. It does not divulge that in 1978, one of them—his artist daughter Pamela—committed suicide at age twenty-eight deep in the woods of the family's SMIP Ranch ("Syntex Made It Possible," later renamed "Sic Manebimus in Pace"); that in his sorrow, he attempted to create something living out of a deliberate death; that this artists colony, incorporating much of SMIP Ranch, would never have been established had it not been for a father's agony in trying to cope with a parent's greatest tragedy: outliving his child.

In 1983, my life took a dramatic turn when my professional bigamy, as a scientist straddling academia and industry, assumed polygamous dimensions with a totally different intellectual flavor, indeed a different social life. These days, I introduce myself as a writer who is still a chemist, which is very different from a chemist who also happens to be a writer. My

*With Diane Middlebrook, Wilanów Palace,
Warsaw, 1982*

life as a research scientist (1942–1991) over-
lapped with that of the writer (1983–?) by only
eight years. Since the former has already been
over-documented in two autobiographies—one
addressed to fellow chemists (*Steroids Made It
Possible*) and the other to a general public (*The
Pill, Pygmy Chimps, and Degas' Horse*)—I shall
start my writer's tale not with my biological birth
(October 29, 1923) but rather with my second
birth: May 8, 1983. After all, not many persons have two birthdays separated by sixty years.

On that day, the love of my life, whom I
had met on Valentine's Day of 1977 (following
my divorce, in 1976, from my second wife, Norma
Lundholm), announced with a tender thunder-
bolt that she had fallen in love with another
man. We were through, she announced quite
unequivocally (though much more elegantly than
stated here); there was nothing to explain, she
informed me, which, of course, inflamed me
even further. My response was typically male,
indeed almost macho. How could she fall in love
with another man when she had me? And how
come I had no inkling? Humorless, self-pitying

revenge—endocrinologically dripping with testoster-
one and adrenaline—led me into two directions: one obvious, the other totally unexpected.

The obvious one was new female compan-
ionship; the unexpected one was an outpour-
ing of poems—albeit confessional, self-pitying,
and even narcissistic—which proved to be an
exhilarating experience for someone who until
then had never written a single line of verse.
Like a typical scientist, who believes that anything worth doing is worth publishing, I discovered a hitherto unknown plethora of poetry magazines that, to my utter surprise, all
had the initial temerity to turn down my sob-
bing lines. But as humorless self-pity turned
into more palatable sarcasm, one poetry editor
bit (*Cumberland Poetry Review,* vol. 3, 1984, pp.
63–64). The first two stanzas of "Lingonberries
Are Not Sufficient" describe in poetic concision what brought my new female companion
and me together.

> When we met
> I spoke
> And you laughed.
> Just laughed.
>
> "Come live with me
> And write.
> I'll feed and launder you."
> You laughed and came.

The "you" in the poem was Diane Wood
Middlebrook, an English professor at Stanford
University. During our first year (1977) together,
she not only spun tales and poetry, but also
completed a book (*Worlds Into Words: Understanding Modern Poems,* W. W. Norton, 1980)—
all of which got me sufficiently hooked on
Wallace Stevens (the subject of her first mono-
graph and of some of her Stanford seminars)
that I attempted to use him as the ultimate
authority on a contentious point of linguistic
idiosyncrasy.

To wit: I am told that I still have residues
of an accent, colored by my mother tongue
(German, with Viennese nuances) and by the
fact that I learned English from a mix of British and American instructors among a sea of
Slavic accents of my fellow classmates at The
American College in Sofia. It is only when I
listen to my voice on the radio or on a tape
do I realize that I speak no language accentless—not even my mother tongue—and most
certainly not others such as Spanish, which I

acquired in the 1950s during my five-year sojourn in Mexico City. But until I met Diane Middlebrook, I suffered under the delusion that my English was grammatically impeccable. After all, it is the only language in which I dream— to me the ultimate criterion of idiomaticity.

"I think we should make reservations already now for Christmas in St. Maarten," I announced during our first communal month. "What do you mean by 'already now'?" she laughed. "It's redundant. It's probably German."

"German?" I hooted until I realized that my non-German speaking critic had simply displayed her innate stylistic *Fingerspitzengefühl.* Of course she was right: *"schon jetzt"* is what every sensible German-speaking mensch would say when a "now" feels naked and incomplete without the security of an "already." But does that make it tainted English?

I enlisted my loyal and literate secretary's help. I asked Guynn Perry, an inveterate reader, to look out for "already nows" in her belletristic browsing. She did not disappoint me, although I have to admit that I used her evidence with the typical droit du seigneur acquisitiveness of a science professor who appropriates his graduate student's findings under the disguise of the first person plural. "Look what we have found," I bragged to my English professor lover. "'I know I'm going to die. You ask him. I feel it *already now.*' That's Leo Tolstoy in *Anna Karenina.* In fact, Anna's own words." Diane didn't even laugh. "A literal translation from the Russian," she said dismissively.

We (i.e., Guynn Perry) did not give up. "What about this?" I persisted. "'*Already now* I feel, as when at the age of twenty I was going to a ball in the evening, that day is a space of time without meaning.'" Diane perked up until I cited "our" source: *Shadows on the Grass* by Isak Dinesen. Diane Middlebrook never sneers, but this time she came close to it with just three words: "Danish, not English."

That's when I raised the ante: If I could produce an irreproachable quote, would she compose a poem containing "already now"? When she agreed (I never determined whether it was amusement or exhaustion that caused her assent) I produced an impeccable source: Wallace Stevens. A few days after Tolstoy and then Dinesen had bit the dust, I handed over a Xerox copy of a page from Stevens's *Harmonium* containing the poem "In the Carolinas." Its first stanza nearly convinced my skeptical judge:

> The lilacs wither in the Carolinas.
> Already the butterflies flutter above the cabins.
> Already now the new-born children interpret love
> In the voices of mothers.

I might have gotten away with this fake because, according to Walsh's *Concordance to the Poetry of Wallace Stevens,* which I had consulted, the word "already" appears in only four poems of Stevens's huge oeuvre. I had simply spliced the word "now" into the Djerassi version of "In the Carolinas" by lifting the word "now" from another poem printed in the same font. But I had overdone it: I had also presented her with a doctored version of Stevens's shortest poem ("To the Roaring Wind") containing two extra words at the end.

> What syllable are you seeking,
> Vocalissimus,
> In the distances of sleep?
> Speak it already now.

It is chancy enough to present a Stevens expert with a tampered line, but picking this particular one was cocksureness elevated to the third power. Weeks earlier, I had started to call Diane "Vocalissima," and this has remained my term of endearment for her ever since. Although she saw through this fake immediately, as a true Vocalissima she paid off a wager she had never lost by presenting me with the following gift I have always cherished:

Sonnet: Auspices

29 July 1977, from the roof—

Already, now, the moon, Diana's sign,
Asserts herself among your darkened trees,
Abandoning the branches one by one.
Gaining the sky she claims your sleeping form;
Dreaming, you do not feel her fluent gaze
Rinsing your face with silver to the rim.

Four months. Is this a sign, this storm of light
Shedding its silent thunder in my blood?
Pagan through love I scan the moving sky
And make of every sound an oracle.
The future seems a tantalizing gift
The moon might open to her priestess here—

The moon is silent. Wind is merely sound.
And yet a benediction fills the night;
My voice, aloud, draws meaning from this hour,
Finding four syllables. Already. Now.

                                 —Diane Wood Middlebrook

Why do I include this "already now" shaggy-dog tale in my autobiographical musings? Is it to demonstrate that I retain a bulldog streak that at times does not permit me to give up when such yielding is long overdue? Or is it offered as evidence for a flickering linguistic childhood residue, awaiting the reviving blasts of suitable bellows? It is the latter, as I will demonstrate in the sequel.

My prolonged exposure to Wallace Stevens during the preceding six years even caused me to indulge in some Stevensiana of my own through five poems that eventually appeared in the *Wallace Stevens Journal*—hardly a household publication venue for an American organic chemist.

As the number of my published poems reached a level where I started to take myself seriously (serious enough to eventually find a publisher willing to publish a chapbook of mine, yet at the same time sensible enough to recognize that it was too late in life to turn into a real poet), I realized that this poetic out-

pouring held useful therapeutic value. I had reached the point where my poems had lost their self-pitying bitterness; to my relief, they had even started to acquire some sense of humor. Starting in the late 1960s, my industrial entrepreneurial activities as well as scientific interest had expanded to the insect field—especially insect hormones and pheromones. Gradually, my arthropodan browsing also turned into a text for my poetic lyre. The following excerpt from a 1984 scientific article by Izuru Yamamoto became the long epigraph to a poem in my *Amour D'Arthropode* series in my chapbook:

> *Erectin, a sex pheromone of the female azuki bean weevil* (Callosobruchus chinensis) *induces the male insect to extrude his genital organ for copulation. The male will also copulate with a glass rod, a tubular piece of aluminum foil, or any other surrogate doused with the pheromone. This presents possibilities for population control with an aluminum foil tube being a simple and satisfactory dummy.*

At a reception in New York City for the Bard College award presentations to Carl Djerassi and John Ashbery (left; Diane Middlebrook is standing in the center)

Three Variations on a Theme by Callosobruchus

1

Blindfold me, Izuru.
Douse me with Erectin.
Then tempt me
With aluminum or glass.

2

Will Pepsi empties,
Empties of Perrier
Be rated G, PG,
Or X?

3

Merrill Lynch?
Buy me ALCOA.
Get me CORNING.
I'm bullish.

But I am getting ahead of myself. Before I dropped revenge as a motive for entering the field of creative writing, with bitterness as its predominant flavor, I turned to literary prose—again a genre I had never been tempted by during the first sixty years of my life. I found my poetry to be too circumscribed a vehicle for my grating, narcissistic wrath. I would write a novel of unrequited and discarded amour, a clever roman à clef focusing on the terrible lapse of amorous judgment by an elegant feminist, who dropped her eminent scientist-lover for some unknown litterateur. My surefire masterpiece's title, "Middles," was based on an epigraph from Nora Ephron's *Heartburn* (1983)—itself a piercing literary stiletto serving as the *pièce de revanche* against her former husband Carl Bernstein, who had abandoned her for a newer model. It is true that Ephron wrote: "I insist on happy endings; I would insist on happy beginnings, too, but that's not necessary because all beginnings are intrinsically happy . . . middles are a problem. Middles are perhaps the major problem of contemporary society." But as my novel's *objet de revanche* was meant to be Diane Middlebrook, I was embarking on roman à cleffery at an extraordinarily transparent level.

Still, over the course of a year, I managed to complete a 331-page long manuscript. Another disaster in my personal *annus horribilis* of 1983 helped. In June of that year, while hiking through a creek bed on my ranch (where I had lived since my divorce from my second wife in 1976), I broke through some rotten timber and fell backward. My stiff left leg (from a knee fusion, many years earlier, associated with a skiing accident) remained immobilized—practically fragmenting. If I had not been accompanied by a group of my graduate students, I surely would have died since the accident occurred in a very steep and rarely visited gulch on my 1,200-acre SMIP Ranch. Although only a thirty-minute drive from the Stanford hospital, it took seven hours and over a dozen paramedics and other rescue personnel to winch me up to the waiting four-wheel-drive ambulance—and truly elephant-sized doses of morphine to blunt my pain. The postoperative recovery kept me in a cast for eight months, which I used in part to start on my magnum opus. The rest was finished on airplanes, in hotels, and at scientific conferences.

I was impressed by my ability to complete an entire novel under less than ideal writing conditions—sufficiently so that I started to explore avenues of publication. Fortunately, my original muse—though now in another guise—intervened. On May 8, 1984, I received a note and flowers from Diane Middlebrook, whom I had not expected to ever encounter again. Her basic message was: "A year has passed. Let's talk." Of course, I accepted; though instead of flowers, I presented her with a selection of the more brutally frank chapters of "Middles" and soon thereafter, with the entire manuscript.

Our rationalization, peace negotiation, reconciliation, and other bridge building took some months, culminating in October of that year in a brief trip to Brazil that we kept secret from everyone—at work and at home. But already during the very early stages of our rapprochement, we realized that we were only removing some mud atop a foundation of granite and that we would never part again. In some silly and yet fundamental way, "Middles" helped: Diane tried to persuade me that the novel was unpublishable on many grounds, discretion being only one of them. I promised never to publish that manuscript if we got married, and marry we did on June 21, 1985. And yet I hedged. I said I would not publish "Middles," but I had not promised not to cannibalize that deeply personal manuscript. How long that cannibalization took will become obvious below.

In everyday life I possess a sense of humor; "Middles," however, suffered from a conspicuous lack of it: Its structure was too lin-

"Opera star Tatiana Troyanos signing a copy of my short story, 'What's Tatiana Troyanos Doing in Spartacus's Tent?' in which I fantasized sharing a hot tub with her while she . . ."

ear; the dialog forced. (I conceded that point, blaming it on four decades of still-too-ingrained scientific writing, which is totally monological.) But as my severest critic pointed out, "Middles" did show occasional flashes of insight, and most importantly, it demonstrated that I possessed a writer's discipline. "If you want to write fiction," my wife advised, "try short stories."

To this day, I congratulate myself for having accepted her advice because short stories are the ideal vehicle for an autodidact: one learns concision; in the process, one becomes cold-blooded enough to kill one's literary darlings; and most importantly for the scientist-writer who hardly ever revised his scientific manuscripts, one acquires the habit of repeated revision. Scientific writing is information transmittal where content is king, and style counts for little.

"Middles," of course, was pseudobiography or—more precisely—autopseudopsychoanalysis. The first excerpt I extracted from it as a vehicle for a short story was almost totally autobiographical. "What's Tatiana Troyanos Doing in Spartacus's Tent?" is my shortest short story and longest title. Eventually it appeared in *Cosmopolitan* (United Kingdom) magazine as well as in German and Italian translations.

Through years of sexual reality, I dreamed ever so often of a woman lover who'd sing while coupling with her man. Once a husky-voiced woman, who'd brought her guitar, started to sing in a stunning contralto. Lying on my bed, exhausted and content, gazing at the naked woman strumming her instrument, I was about to ask her whether she could . . . But then I chickened out; I was afraid she'd just laugh.

Years later, I happened to go to a performance of Monteverdi's *L'incoronazione di Poppea,* set in the time of Emperor Nero before he went mad, with Tatiana Troyanos singing the lead role. About half-way through the love-scene on the couch between young Nero and Poppea, the performance assumed such erotic overtones that I began to squirm in my seat. I don't go to operas for sexual titillation; except for an occasional *Salome* or *Lulu,* it's the music that excites me. But this was different. Suddenly I realized that Troyanos was the woman of my fantasies who'd walked into Spartacus's tent over two thousand years ago. . . .

But the spur to my longest and most lucid dream was *The Gladiators*—Arthur Koestler's version of the slave uprising led by Spartacus. Don't get me wrong: as time passed, as I became a man, there were months, even whole years, when Spartacus did not exist. But the vision never departed totally from my memory. When I had a lover whose climax always ended in such a long-drawn cry that we could never meet in a hotel, I wondered more than once how Spartacus had handled this in his tent on the plains of Campania. And when I saw *Spartacus* at the Bolshoi in Moscow thirty-five years after I'd read Koestler's novel, I felt a pleasure reawakening.

I then dropped "Middles," though only temporarily, as a source of inspiration to turn to *real* fiction as I thought of it then, not fully realizing that all fiction writers are consciously or unconsciously autobiographers wearing masks. My second short story, initially called "Cohen's Dilemma," was my first entry in what has turned out to be my favorite genre for full novels: "science-in-fiction" (not to be confused with science fiction) in which I describe in verifictional disguise the behavior and tribal culture of contemporary scientists. In "Cohen's Dilemma" I wrote about a flawed Nobel Prize with an ambiguous ending—a story that pleases me to this day. I showed the manuscript to Terrence Holt (a writer and English professor, whom I had met earlier during his residency at the Djerassi Resident Artists Program), asking him not to tame his editorial pen. It was the beginning of a long-lasting professional relationship since Holt has served as freelance editor for my five subsequent novels, two of which are dedicated to him.

"Cohen's Dilemma" met the usual fate of a first submission: a printed rejection slip from *The New Yorker.* But the next attempt succeeded: Fred Morgan of the *Hudson Review* accepted what became my first published short story, although he requested that I change the name Cohen on the advice of an editorial consultant of Nobel Prize stature, who felt that Cohen was too common a name for a fictional Nobelist.

Rather than arguing, I proposed Cantor since—for reasons obvious to any reader of my story—the name had to start with a "C"; for personal reasons, it also had to have a Jewish connotation. But the editorial consultant was too well informed. "What about Charlie Cantor?" he inquired, referring to the chairman of the genetics department of Columbia's College of Physicians and Surgeons. I was so anxious to see my first short story in print that instead of arguing that Columbia's Cantor surely carried no trademark on that name, I offered an "s" for the "n." "Castor's Dilemma" proved to be the vehicle that eventually converted me into a novelist.

The first half of 1985 started auspiciously: Diane Middlebrook and I got married on my son's birthday, June 21, followed by a glorious wedding feast at SMIP Ranch, which was attended by many of our Stanford University students and colleagues. Its artistic high points were the "edible art" created by our mutual friend, Sharon Polster, in her catering establishment; commissioned music for three flutes and soprano by John Adams set to lines by Wallace Stevens; as well as a wedding dance created by Rhonda Martyn. My scientific research at Stanford with nearly two dozen predoctoral and postdoctoral collaborators was going full steam and gave no indication of slackening. And my physical health was so good that I was ready to embark on a trek from Tibet to Nepal, prompted by a fabulous trek, four years earlier in western Bhutan, that had demonstrated that I could cope on such strenuous terrain with my fused left knee. But then the gods stopped smiling.

As the oldest member of that expedition, I had to take a physical examination in preparation for the high-altitude exposure. Instead of the anticipated clean bill of health, I was diagnosed with colon cancer. Instead of breathing thin air, I inhaled an anesthetic for over five hours because a team of urologic surgeons had to be called in when my urethra was cut by mistake during the cancer operation. Barely a new bridegroom, I suddenly came to terms with my mortality, even wondering whether I would survive beyond the next few years. What if I had known five years earlier that I would come down with colon cancer? I asked myself during the weeks of onco-prompted self-exploration in the hospital. Would I have led a different five years? The resounding "yes" to that question raised the obvious corollary: so what about the next five years? The second "yes" led me to toy with the idea of embarking on one more intellectual life, one totally different from that of the preceding forty-plus years.

Fiction writing ought to qualify as "totally different" from science, where nothing is supposed to be "made up." The never-to-be-published "Middles" demonstrated to me that I had a writer's stamina, while "Castor's Dilemma," though not yet in print, showed that I could write prose acceptable to a serious literary magazine. I realized that implementation of such a plan would take about five years, because I still had a large research group and many doctoral candidates who had several years of research ahead of them before completing their Ph.D. requirements. It was clear that I could not abandon them, nor was I prepared to drop instantaneously an exciting line of ongoing research.

But I took the first step: without telling anyone, I decided not to take on any more graduate students in my laboratory. I did accept new postdocs, because they only came for one- or two-year periods and because I was not sure yet whether a literary career was actually feasible. I was (and still am) too ambitious to consider the act of writing by itself a consummated literary life, without the external validation of subsequent publication, and I was quite aware of how much I still had to learn in terms of writing. Once more, my wife—though this time through her own professional plans—provided the indirect impetus for my first serious immersion into the waters of composing literary fiction.

Until 1986, I had never taken off during the academic summers other than to attend scientific conferences. Summers are the time when graduate students in the sciences work full-time in the laboratory without taking courses, assisting in teaching, or other distractions. It was only natural that I wanted to stick around the lab. But that summer of full recuperation from my cancer episode was also the period when Diane served as director of a summer program sponsored by Stanford at Oxford University, so—for the first time in my life—I became a faculty husband. I drove her to the Stanford site (leased from Magdalen College), took my morning swim in the private pool of the Maxwell estate at Headington Hill Hall (in 1984, my son, Dale, had married Isabel Max-

well, one of the daughters of Robert Maxwell of Pergamon Press), bought some groceries, and then settled down for the rest of the day to do serious writing in a two-story house on Woodstock Road, which belonged to the Maxwells. The upstairs occupant was another recipient of Maxwell hospitality, the former Prime Minister Harold Wilson.

"Serious writing" meant following my wife's counsel to concentrate on short stories. After the completion of "Castor's Dilemma" and my Tatiana Troyanos story, I had started first drafts of three other stories. I revised and polished them and then continued without interruption in a euphoria of free-flowing fantasizing. I consciously use the word "free-flowing" because I now know that this is the fiction writing mode with which I am most comfortable. I know how I want to begin; I can visualize my main characters; I even have a good inkling of how to end the story. Yet each time, my protagonists change "their" plans; they introduce me to other persons, presumably unknown to me; they take me on side paths.

With his "very first" wife, Virginia, Madison, Wisconsin, 1943

Most significantly, the story ends differently from how I had envisaged it at the outset. I was fascinated by these fishing expeditions into the depth of my unconscious psyche, which started to teach me a great deal about myself. Scientists, I believe, are on the whole not self-reflective. I certainly never was. We are too occupied in analyzing the environment around us through our sophisticated scientific lenses to pay much attention to our own behavior. But now, I started to examine what made me tick as a member of the scientific tribe to which I belonged for four decades. In one way or another, my stories started to assume a psychologically analytical resonance. One example, my favorite short story, will suffice.

Some six or more months before my Oxford sojourn, I had dinner in New York with Gilbert Stork, my oldest friend from graduate school days, now a world-famous organic chemist teaching at Columbia University. Gilbert, who claims never to read fiction and to abhor writing—even scientific papers—is a marvelous storyteller, especially when the subject is one of his automobile misfortunes. This time, he told me about an accident in his wife's car while she was in Paris. Although he had been knocked unconscious, he had suffered no lasting injury. The Toyota, however, was a total wreck. When he called his wife in Paris, promising to purchase a new car, she asked him whether he had recovered the bumper stickers. I could, of course, go on with their tale, but I won't. Winifred Stork's question appeared to me so preposterous (perhaps because I never plaster "Save the Whales" or even political messages on my bumper) that my internal fiction engine started revving up. The following morning, the outline of a professor's car accident and his wife's obsession with bumper stickers had crystallized.

"I still think it's absurd. There I was in the hospital, my arm in a cast, feeling sorry for myself, and still not knowing precisely how I'd smashed up Bea's car." Those were the first two sentences of "The Toyota Cantos" that I started to write in 1985 on the plane while flying to Italy to present a lecture before an Italian Gynecological Congress in Salsamaggiore and then to visit the Gori Collection outside Florence. The Italian connection was important because I had made my hero a distinguished Dante specialist from New York University and his wife a creator of special bumper stickers

"A mock machete duel with my oldest friend, Gilbert Stork, of Columbia University, on a cactus collecting trip in Mexico," 1954

taken from *The Divine Comedy*, which she used in an unsuccessful attempt for coded communication with her husband. I hadn't read Dante for some decades, but in preparation for my story, I scanned Cary's, Binyon's, Singleton's, Sisson's, Carlysle-Wicksteed's, Mandelbaum's, Musa's, and Anderson's translations. Only when I hit upon John Ciardi's colloquial English version did I settle during my Italian voyage on a hyper-detailed re-reading of the entire *Divine Comedy* to construct a spectacular list of potential Dantean bumper stickers that became the centerpiece of my story. To show how seriously I romanticized this first excursion into true belles lettres, I stopped, after my scientific lectures and art visits, for a couple of days in Lérici to weave the most allusive Dante bumper stickers into the fabric of "The Toyota Cantos" while sitting on the balcony of a pension overlooking the Bay of Genoa. And why Lérici? Because that is where Byron, Shelley, and their friends cavorted and where Shelley drowned.

Somehow, I wanted to acquire some posthumous, subliminal poetic inspirations for the best choices of Dante's terza rima to be pasted on my fictitious Toyota's rear bumpers. I used these bumper cantos to explore the inability of a sophisticated, long-married, academic couple to effectively communicate on deeply personal issues. It was the beginning of a journey in which I started to turn into my own shrink.

Ten years later, I realize that my brief description of the genesis of "The Toyota Cantos"—involving a factual incident, followed by detailed "research," and finally freewheeling spinning of a story—is as valid a description of my mode of fiction writing as I can offer. In any event, during that 1986 Oxford summer I completed a collection of eleven stories, which were published under the title *The Futurist and Other Stories.* Considering that the bulk of the work was done in England, it was only fitting that both the hardcover and the paperback versions were published by a British publisher (Macdonald and Futura, respectively).

My writer-cum-faculty husband function at Oxford always ended in the late afternoon, since most evenings we went out socializing or, even more frequently, driving to London to the theater. The following year, both Diane and I decided to repeat such a concentrated summer writing stint, but this time in London— she on her biography of Anne Sexton (eventually a *New York Times* bestseller) and I on an expansion of my "Castor's Dilemma" short story into a full-length novel.

Both of us found London to be a very livable city, ideal for our work and lifestyle. As we did not want to be disturbed by anyone, the eight-hour time difference from our California stamping grounds coupled with our daytime working schedule provided an ideal buffer. We repeated the London summer sojourn in 1988 by renting for the summer a flat owned jointly by the novelists Alison Lurie and Diane Johnson in the Little Venice section of Maida Vale. We promptly fell in love with that area and purchased a flat of our own, which for the past eight years has turned into our summer home and principal writing abode. Writing seven hours a day, seven days a week; sifting through our mail, pre-culled in California by our secretary, only once every ten days; going to the theater or concerts or opera almost every evening; and meeting a new circle of friends—most of them writers of one sort or another—proved to be the ideal setting for a new intellectual life.

In London, I completed my first published novel, based partly on my short story, "Castor's Dilemma." Within weeks of the appearance of that novel's progenitor in the *Hudson Review,* I had started to receive letters about my tale: "Had the postdoc cheated?" "Was Professor Castor thinking of suicide?" "Do you really find it necessary to wash dirty lab coats in public?" These questions inspired the novel as an answer. People working (rather than just posturing) in white coats are bound to get dirty—a fact of life of which white-coated scientists should not be ashamed and which the public should judge on the case's specific merits or demerits.

Before handing my novel over to my London agent, Ed Victor, I headed for the Royal Society Library to confirm the nonexistence of any tumor cell biologist named Castor, since this was the scientific specialty of my novel's tainted Nobelist. To my chagrin, I discovered that such a biologist did indeed exist in Pennsylvania, whereupon I decided without further dillydallying to revert to Cantor. *Cantor's Dilemma* was the title under which Doubleday published the hardcover edition, and—while the novel was reviewed very widely both in the lay and scientific press—neither Charles Cantor of Columbia University nor any other Cantor ever complained to me. Some readers assumed that the initials C.D. of the title were a masked reference to my name, but if this was the case, it was disguised so subliminally that it had escaped my attention.

The overall reception of the novel left little to be desired. The Sunday *New York Times's* judgment: "This novel's rendering of the scientific establishment is so precise that anyone considering a career in science should be required to read it" anticipated the eventual adoption by many American colleges and universities of the Penguin-USA paperback version as a text or recommended reading—an event that has led to annual reprints each year since its launch by Penguin in 1991. But the first couple of weeks following the official release by Doubleday in early October 1989 were hardly auspicious.

The inaugural public reading was scheduled for 8:00 P.M. on October 17 at Cody's in Berkeley, a Bay Area bookstore and seemingly ideal

"My son Dale and daughter Pamela, the year before Pamela's suicide,"
SMIP Ranch, Woodside, California, 1977

launching pad for a local writer's career. My wife and I crossed the Bay Bridge from San Francisco to the East Bay shortly before 5:00 P.M. in order to have a leisurely dinner in Berkeley within walking distance of Cody's Bookstore. I was about to feed a Berkeley street parking meter with quarters when the ground around us began shaking so violently that car alarms within blocks went berserk. We held on to the parking meters until the earthquake subsided, not realizing that we had just experienced one of the strongest local seismic tremors in recent memory—the infamous Loma Prieta earthquake of October 17, 1989—strong enough to have caused a portion of the Bay Bridge and of a nearby elevated freeway to collapse, with significant fatalities. Naturally, the bookstore too had closed. It took us over four hours in horrendous traffic and virtual pitch darkness to return to our home on the opposite side of the Bay. My next scheduled reading at Printers Inc, another well-known bookstore, this time in Palo Alto, was also canceled because of seismic retrofitting. In addition, during the preceding month, my publisher, Doubleday, suffered a major staff and management upheaval that included the sudden departure of the editor and of the publicity person to whom my book had been assigned. When the remarkably wide review coverage of *Cantor's Dilemma* propelled my novel to bestseller status on the Bay Area list, Doubleday was caught unprepared. The modest first print run was quickly sold out, and no one pursued a timely second printing until after Christmas, thus making *Cantor's Dilemma* a short-lived collector's item for the two busiest weeks prior to Christmas. The post-Christmas reprint by Doubleday, though personally gratifying, hardly made up for this marketing bungle.

If I were superstitious, I would have concluded that some omnipotent god of fiction was advising me to return to chemistry. But even if I had been burdened by superstition,

Visit to the Institute of Bioorganic Chemistry, Soviet Academy of Sciences, Vladivostok, two months before boarding the Akademik Oparin *in the Indian Ocean, 1989*

the next omen would have encouraged me to press on.

Exactly ten days after the earthquake disaster, my son Dale and I took off for a round-the-world trip prompted by an earlier commitment to arrive on October 29 in Male, the capital of the Maldives in the Indian Ocean. Curiously, for that particular date, the most direct route from San Francisco was to fly by TWA via New York to Vienna in order to catch, a few hours later, a twice-weekly Vienna to Singapore flight that refueled in Male. Our stopover in Vienna, though measured chronometrically in just a few hours, carried decades-long psychic resonances that I recounted two years later in the shortest, yet most ambivalent, chapter of my autobiography. Under the title *"Wien, Wien nur du allein,"* the chapter described the express tour I gave my son through my childhood stomping [*sic!*] grounds from pre- and post-*Anschluss* days. October 29 was not only my sixty-sixth birthday, but also the day on which we were supposed to be picked up in Male by

the Soviet oceanographic vessel, *Akademik Oparin,* which was on a four-month-long expedition, starting in Vladivostok and ending in Leningrad. I had encountered the ship two months earlier during a scientific visit to the Far-Eastern Siberian Branch of the Soviet Academy of Sciences in Vladivostok, the *Akademik Oparin*'s home port, and was so impressed by its diving facilities (including a decompression chamber) and shipboard laboratories that I managed to inveigle an invitation to participate in a forthcoming collecting trip to the northern Maldives in the Indian Ocean. Once that was accomplished, it was not difficult to convince my Soviet hosts to let me bring my son, who had learned scuba diving with me and had since become an expert diver.

In the late 1980s, Vladivostok was still a closed city. Indeed as far as international fax communication was concerned, the entire Soviet Union was basically non-faxable. But not the *Akademik Oparin,* whose fax machine could be accessed directly from the States via the

COMSAT satellite system. Dale and I were the only non-Russians on board and also the only non-Russian speakers. But by using English, German, or Spanish (several of the scientists and crew had worked in Cuba), we managed easily. Just as we sat down to a welcome-aboard dinner in the captain's quarters, the first officer broke in excitedly with the message, "A fax for the professor." Instead of an emergency message, it turned out to be a photocopy of the glowing lead review of *Cantor's Dilemma* from the October 29 *Los Angeles Times* with "Happy Birthday!" scribbled in my wife's handwriting on the top. "You can't enjoy pleasures like this in chemistry," I told my son.

Cantor's Dilemma produced another enjoyable and much more consequential effect: my first interaction, subsequently ripening into personal friendship, with Gerd Haffmans, the founder of Haffmans Verlag, which has become my German-language literary home as it has served that function for a diverse list of British authors, ranging from David Lodge and Julian Barnes to Stephen Fry and Michael Palin—even Monty Python scripts. By now, Haffmans has published seven of my books in German translation (my short story collection, my autobiography, and five novels) and has worked so fast that even though my manuscripts first have to be translated into German, they still come out nearly one year in advance of their American Ur-texts. *Cantors Dilemma* (only the apostrophe had to disappear in the German title) was especially successful since the *Frankfurter Allgemeine Zeitung,* Germany's most important newspaper, serialized the novel in its entirety over a period of two months prior to the publication of the hardback by Haffmans. The latter also arranged for the eventual German paperback release of all of my books through Heyne Verlag of Munich, one of Germany's largest paperback publishers.

Cantors Dilemma has appeared in a number of other languages, but its German rendition has proved far more important to me than even the English version—not for commercial, but for psychological reasons.

German, or more precisely Viennese-Austrian (though not Viennese dialect), is my mother tongue. That's what I spoke exclusively for the first fifteen years of my life; *Deutsch* was also the language in which I did my first significant belletristic reading as a student in an elite

central European gymnasium-style school, much more advanced than contemporary American public high schools. For instance, by age fourteen, I had already studied Latin for four years; Shakespeare, though all in German translation, had become familiar through his collected works and my *Burgtheater* attendances; books by Charles Dickens, Mark Twain, Jack London, Edgar Allan Poe, and other English-language authors were avidly read—but all in *Deutsch.* Once I took off on a Nazi-prompted emigrant's voyage via Bulgaria to become, at age sixteen, a new American immigrant, my mother tongue atrophied for fifty years: First as a college student wanting to become instantly Americanized; then as the successive husband of three wives who spoke not a word of German; and most importantly, as a workaholic scientist during the postwar decades when English rapidly became the lingua franca of the realm.

As far as I can remember, the last novel I read in German at age eighteen or nineteen was Arthur Koestler's *The Gladiators*, featuring Spartacus as the main protagonist. (Koestler's Spartacus resurfaced, some forty odd years later, in my autobiographical short story, "What's Tatiana Troyanos Doing in Spartacus's Tent?") Half a century later, I read another novel in German, with an attention I had never before dedicated to any other piece of fiction. As I turned the pages of Ursula-Maria Mössner's translation of my *Cantor's Dilemma*, long-forgotten German phraseological nuances bobbed up from some Viennese mental interior that I had assumed had long ago been covered by impenetrable psychic soil on which my adult American persona had grown such deep roots that I had virtually forgotten the original ones. As far as I was concerned, I had become a totally assimilated American, whose entire higher education and professional development in chemistry had been stamped indelibly with "Made in USA."

In hour-long telephone conversations between San Francisco and Ulm in southern Germany, I attempted to convince Ully Mössner, the sophisticated German translator hired by Haffmans, to modify a phrase here or there, using (what I thought) would be a more precise phrasing of my original *Cantor's Dilemma* English text. (Even the word "English" is defined with unimpeachable precision in Germany: all my books state on the cover, *"Aus dem Amerikanischen."*) But I grossly underestimated the stubborn professionalism and diplomacy of the person who has since become my verbal German alter ego. Ully Mössner's polite demurrers ("I'll think about that" or "I'll let you know" without hardly ever amending the text) eventually changed into undisguised hilarity when she stressed that in most instances, my modifications were based on a Viennese of the 1930s, which, though totally devoid of English contaminants so common in contemporary postwar German, still dated me. I finally conceded to myself that in spite of my silver hair, my verbal language age in German had not yet passed the teens.

When the German *Cantors Dilemma* appeared, Haffmans Verlag arranged a reading tour, starting in Berlin. Reading a text aloud in German presented no difficulties and my slight Austrian accent, now even scented by whiffs of occasional Americanisms, certainly did not put off the audiences. Initially, I was worried how I would cope with extemporaneous answers in German to ad hoc questions. But as I proceeded from Berlin to Hamburg, then Köln, Frankfurt, Braunschweig, and onwards, my *Deutsch* loosened almost hourly. Even impromptu live TV and radio interviews in German have long ceased to concern me, especially since—in my experience—the German interviewers and journalists are far better prepared through much more extensive background reading than their American counterparts back home; furthermore, the interviews are generally longer, thus reducing the pressure to produce sound bites in response to questions that deserve considerate commentary. Six years and many dozens of lectures and interviews later, much of my German has returned. On at least one occasion, I even dreamed in German—to me the ultimate testimony that a reviving mother tongue is poking holes in a psychic barrier that, prior to the middle 1980s, I had assumed had become impenetrable. Yet to this day, my German chemical terminology is hopelessly limited. Thus, during a 1996 live, radio quiz show over an East German radio station, I—who had just been introduced pompously as a world-famous chemist and "Father of the Pill"—could not think of the German word for HCN. To my total embarrassment, all I could mouth was a German pronunciation of hydrogen cyanide, which bore not the vaguest resemblance to the correct *Blausäure*. Even the idiomatically English prussic acid—rather appropriate given the radio station's location—had escaped me.

A brief digression: in 1988, I accompanied my wife to the Fifth European-American Conference on Literature and Psychoanalysis, held in the small Austrian village of Kirchberg am Wechsel. A couple of years earlier, she had planted in my mind the proposal that I write an autobiography. She now suggested that an unstructured visit to Austria, in the psychoanalytically literate ambiance of her conference, might just be the occasion for some serious germination of such a project. Her prescience was confirmed almost instantaneously. Of all days, we arrived in Kirchberg am Wechsel on the fiftieth anniversary of my emigration from Vienna! By the end of the conference, the first draft of a memoir, *Freud and I*, had been completed, which after some revision was published in the *Southern Review* (vol. 26, number 1, 1990) and eventually became the first chapter in my book-length autobiography (*The Pill, Pygmy Chimps, and Degas' Horse*).

This autobiography has also been published in Spanish, Italian, and French; but the German translation (again by Ully Mössner) under the title, *Die Mutter der Pille*, had by far the deepest impact. Not only is it the longest version—with two extra chapters and a special foreword—but it finally showed me that I was not a totally assimilated American, that my Central European roots, though deeply buried, were still alive. It is strange that much of that recognition did not occur in Austria, the country of my birth and early education, but rather in Germany—a country I had never visited during my childhood, but had always judged the ultimate Hitlerian source of my flight from Europe. My first visit to Germany had only occurred in 1955 as an American scientist, and all subsequent and relatively infrequent visits were related to invitations to scientific lectures or congresses that were held entirely in English. Except for a smattering of German small talk with waiters and taxi drivers and the occasional skimming of some German newspaper, I considered myself, and acted, like a visiting American. All that has changed because of my extensive visits to Germany in association with the publication of my fiction. The biggest impact, however, occurred when I found myself mouthing, in the translated German of a modern German woman, excerpts from my autobiography that I could only write down in English rather than in German, the language in which the events had actually happened. It took a modern German voice, and a woman's voice at that, to make me come to terms with my European origins.

The reception of my first novel, *Cantor's Dilemma*, prompted me to continue with my "science-in-fiction" mode. The seminal idea for the second volume, *The Bourbaki Gambit*, came to me at Princeton University, where I spoke in 1988 at the retirement party of my friend and close collaborator, Kurt Mislow—at that time arguably the most distinguished chemistry professor on the Princeton faculty. During the festivities—attended by over one hundred former graduate students and postdoctoral fellows of Mislow's, as well as faculty members from at least a dozen other universities—my friend drew me aside to show me a curt one-sentence missive from the secretary of the Princeton board of trustees that he had just received. I could tell that its coldness, its lack of grace, and its succinct legalese framing of the emeritus status under which Mislow would be permitted to

continue with his research in the Princeton laboratories, had grated on my friend. It read: "Dear Sir: I have the honor to inform you that at a meeting of the Trustees of Princeton University held today, you were appointed Senior Research Chemist in your department, without stipend, for the period June 1, 1988, to May 31, 1989. Respectfully yours. . . ."

This letter (reproduced verbatim in my novel, but under another signature) became the kernel of irritation that eventually grew into a pearl of fictional revenge. The blurb on the back of my novel's Penguin paperback edition succinctly summarizes my plot:

> At the age of sixty-eight, distinguished science professor Max Weiss is bribed into taking an early retirement. Frustratingly aware that his best years are not yet behind him, Weiss devises an ingenious revenge in the form of "Dr. Diana Skordylis" [whose archetype is a famous group of French mathematicians who actually have been publishing collectively for several decades under

With the poet Robert Lowell (left) at an honorary degree conferment at our alma mater, Kenyon College, 1958

the nom de plume of Nicolas Bourbaki]—a pseudonym for a partnership between Weiss and three aging colleagues, each with an ax to grind against the scientific community. What the Skordylis group doesn't anticipate, however, is the unbridled success of their venture: the discovery of PCR, one of the most important breakthroughs in contemporary biomedical science [a real invention that was recognized by the 1993 Chemistry Nobel Prize]. Professional jealousy soon threatens Diana Skordylis's life. As the force of ego tests the bonds of collaboration, the reader is treated to a fascinating glimpse inside the worlds of academia and scientific enterprise.

What gave me particular pleasure, beyond my obvious identification with the age group (sixty to seventy-two) of my fictitious protagonists in *The Bourbaki Gambit,* was to write the novel entirely in the first person singular. Scientists are discouraged in their scientific writing from doing that, and I do not believe that in over forty years of research writing, I ever used the word "I." Finally, this artificial cultural shackle of Carl Djerassi, the chemist, was broken by Carl Djerassi, the novelist, with an avalanche of "I's" in *The Bourbaki Gambit.*

I started the novel in London in 1989 and completed it in 1990 during a fabulous five-week residency in Bellagio on the shores of Lake Como at the Rockefeller Foundation's Villa Serbelloni. *The Bourbaki Gambit* was first published in hardback by the University of Georgia Press—with a cover of a stunning Magritte image, "The Sorcerer," depicting a man performing four different actions with four hands—while the paperback was again brought out by Penguin-USA. Just as with my first novel, *Bourbaki* received excellent and wide review coverage from both the general press ("A subtle meditation on the scientific personality . . . an odd blend of literature, philosophy, and science writing, as creative as any organic potpourri that Djerassi might have mixed up in his laboratory"—*The Washington Post*) and scientific magazines ("Probably the quintessential science novel of the past year"—*Science*), which propelled me to extend my original plan of a "science-in-fiction" trilogy to a tetralogy.

The third volume had actually been simmering in my mind for years. *Cantor's Dilemma* and *The Bourbaki Gambit* were meant to illustrate the academic scientific turf, but—as science's racehorses also are known to graze on other pastures—they became the principal venues of my tetralogy's last two volumes. My first two installments dealt mainly with the arcane rituals of an enormously important but basically closed tribe, the scientific research community. Only the insider scientists of that tribe are in a position to describe accurately their own behavioral and cultural idiosyncrasies—to the extent that they even pay attention to them, preoccupied as they are with analyzing the physical world around them. But scientists rarely get brownie points from their peers—the providers of the accolades scientists crave most—for communicating with the public. I am now at an age where disapproval or, indeed, even approval by my scientific peers can do little for my scientific career or self-esteem as I cross into literary terrain; yet I feel strongly as a scientist and a pedagogue that the scientific culture must be illuminated for the broader public that otherwise—largely out of scientific illiteracy—cares little for it. Why not attempt some pedagogic experiments by smuggling such concepts into the conscience of a wider public in the guise of fiction?

Cantor's Dilemma and *The Bourbaki Gambit* deal with practices dear to the egocentric heart of a scientist: publications, priorities, the order of the authors, the choice of the journal, the intimate collegiality and concurrent brutal competition, academic tenure and grantsmanship, the Nobel Prize, even *Schadenfreude*. The scientist's culture and mores are tribal: acquired and transmitted by apprenticeship via a mentor-disciple relationship, by intellectual osmosis rather than through lectures or textbooks. Hence the mentor-disciple relationship in its various manifestations plays an important role in all of my novels, and so does the scientist's overwhelmingly patriarchal clan culture in which my fictional characters move. The problems modern women face as they attempt to enter a previously exclusive male domain are a recurrent motive in all of my fiction.

All of these issues are common to science, irrespective of where it is practiced. Yet I feel strongly that my readers should also become familiar with the nonacademic turf on which such behavioral patterns and actions are played out, even if most of the players are still academics. Thus, in the third volume of my tetralogy, *Menachem's Seed*, I enter the arena of

Four generations of Djerassi males (including grandson Alexander), each generation separated by thirty-one years, SMIP Ranch, 1984

international policy, giving a semifictional account of the Pugwash Conferences on Science and World Affairs (renamed Kirchberg Conferences in my novel). Pugwash is a movement established in the late 1950s that until recently was unknown to the general public and even to the bulk of academic scientists—until it was recognized in 1995 through the award of the Nobel Peace Prize. I had participated in Pugwash for nearly twenty years from the middle 1960s to the early 1980s, during which period I was also heavily involved in bilateral discussions of science policy under the auspices of our National Academy of Sciences with scientists of lesser developed countries. I thus feel qualified to illuminate these activities to a broader public, be it in factual prose or in the guise of fiction.

But there is one much wider area, in which science is practiced and where the behavioral and even cultural patterns differ from those in academic science, namely in industry. Since I had straddled the academic and industrial worlds for decades, I unabashedly consider myself competent to draw on themes and problems from

that milieu for my fiction. The final volume, simply titled *NO*, attempts to fill that gap in my tetralogy's semifictive survey of the scientific scene and does so by focusing on the small, entrepreneurial, research-driven enterprises sometimes collectively referred to as biotech. I made that choice because, in contrast to big industry, biotech companies of the 1980s and 1990s are uniquely American phenomena born out of academia—much of it right in my own backyard: the San Francisco Bay Area. Because of their intellectual origins in educational institutions, these biotech ventures have also generated a series of contentious problems, arising from the interaction of profit-driven enterprises with supposedly nonprofit institutions and (ideally) disinterested individual scientists. These have caused numerous legal, philosophical, and ethical debates that will continue to influence the conduct of science within the academy, as well as the ways it is disseminated into the economy and culture at large.

While a two-letter title would seem to leave little scope for ambiguity, the meaning of my

"Booksigning on the occasion of publication of my first novel, Cantor's Dilemma, *with my stepdaughter, Leah Middlebrook," November 1989*

NO is complicated. It refers to the many layers of the negative expletive as well as to the chemical formula of nitric oxide, an industrial gas and global, environmental pollutant. Yet some of the hottest recent biomedical research has also shown that NO fulfills a singularly complicated and sophisticated function in the human body, where (continuously generated) it serves as a biological messenger, indispensable in a staggering variety of processes, including penile erection. This, in turn, led me to use the therapeutic treatment of male functional impotence as the vehicle for illustrating the role of a biotech company in contemporary biomedical research.

These days, many of my lectures carry the generic title "Science-in-fiction is not Science Fiction. Is it Autobiography?" My answer has to be affirmative. Only by dipping deeply and frequently into the well of my accumulated experience as a scientist can I even dare to attempt the task of explicating my tribe's mores to the outsiders or indeed even those insiders who have chosen to pay little atten-

tion to our many quirks and foibles. Yet my admission that much of it is autobiographical does not mean that the plots are biographical. They are psychically autobiographical, but operationally, the bulk is fiction. And the part that isn't, is generally well disguised.

My tetralogy, provisionally titled "Secrets of the Tribe," deals primarily with the "*how* do you do it?" rather than with the "*what* are you doing?" aspects of a scientist's life. But I have not ignored the *what*—and especially not in the last two volumes. One of the high points of the early part of my scientific career was my participation in the very first synthesis of a steroid oral contraceptive. The question that I and many other scientists active in female reproductive biology have been asked is, "Why is there no Pill for men?"

There is no single, all-encompassing answer to this seemingly simple question because it carries with it a lot of hidden baggage, way beyond straightforward scientific or even commercial considerations. One answer, which to me represents a distillation of all the misconceptions carried by modern women—notably from America and Europe—was offered by the distinguished anthropologist, the late Margaret Mead:

> [The pill] is entirely the invention of men. And why did they do it? . . . Because they are extraordinarily unwilling to experiment with their own bodies . . . and they're extremely willing to experiment with women's bodies. . . . It would be much safer to monkey with men than monkey with women. . . . Now the ideal contraceptive undoubtedly would be a pill that a man and a woman would have to take simultaneously.

I have chosen to tackle the complexity of the problem in my last two novels, which address the question why no male Pill has been created and why no such male contraceptive will be available for the next decade or two, if then. In this place I will not offer a summary of the plots of *Menachem's Seed* or *NO* other than to point out that there are aspects of male reproductive biology which are currently high on the list of research and development priorities in Europe and the United States. These involve the treatment of male infertility, the scientific subject matter of *Menachem's Seed*, and of male impotence, as covered in detail in *NO*.

> "I knew it!" the woman exclaimed triumphantly. "All female reproductive biology means to you is contraception. But when you men work on your own sexual apparatus, all you worry about—"

The woman in the preceding paragraph could well have been Margaret Mead or many other like-minded critics. In fact, such a critic is one of the characters in *Menachem's Seed*, and I am citing her to indicate that I use women's understandable concerns as one of the components in a fairly complex plot. As a scientist, I have never worked in the fields of male infertility or impotence, although I followed some of the leading literature. So is my "science-in-fiction" autobiography? Experientially, much of it is not, but otherwise. . . .

The underlying purpose of the *Contemporary Authors Autobiography Series* is, of course, autobiographical disclosure, so I shall end on that note with a novel, *Marx, Deceased*, which is intimately connected with this somewhat autohagiographic record of my second life. As I stated

earlier, that life commenced on May 8, 1983, and shortly thereafter resulted in my writing the novel, "Middles," whose never-to-be-published status was part of my 1985 marriage contract with Diane Middlebrook. But the promise never to publish a manuscript does not include—in fact, cannot include—a guarantee of expunging it from one's brain. During the intervening years, some aliquots found their way into two of my short stories, "First-Class Nun" and "*Maskenfreiheit*," but the rest simmered for nearly a decade until surfacing in a totally different context in *Marx, Deceased*—a novel seemingly unrelated to my "Secrets of the Tribe" tetralogy. I deliberately say "seemingly unrelated" because, in fact, it does merit reading as a component of my tetralogy.

Marx, Deceased was written and completed after I had finished *The Bourbaki Gambit*—a novel that deals with a phenomenon hardly ever addressed or even considered by scientists: their inability to write under a nom de plume. As I stated in the foreword to *Marx, Deceased*:

> Like scientists, most writers also display a need for approbation by their peers. But areas of intersection are not necessarily areas of agreement: this point of contact between the creative writer and the researcher in hard science, while it reveals some convergences, exposes important differences as well. Novelist Stephen Marx's preoccupation with his own image, is not very different from describing a scientist's hunger for peer validation. In each instance, that urge is both the nourishment and the poison of a creative mind.
>
> But writers also lust for recognition beyond the community of their peers. Unlike scientists, who live and die by peer review, a writer requires above all else the approbation of the general public. Best-sellers are created by the book-buying public, not by the writer's peers. Even the favorable opinions of book reviewers and critics, though craved by authors, are not essential for elevation to the best-seller lists. Here scientists have an advantage: they need not concern themselves with professional critics, because such a breed does not exist in their intellectual world—which, incidentally, also excludes the general public. But the final difference between these two groups, in this regard, is the one that concerns me most, for it is the one that cuts, I believe, to the heart of the matter. It has to do with indi-

vidual identity—with ego, the ultimate source of all this hunger for success. Scientists, I have said, never publish anonymously. To do so would seem to rob the entire exercise of its point as I have tried to demonstrate in my preceding novel, *The Bourbaki Gambit*. But a writer? If one's central purpose is to win general acclaim—the kind of celebrity in which one's individual identity is as irrelevant as the actual deeds or personalities of any of the celebrities whose faces grace the supermarket tabloids—it hardly matters if one writes under one's own name or not [e.g., Eric Blair a.k.a. George Orwell or David Cornwell a.k.a. John Le Carré].

This question of celebrity is not an idle one, because, ultimately, it goes beyond ego to the quality of the work itself. What kind of celebrity we pick has everything to do with what we write. If a novelist had to choose between best-seller status, on the one hand, and critics' choice on the other—to sell thousands of books for a couple of years (followed by the oblivion of the remainder bins), or to be neglected by the general public now, but still to be read half a century later—in other words, as Flaubert put it, choose between audience and readers, which would it be? Such a choice is a formidable test of a writer's self-esteem, a test to which my fictional author eventually subjects himself.

But does he pass it?

I end my autobiographical account by pointing out that my fictitious character, Stephen Marx, is the author of thirteen novels, the last of which bore, mirabile dictu, the title *Cohen's Dilemma* and which dealt with a flawed Nobel Prize. In my novel *Marx, Deceased* I have Stephen Marx say the following:

> To me, the ultimate truth is fiction. In ancient Greece, whenever lawyers met after some interesting case, they teased each other with "What if that had happened?" "What if he had done . . . ?" "What if . . . ?" Supposedly, that was the origin of fiction. In any event, that is how I write. I do serious research; I collect the evidence; and then I proceed with "But what if . . . ?" It is a god-like feeling, creating people and situations, passing judgment upon the creatures of your imagination. But unlike a god, I am very sensitive to judgment of my own work. Preoccupied with wanting to know what people *really* thought, I felt only posthumous evaluations would give me that insight.

Stephen Marx's obsession to be a fly on the wall and observe what people really say or think about him is surely shared by other ambitious and active fantasizers. But in my novel, Stephen Marx, a well-known New York writer, actually manages to stage his death in a plausible sailing accident. Holing up in San Francisco under a genderless new name, Marx writes and then publishes his fourteenth novel as a first novel under the nom de plume of D. Mann. As perceptive readers of this autobiographical sketch of Carl Djerassi may already have anticipated, the title of D. Mann's first novel is also "Middles."

Readers should note that these lines are written around the time of my literary bar mitzvah and that I have not broken my premarital promise never to publish Carl Djerassi's "Middles": It only appeared as snippets of a novel-within-a-novel under the title *Marx, Deceased*. Not a bad way of embarking on my literary teens at the chronological age of seventy-three!

BIBLIOGRAPHY

Fiction:

The Futurist and Other Stories, Macdonald/Futura, 1988.

Cantor's Dilemma, Doubleday, 1989, Penguin-USA, 1991 (paperback).

The Bourbaki Gambit, The University of Georgia Press, 1994, Penguin-USA, 1996 (paperback).

Marx, Deceased, The University of Georgia Press, 1996.

Menachem's Seed, The University of Georgia Press, 1997.

NO (German translation), Haffmans Verlag, 1997.

Nonfiction:

The Politics of Contraception, W. W. Norton, 1979.

Steroids Made It Possible, American Chemical Society Books, 1990.

The Pill, Pygmy Chimps, and Degas' Horse, Basic Books, 1992.

From the Lab into the World: A Pill for People, Pets, and Bugs, American Chemical Society Books, 1994.

Poetry:

The Clock Runs Backward, Story Line Press, 1991.

Scientific monographs:

Optical Rotatory Dispersion, McGraw-Hill, 1960.

(Editor) *Steroid Reactions: An Outline for Organic Chemists,* Holden-Day, 1963.

(With H. Budzikiewicz and D. H. Williams) *Interpretation of Mass Spectra of Organic Compounds,* Holden-Day, 1964.

(With H. Budzikiewicz and D. H. Williams) *Structure Elucidation of Natural Products by Mass Spectrometry* (2 volumes), Holden-Day, 1964.

(With H. Budzikiewicz and D. H. Williams) *Mass Spectrometry of Organic Compounds,* Holden-Day, 1967.

Numerous poems, memoirs, and short stories have appeared in literary magazines, including the *Crescent Review, Cumberland Poetry Review, Exquisite Corpse, Frank, Grand Street, Hudson Review, Kenyon Review, Michigan Quarterly Review, Midwest Quarterly, Negative Capability, New Letters, Poet & Critic, South Dakota Review, Southern Review,* and *Wallace Stevens Journal.* Work has also appeared in some anthologies and various issues of *Der Rabe* (in German).

Djerassi's fiction, nonfiction, and technical books have been translated into Chinese, Danish, French, German, Italian, Japanese, Portuguese, Russian, and Spanish.

Edward (Halsey) Foster

1942-

Edward Foster (right) with Gene Blanton at Vaux-le-Vicomte, France, summer, 1996

One December morning when I was seven, I went down to the kitchen and found my grandfather, very angry, poking with the tongs at coals in the stove. Sparks were flying onto the floor.

My brother and I had been in bed with my mother and one of my aunts, telling jokes. It was the first time we had been able to laugh since my father's death a few weeks before.

Their laughter came down the stairs, and my grandfather tried to talk, but his voice was slurred. I stood there, more bewildered than afraid, as he dropped the tongs into the fire and collapsed onto the floor. He lay still for a moment and looked toward me with eyes as empty as my father's had been when he died.

I ran upstairs and got back into bed with the others. I didn't want to believe that what had happened to my father was happening to my grandfather now. I'm not sure how long it was before I went back to the kitchen. My grandfather was lying where he had fallen, breathing heavily next to the stove. He reached toward me, but I backed away and ran to get my mother.

Today I would like to believe the stroke was so severe that he did not notice, or at least did not remember, that I had left him alone, but I knew even then that I had done something terrible.

"Grandfather Foster in one of his serious moods so troubling to me as a child." With him is Foster's father and grandmother, 1938.

When I was young, I spent much time in the hospital because of asthma and other ailments, and when I was there a month later, the nurses said I could visit my grandfather in the ward where he was recovering. I didn't want to go but couldn't tell them why. One afternoon they took me to him, and he told the nurses to go away. They did, and I expected him to punish me. But he seemed happy I had come.

My grandfather lived seven years more, and if he held me accountable for deserting him that December morning, he never showed it. Still, I believed at the time that he knew what I'd done, and this belief, together with the guilt I felt in connection with my father's death (as I will explain later), made me a very unhappy child. I was afraid I might do something awful again, and not wanting people to know what I was really like, I became secretive and apprehensive.

My grandfather was an Edwardian gentleman; this had been the fashion when he came

of age, and he never changed. We lived in a small New England town—Williamsburg, Massachusetts—where most men were either farmers or factory workers, so he stood out plainly, and that was what he wanted. His full name was John Clark Foster, but he styled himself J. Clark Foster and asked his friends to call him Clark. He demanded respect and got it, at least outwardly, although people must have had their reservations. I'm sure there was considerable gossip. It was well known that he had wasted an inheritance from his father, a minor but successful inventor, and another from his grandfather, a Scotsman who had invested in Manhattan real estate. In fact, my grandfather had chosen Williamsburg originally as a summer residence and moved there permanently only when he could no longer afford two homes.

He then took a job in some administrative capacity—I'm not sure exactly what—at a local factory but was fired for embezzlement. There were also rumors of misdealings in a social club of which he was a member, but I've never been able to learn the details.

My grandfather lost his inheritance largely by gambling, and I suppose embezzlement was for him a kind of gambling, too—gambling, that is, that he wouldn't be caught. He believed in luck, as he told me many times, and he had reasons: his father—the man for whom I am named—had shown him what good fortune could do. With great ambition but no education (he came from a family of cobblers who didn't believe in schools), my great-grandfather had decided to become an inventor, and after making a small fortune from a device for cleaning rugs, he tried to invent a perpetual motion machine. Instead he invented a strange but lucrative contraption he called the "Well-Curv." I've never seen one but have been told they were found in rural areas throughout the Northeast as late as the 1930s. The Well-Curv had a set of buckets strung along a continuous length of rope which was lowered into a well; in the more elaborate models there were cranks and gears, and when these were set in motion, the Well-Curv brought up buckets of water, tipping them into a system of troughs and pipes through which the water flowed to the kitchen. The invention sold well. My great-grandfather knew little about physics, but ingenuity and luck made him comfortable, if not rich. He was able to send his son, my grandfather, to private schools and to Yale, which my grandfather soon abandoned, however, as he had little interest in formal education.

Many years after he was fired, my grandfather became the groundskeeper at the local cemetery (primarily, he said, so that he could be near his wife's grave) and once took me into a tomb there and opened one of the vaults, telling me that this was where we all end. My grandfather was no ordinary man.

I think the tone and character of much that I am was determined by him. Certainly no one in my childhood fascinated me more. On the surface his behavior was very mannered, but his interior was perfectly still, like a cat's. He would tease me by saying that I should become an Episcopal priest, for I loved the rituals in that church, but the reason I loved them was that he had taught me to. He adored ceremony, and his enthusiasm was infectious.

My grandfather had ornate manners when the occasion permitted, but he could be impu-

"Grandmother Derosia at a family picnic in 1960. Her face has its characteristic expression: gentle but determined, slightly troubled but conscious of higher, spiritual truths she learned from Mary Baker Eddy."

dent and outrageous as well—living graciously, for example, long after the scandal, in a large Victorian home across the street from his former office. In his last years he dressed in a three-piece suit and flamboyantly walked about town swinging a gold-headed cane. He styled himself flawlessly. Beyond the surface, however, there was little humor; I think that at heart he was a very serious man, and his long silences would have frightened any child. I would sometimes hide under my bed when I thought he was in one of his strange moods.

One of his stories (and it may hold the key to his complexities) involved waking at night at his boarding school and finding the dormitory in flames. He escaped, but some of his friends did not. I believe that memories like this can make one a gambler, persuading one to trust one's luck, knowing that in the end it won't matter whether or not one wins.

I started writing because my father asked me to. Perhaps it was because he needed quiet that he bought me the notebook in which I began copying nursery rhymes and then imitating them. My father was sick much of the time and needed to take long naps, so my brother and I had to remain quiet for an hour or two every day in our rooms. But perhaps my father gave me the notebook simply because he was so restless, forever proposing new things for me and my brother to do.

My father, Edward Clark Foster, had been a pianist. He studied at the New England Conservatory of Music, and his recitals, one of his aunts told me, were well received. He was also a doctoral candidate in English literature at Clark University but returned home to support his parents when his father lost his job. Williamsburg was very small, and there weren't many jobs, but the high school needed someone to teach physics, and he was hired, although he knew little about the subject. But, then, neither had his grandfather.

He was, however, a knowledgeable geologist and mineralogist and was the first to identify a certain semiprecious stone he named Goshenite in honor of the town—Goshen, Massachusetts—where he had found it. He published a scholarly piece about lead mines, founded a local geological society, and worked one summer as a geologist for Kodak. He also continued to play the piano—Rachmaninoff and Chopin mostly—and organized a village band for concerts on summer evenings. He taught me to conduct, and when I was five or six I actually led the band in some Sousa marches—or thought I did, although more likely the musicians were following him, standing behind me. But it was a splendid experience for a little boy to think that people were applauding him.

My father, it seemed, pursued every whim and opportunity that came his way: he was not only a musician, geologist, scholar, and teacher but also the town clerk, the local justice of the peace (conducting weddings in our living room), a notary public, and a volunteer fireman. He was a good photographer, enjoyed building things (such as the bookcase next to me now), and liked to hunt, fish, and camp in the woods. He gave music lessons, organized a Boy Scout troop, and coached basketball for the high school. He was also a serious reader, as his doctoral ambitions suggest, and had much affection for Henry David Thoreau's *Walden.*

"My father in his early twenties working at a boys' camp. Looking youthful, collegiate, and handsome, he has the energy and joie de vivre that would carry him through many disappointments."

When I was five and my brother Roy (or "Skipper," as we called him then) was three, my father took the family to live in a two-room house, one room above the other, in the woods about a mile from the nearest road. (My grandfather, who would have nothing to do with the woods, stayed behind at a hotel.) Ostensibly we moved there because there was nothing else available in town, but I imagine the reasons were more complex. I remember him there reading to my brother and me from *Walden* (particularly the passage about the battle of the ants). The words didn't mean much then, but they came back years later when I read Thoreau in high school.

Today my brother and I agree that living in the woods was the only time we were truly happy for any length of time; we had little supervision and were free to roam in the forest as long as we stayed within certain generous boundaries.

The house had never been properly finished, however, and one morning in November we woke to find snow falling through the chinks, making white lines across our blankets. Skipper and I pretended to be wearing prison clothes, but our parents did not think it as funny as we did, and within a few days we were living in an old, one-room schoolhouse, with a good roof, on the edge of a marsh. That, too, was a grand experience for my brother and me—we could hunt frogs with our popguns—but I think my mother had experienced more than enough rustic life (the only place to cook in the schoolhouse was the fireplace), and very soon we moved into a large white house near the center of town.

A few months later, fighting a fire in the house across the street, my father experienced terrible chest pains, and we assume now that he had a heart attack. But the doctors weren't sure, and although they gave him countless tests, they couldn't explain why he seemed to be growing progressively weaker. Finally, with the shrewd insight reflexive in country doctors, they decided the problem was either his teeth or his heart. They decided to treat the teeth first, as that was easier, so he went to the hospital and had them pulled out.

He came home one Sunday in late November and went directly to bed, too weak even to come downstairs for meals. I envied the attention he was getting, and that Tuesday I pretended to be sick and stayed home from school, writing in my poem book in bed. I remember that it was a bright sunny day, and I wanted to go outside, but my mother said that if I was too sick to go to school, I was too sick to get out of bed. She went into her bedroom to talk with my father and shut the door.

Then there was a terrible commotion, the door opened, and my mother ran down the hall, telling me to stay where I was; my father, she said, was sick. It had always been a nervous household, and since my brother and I were sick to our stomachs from time to time, my mother kept a basin under the bathroom sink for us to throw up into. I thought at this moment that my father must need the basin, so I went and got it. My mother, seeing what I was doing, shouted at me: "He's not sick like that." But I took the basin, not knowing what else to do, and entered their room.

My father was in agony, and I do not think that at first he knew I was there. But when he saw me, he looked at me desperately, I think, as if asking me to come near. But I held back. I had never seen death, but I read years later that when we die our eyes cloud and the pupils dilate, and as I watched that morning, in a great panic, this happened to him. It is a moment which I recall most days; I dream about it and think about it, reconstructing second by second what happened. It was many years before I could admit to myself what I had seen, but from the first, I would run over the event again and again in my mind, knowing that I had done a terrible thing by not going to him when he looked at me in that particular way.

At the time, I was simply terrified. Understanding nothing, I ran to my room and climbed under the bed with my poem book and tried to read it—it was the only thing I could think of to do—but I was shaking too much to see the words. I could hear my mother in the hall beginning the Lord's Prayer, over and over, and I thought I should try to reach God, so I climbed on my bed and raised my hands to the ceiling to beg for help. The front door slammed open, very loudly, and a doctor ran up the stairs. He went with my mother to the bedroom, and they closed the door. It seemed a very long time before they came out and my mother told me that my father was dead.

Soon after, my grandfather came home from the cemetery and went directly to his room. I wanted to talk to him, but he said almost nothing to me until the day of the funeral, when he told me that someday he would tell me what death was—although in fact he already had the day he took me into the tomb. He said very little to any of us between that day and the morning of his stroke, and there were few opportunities to talk with him after he was released from the hospital, for he spent the rest of his life first in a nursing home and then on a farm far from where we lived.

To make the down payment on the house, my father had cashed in his life insurance, so that when he died our only resource was the house, an old car, and the furniture. One warm spring morning the local auctioneer set up his tent facing the veranda. He put his podium at the top of the steps to the veranda, and one by one, our things were carried out the door and sold—sewing machine, kitchen table, piano, books. My father's gems and semiprecious stones were sent to Clark University. (I went there to see the collection many years later, but no one remembered where it had been stored.) We kept for ourselves little aside from photographs and my father's childhood toys.

A few weeks later the house was sold, and we moved to an industrial city, Pittsfield, Massachusetts—a very ugly place—where we lived for a year in a tiny, four-room house surrounded by tenements. The General Electric plant was at the end of the road. My mother worked first as a domestic and then sold cosmetics door to door. I remember very little about that year—and nothing that was happy. My strongest memories concern my brother badgering my mother to buy him leather boots and a black denim jacket. Finally, she gave in. We had very little money, so these things were considered major purchases. They were also things I'd wanted myself but had been afraid to ask for.

Children do not fully understand the secret language of clothes, but the fascination is there, and I envied my brother for getting the things I wanted myself. It was as if he were becoming the person I wanted to be. We had always been rivals, but the rivalry now became hostile, and we fought much of the time. I bloodied him only once, and he never seriously injured me, although he could have, being much more muscular.

This miserable year ended when the Williamsburg superintendent of schools asked my mother if she would return and teach sixth grade. The pay was poor, but the job was better than ringing doorbells, and it allowed us to escape the factories and the tenements.

My mother had taught in Williamsburg before she married and would have continued, but state law at that time said married women could not teach, for there were not enough positions for both married and unmarried women. The law argued that since married women had husbands for support, jobs should go to those who had to support themselves. My mother had been to college for only two years, which was considered adequate for a grammar school teacher in the 1930s when she began teaching, but in the 1950s the state changed its mind and said that grammar school teachers must now have four years of college. Consequently each year the school board had to get her a waiver from the officials in Boston. After many years the board felt the state would no longer make difficulties; by that time my mother was the principal of all three schools in town, but she worried until she retired that someone malicious would make trouble.

My father and, more particularly, my grandfather dominate my earliest memories, but my mother very soon took hold of my life in her own way. She became effectively my conscience, and when I was a child, I would have ventured very little without asking myself first whether it was something of which she would approve. My mother is a single-minded, determined woman. Her dedication to teaching is a clear instance: she would leave for school while my brother and I were still eating breakfast and not return until dinner, then spend the evening correcting papers and preparing classes for the next day. She granted my brother and me much freedom; no one among my friends had as much, but, of course, we were expected to do the right thing. And, in general, we did.

The importance to my mother of books and art affected me as much as her conscience and her determination. She had studied drawing and painting at college and kept portfolios of her work in the attic of the house where we lived during the last months of my father's life. I was forbidden to go there alone because of splinters and nails poking through the floorboards, but sometimes when we were supposed to be quiet so that my father could sleep, I would sneak up there to look at her works; they were mysteries to me, for I didn't know how things so lovely could be made. There

"My mother with silk stockings and a carnation. As beguiling and youthful as she seems, there is already a great determination around the mouth and eyes."

was a charcoal of a forest at night that particularly fascinated me. I tried drawing something like it in my poem book but couldn't do anything as satisfying. The portfolios disappeared after my father's death, and I don't know where they went.

My mother, like my father and grandfather, read during much of her free time (there were books throughout the house), and my respect for literature is one result. She worked so much that on many days my brother and I had little contact with her except at mealtimes, but there was always, just before bed, the special intimacy of hearing her read to us from such books as *Treasure Island*, *Gulliver's Travels*, and *The Secret Garden*, which must have been her favorite, for we heard it many times.

Sometimes we had two parents, for my Aunt Betty, my mother's sister, who worked at a hospital near Albany, would stay with us weekends as well as during her vacations and holidays. She was much stricter with us than our mother and had definite ideas on how boys should behave and how they should dress and comb their hair. She liked pressed trousers and polished shoes and did not allow boots in the house. You could never argue with her on these matters, and so it was necessary to change clothes secretly and slip out the back door when we went off to see friends.

But she was very generous, too. My mother could not afford a car, and so it was my aunt who took us to see the ocean, Boston, New York, and other places that were wonderful to children. Further, my aunt and another of my mother's sisters spent much time painting or working with clay. My brother and I might have turned out very differently if my mother and her sisters had been concerned with sports or gossip rather than books and art. As it is, I've never watched a baseball game to the end; it was something that none of us would do. When my father was alive, we played softball with him, but the equipment disappeared in the auction. My brother played basketball in high school, but otherwise sports were of little interest to our family.

Behind my mother and her sisters was Grandmother Derosia, whose religious bias affected us all. She had grown up in terrible poverty (newspapers were used to keep the wind from blowing through cracks in her bedroom), and she had little trust in the material world, which she came to think, after reading Mary Baker Eddy, was an illusion. My grandmother would lecture me on the "errors" of "mortal mind," a fundamental notion in Christian Science but one I could not understand. I certainly did understand, though, that sickness of any sort constituted an "error" of "mortal mind," which is to say, it didn't exist. But I had spent too much time in oxygen tents and emergency wards to believe that. Still, I was very taken with her vision of a world built of love and utterly beyond the one we saw. I suppose her insistence that the physical world was not the ultimate one made it easier for her family to cultivate interests in books and art. Christian Science is solidly indebted to Ralph Waldo Emerson, German idealism, and gnostic convictions, and I doubt that my own curiosity about these matters would have developed had it not been for her.

Williamsburg was a more congenial place to live than Pittsfield, but this was the 1950s, and the country belonged to "normal" families—meaning a father who worked and a mother who didn't. Ours was the only "incomplete" family in the town, and we felt it strongly. People could be quite cruel, especially when they were most patronizing—as when giving us clothes their children had outgrown. In the 1950s one was supposed to be "well adjusted," and we most certainly were not. But even in such a small town we were not the only oddities, and my brother and I had friends with whom we did things like perform plays, tell stories, and publish a newspaper on a small handpress I was given one Christmas. There were no televisions in any of my friends' homes; in fact, there was none in town until I was ten or eleven, and even then it was something we watched only as a curiosity. Several of those friends are now successful: one directs a repertoire theater, another is the stage manager for the San Francisco Opera, and a third writes books for children.

The gossip networks in Williamsburg, as in all small towns, were byzantine; without television to occupy spare time, most people spent their leisure talking about others, and no one's life was private. My mother usually didn't gossip—she was too busy for that—but I knew that she would soon hear if I did anything wrong. There was little chance I would, and I certainly would not have done anything illegal, for my mother's moral presence was always a force to be reckoned with. Nonetheless, when I was twelve and became an adolescent, I was fearful, as children at that age often are, that people around me could hear the terrible things in my head.

In addition, I still believed that I had failed my grandfather and my father and that my misery was somehow my punishment; I believed I should stay away from people, and aside from my close friends, I did. I spent long days in the woods, where I felt no one would hear my horrible thoughts. I also explored local caves, where I could be more certain of being alone and keeping my thoughts unheard. Of course, local people thought it was merely another healthy interest, and a reporter did a couple of articles about me and my caves for the county newspaper.

A reprieve from this paranoid foolishness came from the town librarian, who hired me to "keep an eye" on the library when it was closed. This meant that I had a key to the building and was supposed to go there every day she didn't, "just to make sure things were okay," and soon I was spending my time in the empty library rather than in the woods or in caves. The librarian's deeper purpose, I assume, was to keep a very odd boy out of trouble.

I was not supposed to turn on the lights, for people walking by might think the library was open, but in the gloom I discovered *Wuthering Heights*, Dickens, Agatha Christie, a biography of Douglas Fairbanks, picture books of flowers and birds, local histories, and much more. The most important was a tiny leather-bound book—Manoah Bodman's *Oration on Death*—published in Williamsburg in 1817. It was a collection of poems and an account of the author's struggle with Satan, who for decades had deluded and tormented him, assaulting him in his bed, in the street, and in the woods. Bodman was a great visionary. Local histories

"Eighteen months old and looking cocky and spoiled. The irises behind me were grown by my grandfather, who saved the best blooms for his wife's grave."

said that the townspeople had considered him a madman and a crank, but that did not trouble him: he was engrossed in business more important than theirs, for his war with Satan was real, a cosmic battle for his soul. Bodman was a powerful writer and would have interested any child with an imagination, but he was especially critical to me, for he had lived where I did. I knew the places he mentioned, and not only were the names of the people familiar, I knew where they had lived and where in the cemetery they were buried. Checking town histories and obituaries, I discovered that Bodman had died in the house in which I was born. Since the *Oration* was a rare book, the librarian would not let me take it home, so I spent afternoons copying out passages of the narrative and all of the poems. Bodman so occupied my mind that I would stay up all night thinking about him and fall asleep the next morning in school.

For many years I tried to have the book, or at least the poems, republished. Occasionally I would find someone as excited by Bodman as I—the poet Lewis Turco, for example—and at last I was able to get one of the poems included in John Hollander's anthology, *American Poetry: The Nineteenth Century* (1993), published by the Library of America. One person who reviewed the book said that the closest Bodman had come to poetry was the day he was baptized—a clever thing to say but not true. The reviewer remains among those I hate most.

I believe that Bodman deserves attention, although I realize now that much of my early enthusiasm was quite personal and subjective. Bodman's inner troubles bore an affinity to my own, particularly his belief that he was horribly corrupt and must avoid people. And he was a writer from my own town, and that was very important, for it meant that someday the things I wrote might be published, too.

Meanwhile, my teachers had come to the not very surprising conclusion that I had problems and was a bad influence. In seventh grade we were asked to elect one of three programs to follow during the next five years: college, commercial, or, the least difficult, general. I chose "college" but was assigned to "general" with the provision that if I worked hard I could move up to "commercial"—this in spite of my being second or third in the class. The school's attitude to my brother was equally bleak, and although he was the class valedictorian, he spent his first college year, on the advice of his guidance counselor, at an obscure school training to be a basketball coach. The next year he chose his own school, eventually completing a Ph.D. in physiology and securing a position teaching and doing research at Berkeley. I confronted the guidance counselor many years later, asking him what he thought of my brother's success, but he only looked confused.

I asked my mother a few years ago why my teachers treated me as they did, and she said it was because they thought I believed I knew more than they. In reality, the problem was the opposite: I felt that I was a very wicked person and that this was why others treated me the way they did. Shortly after I was assigned to the "general" program, the school psychologist examined me and decided that I might do better at a boarding school. He arranged for me to attend, on scholarship, Williston Academy, where I lived, aside from school vacations, for the next five years. Most boys there came from privileged backgrounds and had no interest in me, but there were a few whose lives had been like my own, and we became friends. There were also teachers—or "masters," as they were called—whose influence on me would be crucial.

In my junior year psychologists gave me a battery of tests and summarized the results in a "profile" that said that I was inordinately self-confident and "touchy, suspicious, and easily irked by other people," that I had "serious adjustment difficulties" and was intellectually serious and independent (not necessarily a good thing in those years when intellectuals were dismissed as "eggheads") and "subject to apprehensive fears or worries," and that I saw life "through daydreams and uneasy retrospection." The tests found that I might be a successful "author-journalist," but that I should also consider a career as a lawyer or an "advertising man." On the other hand, my interest in music was "momentary" and an "escape."

It was not, or at least it hadn't been. Shortly before the profile was written, my music teacher had been arrested as part of a homosexual "ring," so named by tabloids, one of which headlined its account "Sex Scandal Rocks Quiet College Town." That "scandal," one of the last great government-sponsored persecutions of homosexuals in this country, centered on Newton Arvin, the distinguished literary critic, Smith College

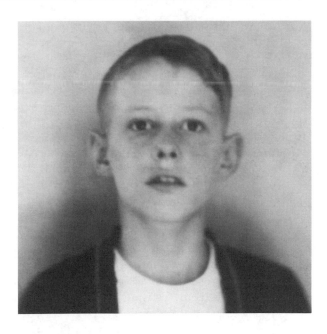

"Ten years old in a photo taken in a booth at a penny arcade. I'd not yet learned how to pose for photos, and the bewilderment and perplexity in the face truthfully express the person I was at the time."

professor, and, for many years, companion to Truman Capote. Zealous officials extended their investigation into the lives of other men in the area, who were then "exposed." My teacher simply disappeared from the school, but I was told privately by the headmaster (who surmised correctly that this teacher and I had been very close) that although what had happened was a "tragedy," it would be best not to talk about it—or indeed mention my teacher's name on the campus again. I would have no idea what happened to my teacher, in fact, were it not for classmates who found him working in a bookstore in Harvard Square. When he realized he had been seen, he ducked down the stairs, obviously wanting to be left alone. It is out of respect for this apparent wish to "disappear" that I do not name him here, but I testify that his effect on me was profound.

He knew, for I had told him very early, about my father's interest in music and so he made me one of his acolytes, taking me to concerts, giving me music scores and books about music, teaching me basic rules of musical composition, and encouraging me to write my own music. I'm sure that what I did was not very good, for I knew very little about composition, but he was encouraging and turned me over to Alvin Etler, who lived nearby and was then well known for works commissioned and performed by the Boston Symphony Orchestra. Etler was fully as kind, but not long after I met him, my teacher was implicated in the "scandal," and suddenly my interest in music became an issue for certain vocal and self-righteous students.

Homosexuality was thought to be a terrible sin in boys' boarding schools at this time. The headmaster no doubt thought he was being helpful in telling me not to mention my teacher's name. Fellow students would question me about my "friendship" with my teacher, and it did not help that he had also been my dorm master, living across the hall. In that pressured world, my interest in music eventually became "momentary" and an "escape," although it took almost a year before I was worn down sufficiently to abandon afternoons with the piano and take up lacrosse instead. In the end, I was a coward, and the one a coward hurts most is himself.

My music teacher was replaced in my affections by another Williston master, Horace Thorner, a skilled poet and translator. I thought him physically ugly and vain (he once told me he had "noble features"), and he had the affectations of a Boston Brahmin (which he was), but beyond the vanity and affectations, he was a loving man whose nature is perhaps best indicated by a line in his translation of *The Rubáiyát* of Omar Khayyám saying that his "Friend" is his body, "upon whose Sword my Soul needs must depend."

A few years ago, reading through Jack Spicer's papers at the Bancroft Library, I found a scrap on which was written "Edward Thorner" with what I assume had been his Boston address and telephone number. "Edward" was Thorner's real first name, "Horace" being the name he used as a poet and a teacher. I assume that Spicer and Thorner crossed paths when Spicer was living in Boston in the mid-1950s (the paper is mixed in with letters and notations from that period), but it is curious

"My mother and handsome brother Roy, then twenty-two, visiting the Maine coast for the last vacation the three of us had together"

that Spicer should still have had the paper ten years later when he died. Were these two heroes of mine perhaps lovers, even briefly? I would like to think so. Certainly one can't imagine they had much to tell each other about writing, for their respective poems couldn't be more different; Thorner's model was A. E. Housman, a poet whom Spicer would have abhorred.

Thorner was very important to me after the scandal, when there were so few people on the campus, aside from a few classmates, with whom I could talk openly. Like all good poet-teachers, he never insisted that his students imitate his own work, but the poets he admired and whom he encouraged us to read—Housman, early Yeats, French symbolists—were all masters of the devious, poets who suggested feelings and ideas that could not be expressed directly. Thorner freely loaned us his books, and I always had a few in my room. I loved in particular his three-volume set of *The Divine Comedy,* illustrated by Gustaf Doré, and kept it a whole year. Thorner left the set to me in his will.

Thorner collected furniture, and his apartment was a decadent's dream—tapestries, overstuffed chairs and divans, Oriental carpets. He preferred candlelight, played the piano on a baby grand in his parlor, and scented his rooms. It was an elegant concoction of late romantic, decadent traditions and styles. Neither I nor any of the other students he favored had any knowledge of the history behind tastes of this sort or any understanding of how valuable many of his possessions were, but it was thrilling to be invited to his home.

Another faculty poet, Richard Henchey, was writing the poems he would publish in a collection called *Existential Nerve Cell* (1964); he showed them to me and other students, and we considered this an honor. There was also an aspiring playwright, Ellis Baker, on the faculty. He had been to the Bread Loaf Writers' Conference several times, and the year I graduated from Williston he got me a job there waiting on tables, so that I had the exhilarating experience of listening to Robert Frost and having my poems praised by John Ciardi. In fact, that was altogether too much for a seventeen-year-old, and I left the conference quite certain that, in time, I would have my Nobel Prize.

Destructively overconfident, I entered Columbia University that fall, believing that I would be having classes with Allen Ginsberg and Jack Kerouac. In fact, the only thing I knew about Columbia, aside from the fact that it was in New York, was that Kerouac and Ginsberg had gone there. Nor was I alone in choosing Columbia for that reason. Ron Padgett, who was a year ahead of me, told me many years later he had told the admissions office it should have given Ginsberg and Kerouac an honorarium since they had been, however inadvertently, the best recruiters the college had. What all of us overlooked was that Kerouac had dropped out and Ginsberg had been suspended.

I did my graduate as well as undergraduate work at Columbia—a cold, impersonal institution which at first I despised. A film currently being made about writers influenced by Kerouac contains a sequence in which I appear, maniacal in motorcycle gear and striding around a dock in Hoboken, ranting about the horrible experiences I had there. In fact, I had no teachers at Columbia as caring as Thorner; rather, they were phantoms, it seemed to me, for I rarely saw them except in class. I remember one professor recommending that I take his course when in fact I already had. And there was the distinguished professor of modern poetry who allowed that Marianne Moore was respected, although he didn't know why and had nothing to say about her. And then there was the distinguished scholar whose best class, in my opinion, was the one in which he described mnemonic devices for remembering addresses and telephone numbers.

However inadequate the teaching seemed to me, the Columbia curriculum was good, built on a foundation in Western culture and civilization. And yet I had not expected to be writing papers on Locke or Hume, to cite two figures I learned to loathe that first year, and so I disappeared from the campus for long periods, failing courses and discovering that, aside from the financial office (which reduced my financial aid from a scholarship to a loan), no one seemed much concerned. Columbia made adolescent rebellion pointless since there were so few people who noticed or cared what one did—which may be why student uprisings in the late 1960s had to be so fierce. Truly, one had to "capture" a building or take the dean of admissions hostage in order to get attention.

There were a few professors who *did* take a great personal interest in their students—Carl Hovde, for example, who let me live with

Foster at age seventeen

his family for several weeks when my emotional problems were at their worst and I was unable to care for myself. When I started teaching, I tried very hard to model myself on him. He is one of the few college teachers I've known who was deeply concerned about his students personally as well as academically, and this quality surely had much to do with his being chosen dean of Columbia College in the wake of the student riots in the late 1960s; he could be counted on to listen to students rather than expecting them to listen to him.

I had come to Columbia hoping to write poetry and fiction, but in literature classes one heard such irritating silliness as "We live in a silver age, not an age for poets but an age for critics." The critic-poet Randall Jarrell had written something to that effect, and it caused a great controversy. But he was wrong, as anyone who spent time in bookstores should have known. There weren't many prospective critics among students in those classes, but there were many who have become respected poets and novelists: Padgett, David Shapiro, Bob Holman, and Paul Auster, to name four among dozens. Some

of these were inescapable presences on the campus. Padgett, for example, glided about dressed in black, being very serious, and became one of my heroes. I tried to imitate him and failed thoroughly. There were others savagely getting their thoughts into verse or novels, but I don't remember any of them saying "This is a silver age, so I must become a critic."

Eventually I started blacking out (perhaps from drinking too much). Friends took me early one morning to an emergency room, where the doctors huddled and decided my problems were psychological. They referred me to a psychiatrist, who prescribed medicines that did marvelous things to my body, but the real joy was meeting regularly with him, since he *seemed* to care. Perhaps he did, but one day a fellow student, who had also been one of his patients, stopped me to say that our psychiatrist had killed himself by swallowing carbolic acid. By that time, however, he had imbued me with one idea, a fatal one, as it proved: namely, that it was best to be "normal," by which he meant married. It was the only specific advice he ever gave.

Months later, walking along Amsterdam Avenue, I felt, for no reason, transformed and happy. The inner trouble was, for the moment, gone—as indeed the psychiatrist had predicted. From that point on I learned to turn Columbia's shortcomings into virtues, for I realized that if no one cared what I did, I could do whatever I wanted: I was free to please myself as long as I passed my courses and remained discreet. I could even, if I wished, transform myself into someone new.

My mother regularly sent money, and I had scholarships and loans, but it was not enough to cover all the bills, so I bartended at private parties, tutored rich families on the East Side, and worked freelance for newspapers and a company specializing in soft-core pornography. (I wrote captions for pictures of big-breasted women, a difficult assignment, as I did not care for them at all.) For newspapers and magazines, I continued as "Edward Foster," but I became someone else for other jobs. When calls came from people who had been referred to me for the first time, I said, when I thought I could get away with it, No, my schedule is full, but I have a friend, Samuel Retsov, who can do it for you. (Sammy had been my boyhood nickname, and Retsov is Foster spelled backwards.) Strangely, I was never caught; even when I bartended at parties attended by people for whom I had worked as "Mr. Foster," no one noticed, as far as I know. Perhaps they were too drunk. With my new identity I was able to establish all sorts of liaisons entirely without guilt. I could go home with people I met at the parties and assume a thoroughly fictitious personality. Given the way the world works, no bar mitzvah or confirmation could have made a better rite of passage.

I began using "Retsov" and other pseudonyms to submit work to little magazines, where it was accepted and published, but Columbia's obsession with critical theory was having its poisonous effect: there was increasingly less work to submit. The summer I graduated from Columbia, I went to England thinking that I would throw away the return ticket if I could find a job there. I'd read *Wuthering Heights* many times since discovering it at the Williamsburg library and imagined I could find work in Yorkshire, in Brontë country. When I got there and sprightly presented my plans to the director of the Brontë museum, she said, sweetly, that although she'd like an assistant, I'd need British citizenship if I were to be paid. I had some money with me—not much, but enough for a cheap room until the return flight—and spent my time on the moors, once getting lost and being rescued by farmers who told me to stay on marked paths in the future.

Returning home in August, I found a letter from Columbia: without my knowledge, three of my professors had arranged for me to enter the doctoral program in American literature. And there was financial aid, too. So I became a student again instead of selling insurance, teaching high school, or working full-time for the pornography publishers—the only "opportunities" I considered realistic at the time. And as the war in Southeast Asia intensified, I found an even better reason for being a graduate student: avoiding the draft. I was also glad to be in New York again, where one could pursue one's private affairs without being scrutinized and judged. Aside from two years in Turkey, I have lived in New York or its environs ever since.

Many of Columbia's graduate students were women who would stand among the most effective theorists and writers in the first wave of modern feminism: Lillian S. Robinson, Sandra M. Gilbert, Kate Millett, Lyndall Gordan, and

Rachel Blau DuPlessis, among them. The graduate students in American literature were almost all women, and the question they kept asking was why the works we read were almost all by men. American literature at Columbia meant nineteenth-century American literature (everything else was "colonial" or "modern"), and the only woman on the syllabus was Dickinson, slightingly referred to as "Emily." I decided to read my way through everything in the Columbia stacks by nineteenth-century American women; that meant thousands and thousands of books. I did not actually read all of them, for many quickly proved intractably sentimental and sweet, but there were some wonderful finds. The books I wrote on Catharine Sedgwick (1974) and Susan Warner (1978) were the result.

These and other critical and biographical works that I published over the next several years were quite well received, but the reputation they gave me had its price: I was soon telling my students that we lived in a silver age, etc. Worse, I believed it. The best received of these books was *The Civilized Wilderness* (1975), which is still in print, although I can't imagine who would read it now. It was intended as a subtle attack on the myth-symbol school of criticism, a very hot subject at the time, but the book was much subtler than I thought since it was prominently disparaged in a professional journal as an exemplar of the thing I had tried to attack. Still, whether or not I was understood, my ego could only swell with the attention. I found great delight in opening an admired journal and seeing my words and ideas gravely discussed.

But I had stumbled onto this kind of writing by accident, and in retrospect I doubt that I ever much cared, really, whether my work was on the "cutting edge" or whether a paper was accepted for the Modern Language Association's annual meeting. I have good friends whose diligence as academic critics has paid off, for they are well known in their fields, well salaried, and tenured. To be sure, I did care, hugely, about the subjects I chose for books and articles, but that in itself was not enough motivation to pursue a conventional academic career. I wrote virtually no poems between 1968 and the late 1970s, and although by that time I was a widely published professor, I was back in that desperation that had sent me to my suicidal analyst a decade before.

When I was still seeing the analyst, I had received an invitation from a friend's sister, Elaine Dunphy, to attend the Winter Carnival at Middlebury College, where she was a student. Could anything have been more "normal" or closer to what the doctor ordered? As soon as she graduated, Elaine moved to New York, and we were married the following summer. The marriage lasted twenty-eight years, and even now we choose to live within a few blocks of each other. But much of that marriage was sustained by the problems of rearing children and maintaining a household as well as a willingness to leave each other's private lives alone. No matter how much one may respect another, marriage is difficult to pursue on a psychiatrist's recommendation that one be "normal."

When our children—Katherine Hearn Foster and John Clark Foster—were young, we bought an old farmhouse in Cummington, Massachusetts, and spent the next summers renovating it. Cummington is a tiny village—fewer than six hundred residents—but quite important in American literature. William Cullen Bryant was born there, and his house is now a museum. The Cummington School of the Arts, founded in the 1920s, brought Marianne Moore, Robert Lowell, William Carlos Williams, and other poets to the town. The Cummington Press, the most distinguished small publisher in the country at midcentury, issued major books by Williams, Lowell, and Wallace Stevens. From the hill behind our house I could look out toward the homes of Richard Wilbur, William Jay Smith, and Ralph Ellison. It seemed, without much exaggeration, as if there were a book being written in every house on our road except ours. And others knew it; visiting us one weekend Alice Notley wrote her poem "Cummington," which begins: "They write about the weather when they live here," adding, "if they write."

Carl Hovde had a house in a neighboring town, where he was working on a new edition of Thoreau's *A Week on the Concord and Merrimack Rivers,* and Hovde's project brought back memories of my father's enthusiasm for Thoreau. Horace Thorner, whom I hadn't seen for several years, lived nearby. I visited him often, listening to him talk about his "collected works" and the tapes he was making of himself reading his poems. Then one day, very despondent, he came to dinner and said he'd always thought himself a "poète maudit," but now he knew he was really a "poète manqué." No one

cared what he had written. He had thrown his tapes and most of his manuscripts into the fire: there would be no "collected works."

He wanted support, but I was preoccupied with sheetrock and spackle and callously replied, without sympathy, that he would probably be back at work soon. "Oh," he said, with the irony that comes naturally to prep school teachers, "you mean you still compose?" I babbled things about supporting a family, repairing the summer house, all the obligations. "Well," he said bitterly, "you'd better give your home a rest, or you'll be manqué, too."

I didn't see him much after that. He eventually went back to his "collected works" and published a few volumes; the rest were published after his death by a friend.

By the late 1970s I was drinking heavily again—as much as half a fifth of Scotch to get through the night. Writing of any sort was impossible. Walking down Broadway one afternoon, I collapsed at 96th Street. People were unusually solicitous—do you need an ambulance? can I help you over to the bench?—but I found I could not speak until I got home. A colleague who was aware of what was happening suggested I apply for a Fulbright, which would allow me to leave the country for a while. I applied and was accepted for an opening at Moscow State University, but complications developed within the Soviet bureaucracy, threatening Fulbright applications. Officials in Washington called just before the school year was to begin and asked if my family and I would go to Turkey instead. In truth, I did not know then where Turkey was, except that it was in the Middle East. Certainly I didn't know that the country was in the middle of a civil war.

The plane landed in Ankara late one September night. The airfield was massed with gendarmes and military troops. We were taken in a black limousine to a hotel that looked like a shabby set for *The Third Man.* An official took me aside, gave me Turkish lira, and said never to allow either my wife or my children to answer the door. I mentioned this the next day to another Fulbright professor as a strange custom. No, he said, the official was not talking about customs but the current method of assassination: the doorbell would ring, and whoever answered would be shot. Americans were considered good targets by certain extremist

"With Elaine, Katherine, and John, two days before we left for Turkey. Katherine seeems as bemused and serious as she is today, and John has the sense of humor he has never lost."

groups. A U.S. naval officer was shot walking along the most fashionable street in Istanbul, and an American teaching in southern Turkey was also shot, together with his wife and children. The English-language newspaper regularly listed the week's victims.

My first day at the university, I looked out the window to see students firing guns at each other. Gendarmes with machine guns guarded the classrooms. One day I was warned by the embassy not to go to the university. That day men with machine guns, looking for the American, stopped the bus I usually took to the school.

Why did we stay? For one thing, conditions that seem intolerable in retrospect (repeated talk of assassination, students shot, tanks rumbling in the streets) came to be accepted as the normal state of things, no more extraordinary than the possibility of being assaulted in Central Park. But the greater reason involved the seductions of Islamic and Turkish culture: although much of Ankara looked like European steel-and-concrete cities built or rebuilt after the Second World War, the similarities were

only on the surface. The culture worked on principles foreign to the West and thereby called into question any sense that our own traditions, language, and culture were natural and inevitable. The effect might have been less had we spent the year in Damascus or Cairo, where discrepancies between the two cultures were more immediately clear. But a world that seems familiar and then gradually reveals itself to be radically different can be perversely alluring; gradually everything that one takes for granted—values, traditions, even one's language—loses its reflexive certainty. There is a masochistic pleasure in finding that whatever one has thought natural and inevitable is only another construction. Americans living in Ankara for business or political reasons and Americans assigned to the air force base outside the city avoided intimate contact with the Turks. I would see them transported around the city in special blue American buses, but I knew very few of them. I didn't want to know them, for they reminded me of values and convictions which I wanted to forget.

The critical moment in this divestiture came early one spring morning. My wife had returned to the United States with the children because her mother was ill, and I had been alone for many weeks. The political situation was bad, the university was closed, and embassy officials said not to leave the apartment except when necessary. The pop-pop-pop out in the street was not fireworks. I had spent several nights drinking, then sleeping through the day. That particular morning, listening to the call for prayer from the mosque down the hill, I felt suddenly transfigured, as if everything had abruptly altered its appearance. Perhaps I was simply poisoned from so much alcohol, but I believed, or wanted to believe, that the experience was deeper. Whatever the cause, I felt as if I had been unburdened of all the values and expectations with which I had previously measured myself. Even more strongly than the day at Columbia I realized I was free to do as I wished, I felt unaccountably independent, and this was a good thing: I felt distanced from everything, and it didn't matter. The early morning call to prayer had been the final shattering of all the demands for the "normal" or "well adjusted"—the chimera that promises happiness if we will only do as others expect.

I began thinking about my father and grandfather and felt as if I understood them for the first time. Their secret, it now seemed, had been a capacity to be alone. My grandfather, in a village of tongue-clicking gossips, had strolled about with his gold-headed cane. And my father, whose luck ran out the day filial obligation brought him home, had refused to be just another well-adjusted father and son and, indubitably eccentric, moved his family into the woods and ran about wildly being a geologist, musician, town clerk, fireman, and scholar. But neither man opened to public scrutiny whatever he was at the core; that part was private, available to no one but himself. It was clear, however, that neither would have been satisfied doing merely what was expected of him; their motivations were elsewhere. In effect that morning I felt that I not only understood my father and grandfather for the first time but knew as well how to emulate them.

Of course, I also knew that doing so would have its penalties; the world can take revenge on the peculiar and the odd—as my music teacher, Bodman, and Thorner had discovered. Cruelty, ridicule, and indifference are

not greatly damaging, however, if one can still produce an *Oration on Death* or a "collected works." And there are ways to evade an overly attentive or indifferent community: my father moving to the woods, my grandmother imagining spiritual ecstasies, my grandfather constructing a persona from sheer style. Each of them avoided the expedient, the expected, the politically correct.

In 1992 I published an essay, "Poetry Has Nothing to Do with Politics," arguing that poetry which obeys a community's expectations is not poetry at all. That isn't news, of course; a thousand essays have said the same. Friedrich Schlegel argued, for instance, that "every honest author writes for nobody or everybody. Whoever writes for some particular group does not deserve to be read." But among academics and many poets in this politicized era, the argument is heresy.

David Landrey and Bilge Mutluay collected a series of responses to my essay, publishing them in a book entitled *Poetry and Politics* (1993); most of the essays were negative, one poet saying he was "saddened" by the title of the essay (I gathered that he hadn't read further) and insisting that "poetry is political to its very bones." A widely published professor argued that my position was "a political stance of the highest order," but I still don't understand what he meant. I think he was saying that we are all essentially political, and the most political are those who try not to be political at all. Be this all as it may, I still argue that whatever poetry borrows from the language of politics or however politically effective it may be, its core is closer to the solitude and suffering in, for example, spiritual afflictions like Bodman's.

Much of the controversy the essay provoked came from those who did not like the title (borrowed, as it happens, from Jack Spicer). Some claimed that the essay and its argument are elitist, but the opposite is true: they are Emersonian and democratic. By politics, as the essay makes clear, I mean the prescriptive orders of an individual or a community. Emerson denied that any action was correct except that which rose spontaneously: "The only sin," he said, "is limitation." That means that each person is free to make his or her own determinations. In turn he or she will be a threat to conventional communities, but my own experience with conventional communities has been that in their assurance they are oppressive and cruel.

The books I published during the 1970s are politically conservative; I was in effect taking issue with the left-of-center politics that viewed all values as contingent. In defending Catharine Sedgwick or Susan Warner, I looked for "literary excellence," as if that immutable standard existed outside the critic's head. My books after 1980 began with the opposite assumption, arguing, for example, that William Saroyan, Kerouac, or Spicer are interesting precisely because of the ways in which their work violates standards; they were discovering new ways to speak, and new ways to speak make it possible for new things to be said. As Ted Berrigan repeatedly pointed out to me, however, no good writer does that until he or she knows what the standards are: disruption is not by itself a good prescription for writing.

I had seen Berrigan around the campus when I was an undergraduate at Columbia. He was not a student but a friend of Padgett's, writing term papers for income while publishing in the Columbia literary magazine. I might have forgotten him were it not for a phone call one day from Allen Ginsberg (with whom I had corresponded but whom I had never met) saying Berrigan needed a job. Ginsberg had heard that my university, the Stevens Institute of Technology, was looking for a "distinguished visiting professor," and he thought that Berrigan, who had taught at various schools, should be considered. I liked Ted immediately, and he was hired and became a close friend—as close as any friend I'd ever had—until his death three years later. I spent time in his office whenever he was there and, after his appointment ended, visited as often as possible at his apartment in Manhattan.

Like Spicer on the West Coast, Berrigan was one of the great teachers of poets, partly because he had no interest in teaching any poetic style or technique. Ted did not want copies or clones. He was a true Emersonian, insisting that each person write exactly as his or her own personality, necessities, and "gods" (a favorite word with him) dictated. But he insisted that a poet's dedication to the work be absolute. Padgett wrote in his memoir of Berrigan that "Ted's passion for writing was everyday and always. . . . It was something you did when you read the sports page or ate a donut." As Alice Notley said, "You did it in your sleep too, in your dreams when you were asleep."

Ted was relentless in this. He didn't much care who your gods were as long as you had gods and they did things for your poetry. He made much of the so-called New York School of Poetry, in which critics gave him a leading role in the "second generation," but he did so mostly for publicity and to keep the critics happy. Although he learned much from first-generation New York poets like Frank O'Hara, John Ashbery, and James Schuyler, his poems are rooted in his Irish Catholic, working-class, New England sensibility: that was where he found his gods. He had wide tastes, even praising conservative formalists like Conrad Aiken and Robert Frost. They were much more provincial than he, however: Aiken's collected letters includes one in which he takes Ted to task for not being more attentive to poetic conventions.

Ted was in fact as knowledgeable about these conventions as any of his peers: he knew the rules before he broke them. But he knew that one had to break rules in order to discover new territory, and for that reason he didn't want anyone merely imitating him any more than he wanted to imitate Aiken. Respect was one thing, imitation another. He saw poetry as a democracy in which each poet pursued his or her own bent. Anything was acceptable as long as one was wholly committed to one's art. It was clear that I had to agree with him on this point if we were to be friends.

He made one exception: my infatuation with motorcycles. I have never liked cars but can spend an afternoon reading a motorcycle magazine with all the piety of a monk reading the Bible. Ted had vicious back problems, so I was never able to take him for a ride on a motorcycle, but I think I was able to convince him that executing a perfect turn on a mountain road at seventy or eighty miles an hour requires the same precision and delicacy as executing a perfect turn at the end of a line of poetry. In fact I believe that's true, although I've known few poets who liked motorcycles, and most of my motorcycle friends are more interested in beer than in books. Poetry and motorcycles both require sharp reflexes, knowing exactly and intuitively what to do at a given moment.

In part, being able to do the right thing is a matter of luck. The most serious accident I've had with a motorcycle involved dismounting when moving at sixty or so miles an hour. A car suddenly stopped, broadside, down the road, and there was no way to avoid it. You can't survive accidents like that, as any motorcyclist will testify, and I have no memory of the time between the moment when I knew I had to get off the bike and the moment, on the ground, when I knew I was alive and could see the bike furiously skidding into the car. But that's what happens in poems, at least in my experience: the right words are suddenly there, although one doesn't know where they come from. Ultimately it all depends on luck.

I thought of Ted as an older brother, one whose advice could always be trusted, but William Bronk, with whom I became close at this time, was my new "father," for in his work I found an identity congenial to my own. There are three "gods" in my pantheon: Jack Spicer, Constantine Cavafy, and Bronk. Spicer, whom I had been reading since the 1960s, led me to symbolist poetics and poetry as dictation—poetry, that is, devoid of personal intent. Cavafy,

whom I knew only in translation, showed me ways in which history and one's private experience could be used without making a poem needlessly political or personal. But Bronk was the most important of all, for he was at the same time a caring friend and the harshest critic I'd known. He showed me, like Cavafy, how poetry could use one's experience without being personal and, like Spicer, how poetry could depend on necessities outside one's own inclinations and presumptions.

Some years ago a poet (a very political poet) unsympathetic to poetry of this kind called it gnostic, as if gnosticism were a sin. Amused by the passion in his argument, friends and I adopted "gnostic" to describe what we do, but actually the word is misleading. A better adjective would be one common among nineteenth-century poets and critics, "disinterested"—in short, poetry that does not have some ancillary intention but that tries to take its place in the world as naturally as a rock or a stream. Poetics in works of this sort depend, as Ted would

Foster "in 1984 with a brand new GS 850, the most recent addition to a long string of joy machines and the one on which I was nearly killed two months later"

say, on "getting all the words inside you" and then letting the work itself assume its perimeters. In an extreme form, this is what is meant by "dictated poetry," where the real source is unnameable and prior to language. Spicer was inclined to call the source "East Mars," but this was only to satisfy, or mystify, his critics. Essentially what he and others whom I admire require is that the poet abdicate any self-conscious control over the words. As Bronk remarked in an interview:

> I have repeatedly had the experience, when the poem gets written down, of saying, oh, God, no, I don't mean that—but hesitating to change the meaning because it seems to me the way it has to be said—and then only later, maybe the next day, two days later, the next week: yes, I guess that's what I do mean. But the initial rejection of what the poem is saying because it seems to me something that I don't particularly want to mean, a meaning that makes me uncomfortable or embarrasses or contradicts something else I've said or whatever. Having to accept that when I've lived with it for a little while. . . . Admitting, yes, yes, I guess that is what I mean.

As an instance of this, I offer "Salt," which is not one of my poems that I prefer but is one that seems to satisfy many people; they write to me about it, and it has been published in Turkish, Russian, and Chinese translations. The poem began on Christmas in 1989, when I was walking with my brother, my son, and others up the hill behind my mother's house. My son and brother were discussing some serious but personal matters, and I was eavesdropping, occasionally adding a word or two. As we walked along, we passed a neglected house with a plastic angel over the door, and I heard in the back of my mind the words "autumn's angel." We branched off into the woods where snowfall from the week before was crisscrossed with animal tracks, including some which I took to be a rabbit's followed by a dog's. Again there were words: "fear in tracks across old snow." When we got back to my mother's, I wrote down these and other phrases I had heard—or overheard—during the walk. Over the next months I listened again and again to these words and rhythms until the poem took this form:

This frigid morning you,
form rising,
seemed the autumn's angel,
kinder than I would ever be,

But when your hands reached mine
my tongue could taste the salt,
and we consigned our words
　　　　　　　to none.

Your fingers were the frozen branches
　　　　　　budding in the sun.

Set up, it always ends that way,
fear in tracks across old snow
the details that we had to know.

Because it is my job, I teach courses in critical theory in the graduate school at Drew University and at the Stevens Institute of Technology, but I don't have much sympathy with the subject and use it to show how inadequate the critical mind can be. As the poet Witter Bynner said, "The creative and critical faculties do not combine." Most criticism is pernicious, I think, as inferior to poetry as theology is to revelation, but one would never know this from the critic, addressing poets as if he were seated on the papal throne. The New Criticism has been out of fashion for twenty or thirty years, but it taught a more profitable way to read poems than do theorists who reduce literature to programmatic politics or who talk about "indeterminacy" and "deferred meaning." Poetry does indeed have meaning, as anyone can discover who reads attentively, and it is neither indeterminate nor deferred. Much New Criticism was merely reactive and academic, but it could make one read attentively, which is the best way to discover how silly theoretical babble can be.

I taught at the University of Istanbul in 1985–86 and lived on the Bosphorus near the site of a temple to Hermes and a short walk from a spring that had once been sacred to Apollo. I spent many afternoons with the Armenian poet "Zahrad" (Zareh Yaldijian) at his shop near the Süleymaniye mosque and with a group of young Turkish poets. But my principal object that year was to construct a life that, as Ted wished, admitted only poetry.

Returning from Turkey, I began work with Joseph Donahue, Zoë English, and others creating the journal *Talisman*. The first issue appeared in 1988, and it is as good as any journal committed to important new work in American poetry. Most issues include essays about, and an interview with, a contemporary poet whose work is outside mainstream or conservative traditions. The interviews from the first ten issues are collected in *Postmodern Poetry* (1994), which is dedicated to Ted's memory, and delineate the current landscape in American poetry outside the mainstream; the poets include, among others, William Bronk, Clark Coolidge, Susan Howe, Nathaniel Mackey, Alice Notley, Ron Padgett, John Yau, and Gustaf Sobin. With Leonard Schwartz and Joseph Donahue, I edited the anthology *Primary Trouble: An Anthology of Contemporary American Poetry* (1996), which proposes that no single tradition dominates American poetry, and that American poetry follows tendencies as diverse as its practitioners. The academic idea of tradition no longer holds much meaning; in its place is the democratic model Ted admired.

I founded Talisman House, Publishers, in 1993, and it has become one of the chief literary publishers in the country, with titles by, among others, Dodie Bellamy and Sam D'Allesandro, Ted Berrigan, William Bronk, Joseph Donahue, Michael Heller, Mark Jacobs, Stephen Jonas, Gerrit Lansing, Alice Notley, Geoffrey O'Brien, Douglas Oliver, Simon Pettet, Leslie Scalapino, Leonard Schwartz, Jack Spicer, Gustaf Sobin, and Rosmarie Waldrop.

Literary publishing has always been an unpredictable business in America, but it is particularly problematic now. It can take much time for serious works to find their audience, but "superstores" and chains, which now dominate the book trade, stock titles only for a few months. These stores may use books like Talisman's to give their shelves an aura, but the real sales are in calendars and cookbooks. Furthermore, major publishers have resources, financial and otherwise, that no company like Talisman has. Yet Talisman succeeds: the pressures are enormous, but we work harder and are grateful for lengthy periods of insomnia.

At the same time that Talisman began to prosper, my marriage was ending. It was necessary to sell the house in New Jersey, directly across from Manhattan. With my half of the income from that sale, I was able to buy a larger, much more substantial house in what the real estate agents call Jersey City's "historic downtown district." In fact that area is a remarkable survivor of the brownstone and brick-front neighborhoods that were once common in New York and vicinity. It is a wonderfully mixed community with substantial gay, Hispanic, and African American populations. More important, the historic district is only one subway stop from Manhattan, and the house itself is huge, big enough that two floors can be rented to help with taxes and upkeep, while a third can be committed largely to editorial and storage space for Talisman.

During the years that these transitions occurred, I wrote my books on the Beats and the Black Mountain poets, published in 1992 and 1995, respectively. My selected poems, *All Acts Are Simply Acts*, appeared in 1995, and the following year a long poem, *Adrian as Song*, was published. From 1991 to 1995 I was the poetry editor for *MultiCultural Review*, which provided me with an opportunity to write essays on poets outside the mainstream, like John Yau, Mary Fabilli, and my friend from Columbia, Bob Holman. And there were opportunities as well for readings and lectures in this country and in France, Italy, Spain, Slovenia, Turkey, Russia, and elsewhere, as well as an appointment to teach at the summer institute of the Jack Kerouac School at the Naropa Institute. My motorcycle trip there in 1994 was the beginning of *Code of the West*, a first version of which I read as a lecture the final day of the summer.

I do think Ted was right: if one is to be a poet, one must do things related to poetry even when one sleeps, and they must be done well. As Williams told Ginsberg, "In this mode, perfection is basic." Poets can be rigorous critics of each other's work. I have heard many generous things from readers about "Salt," but the first criticism came from a poet who told me I should have "tinkered" more with the final line, and he was right. Some poets, it is true, feel that only their own work is worth their time and will read someone else's merely to see what can be borrowed. I spent an afternoon recently with a poet, one of the best, who dismissed as "not really poets" Robert Duncan, Charles Olson, and Ezra Pound. "Do you like Shakespeare?" I asked, irritated. "Not all of it," he replied, "though I used to read the sonnets."

Walking through a park near my house a few weeks after moving to Jersey City, I met the artist Gene Blanton, who lives with

"With William Bronk, the greatest English-language poet of his generation I would argue, in 1988. Although his poetry is somber and ascetic, the man himself, as the photo makes clear, is genial and kind."

me now. Each night around eleven, he and I begin our rounds of the "historic downtown district." We are, like Thoreau, "self-appointed inspectors of snow storms and rain storms." Gene may be generally more optimistic than I am, which makes us a good match. He can say things are better than they seem, I can say they're worse, and we can settle for something in the middle. But in fact there is not much reason for complaint: today my daughter Katherine is in charge of props for the New York Public Theater and Shakespeare-in-the-Park; my son John lives with me, is in graduate school, and teaches in college; my brother is planning to buy a catamaran and sail around the world; and my mother and aunt (now eighty-five and ninety, respectively) are doing fairly well.

So this morning, things are fine. Gene is here, and there is bright sun in the backyard.

Last winter I thought I'd have to sell the house in order to pay Talisman's printing bills, and perhaps next year I will. But a few months ago an anonymous check arrived, enough to make printers and lawyers and collection agencies happy for the moment. This check, like others that have arrived as mysteriously over the years, was sent by an accounting firm acting on behalf of an individual who asked not to be named. So Talisman books continue to appear—there will be a dozen this year as well as two issues of the journal. And another Talisman project is scheduled for next year, a bi-monthly magazine devoted to reviews of poetry and articles about poets.

William Bronk says in a recent poem, "Among Ourselves," "No one is safe from the world, or missed by it." Which is true, although I would like to believe that the poem I read early this morning will be a sufficient reprieve, for now. And then I will try to find a way from that reprieve to another, and in this way imitate my grandfather, sashaying past his neighbors with a gold-headed cane.

BIBLIOGRAPHY

Literary criticism:

Catharine Maria Sedgwick, Twayne, 1974.

The Civilized Wilderness: Backgrounds to American Romantic Literature, 1817–1860, Free Press/ Macmillan, 1975.

Josiah Gregg and Lewis Hector Garrard, Boise State University Western Writers Series, 1977.

Susan and Anna Warner, Twayne, 1978.

Richard Brautigan, Twayne, 1983.

William Saroyan, Boise State University Western Writers Series, 1984.

Jack Spicer, Boise State University Western Writers Series, 1991.

William Saroyan: A Study of the Short Fiction, Twayne/Macmillan, 1991.

Understanding the Beats, University of South Carolina Press, 1992.

Code of the West: A Memoir of Ted Berrigan, Rodent Press, 1994.

Understanding the Black Mountain Poets, University of South Carolina Press, 1995.

Poetry:

The Space Between Her Bed and Clock, Norton Coker Press, 1993.

The Understanding, Texture Press, 1994.

All Acts Are Simply Acts, Rodent Press, 1995.

Adrian as Song, OASii (Israel), 1996.

Editor:

Hoboken: A Collection of Essays (with Geoffrey W. Clark), Irvington Publishers, 1976.

Postmodern Poetry: The Talisman Interviews, Talisman House, 1994.

Primary Trouble: An Anthology of Contemporary American Poetry (with Leonard Schwartz and Joseph Donahue), Talisman House, 1996.

Other:

Editor of journal *Talisman: A Journal of Contemporary Poetry and Poetics,* 1988—. Poetry editor of *MultiCultural Review,* 1991–95.

Richard Harteis

1946-

WINDOW ON THE BLACK SEA:

A Fulbright Year in Bulgaria

Richard Harteis, fiftieth birthday, August 18, 1996

Varna
July 5, 1996

A red-letter day, though in post-Communist Bulgaria one still cannot use the word red without raising the specter of Bulgaria's political past (and possibly its future, depending on this fall's elections). I have come to the Black Sea for a little working vacation before packing my bags and saying farewell to the most extraordinary experience of my life. This summer I will be fifty, the year one takes stock and prepares for what he hopes will be

the second half of his life. And this is certainly the place for such a retreat.

I am sitting on the ninth floor of the rest house of the Union of Bulgarian Journalists, and below my balcony the Black Sea swells exquisite and aquamarine out to the horizon. Little microplanes glide by like lazy pterodactyls, an occasional hydrofoil cuts across the water, and though I can see the bathers bobbing in the glassy sea, this high up the only thing I can hear is the gentle surf crashing below me. The world divides, they say, into morning people and night people, those who love the mountains and those for whom the ocean is paradise. In a fairly long life of searching for the ultimate beach, I believe I have found it in the Golden Sands of Varna.

One thing I wanted to do while I was here was to write a love letter to Bulgaria in preparation for the ceremony at the end of the month in which I will be given Bulgarian citizenship. During this past year as Fulbright poet-in-residence at the American University in Bulgaria (AUBG among friends), I rose to the occasion of writing a commissioned poem only once, when a colleague asked me for a tribute to his sixteen-year-old arctic terrier, Lady. But the gift of citizenship calls for an official thank you, and while I've never tried a serious "public" poem, today, for better or worse, I finished my best effort and sent it off to Krassin Himmirski, an AUBG colleague, for translation.

On June 18, President Zhelev signed a special decree bestowing citizenship on me and my friend William Meredith for our work in the culture here, the first Americans ever to receive such an honor. I will pick up the little green passport when I return to Blagoevgrad, but at the end of July the president will join us at a celebration given by the St. Cyril and Methodius Foundation to make it all official. Orpheus House will launch William's new and collected poems, his portrait will be given to the foundation library, and we will receive membership in the Union of Bulgarian Journalists. What a way to end the year. Like the parasailors drifting over the Black Sea outside my window, I am filled with a sense of elation and a certain valedictory nostalgia as well.

Was it only this May we all marched in our black regalia into the heroic square in front of the former Communist party headquarters which now, with no little irony, houses the American University? As the commencement speaker recited her litany of injunctions to the future leaders of Eastern Europe, I drifted into my own ruminations on how fast the time had flown. I felt the same sense of lacrimae rerum, the same formal appreciation of life and its passing that makes the elderly so emotionally liable when a beautiful bride and groom kiss at the end of the wedding ceremony. One of my students who had done brilliant work in my translation class, but had insisted on a formal distance throughout the year, came back from the dais, held his diploma on high, and, from beneath his mortarboard, gave me one

Richard Harteis and William Meredith meet with President Zhelev to receive Bulgarian citizenship, July 1996

of the goofiest grins I've ever seen in my life. And I cried, of course.

A little over a year ago, I sat at my desk wading through a pile of Fulbright application materials like a nervous senior applying for graduate school, wondering what the future might bring. It had been a very long Connecticut winter, and I had a serious case of cabin fever. Yet another midlife crisis, I had reached one of those watershed moments a caregiver occasionally arrives at when you desperately want a change of pace in your life, a little glamour, a little relief from your responsibilities.

In 1983 William sustained a major stroke the night before he was to read at the centenary celebration for the Brooklyn Bridge. In the morning, I thought he was just playing around when I couldn't pry his mouth open to give him his pills. The first two years after the stroke he sustained that night, William had virtually no movement or speech—a particularly ironic and difficult fate for a poet. But in the thirteen years since then, he has made much progress and even managed to put together a collection of poems in 1989 which won the Pulitzer Prize in poetry. We have represented the United States at poetry festivals in Macedonia, collaborated on Bulgarian translations, taught together at various writers' conferences. We travel a great deal and have good friends all over the world. In many ways life has been extremely generous to us, but half of our twenty-five years together has seen much hard work for us both to keep the old sweetie going.

Before William's illness, he was awarded Bulgaria's gold medal for literature to thank him, in part, for the invitations Bulgarian poets received when he was the poetry consultant at the Library of Congress and for introducing American audiences to Bulgarian literature. Over the years, I accompanied him on a number of visits to Bulgaria for international writers' meetings, and while I am not the household word William has become, my own work has received its share of recognition here. I felt my anthology of Bulgarian poetry, *Window on the Black Sea,* and my work as editor for *Orpheus* magazine gave me further credibility as I filled out the Fulbright application forms. I hadn't taught in a number of years, but I could audit some summer courses to see what American Studies was all about these days. If ever there were a year I might win such a Fulbright grant, this seemed to be it.

I wondered, however, if it were fair to go traipsing off to Bulgaria and take William from all his friends and his pleasant life at Connecticut College where he taught for nearly thirty years. And at seventy-six, with his past heart troubles, I had to consider how sensible such a trip was from the medical point of view. His health was stable, and his doctors had always encouraged me to help him live his years to the fullest. But I wasn't sure how easy it would be to pop into a good emergency room if the need arose in Bulgaria, or how we'd get the many sophisticated drugs he takes daily. I remembered the time William developed appendicitis the night before we were to leave Haiti where we'd been visiting old Peace Corps friends. The embassy doctor thought we might risk flying home in the morning, given the uneven health care in Port-au-Prince. But my heart sank when, halfway over the Atlantic, his pain seemed to disappear. The appendix had

ruptured, of course, and by the time we landed in Miami he was very grey and deep in shock. Six weeks and five operations later, he was miraculously on his way home, having used up several of his nine lives. I doubt he would have survived such an ordeal in Bulgaria.

During that awful recuperation period, my friend Bill Barrett came down from D.C. for a while to spell me at William's bedside and enable me to take care of business. And last spring, as I was wringing my hands over whether or not to apply for this Fulbright, my old bud turned up again from D.C.

"I don't want to bring William home in a box," I told him.

"You won't, you'll bring him home in a jet," Barrett said.

"William says Bulgaria is best. He wants to go and eat yogurt and live to be a hundred like a Russian peasant."

"Well, hey. Go man go."

I sealed up the application and carried it out to the mailbox. All the petals had fallen from William's favorite weeping cherry tree in the yard. Robins and blue jays had stripped the red and white threads of a martinitza, a traditional Bulgarian talisman tied to a tree after you have made a wish and when you see the first bird of spring, that I had tied to the tree for luck. A good sign. I could only wait and see how the lottery would play out.

When the grant letter came later in the summer, I still had reservations. The single requirement I had for accepting the fellowship—a ground-floor apartment or building with an elevator—seemed to daze the bureaucrats administering the program in Washington. Every two weeks my university assignment changed for mysterious reasons. One day a lady called out of the blue informing me that she was my new boss and wished to fax a list of books she expected me to purchase with my book allowance for her literature courses. And when things seemed finally fixed and I had made the myriad arrangements required to keep three houses running, the dog in good health, and all the bills paid, I was informed that the assignment had changed yet again and I would need to leave a month earlier than planned to get to the American University in time for classes. English classes at that, and not the American Studies courses I had prepared for all the hot summer long by auditing classes at the University of Connecticut.

*The four American poets at the Struga Poetry Festival, Macedonia: Dick Holmes,
William Meredith, Peter Liotta, Richard Harteis, 1994*

Another Balkan story, as the saying goes
here. But this time the mysterious machina-
tions proved to be very lucky indeed. For many
reasons, I can't imagine having spent this year
anywhere else except the American University
in Blagoevgrad. The reception William and I
received was phenomenal, and teaching there
proved to be "a really great gig," as my colleague Dana Wilde explained when he popped
his head into my office that first week to introduce himself while I unpacked books and
set up shop.

Blagoevgrad is a beautiful little town of about
eighty thousand people, an hour and a
half south of Sofia on the main road to Greece.
During the Communist regime of Todor Zhivkov,
it seems to have been designated a kind of
regional capital or diplomatic center and was
given a modern face-lift of Stalinist proportions.
An enormous central plaza dominates the town
with cascading fountains, municipal buildings,
theatre, opera house, and heroic sculpture. The

revolutionary Haiduk, Gotse Delchev, stands firmly
fixed on the edge of the future, while another
poet revolutionary for whom the town is named
sits as calm as a Buddha, meditating on the
past. A great stone angel floats over ranks of
Russian soldiers coming like the storm to liberate Bulgaria from four hundred years of the
Ottoman Yoke.

At orientation, a linguist pointed out to us
that virtually every word in Bulgarian which has
been borrowed from the Turkish has a negative connotation, guaranteeing that their hatred for this period of domination will survive
as long as speech. The French poet Lamartine
passed through the country at the time and
wrote about the Turkish oppression. As a result, the house he visited in Plovdiv for a week
or two has now become a museum in his honor.
The Ottoman Yoke has become the great central event of Bulgarian history and culture, and
those Bulgarians who resisted Turkish rule live
on in legend as heroic national forefathers.
Zhivkov made a concerted effort over the years

to eradicate the vestiges of the Turkish culture that remained by forcing ethnic Turks to change their names and outlawing Turkish speech and dress. In 1989, just before Zhivkov finally fell from power, almost four hundred thousand Turks fled or were forced to flee Bulgaria to great international outrage.

(William and I were guests of the Writers' Union during that time, and I wanted to get a true picture of what was going on from our ambassador before meeting with our Bulgarian hosts. I felt it necessary to make a statement about the situation lest we seem insensitive or our visit be used for political reasons not of our own choosing. Ambassador Polansky kindly came along to that meeting to wave the American flag and give some moral support. And it seems to have been Ambassador Polansky, in fact, who somehow managed to get the newly vacated Communist headquarters building at the head of the plaza in Blagoevgrad to house the American University.)

The tree-lined streets radiating off the central plaza in Blagoevgrad are filled with cafes and boutiques and have also been designated pedestrian walkways. Despite the economic crisis, in the evening the streets are filled with miniskirted girls dressed to kill and teenage boys in scruffy jeans and sweats, dressed to be killed. One cannot imagine how they manage this sense of dolce vita when the average monthly salary now is just fifty dollars. In the golden Indian summer days of September and October (in Bulgaria it is called gypsy summer) with chestnut leaves falling about, you could be strolling the charming streets of Aix-en-Province or any provincial European town you can imagine. William uses a wheelchair for long distances such as airport corridors or shopping malls, so the pedestrian setup in Blagoevgrad made it possible for him to use the town to a degree not usually possible in European cities, given their general disregard for the special needs of people who are physically challenged. If you set out in a wheelchair you'd better be sure your stop on the tube has a lift that works, or that the museum is accessible for wheelchairs. I remember learning these hard lessons the summer we were visiting London and William broke his hip. But in Blagoevgrad we can amble along with the pedestrians, checking out which restaurant we might like to try that night, or wheel over to the huge open market on Saturday morning and meander

through stalls selling everything from leeks to light bulbs.

Before we arrived in Blagoevgrad there was a flurry of e-mail over apartments. The best the university could do was a ten-step-up apartment on the ground floor of Blok 43 in the Oktomvri Complex on the outskirts of town about a mile from the campus. Oktomvri looks a little like bombed-out sections of the Bronx—a maze of potholed streets through dilapidated cement towers each with a communal dumpster crawling with alley cats. But it suited us just fine. Taxis cost about fifty cents to any point in town, and, as is the usual case in Bulgaria, the apartment assigned us inside Blok 43 proved to be a charming two-bedroom, two-bath flat with formal living room, glassed-in terrace for drying laundry, and a large kitchen/dining room with another small terrace which we used as a root cellar. Depending on how badly the cat was misbehaving she was alternately exiled to the kitchen terrace (dubbed the winter palace by our translator) or her summer palace off the living room. And to the amazement of all who visited us, we even had a little laundry room with a washing machine.

The apartment came with a hyperactive landlord named Dr. Kostovi, who was so honored to have William Meredith living in his son's apartment he went to the limit to make us happy, including hijacking one of the phone numbers reserved for the socialist party election committee so that we might have a tele-

Blagoevgrad, the Bazaar

phone. With the help of our able translator/ girl Friday, Julie, we found the excellent Tanya, a Russian-looking woman with hands bigger than my own and a heart as big as Texas who kept the house spotless. When we told her we really were going to return to the United States in August, she just stared at us like an unbelieving child and let the tears flow, unabashed, down and down her broad cheeks. She only cheered up a little when we told her we would let her keep the cat hostage until we returned to Bulgaria next spring.

Early on in our stay, I called home from the office and heard a cat yowling in the background. I found this strange, since we did not have a cat at the time. Julie and William had adopted a kitten from the street, it turned out, and were giving it its first bath. She's a nice little cat, not so little anymore, in fact. We gave her a pot to stand on, and she stretched herself out like an alligator all through the winter at the kitchen window until now she can jump with ease down into the street below. I even wrote a companion poem to the paean for my colleague's arctic terrier which I risk folding in here to spite the editor of *Literary Forum*, who rejected it recently with an enlightened, "I don't do animal poems."

Spring

for David Fisher

Red petals lie strewn on the kitchen table
like the leftovers of a cardinal the cat
has had for breakfast. The zinnias were
amusing for a while, but now she's
bored and stands on tip toe, paws fixed
to the wooden sill, taking in the blok.
Her tail traces lazy question marks on the
morning air as her window world wakens.

A gypsy girl wheels a perambulator
up to the dumpster to rifle through
the steaming garbage for tin and plastic
treasure. The cat would like to help,
and taps at the window, but the girl
can not hear her and wanders away.

The cat begins to sing, is teaching
herself how to chirp, against some
future day when she graduates to the
garden, and can surprise the birds
at their own game. But she can't get it
quite right, purrs with a Bulgarian accent.

The streets are turning into mud again.
She remembers mud, like walking on velvet,
just last fall when she was a kitten,
before the man took her out of the rain,
to guard his kitchen—that poor excuse
of a dog marks a patch of dirty snow
with his yellow signature. She narrows
her eyes in derision like a cat. "One day,
we'll meet," she thinks.

Now children dressed in uniform begin
to pour out of the blok's cement towers
like blue corn from a silo and poke
their way to school. The far off
mountain which earlier glowed pink,
electric with the snow and sunrise
has dimmed. The night shift is over.

It is time to fold herself into a ball
in front of the radiator and wait for
the man to open the delicious can—
fish, chicken, what will it be? She'll
rub against his legs like silk, in
gratitude, anticipation. And more.

What can it be lately, this hunger
welling up in her the way, incredibly,
the tips of the trees have begun
to swell into delicate green fingers
under which she aches to play.

Well, in any case, having established our little domestic physical plant, I was now able to begin my work at the university. It had been years since I'd experienced one of those

"A devil to get started, but gets great mileage,"
Oktomvri Complex, Blagoevgrad

heartthrobbing first days of class when you hand out your syllabus with all the aplomb and nonchalance you can muster, while forty eyes train on you like gestapo klieg lights taking in every crease in your trousers, the slightest twitch of an eyelid. Teachers who have been at the game all their lives tell me the butterflies you experience on the first day of class will fly about your stomach until the day you die and retire to the great faculty lounge in the sky reserved for emeriti professors. The adrenaline keeps you sharp, better able to engage them—not a question of fight or flight. And a good night's sleep for a teacher the night before he meets his first class is out of the question, of course. Fortunately, this is a trade secret unknown to most students.

I had heard about how brilliant the students at AUBG were, which was reassuring since these are the easiest to teach. In America we believe everyone who wants a university education should have it, regardless of their abilities, which makes for an awful lot of remedial work at the lower end of the class roster. In Europe there is no shame in going to a trade or technical school, and the students who make it to the university generally belong there. The American University in Bulgaria then was to be a magnet school for the best and brightest students in the Balkans, similar to the American University in Beirut. George Soros, the billionaire philanthropist from Hungary, took a particular interest in the university as a vehicle to bring about democratic institutions and change in Eastern Europe after the fall of Communism. As a result of his patronage and support from the American government, virtually all the students at AUBG are on full scholarship. Their SAT and Test of English as a Foreign Language scores tend to go off the chart.

But testing in the top one to three percentile does not necessarily make for a well-educated student, of course. To a great degree, education under the socialist system meant memorizing a vast amount of information and spewing it back at final examination time. The professor stood at the podium professing—disdaining questions or like interaction with students. Attendance was not even particularly required—if a friend took good notes you really didn't need to turn up at all, especially if the friend was willing to help out at examination time.

Richard with true Bulgarian national symbol

This is one area where Communist theory seems to have taken genuine hold. It is very difficult to convince Eastern European students that plagiarism is stealing, or that cheating is not merely cooperative effort between colleagues, especially when the professor wields all the power and getting a diploma is a little like winning a war. Learning how to solve problems, how to ask "why?" how to think independently, and educating students through dialog were alien precepts in the old days—which is not to say the students do not have their private thoughts and opinions.

An American poet friend married to a Bulgarian writer once described this country as a nation of masks. A question in the classroom, for example, is often met with an extremely beautiful, deer-caught-in-the-headlights expression, revealing nothing of what might lie under the jet-black hair or behind the deep-blue eyes, faces with all the animation of a department store mannequin. And it is exasperatingly difficult to get a sense of whatever emotion might attend a response to the question.

But in defense of my soon-to-be fellow countrymen, one has to admit how understandable this is. Just as they were forming a modern nation after four hundred years of Ottoman Yoke, in came the Russians for fifty years of another kind of yoke. In a world where Big Brother really was watching you—sometimes through the eyes of a neighbor who would report any deviant, antisocial behavior like criticizing the government or blowing your stack at a fellow worker who screwed up the day's work, it probably was best to keep your own counsel—flat affect as a defense mechanism, if you wish. With no chance of escaping, no California on the distant shore to which one could always flee and start a new career, a new life, one could not easily afford the luxury of telling someone off in public. You did not burn your bridges with people because you would be living with them for the rest of your life, and you could never be sure what power an enemy might one day hold over you.

Another friend, a Bulgarian poet, described his intellectual life under the previous regimes as a kind of schizophrenia. He and his friends retreated into a world of music, books, and radio communication from the BBC, completely ignoring the official public life of the country, which they considered a great lie. I wondered for a long time what the strange electrical outlet in our apartment was for, for example, and it turns out to be the plug for the cheap little white radios you see all over the place which piped in the official music and news to each apartment. Every building was wired, Orwellian fashion, for your morning dose of newspeak. On the road to Sofia from Blagoevgrad there is a sprawling field of radar antennae and equipment which was the jamming station keeping decadent Western TV programs from beaming into Bulgaria. And there is a prison camp on an island in the Danube popularly known as Sunny Beach where dissidents were imprisoned and sometimes beaten to death. Despite the heartbreaking beauty of Bulgaria, the nineteenth-century fields harvested by hand by peasants in brightly colored clothes and all the extraordinary charm of the country, it seems poor Bulgaria was not a very pretty place to live at some very important levels in the past. My hippie generation used to snicker at Ronald Reagan's dinosaur vision of Russia's "evil empire," but the longer you live in this particular outpost, the clearer it becomes how people suffered here. Bulgarians themselves will tell you they are damaged goods, that a generation has been lost, and the self-pity implied in this idea proves the point to a degree. It is the logic of childhood: we have a bad time and now you in the West owe it to us to make life happy once

Nicky, Kalina, William, and Richard at the Plovdiv sport center

again. But the euphoria which swept the country in 1989 when hundreds of thousands lit candles in street demonstrations and brought down the government has dissipated. People felt that simply changing the government would bring about an affluent Western "lifestyle," when, in fact, the opposite has occurred. The average monthly salary is so low and inflation is so bad people are virtual prisoners in their own country, unable to afford travel even within Bulgaria. People have to grow their own food to survive. A country that used to be the bread-basket for Russia now must import grain from the United States. And so the little "red grand-mothers" all over Eastern Europe are going to the ballot box and returning the old Communists to power. The trains didn't necessarily run on time in the old days, but there was no such thing as Mafia terror on the streets, their meager pensions sufficed, and there were no breadlines.

The cynicism young people feel for politicians is more than just the cynicism of youth. A parallel "generation X" has grown up on this side of the world, trying to figure out how to get an education that in the past was guaranteed, unsure how they will make a living in the future, angry that they have been blacklisted and cannot get visas to the West. And so, in some of the brightest young people, there is a defiant pan-Slavism at work, a pan-Slavism in designer jeans, if you wish. At one point, after reading our poems at the newly established Slaviani Institute, we were invited to teach a minicourse in American poetry. The institute is seen by some as the Russian version of the American University, though the rector claims his goal to be the appreciation of Slavic culture in a Bulgarian context. The first day we came to teach, we happened to push the wrong button on the elevator and got off by mistake on the uppermost floor. There, sitting like so many Anthony Perkins in a Psycho attic, were enormous statues of Lenin which seemed to have been placed in storage until the political winds blew a little more favorably to the East. It was like walking through a Fellini movie.

I came to Bulgaria as an English teacher, of course, and it was not my job to inculcate the American way of life. (One born-again AUBG professor who began heavy-duty proselytizing in the classroom a couple of years ago was apparently run out of town on a rail.) In fact, my politics have always drifted a little to the

Sailing on the Black Sea

left of George McGovern and Eugene McCarthy—socialism is not necessarily a dirty word in my lexicon, though the word Socialist in Bulgaria is just the new moniker for the old Communists who have popped up like mushrooms after a heavy rain. Anyhow, one definition of politics is simply how people live together, and in this light, it would have been impossible not to have touched on political issues in a literature course.

I recall a student from Albania who was exceptional in his ability to turn Western values on their head and confront me in class with the most bizarre interpretations of the works we were reading. It was really wonderful to have someone who would speak his mind so freely, but sad, too, that the very large chip he wore on his shoulder came from his sense of living "in exile," at a university whose philosophy he did not espouse. For him, the arsonist father in Faulkner's "Barn Burning" was the hero of the story, a victim of the civil war. Auden's "Unknown Citizen" satirized fas-

Harriet Fulbright visits Sofia

cism and Western consumerism and had nothing to do with the socialist state. This student had a particular antipathy to modern psychiatry and any reference to the dark healer; Freud in our class discussion invoked his deepest scorn. The one story he did approve of was Crane's "The Open Boat." The long-suffering oiler who spelled his shipwrecked colleagues at the oar without complaint was a model of social brotherhood and responsibility. And who could disagree with that? I'm not here to lay down the "truth." Talk to me. If the oiler's the hero, what do you make of the journalist in the lifeboat?

While I am not fervently religious, it surprised me the degree to which atheism, or secularism at least, had successfully taken root in the minds of my students. If they chose to write a paper on abortion, say, or euthanasia when given an assignment in argumentation, invariably the woman's right to end a pregnancy or an individual's right to end his life were seen as unquestionable. An American student would at least tip his hat to the opposition, would acknowledge that some people consider such termination of human life immoral. The Bulgarian students respected Orthodox Christianity and might even attend services on the big holidays the way young couples on a date swell up Catholic churches at Christmas and Easter in the United States after everyone has had his share of turkey or ham at family dinners. But Orthodoxy is seen as a unifying cultural force which kept Bulgaria a nation during

the Ottoman Yoke, not the sacramental focus of one's spiritual life. The king, on the other hand, is a different matter.

When he returned from exile in Spain for a visit this spring, thousands upon thousands of young and old flocked after him in every city he visited like the Pied Piper come to Hamelin. For the young in particular, he is the only hope, the royal father of every fairy tale who will make it all come right in the end. And who knows, they may be right. I certainly went flying after him with the crowds when he came to Blagoevgrad.

I wonder as I write this if I haven't painted too bleak a portrait of my countrymen-to-be, the life here in Bulgaria. I will carry myriad beautiful images of this place when I must get on the plane next week. Translation student Tenyu Boyadjiev's face, open as a flower, gentle and brilliant all those afternoons we sat together in my office and he led me through the intricacies of Bulgarian poetry. Nita Luci, golden hair and grey business suit sitting in the Budapest City Hall for the opening of the student conference as though she owned the place, and how hard she worked at revising her essay to win the competition. The damn fleet of work-study geniuses who could fix any computer problem in an instant while you looked on, mouth agape like a stunned brontosaurus. The Pierrot-like face of our driver Vasil as he carried us two thousand kilometers around the country on a book tour the media dubbed Pink Floyd II—his good will and calm good manners that enabled us all to remain friends by the hectic end of the journey.

And over the years I've certainly seen many acts of political courage. I remember sitting in a hotel lobby with Blaga Dimitrova once, shortly before the government fell in 1989. She had just come from presenting the parliament with an open letter signed by many Bulgarian intellectuals demanding that the government stop its intimidation of writers. The police had recently confiscated all of Peter Manolov's works, for example, on the pretext that it was decadent and scatological, when everyone knew his real crime was his work as a human rights activist. Manolov had gone on a hunger strike and was not faring well. Blaga's husband had just been arrested and interrogated for twelve hours. "Aren't you afraid to be seen with me here?" I asked her. Public contact with a Westerner would certainly do her no good. "They know where I live, they know what I think," she said. "This has all simply got to stop." And Bulgaria saw even greater nerve after she became vice president of the country.

Several nights ago I sat in the baroque theater on the central square in Varna for one of the opera events staged for the International Music Festival each summer. Two exquisitely beautiful little girls sat to my right dressed in similar blue polka-dot dresses with black lace hems. They listened to the chorus of *Nabucco* in ecstasy and didn't take their eyes off the heroine when she sang. They politely refused my offer of a Tic-Tac, but their dark eyes lit up and quiet smiles broke through their formality when I offered a complimentary program. After the music, William and Nicky and I met Tiho, a former AUBG student who works as a banker here, and we all sat out under the trees at a cafe drinking white wine late into the night, discussing Bulgaria's future. Nicky had been swimming that afternoon and gave me a shell he found on the beach. "Listen," he said,

holding the small conch to my ear. "The Black Sea." And at that moment, I would not have been anywhere else on earth.

How one interacts with the host country was certainly a key topic at the orientation we were given before leaving Washington for our teaching assignments. And it seems to be a perennial subject when Fulbrighters get together. This year is the fiftieth anniversary of the program, and there have been celebrations all over the world, in part to buoy up political support and counteract the Republican Congress's financial cutbacks. The entire Fulbright program budget for the past fifty years apparently comes to less than one day's operating expenses for the defense department, but this sort of statistic gets lost in an election year.

One such conference, "Understanding Differences and Building Bridges," was held in Sofia this May, and I had the pleasure of interviewing Senator Fulbright's widow, Harriet Fulbright, who actively supports the program and was visiting us. I sat with this extraordinary woman

Hungarian Fulbright director Hubba Bruckner, former Bulgarian vice president Blaga Dimitrova, Richard, William, and former U.S. ambassador Jack Perry, in Sofia

at a penthouse cafe overlooking the golden domes of Alexander Nevski Cathedral. And while I am not a professional journalist, nor did I use a tape recorder while we talked, I tried to keep careful notes on our conversation.

She described the goals of this educational exchange program one would expect: mutual understanding among nations and different cultures, and the increased chance for peace that might attend such understanding. She quoted Michael Sandel's book *Democracy's Discontent,* on the importance of thinking globally but acting locally, how the PTA was as important as the WTO, perhaps even more so, how important it was to act, to do something to bring about change. But I felt it important to pick up on a question that had come from the floor in the morning session which asked if the Fulbright program and others such as United States Information Service were not indeed just tools of American foreign policy and a kind of cultural imperialism. "Yes," she admitted, "but in the best sense of the word." When scholars come to a foreign country from the United States, she explained, and they are completely free to criticize what is wrong with their country, when the United States actually funds such criticism, this can only be seen as a good model for freedom in the host countries. I thought of my previous year as a Fulbrighter and, indeed, in the hours of orientation, in the contracts I signed, and interaction with administrative staff, never once did I get any impression that I was expected to tow the political line or wave the American flag in the classroom.

If anything, it seems that America benefits more from programs such as the Fulbright exchanges than host countries. I was discussing this idea with the Fulbright director, a really lovely guy named Hubba Bruckner, in Budapest this spring. Hubba had arranged for me and William to give several poetry readings in Budapest and Debrecen when I brought three of my students to the Civil Education Project Conference. I mentioned to him that I had served in the Peace Corps in Tunisia for two years, and he said he saw the Fulbright program as a kind of extension of the Peace Corps ideal. Volunteers return from their foreign assignments and become windows on the world through which both countries get to know each other. They are like so many Lemuel Gullivers, returning from their travels with far greater

insight into their own native land for having made the journey.

I thought of how many of my fellow Peace Corps volunteers took their overseas experiences back home into government service or legal practices in the local communities or international commerce. Given our relative isolation as a nation and our penchant for looking inward, it seems this program more than pays for itself for the insight and connectedness it gives us to the world. Understanding differences is a crucial first step if we are to speak to each other across the barriers of language and culture.

Oddly, the longer I am in Bulgaria, the greater those differences seem to me, but the paradox is not unlovely. This morning the chambermaid handed me my laundry and broke into tears. "My sister died and she was only fifty and a half," she said, out of the blue, trying not to sob. I hadn't noticed the black scarf about her neck, and my cheeriness triggered the sad outburst. I'm not sure this would have happened in the United States.

Once, poet Lyubomir Levchev took us to visit the enormous caves of Madara, and we came across a man dressed in animal skins carrying an ax. This was not a Disneyland tour guide, however, but a Bulgarian historian named Todor Riznikov who had had it with contemporary society and was now living as a hermit. A friendly hermit. He showed us around his cave, asked about things in Sofia, and at one point picked up a little red serpent that seemed to be following us and crooned to it, "come along pepe, come along now," and tossed it into the bushes. I later discovered it was a pepelianka, the most poisonous snake in Europe, and though he had been bitten a couple of times, he still considered the snake a brother creature.

There is a blind soothsayer named Aunt Vanga who lives in the village of Rupite near the Greek border and is revered by Bulgarians as a saint.[1] People come from all over the world to find out about a lost child, to be healed of an illness, to learn the future. She lives in a little cottage beside a strange temple raised in her honor at the center of a dead volcano. She shouts at you as though you were hard of hearing in a brawling peasant dialect which most

---

[1] Aunt Vanga died in August 1996.

Visit with blind soothsayer, Aunt Vanga

Bulgarians cannot understand. A translator stands at her side decoding the cryptic messages that come from another world or different dimension.

She encouraged us to ask her detailed questions when we visited, but I was reluctant to know my future. I did ask if the Fulbright year would be extended, and she assured me it would be. You must always give someone a gift when you meet them, she told us, and William must eat honey and yoghurt every day. I felt a remarkable affection for the old woman, and after our visit I gave a favorite Buck knife I happened to be carrying in my bag to the young journalist who had arranged our visit. "How did you know I collect knives?" he asked, astounded. William often acts as my writing coach and has limited me to three poems for this piece. Perhaps the account I wrote of our visit might qualify here.

Rupite

Vanga rests in the eye of the volcano,
the great red eye of day, the third eye
if you wish, the sweet panorama of time:
a tear, an icon, a feather—a little
boy wields his sword in the sunlight, and,
"give his father your knife, perhaps they
will gut a deer one winter day and crawl
inside for warmth, come back to me when
there are cherry blossoms, place a gift
in my temple, a million dollars, a
new penny. Where were you born?"

At her garden gate supplicants wait
like repentant crows, chastened vultures
as we enter, snowy, into the inner sanctum.
"Vanga help me out of this darkness,"
they would cry if they had tongues.
White turkeys mock their pain with loud
gobbles, roosters crow with impunity.
A cloud of steam rises over the ponds,
a sulphurous mist, Delphic, the shape
of anything you might wish.

"Hey, where is your wife; is this icon blessed."
"only with my heart, Auntie, I bring my friend
    instead."

The red logs agree; "hey, you will have great
    success."
But will I be wed to these mountains, Vanga?
    I could weep
for their light. Am I to be born again?

The question goes unasked, floats to the bottom
of the mineral pools into slime—the moment cold
suddenly, as on another winter day, a
beautiful boy in the shape of a beautiful boy
presented me with the temple of his body,
    and I
in awe, stood mute at the door, frozen like a
stone lotus at the Buddha's feet.

The cherry blossoms are sweet, insisting.
In your village once a robin covered the lost
children who had strayed too far from home in
cherry blossoms, Na li?

Yes, yes it's true Auntie, but she spread a blanket
of strawberry leaves, and the children never
    woke—
herbs take us into and unto the end of time,
did you say, Auntie? In this middle moment, this
rosemary afternoon, this aquamarine crystal
of a day—I kiss your hand in sad reverence,
    hey.

The boy thinks to himself, how like the edge of
the moon this blade, white, clean, cutting the
night as though it were the throat of sacrifice,
and he carves the bread.

This strange culture, this beautiful Bulgaria, not East, not West, Europe and not Europe. How I have come to love it. Travelling back and forth across the country, I have come to feel like a citizen, have taken Bulgaria into my blood. Eliot says that speaking a foreign language is like having a second soul, and though I am hardly fluent in Bulgarian, I sense an expansion of spirit for the sake of this past year and everything I have experienced. Sometimes in my dreams, I am swimming with Nicky again far out into the Black Sea on our way home from the disco, bobbing in the aquamarine water until the coral sun breaks the horizon and pushes fully into morning. Or I am having coffee with William at the ice fountain in Malyovitsa, and the white peak of Rila Mountain burns against the purple sky. Or there are acres and acres of sunflowers, the entire valley golden with sunflowers, where we stop and gather up bouquets, our arms green and sticky and golden with sunflowers.

There have been many moments I will not forget, moments that bring my experience with Bulgaria to a kind of completion.

One day last October, William and I sat looking out over the golden onion dome of the Russian Orthodox church in Sofia waiting for our host to come into the living room. Gerogi Djargarov entered, frail, cachectic, and in pain with an obvious cancer, but dignified and straight as a cyprus. The brilliance and good humor of the eyes remained. He asked polite questions about my work, seemed anxious to get the record straight about his own role as Zhivkov's vice president.

I reminded him of the time years ago when he had commanded William's presence for an interview. Both men had fought against fascism, both were poets, both even the same age. We had had a difficult schedule and William was just out of hospital from a heart attack, so when I was forbidden to attend their meeting, I informed the security guards that for health reasons it must last no more than twenty minutes. An hour later I threatened to burst down the door, but the beefy guards simply ignored me. William emerged ashen and elated from the visit, and I took him away in a fury.

"They thought you were a journalist," Djargarov said, his eyes dark with compassion and apology. Despite his pain, he walked us to the door. I took in his frailty, his courage, and his integrity—despite the political past. I thought of William's frailty, my own, how all things must pass, and my own eyes filled with tears looking into Djargarov's. This spring, Lyubomir taught me a Bulgarian custom I had not known before. When someone mentioned Djargarov's name at dinner, Lyubomir spilled red wine in memory of the dead, and Djargarov's spirit passed among us for a while.

Last winter I sat in front of a space heater at my kitchen window one morning preparing classes. As I reviewed a simple D. H. Lawrence poem and the mountains came into the morning light beyond the town, I thought of my old friend asleep in the back bedroom and grew acutely aware of my own existence beyond time, beyond its present physical state, an otherness beyond words, like watching someone in a room who is not aware of your presence. Lucky and sad and beautiful to go out of one's body this way. And rare. It doesn't happen unless you are willing to investigate unfamiliar territory.

Fortunately, this will not be the end of my friendship with Bulgaria. As I turn fifty and begin the second half of my life, more and more of it will be spent in my second home. Very strange, to acquire a second homeland in the middle of one's life. The press here has found it curious that two Americans are being given citizenship when so many young people are trying to go to America. In today's poem,

Caveboys Todor Riznikov and Richard Harteis, Madera

I've tried to answer the question they ask so often: Why do you wish to become a Bulgarian citizen?

Because (A Garland for Bulgaria)

from early summer,
red poppies pave the way
from Sofia to Russe,
Shumen to Smolyan
and Babushkas
dressed in black and white
bend to the hot July fields
harvesting grain—mirror
images of the storks,
dressed in black and white
gleaning after them.

And in Blagoevgrad
Infinite hexagons flag
the walkways through
the maze of bloks, each
cell fitted like
the other, each worker
colleague buzzing about
his own business, but
humming the music
of the hive. While,

because this summer, only
imitation Addidas can
be found in the shops,
teenagers stroll the gentle
evening in uniform leisure,
like a field of sunflowers,
heads bobbing with affirmation
and affection from side to side
the way gravity spins counter
clockwise south of the equator.

And because once I
fell in with a man,
jogging beside the tracks
through a forest of purple
thistle, whose chest was
carved ivory. And when
we stopped, we lay in a
wheat field—spent—
and he smiled
and kissed me
and ran away.

And up the road
the king's heart,
the king's faith burn
bright in the Rila Monastery
under the eyes of St. Jean
and the eagles circling
his mountain aerie.

William, Gerogi Djargarov, and Richard at Writers' Union house in Varna, 1994

And because history has fashioned
centuries of stone into the
mountain mosaic of Plovdiv,
and golden domes rise over Sofia
like the promise of morning and
in Varna two ancient ghosts
smile up through museum glass
at us with the melancholy of time.

Or, because in Veliko Turnovo
the flushed face and black eyes
of a girl swept by us, up the hill
like Joan of Arc against the infidel,
like another who with only
his breath and bagpipes
forced a wild Rhodopo song
into a rhapsody of desire.

And because once the full moon
was a magnet, pulling our
little train through the night
to Varna, waiting like a calm
bride by the sea, and flooded
the valleys with golden light
while my countrymen slept
under the Balkans
mistaking my love
for the train's distant whistle
at the edge of a dream.

Because in Sandanski
and Hissarya
sulphurous clouds rise
over the mineral baths
and brazen youth float
in and out of the mist
with bold smiles and genitals
like fallen angels
in Dante's Inferno
tempting the doomed onanists
leering at the water's edge
to release.

And because in Sopot
Natalia administered
little wet kisses
and glued a firefly
to each forehead
so, all night long
we sat like beacons,
stars bursting about
our eyes, shining below
each golden third eye,

And summer held her breath
in the silent trees
for the love of these
phosphorescent aliens
who had landed
winking and blinking
in her dark garden

And because riding home,
a late afternoon haze
drifted across acres
of lavender
carpeting the canyon
and the Balkans floated up
like blue ribbons
tethering the purple earth
to the troubled sky.

Because in Bourgas
on the Black Sea
my lover's chameleon eyes
grew aquamarine,
gleaming plate-glass,
each morning
as the sun rose on
our lovemaking. Grew

by day, as tacky and true
as the regal-cobalt-Elvis
eyes a road-side artist
hawks at Graceland

and with the moon,
panther green,
impossibly emerald,
stalking me through the
black velvet jungle
of our passion.

And because once
after a plebeian supper at
Caesar's Club and Restaurant,
Lydia studied the busty Venus
in the lobby and opined,
"Affreuxdite."

And even because no one
has repaired the broken bench
waiting at the edge
of an abandoned court
for the fields to turn again
to Mars, while a leopard prowls
the lonely sky, dappled dark and
moonlight, crouching over the night,
his luminous blood coursing
with hunger and solitude.

BIBLIOGRAPHY

Poetry:

Fourteen Women, Three Rivers Press, 1979.

Morocco Journal: Love, Work, Play, Carnegie-Mellon University Press, 1981.

Internal Geography, Carnegie-Mellon University Press, 1987.

Keeping Heart, Orpheus House (Sofia and Paris), 1994, bilingual edition, 1996.

Fiction:

Sapphire Dawn, www.galaxymall.com, spring 1997.

Nonfiction:

Marathon, W. W. Norton, 1989.

Editor:

(With William Meredith) *Window on the Black Sea,* Carnegie-Mellon University Press, 1992.

Translated poems and assisted in the editing of *Poets of Bulgaria,* Unicorn Press, 1986. Contributor of poetry, short fiction, translations, and theatre pieces to literary and trade magazines.

Marvin R. Hiemstra

1939-

This brief autobiography is a sincere thank-you to everyone and everything making an appearance in my life and, most of all, to the Resplendent Cycle of which I am privileged to be an infinitesimal part.

TRIUMPH ONE—RUSTIC STRONGHOLD IN A TRULY HORRENDOUS WORLD—1939 to 1947

Cozy Earth Corner—Half-section farm in the middle of absolutely nowhere Iowa.

Profound Space—Rambling old house: a gallery room with three windows—each a different view of the world, gigantic elms with petite green tree frogs, pet graveyard I demanded and, with great devotion, maintained.

Library Opens—Intelligent and complex radio programs alive with stunning vocabularies, twenty-five magazines, from *Saturday Review* to *Farm Journal* to *National Geographic* to *Life* (devious manipulator of the mid-century U.S.A. lifestyle), an almost complete natural world (my father refused to allow crop dusting so every wild creature in Iowa moved in: our crops did better than most because multitudes of appreciative birds wiped out the corn borers and other insects).

What Happened:

❖My grandparents lived ten miles away on a remote hilltop farm: a glorious subsistence pioneer paradise with a smokehouse, wren box under the eaves, and goldfish keeping the horse tank clean. Their love-filled summer kitchen became the dream setting for my most telling poem, "Locus Classicus" from *Dream Tees.* Herbert Gold enjoyed that "poem, whose sentiments I like—and that strong first stanza with the catfish, the iron cookstove . . . and the carrot cakers equaling the two on the sun porch."

The author at Eagle Falls, Lake Tahoe, 1993

I am sitting all alone at a solid old oak round table
in a splendid summer kitchen: invincible porcelain
and iron cookstove, jam-packed pie safe (an angel
was once arrested trying to break it), just caught
catfish swimming in a bucket. I am humming "Dixie"
while I spread butter frosting on a round carrot cake.

Hiemstra's maternal grandparents, about 1900

A wonderful person smiles through the screen door,
a smile and look more wonderful than anyone
has ever given me. I smile back and pull out the chair
next to me.

The wonderful person comes in, sits down, and speaks,
"You know something. There are one hundred kinds
of love in this world and the one most highly advertised
(activities on top of and/or between the sheets)
is merely one of the hundred. What we are doing right
now cutting into this delicious carrot cake is just
as satisfying as what those two are doing on the sun
porch! Gee, they've been out there a long time.

I do not happen to be this or that or any combination
of the above. I am just a complete person and I have
picked you, another complete person, regardless of gender
or theological woof or alleged ancestral warp to love
and respect. What more do you want?"

❖When I was four, my Great Aunt Lizzie from Cortland County, New York, came to visit. Since my parents and brother, all much older, were tangled in their own battles, Aunt Lizzie was the first person who really communicated with me directly in words. My grandparents had already communicated with me, magnificently, in actions.

That cold, dry, barren February Aunt Lizzie took me outside to help collect the twigs that were to become splendid bushes and trees on her New York State farm. My curiosity burst. "How do you know what plant it is by just holding a twig?" I cried. Smiling—Aunt Lizzie explained everything, and exactly why she was absolutely thrilled to have that particular blackberry bush.

I learned how amazing twigs in winter (bare and ugly and cold) really are. They are alive: potentially important and beautiful and delicious and the words that described those twigs are just as important and just as beautiful and just as delicious as the twigs themselves.

I began to understand. **Words can do anything.**

❖ From the beginning animals returned my love a zillion fold: a half collie/half shepherd who was my loyal friend, a flat of rainbow-feathered bantam chicks my grandmother gave me to raise, cows I brought in from the fields.

My dad began farming with an immense pair of Percheron horses. When he bought tractors, the horses were kept (most farmers had them slaughtered). I loved that team and they loved me. When I was in the yard, they would amble to the fence. I would climb the fence with great difficulty, scramble onto their backs, and sit happily singing for hours.

❖ I can clearly remember my very first all-consuming passion for another human being. A young trucker took off his shirt after unloading some dusty corn and I, at five, was stopped in my tracks with the incredible beauty and incredible satisfaction in observing a perfect torso.

❖ Liberty Corner was a one-room, eleven-student country school and Johanna Rouwenhorst was a teacher and human being of amazing quality. I, a bright and obnoxious little parrot, wanted attention desperately because I was pretty much ignored at home. Miss Rouwenhorst gave me my first compliment when I spouted a radio show phrase, "What a captivating coincidence!" in a proper context.

She was always brilliantly and appropriately positive. I learned the right behavior to expect and to accept. What a gift! Throughout my life the inevitable horrors are always workable, because I know without thinking what is acceptable and what is not.

I was able to reconnect with Johanna Rouwenhorst at the time of my Pulitzer Prize nomination for *Dream Tees*, decades later, and thank her for helping the sun to shine in my life.

TRIUMPH TWO—DUTCH TOWN ON A SQUARE—1947 to 1960

Cozy Earth Corner—Fancy cattle farm spread on the city limits of Pella, Iowa.

Profound Space—A sprawling house radiating tremendous good energy to balance out a barely functional family, lavish grounds (immense maple trees, clipped hedges, endless lawn) which I maintained during the blistering summer months.

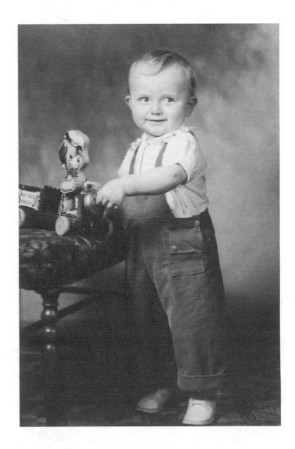

As "Kewpie prototype," late 1940

Often after I scooped corncobs out, I hopped up into the bunks and sang and tap-danced "Oh, what a beautiful morning!" to a captive audience of four hundred beef cattle, patiently waiting for me to shut up and feed them.

Library Open—A picture-book town with four thousand very sticky, *largo*, low blood-pressure Protestants. Betty Wells, Des Moines talk-show hostess, always knocked me out as I was washing dishes after lunch with her signature gush, "You can do anything you want to do if you really care enough." My first bookcase at age eleven and by high school (courtesy of *Saturday Review* and *Time* and frantic notes direct to publishers—Iowa had no real bookstores then) my shelves groaned happily with Carl Sandburg, e. e. cummings, the radiant King James Bible (the Trinity's favorite pied-à-terre. If Christianity were only practiced as it shines with Love and Understanding in that Holy Book!), William Carlos Williams, Archibald MacLeish *J.B.*,

Dmitri Shostakovich's Symphony No. 10 (this miracle entered my life when my friend Tom went to summer music camp in Iowa City and heard the university symphony prepare it. No. 10 remains my absolute musical bulwark), and a tidal wave of philosophy and psychology books. Most important, David Vos and an intelligent gang of friends put together *MRH*, my first volume of poetry, when I was nineteen: a surprise hidden in a church tower.

What Happened:

❖ My ancient piano teacher, Hatie Cox Van Cleave, was the daughter of a Civil War drummer boy who at age ten spent the last year of the war in military prison. What a blessing she was!

Diane Wang observed, "Poet, Spare that Poem," my hard-hitting War between the States eulogy, "helps us remember what real poetry is all about."

A poem wants to go down
deep into the soil.

A poem deserves the right
to grow like Topsy and to enjoy the ultimate pleasure,
standing in the sun —   complete and dazzling   in bloom

for all to see.
A poem is a tough, magnificent southern magnolia
grandiflora   home in its time to 474 bluebird nests,
221 happy raccoon families and 49

bloody
coon hunts, home to 4,751,236,011
born pushy   social   insects,
tickled to death by 301 sharp-witted and persistent pileated woodpeckers,
final home to one

gravely wounded
Civil War soldier
who, after excruciating pain, died
happily
hallucinating and clinging
with his last strength
to the magnolia trunk
believing he was walking
home to his mother's
supper call   after a long
day plowing   the spring fields.

Hatie Cox Van Cleave actually understood life. She would become, without notice, a sibyl who could make Maria Callas plead for a Kleenex. In the midst of "one *and,* two *and,*" an uncanny voice would proclaim, **"Your music will save you, lad!"** and it did. She introduced me to Bartok, Ravel, Brahms, Poulenc, and all music.

❖ There was one Japanese family in Pella quietly thriving amongst a telephone book jammed with more-than-a-mouthful Dutch names. The daughter, Tomi Ikuta, a talented silk screen artist, noticed that I was an artistic nut about to crack and asked if I had seen the Des Moines Art Center. I, a seventh grader, said I'd love to go. Thus began my incredible love for and need of the visual arts in all forms.

The Japanese mother, a Shinto, was spotted by me (driving a tractor through town early one morning) on the fire escape of the family's above-a-store apartment blowing a large conch shell with silk cords attached. I was astounded

With Prince, 1945

although I didn't understand why at the time. A door to a sacred corridor in a previous life had opened.

Years later when I became obsessed and nourished by the Japanese culture before 1850, I knew exactly when that world of understanding and simple respect for the spirit, the kami, in absolutely everything had so gently entered my vision in this particular lifetime.

❖ During a routine medical checkup in Des Moines, my third year of high school, I announced to the sleepy doctor who was about to take my blood pressure that I felt strong affection for men and **I was not leaving his office** until he referred me to a psychiatrist. How did I ever have the guts to do that? The wide-awake doctor talked to my parents.

Two years of blissful uninterrupted free association and 137 choice Havana cigars later— Dr. Paul T. Cash announced that I was definitely better balanced than most, bright as the sun, and that I wouldn't really have any trouble with my life, but I should always remember that some people are pretty stupid, unable to deal with the full spectrum of life, and, consequently, prone to vicious behavior. That no-nonsense understanding has allowed me to happily withstand (and often just ignore) a lifetime of illogical discrimination.

❖ At that period Central College in Pella was an intrepid, tiny institution doing its best with no money. The Drama Department consisted of a one-man power force named Maurice Birdsall. He produced miracles: growing up in Pella one went to all **better than professional** college plays (*Bell, Book, and Candle* helped me give Good and Evil a powder, once and for all). During my two years at Central I was heavily involved in theater: invaluable for my present performance activity.

❖ Knowing that I was too much for Central College, Hatie Cox Van Cleave's brother, whom I scarcely knew, insisted I come to see him. Having investigated the program thoroughly, Henry Cox informed me that the State University of Iowa Writers' Workshop should be my next step. I transferred, with great elation, to Iowa City. Thank God for people who care!

TRIUMPH THREE—THE RIVER THROUGH ATHENS—1960 to 1962

Cozy Earth Corner—State University of Iowa at Iowa City.

Profound Space—First year in Quadrangle Dorm: second level—an unbroken square around which at 3:30 A.M. I ran whacking each door with a hammer and Ed roller-skated behind me: we created a Stockhausen brouhaha waking everyone, who blamed and tried to punch out their neighbors (Ed and I were already back at our rooms, pretending to be just awake).

Second year in Ada Wolff's rooming house— she really understood me. Monumental walnut and marble Victorian furniture soon appeared in my room: heaven with a bay window and the eagle from my Pella gang, hovering on top of the brass bed.

Ada had outlived three husbands whom she visited in the cemetery with flowers each weekend (the same cemetery where my audacious and wonderful friend Dana ran naked after each spring rain because the walks were alive with earth worms). Ada assured me that I would have been the fourth husband if the Secretary of Chronology and the Secretary of Genes had been a little kinder.

When I stayed up reading and typing all night, which was often since I achieved decades that year, about 2:30 A.M. I would open the door to a knock and be greeted by a strawberry shortcake à la mode on a tray. I would polish it off, write a thank-you to Ada, and get back to work.

Merci

Sound asleep
on my typewriter
a kind knock
brought me back
to coffee, fresh
peach pie, and
a Verlaine jig.

Dana didn't like my name so she dubbed me Greg. I soon discovered that I had a complete and amazing double life with twice as many friends. Greg could do things Marvin would never dream of and vice versa. My sense of multiple

As a "guileless high school graduate," 1958

perspective bloomed—if I could be two different people at once, a poet could be a whole shining world at once and love it.

The University Theater Department featured David Thayer, who created special lighting effects far beyond the imagination of a serious visionary arctic fox. The production of August Strindberg's *The Dream Play* was worth several top-of-the-line lifetimes. I went to every performance of every play and learned, learned, learned. Studio Theater did a heart-crumbling and priority-smashing Tennessee Williams, *Camino Real.*

Library Island—William Faulkner *As I Lay Dying,* Count Baldassare Castiglione *The Courtier,* Charles Baudelaire *Les Fleurs du mal,* Henry Purcell *Dido and Aeneas* (if only there were more frequent rainstorms with convenient cozy caves), Rainer Maria Rilke *Das Buch der Bilder,* Aaron Copland *Appalachian Spring* (what it means to be blissfully alive), Ovid *Metamorphoses* (a dazzling fountain of poetic technique/realization), and individuals: Peggy Wyse, David Holtz, Patricia Smith, Dana Walford, Roy Proctor, Harald Hoeffding, Pierre André Larocque, Joseph Tuttle, and Rodni Rexach, among a multitude of glowing spirits.

What Happened:

❖ I plunged into two years of fierce and focused study: literature and life. My terrific Understanding Poetry teacher, Edmund Skellings, actually taught poetry with a solid naturalist's understanding of the devious volcano that hides, ready to blow, beneath every real poem.

❖ Iowa City, at that point in time, was very much like Athens with Plato on permanent sabbatical—a vortex of creative energy with no "shut up, smother your mind, and do unpaid research for me" leaders to limit the brilliance.

❖ Summer between my junior and senior years I escaped to work in New York City and so learned early that I wanted a life of more than art-filled indulgence. My job in a small hotel (home to ladies, gentlemen, and others, weekly scheduled assignations, and assorted nut theater types) resulted in my hotel poems, *On the Way Up,* which became my B.A. Honors in Creative Writing project under Donald Justice.

TRIUMPH FOUR—IRONIC LIMESTONE COLUMNS—1962 to 1966

Cozy Earth Corner—Indiana University, Bloomington, a colossal Liberal Arts Knot Garden.

Profound Space—Well-loved, pre-1900, graduate student apartments: the last, two perfect fifteen-foot cubes with fireplace: kitchen and bath attached, welcomed aspiring celestials to midnight poetry and folk-tale parties and delighted friends to scrumptious dinner parties with menus I created, recipes still lovingly prepared around the globe.

My bed, center of second cube, was gleefully circled by shining upstairs neighbor, Delia Bell, on her brand new moped which roared me awake early one brilliant sunny morning.

Campus, town, and surrounding area had evolved magnificently from the original natural world. The countryside was dotted with abandoned Victorian farm houses which were heaven-sent for people like me just learning how to make love. The nautical conceit in this autobiographical poem, "Wind and Two Young Barn Owls" from *I'd Rather Be a Phoenix!* was inspired by an outrageous J. M. W. Turner painting in the Tate Gallery, *Orange Merchantman Going to Pieces,* a cargo ship breaking up in a storm with oranges sprinkled all over the waves.

> Spring! A clear, deep gallon jug of hard cider
> did it. Just half-full was enough. We took over
> the boarded-up Early Victorian guarded
> by loyal irises, ancient in saffron and indigo.
> That house was lonely, abandoned except
> for the wind and two young barn owls
> in a hollow of the black oak
> dreaming of the Sphinx on roller skates.
>
> Near sunset looking down from our attic hideout
> on the apple blossoms just beginning,
> we shared a simple basket of supper.
> I asked you for a second glass.
>
> You tipped it, our rough molded crystal jug,
> and the miniature tempest struck! Man the ballast!
> Life craft down quick! The dying sun
> through a sparkling amber violence
> is more beauty than I can get at alone.
>
> Frantic maelstrom of the jostled deep is over.
> The calm foams into my anxious
> glass. I am not alone. You
> are both the wind wild unruly
> ferment and the delicious
> wake, so easy after the brilliant storm.

Like many university towns Bloomington thrived as an amorous milieu and I relished my first two considerable relationships, each about a year in duration: number one, an unmitigated jerk; number two, a centered being. Consequently, I understood and I was ready when the real love of my life appeared a few years later.

Library Island—Vladimir Nabokov *Speak, Memory: An Autobiography Revisited* (original title: *Conclusive Evidence.* **At best we can only be a metaphor of what we are**), Robert Laxalt *A Man in the Wheatfield,* Arthur Machen *The Hill of Dreams,* Walter Pater *Imaginary Portraits* (no one knows how to **literally** illuminate detail better than Pater. My M.A. thesis on *Imaginary Portraits* was an invaluable exercise, not unlike learning how to facet emeralds), Benjamin Britten *Peter Grimes* (one of the finest examples of style embodying content in an absolute fusion and an absolute communication), Mark Twain *Pudd'nhead Wilson,* Iona and Peter Opie *The Lore and Language of Schoolchildren,* Antti Aarne and Stith Thompson *The Types of the Folktale,* and resplendent individuals: Jean Martin, James Lee White (with whom I shared sublime metaphysical discussions and whose persistent Velcro Angst inspired my brightest affirmation: "I always face the world with a sincere erection!"), Olive Fredericks, George F. Byers, Tom Waechter, Georgia Rodgers.

What Happened:

❖ Herman B. Wells had created Indiana University, a miraculous and magnificent citadel to culture, with tremendous wisdom and sheer brilliant willpower.

Any student, laced with curiosity both above and below the waist, was treated to a superb Cornucopia of Civilization: a professional and exhilarating opera production each weekend (Ross Allen served as the ingenious opera stage director, creating some of the most dynamic crowd scenes and poignant solo moments in the history of theater, musical or otherwise. My performance technique owes much to his total concepts: both ruthlessly logical and intensely human), first-rate musical and theatrical events (the resident Beaux Arts Trio included, and happily still includes, Menahem Pressler, a transcendent classic paradox, being a superb pianist who is both flawless and spontaneous), a library system that was accessible and outstanding (I spent four years of intensive self-directed reading in addition to the strenuous course requirements), and, generally speaking, a university that was wide open to the best in all its diversity.

❖ Thank God, poetry had not yet been institutionalized. Willis Barnstone was on the faculty, but in a non-poetic capacity. The one visiting poet I remember in the four years was Anne Sexton, who managed to draw about seven students and twenty male faculty members (in yardstick lapels and ties). Anne ranted until (because of the alleged heat) all male faculty members took their coats off so she

could check out the best physique possibility for her post-reading enjoyment.

❖ Extremely well-tempered into a radiant lifelong independent I finally left Indiana University (after satisfying semesters of teaching Freshman Composition, intensive study with an M.A. in Victorian Literature and a zillion additional course hours) terminally bored with academic politics (higher than Everest stacks of mindless hatred balanced by only short stacks of cash) and dashed off "to Europe never to return, alas . . ."

TRIUMPH FIVE—EUROPA EST—1966 to 1967

Cozy Earth Corner—Northern Europe, the tough cradle of my origin (on paper I go back to 1426 in Friesland, brisk and forbidding northern coast, and, in reality, to a forest shaman's smile 527 B.C. near what is now Bremen, Germany).

Profound Space—Amsterdam, third-floor room overlooking Vondel Park, in blissful exile from the unimaginatively vulgar, and often amazingly redundant, Collective Unconscious in the U.S.A.

I felt an overwhelming need to touch the greatest achievements that my ancestors had produced and so thoroughly delighted in. For one splendid year I did just that. I spent every waking second glued to the art museums and architectural triumphs of northern Europe. I have never felt more at home, before or since.

Special Library Island—Emily Dickinson (she didn't reach out to me until I was over there. Here is "Write Success into Your Résumé" from *In Deepest U.S.A.*),

> Simultaneous Reincarnation
> is efficiency
>
> at its best!
>
> It doesn't happen
> often, but when it works,
>
> Civilization pulls down
> the black crepe and shrieks
>
> with delight.

Think of the advantages

if you could
be a white Bengal tiger,
a cross/dressing Zuni
shaman, and Miss Emily Dickinson
at the very same time
on the same
hard-working soul.

Just think
of what you'd learn,

think about it,

and the sharp-edged
vocational skills
you'd have

for the next

time around.

A. Koolhass *Niet Doen, Sneeuwwitze,* Charles Ives (Concertgebouw audiences worshipped him, like Bach—I realized that he is America's most profound humorist), Christian Morgenstern *Galgenlieder,* Richard Strauss *Elektra,* George Balanchine *Prodigal Son,* Victoria and Albert Museum, Cologne Cathedral Treasury, Rijksmuseum, and beneficent mentors: Ernst Budde, Gerard Beerling, Hans Linka.

What Happened:

❖For the first time in my life I could step out of myself and begin to nourish the ultra-cosmic perspective essential for a writer. Only in the summer after my return to the U.S.A. was I, for the first time, beginning to see clearly my own creative vision. There's no point crying over spilled time.

❖I met two European men, appropriately enough—one Dutch, one German, whose full and affectionate lifestyles were really worth emulating. To that point my only valid role models had been Gertrude Stein and Alice B. Toklas. These excerpts from "Aesthetics of Survival Course No. 49—Advanced Rose" in *Dream Tees* hint at the elucidative creative power: unique to that once-in-all-of-time team.

Prof. Garden: For your next assignment—arrange alphabet blocks in various combinations until you build a perfect rose. . . .

It must open to the unsuspecting sun like a rose,

cuddle up and scream and lust softly like a rose,

pose at a moment's notice like a rose would pose,

lecture on Blooming Tingle just like a rose would,

but never never never never never never never fade on you.

You'll have all the time you need. . . .

Wisteria: How's that again? . . .

Lily: What about reincarnation?

Prof. Garden: Reincarnation works until one gets to Gertrude.

Hollyhock: Stop! I broke my point.

Prof. Garden: Time, our finest artist, waits
for no person or point. Don't interrupt!

Reincarnation works until one gets to Gertrude.

Gertrude was Gertrude, thorns fully adjustable, totally committed to being Gertrude. (Rose stems with heavy thorns form a grid within huge chalkboard frame)

In the sweet by and by she would definitely resent not being Gertrude.

She would not stand for it, not for a minute and certainly not forever!

Gertrude was and is and always will be an immense cubist patchwork rose window
quilted teacosy—always hot!
(Rose blocks attempt to form a rose window. One block keeps falling out, struggling back into place, and finally sticking—to great applause from fellow rose blocks) That is Gertrude
is a rose is a Gertrude is a rose
is a Gertrude is a rose is a Gertrude . . .
is a rose is a Gertrude is a rose

with polished Baroque dew drop
on a petal reflecting an apron
full of strawberries, just picked
by Alice, and assorted soft saints

(Saints skip across chalkboard)

and three extremely forward gears
with no reverse in sight (1917 Red
Cross truck roars madly across)

and a sky blue lectern cruising
with a smile through a sky blue sky
and one amber eternally outraged
bumblebee button (Bumblebee, fists
in gloves, boxes with bee intensity).

Gertrude is a mighty rose
forever wide open (Blue sky back
light turns into a gigantic rose
covering all of space)—so why
close if you have a good thing going
forever? . . .

Their enlightened and affectionate example
was an absolute lifesaver for me (and legions
of others), but I needed something more specifically applicable.

At that time the male human in the U.S.
huffed and puffed toward only one and/or
two supreme goals: lots of zeros in the bank
and ten-minute flings with whomever and
whatever crossed their bar path.

Only in Europe did I discover men and women
with full, balanced lives consisting of many
actively enjoyed dimensions. "I admire the diligence with which you give yourself to the
world." The United States howled and bel-
lowed about SEX, but only held the vaguest
understanding of the concept of LOVE. For
me Europe was a sunlit kingdom of enlightened and positive reinforcement.

❖Artistic creation and presentation live in Europe for every individual, whether that individual has several university degrees or drives
a taxi or both. Europeans have opinions and
genuine feelings about art, music, and literature.

The average U.S. human is absolutely terrified to have any opinions and feelings about
art, music, and literature. A work of art is
acceptable only if it is introduced by a full-
page ad in *The New York Times.*

I love *The New York Times,* but if I tell some-
one how much I like a play or a recording,
I will receive the same canned response:
"Sounds great! Which critic said that?" When

I serve them the cruel information that the
words are mine, I am given a sneer and a
tedious backside charging off.

How can people enjoy anything if they do
not allow themselves the privilege of their
own opinions? How can any creative person
create anything unless he or she has spent a
lifetime nourishing her or his own unique
opinions?

❖The Dutch social dynamics taught me so much.
Because the Netherlands is jam-packed with
people, the people know they must reinforce
each other's identity at every opportunity by
honest acknowledgment.

A writer stands only if he or she does the
same. A writer must honestly acknowledge the
real world and, most important, **the entire
world** of his or her own personal vision. Many
do not. Wallowing in Group Think they blithely
write to current spec. The unfunctional results repeatedly rip very ugly holes in the
Tent of Civilization.

TRIUMPH SIX—DAZZLING BAY AREA: IN HOME AT LAST—1967 to 1985

Cozy Earth Corner—Someone in Europe informed
me, "You are obviously in serious transition.
What are you doing here? You could be living
in San Francisco."

Profound Space—Little hilltop home: bonsai deck
and Japanese room with silhouette garden . . .
intrepid and joyful legions of books.

Library Island—Carl G. Jung *Dreams, Memories,
Reflections* (the document most essential to my
life, that book opens new doors at every reading. Each day I give myself complete permission to discover my own personal vision, however difficult or terrifying that process might
be. Without *Dreams, Memories, Reflections* and the
Limitless Sources of Understanding related to
it I would never be able to do so. Most bodies
in the U.S.A. sneeze in synch: convenient for
the Advertising Smear Doyens, but problematic
for the very slow Crawl of Civilization since
advancement usually comes from the individual),
Walt Whitman *Leaves of Grass* (and most crucial The Preface to the original edition), Florine

Stettheimer, Pablo Neruda *Bestiario,* Martha Graham (unlimited and fanatical courage is required for anyone in the U.S. artistic world and Martha Graham's example makes anyone's problem as a writer and/or artist look petty, indeed), Richard Strauss *Die Frau ohne Schatten* (it is always a comfort to know that myth with a capital M is still allowed in twentieth-century opera), Lyonel Feininger (if one could only live in the enlightened and color-washed world of his paintings), Max Beerbohm *Zuleika Dobson* (this neglected total masterpiece presents the vagaries of human relationships in terms both extravagantly amusing and profound as a Renaissance cameo), Gwendolyn Brooks (when all the political attitude nonsense is washed away by time, her poetry will always be known for its metaphysical and human completeness), Lafcadio Hearn, and San Francisco individuals: Allan Yeager, Paul Grant.

What Happened:

❖ I met Lloyd Neilson a few weeks after I arrived in California, early autumn 1967. It was time to settle in and start a home. At this writing we have shared almost thirty years: learning and creating and enjoying the world every minute of the way.

❖ Other side of the Rockies the natural world usually appears only a pathetic remnant; in California much of the natural world has survived: vital balance and raw beauty. The multitude of natural environments in California often serves as prototype for my poetic fusions. "Ribbons" from *Dream Tees* is based on a rare dream phenomenon, a dream that directly replays a life experience.

My dream is a fresh from the fog path of bay
leaves, original earth, Spanish fir, mustard
slugs, and five finger ferns thriving forty nine
feet up from the ground in the charcoal spear
of a burned out redwood. At the end of the path
in a hard earned clearing I face the ruins
of a solid cabin built with the blazing energy

of love long ago. Cabin burned. Brook stone
fireplace did not burn. Redwoods did not
burn. Brass bedstead did not burn. In the sorrel,
wild strawberries, and trilliums under the brave
green tarnished, black smoked bedstead
little yellow and black ribbon snakes stretch out
lazy in the warm sun they love so much.

❖ Animals have always been the touchstones of my life: if an environment is not suitable for animals, it is not a valid environment. Lloyd and I have always shared our lives with a cat in charge and our lives have been enriched beyond all measure. With immeasurable joy I have written three cat books. Hilary Knight proclaimed *Sun Cat* "really charming." Wayne Koestenbaum called "Trio" from *Cats in Charge*—"delightful and visually arresting."

TRIO

This morning I danced once again—
I've done it all my life—
to the Emperor Concerto,
originally written to help
God feel better about things.

During the *Adagio un poco mosso* I
gave Juniper an exorbitant back and all
around wrong way/right way rub.
Living room floor turned
into one magnificent cloudscape
of white, fluffed out, winter fur.

Juniper, Beethoven, and I
were all together   **in Heaven.**

Barbara Roth delighted in *San Francisco Cats: Nine Lives with Whiskers:* cat "comments about humans are so fine. What a wonderful guise for putting all us tacky people in perspective!"

❖ In 1976 Lloyd took the name Juniper Von Phitzer, the names of three of our cats, and established Juniper Von Phitzer Press for the purpose of producing and publishing my *I'd Rather Be a Phoenix!* a fabulous large-format limited edition book with each poem illuminating a bird motif. Archibald MacLeish called that book "a true signal of good will."

Juniper Von Phitzer Press has become an international award-winning fine arts press and I am blessed to have so much of my work presented in breathtakingly beautiful and appropriate settings. The designs of all Juniper Von Phitzer Press books are unique and created to manifest the content.

Because the West Coast has received shiploads of goods and ideas from the Orient over the decades, treasures beg to be discovered. This selection from *Seasons: Eager Blossoms, Summer Mountains, Autumn Dazzle, First Snow* suggests the remarkable ability of the Japanese mind to focus on the detail most essential in a particular moment.

> Snow on the wooden
> bucket rim
> is thick
> as my thumb.
>
> Pine tree proudly slips
> into a new white
> green needle print
> winter kimono.
>
> Ducks,
> absolutely furious,
> curse
> the frozen pond.
>
> Frost discovers
> a spider web
> carefully hidden
> in the eaves.
>
> A snowflake scares
> the cat
> who is pretending
> to be asleep.

And I knew immediately I wanted a Japanese room . . . that is, Japan before 1850 (probably one of my happier previous lives), and, slowly but surely, Lloyd and I created that room, a sublime space in which the components may shift daily according to need and aesthetic vitality (the antithesis of our Western approach—screwing everything in a room tightly in place, shining a spotlight on each item, and leaving everything in position for two years until the next move or the next decorator). The *tokonoma,* a display alcove, encourages one to rotate objects for the day and the season showing love and respect for the constant and inevitable changes in life. My work study snugs down in a cubicle within the room. That relaxed, numinous, thinking space holds me gently and firmly in a relaxed, numinous space.

People walking into the Japanese room for the first time always say, "Are you a Buddhist?"

I say, "Yes, along with every other religion in the history of the world I've had the privilege to study."

I always have been an Absolute Ecumenical and can never understand why so many waste their lives (our lives do have time limitations) polishing hatred in the name of a religion dedicated to love and understanding.

Consequently, religion has received a very bad name. One can not even use the word prayer because so many practitioners have defiled the word, demanding a high-gloss banana peel in a competitor's path or much worse.

I tell people I send them good energy every day. They can deal with that. **The process is imperative**—as the Pueblo de Taos Indians humbly request the movement of the sun through the sky each day. We all must send good energy out at every opportunity. If we do not, the consequences are unthinkable.

The Proverbial Answer is a simple one. When an individual has the heart and pluck and honesty to acknowledge and develop a purpose for being, a genuine spiritual position comes naturally to that individual. If one must depend completely on the sorry thoughts of someone else, no valid spiritual position can possibly exist.

TRIUMPH SEVEN—LOTUS BUD OPEN— 1985 to 1997

Cozy Earth Corner—Genius Loci, the Spirit of San Francisco, has become my true haven.

Profound Space—I am revitalized in our hilltop home. My real Profound Space is everywhere I perform. There is a positive flow between my audience and me that is much greater than the both of us.

Happily, my most frequently quoted affirmation is one of my most intrepid observations: "I write to communicate and I perform to communicate and that communication takes on a wonderful life of its own. One of the joys of being an artist is the constantly renewed revela-

Hiemstra with Lloyd Neilson, his partner of thirty years, and Von the cat, 1996

tion that the artist's creation is always much, much more important than the artist."

Library Island—Martin Buber *Ten Rungs: Hasidic Sayings* (no words can describe the sacred importance of this book), Antonio Gaudi (delicious architecture that celebrates the crinkumcrankum of human existence), Theo Dorgan *Rosa Mundi* (a young poet of incredible achievement and incredible promise), Sallie Middleton (a painter who as the only psychological naturalist I know serves as a superlative champion of the Natural World), Greg Sarris *Mabel McKay: Weaving the Dream* (Native American wisdom and spirituality is finally reaching non-Native Americans who are in desperate need of it), E. F. Benson *Ravens' Brood,* John Cowper Powys *Porius* (only Powys deals with the full range of human feeling and desire), Lucia St. Clair Robson *The Tokaido Road,* Samuel Beckett *Happy Days,* Allan Kaprow, Wayne W. Dyer *Your Sacred Self,* and individuals: the amazing, multi-personality Samuel M. Steward (spent Christmas with Alice B. Toklas every one of those difficult after years),

Mary Milton, Todd Ostling, Mary Berg, David Allen, Carole Garcia, Ed Hutchins, Carl Martin, Doug and Margaret Stow.

What Happened:

❖ In 1985 I was one of the Poetry Competition winners at the Montalvo Center for the Arts and we were all expected to read. I considered poetry readings dreary aberrations at best. I decided there must be a way to do it right. I rehearsed my three short poems every day for two months. At the event, I received a roar of elation. I did my first solo performance at Villa Montalvo, spring 1986. My life as a performance poet began. "Final Thoughts of a Dying Paperweight" was one of the winning poems.

> The amount of joy in this room would be completely covered if a fly put his foot down . . . one day Louise said to Manjit, "Your ears are getting long,

Hiemstra in a Japanese garden, 1996

just like Buddha's!" . . . I will not have died in vain if I've just kept one good image from blowing out the window . . . a toothpick's lot is not an easy one . . . in certain remote areas where hate is scarce, love is often the only means of artistic expression . . . always pretending to diet, Mari hides her pie in a cup . . . there is some hope for mankind, however slight . . . Drat! I'll never see the northern lights . . . Bill loves to shout, "IF IN DOUBT OR DIRTY, JUST CLIMB TO THE TOP OF THAT TREE AND WASH YOUR HANDS IN THE SKY . . . SKY . . . SKY . . . SKY . . . SKY . . . SKY . . . SKY . . .

I have since appeared all over the United States with glowing response and will soon leave on my fifth European tour.

Julie Jensen reviewed a 1996 live performance of *In Deepest U.S.A.:* "Marvin Hiemstra can become an earthquake or a mountain, have an existential conversation with toucans or probe the psyche of a worm. Not since Mark Twain has an American writer and performer presented the American twists and eccentricities with so much delightful honesty and so much love."

❖My first CD, *In Deepest U.S.A.,* has just appeared (three more are planned) and the success has been quite remarkable. From Joseph Leonardi's urbane critique, *In Deepest U.S.A.* "guides you on a charming tour through the backroads of the American psyche!" to basic utilitarian results—Jannie Dresser found the CD excellent medicine for postop recovery, who could ask for anything more?

❖One does yearn for an ever larger audience and yet I have always received a tremendous response: letters, calls, handsome reviews, heartwarming delayed reactions, so I know my work communicates and lives and often transforms.

I once overheard one audience member whisper to another, "If you can't find it in Marvin's poetry, you're better off without it."

My projects for the future include a second volume of dream poems, *Dreams on the Line,* a *Collected Marvin,* more broadsides in the *Signed Drollside Subscription Series,* and more books about cats, the constant joy and revelation in our life.

My newest performance, *In My Forest Trees Sing,* puts the audience into a landscape of bliss. Tom Waechter noted, "When we can't see the top, we are certain it is there just because these trees have a foundation we trust. . . . This amounts to rather a tribal understanding that even the children present seemed to understand." *In My Forest Trees Sing* comes from my heart because trees have always been absolute top on my list. Animals are number two and, on a very good day, humans come in number thirty-seven.

❖Unfortunately, the County Fair Champion Poetry Prize syndrome is still the norm in the U.S.A. One poet, often with the fattest bottom, wins. All others lose and are shot immediately. The winning poet is shot the next day.

If more Americans would allow themselves the simple pleasure of opinions, all poets could be enjoyed. I love and respect every poet: quite dead, alive, or still to appear. "Leaves are forming everywhere even while I speak." It keeps me going to know that poets everywhere around the world are writing right now, no matter what the situation.

There is great hope in the fact that poetry in the U.S. is experiencing a tremendous boom: books, CDs, and reading/performances everywhere. Eugène Delacroix believed that the first virtue of a painting is to be a feast for the eyes. I believe that **the first virtue of a poem is to be a feast for the heart.**

SELECT BIBLIOGRAPHY

Poetry:

MRH, Nina and Ohva Publications, 1958.

I'd Rather Be a Phoenix!, Juniper Von Phitzer Press, 1976.

Cats in Charge, Juniper Von Phitzer Press, 1989.

Dream Tees, Juniper Von Phitzer Press, 1991.

26 Compliments, Juniper Von Phitzer Press, 1991.

Redwood Burl, Juniper Von Phitzer Press, 1992.

Seasons: Eager Blossoms, Summer Mountains, Autumn Dazzle, First Snow, Juniper Von Phitzer Press, 1993.

San Francisco Christmas Streamers, Juniper Von Phitzer Press, 1995.

Snow on Golden Bamboo, Juniper Von Phitzer Press, 1995.

Worm Fiddling in Florida, Juniper Von Phitzer Press, 1996.

Prose.

Sun Cat, Juniper Von Phitzer Press, 1986.

Golden Gate Treasure, Juniper Von Phitzer Press, 1987.

San Francisco Cats: Nine Lives with Whiskers, Juniper Von Phitzer Press, 1991.

STAR MOLEN: 1649–1949, Juniper Von Phitzer Press, 1994.

Boxing with Compass, Juniper Von Phitzer Press, 1996.

Collage performances:

In Deepest U.S.A., Marvin R. Hiemstra, 1994.

Deeper Still, Marvin R. Hiemstra, 1995.

In My Forest Trees Sing, Marvin R. Hiemstra, 1996.

Other:

Signed Drollside Subscription Series (poetry broadside), Truly Droll Inc., 1991—.

In Deepest U.S.A. (compact disc, with music by Doni Harvey), Zippy Digital, 1996.

Contributor of poetry and prose to anthologies, including *Emperor of Dreams,* Donald M. Grant, 1978; *A Harvest for Thanksgiving,* Juniper Von Phitzer Press, 1986; *The New Poet's Anthology,* Cherryable Brothers, 1987; *A Pair of Roses—Gertrude Stein and Alice B. Toklas,* Juniper Von Phitzer Press, 1993; *Parnassus of World Poets,* Devaraj, 1994; *Hands,* Juniper Von Phitzer Press, 1996; *Dutch Touches,* Penfield Press, 1996; *One Hundred Years of Klarkash-Ton,* The Averon Press, 1996; and *Marilyn, My Marilyn,* Pennywhistle Press, 1997.

Contributor of poetry and prose to periodicals, including *Abstract, East/West Review, Knickerbocker, The Microbibliophile, The North American Review,* and *Nyctalops.*

Leza Lowitz

1962-

Leza Lowitz, Tokyo, Japan, 1993

i.

As a child, I wore oversized glasses, adult glasses that swallowed up my small face and framed my already sizable eyes in gargantuan mock-tortoise cat's eye triangles. When one of the wings broke (how I love that word to describe those delicate arms that first kept me pinned to solitude like a butterfly to the cork board, and later released me through the discovery of words), I graduated to a shimmering herring-blue pair studded with white rhinestones, though my face had not yet filled out enough to fit them. Both were given to me more by default than by design—the story of my life—for we lived on a navy base, and there were, presumably, no children's glasses to be found there. So I wore adult glasses throughout my childhood and saw the world through strange and sidelong eyes.

I cannot say those glasses made me a writer. They made me something of an outcast, which led me to seek solace in books.

ii.

I began my life as I shall no doubt end it: among books.

—Jean-Paul Sartre, *Words*

Every writer is first a reader. My childhood, perhaps my creative life itself, seemed to

*Grandmother Evelyn Weissman Lowitz,
about 1920*

begin when my grandfather, Samuel Lowitz, read to me from *1001 Arabian Nights* and *Grimm's Fairy Tales.* Entranced by the cadences of his gentle voice and the enchanting worlds it delivered, I learned of sultans, princesses and princes, winged horses and wizards, magic cities and labyrinthine quests. However impossible they seemed, these quests were sometimes successfully completed.

In love with words, my grandfather cut out articles from the newspaper and underlined pertinent sentences in red pen with a steady ruler held underneath—horoscopes, cartoons, a myriad of proverbs, advice columns, and words to live by.

The Rubaiyat of Omar Khayyam, a tale in linked *haiku*-like verse, was my grandfather's favorite book. Perhaps befitting for a man whose favorite poem was, however beautiful, an ode to the powers of alcohol, he drank heavily. Even now I hear accolades for his dry-as-the-desert martinis, "the best this side of Des Moines, Iowa," where he was from. My grandmother, Evelyn Weissman, had apparently been engaged to marry a Harvard-bound pre-med student from a good family, but my grandfather played jazz clarinet, and when they met at a speakeasy, she fell in love with him instead.

My grandparents seemed to live the fairy tales I was read from. They traveled around the world, bringing dolls from every country in traditional dress for my sisters and me. Soon I had an enviable collection of Japanese girls in kimonos, Greek men in starched white skirts and red tasseled fez, Russian maidens in peasant skirts and flowered scarves. I lined them up on my desk and stared at them as I did my homework. It wasn't the dolls that I liked— I doubt if, as a child, I'd ever really played much with dolls. Rather, it was their almost mystical power as symbols of a vast world away from the home I had already decided to escape from that made me await each souvenir from their journeys and dream of making such journeys myself.

That faraway fairy-tale life became mine for a time when the family moved from San Francisco to Key West, Florida, where we lived on a navy base, the lights of Cuba both beckoning and threatening over the fathomless waters of the Atlantic.

iii.

It was 1967. I was a navy brat living with my parents and two sisters in a corrugated metal-roofed naval base home. We had a Styrofoam pond full of goldfish that would upturn during hurricanes, dumping the fish on the wind-devastated lawn in their wake. The southernmost tip of the United States was a place full of lights and mysteries, stories, tragedies, intimations of injustice (class, racial, religious) and the ghosts of literary heroes like Tennessee Williams and Ernest Hemingway looming somewhere unseen in the sultry skies. The locals were also otherworldly, mysterious: Suzick, a woman with a French last name who lived alone in a wind-swept pastel-colored house down the beach and painted our portraits onto tiles. Renee, the animated Cuban friend of my father's who always brought armloads of Coors beer. A bearded old man who sold conch and bits of frosted green-and-blue glass made soft by years of salt-water sea on the corner of the beach.

We'd glue the glass and shells together with resin for sea paintings. I do not know which is the truth: if the glass went into my sister Robin's eye or my own, one day when we were breaking glass with a hammer for our "sea pictures." I do remember wearing a black patch over my left eye for a time in my childhood. It was possibly a very short time, but seemed interminable. In childhood, seeing was always obstructed.

My father nailed a sting ray on the palm tree in our backyard, a small steel-gray crucifix that turned to brittle bone in the hurricane winds. There were piñatas on birthdays, a salt-water pool, the Conch train that traveled through town tooting its tinny horn, and a small theater where I dressed like an elf and ushered people into a dark world of Punch-and-Judy shows. My father had parties where he used to barbeque shark in an old oil drum in the backyard. We played on the lightning rod between hurricanes.

My parents were happy, then.

iv.

I am the youngest of three girls, each a year apart. Robin was the "smart" one, Leslie was the "creative" one, and I had no such role to conform to until later on, when I became the "pretty" one.

My father was the navy-base psychiatrist and had to determine who was "sane enough" to fight. Young men would call him up on their way to the roofs of buildings, threatening suicide. Calling their bluff, he would tell them to "tough it out." Sometimes they did not.

It seemed I was always alone, chasing the marines in training as they jogged down the beach in morning exercise, my black Labrador in tow. Maybe I was the last child they'd see on American soil. Who did they see when they looked at the little girl and her dog, drift-wood between its teeth?

I cannot say I was a timid child; rather, mine was a mixture of fear and fascination of the often violent, unknown forces around me. There was neighboring Cuba and the not-so-distant threat of war, there were the young men being sent off daily to their deaths in Vietnam, and there were the more mundane dangers of stepping on sting rays or rusted fishing hooks and nails that had been washed ashore. Threat of the dreaded lockjaw (mouth forever open, unable to talk) was enough to make anyone stop walking barefoot anywhere, though I never saw anyone with that awful condition and wondered if it was something my parents had made up. Not being able to talk was the worst imaginable punishment for me. It was one I was later to suffer often.

There was only one school in the small town, and it was Lutheran. Being Jewish, I did not pray with the other kids, and I used to talk incessantly during prayer time to whomever would listen. I loved to talk. I was often punished for this, had to press my nose against the desktop during class. But the smell of the wood entranced me and in the enforced silence I dreamed up stories, imagined all the places I would go when I got old enough.

v.

When my father's two-year term was up, we packed the car and drove across the country back to San Francisco, California. The trip was long and uncomfortable, and there was always heavy traffic, hurricanes, or some other act of god or nature to add to the mix. The suitcases, made of an odd resin-smelling plastic, were strapped to the top of the old diesel Mercedes. Two or more of us were inevitably fighting over something, which led to our parents fighting. Perhaps to disabuse myself of that empty new label I disdained ("the pretty one"), I developed a talent for rebellious language that was anything but. The car was pulled to the side of the highway, the three of us were pulled apart from a tangle of arms and hair, and I was pulled out and beaten on the open back hatch in front of the passing cars—the first of such punishments I was singled out for. I was to remain silent for the rest of the trip.

It would take us a week to reach California.

We drove for hours upon hours, stopping only for fast food or if one of us had to use the toilet. Suddenly, as if by the force of my held-back words erupting, the suitcases blew off the top of the car and crashed to the highway, spilling clothes, books, and dolls out onto the road. My father sent us all out to collect the debris. I laughed and cried as I picked the clothes up off the highway.

Key West was the last place of my innocence.

vi.

We moved back to San Francisco, where I'd been born in late December of 1962. We lived in a brown-shingled Victorian house on Walnut Street.

My mother took me to the public library off Sacramento Street. It was a huge, domed building with a rolling lawn that looked majestic and presidential. She took me to an after-school Jewish reading club where we read Jewish books and had to write reports on them each week.

Each birthday, she gave me books. My favorites were those by Roald Dahl, whose oddly sadistic humor seemed to me, at least, a realistic portrayal of the cruel ironies of the world. And it was through Carl Sandburg's *Complete Poems* that I discovered a word as funny and onomatopoetic as "rutabaga." So comical and playful, what did it mean? Was it a real thing? I also loved Lewis Carroll, saw that through invented words, one invented worlds.

My mother was a Girl Scout troop leader. While her education of her daughters at home was mostly Jewish, she took the Girl Scouts on multicultural expeditions. We went to small Buddhist temples tucked away in Chinatown's back alleys, where we lit incense and were given tours by local actors such as the man in "Flower Drum Song." We visited the Japanese Tea Garden with its bright-red serpent-like bridge and cherry blossom trees in full bloom. She took my sister Leslie and me to the de Young Museum, where we fired Japanese *raku* pottery in an oil drum filled with red-hot hay. Hearing languages I could not understand fascinated me.

One night when we were out to dinner, our house was set on fire by an arsonist. He left a note saying his Boy Scout troop had dared him to do it. Because we were Jewish? I never learned the truth. There was a family of ten two doors up, a Chinese family with the name McDonald, whose eight children hauled buckets of water up and down the stairs, passed between them like a perfectly choreographed Chinese fire drill. They put out the fire in our absence.

The neighborhood girls and I escaped into an exotic realm of basement mysticism. There, we hung beaded curtains and celebrated the Chinese new year with popping firecrackers, held

Evelyn Lowitz (far right), with Rose Kennedy (second from right) and two other organizers of John F. Kennedy's presidential campaign, Chicago, 1959

seances and levitated each other with two fingers under the elongated spine. Outside, my older sister, Robin, was pulled into a moving car. There were gunshot sounds in the night; my father found a wallet in the bushes of our house. He then decided that San Francisco had become unsafe. We moved, of all places, to Berkeley.

vii.

I came of age in Berkeley in the 1970s, was bussed to the utopian educational experiment called Malcolm X Elementary School. Since I was small, I wore glasses, and, worst of all, I was white, I was often beaten up.

The school was originally named after Abraham Lincoln, but when it was discovered that Lincoln had kept slaves, the students had a revolution to change the name. There were three choices—Harriet Tubman, Dick Gregory, and Malcolm X. I voted for Harriet Tubman.

The one saving grace for me (and it was a great one) was the fact that we were visited in home room by the likes of wiry James Baldwin coughing out invectives against racist America like an ailing carburetor, and by Angela Davis (had she really murdered someone?), and Maya Angelou dressed in a many-colored *dashiki* singing out her poetry to an auditorium of partly entranced and partly terrified sixth graders. Halfway through the fifth grade I had a revelation in the form of a tough black boy named Rufus Gupton. He asked me to help him with math (my worst subject, ironically). In exchange, he would be my bodyguard. A deal was struck. I was never beaten up there again.

Up on campus, the older generation was having its troubles—tear gas in antiwar protests, elusive serial killers, a kidnapped heiress who became a back-street revolutionary. It was a far cry from the quiet midwestern towns of Davenport, Iowa, and Rock Island, Illinois, where my father and mother, high school sweethearts, had grown up. Their marriage was suffering under the strains.

viii.

Violence, or the threat of violence, has colored my life since I can remember. The American landscape I knew as a child was riddled

"*My parents, Donna and John Lowitz, at their wedding reception,*" *Rock Island, Illinois, 1958*

with uncertainty and fear. While I was quite fortunate not to have grown up in a place where violence was direct or immediate, it always simmered beneath the surface.

My mother wore a peach-colored ribbed wool turtleneck and a pendant that said "War is not healthy for children and other living things." On the back was the name of a POW and the date he was last seen in action.

In the fourth and fifth grades, it was racism and bussing. In the sixth grade I was shaken down for milk money. In the eighth grade I was surrounded by a girl gang and robbed of the Navajo turquoise ring my grandmother had given me. "I can't get the ring off her finger," my attacker cried. "Bite the fucking finger off then!" said her "girl boss" with a wicked laugh. I got the ring off.

My parents were usually off in Europe.

Later, in my adult life, I was attacked again. Always in Berkeley.

Once as I was jogging through the School for the Deaf and Blind. It was an awful place to be attacked. No one can hear you scream.

Once I was jumped from behind on Tunnel Road, a busy freeway thoroughfare. The attacker tried to pull off my purse, but it was wrapped over my head and around my shoulder and he could not get it off. He cursed at me. I cursed at him. Cars drove by but no one stopped. Later, when the police came to take the crime report, the neighbors admitted they had heard me scream. "You didn't call for help," they said.

ix.

I wanted to be an actress, to escape to the world of theater I had discovered in the Punch-and-Judy shows of Key West. I had a pink Art Nouveau poster of Sarah Bernhardt hanging over my bed, and I dreamed of her glamorous life and mysterious death.

But as before, real life always had more drama than the stage.

Ninth grade. Crossing University Avenue one Saturday afternoon, coming back from Taco Bell after a break during rehearsal of the drama club's performance of *The Madwoman of Chaillot*, my friend S. was struck by a beat-up Buick Impala barreling down University at seventy miles per hour, drunk driver behind the wheel. She flew twenty feet into the air, both shoes coming off from the impact. I tried to give her mouth-to-mouth resuscitation, but her face was a horrible mess of skin and bones and the blood bubbled up in her mouth as I pressed my lips to hers. She suffered brain damage and never fully recovered.

The war finally ended.

Vietnam vets came home and hung out at the high school. My girlfriends and I thought they were cool, had seen and experienced something so dramatic and unspeakable it made them heroes in our eyes, far more interesting than the boys our age. They picked us up in their yellow Chevy Novas and drove around sock-footed in the Berkeley Hills, guns in the back.

In the tenth grade my friend K. slit her wrists.

That year I lost my virginity to an older boy I never saw again, never wanted to see again. Somehow, we all survived.

x.

In our household, words were usually weapons, certainly double-edged swords.

My parents had a running joke between them, a hostile one, it now seems. Each Chanukah or birthday, one of them (usually

On the playground of the Jewish Community Center, San Francisco, 1966

my mother) would receive a brass or iron handle, a doorknob of some sort, which changed in design and material with each new year. This gift, intended to give a message, was a pun, a reminder for my mother to "handle" herself.

Words.

The note the Boy Scout arsonist had left on our door.

The names of the prisoners of war on the back of my mother's pendant.

The burning of draft cards.

Words were powerful weapons, but they had also been my salvation.

Yet they always seemed to get me into trouble.

Then they were taken away.

I was often grounded for days, weeks, sometimes months at a time. I was to go directly to my room, speak to no one, not even by phone.

Being robbed of the ability to use words, I did not use them well when my "groundings" were over and my ability to speak was "restored." Having discovered their power, I disabused myself of any politeness and repeated at home the most vile, base language I had heard at school. This did not go over well with my father, and my mouth was often washed out with soap, usually in the kitchen, where he'd grab me by the throat and cram the bar of soap into my mouth. I'd clamp my teeth so tight against each other that I had to breathe with a sucking sound, but he simply ground the soap harder against my clenched teeth. Bitter, chalky, gritty, sharp chemical hell is what I remember—a horrible invention called Lava soap.

Naturally, the punishment only made me bolder. I didn't care anymore what happened, because what happened was always the same. I became bolder and bolder.

"Rage is to writers what water is to fish," wrote Nikki Giovanni.

I hated my life, my family, my father. He chased me around the house. Once captured, he hauled me onto the oak stairwell, where he'd put me over his knee, take off his belt, and strap me with its brass buckle.

My mother seemed distraught about what happened but unable to find a way to go against my father or to stop it.

This brutality. Why was I the only one who received it? Surely not just because of what I said.

Later I came to realize that it was the courage to speak that I was being punished for— surely I spoke for the others with my childish protests against my father's iron-clad control.

The author (center) with sisters Robin (left) and Leslie, Key West, Florida, 1968

"Don't write about that in your autobiography," my sister Leslie admonished me just this week. "You'll seem like an abused child or something. It didn't really happen *that* often."

"How often does it have to happen?" I asked her.

xi.

I was let out of my room whenever there was a party, which was often. For as long as I can remember, my father loved to throw parties. In Key West they were smoky backyard barbeques; in Berkeley they were Gatsbyesque southern-style lawn parties spread on tables around the pool. My sister Leslie and I would be enlisted (always a part of the punishment) to carry huge platters of food up and down the stairs, and to serve the guests graciously. Somehow, Robin always managed to escape these affairs by locking herself up in her room to study (voluntarily) or heading off to debate team.

"What lovely daughters you have—and so helpful. So well-behaved!" the guests would comment.

How could they see what our parents could not?

I suspected I was some sort of witch.

I was sure of it.

I tried to send telepathic messages for someone, anyone, to save me. Once or twice the screams were so loud that the police or a concerned neighbor would knock on the door and ask if everything was okay. I always seemed to be the one to answer the door, but I never knew what to say. There was so much that was not okay I did not know how to begin to tell them, so I always just closed the door and walked sheepishly away.

While my sisters were off at debate club or on sprees of juvenile delinquency, I was locked in my room. It was there that I began to write. I wrote about everything in small black and red-bordered journals I had bought with my allowance in Chinatown (a bargain at $1.50) and filled them up with woeful tales of an unhappy childhood and dark poems about ravens and cliffs and misunderstood little girls who jumped off of them. I never filled these journals with the words I'd been forced to swallow in mouthfuls of soapsuds. Never. This was a sacred place, a place to resurrect all the wrongs of the outer world. I wrote about princes and princesses, poor waifs and plucky heroines who escaped their dark prisons, echoing back to the fairy tales my grandparents read me and the worlds that seemed so far away from my own. I thought of my grandparents, whom I believed had managed to escape, to travel the world, to live a good life!

I started writing because, locked in my room, I had no one to talk to.

So I wrote instead, and I read. For days, weeks, months at a time.

Someone asked me recently if anyone had encouraged me to write when I was young. I had a teacher in the eighth grade—her name was Addie, and she taught creative writing at Willard Junior High. It was the only time in the day where there was peace, no screaming parents or tearful children—as much a miracle as the writing itself. She served us each a cup of Lipton tea, and we got two squares of graham crackers. She would give us a topic and we would write for half an hour without interruption. Sometimes she played classical music as we wrote. Sometimes we read our compositions aloud in class, and everyone clapped according to the class rules. It was the most magical place in the world. I never missed Addie's class.

The poem that changed my young life, I must admit, was Rudyard Kipling's *If.* I copied it out on a piece of paper, substituting "boy" for "girl" and "man" for "woman" at the poem's end. If someone as far away from my own experience as a British man in colonial India could speak to me, a Jewish-American girl in northern California, then there was hope. Words were a bridge, the life buoy I'd been looking for, the way out of my locked room.

Flannery O'Connor wrote that anyone who'd survived childhood had enough material for a lifetime. Not all my childhood was miserable, but the unhappy times were what burned into memory and shaped me. If I hadn't been so miserable, hadn't traveled in the world of mind or books (every unhappy child's savior), I might never have braved the larger world or become a writer. One always becomes a writer.

A need to speak, to not be silenced, to have faith in something, to believe in the power of words and the ability of stories to speak where the heart cannot.

To have to tell one's story.

That is what made me a writer.

xii.

My parents began fighting more frequently. My father began to drink more, too, like his father before him. Sometimes he'd fall flat on his face or scare my sisters and me (deliberately, we thought) by weaving in and out of various lanes as he drove his Datsun convertible across the Bay Bridge. We sat in the back. There was no roll bar. I'd lean back and look up at the gray steel rungs of the upper deck whisking past above us and imagine they were Jacob's ladder, imagine that if I died at least I'd find a way to climb up to heaven.

My mother tried to raise three increasingly miserable daughters while working. She taught cooking at senior citizens' groups in churches and community centers, worked for WIC, and wanted to go back to school for her master's degree in nutrition, but when she asked him for permission, my father refused to "let" her. He felt she should be home with us during our "difficult teenage years." So she started to see a therapist, discovered feminism, cut her hair short, and took to smoking Virginia Slims and listening to Helen Reddy. She plotted ways to leave him.

xiii.

While my mother had given me books and instilled in me a love of reading, one good thing my father gave me was music. He loved music, loved to sit in a big leather chair and listen to Rachmaninoff, Beethoven, or Chopin. It was his most enjoyable hour, smoking a cigar and humming to the music emanating from his earphones. Other times, he would blast the music through giant speakers and the sheer force and intensity of these symphonies, their absolute emotional power, transformed the space. It was usually so loud that we could not speak, ergo, could not fight, because even our screams would not be heard. When my father listened to music, there was peace in our house.

I will always have music in my life.

xiv.

My mother eventually left my father and, finances being what they were, could not take us along with her. She took our eldest

(From left) Leslie, Robin, and Leza, Los Angeles, 1970

sister, Robin, the well-behaved one who had had a bat mitzvah. (Neither Leslie nor I had, feeling spiritually unconnected to Judaism and unworthy of the shower of gifts that came down on the occasion.)

And so my middle sister, Leslie, and I stayed in the huge house with my father, who was never home, off dating a string of women and calling occasionally from some mysterious location just to let us know he was still alive.

Leslie and I had unwittingly inherited our father's party bug. Our father disappeared for weeks at a time. We were fifteen and fourteen years old. Left to our own devices, we created a "Hotel California," which became legendary in the Berkeley Juvenile Delinquent Underground. We had lots of boyfriends—Panamanian, Chinese, African-American. We rode in hot-wired cars and shoplifted candy-flavored lipsticks. I got D's and F's, cut classes.

In tenth grade I took acid. Natural Man, the Zig-Zag Man, a bearded Che Guevara. We placed the small squares on our tongues and let them dissolve. When nothing happened

after a while, I asked for another hit. We went to see *Star Wars*. It was a roller-coaster ride. At home later that night I couldn't sleep and watched the digital indicator on my first stereo receiver blink off and on like the harbor lights of a miniature city. My arm turned into a snake, fell off, and slithered across the room.

In junior high I met a sharp-tongued, raven-haired girl named Helen Taschian, who by then had become my best friend. Her father was a professor of Russian, her mother a sharp-tongued blond who was a wonderful cook. I spent the night often at her house. We bathed together, plotted our rebellions. Helen and I raided our houses for junk, then sold it at the flea market to support ourselves.

No one seemed to notice that anything was missing.

No one seemed to notice much of anything.

There were always people staying in the house, people who would appear suddenly and without fanfare, working off some debt to my father or helping him pay the mortgage. They'd just suddenly appear and be sleeping in my sister Leslie's canopied bed (she had the best room in the house). We found ourselves roommates with a mathematician from Hungary. A crazy Israeli artist who worked as a carpenter and whose creations always looked like the Winchester Mystery House. A handyman con man. A tile layer who loved to break into my father's wine cellar. A psychologist girlfriend who grew marijuana in the music room and harvested the plants in huge black plastic garbage bags hanging upside down in my father's closet—bags that mysteriously disappeared and that my sister and I were accused of having stolen.

That did not go unnoticed.

To this day, we maintain our innocence.

xv.

My father kicked me out of the house more than once when I was fifteen—my stuff piled up on the doorstep the way the clothes had spilled out onto the highway in our cross-country trip from Key West.

If nothing else, I had learned from my parents how to survive.

I got a job as an ice-cream scooper at the neighborhood Baskin-Robbins, though I was technically underage. (Hiring age was sixteen.) I moved around a lot, spending the night at Helen's or with a boyfriend's family or sometimes at my mother's new apartment.

The optimism and magic of Kennedy and the first man on the moon were promises destroyed by Vietnam, Watergate, Nixon, and later the Challenger disaster.

The flea market became my home away from home.

xvi.

I was an utterly nihilistic teenager, my head full of radioactive warnings and doomsday scenarios of an all-out nuclear war (I prayed for the epicenter). Nothing impressed me. Nothing really even moved me, but somehow I felt at home at the flea market, where things had chips and imperfections, where they smelled of dust and rust and mold and a mysterious life force that had no name. The flea market was a place unafraid of death in a time the coun-

try was wholeheartedly celebrating its sanitized-for-television Bicentennial "birth."

What one found at the flea market: boxes of buttons, old tools, beads, license plates, cowboy boots, Fiestaware or Bakelite jewelry. To enter those booths was to enter small worlds made up of the detritus of the modern world, T. S. Eliot's "fragments shored against our ruins." Each booth was like a different slide in a magic lantern show, someone's personal universe in disarray. Up for sale. No questions asked.

Helen and I went there almost once a month, while our friends spent their Sundays wandering the Hilltop Mall. The mall seemed to insulate us from life, and, as rough as real life sometimes got, it was where we were most comfortable. We'd arrive with the others before dawn, their cars loaded down and roped up with belongings like a scene from *Tobacco Road.* Sometimes we didn't even have a chance to unpack our boxes, since the other "vendors" would start to rummage through them to get the best deals, which they'd turn around and sell that very day.

Going to the flea market was a little like playing jacks in the age of Nintendo. Low tech. Up to chance. Close to the ground. Subject to dirt and rust.

The flea market was nomadic. It was portable. It could be anywhere—a bird market in a Paris metro, a Shinto shrine in Tokyo, a Zen temple in Kyoto, or a drive-in theater in Alameda County, California. The flea market was the closest thing America had to the European marktplatz or the Arab souk. Yet it was truly multicultural, peaceful.

First there were the smells—of Chinese jasmine or Indian sandalwood incense mingled with the sharp vapors of home-cooked hamhocks, chitlins, and greens from the Soul Food Kitchen, or the heavy spice of chili oil from the chop suey and egg rolls fried up in the Lotus Garden trailer's rusted iron woks. Then, there was the fact that you could sell anything, or buy anything, too.

Philosopher, gambler, poet, martyr, children from busted-up families—we were all there, haggling and bantering. The flea market was a place where the "Other"—the exotic, eccentric, the marginal—found a place. Things that fell through the cracks fell there. No one asked who you were or why you were there: being there was enough of an indication that you belonged.

What Helen and I didn't sell we gave away. What we couldn't give away, we left in a "free box" or broke. We wanted to smash our pasts into a thousand pieces, break away from the histories that tied us down. The flea market was our source of redemption.

Are we the sum total of our experiences? Or are our experiences the sum total of us?

Life leaves behind a fingerprint—memories of the past.

One thing I never sold were books. I hoarded them.

xvii.

In high school I joined the drama club. We looked to the not-so-distant avant-garde past, put on plays by Durrenmatt and Genet. I still vaguely wanted to be an actress, but my mother encouraged me to do something practical. She insisted I take typing, that if worse came to worse I could be a secretary. So I took typing while most of the girls were taking wood shop or auto shop. And I discovered Zen.

Berkeley High. I will never forget when a fellow senior named Drew Zavatsky gave me a copy of Shunryu Suzuki's book *Zen Mind, Beginner's Mind,* and told me my aura was yellow. Yellow, the color of intelligence!

I had never before thought of a color as symbolic of a quality, never imagined that a word such as "yellow" could be seen to represent those qualities through something as ephemeral and beautiful as an aura, which could not be seen.

I had never thought of myself as intelligent, either. Never been told by anyone that I was.

I did not know which was the bigger revelation.

With that brief moment of encouragement, I began to study. I got straight A's my senior year of high school.

Because of that fortunate turn of events, my grade-point average was high enough to help me get into college. Now all I needed was the money.

xviii.

My parents finally got divorced. I cannot say their divorce was any more traumatic than the marriage that had preceded it.

In her divorce settlement, my mother gave up most of her alimony payments, altruistically negotiating that my father pay for our college educations instead. My father agreed, but conditionally—offering us each the price of going to a local school such as Berkeley. He wanted us to stay close to home.

My mother went back to school and got her master's degree in nutrition. She worked in the food-service industry. She eventually remarried.

From my mother I learned the high price of being true to yourself, and the even higher price of not.

Words to live by: my mother always said, "Can't never did."

There are those who say, "You grew up in Berkeley in the late 1960s and early 1970s? What an exciting place to be."

I couldn't wait to get out of Berkeley.

My sisters before me had felt the same.

xix.

A turning point in my life came when I graduated from high school. I had saved enough money from work, flea market, and babysitting to go somewhere for the summer, and when I saw an ad in the *Daily Californian* for a student trip to Paris, I signed up. I took off with a teacher from Cal and a group of twenty students. We lived at the Cite Universitaire, read Sartre and Baudelaire in the original, hung out at Pere Lachaise cemetery amid the ghosts of Colette, Chopin, Moliere, and Jim Morrison, and, most important of all, I experienced life away from America for the first time.

xx.

My oldest sister, Robin, had gone to Brandeis two years before, and Leslie had gotten accepted to the Pratt School of Art. As soon as I returned from Paris, I followed them eastward.

I went to college at seventeen. I had been accepted to New York University's School of Dramatic Writing in 1980—the first year of its inception. Because of my mother's limited income, I was able to get work-study and student loans. I lived in the Rubin Dormitory on Fifth Avenue and East Tenth downtown. I went to poetry readings and worked the Bobst Library midnight shift and at the huge Barnes and Noble store on Fifth Avenue and West Eighteenth to pay the remainder of my tuition and board.

I wrote poems and one-act plays, made crude Super-8 films. In class I studied Plato, Artaud, and Peter Brook's *The Empty Space.* My film teacher taught us eighth-century Japanese poetry, emphasizing its cinematic aspects. Outside of class I combed the stacks of the Bobst Library, discovering books of poetry. I was particularly drawn to the objectivist poets—wandering, alienated seers who took the world on its own terms.

I no longer wanted to be an actress, no longer wanted to be a victim (as I then saw the trajectory of my whole life) so I took up Okinawan martial arts, answering an ad I saw in the *Learning Annex* brochure. (It seems that most of my adventures in life were the direct result of answering newspaper ads. Having few contacts and a tremendous desire to learn, I found them an effective, populist method of exploring the world.)

In a small *dojo* on East Eighty-sixth Street, we read Zen texts and chanted the Heart Sutra in Japanese, sat *zazen* and did running *kihin* meditation, sometimes barefoot in the snow in Central Park. I was drawn to the discipline, the ordered world in which I experienced the deep, soothing rhythms of the guttural chants I could only understand instinctively. I fell in love with the Orient, with Japan. It was an imaginary Japan, but I fell in love with it nonetheless.

And I fell in love with the Zen "koan," the possibility of an answerless question, a life where the inquiry was more important than the answer.

Coming from a household of noise, I fell in love with the silences.

Finally, home seemed far away.

xxi.

Ronald Reagan was elected president, and after a few years in office, my student aid was discontinued and work-study programs drastically cut back. I still had two years of promised tuition from my mother's divorce settlement, but asking for money from my father was difficult, and getting it came with so many

strings attached that my sister Leslie eventually dropped out of college rather than fight it.

But I'd learned from my mother how much a college degree could really cost, and I was determined to get mine. Without work-study and student loans, staying on at NYU was impossible, so I transferred to Hunter College, where tuition was much cheaper.

I had to find work again. I combed the bulletin boards and classified ads endlessly. Finally, I found a sign up in the student employment office for FROM—the Foundation for Research into the Origins of Mankind—right on Forty-second Street. I called the number immediately. Nadine Russo, the office manager, said that there were already fifteen interviews scheduled and that the position would surely be filled after one of them. I convinced her to let me visit the office so I could see what the foundation was all about. She agreed. I was hired on the spot.

It was the fund-raising organization of Richard Leakey, the anthropologist from Kenya, son of Mary and Louis B. Leakey. I worked there for years, writing for the newsletter, sending out mass mailings, borrowing fake pearls and buying used velvet dresses for two dollars at the Salvation Army for the fund-raising benefits we held for the rich high-society patrons.

I saw how ironic life was, how one could do two paradoxical things such as digging in the hot earth for bones under a sweltering sky and swimming among socialites at five hundred dollars a plate. Fifth Avenue fund-raisers all for the same goal—furthering one's life's work and making a contribution to society.

Then my grandmother Evie took ill.

I moved back to Berkeley to be by her side as she died.

I applied to the University of California at Berkeley as a transfer student and was accepted.

xxii.

I lived with my father and stepmother (he had since remarried) in the "Hotel California" house. I had to pay rent and keep my food on a separate shelf in the refrigerator, at my stepmother's instructions. She was an eating-disorder therapist who made me replace anything I'd eaten immediately after it was gone. She was fifteen years younger than my father.

After a long battle with cancer, my grandmother died, just as my grandfather had a few years earlier.

I was distraught over my grandmother's death: she had been my role model, my link to possibility, and now she was gone.

In my junior year in college I met a man some years my senior who had recently quit his job and had money from a profit-sharing plan he wanted to spend traveling. Happily, I took a year away from school (and Berkeley), and we traveled in Europe, Eastern Europe, Greece, Israel, and Egypt, driving an old car we'd bought in Germany.

He'd been studying at the Goethe Institute in Heidelberg. His classmates were students from Greece, Yugoslavia, France. They said, "You must come visit our country and stay with us," and so we did. We stayed with them in their family homes and lived how they lived—going to market, cooking, going to neighbors' homes and family affairs.

In Germany I went to Dachau. As I crunched along the pebbles where so much blood had been spilled, I wrote a long, abstract poem. When I returned to school, I submitted it to the UC Berkeley Yang Poetry competition, and, to my surprise, I won third place. It was the first contest I'd ever entered, the first prize I had ever won for anything I had written, and certainly the first time I had ever been paid any money for my efforts. Seventy-five dollars was an enormous sum of money to me, particularly for something I'd written. I tacked the check to my wall until one day before it expired. Then I cashed it. I desperately needed the money.

Once again, having taken typing at my mother's urging held me in good stead. I got a part-time job as a receptionist/administrative assistant at a public relations firm in San Francisco, also from a newspaper ad. I lived in an apartment on Russell Street in Berkeley sublet from one of my father's ex-girlfriends. The rent was $150.00 a month. At school, I took James Breslin's wonderful class on modernism, where I was stunned by the brief poems of Ezra Pound, William Carlos Williams, and the verse of Wallace Stevens—how could one pack so much into such a stanza? Gertrude Stein was a revelation. I took a fantastic class from Michael Bernstein on Proust, Joyce, and Celine. I was enraptured by Ann Banfield. Her class on philosophy and literature introduced me to Voltaire, Leibniz, Barthes. Robert Hass, then a lecturer, taught me Bantu and Japanese poetry and encouraged my writing in a poetry workshop.

I graduated from UC Berkeley in 1984. Then I was truly on my own.

I couldn't find a "real" job—my punishment for having been an English major, against my parents' urgings to do something more practical.

I wanted to move back to New York and work in publishing.

My grandmother had left me a small sum of money. I used it for my ticket to New York. I intended to stay for two weeks to see if I could find an apartment and a job. It was as long as the money I had would last.

But I could type about 100 words per minute, thanks to my mother.

xxiii.

I stayed with Richard Ruben, a dear friend I'd met at Hunter College. After two weeks of apartment hunting and fruitless job interviews, at 4:30 on a Friday afternoon, the day before my scheduled departure, I was sent into the office of a very young vice-president for a major motion-picture video company. He looked at my resume, sized me up, and said, "You're the same as every other person who's walked in here. So why should I hire *you*?" I sat for a minute, took a deep breath. Having nothing to lose, I surveyed his desk and said, "Listen. Your desk is a mess. You don't have time to find anything, let alone time for this interview. Your phone's been ringing incessantly (I had seen the red light blink each time an incoming call came in). You want someone you don't have to think about. Someone who can take care of things you didn't even know needed taking care of. If that's the kind of person you want, hire me. If not. . . ." I extended my hand and got up to leave. He said, "When can you start?"

I flew home the next day as scheduled, packed my bags over the weekend, and reported to work Monday morning.

I eventually got a room in a Chinatown loft shared with three students—of film, fashion, and music—through an ad in the *Village Voice*. Rent was $250.00 a month. For two years I worked as an executive secretary to the vice-president of acquisitions at CBS/Fox Video. Since my boss was buying properties to take to video, I acted as a first reader of hundreds of scripts and treatments, but I wasn't writing at all. I was "too busy making a living to write," and, beyond that, there were so many layers of self-doubt preventing me from putting pen to paper that I had given up.

Deep down inside, I still wanted to be a writer.

I saw my parents during homecomings.

The farther away from home I got, the more my desire to write surfaced.

The longer I stayed away, the more possible, and necessary, it seemed.

xxiv.

I knew the secretarial road was a dead end for me, so I applied to and was accepted to the M.A. program in creative writing at San Francisco State University at the encouragement of my then-boyfriend. He was from New York and was living in Berkeley. I was from Berke-

ley and was living in New York. I knew I couldn't be a secretary forever, so, with his encouragement, I moved back to the Bay Area to go to graduate school. Once again, my parents discouraged me, urging me to do something more practical, but since it was my money and my dream, I did what I wanted.

My homecoming was painful. It seemed that the family dramas I had escaped had continued to play themselves out in my absence. Coming home, I was once again drawn into the maelstrom. My parents didn't speak to each other, used my sisters and me as messengers. Around my father, I instantly became a child.

I answered an ad in the *Bay Guardian* for office manager for the Center for Human Development, a drug prevention center that worked in the San Francisco public schools with the police department. My boss, Maryann Fleming, became my mother-figure and friend.

At night, I took workshops in poetry and fiction. Criticism discouraged me, but never debilitated me. Amidst this exchange of ideas, I began to truly explore the boundaries of writing, the boundaries of my self and self-expression.

Lowitz and her husband, Shogo Oketani, Rudoiso, New Mexico, 1994

I was not able to choose genres. I am still not able to choose, and don't see why one must.

I wrote a poem about my grandmother's death and submitted it to a contest offered by the Browning Society in the dramatic monologue through the Poetry Center. Expecting nothing, I won first place. Then I found myself at a luncheon at the California Commonwealth Club with older women in white gloves and pillbox hats, just as my grandmother had worn. She could have been one of them. I felt she was there.

The following year, I transformed my adolescent experience into poetry by identifying with another adolescent, one far less fortunate than myself. I imagined myself trapped in my room with my diaries as Anne Frank had been trapped in her hiding place, and I wrote a dramatic monologue in her voice and submitted it to the Browning Society. To my total joy, I won first prize again. For the first time in my life, someone *else* cried as I read the words I had written.

Coming to Light

Anne Frank House

Through the window I see familiar rows
Of hearth-filled houses,
Colors that become an awning of August lights
Moving across the darkness.
Then, as if by accident, my eyes come
To your house, to the house where you once lived.
Though I've been there before, now I can only imagine
The small cluttered studio
With its smell of linseed oil and turpentine
Where you weathered *The Night Watch,*
Rembrandt, where you painted the Jews,
Rembrandt, where you saw something
Much greater than
Sunshine, moonlight, or pure dawn
Through your tired curtains—
I'm certain
I can see you now,
Moving slowly from your easel, paintbrush in hand,
Coming to the light.
I know your splashes of red, orange, burnt sienna,
They are the colors of my dawn.

In my dreams I see flip-book images
Of breasts and buttocks, women turning their heads
As if in conversation, perfect in their incompleteness
Bereft of their own voices.
From you I learned this, that first
We must come to know our bodies
Then we just come to wonder

What is this nakedness we've learned to fear?
Fear for me is just a common trick of life:
"To be interrupted just as you are
Thinking of a glorious future!"
That I learned too,
Better to have thought and imagined
Than not at all.

If the hand of destiny should seize me in this game
Pull me down by finger, arm, hand, hair, skull
Even by dream—
You, Rembrandt, will you wait up for me?

You come to me now
Smuggling in this night.
You bring the light
Slung over your shoulder
Like a burlap bag
Of scavenged scraps.
Perhaps
Your angel falling upon this house,
Heading down like a child,
Whistling its song of awakening
Would know instinctively how to land.
The bed I cannot toss around in scolds:
You cannot really know sleep, Anne.
You cannot really grow, no!
And this chair in which I sit
Parts my hair for me now.
Hasn't that grown to the ground?
It's all been turned upside down.

I am fourteen, spinning like a top
And this will be the only sound
I will sound tonight.
I want to proclaim the getting of words
From stars across the sky:
Each one settling in my heart like a dandelion.
We have learned to speak in gentle whispers—
Words, sighs and smells fly back to me
In these dreams,
Though sleep offers itself barely to me now,
Itself a beggar with none to spare.

Your light comes back to me
A snake dressed in plain shingles
Of uniform green
Coiling me into quiescence.
It enters my daymare
Wearing bright colors, garish for the dance.
Puffing up in swells of
Red, orange, burnt sienna
Vying for me, sliding into me.
I wake up silently
To rub myself against these walls
To loosen the coat of night,
But the darkness grows louder
And I am grabbed by hands I cannot see.

Me? Yes, my name is Anne.
I used to be Hannah in Hebrew.
It was here, in this house, that I learned
Of rhymes and lines,
Sticks and stones and the breaking of bread.
We had our moments of bread:
Of creativity and light,
And we had our moments of matzo:
Suffering.
And Hannah alone means beauty and courage
And most of all
Grace,
That's what you said.
You called me . . . Hannah in my dreams.

It was as if all the blue canals fled past our door
Thieves in that moment, crashing into one another
Too late in each other's history.
Like a succession of folding screens,
We are here now,
Opening, closing in the nadir of darkness.

In here, the pencil marks I put on the wall
To see how tall I've grown
Are light, mark history, say;
Look, I was here. I thought, I sang, I shook,
Embraced my fears.
Hidden deep in leaden grey moldings,
Lacquered once-white trim
Is the lullaby I sing without remorse,
And the no-longer tales of smelling gingerbread
Or lavender or herring or hair or perfume or river,
The smell of the newly born,
The breath of first deaths.

xxv.

I explored my fascination with Japan by minoring in Japanese literature, but it was not until the summer of 1987 that I first went to Japan.

My boyfriend had gotten a grant to go to Kyoto, so I went with him. We swapped apartments with his Japanese friend and stayed in his grandfather's old fuel shop in Kyoto. It was 110 degrees and hellishly humid. I spent most of my time teaching and writing in air-conditioned cafes. Through an introduction by the poet George Evans, who had given a wonderful reading at San Francisco State, I traveled up to the northern hills of Kyoto to meet the poet Cid Corman and his wife, Shizumi. Cid's poems—so full of breath and silence—reinforced the power of brevity. That each word, carefully chosen, could be worth an entire epic. That hot summer in Kyoto was as much of a

revelation as the summer in Paris after high school graduation. In travel I found freedom. In freedom I found permission to write.

xxvi.

Back in San Francisco I finished up graduate school while working for the Condé Nast magazines *GQ* and *Mademoiselle* as an advertising assistant. We lived in the Upper Haight. I wrote a short story and sent it to the PEN Syndicated Fiction Award, and wrote my thesis half in poetry, half in fiction. My poetry advisor, Stan Rice, moved to New Orleans at the phenomenal success of his wife Anne's vampire books, and my beloved fiction advisor, Michael Rubin, died of AIDS. I was an "orphan" upon graduation from San Francisco State, but was hired to teach creative writing there. I won the PEN Award, just from having sent my story in over the transom. (When later speaking with some famous writers who had also won the award that year, I learned their stories had been solicited by their agents, "promised.") I met an agent who later became my mentor and friend, Bonnie Nadell, and she encouraged me to write a novel. Halfway into my first semester, my then-boyfriend had another opportunity to go to Japan. I quit my job to accompany him. As before, I went where my lovers' opportunities led them, hoping to find something there for me as well.

Before I left, I wanted to read everything I could find about Japan, particularly the work of young women poets. When I went to the bookstore, there was a 1972 book by one of my heroes, Kenneth Rexroth, which contained the work of ancient and modern Japanese women poets, but few contemporary works. When I told Kathleen Fraser, a professor and wonderful poet at SFSU, that there were no contemporary women poets in translation, she encouraged me to try and translate them myself. Of course I couldn't, I said. "Who else will?" she replied. She gave me the name of a woman in Tokyo who was the translator of Adrienne Rich. In my life, whenever I was encouraged by someone I respected, I tried my hardest to live up to the potential they seemed to invest in me. The more challenges life threw at me, the more I felt I wanted to achieve.

So I moved to Japan, again with no money and no prospects for work. But somehow I trusted that I would find it. I knew by then that I was resourceful enough to make it happen, and if it didn't, then it wasn't meant to be.

xxvii.

In Tokyo, I immediately looked up the feminist scholar and critic Momoko Watanabe. As it happened, Momoko was busy, but referred me to a young critic and poet, Miyuki Aoyama, who was the translator of H.D. and Erica Jong. We got along like sisters and began to put together an anthology, but since we were young, virtually unknown, and had no publisher, it was an uphill climb in a country of protocol and hierarchy. But that was fine for us; we'd wanted to challenge the limits of those values in the first place. Including poets who were famous side by side with complete unknowns, it was definitely an "American-style" collection.

I hated Japan for the first three months, was ready to pack up my bags and return to America. I struggled with the language, taught 7:00 A.M. classes to salary men at the Nissan Automobile Showroom, choked for breath in packed subway cars. I taught English seven days a week, started a novel on the weekends and threw it away. My boyfriend had everything set up for him—Fulbright grant, no need to work. I always felt in his shadow.

I learned from my mother's hard lessons that I couldn't truly be with someone else until I knew who I was—my strengths and weaknesses—until I had a career that I was satisfied with. I did not want to make the same mistakes my parents had made. Indeed, I spent many years working on myself in various forms of therapy to this end. My boyfriend and I could not seem to get along; I eventually moved out on my own in Tokyo.

He eventually went home to America.

I had nothing to return to, so I stayed.

xxviii.

I lived in Yanaka, a section of Tokyo that had survived both the great Kanto earthquake of 1927 and the American fire bombings of the Second World War. As a result, much remains unchanged. Small wooden houses, ancient temples, tiny twisting alleys lined with potted plants and vociferous stray cats. Neighbors kept

Leza and Shogo, Mill Valley, California, 1996

a watchful eye on everything as they swept their front porches daily and chatted. I had the good fortune to be the neighbor of the writer and foremost Western authority on the Japanese film, Donald Richie, who generously took me under his wing. He became my mentor, my close friend and teacher on all things Japanese.

Through the American sculptor Charles Worthen, I learned that *Art in America* was looking for a correspondent. I visited many art galleries and museums weekly in order to write the monthly column, and was eventually hired. These reviews grew to a weekly column in the *Asahi Evening News,* and, through the good graces of Mr. Richie, regular poetry reviews in the *Japan Times.* There was a thriving literary community, and I contributed to the journals *Mānoa* and *Printed Matter.* I wrote essays, entries in a "Japan diary" that were broadcast monthly on NHK radio. For the first time in my life, I was being paid to write! Everything snowballed— the more I wrote, the more I was asked to write. Further, I met artists such as the Austrian Edgar Honetschläger, with whom I collaborated on a film. Exposure to artists such as

Toshikatsu Endo, who uses all of the elements of nature—water, fire, earth, air—in his simple works, reinforced the power of silences, the empty spaces that shape life. This echoed something I'd learned in meditation, in Japanese poetry, and in the poetry of Ezra Pound, the objectivists, and Cid Corman. It also went against everything I'd been brought up having experienced. It was a welcome relief and a tremendous breakthrough in my craft and confidence.

Providence intervened again. I met a man, Motoyuki Shibata, at a bookstore after we had struck up an accidental (nothing is accidental, I firmly believe) conversation about American writers. We became friends, and he later offered me a job teaching writing at Tokyo University, "Japan's Harvard"—a job I could never have gotten if I had tried. My M.A. in creative writing—virtually useless in America—was a ticket to a decent job in Japan.

xxix.

Miyuki and I continued to search out women poets for the anthology. We still had no publisher and no money and no prospects of either, but were determined to bring our book into fruition. We continued to translate the poems—wonderful, brave *haiku* and *tanka*.

Professor Makoto Ueda of Stanford said translation was a form of literary criticism as well as artistic creation, but it was Baudelaire who said that poets are the "universal translators" because they translate the language of the universe—stars, water, trees—into the language of humanity. For me, translation was a kind of midwifery. I myself was being reborn.

We were lucky to find a wonderful publisher in Stone Bridge Press right in Berkeley, California. Then we received a grant from the National Endowment for the Humanities to continue the project into a second volume. The first volume, *a long rainy season,* later received the prestigious Benjamin Franklin Award for Editorial and Design Excellence at the American Booksellers Convention in Chicago in 1995.

And they said it couldn't be done.

xxx.

My childhood had seemed chaotic, violent, everything upended. So it was not a sur-

prise that I eventually found my adopted home in Japan. Japan's codified manners and age-old traditions did not seem confining to me at all. I sensed in them a foundation I'd been lacking.

In Japan, everything has its place—and there's a place for everything. Having never had rules or regulations, borders or boundaries in my life, I found it truly revolutionary to abide by them. The inkling of this I had gotten in karate class in Manhattan had proven correct. Rules and codes didn't stifle me as they did so many other westerners who visited Japan. On the contrary, I flourished under them, feeling safe to finally explore the chaos within.

Five years passed like the blink of an eye.

xxxi.

While some of my favorite writers were exiles or expatriates, such as Milan Kundera, Anaïs Nin, Paul Bowles, and Primo Levi, or travelers on the road of life or in the mind, like Rimbaud, Kerouac, and H.D., after five years in Japan, I decided that if I didn't come back to America, I never would. I was not quite ready to be an expatriate. I was not quite a writer in my eyes either—having yet to publish a book of my own work. I had to return home one last time to see where my home truly was.

Inexplicably, after I had decided to leave Japan, I met Shogo Oketani, a young Japanese poet, novelist, and translator, on the night of a monsoon downpour in the height of the summer rainy season. The American jazz trumpeter and composer Wadada Leo Smith was touring Japan, and had invited me to his concert in Yokohama at a dark smoky jazz bar. Shogo loved free jazz, had known Leo for ten years. We fell in love the moment we met.

He was quiet, respectful, mysterious, fiercely intelligent. I couldn't have found a better partner if I had tried. I felt guided and blessed by a mysterious force. Was it my grandmother's spirit?

In many ways our childhoods mirror each other's. We were both rebels of a kind, difficult brooding kids who found solace in books and the martial arts (he had studied karate, kung fu, and judo). He was intrigued by Western culture, I was intrigued by Eastern. Yet at heart, he was as Japanese as I was American.

Leza Lowitz and Shogo Oketani, Mill Valley, California, 1996

Shogo introduced me to his parents. His mother was a formidable creature. For one, she was a master of the tea ceremony. She was also a schoolteacher who had raised three children while maintaining a career—unusual in any country, extraordinary in Japan. His father is a literary critic and professor of British and Russian literature who still uses fountain pens and writes calligraphy with horsehair brushes. He wears kimonos and roasts Japanese sweet potatoes over a fire in his backyard. Somehow, the twentieth century seems to not have arrived in their household. Not now, not ever.

I felt I had known them forever. They welcomed me into their home.

But I knew I couldn't stay in Japan—nor did he ask me to. I had lived too much of my life for other people, men, coming and going at their urgings and according to their opportunities and schedules, and I could no longer live that way. He seemed to know that instinctively and to honor that.

He had been working as a journalist for the same newspaper for twelve years. He was also *chonan*—the oldest (and only son) of a close-knit Tokyo family. Quitting his job and coming to America would have been out of the question.

In 1994 I moved back to California, took a studio apartment in downtown San Francisco.

A year later, Shogo came to America to be with me.

I finished my novel.

He finished his.

xxxii.

The artist Joseph Beuys, a fighter pilot in World War II, recalled being shot down over the Crimean Peninsula in winter. He was discovered by Tartars who saved his life by covering him with fat and felt—two materials that would become essential to his art. Perhaps that experience made him an artist. Perhaps his artistic life begins in the middle, with felt and animal fat.

My story begins with each new journey. With each new journey, the past recedes.

And now, to revisit the past, to find the links and threads . . . the silencings and the silences. And all that came between.

"The following of such thematic designs through one's life should be, I think, the true purpose of autobiography," wrote Vladimir Nabokov in *Speak, Memory*.

To imagine the past, even, is a fictional act, an authorial act. One's memory of an incident may not coincide with another who was there to witness it, but that is the transformative power of both memory and literature.

Rashomon-like variations on reality.

Life becomes fiction in retrospect.

We decided to get married, something I never dreamed I would do.

xxxiii.

Shogo met my mother's mother, an immigrant born in Ludsk on a day she cannot remember, and made blintzes with her. "He's a nice boy, but I can't understand him," she said in her thick Yiddish accent. They spoke through their cooking, preparing this meal.

Learning each other's language, communication is stripped down, only the essential calls out for voice. So unlike my past, my family, where words were usually arguments, when a simple conversation could turn into a test of wills, where unspoken resentments surfaced.

I do not wear glasses anymore.

I no longer use words as weapons.

I no longer keep my journals in the closet.

We learn to read between the lines, to find ways to communicate beyond language—reading instead the language of touch, the subtle shift in facial expression, the way the body is carried. We live and work together.

Shogo writes in longhand, filling out the tiny squares of the paper with Japanese ideograms, drawn in a river of fountain-pen ink. We have a quiet life, a respectful life that is at once small-town and global. Often, there is a knock on the door, and friends from Japan, Canada, Europe, or other parts of America appear.

Through translation, our world becomes both bigger and smaller at the same time. Spanning ages, continents, and languages, translation, like love and poetry, is a metaphor and a gift, a bridge between worlds and genres. Opportunity comes from community, connectedness. Nina Zolotow, a writer friend from graduate school, calls. She is starting her own small press. Do I have a manuscript? Through the help of Nina and her family (graphic designers and eager students of book production), my first book of poems is born.

All of the tables in our house eventually become desks—cluttered with books, sometimes his, sometimes mine.

My writing style, like my life, is constantly changing. Not searching for a voice, but exploring all the different possibilities of voices within and without. From the French women writers Colette, Anaïs Nin, Marguerite Duras, Annie Ernaux, I learn that life and art are braided together. Confession, autobiography, is not distinct from fiction. Through Proust and Nabokov, Kundera, and many others, I learn that fiction can be poetry and song. From the solid ground of a supportive partnership, I learn that which was impossible can be possible.

The Marriage

Cutting trout, your hands turn bloody
stuffing the gut with miso paste and butter,
they slip and slide. Slicing bagels or
slicing onions, sometimes we cry because I cry.
At dinner, a good omen—
there's always the fish that ate stones
from the bottom of the river, so we pick
them from the trout's soft belly,
pile them on the edge of the rough blue plate
like a blessing in the rain. Later we work on
a Japanese love story, find "the country of my birth"
to be an untranslatable phrase. From here, we'll write
the story our way, follow the hero's exile to the
   new world
and toast together—you saying *l'chaim* and me, *kanpai*.

I do not know how long we will stay in this country. Perhaps forever, perhaps just another year. We would like to go to a place where we are both foreigners. Or perhaps this is such a world, one we can create daily.

As I write this, whole new worlds open up, while old worlds close like folding screens behind me. I leave my past and enter the future. I carry my past with me, in me, but now it does not carry me.

*

There is a great sense of fortuitousness in being asked to write my autobiography at the age of thirty-three, when I am just beginning to be the writer, the person, I always wanted to become, just beginning to live the life I'd always hoped was possible.

"The last bond between me and the world I come from has been severed," wrote Annie Ernaux in *A Woman's Story.*

My past, the world I come from, has made me the woman I am today. There is nothing I would change about my past, except for everything.

A millennium ends.

I am grateful for my freedom.

All across the world people die for what they have written, prices are placed on writers' heads for the words they put to the page.

I am free to write what I wish, free from the bonds of the past and free of political persecution, free to know that with each word blood, and hope, begins fresh.

In committing to words my life, I am honoring and breaking with my past, opening the pages of the future to the unwritten chapters yet to come. . . .

BIBLIOGRAPHY

Poetry:

Old Ways to Fold/New Paper, Wandering Mind Books, 1996.

Contributor of poetry to *Athena Incognito, Electric Rexroth, Five Fingers Review, Hummingbird, Japan Environment Monitor, Kyoto Journal, Nexus, Noctiluca, The Plaza, Poetry Flash, Poetry Kanto, Poetry: USA, Prairie Schooner, Printed Matter, Seien, Shearsman, Tokyo Today, Transfer, Tsubushi,* and *Word/Woman Broadside.*

Novel:

Hachiko Plaza, forthcoming.

Contributor of fiction to *Prairie Schooner, Transfer, Sequoia, Edge,* and *Printed Matter.*

Other:

(Translator) Gomi Taro, *The Essence of Japanese* (textbook), Metalogue, 1994.

(Translator with Junko Abe) Kato Shuichi, *Japan: Spirit and Form,* Charles E. Tuttle, 1994.

(Editor and co-translator with Miyuki Aoyama and Akemi Tomioka) *a long rainy season: Haiku and Tanka,* Stone Bridge Press, 1994.

(Editor and co-translator with Miyuki Aoyama) *Other Side River: Free Verse,* Stone Bridge Press, 1995.

(Editor) "Towards a Literature of the Periphery," *Mānoa,* University of Hawaii, 1995.

Beautiful Japan: A Souvenir, photographs by Narumi Yasuda, Charles E. Tuttle, 1996.

(With Edgar Honetschläger) *Milk: The Stone in the Crook or How to Go Blind* (screenplay), Fischer Film, 1996.

Sound recording of *a long rainy season* produced, with music by Christopher Yohmei Blasdel, Kokopelli/Okelo Productions, 1997.

Contributing editor of *Mānoa* and *Printed Matter.* Work has appeared in anthologies, including *World's Edge,* 1991; *The Breast,* 1995; *Prairie Schooner,* 1995; *The Dome of Creation: Fiction by North American Women Living or Traveling Abroad,* 1997; and *Broken Bridge,* 1997.

Contributor of literary criticism to *All Asia Review of Books, American Literature Society, Asahi Evening News, Far Eastern Economic Review, INK, Japan Times, Mainichi Daily News, Mānoa, New England Journal of Medicine, Oakland Tribune, Poetry Flash, San Francisco Chronicle, San Francisco Review of Books,* and *Study of Current English.* Contributor of art criticism to *Art in America, Asahi Evening News, Feminist Art Review,* and *Sculpture.* Has translated works for *Harper's, Kodansha's Manga Shop, Ms., Tokyo Journal, Tokyo Today, WINDS, Yellow Silk,* and *ZYZZYVA.*

David Meltzer

1937-

Have memory washes—blips or tricks of time where I've told people I remember being in my mother's womb—a vivid memory of pink light, pink shadows, a bath-warm climate.

Born in Rochester, New York, in 1937. Both my parents were classical musicians—my mother, a harpist, a prodigy from Los Angeles, met my father, a cellist, at the Eastman School of Music. Both were scholarship students since both came from working-class backgrounds. My father was the first son of Polish Jewish immigrants born in America and set up a household with my mother without (I've been told) divorcing his first wife. (I've also heard that he hadn't married his first wife.) There are secrets and mysteries in all families optical illusionists unravel as subtexts for larger brave and tragic fictions.

"You Shoot & We Do The Rest": Rochester was a town defined by a camera secondarily amplified by ocular devices manufactured by Bausch & Lomb. I too was a seer, a looker, obsessed by the alphabet, learning the letters at three, calling out their names wherever and whenever I saw them. At four I began putting letters into words and started reading books, magazines, newspapers, billboards, calendars, anything with words on it. My parents knew the local librarian, who, though I was too young, let me borrow books from the children's section. I'd drag my red metal wagon back home piled with books I'd read over and over and then go back for more. Apparently I read all the children's books on their shelves, and the librarian let me borrow grown-up books under her selective eye.

My father decided to leave the Rochester Philharmonic and go to Manhattan to try his luck as a comedy writer, sending for us after he'd gotten hired as a writer on a radio show. We arrived in Manhattan in 1941, lived on the tenth floor of a walk-up apartment building at the end of Central Park, where my sister and I would throw pieces of paper out of the window of our apartment and step over drunks in the foyer doorway, where my mother burned herself plugging in a hastily wired lamp and the smell of her shocked flesh stung the air for days, and where my bottom bedsheet was a galaxy of blood stars from bedbug bites on my back, and where cockroaches in battalions marched back into cabinets when the kitchen light was turned on. After a few months we moved to Brooklyn into a railroad flat on the first floor of a two-story building on Linden Boulevard and East Fifty-second Street. Around the corner was a synagogue and down the block was an Italian Catholic community. On Saturdays half the neighborhood was in *shul,* and on Sundays the other half was at church. It was a community of first- and second-generation immigrants; the languages on the street were Yiddish, Russian, Polish, Italian, and American. It was a left-wing neighborhood; many people belonged to socialist trade unions, others were active in the Communist Party. The corner grocer's daughter recruited me to slip CP/USA fliers under neighborhood doors. Worlds collided on Friday nights when the Communist Party storefront held its meetings while the synagogue had its services.

Grew up in Brooklyn watching World War II play weekly at the neighborhood theater in newsreel footage of bombers bombing munitions factories, phantasmagorical night fires, Nazi commanders congratulating Hitler dancing in his boots, Japanese soldiers burnt out of their cave by Yank flamethrowers, Soviet soldiers shaking gloved hands with American GIs, generals, maps, parachutists, fighter pilots dogfighting enemy planes, shooting them full of bullet holes and they flip over, exhale smoke coils, and nose down to death below, blitzkrieg falling buildings and fire, V-2 rockets landing anywhere killing British civilians. Movie stars playing marines, sailors, GIs, pilots in love with gorgeous movie-star women writing passionate V-mail to each other. Heroic self-sacrificing deaths, heroic impossible fantasy revenge slaughter of Germans and Japanese by movie-star loner avenging a buddy's death, multicultural platoons outmaneuvering a mammoth enemy army despite all odds, and only a few tragic soliloquy deaths. All of it culminating in 1945 (I was eight) with A-bomb test explosions on a Nevada desert and a crane shot moving over rows of bones, shoes, eyeglasses, gold fillings, watches stacked in pyramids on the grounds of liberated concentration camps. The silence of the Holocaust, the Shoah, and the loud stop-time light-beyond-light blast of A-bombs ended my radio movie books and comic-books childhood. These two impossible facts stood out like unrepairable broken bones and could not be understood through familiar moral codes taught at school and reiterated in communities of spirit.

I was a bright kid, a high IQ kid, an early candidate for an experimental University of Chicago program recruiting smart kids barely in high school into college. My parents said no, Chicago wasn't the place for me, while they were in the intermission of their divorce operetta. I left home for the first time when I was thirteen and shared an abysmal but bohemian room in the Village with Lee Stewart. Lee like me had been a kid star on radio. He was an actor on *Let's Pretend,* while I sang songs on the *Horn & Hardart Radio Hour* with "Uncle" Ed Herlihey. Lee was gay at the time and hustled for money. He introduced me to the gay culture of Greenwich Village cafeterias. I was straight but fit in the same margins they occupied, and everyone was, it seemed, an artist of one kind or another, deeply broody about sex and self, double- or triple-crossed, and/or marginalized in one rut or another in postwar bohemia. (Sometimes Walter Winchell in a squad car would come into the Waldorf Cafeteria to get some dirt from gay informants.) Our plan was to write great poems in that crappy room, subsisting on saltine crackers and tap water, happy to inhabit all the cultural history around us and waiting for it to embrace our beginner's luck.

I became a poet when I was eleven years old. No doubt about it. The moment of the first poem was it. Yet poetry took me by surprise, it ambushed me. Up to that moment I had no real idea of what poetry was or what it was supposed to do. I knew it didn't fill the entire page like fiction did; it had to rhyme like *Hiawatha* or *The Rime of the Ancient Mariner* (which our fifth grade class at P.S. 232 memorized stanzas of to recite in class). A citywide schoolwide contest celebrating the fiftieth anniversary of the New York subway system was soliciting poetry, prose, graphics. Carole Grossman sat across from me in Mrs. Callahan's sixth-grade class. She had round red lips, curly blondish hair, and pale blue eyes peering distantly through pink-framed glasses. When Mrs. Callahan asked for poetry volunteers, Carole looked at me, the self-proclaimed genius, and without hesitating I raised my hand. Any kind of style? I asked our teacher. Whatever you feel most comfortable with. It can be in rhyme or free verse, which doesn't have to rhyme, said Mrs. Callahan. God bless Mrs. Callahan.

Carole Grossman looked at me in a way that said, you'd better try making that poem because if you don't you'll never be allowed into my living room again. There we would help each other with homework and sometimes melodramatically recite passages out of her hefty one-volume complete Shakespeare. Other times she would go to the upright piano, sit on the round stool before the keyboard, and play "Malaguena," which she knew was a favorite of mine. It amazed me how she could open a book of music, spread its pages flat against the piano, and play.

When I got home I asked my father what "free verse" was. He told me that it was probably poetry that didn't rhyme. Is that all? He thought a bit. Well I'm not sure; I know it doesn't rhyme but that each poem develops its own particular rhythms and has different line lengths. He went to a bookcase and pulled out *Magic Casements,* a poetry anthology edited by Louis Untermeyer, and showed me "Patterns" by Amy Lowell, which I read to instantly absorb the sense or essence of free verse. All I can remember is the last line: "Christ! why must patterns be!" It sounded like something I could work with.

That's a free-verse poem, said my father. Why don't you read more to get a better idea of what it's all about?

I didn't have the time. To be honest, I should have said I wasn't interested in anyone's work except my own. I decided to invent poetry for myself in my own voice and rhythms. Just like that.

The first poem that came through me was about the subway system. I say that the poem "came through me" because I had no clear idea of what I wanted to say or how I was going to say it. Everything happened suddenly. I started writing and then automatically began thinking in a different way about words, meanings, repetitions, the sound of language. It rushed out faster than my typing ability could deal with, but I kept at it, figuring I could unscramble it all when it was over.

The subway surged and flowed through underground tunnels beneath a city whose buildings soared to the sky, moving through arterial passageways carrying "the life's blood of the city / the people" (the only lines I remember).

It was as if I were singing, speaking, and acting all at once. An inner voice took over, snipping off lines where it felt they ended, extending them when it felt the voice needed more room. Another compartment of self was aware how the poem wanted to make the subway both real and metaphor. I realized poems could deal with actual things and yet suggest ideas beyond the actual.

My poem on the subway system went on for ten pages describing the whole process as best I could, including a loud hymn to the rush-hour crush and ending with a new day slowly and dramatically dawning as the whole thing started all over again. When I was finished, I knew it and sat back in amazement at what I had done.

Moved to Los Angeles with my father in the '50s. For a while we lived in a genially run-down hotel off Hollywood Boulevard. During the day he looked for work in television while I hung out at bookstores, the Hollywood Public Library, went to movies, looked into jazz clubs with afternoon sessions (unbelievable to this seventeen-year-old bebopper used to the New York night life of Birdland and Bop City, hearing Bird, Monk, Powell, Lester Young), and schemed my flight back to New York.

Whatever I'd imagined Hollywood to be was challenged by the mediocre facts before me. Listening to the radio in Brooklyn, Lux Radio Theater, the Academy Awards; watching movie stars in movies about Hollywood at the Rugby Theater on Utica Avenue; the star-studded preview presences filing into Grauman's Chinese in the *Movietone News;* reading movie magazines at the local candy store, looking through the thick, green-covered annual movie issue of *Variety* my father brought home—all added to my colossal dream of Hollywood. Hollywood and

Vine was an imaginary yet familiar intersection through its reference on radio, especially on *The Jack Benny Show.* My vision of Hollywood was enormous (something akin to Technicolor shots of nighttime Las Vegas), a vast bright city of celebrity. I wasn't prepared for a few flat blocks of gift and souvenir shops, hamburger joints, department stores, two ornate movie palaces (Grauman's Chinese and Pantage's Egyptian) plus a handful of ordinary neighborhood movie theaters, a couple of bookstores, and everything closed down around ten o'clock at night. The flat small strip of my imagined utopia was the first disjunction this Brooklyn bebopper experienced in '50s Hollywood. The second was the apparent absence of any kind of meaningful cultural life; it wasn't the Village, there weren't any artists, poets, startled or numbed-looking intellectuals, no cadres of animated intellectuals smoking, drinking coffee, talking philosophy, politics, and sexuality; the bookstores sold best-sellers, not eccentric handmade avant-garde titles; at the Pickwick Bookstore I'd go to the New Directions shelf as a paper oasis, a shrine, to thumb through Kenneth Patchen books, which were published by a small independent press, and small books by Anaïs Nin (published by her husband) with surreal biology free forms floating on their covers. Hollywood Boulevard was the main stem of a lazy burg low to the ground in the shadows of towering alien palm trees. Coming from the nonstop energy of New York, skyscrapers, all-night movies, music, museums, galleries, bookstores, cafeterias to sit in and rethink the world, Hollywood might as well have been a silo in the middle of an Iowa wheat field. Beneath radiant postcard-blue skies I felt like a skulking teenage vampire. The place seemed populated by either incredibly beautiful young tanned men and women looking like movie stars or movie extras, or ancient men and women sitting on bus stop benches decorated with advertising for mortuaries and grocery stores.

At the corner of Hollywood Boulevard and Highland Avenue was an open-air newsstand where I leafed through little magazines of the period. One day I looked into the saloon at the corner because I heard fragments of jazz piano punctuate the noon drone. Seated on top of the bar, an island in a long dim-lit narrow room, was a heavy black man playing piano to an audience of four or five mid-morning boozers neither listening nor talking to each other. It was the blind jazz virtuoso Art Tatum.

Outside of inventing poetry for myself, the other major art event in my postwar kid life was bebop. Since my parents had been musicians, there was an eclectic collection of 78 rpm records at home which I free-ranged through, plopping platters onto the sturdy turntable of an Ainsley-Crosley console in the living room. Through the twill-grilled speakers I heard (over and over again) Casals playing Bach sonatas, Duke Ellington, Billie Holiday, *Rhapsody in Blue,* the Rhythm Boys, Albert Ammons and Pete Johnson, Louis Armstrong. Sent to a camp in Maine the summer my grandfather was dying of lung cancer, I ditched swim time to goof and read in my barracks when I first heard Charlie Parker soloing over the PA system and walked down to the mess hall where kitchen workers were setting up for dinner, playing Bird at full volume into birch-filled Maine woods. Many of the workers were veterans and hipsters, and I started hanging out there every afternoon to listen to their records of Parker, Gillespie, Monk, Powell. As soon as I heard the music I knew it was talking to me; it was telling me what I couldn't tell anyone in words.

My father liked the music too and took me to the Royal Roost and Birdland to see and hear beboppers in the first heat of their revolution. Bought a beret, a chartreuse cardigan, got me a uniform, enlisted in the bebop platoon. The music showed me more about poetry than the anthologies. It demonstrated articulation, phrasing, dynamics, how to use silence, how to fill up a page with elaborately multifaceted ideas and images à la Charlie Parker or compress complexity into stark condensed heartfelt brevity à la Miles Davis.

Because I'd been accelerated in school in Brooklyn, tracked through what they called "special" classes, by the time I was in eighth grade my course load was the equivalent of a second-year high school student's. When we moved to Hollywood, that system wasn't acknowledged, and I was in no hurry to go to any Hollywood school, figuring that a town so culturally stagnant had to have miserable public schools. Instead, I took what I called "my sabbatical" and got a job working at an open-air newsstand on Hollywood and Western Avenue run by an old immigrant Jewish lady. My father rented one of those *Day of the Locust* pink stucco cottages off Sunset Boulevard. Our landlady, Mrs. Knowles,

always dressed in white silk carrying a white silk shoulder bag with "Faith-Healer" embroidered on it in burgundy thread. At the newsstand I was able to smoke cigarettes, pilfer candy bars, read paperback novels by Faulkner, Celine, Huxley, Wright, James T. Farrell, Dos Passos, Willard Motley, talk with a constant cast of characters: gamblers, actors, gay men, hookers, sadsacks, psychos, starlets, cowboys, fanatics (religious or political or both). Those encounters served as my junior year of high school.

My father, in between work, tried reviving my musical career and schlepped me to various talent shows on local TV. I wound up winning one for a few weeks. It was a show where the talent was evaluated and judged by a rotating panel of show-biz experts. The panel that nixed my final stairway to stardom was led by Harry Belafonte, who thought my outside version of "Summertime" too wiggy for the Top 40. On another talent show my "prize" was an audition for a local R&B label which never panned out. We went to the third floor of a building on Sunset Boulevard above Fairfax Avenue, talked with a sharp sweaty guy who said I was "interesting" and that he'd call back. He never did. In any event, I was seventeen, writing poetry by the ream and a long experimental novel, overwhelmed by my first reading of *Finnegans Wake.* I had a job that suited me which my father thought was a waste of time. I'd go to Ray Avery's Rare Records on Hollywood Boulevard when I got paid and pick up the newest ten-inch jazz LPs. In those days it was possible to have all the jazz LPs extant and barely fill up a small orange crate.

My father was writing an act for Buddy Lester, who was a fellow hipster; we'd debate the differences between Parker's style of alto versus Lee Konitz's. I'd work my day gig (or sometimes night shift) at the newsstand, come home, go to my small room with glass doors facing an overgrown conglomeration of southern California exotic shrubbery, get into bed, light up a cigarette, and read until dawn. Reading everything that looked interesting, I accumulated a huge library of paperbacks—Bantams, Signets, Pocket Books—as well as continuing my fascination with postwar science fiction. And playing ten-inch jazz LPs over and over on my portable phonograph. (It's remarkable how attentively one listened to music then.)

We moved to a larger house off Santa Monica Boulevard near Western Avenue and were joined by two of my sisters. It was furnished haphazardly with run-down stuffed chairs and sofas and creaky straightbacked chairs and a small piano with hard action; funky but comfortable. It had a large backyard with carp pool filled with weeds. I left the newsstand to work as a messenger boy for RKO Radio Pictures that summer while writing another novel and poems on a daily basis. My boss was a grouchy paternal man with leg braces, thick horn-rimmed glasses, a few jet-black strands of hair seemingly glued over a shiny suntanned skull dome.

Returned from my exile to high school, Fairfax High. I was seventeen going on eighteen and a sophomore. Met a group of fellow marginals who were artistically and politically alert; started dating, fell in love with a girl who lived with her mother a couple of blocks from school. We'd go to Peggy's apartment since her mother worked days and neck furiously, eat, talk, listen to records. At nights we'd go to the Coronet Louvre on La Cienega Boulevard, a film repertory theater run by Raymond Rohauer. There we saw an enormous range of classic and experimental films. Across the street from the theater was a bookstore run by Norman Rose where we'd hang out before the movies began, reading all the experimental magazines and books he stocked. There was always an intriguing group of people at Norman's store who all knew each other and would, after a while of chitchat, go into the back room. It was there and at the Coronet I first saw the artist Wallace Berman and his beautiful ethereal wife Shirley. I found out later that the back room was where the artists and hipsters would go to turn on before going across the street to watch the movies.

Peggy wanted to be a sculptor and was working part-time at the May Company, saving money to rent a studio on Santa Monica Boulevard behind a fiberglass car body shop a couple of blocks from Fairfax Avenue. It was a narrow run-down shed with uneven wood-slat floorboards. Peggy brought her sacks of clay and shaped small figurines. There was an old Goodwill mattress on the floor that we'd lie on to talk and caress. Her sculpting career and her money ran out almost simultaneously as her studio began serving as a free-floating open house for local artists and hipsters. Peggy reevaluated her tentative artistic yearnings after talking shop with so many full-time artists, getting firsthand field reports of the mixed pleasures, struggles, and

instability intrinsic to their work. Ed Keinholz became the next tenant and within a week had constructed a sturdy studio from lumber and materials scavanged out of alleyways. Ed was an amazing hunter-gatherer of abandoned objects and would forage the urban terrain on a daily basis. He brought a no-nonsense do-it-yourself approach to carpentry as well as automobile repair. A big burley Falstaffian man from the Pacific Northwest, he could drink prodigious quantities of beer while working on floor-to-ceiling constructions while listening to the radio while bantering with other artists and civilians who started hanging out at the studio. Genial, wickedly funny, generous, Ed had enormous energy, worked and partied hard on a nonstop basis. His studio became my full-time hangout. I moved out of the home I was living in with my father and sisters to rent a one-room shack behind an old wooden two-story rooming house. It was next door to Rare Junk, an antique shop whose outside was painted black, run by a beautiful and crazed blond Latvian émigré who looked like a pint-sized Ingrid Bergman and her tall blue-eyed blond crew-cutted actor boyfriend (his biggest part was in *State Fair*). I did part-time work for them "antiquing" Ming Dynasty horses. I'd roll newly baked and glazed clay clone ponies into dirt and twigs, let them settle, scrape off debris, and work the rest in. A few more passes and the nags looked prehistoric. They sold lots of those faux Flickas. They were constantly fighting with each other, and she was a tiger. I remember going to work one morning and finding an ax buried deep in the back door. She'd been chasing him around with it earlier, screaming Serbo-Croatian and mangled English, and finally threw it full force into the door he closed before it hit him in the chest.

A stream of people passed through Ed's studio, and it was there I met Wallace and Shirley Berman, Robert Alexander, Dean Stockwell, Dennis Hopper, Diane Varsi, George Herms, and other artists like Craig Kaufman, John Altoon, John Kelly Reed. Alexander and Berman were my mentors; these two Jewish hipsters were best friends but an odd couple. Berman was small and lithe and talked gnomically and sparely; for him, anything was filled with potential mystery and/or strangeness, the material world was oracular. Things were "cool" for Berman whereas everything was decidedly hot for Alexander. A tall, dark, flamboyant man, a terrific talker and great storyteller, he was also an energetic self-destroyer. (I first met him at Ed's studio after he'd gotten out of Lexington, kicking heroin under the government's supervision, sitting on the floor mattress drinking down a half-gallon jug of Thrifty's red wine.) Both men were exceedingly inspirational, helpful, and supportive. Keinholz's studio was my university, and Berman and Alexander were my advanced degree.

I went to Los Angeles City College for a year but felt out of place either knowing or not wanting to know all they were teaching. I met Idell and Lee Romero in a poetry workshop class; they were haiku wizard heads who got me into the haiku form as well as Japanese culture and R. H. Blyth's four-volume compilation of haiku. One night after class they took me up to their pad in the hills and we sat in their living room lit by a red bulb, smoked grass, and listened to a newly issued Charlie Parker memorial album on Savoy. After a year at City College, I went to UCLA and only remember one course: a philosophy in modern literature course taught by Hans Meyerhoff.

The shack I lived in behind the rooming house was connected to a row of other shacks inhabited by often demented souls living on a tight budget. One guy, an alcoholic vet, would get so deep into the bottle he'd pull out his .45 and wander around the yard threatening to kill anybody, even himself.

I had a series of jobs to pay the rent and get food, though in those halcyon days in L.A. dumpster-diving was sweet. The produce department of Ralph's Supermarket, a few doors down, threw out fruits and vegetables with the slightest defect or imperfection. The '50s was an era of seeming abundance, and if, for instance, a tomato had the slightest dent it was exiled from its display case under bright cosmetic lights and dumped into the outside bin. I'd go there every evening and have my pick of primo produce.

Ubiquitous "odd jobs" got me by: buttonhole cleaner at Missy Suits in L.A.'s downtown garment district; short-order cook at the Peppertree Gardens across the street from L.A. City College, a burger joint run by two actors, one of whom initiated me into the wonders of Duke Ellington. (As a bebopper, I was fixed in that time zone until introduced to the glories and history preceding Bird and Diz.) Dishwasher at the Kit Kat Café down the block from my pad; played young Christ in a tableau in the Pag-

eant Play and doubled as an extra in crowd scenes; collaborated with science-fiction writer Jerome Bixby, who lived in the rooming house, doing ghostwriting for a ghostwriting agency on Sunset Boulevard; churned out a fistful of science-fiction stories that I gave to Forest J. Ackerman, Jerry's agent, who became my agent and gradually, over a seven year stretch, sold them all; picked strawberries on Vashon Island in Washington during a summer I accompanied a friend and his new bride on their honeymoon; and always writing poems and stories and novels.

At John Altoon's studio (near the Ferus Gallery on La Cienega Boulevard) was introduced to his friend Robert Creeley's work in issues of *Black Mountain Review* and typescripts Creeley sent John from Mallorca. I found the magazine revelatory with works by Charles Olson, Fielding Dawson, Robert Duncan, who were news to me. Its squat unconventional shape reminded me of *transition,* the Continental magazine of experimental writing from the '20s. (I used to hang out at the Gotham Book Mart in New York and read through files of *transition, Little Review,* and the more recent *Tiger's Eye, View, Neurotica,* a particular favorite. They were scrapbooks of a counterhistory I identified with. In the post-World War II era I became fascinated by post-World War I writing and culture, triggered by reading Malcolm Cowley's *Exile's Return* and Frederick Hoffman's *The Little Magazine.*)

My on-site education by artists was amplified when I fell into a zone of '50s L.A. jazz culture. Paul and Carla Bley had an apartment over a garage on Santa Monica Boulevard. At nights musicians would, as they say, fall by and jam without disturbing the commercial activity of the street, which closed down at six. Precursor of the New York loft scene of the '60s, the Bleys' circle of players included bassist Charlie Haden, vibist Dave Pike, tenor saxophonist Warne Marsh, and soon Ornette Coleman and Don Cherry. Paul's trio had a regular gig at the Hillcrest Club to which he added Coleman and Cherry. The newly formed quintet played a few nights before they were all fired. (It was a calculated risk Bley took and never regretted.) Musicians would literally play until dawn, and whoever was in town in a similar musical orbit would fall by and sit in. It was paradise for me: intimate, friendly, music-centered, very little chitchat between numbers or during brief rest breaks. The music was all that mattered; a ritual feeling about those long nights suited my spiritual needs perfectly.

(Became friends with tenor player Warne Marsh, who was an early jazz hero in my teenage pantheon through his work with Lee Konitz in the Lennie Tristano Quintet. Had thoughtful talks about poetry and music with Charlie Haden, who was my contemporary; we were both relatively new to L.A. A little later, when I wound up in San Francisco, I saw Charlie again; he was, at the time, rooming with bassist Scott LaFaro. Remember meeting avant-garde composer-player LaMonte Young at a jazz club on Sunset Boulevard that had open Sunday-night jam sessions. He was playing an alto sax, wore strong glasses and a Buffalo Bill mustache and goatee.)

Was scraping by, in and out of work, living off handouts from my father, Dean Stockwell, John Altoon, Bob Alexander, and others. Sold my first story to a sleazeoid "girlie" magazine for a hundred dollars given to me by my agent in a lei of one-dollar bills. Was in a difficult relationship with the wife of a jazz musician and was getting restless; was hanging out with young actors (Hopper and I turning on, on the tarred roof of a Sunset Boulevard folk club talking Thomas Wolfe) and former child stars (Stockwell put the first of a two twelve-inch LP set of a Bruckner symphony on the hi-fi in his sparsely furnished living room, which we listened to as intently as a jury verdict); living a drifting hand-to-mouth ballet was getting me down.

John Reed, myself, and other young artists got a job hanging the annual Barnsdale Park art exhibit, which took all night and paid well. With that money I decided to move up to San Francisco. Norman Rose was managing a book warehouse and had a job for me (as well as a place to sleep in his pad). I left L.A. at nineteen (going on twenty) with Wallace Berman (who was going for the weekend). We flew up together, taking turns going into the airplane's tiny toilet with a glass porthole to turn on. (There was a bright full moon vibrating in an intensely clear night sky; as my eyes got clearer so did the designs on the moon's surface, which I stared at through the round window for a brief eternity.)

Moved cartons of books around at Paper Editions during the day and at night went into North Beach's hipster and beat culture (as yet neither discovered nor publicly invented). Bohemians, artists, poets, drifters lived in modest comfort (cheap rent and food), accepted and/or tolerated by the Italian residents. I'd walk into North Beach through Chinatown to eat great cheap filling food in noisy basement restaurants; usually slurped up a big bowl of war wonton.

Was laid off after a couple of months and went back to borrowing, cadging, hustling money off friends and relatives, spending more time in North Beach, especially at the Coexistence Bagel Shop, where I became friends with one of the countermen, who would lay thick sandwiches on me and endless cups of okay coffee. "Mad Alex," David Whitaker, and Tina, my future wife, sat in the window seat and talked for hours joined by other beatnik philosophers drawn into Alex's orbit. He was a tall thin African American who always wore a long Raskolnikov-style overcoat (no matter what the weather indicated), expounding and gesticulating a convoluted and wildly heady teaching to the initiates, who understood each nuance without being able to translate it to outsiders, who heard it as lunacy of the most elaborate design. African-Jewish-American poet Bob Kaufman used the Bagel to write poems and manifestos on the wall. Young artists like Joan Brown and Manuel Neri ate there; Neri once paid me ten dollars to write two love poems for a woman he was courting, and I found out, years later, they didn't work. Made friends with a loosely connected group of hipster filmmakers like Jordan and Jane Bellson, poet and filmmaker Christopher Maclaine (who was funny and tragic and later, when methamphetamines hit the scene, became an early victim). Tom Albright, working for the *San Francisco Chronicle* reviewing records, would lay classical LPs on us. Later he became their art critic and a significant and lucid historian of the Bay Area art scene. There were ongoing quasi-salons and parties I'd go to hoping there would be food or drink or both. Spent a lot of time at City Lights Books, checking out the new little magazines and small-press poetry books and talking with Shig, a wry Japanese American sage who was Ferlinghetti's right-hand man at the shop for years. Jack Spicer and his clan drank, bitched, gossiped, and talked poetry at Gino & Carlo's on Green Street. On Sunday afternoons at Joe Dunn's apartment there was a combination poetry workshop and salon unofficially chaired by Spicer and Robert Duncan.

Joe was a Boston transplant who worked at the Greyhound bus terminal on Seventh Street in an office that had a mimeograph machine he used (when no one was looking) to publish poetry chapbooks under the White Rabbit Press imprint. Spicer and Duncan team-taught my graduate course in poetry and poetics.

*   *   *

[*Aside:* My race down Memory Lane is beginning to resemble a familiar aspect of the autobiographical genre, which becomes a litany of magic names whose shells contain seeds of buried narrative and complex relationships unexplored and unrevealed. Apologies. This isn't Proust or Mandelstam.]

*   *   *

At Joe Dunn's salon a group of younger poets (Brautigan, Joanne Kyger, George Stanley, Harold Dull, John Kelly Ryan, and other visitor-participants like John Wieners, Michael McClure, Ed Dorn) would read recent work for group critique, ultimately waiting for either Duncan or Spicer to address their work. Spicer wanted the poem spare, condensed, mysterious, vernacular; Duncan wanted the poem expansive, rhetorical, rich with reference and allusion. They practiced to opposite metronomes. Exposed to both approaches and being able to choose one method over the other or to seek ways of combining them was a major learning experience for me. Being in the company of poets and peers was also new for me since L.A., like Rochester, wasn't a "word" town but an "image" village with a strong visual bias fundamental to its economic existence. San Francisco was then and is now one of a handful of major literary cities in the United States. I was a young poet in the first-wave heat of blinking flashbulbs inventing the Beat; studying with the primary figures of the Berkeley-based San Francisco Renaissance; listening on KPFA every week to Kenneth Rexroth, who was part of an earlier activist arts culture that flourished in the Bay Area during the Depression, talking holy this and that with Allen Ginsberg; eating cream cheese sandwiches made at the Bagel Shop by Robert Stock, who belonged to a group of formalist poets (Daniel Langton, Michael Greig) who were part of Weldon Kees's circle; and later learning from Lew Welch and Philip Whalen. It was heady stuff.

My first book of poetry was published in 1959, a two-poet debut shared with Donald Schenker. Don and his wife Alice hand-set the book in the basement of Michael Greig's house, working on a small handpress that belonged to Weldon Kees. Our book was called, simply, *Poems*, and was printed in a small edition with an extra ten copies hand-bound and "signed by the blood of the poet." We pricked our thumbs and spritzed blood drops on each colophon. My next and first full-length collection, *Ragas*, was published by the Discovery Book Shop with a cover by artist Peter LeBlanc. I was working at Discovery at the time, learning the used-book trade under the wily guidance of Frederick Roscoe. The shop was a few doors down from City Lights. Up to that time I'd been the janitor at the Coffee Gallery, a bar and club that Tina and I often performed at. (Tina also waited tables there.) Wallace and Shirley Berman, George Herms, Robert Alexander were living in the Bay Area; the Bermans lived on Scott Street, where their apartment became a locus for poets (John Wieners, Michael McClure, Kirby Doyle, Robert Duncan) and artists (Jay De Feo, Jess, Larry Jordan), and then moved to Larkspur onto a houseboat. George and Louise Herms moved from a North Beach basement into a landlocked funky barge in Larkspur close to the Bermans. In 1965 Berman devoted an issue of *Semina* to my work *The Clown* and Robert Hawley's Oyez Press published *The Process*, which I feel was my first integral collection of poems. But I'm accelerating the chronology somewhat.

There was jazz and poetry. Ferlinghetti and Rexroth were reading down at the Jazz Cellar (and Kenneth Patchen was working with a Canadian sextet back east). It was inevitable that I get involved and soon became a regular performer at the Jazz Cellar backed up by the house band (which often included saxophonist/flutist Leo Wright). As a young hipster I thought the older poets were stiff and outside the music's rhythms and vocabulary, i.e., they didn't swing. What they were doing was more like Schoenberg's *sprachstimme*, reciting verse against a musical background. Being young, arrogant, unquestioningly sure of myself, I decided to improvise poetry as another soloist in the jazz band. I'd bring poems in outline, like a head arrangement, and fill in the rest while the music worked behind me. Because I'd been a kid singer on radio I wasn't afraid to use my voice as an instrument. For a while I was in my element and many poets came to hear me, including, as part of a North Beach tour, William Carlos Williams. I became aware of a division between high and low culture when some poets thought performing poetry this way was impure and I wasn't sharp enough to remind them of the poem's origin as song. It didn't stop me, but I began to be more conscious of cultural politics and the clannishness of poets.

Jim Dickson, Lord Buckley's manager, was in town and caught my "act" at the Cellar and flew me down to L.A. for a combination gig and recording session at the Renaissance on Sunset Boulevard. Exhilarating to be backed up by Bob Dorough on the piano, a bass and drummer whose names are impossible for me to access, and the great post-bop tenor player Allen Eager. The audience was filled with movie people and artists; top of the world. After the performance, we spent the rest of the night in the club recording material for Dickson's Vaya Records. As it turned out nothing was ever issued. All that's left is a sandblasted-sounding twelve-inch acetate.

By this time Tina and I were living together, sharing a single army cot in a former radio repair shop on Larkin Street we rented. Its prior tenant, Norman Rose, had painted the two rooms white; it was zen-spare, which was okay for us. (We were in love for nearly thirty-eight years before her recent death of ovarian cancer and raised three daughters and a son. Tina was the center of the rhythm and harmony of our lives.)

From the mid-1960s onward, we performed together either as an acoustic duo singing a weird mélange of folk, country, blues, and jazz material or as members of various string and bluegrass bands, including the Snopes County Camp Followers. We were a part of the Bay Area folk "revival," participating with musicians and performers like Janis Joplin, David Crosby, Dino Valente, Jerry Garcia, Eric Anderson. At the outset of the "psychedelic" moment, Sam Charters (poet, musicologist, record producer, musician) signed Tina and me to Vanguard Records to make an electric album, though up to that time we performed on acoustic guitars. We formed a rock-and-roll band, the Serpent

Power (with a nod to Arthur Avalon), to make our first record, bringing out from the East Coast the poet Clark Coolidge to be our drummer. Clark was a jazz-trained drummer, and my guitar concept was more jazz and experimentally oriented than straight-ahead rock-and-roll. We rehearsed for a couple of months and recorded our first album at Sierra Sound, a studio on the borderline between Berkeley and Oakland. We recorded our first album at the same time Country Joe and the Fish were recording theirs. Our bassist and rhythm guitarist were a few years younger than we were and were rock-and-roll veterans, having played and toured with the Grassroots. They left the band after the recording session. Tina left the band after listening to our album and after our debut performance at the Fillmore Auditorium. This left Clark and me to re-form a working band to prepare for the second Vanguard album. Serpent Power gigged regularly at North Beach bars and played benefits and concerts. We were an eccentric group with Clark's complex polyrhythmic drumming style, my often spiky guitar improvisations, Jim Moscoso on bass yearning to play with a funk band, Bob Cuff (formerly with the Mystery Trend, the San Francisco Art Institute-based pioneer art rock group) on rhythm guitar, and joined by poet Daniel Moore on *shenai* (a Chinese reed instrument producing oboe and soprano sax sounds), conch shells, and various bells, Christian, a tenor sax player learning how to play on the gig, and J. P. Pickens playing free jazz amplified five-string banjo. We developed extended improvisations around blues modes, and like I did in my days at the Jazz Cellar, I'd improvise lyrics. Our sound was neither standard-issue rock-and-roll nor paisley psychedelia, but we did, in our own low-rent way, gather a following of devoted groupies and fans who were, as we were, not from the company store. Through performing we developed what we thought was a tight yet open music. We hoped Vanguard would record us live in one of the clubs we played at. Charters caught a set and told us it wouldn't work, we weren't going to sell records with what we were doing. After almost a year of playing and anticipating the record session, the band disbanded.

The second album on Vanguard, *Poet Song*, was composed primarily to showcase Tina's magnificent voice. A string ensemble from the Oakland Philharmonic was hired to play arrangements by Ed Bogas. Sam also suggested adding a few tracks of my poetry backed up by multitracked guitar.

A young couple from Mill Valley wanting to locate in San Francisco swapped their tree house in a redwood canyon for our railroad flat on Jones Street between Union and Filbert (one of the city's steepest streets; the air heavy with clouds of burnt tire rubber off cars panicking as they went down it). Suddenly we found ourselves in the "country," on welfare, with three kids. I supplemented our income writing erotic novels for an L.A. publisher. I wrote ten in a year and half, using the genre as a direct form of political intervention. This was the Sixties, and I thought pornography was the right form of address to the Vietnam War, racism, economic immiseration.

From Mill Valley we moved further down the coast to Bolinas, which, at that time, was a literary hot spot. Joanne Kyger, Robert Creeley, Bobbie Louise Hawkins, Tom Clark, Bill Berkson, Lawrence Ferlinghetti, Ebbe Borregaard, John Thorpe, Duncan McNaughton, lived there, and the flow of visiting poets, especially in the summer, was hard to keep up with. Robert Kelly, Philip Whalen, Anne Waldman, Richard Brautigan, Brother Antoninus/William Everson, Lewis Warsh, Jim Brodey, Lew Welch, Robert Duncan, were some who passed through one summer. It was sometimes like living in a literary anthology by the sea.

While Tina was teaching at the Bolinas School, I was doing writing odd jobs: an anthology of classical kabbalistic texts, a book of interviews with San Francisco poets, a collection of cross-cultural writings on the birthing experience. We were saving our money to leave the States. We were planning on going back to the Old Country to live in exile.

Wanting our kids to get a sense of the landscape we were abandoning, I set up readings across country. We piled into a used station wagon, stuffed to the hilt with possessions impossible to let go of. By the time we got to Great Britain, we'd jettisoned much of our baggage. Hired a cab to Camden Town, where the Benvenistes lived. Asa was a poet and printer who had published a collection of mine, *Yesod,* under his Trigram Press imprint. His wife Pip was an artist and filmmaker. They miraculously and graciously took us all in.

The exile lasted about a month. Tina got discouraged trying to find a place for us to live, our daughters were getting panicky about the prospect of going to British schools. They'd been loosely educated in primarily free-school settings and were amazed and daunted by how British kids seemed to talk in complete sentences and even complete paragraphs. On the other hand, I was settling in, wandering around London, spending time in the British Museum library, feeling for the first time unburdened by the weight of the States. Our savings were being quickly eroded, and at a family meeting we decided to return.

We had no credit, just what was left of our savings, and by luck (or destiny) found a funky house in the East Bay, assumed a low-interest FHA loan, and suddenly became owned by a mortgage and truly settled in one spot.

Tina took up teaching music in preschools and day-care centers, our daughters entered the maelstrom of adolescence, and I taught creative writing for three years at Vacaville Medical Facility, a state prison.

Poet Duncan McNaughton called to invite me to be core faculty of an M.A. program in poetics he and Louis Patler were inaugurating at New College of California in San Francisco. The program's faculty were practicing poets, Robert Duncan, Diane DiPrima, McNaughton, Patler, and myself, supplemented over five years by visiting poets and adjuncts like Michael Palmer, Anne Waldman, Judy Grahn, Robert Grenier, Lyn Hejinian, Robert Creeley, Susan Howe, Nathaniel Mackey, Michael McClure, Leslie Scalapino, Philip Whalen, Gregory Corso. Working with Robert Duncan was an endless delight, and he was central to the program's intelligence and spirit. Though contending with a life-threatening illness, Robert devoted his considerable enthusiasm and brilliance to students and faculty with generosity and excitement. It was a remarkable group and a rare and unique program.

So what happened next? This incomplete and superficial ramble makes my life look like a suite of sound bites or fast-food blurbs à la *People* magazine or *Entertainment Weekly.* "What I Did on the Road of Life": a collection of picture postcards annotated with obligatory highlights and brag. How are you? I am fine. Liturgical social banter of revelation and avoidance.

What's left out? For many years edited and published an irregular journal called *Tree* and

Tree Books (press). It was an attempt to somehow relate classical Jewish mystical texts to modern and postmodern poetry and prose. In the last few years began performing again with Clark Coolidge and Tina in a group we called Mix, blending improvisatory music with poetry and backing up Tina on vocals from the jazz standards book and accompanying her song versions of various contemporary poets' work. Got tapped as a somewhat Beat figure (definitely on the B list) and thus attended a couple of conferences on Beat Gen flimflam. Rhinoceros/ Masquerade Books reprinted some of my erotic fiction from the '60s which my students read with mixed results. Our first album, *Serpent Power,* was reissued on CD and went quickly out of print. Compiled a polemic anthology of jazz texts, *Reading Jazz,* to mostly favorable reviews, and am at present assembling materials for a companion volume, *Writing Jazz.* Where the first collection demonstrated the white construction of jazz as subject and object, the second volume presents jazz from African American perspectives and is profoundly different from its predecessor in intent and direction, though still a form of polemic collage.

Am still teaching at New College of California, in both the undergraduate humanities program and the graduate program in poetics. Like a personal ad, am a widower living with an eighteen-year-old son who spends most of his time before a computer either at work or at home. We watch Japanese *anime* features; listen to wide bandwidths of industrial rock; and talk about how lousy the immediate world is (from obviously different historical platforms) and how intentionally (and unintentionally) gruesome the upcoming millennium looks. I don't know about him, but I'm still hopeful. We also e-mail each other wise and foolish jokes from the vast labyrinthian storehouse of folklore from cyberspace, an expanding ineffable space of the known.

Future projects? Like all writers and poets I probably enjoy planning books more than writing them. Want to write a cultural history of the California arts scene from the 1950s to the '60s using artist Wallace Berman as my focal point. Have another book of poetry almost done comprising two long sequences, *Reds Versus Feds* and *No Eyes,* which Black Sparrow promises to publish maybe in 1997 or 1998. Am writing two erotic novels (*Boff* and *Lamb*) since I still feel this genre, like science fiction, allows writ-

ers room to rant and speculate and criticize outside the shadows of regulating high culture can(n)ons.

—*David Meltzer*

BIBLIOGRAPHY

Poetry:

(With Donald Schenker) *Poems,* privately printed, 1957.

Ragas, Discovery Books, 1959.

The Clown: A Poem, Semina, 1960.

Bazascope Mother, Drekfesser Press, 1964.

Station, [San Francisco], 1964.

The Blackest Rose, Oyez, 1964.

In Hope I Offer a Fire-wheel: A Poem, Oyez, 1965.

Oyez!, Oyez, 1965.

The Process, Oyez, 1965.

The Dark Continent, Oyez, 1967.

Nature Poem, Unicorn Press, 1967.

Journal of the Birth, Oyez, 1967.

The Agent, Essex House, 1968.

How Many Blocks in the Pile?, Essex House, 1968.

Round the Poem Box: Rustic and Domestic Home Movies for Stan and Jane Brakhage, Black Sparrow Press, 1969.

Lovely (Book 1 of *Brain Plant;* also see below), Essex House, 1969.

Healer (Book 2 of *Brain Plant;* also see below), Essex House, 1969.

Out (Book 3 of *Brain Plant;* also see below), Essex House, 1969.

Glue Factory (Book 4 of *Brain Plant;* also see below), Essex House, 1969.

Agency, Essex House, 1969.

The Martyr, Essex House, 1969.

ORF, Essex House, 1969.

Poem for My Wife, Maya, 1969.

Yesod, Trigram Press, 1969.

From Eden Book, Maya, 1969.

Abulafia, Unicorn Press, 1969.

Letters and Numbers, Oyez, 1970.

Bronx Lil/Head of Lillin S.A.C., Capra, 1970.

32 Beams of Light, Capra, 1970.

The Brain Plant Tetralogy: Lovely, Healer, Out, and Glue Factory, Essex House, 1970.

Star, Essex House, 1970.

Greenspeech, Christopher Books, 1970.

Isle Vista Notes, Christopher Books, 1970.

Luna, Black Sparrow Press, 1970.

(Editor) *The San Francisco Poets,* Ballantine, 1971.

Hero, Unicorn Press, 1971.

Knots, Tree Books, 1971.

Hero/Lil, Black Sparrow Press, 1972.

Tens: Selected Poems, 1961–1971, McGraw, 1973.

The Eyes, the Blood, Mudra, 1973.

Bark: A Polemic, Capra Press, 1973.

(Editor) *Birth: An Anthology,* Ballantine, 1973.

French Broom, Oyez, 1974.

Blue Rags, Oyez, 1974.

Harps, Oyez, 1975.

Six, Black Sparrow Press, 1976.

(Translator with Allen Say) Shiga Naoya, *Morning Glories,* Oyez, 1977.

Two-Way Mirror: A Poetry Note-Book, Oyez, 1977.

The Name: Selected Poetry, 1973–1983, Black Sparrow, 1984.

Arrows, Selected Poetry, 1985–1990, Black Sparrow Press, in press.

Poetry appears in anthologies, including *The New American Poetry: 1945–1960,* edited by Donald M. Allen, Grove, 1960; *Beatitude Anthology,* edited by Lawrence Ferlinghetti, City Lights, 1960; *Junge Amerikanische Lyrik,* edited by Carl Hanser, [Munich], 1961; *The Real Bohemia,* edited by Francis J. Regney and L. Douglas Smith, Basic Books, 1961; *On the Mesa: Anthology of Bolinas Writers,* edited by Joel Weishaus, City Lights, 1971; *Mark in Time: Portraits & Poetry–San Francisco,* edited by Nick Harvey, Glide, 1971; *A Caterpillar Anthology: A Selection of Poetry and Prose from Caterpillar Magazine,* edited by Clayton Eshleman, Doubleday, 1971; *Visions of America,* edited by David Kherdian, Macmillan, 1973; *John Keats's Porridge: Favorite Recipes of American Poets,* edited by Victoria McCabe, University of Iowa Press, 1975; *A Big Jewish Book,* edited by Jerome Rothenberg, Doubleday, 1978; *Calafia: The California Poetry,* edited by Ishmael Reed, Y'bird, 1979; *Convivio: A Journal of Poetics from New College of California,* edited by John Thorpe, Tombouctou, 1983; *Stories and Poems from Close to Home,* edited by Floyd Salas, Ortalda, 1986; and *Exiled in the Word,* edited by Jerome Rothenberg and Harris Lenowitz, Copper Canyon Press, 1989.

Audio recordings:

Serpent Power, Vanguard, 1968.

Poet Song, Vanguard, 1969.

Re-Runs, S-Tapes, 1980.

David Meltzer Reading, Membrane Tapes, 1981.

Nurse, S-Tapes, 1982.

(With wife, Tina Meltzer) *Just Folks,* Living Room Tapes, 1985.

(With Tina Meltzer) *Faces: New Songs for Kids,* Folkways Records, 1985.

Just Standards, Living Room Tapes, 1986.

For, Living Room Tapes, 1987.

Stars, Living Room Tapes, 1988.

Contributor to audio anthology *Poets Read Contemporary Poetry: The Before Columbus Foundation,* Folkways Records, 1980.

Other:

(Editor with Lawrence Ferlinghetti and Michael McClure) *Journal for the Protection of All Beings #1: A Visionary and Revolutionary Review*, City Lights, 1960.

We All Have Something to Say to Each Other: Being an Essay Entitled "Patchen" and Four Poems, Auerhahn Press, 1962.

(Contributor) *Notes from the Underground Press*, Underground Press, 1964.

(Editor) *Golden Gate: Interviews with Five San Francisco Poets*, Wingbow Press, 1976.

Bolero, Oyez, 1976.

(Editor) *The Secret Garden: An Anthology of Kabbalistic Texts*, Continuum Books, 1976.

Abra (juvenile), Hipparchia, 1976.

(With Robert Duncan) *Wallace Berman Retrospective*, Fellows Contemporary Art, 1978.

(Editor with Lawrence Ferlinghetti, Michael McClure, and Gary Snyder) *Journal for the Protection of All Beings*, City Lights, 1978.

(Editor) *Birth: Hymns, Prayers, Documents, Myths, Amulets*, North Point Press, 1981.

The Art, the Veil, Membrane Press, 1981.

(Editor) *Death: An Anthology of Ancient Texts, Songs, Prayers and Stories*, North Point Press, 1985.

Reading Jazz: The White Invention of Jazz, Mercury House (San Francisco), 1994.

Writing Jazz, Mercury House, 1997.

Editor with Jack Shoemaker, "Maya Quarto" series, Maya, 1966–71. Author of column "Green Atom," *Los Angeles Free Press*, 1969. Contributor to *American Book Review, Caterpillar, Co-Evolution Quarterly, Haight-Ashbury Literary Journal, New World Journal, Oyez,* and *Yale Review*. Editor, *Tree* (annual), 1970—.

Sarah Menefee

1946-

Sarah Menefee—"Self-portrait," 1994

Where does it start? Before language, in the reception of the bright world, running out into it. My beginning, before I remember. Always there in the kinesis of the language, in the tendency to locate the occurrences of the poem in transit, on the street moving. I ran down the streets of Chicago before I was a year old, snagging cigarette butts out of the gutter to put in my mouth, the unfurling of the poetic line across the page. It goes back to the mystery of coming into the body of the world, to come out of mystery into all-this.

I back into this with trepidation: the poetry insists on the intimate, not the personal. To center it, as Jack Hirschman says, in the "spine": Birth-Love-Death: "To put a skin around it." Down through the words into their great collective meanings (to understand, to stand under), a game best played by the anonymous.

The poetry is usually not far from the nightly dream and the daily jottings: "5-19-96—When we get older we enjoy food more and more, the taste of it, eating. More outrageous that there's hunger! A guy has a newspaper of fish and chips open eating on top of a newspaper box, down on the corner in the sun. The smell of hot greasy vinegar, ah! He's allowed to buy them but not to eat inside."

I found poetry as a way for the heart to speak.

A first memory: in the bathroom mirror, looking at blood on my tongue, surprise not pain, the red of it. I've climbed up and tasted my father's razor blades, am painting with my blood on the sink. And the beautiful purple tincture swabbed on my throat for a terrible diphtheria at fifteen months so I had to learn to walk again. Back up, flinging forward, shedding my clothes behind me, running naked into the world.

They named me Sarah. There had just been Nagasaki and Hiroshima. And that other holocaust, that unthinkable abyss.

During the war my mother had nightmares of running from bombs falling from the black sky, as they were all over the world, in terror. She was pregnant with my sister when my father was inducted into the army in 1943, sent to boot camp and intelligence training; my sister, Ann, was born in October. My father was stationed in Saipan till the end of the war. I was conceived on his return, born in late September of 1946, my brother Joseph in early 1948, and my brother Paul in 1954.

Later on I remember seeing snapshots my father or somebody else had taken in Saipan, of a family in front of a hut, the little boy naked below the waist, and another of a hole in the ground where people had been incinerated trying to hide.

My parents, known to their friends in those days as "George and Mary," were both students when they met, my father at the University of Chicago, my mother at the Art Institute.

My father, George Herman: his stories about the Manhattan of his boyhood, going to the automat ("the coin-blackened hands of the woman who took the money"), later walking up Broadway to Union Square to listen to the orators on their soapboxes. Family history somewhat occluded by the trauma of steerage, an infant smothered in his grandmother's arms, her going to the rabbi for a divorce, then poverty forced her to put my grandfather Joseph and his sister into an orphanage. He, Joseph, was born in Latvia, became an electrical engineer, and married my grandmother Sue. She'd been brought to this country as a young child also, born near Moscow of Lithuanian parents. She was pretty and dramatic, a great mimic and a "foxy" dresser, worked for many years as a secretary. My grandfather, by all accounts a wonderful man, was out of work for a time during the Depression, and this caused some conflict.

An earliest memory of my father's: of a swordfish dead on the beach at Asbury Park, touching its sword. My father has been a poet for many years.

Mary, my mother, I think of always as a young girl, with a "bleeding heart" as she would say, running through the small-town streets of Springfield, Illinois. She is full of funny stories, with a touch of the Midwest gothic, about those times, the twenties and thirties of this century. She was the third of three children, and her mother divorced her father, Jack Kiser, a salesman who had a hard time of it during the Depression, when Mary was in her teens. My grandmother Inez's father was a housebuilder who followed the frontier, then settled his family in Oklahoma Territory; he'd as a teenager fought in the Civil War and done some time in Andersonville Prison. I was very close to my grandmother, who lived to be 102.

My mother tells of "nutting" in the woods, knocking black walnuts out of the trees and putting them in gunny sacks, the whole family. She picked blackberries, lilacs, and such, and sold them from door to door. Money was scarce. She was skinny and shy and romantic, and loved to make things. She became a great swimmer and a champion diver. She's been an artist all her life, an accomplished painter.

My parents married in 1941. My mother wanted to start having babies right away.

I try to understand who my parents were then, before we came along. I try to put it together from stories they tell, about the early

"Blowing bubbles: My mother, Mary, holding me, and my sister, Annie," Chicago, 1946

part of the marriage, before it fell apart. Eating once a week at a cheap Chinese restaurant. Complicated, sensitive, soulful people.

Birth. From the paradise of the womb, to the light, the golden light of autumn, to the milky breast, to the finding of the body and the body of the world. When my head emerged I began to scream. I was a fat, colicky, keyed-up, active female infant. Very early to walk, late to talk. Running and peeing into the gutter, tasting everything. How constantly infants appear in my dreams, not "my" baby, or myself, but infancy, full of beginning.

Aside from some black-and-white movies of that era, noir, nothing is as evocative for me as a city pavement, what is written upon it ("see how the mulberries stain the pigeon turds"). The city is the first context. An alley behind the apartment on Fifty-seventh Street, rats in the garbage cans behind the Chinese restaurant down the alley, sooty bricks.

Chicago: Hyde Park, the Midway, Jackson Park, Lake Michigan's soft gray-blue stretch fading into the sky and its beach and pier. Four beautiful harsh seasons. I played around a railroad bed with the tiniest round cinders I called my "cinder babies," looked at them so intently, perfect worlds.

Inside, the matrix, floors my mother painted red. My sister has gone across a busy street to buy us candy lipstick while I wait on the curb.

She is sensitive and articulate, careful with her possessions while I wreck all around me. My brother I play with, great partner in ever-escalating mischief. At ages two and three we run away together on two adventures, the second time across busy city streets. The moil of human traffic amidst the gray buildings and the sky full of weathers, primal.

My father finished school and got his first teaching job, as an instructor of English at the University of Alabama at Auburn. In late summer of 1950 we bought our first car, and headed South.

What can I choose to represent this place? My seven-year-old sister asking my mother why all the garbage men were Black. The answer my mother gave was to read from history, stories about Klan terror, and I listened. I see the terrible night riders torching the poor shanties, those unpainted shacks that still ringed every little town. We had a little taste of it, being from the North and not respectable. I remember the looming presence of a cop, called on us when my parents were fighting by the neighbors who loudly beat their children for playing with us. Yet they did, and we ran in gangs and adventured as children do no matter what.

"My father, George, with Annie, and me on his lap," Chicago, about 1947

When my father got a job for the following year at Kansas University, we shook the bloody-red mud of the place (that we'd so loved to play in) from our heels, and moved again.

Lawrence, Kansas. A converted army-barracks apartment complex called Sunnyside. School began, the fifties, that grueling decade: the Korean War (more poor incinerated Asian people), the McCarthy era. Kindergarten was for me a signal of what was ahead. The teacher slapped us around to keep us mustered into silent order: boot camp. By second grade or so I had a gang of younger kids I'd send into the corner store to steal licorice, while I stood outside keeping my eye on the street. We also hatched a plot to take over the classroom and bump the teacher aside, never carried through but rehearsed so vividly it was as though we'd done it. I also remember being taken on a school outing to a jail, looking at the men behind bars looking back at us, being filled with bewildered embarrassment about it: a lesson. Stories about "Bleeding Kansas" and the burning of Lawrence, the guerrilla war that took place there, John Brown. Of a Black child, a boy in fourth grade (where my teacher would announce that I was at the top of what she called her "black list"), tormented by read-aloud racist stories and mocking remarks, squirming shame.

Walking to school on rainy mornings, autumn leaves wet on the sidewalk, a sight that still evokes absolute happiness. School also a social world, other kids. After school we ran around without adult supervision. In fact, it always shocked me when one found out something we'd been up to. Little "sex" clubs, girls only. I often couldn't tell dreams from waking life. I thought that when I dreamed I went to a place on top of the clouds, and that I could will myself to have "erotic" dreams if I concentrated.

I remember what moved inside me the first time I was told, by another kid, about death, trying to imagine that; and that I would bleed "down there" when I was twelve.

I associate this time of childhood with the Yiddish and made-up Yiddish my father used for parts of the body otherwise unmentioned, and as endearments, so that Yiddish is for me (and objectively!) deeply expressive, intimate, and playful. The dialect I was hearing was Litvakian, as I recently discovered. My father, the poet, liked to riff and play with language,

"A most wonderful event": Sarah, with newborn brother Paul, Lawrence, Kansas, 1954

mess it around, in a way I've always loved. Likewise my mother was witty and loved to use wordplay and slang ("a terror to rats!").

I remember a tantrum, banging my head on the floor, not knowing why I was doing it. I did a dance out in the dust, imitating a fly, cleaning legs and wings and head, buzzing around. Listening to my mother read to us from Grimm's fairy tales, "seven in one blow" flies killed to outwit the giant. I liked to be sent out to the garbage cans on our building's back porch to swat flies in the heat. There's a drawing my mother kept, a school exercise illustrating the words "Go Down": flies falling from a naked light bulb, singed. Later, at age eleven, my first "real" story was a description of the death of a fly. Issa, one of my favorite poets, writes: "don't strike! the fly wrings its hands, its feet."

At age nine I fell in with some Baptists, a blind evangelist who "converted" me with wonderful stories about being hit by lightning and such. About that time I wrote my first deliberate poem, about the five emotions. The poem is long gone, but I remember how it felt writing it.

Reading: first the usual childhood fare, weeping for Black Beauty and Bambi. Scenes I remember, epiphanies. When the landowner sets

his dogs on the serf's son, from *The Brothers Karamazov,* read at eleven. Later, through adolescence and college and beyond, going up and down library shelves; the writers that interested me were those that married heightened emotional drama with vivid description. Even in philosophy: Kierkegaard, Pascal, Rudolf Steiner. In college I read a lot of "hermetic" stuff, and existential psychology. Binswanger: I liked the "case histories." Rimbaud's plate of ham, Blake's Ghost of a Flea (his rose!), Gilgamesh and Enkidu, Kafka's roach, Christ's trial, Aesop's crow, and on and on. But I'm getting ahead of myself.

Reno, Nevada: a radiant place in my solar plexus. In the south center of that state nuclear bombs still tested above ground. A location in recurrent dreams of the most ecstatic red desert, mountains of bare red rocks that when I climb I'm overcome with the most intense ecstasy. Or am going there, trying to get there, traveling toward, down the years.

We moved there as I was about to turn eleven. I would live there off and on for the next twenty years, most immediately my junior high and high school years. Adolescence: radiant empty American loneliness, the heart of my poetry.

Age twelve, my seventh-grade friend Peggy, granddaughter of a white sharecropper, taught me the "facts of life." We ran around inseparable, downtown our stomping ground. Those late-fifties horror movies, meeting boys in there, "making out." She taught me the words that went with what men and women do. Rehearsing the mysteries in talk and imagination, a potent poetry. This "climaxed" with my first sexual experience, in a car of course, at age fourteen.

Then Cathy, my best friend in high school, a lovely irreverent girl, oldest of nine children of a single mother, who lived in low-income housing not far from our tract home. We spent a lot of time roaming around together, passing long notes between classes. Otherwise I hated high school and its social arrangements. I treated this common adolescent misery, and the pain of a three-year "semi-affair" with a married man, with bourbon from the bottle at home and at a downtown bar after school. I kept these things secret, even from my friend; they were taboo, despite our cheerful smuttiness in the back of the bus, those "banging on Lulu" songs. As for poetry, I was writing behind my textbooks in the back of class, as yet imitations, exercises, play. I had the sense that this would be something I would always "do."

I started working weekends through my senior year, and full-time the following summer, as a nurse's aide, so I could afford to go to college out of state.

"A hospital is like a casino," my stepson Maynard said recently, "someone always coming by with a tray." Where people are out of themselves, divisions dissolved by pain or alcohol. I worked on all the floors: cleaned up after childbirth, threw the placenta away, prepped the dead and wheeled them down to the morgue, and everything in between. Then I asked to be put on the geriatrics ward. I saw what the old have in store for them, especially those with no money. Sometimes I still have the nightmares: "up and down corridors blocked by beds of the cadaverous old hooked up to bags of dusky urine shitted-on drawsheets great craters of bedsores." Many of these old people had been warehoused and abandoned. I liked to hear their stories, some of them moving indeed.

I spent two and a half years at the University of California at Santa Barbara, struggling to be a painter and failing to do much of anything else except what we did then in the sixties, we of a certain age and background too immature and self-involved to engage the political, as it was happening then: the escalations of a horrible war registering as nightmare and body count, a lot of talk about leaving the country.

I find it's hard to "tell" what happened during this period of my life, because a certain undefined project, inchoate and urgent, was so at odds with what seemed to be expected of me, that in itself pretty undefined. Though I very much enjoyed having lovers and friends, was especially close to a few of my teachers, I began to experience the institution as a sort of anthill. I stuck to the painting studio when I wasn't running around with those ubiquitous companions marijuana, mescaline, and LSD. By autumn of 1966, turning twenty, I was bad-tripping, "breaking down," medicating myself from the vodka bottle.

I think of the Groucho Marx line: "I see you're having a nervous breakdown. Why don't you pull yourself apart?" That was the sense of what this project was, that I'd been working

on since the age of sixteen or so; that something needed to break apart and be put back right or dissolved or burned away, a passage: "the stars shot down / rays of pain to burn me alive / my body gave off the smell / of roses half of California with me inside." I spent two weeks in Camarillo State Hospital, a comradely place full of every human unstuck piece of the time, elderly poor who would nowadays be on the streets. All there with no assumption of power, an important place in my memory.

That was my graduation. I left school and moved back to Reno.

I met my husband, Bob Menefee, thirty-nine years old, and his three-year-old son, Maynard, the following summer. I was living near downtown Reno, working as a nurse's aide at the county hospital. I then, a rather complicated divagation, moved to San Francisco for a short time, working graveyard in a hospital there, living in a room near Union Square. At the end of November of 1967 he came and picked me up, and we started our traveling.

My husband was a gambler, tried to do that for a living, as well as an obsession, offended as he was by the life doled out to him as working class and nearly illiterate. He shared my rather confused contempt for "respectability" and its hypocrisies. His squandering of money taught me not to cry over its going. He used people all along the way to keep his journey going, until it killed him. Along the way there was no material or social base from which to create anything but the next trick of survival. Having experienced that condition, I see the domestic ruins of a whole new class created by the time we inhabit, and understand in a small way its most intimate features.

My husband was someone who could tell me certain things about his life and experiences that lit up very vivid pictures in my mind. He used this ability, the artist and poet he naturally was, to persuade people to either shake off their routines and fall in with his adventures, or at least help keep him going on his. I was certainly good for this. And he would help me figure out what to do with my life: "somebody to love."

I began to work, in Reno, Las Vegas, and elsewhere in Nevada, in the casinos, as a gambling shill and a cocktail waitress. Danced in a bar in Miami, dollar bills in my panties and bra. And so on. Stories heard in these places of "sin," intimate yet impersonal, stories and secrets, passing through. And the camaraderie of the workers. We called the clubs "toilets." People were always saying "there's gotta be a better way." The sense of being trapped yet transient, a loose piece, no bones about it, though you could hustle up good "side money." And then the guy cruises through and takes the tips off your tray to run them up next door. Moving in the middle of the night. Seeing how far he could get on wit and trickery, an old story; the messenger between the worlds, mercurial. You can expect to be fucked over, sometimes have an interesting journey of it. In its American incarnation.

He lived for the moment when we would pull into some small Nevada town broke and out of gas, lay a last dollar on a roulette number, and hit enough for a fleabag room and some gas to continue on. Much of the time we were moving around this way, often sleeping in vehicles or out beside the road. Maynard told me recently that he used to think the Vagabond Inn, with its logo of the hobo with

bundle and stick, was a place where "transients like us" could stay without paying, but we never stopped.

Maynard spent his life in this proto-homeless condition, hundreds of different places during his childhood. A tough life: "The Nevada desert is no place to be broke down," he says. Five of these years I shared. I fell completely in love with him, as one does a child, and tried to mother him, dearly loving the trying of it. He was and is a remarkable soul who has always seemed to know way more than he should. Close to an endlessly inventive source of creativity in him, I exploited that delight.

Bob and I divorced in January of 1972, paid for by a woman who'd sold her house to go off with him. I signed the papers on an empty twenty-one table in the Primadonna Club where I was shilling. After a short time we got back together, and remarried. He left again a month later. "Between the Watergate courtroom faces and the firebombing of the Inglewood SLA hideout I moved to LA when he left me after our second marriage . . ." (from "Hollywood").

"On the road": With Bob and Maynard Menefee, 1970

I knew I'd better get out of Reno or I'd fall back in with him the next time he came through. My dear friend Marguerite, who'd been my college roommate, was now married and living in North Hollywood. I stayed with them for a week, then moved into an apartment building with a pool (one of the few places I've ever rented that's actually had a bedroom!) in the middle of the Hollywood flats, a few blocks from Sunset. I lived in Hollywood and near downtown L.A. for the next year and a half, in about four locations, working as a two-buck-an-hour insurance clerk for Blue Cross of Southern California, a high-rise pink-collar sweatshop.

Through two lovers I had there—the first, from Watts, I was terribly in love with; the second, from Detroit and Mississippi, I lived with for a while—I experienced a little bit of the Black world, post-Watts uprising. I heard and saw things there that helped me shake off a certain oblivious innocence ("You're as innocent as a *worm*," my second lover said), and later helped me understand the context of the explosion and uprising of 1992. There were stories of cop beatings in South Central, and of course less dramatic things—poverty, a history, a community, and a culture. The sense of the enormous human habitation there that isn't "Hollywood" or fame.

My lover, an artist who'd done time in prison and had become politicized, was messing around with heroin. His young friend, at the time sleeping on my couch, whom I also loved and called "little brother," died of an overdose in the alley behind a halfway-house apartment where we used to visit and drink sweet wine; this led to busts of other friends and jail terms. Police helicopters flew over at night shining spotlights down on the roofs of Mariposa Street, across the street welfare housing, full of beautiful children, immigrants. For a time things were violent and full of anguish. I then fell into another relationship, which was ruined by lack of love on my part and much alcohol ("anger is hundred proof spirit of pure distilled tears yes we are a very spiritual people lord").

By the second summer, with its pall of hot smog, I was ready to leave this place that "could be a paradise," as a comrade said years later as we visited homeless camps in a hillside park, a pan of red chile meat on a blackened rock, and the downtown canyons with their alleys of "cardboard condos." This monstrous beautiful place.

My plan was to move to San Francisco, but I ended up in Reno again.

I need to mention at some point Vietnam—that terrible background of horrifying images and nightly body counts, year after year. I was not involved in protest during the ten years it ground horribly on, but had ongoing and repeated nightmares, though I'm not sure exactly when they commenced or stopped. They were so heightened and terrifying that they didn't seem to be coming from me but *into* me, as though real suffering going on in the world was going on inside me, in real time, unending and unbearable horror, as it must have been for those caught in the relentless nightmare the war was (and that still hasn't ended for those who were involved; I've known and loved a few). "In that self-absorbed time," I wrote, trying to describe these dreams, "somehow receiving the real agony of whole numbers of people, unleashed by those images and body-counts, year after year, that's how it felt, the terror and pain were multiple, it is utterly indescribable and I have not been able to write it, terror, terror and burning and mutilations the hideous suffering even of the trees and all other beings that were maimed and burned." This has been difficult to "deal with" in the poetry directly, except as something always in the background, a line or two ("I shiver and in dream that night / restore the lines of tenderness the poem was missing / through endless nightmares of, tortured Vietnam"). Certain photographs: "bent into the crippling hell of a tiger cage / with a look of fierce anguish that struck my heart numb / 'when I got out of the army I wanted to be a woman.'" Poems written ten and more years after the war was over. At the time, the nagging sense of the horror of it as life went fumbling on, and the nightmares.

After leaving Los Angeles I visited Reno, and unwisely popped into the Primadonna Club, where I'd been working before I moved away. They offered me my job back, and it was all too easy to accept. So there I was, "stuck in Reno" for another four years.

I worked for a while at the Primadonna, on graveyard, then in various other casinos, in and out of "relationships." The last of these, with a crap dealer who was a poet of sorts, and a rather tireless and sometimes violent alcoholic, lasted for three years. We fought and drank together, and traveled, to Mexico and all over Peru.

These two looks outside this country were very important to me, especially the experience of Peru, that omphalos in time and space, one of the poorest and most starkly beautiful places on earth. I fell in love over and over there, with the people, the place, the spirit, the depth of time that was timeless, and the sense of history brewing. Also with the children ("child bent running under millennial luggage"); the red graffiti and hammer-and-sickle scrawls; the beggars and ragged coca-heads and squatters camps familiar forward through time, so as the process unfolded here it looked the same, though very different too; one reverberates with the other always, and all other places not seen: the true Internationale. I believe that what I experienced there, as well as in Mexico ("it's always the poor who help the poor in Mexico"), helped liberate me from something I was stuck in, a chauvinism, to at least imagine moving through the world in a certain way.

Echoed in Peru were the two primal landscapes that have most defined my life: the desert mountains that I keep inside, an enormous ecstatic place, and the coast, the Pacific.

Nevada: a place of tears, of vodkas, of know-nothing and small decencies. I worked in its shabbier casinos, built in a second big wave of construction underway then: the King's Inn, the Plantation Club, the Bonanza north of town, a hangout for construction workers and cowboys (one told me his horse would never lie to him). I was still young and receptive enough, turning thirty, to sit at the bar and listen to the stories: Freddy the Freeloader, Paiute Stanley, Johnny Love the pimp, and so on—many I've written about here and there, Nate the shill.

I was now ready again to leave, to "be a writer." Propelled by a last burst of turbulence, I moved to San Francisco.

San Francisco: late August 1978. I found a small studio apartment, where I've lived since, on Sacramento Street, right off Polk, on the bottom of the west flank of Nob Hill, in Polk Gulch. On the rocky lip of the city with its quartzic light buildings in the moving weathers between the waters of the Pacific and the Bay.

That November the mass murder at Jonestown occurred, a profound, terrible event particularly in the psyche of the Bay Area, like a black hole into which much was sucked, leaving the fabric of things altered, recurring often as

Reno, Nevada, 1975

an image in my poems. The following week the city hall murders of Mayor Moscone and Supervisor Harvey Milk, fire in the streets. A sense of something undefined but from now on different, the early-dark evenings boded: "the dead of Jonestown knocking about our hearts and you unknown to me when the days got shorter in an autumn cloud you were releasing fierce words into the city." I felt I was being thrust into history in a certain way. Just to say "Jonestown" tells of a whole process: the running of the "poor and unwanted" from the city, from their neighborhoods ("walking up and down laughing and crying / used to be her neighborhood"), out of existence—one that continues, greatly stepped-up, into the present.

I won't go into anecdotes about this part of my life: a seeking and thrashing about, loneliness and alcohol, but also friendships and exploration, and poetry, lots of it. Getting to hear and know so many poets, some weeks a reading just about every night, listening, finding out. I'd audited a couple of courses that first fall at New College, a stucco ex-mortuary on Valencia Street in the Mission District, had been encouraged to apply for a government grant to study there in the Poetics Program. This paid my tuition and a living stipend, enough to get by working part time for the next three years: in a bookstore, as a day-care aide, and as a file clerk in a downtown law office (barely squeaking by).

The New College Poetics Program, led by Louis Patler and Duncan McNaughton—and, a couple of years into my stay, the Master's Poetics Program headed by Robert Duncan and Diane DiPrima—represented the confluence of some of the best *working*, nonacademic poets this country has to offer. The tendency was the "hidden tradition," poetic gnosticism, very attractive to me but also sometimes troubling, probably more a reflection of my own inarticulate lacks. I found what I was given and was able to absorb immensely liberating, helping me to break with old constraining habits. In any case, the experience taught me to be a poet: the immersion in the poetry and poetics, in the works and words of other poets. Especially important to me as teachers, poets, and friends were Duncan McNaughton, Larry Kearney, and David Meltzer, and many many others. Duncan McNaughton in particular helped me find what is called, rather tritely I guess, my "voice." His classes were structured as a company of friends speaking of the deepest places of poetry, whether occasioned by a "myth" or other texts: deep meditations on love and gnosis as the practice of poetry, working through the heart's texts and the "plain tale" (Kerouac). David Meltzer's teaching of the Kabbalah also wonderful, impeccably treated in its historical and cultural context as well as for its utter poetic suggestibility (later I've had much access to this through Jack Hirschman, a translator of many kabbalistic texts, and an old friend and cohort of David's). Also of course Robert Duncan, a diamond that threw off sparks that could both illumine and burn, his human presence, wit, and responsiveness. As muddled and hesitant as I was (or lazy, unsure, and hungover), I was able to learn and receive an enormous amount from this privilege and encouragement, the special "occasion" in time and place that this coming together was. I probably wouldn't be a poet without it. "An alchemical pastime, an Alexandrian pastime," as Duncan McNaughton says. What is received that way is later felt as gratitude, with the desire to reciprocate, figure out how to do so.

I also splashed around in the beatnik waters, North Beach, more a street scene, bar, cafe, and open readings, so for me more comfortable and "free" (for a while I just observed from the bar, where I felt at home), though with a sense of having seen better days, as the neighborhood gentrified. I got to know Bob Kaufman, his piercing, radiant visionary later poetry, published in *The Ancient Rain* in 1981. How wonderful his presence, his friendship, and what he represented (so often distorted by racism, privilege, and others' projections). He never stopped being a street poet in every sense; for me, as for so many others, a fountain, an ether that went through the streets collecting eighty-sixes. The end of something dirty and pure. Generally, the scene's sweet sad lack of a forward thrust that left us with our alleys and brandies, friendships, hijinks, and lots of poetry.

What was the core of me then? An impatient waiting, a floundering into the space of the abyss of Jonestown, a need to find a context, to act in some collective way that nothing was giving me (though in some measure all of it was); I was becoming desperate, in that time when "the door of the heart begins to open at thirty-five, in pain, with a breeze that blows through, and a cord of feeling that extends to the heart of another, and out into the spaces between the stars."

The early "Reagan years." Homeless people, unnamed, were beginning to appear in the streets. Polk Street was already lined with homeless youth, young hustlers, "boys for sale leaning against the walls of boutiques I pass in the night with aching breasts." Now came others, seemingly out of nowhere, carrying tattered blankets or bedrolls, going through the trash cans for something to eat. We watched from behind the cash register in the bookstore where I worked, called them "loonies," not understanding.

"He used to be young and attractive not so long ago the sick boy hustler who goes by wrapped in a blanket that trails behind in the mud his bare feet cracked and indecent past groaning walls and gutters flowing with blood." Written in the very early eighties, on a scrap of paper at work. A quick sketch that became a poem as I wrote it, the rhymes unconsciously arising, not bothering with line breaks. The important thing for me was to try to capture a wink of living reality, suggest the terrible truth it represented. The final image is in my mind a faint echo of the last lines of Blake's "London": "And the hapless Soldiers sigh / Runs in blood down Palace walls" (millions of homeless Vietnam vets; just the other day a cardboard sign lettered "Gulf War veteran"). Suddenly the ending of a process (the era of capitalism) was

At a Union of the Homeless action, San Francisco, 1987

creating conditions whose human results—hunger, homelessness, migrations and internal exiles, beggary, poorhouses a.k.a. shelters, and so on—looked the same: new to our eyes but nothing new at all. "Hark hark the dogs do bark, beggars are coming to town . . .": a nursery rhyme with Elizabethan roots, beating time in my heart. Before I had any explicit understanding of any of this, it was walking into my poetry, "walking along in hunger and want / pain and deprivation warping your limbs." It appeared in the first such poems with "blackened feet first sign of gangrene early in the decade." The image of sore feet ("lame maimed and limping always the same"), again and again, through the sleepless death march of this existence, running through everything I wrote. I saw the symptoms. I needed to understand the cause.

About some emotional misadventure or other (my still having the bad habit of meeting men in bars), my dear friend Jeanette once said, "It's like a storm through your life." Such those wonderfully wet years, one storm after another passing through. My husband came riding one of them, and after that Maynard came to stay

with me for six months, went to New College for a semester. I little knew what I was about with a seventeen-year-old kid/man, out on those howling streets himself, having inherited every genocidal poison and carnival ride designed for the children of his class. His father's life already being swallowed by Saturn's black rings, as it appeared to me in a dream then: he died a few days short of his fifty-fourth birthday, July of 1983. He'd been living in the back of a station wagon, up and down the coast and deserts of California, till his last days spent in the veterans' hospital near the ocean in San Francisco, where I was able to visit him, and to some extent say goodbye.

I pictured this time, at the time, as ruled by the mercurial, a bitter sludge settling to the bottom, nigredo. The wonderful rainy seasons, sheets of gurgling water running down the hill below my window as I sat on my bed writing the scattered narratives of memory and the moment. And part of everything from then on, the awareness of people out there in the rain, the slow torture of it: "with all these storms I keep catching the same pneumonia."

On Halloween in 1983 I met my mate, Jack Hirschman. He brought me into the political work and solved the weeping-in-loneliness that had carried through a lot of years. I look back along the thirteen years we've worked together as poets and revolutionaries, and certain continual symmetries are made that develop through my poetry and my work in the world. That is the vantage from which I see things now, as though everything *led up to.* Now I had a lover and companion, one conscious of the global process of spirit that bursts out of holocaustal abysses. Anything I can now say about my life is magnetized around this point, this turning. From the time we began our deep conversation of love, my lines began to unsnarl, as though the heart chakra was opening its petals, leaving spaces between them for the breath, or light, the silence that is the quality of the light itself. The process has been most workaday and delirious, full of laughter and body. The text has been the developing objectively revolutionary movement, first unorganized and seemingly inchoate, the survival movements, the homeless struggle, in which I've been engaged.

Jack also became my teacher in the true sense of equality and mutuality; we began our work together, which would sharpen my own self as a poet while immensely expanding my sense of the boundaries of poetry into the world, the expression of its striving and transformation, of the poet's role of "prophet" in the sense of seeing-what-is, the naked face and meaning of it into the future. The profound humane and fiery internationalism of this man, his gentleness and ferocity for justice, the absolute brotherhood of his generosity, a revelation to me. All of that in his poetry, the great living body of it.

To have found such a lover and friend seemed an utter miracle; having this as a foundation, anything seemed possible. I dropped the anodynes, which I no longer needed. I entered the *conscious* body politic.

The watershed of my life was when I joined the Communist Labor Party (CLP) in early 1984, and began to understand the meaning of "com-

At the site of a housing takeover on Polk Street, San Francisco, 1993

rade" in its sweet American sense. This work gave me the theoretical and historical background and understanding I'd been looking for. I saw that this wasn't a speak-for-them sect I'd rather ignorantly associated with left politics. Here, the people I'd always considered the basis for dissent and change, those most oppressed and resistant, were not only members and fighters, but leaders, developed as true proletarian intellectuals. Exemplary of this is CLP founder Nelson Peery, a retired bricklayer who's been at the heart of the Communist revolutionary movement since the thirties—one of the foremost Marxist theoretical, historical, and visionary minds working in the world. One who not only wrote but organized and taught, spent his life working with others to build an organization capable of its mission in the times ahead. Together, the comrades have built a body of theory and practice that both predicted the features of the current crisis and disintegration of the capitalists' "social contract" and gave them the strategy to build an organizational vehicle able to unite and educate the leaders of the scattered struggles. Nelson Peery's powerful, novelistic memoir *Black Fire: The Making of an American Revolutionary* was published by New Press in 1994. The qualities I mention of Nelson's are shared by all the comrades in this work (including his wife, artist Sue Ying), too many to enumerate, but each uniquely a point of transformation in this time, whether at the national office in Chicago or in various cities and towns across the country. This work and organization, contrary to popular orthodoxy, has been very supportive and conducive of the freest liberty of expression, full of all kinds of poets and artists: the work itself greatly helps that aspect of the self to flower. Furthermore, its fight is for conditions that will set us all free to express our fullest dreams and aspirations.

In 1986 my first book, *I'm Not Thousandfurs*, was published by Curbstone Press. For over ten years now, Curbstone's Alexander Taylor and Judith Doyle have been not only our publishers but friends and comrades. Both my books (a second, *The Blood about the Heart*, was published in 1993) were hand-printed and bound by Judy, an artist, a loving, beautiful compliment. Most important has been the company one is in by virtue of being a "Curbstonista," as Sandy calls us—many of the greatest revolutionary poets and writers of Latin America and

the United States. To name but a few: Roque Dalton, Ernesto Cardenal, Claribel Alegría, the incomparable living master Roberto Sosa of Honduras (we'd the pleasure of reading with), Jimmy Santiago Baca, Edgar Silex, devorah major, Victor Montejo, and on and on. Curbstone also brought out two important collections of Jack Hirschman's poetry (of the more than seventy-five books of poetry and translations Jack has written), *The Bottom Line* and *Endless Threshold*. Jack and I are each other's editors, a real inspiring labor! The superb political poet and dramatist James Scully, the editor of the important Art on the Line series with Curbstone, was instrumental early on in introducing us to the Curbstone "phenomenon." And we had the prideful joy of bringing the poetry of our comrade Luis Rodriguez to them: they published his book of poetry *The Concrete River* and then the "powerful, lyrical, brutal" memoir *Always Running: La Vida Loca: Gang Days in L.A.* And now just out another book of triumph, struggle, and revolution, *Each One Teach One* by Ronald Casanova, also a comrade and friend. From orphanage to homeless childhood in Harlem streets, through psychiatric torture and addiction, to the most basic necessitous organizing while living in Tomkins Square Park, resisting the brutal sweeps. Also the three-hundred-mile barefoot march of rags to the '89 Housing Now Rally in Washington D.C., organizing with the Union of the Homeless and the League of Revolutionaries for a New America, and wherever the poor and oppressed speak for themselves. These especially are some of the people, the writers, who have influenced and inspired me. As I write this, a terrifying and visionary novel about the Vietnam War and its aftermath, by our friend Scotland-born San Francisco writer John Mulligan, called *Shopping Cart Soldiers,* is forthcoming from Curbstone; I expect it will be well known by the time anyone reads this!

Both Jack's Curbstone books, and my second, were translated into Italian by the Italian poet Bruno Gulli, and published in beautiful bilingual editions by Raffaella Marzano and Sergio Iagulli of Multimedia Edizioni, in Salerno. Jack and I toured Italy together in 1994, my first sight of Europe. Something new but of the aftertaste of the *partisani* was particularly strong there, embodied by the many friends, the best of this generous, warm, and communicative culture: Sergio and Raffaella, dearest Sandro Spinazzi who facilitated Jack's first tour in 1993,

Maynard Menefee, San Francisco, 1995

Anna Lombardo, Mariella Setzu of Sardinia (translator of my chapbook *Questa Mano Peritura/This Perishable Hand*), and the incomparable working-class revolutionary poet Ferruccio Brugnaro. And again in 1995, back through Italy ("where all is close to Africa and always beginning," à la Pasolini), and also to London and Bristol for readings, and a week in Paris (decay in the midst of the artfulness of culture, the weight of it: "lifted shirts and withered stick-thighs pissing onto rue de St-Germain / high above a gargoyle bites off a living head"). The sense of the human everywhere, culture, both a wonder and a delight, and a burden, deeply familiar on some level yet strange and different. History everywhere, everything more conscious, including political polarization, class consciousness. Yet the same attacks on immigrants, the scapegoating, an upsurge of fascism, and mass organized resistance, thousands of people in the streets both protesting and striking against fascist political and economic policies. One could (a good way to pick up some of the language) read it in the graffiti on the old walls of Europe. "This is where capitalism was born," a

young writer and communist, Ivan Carlot, said to me, as he touched the Renaissance paving stones of a Venice piazza, "and here is where it dies, eating from the garbage. The buildings are *borghese*, but the light is *proletario!*"

In 1986, because of my interest in the question of homelessness, I was introduced to organizers from the National Union of the Homeless who were organizing a local in Los Angeles. Inspired, I began to go to food lines, shelters, and the streets, talking up the idea of founding a local here. The founding convention of the San Francisco Union of the Homeless took place in April of 1987, followed by a three-month shelter strike against abusive conditions in a local church- and city-funded shelter. "It's like we grabbed hold of a whirlwind," a homeless member later said of that period. The local union didn't survive as an entity, but the movement by necessity continued as conditions developed and worsened.

Since then I've participated in various organizations and activities, helped found a few. I was brought to trial in 1991, one of many hundreds arrested with the antihunger group

*Sarah Menefee and Jack Hirschman (photo taken by their close friend
Maria Letizia Gabriele), Padua, Italy, 1995*

Food Not Bombs, for feeding the homeless "without a license"; the charges were dropped on jury-selection day, after six months of legal harassment. I've taken part in numerous housing takeovers and organized squatting support with Homes Not Jails and others; protested the criminalization of poverty through "anti-lodging," panhandling, "loitering," camping, and other mean-hearted and illegal laws; led civil disobedience protests against the sweeps of homeless encampments at Civic Center Plaza and elsewhere; organized "visits" to two mayors and a HUD official's house (since they roust us where we live); and so on, all through the last half of the eighties and nineties. I've seen the inside of jails on numerous occasions, and this has been most instructive, frequently a part of my poetic imaging ("the one arrested with us

who cursed and howled for her confiscated bed was down at the curb in my dream singing so sweetly"). I am constantly inspired by the ability of those in the most dire and minimal circumstances to express themselves eloquently and poetically. I do not "speak for" anyone else, since that isn't necessary, but these heard voices echo through my work.

Two historical vortices at the beginning of this decade were the Oil War in the Persian Gulf (and the recent brutal repeat), the virtual-reality horror of the sheer tonnage of the bombings and their aftermath, the outburst of rage and protest ("a crowd of ten thousand that takes its own streets for peace is not a mob but a serpent with shining scales and mind of flaming Omega"), and the Los Angeles Uprising of 1992, with its explicit, all-color, spontaneous acts of reappropriation. "A vigorous running, a tray of diamonds I saw go by the old order's ashes. Oh let them appear on every young earlobe!" This especially signaled the need for more organization, consciousness, and collectivity: that has been the framework of the life as it goes forward, demanding the mutually educative. In 1993, the Communist Labor Party dissolved in order to reform into a more broad-based, nonsectarian organization capable of accommodating this developing objective process. In 1994 we adopted our present name, the League of Revolutionaries for a New America.

The poetry is intimately related to all of this, for me not so much by directly providing a "subject," as a constant attention and obsession that throws up its shards of dialogue, image, dream, and even "little scraps of back-talk gathered together." Emblematic of this historic reality, the formation of a new class out of the disintegration of old arrangements. The humor, patience, rage, and consciousness of those most affected, amidst the terrible conditions, as a fragmentary and halting suggestion of something new: "when everything cracks and crevices does fire and light come out?" The little utterances and scraps of scene or speech or drama are hard-pressed to contain this, but poetry, if anything, might try to.

October 1996

My friend Louise Vaughn, sharecroppers' daughter, public housing and antipolice brutality activist, poet of street agitation, said this month: "I have trouble hugging a tree when so many of my people have been the strange fruit hanging from one." I hear the echo of old Bertolt Brecht in her words. What my friends tell me keeps me a poet, receiving what I need to hear.

Recently in a dream I see from space the globe of the earth, the tactile topologies of its mountainous places. A rip or a gash, the Red Sea or the Persian Gulf, red like a wound and hot. Panning back, I see a series of worlds and heavenly bodies forming a double helix.

To have been given this drop of life, and poetry. . . .

BIBLIOGRAPHY

Poetry:

I'm Not Thousandfurs, Curbstone Press, 1986.

Please Keep My Word, Worm in the Rain Publications, 1991.

The Blood about the Heart, Curbstone Press, 1992.

Questa Mano Peritura/This Perishable Hand, Multimedia Edizioni, 1995.

Menefee's poetry appears in several anthologies, including *Poetry Like Bread: Poets of the Political Imagination,* Curbstone Press, 1994, *A Night at the Palace: A Benefit for Visual Aid,* in *Cups, a Café Journal* (San Francisco), 1994, *Would You Wear My Eyes? A Tribute to Bob Kaufman,* Bob Kaufman Collective, 1986, and *Beatitude 33: Silver Anniversary Edition,* in *Beatitude* (San Francisco), 1986. She also has contributed to numerous periodicals, including *Acts, American Poetry Review, Baltimore Sun, Beatitude, Channel, Collision, Compages, Conjunctions, Deluge, Erbafoglio, Exit Zero, Flit, Foot, Gas, Ink, Left Curve, Minotaur, Northern Contours, Oro Madre, People's Tribune, Poetry USA, Prosodia, Queen of Heaven, Real Fiction, Siren, Temper, Volition, Whispering Campaign, Working Classics, The World,* and *Worm in the Rain.*

Sheila E. Murphy

1951-

Sheila E. Murphy and her brother Tommy

Prior to my birth, my mother shaped the sounds of vocal music in classrooms and on stage. Six weeks before I was due, she gave birth to a three-pound, eight-ounce daughter who was all brown eyes.

My first several weeks were spent in an incubator under the care of Nurse Molnar at St. Joseph's Hospital in Mishawaka, Indiana, roughly ten miles from the University of Notre Dame. There, my father spent his whole career, first as professor of finance and later for some thirteen years as dean of the College of Business Administration.

I was a first child, initially frail due to my prematurity. My incubator time may have im-printed my experience of living on light and love from a remote source. To this day, I find institutions comfortable and comforting.

We lived out in the country on a few acres which allowed Mother to garden. In the yard were sour cherry trees and one sweet that I would climb. We had raspberries and strawber-ries. I caught butterflies, wore starched nylon dresses until my mother reluctantly purchased for me a pair of blue jeans with a little matching shirt. As the story goes, I refused to take them off, even on my way to sleep.

I was a serious child, surrounded by laugh-ter. These were post-war years. Most of my father's students at Notre Dame were his own

*Murphy with her parents Thomas T. and
Bernadean F. Murphy*

age. My parents entertained in the country house
we had on East McKinley Highway, formerly a
restaurant. In the long living room were sheer
curtains and fluffy white rugs and a Weber grand
piano that my parents bought before they had
another stick of furniture. My mother played
and sang. She'd grown up with a father whose
passion was the fiddle. My grandfather Bernard
Flynn (we children called him "Boo Boo") was
an ingenious and eccentric man who owned a
farm twenty miles south of Grand Rapids, Michigan. His wife, my grandmother, Cecilia Haley
Flynn ("Peetie" to us) was a sparkling and
magnetic presence who could make a person
feel more welcome than anyone I've ever met.
Her enthusiastic, trisyllabic "Oh-my-yes!" was happy
and musical and loving. She and my mother
had the same variety of green thumb.

We would visit Peetie and Boo Boo often.
I followed Boo Boo everywhere: Rode with
him on the tractor, walked with him through
the barn, and fractionally took part in doing
chores.

At age two, I announced to my parents
that I wanted a brother. Not a sister. One day,
I went to visit Peetie by myself while my brother
was being born. I remember being taken to a
restaurant in Kalamazoo by Peetie and Romaine
("Manie"), my mother's youngest of three sisters, who with her husband Ed lived with us
at the time. Manie and Peetie observed that
another little girl in the restaurant was kneel-
ing on her chair and that "Sheila would *never*
do that." I was formed that way, responsive to
praise.

I went home to find a glowing baby boy
so perfect looking in his crib that I reached
down to touch his pretty head. (His birth was
June in 1954.) My Uncle Ed said not to touch
the baby's head. I announced, "He's *my* brother.
I can touch him if I want."

With Tommy in the yard, I tossed toys into
the playpen. Because he could not talk, I didn't
know what else to do with him. We had another little brother come along some fifteen
months after, Cornelius Sean ("Neil"). He was
named after my father's cousin-brother Cornelius.
Neil was a little dose of rugby. Muscular and
independent and humorous, constantly loved.
Full of magnetic energy. Tommy was a prince.
I was in charge. Removed because of the mere
three years between Tommy and me.

I attended kindergarten at St. Mary's Campus School at St. Mary's College, the women's
college adjacent to the University of Notre Dame,
where Sister Teresa presided. My dad would
pick me up and take me to his office, where
his wonderful anchor of a secretary, Mrs.
Coleman, would preside. I loved all that paper, all those pens.

My father thought with his ears. He mim-
icked people all the time. He loved words. And
his Irish heritage made him tell stories more
than once. (He was second generation Irish,
both his parents having come from Castle-
townshend near Skibbereen in County Cork.)
Once, while we were driving to or from my
school, he made up a story about a little girl
named "Cities Service" (lifted from a gas-station
sign to complete his didactic exercise) who leaned
on her car door and fell out "and now her
father looks for her every Sunday."

First and second grades were located less
than a mile from our country home. Miss Cowan
and Mrs. Chapman, respectively, taught me those
grades. I learned to read and write like a champ,
and would rise early each morning to get a

head start on my books. Unlike any of my peers I've had the guts to ask, I have memories of loving books on Dick and Jane. The farm visits they made brought to mind the hay smells of my grandparents' farm. I had seen corn and horses . . . chickens . . . ducks swimming in the pond.

In 1959, when I was eight, we moved to Oak Ridge Drive in South Bend, a mile from the university, in a neighborhood called Wooded Estates. Where we had been secluded in the country, we were now glutted with a supply of families with children, all of whom descended on our yard at once. This was my mother's view. I was happy to be among children, having felt isolated in the country. Over the years at Oak Ridge Drive, I found myself coaching football rather angrily with neighbor kids. One rather formative comment made by my mother was, "Darling I will always love you, but others may not, so you must be nicer to them."

Daddy's father, Pop Murphy, visited us from Brookline, Massachusetts, every summer until he was no longer able. Pop Murphy had a sparkling personality and a temper that justified the adjective "Irish." He constantly played pranks on anyone who might fall for them, traipsing to the neighbor's house to make a phone call for one of us and then barking like a dog

A young Sheila Murphy with her second cousin Helen J. Keily

when we got on the phone. He taught me my colors on Mother's plastic clothes pins.

Unlike my previous three years of schooling, third grade with a particular nun was tense. One of the apparent motivations that my parents had for moving to South Bend was that my brothers and I would be able to attend St. Mary's Campus School, where I had gone to kindergarten. The rest of the school proved not to resemble the warmth of Sister Teresa's kindergarten. The nun who taught third grade had a reputation for being a terror. She routinely and with sadistic flourish would dump out people's desks all over the floor if she detected any hint of clutter. So I lived in trepidation that such a fate might befall me.

My father's Irish version of schmoozing was applied full force during this time in my life. If ever there was a man who loved to buddy around nuns, it was my father. They treated him like the king's cousin, and he loved it. The pattern was circular, and mutually feast-inducing.

So Sister X did not dump out my desk. I survived what would have been poisonous humiliation to my tender, serious, small soul. One day when I was much younger, still at the McKinley House, my mother saw me weep over a Christmas song and exclaimed, "Oh, my poor baby, you're just like me!" Any toughness added since has been of sheer necessity.

At age ten, in fifth grade, I became eligible to enroll in band. My mother and I conferred about my choice of an instrument. I think I harbored a hankering for brass, but we looked over the picture book and landed on the flute. My lips were perfect for it. It was considered a nice instrument for a zgirl. Despite that predictable coincidence, I've not regretted the choice.

My personality seemed tangible in flute playing. I was known for my performing, my improvisation, my obsession. I practiced maybe five or six hours a day, at no one's urging. I played with considerable force and a vibrato. I played better than I really was. The inconsistency was frightening.

I was given a great deal of encouragement for each of my interests, especially the music. Aside from my early discipleship of my grandfather Boo Boo, I earned his vote of confidence just by being a musician. The only people who counted, according to him, were musicians. Everyone else was merely tolerated. Whenever we visited the farm, someone would "persuade" Boo Boo to play the fiddle, and mother would accompany him on the out-of-tune upright piano. She played with intelligence, as did he. They seemed to share a sweet, spiritual kind of understanding.

I was very good in school. And very good in music. It was at around age ten that I also taught myself how to be popular. I worked at it methodically, recognizing early that "personality" was the master key that made most things possible.

My first experience with "speaking up for myself" occurred in seventh grade, when faced with another difficult nun who told what I considered a lie to the class. She asserted that public schools were terrible places where students were allowed to run wild all day and learned practically nothing. I raised my hand and stated that many of my neighborhood friends went to public schools and that my mother had taught in public schools. These places were not as Sister described them. She retorted, "Well, if you like them so much, why don't you go there?" I assured her, just as forcefully, that I would if I'd had any choice.

It was not until high school at St. Mary's Academy that learning came to life in a lasting way for me. Although I fought being separated from neighborhood friends who would go to the local public high school, St. Mary's was a splendid place for me. An all-girl, private (mostly day) school, the academy attracted outstanding teachers and intelligent young women, many of them university faculty children or the children of corporate officers.

Several teachers at the academy influenced me in important ways. Then Sister Miriam Edward, who taught French, taught me that my ear was flawless. She had the same quality and thankfully recognized it in me. Mrs. Syburg, head of English, taught excitement, humor, sense, and depth of human feeling in her class. She could tell a story gloriously.

Mrs. Walton was a Plath fan and instilled in us the love and magicality of the literary life. It became clear to me in high school that the people most uniformly revered were poets. There was a student in my class who was known to be a poet. It was understood that she was the resident genius. Above the rest, a junior member of the faculty.

Among the most heartening experiences in the still early part of my life were two: First,

upon graduation, I was awarded the Eleanor Perry Engels Award for the student "most alive to the world of ideas and the needs of others." The second was the outcome of the advanced placement test in English. Mrs. Walton had giftedly prepared us for this national exam by requiring us to read important works in several genres and write timed practice essays in response to questions we had just seen for the first time. On the day the scores were to arrive in the mail, I knew I needed a "3" (of "5") to test out of some college courses in English. I received a call from friends who received a "3" and a "4." Both of these friends were bright. I hoped for a "3." To my utter shock, I scored a "5." Only two in the class of eighteen or twenty achieved this: Myself and the acknowledged genius.

At around this time, I had begun to wonder whether I might not be highly intelligent. I sensed my ability to read with understanding. And more than anything, I wanted to write. I had begun to try to do so, secretly. In my room upstairs, late at night, when all the beautiful outdoor sounds or the comfortable heater sang its warmth to me. I was fearful of being found out. The work would inevitably be too personal. One night while staying over at Manie's, I scribbled a poem about snowflakes and inadvertently left it beside my bed. Manie found it, asked me if I'd written it, and I denied that I had, saying I'd just copied off something I'd remembered.

Later, during high school, I began submitting poems under a pseudonym. Luckily or not, I received an acceptance. My dad approached me about this, seeming interested. I shuffled and changed the subject.

In college, I continued this pattern, creating numerous pseudonyms while also using my own name. There was another student, an older male, who appeared also to do this. I've since conjectured that only two actual persons had written poems for the college's literary journal, which listed a string of literary-sounding and sophomoric-sounding appellations.

College began another chapter altogether. My parents, always protective, offered me two choices of colleges that I could attend: St. Mary's College or Nazareth College in Kalamazoo, Michigan, where Mother attended both high school (Nazareth Academy, a boarding school) and Nazareth College. Both were all-women's colleges at the time. Midway between my college career, two things happened. Nazareth became coeducational, and Notre Dame began admitting women.

Although, to all appearances, my choice between St. Mary's College and Nazareth was tipped in favor of the less fruitful selection, I required the privacy and independence that going away to school would provide. Nazareth had obviously changed rather dramatically between the time my mother was awarded her diploma "summa cum laude" at age nineteen and my arrival on the scene in 1969. The Vietnam War was raging; dope was being smoked across the land, and beer flowed. Some of the girls enrolled were "problem" girls. The era also featured "sensitivity groups," which amounted to the mutual administration of an overdose of honesty that effectively killed spirits galore.

In classes, I excelled, double majoring in music and English, with a hefty dose of performance in my flute minor and nearly a minor in philosophy, as well. When I took my comprehensives for the English major in my junior year, the then department head remarked, "Sheila Murphy's way up here somewhere, and then there are the rest of us." I sailed through the required essays. Still wanting to write. Still locked up tight.

I was "in" everything musical: Madrigals, chorus, small ensemble, and a trio of flute, oboe, and clarinet. True to my era, I concurrently maintained a full-time partying schedule with my wild friends. The double life was tiring.

My senior year saw a major flute recital with a Bach, a Mozart, a Hindemith, plus a work I wrote for flute alone with dancer. My family and hometown friends, as well as school friends, were there in droves to support me. My flute teacher was a socially clumsy, dry man, in stark contrast to the teacher I had had since seventh grade in South Bend, Mr. Opperman. This college teacher lacked the verve and passion Mr. Opperman possessed. I could not help feeling that the celebration would have had more punch had Mr. Opperman been my guide. Regardless, the event went off, with me in my brightly colored, Hawaiian floor-length dress, and hoards of enthusiastic friends and family.

Midway through that year, I received news of having been awarded a Michigan College Fellowship to pursue graduate study in English at the University of Michigan. In Ann Arbor, where mother, too, had received her master's

Murphy with her brothers Tommy (center) and Neil

degree, I felt very well equipped academically, but definitely out of touch with myself. The "overcelebration" syndrome was in full flower, continuing the dual life of academic prowess and escape.

While at Michigan, I realized that I needed a break before going on for the doctorate, which I would surely do. My parents helped me write letters to community and junior colleges, seeking a faculty position. I remember my father's wonderfully uplifting words about job seeking: "You only need one!"

I did find one. In a little community college in the upper peninsula of Michigan. I was twenty-three and taught English brilliantly, as if by nature. Two weeks into the job, I suffered a car accident that put me out of commission for two weeks. My parents came up to stay with me. I had a severe concussion and had broken my clavicle. Upon return to teaching, I resumed a life that felt too quiet and secluded for my twenty-three-year-old sensibilities.

My dean who had hired me was preparing to retire after my second year at the college. He treated me as though I were his daughter. He helped me secure a fellowship in educational administration and supervision, emphasizing community education, saying: "You could stay on here forever, but I think you need to pursue a doctorate. You have much greater potential." I followed through and secured a full ride for the first year of a program at Arizona State University (ASU) in Tempe, Arizona. I moved to Arizona, first living in a small student apartment in a high rise near campus.

During my first week of class, I found myself in three of four classes with a woman then named Beverly Pergeau (now Carver, her own name), who was herself a school professional and a graduate of Harvard Graduate School of Education, returning to ASU for her doctorate. Bev was in the process of ending a very difficult marriage of seventeen years. She and I participated in the same work groups in class and paired up on assigned collaborations.

I would frequently go out to Bev's house on what was called The Ranch in then North Scottsdale. She served sparkling cider and "gorp" (Virginia peanuts, slivered almonds, shaved coconuts, and raisins). She treated me like a princess. Time passed in the program. We became close. Beverly played the piano, had practiced dutifully, methodically, and generally vigorously. Her touch was as sheer and light-graced as my mother's curtains.

One day, en route to a school-related retreat in Apache Junction, Arizona (Bev was driving the white Monte Carlo) I read her a poem that began, "We nurture frames of silk. . . ." She listened very carefully, then shared a couple of adjustments she would recommend. We worked together on the piece while she drove. The poem improved. I learned. Bev was a gifted teacher who had been watched by teachers from all over the country. Apparently, her lack of previous study in poetry per se made little difference. Where I could see and hear nuances of inflection, she perceived structure brilliantly. Her mind was gorgeously organized, and she had honed that organization over years of meticulous, disciplined practice. This exercise proved a natural extension of our writing papers together for university courses, seemingly without effort.

As the second of our school years was drawing to a close, my living situation was about to change. Bev invited me to come and live with her. Following the divorce, her daughter planned to live for a time with her father and his new wife.

In May of 1978, I moved in with Bev to a house on East Camelback Road, several miles south of her home on The Ranch. We had a swimming pool in back and plenty of room. More furniture than we could use, with the move from a huge home to a still good-sized but less spacious one.

At some point, perhaps even incidentally, I shared with Bev that my friend from northern Michigan, poet and social researcher John Beck, had told me about a small press that would consider eleven-page chapbooks in poetry. I told Bev that I had pages and pages of fragments, but nothing finished. The bottom line was that I didn't know how to finish poems. She asked to see them. I brought them out, and we worked at the white kitchen table, with Bev coaching me toward completion of the poems.

John had begun to send his poems to literary magazines. This was new to me. To this point, we'd spent hours on the phone, introducing to each other the works of various poets. I would follow up, and we would talk again, with mutual references to top-flight books.

John one day mentioned a magazine called *Salt Lick* that was listed in the *International Directory.* The idea, he said, was that "this guy will send you back great stuff, even if he doesn't take the poems."

I sent (for the first time since my incognita appearance in an early woman's magazine). Jim Haining wrote back: "Like these poems enough to print." Haining, the editor in Quincy, Illinois, took "The Mail" and "Solipsism." Then mentioned that I ought to send him more. He liked to print a good-sized gathering, rather than snippets of an author's work.

This occurred in November 1978. Bev bought me a rose and a little card about being published, here's to many more, etc. I was twenty-seven.

The timing could not have been more perfect. The factors connected with this (learning the craft/completing a poem/then having a poem accepted) fueled me for many blessed hours of productive activity in poetry.

I would sit at my manual upright typewriter that Dad had bought from the university when I was in high school. I would churn out poems as best I could. Although I'd tried to do this for literally years, I felt suddenly fluent for the first time.

Jim Haining's *Salt Lick*/Lucky Heart Books represented a tremendous publishing effort, offering work by Gerald Burns, Michael Lally, David Searcy, and others. Yours truly didn't even know at the time how deliciously flukey this success was.

I sent poems to other places and enjoyed additional success. Something had started for me that felt more right than any previous endeavor. It seemed that anything might be possible in poetry, and on my own terms.

My earliest poems were direct and fresh and plain spoken, often reflective and philosophical. The accessibility of such early works as "Eucalyptus" gave them broad acceptance and helped bolster my confidence about learning and creating.

What felt strange to me, both at the time, and later in retrospect, was the degree to which some editors like Jim could see ahead. The few pieces of mine that he saw so early would not have given enough clues to most people, certainly not to me. That sort of perspicacity earned such individuals the title "editor." The challenge, of course, involved their seeing before I could distinguish what was working and what was not. In a haze of prolificity, I tried to spin straw to gold.

In September 1979, we moved to a condominium on East Monterosa Street in Phoenix. Newly converted from an apartment dwelling, this was a cozy place quite near most things we needed to reach. The poem "Rosie" came from the direct experience of having the previous tenant walk through apartment #5 with a realtor.

At around this time, Bev persuaded me to attend a poetry reading at the Phoenix Public Library. I had never read a poem aloud before. It turned out to be an important thing to do for learning, listening to others, and for becoming part of the writing community. The poet David Chorlton, also a gifted visual artist, was active in the community. He promoted my participation and invited me to read in numerous programs, sometimes including flute music in performances of works by him.

Bev and I likewise went to hear Will Inman read. Neither of us had ever heard of him. Bev encouraged me to write to him. I did. He wrote back, fierce at first, and later generous, eager to respond and advise, always fiery.

Correspondence became a huge part of my life. So did submitting poems to magazines. I wrote a great deal, sent a great deal. Bev produced a system for me that I have consistently maintained, noting where and when poems were sent, accepted for publication, according to dates and places, and copies of accepted poems.

Early in my reading/writing career, I was attracted to the writing of Heather McHugh. I learned that she was to be teaching at the Aspen Writers' Workshop. Bev insisted that I go for the two weeks. It is the only such workshop I ever attended. Heather turned out to be a brilliant reader and discoverer/opener of text. She was energizing and encouraged me, declaring that I had both the intelligence and the music. Delicious words to hear.

The living arrangements involved four-person apartments. I stayed with Myra Shapiro, Joyce Richardson, and Gail White. The two weeks were splendid. I found the time inspiring. My friendship with Myra was the most lasting and valuable result of the time there.

In late 1980, Bev and I received our Ph.D. degrees from ASU. Our postal carrier at the time, named Mel, ceremoniously came to the door and presented our diplomas, calling us "the two doctors." We actually did go through the official ceremony in December, but this informal one most touched us.

Three weeks later, I was working a full-time position with the international headquarters of a large hotel chain headquartered in Phoenix. During my twenties, I had worked at my father's hotel under the same brand name, which he and several partners built as an investment. This had provided me substantial background in hotel work. That experience, combined with college teaching and a new Ph.D. degree in educational management and leadership, made me marketable, apparently.

I was hired by and reported to a very strangely charismatic older woman who was pushy and wanted to be part of everybody's life. The job involved presenting training programs to general managers who came to our training center from places all over the world, although primarily from the United States. For all this woman's faults, she could dazzle a group short term. I learned.

My life came to comprise a wonderful mixture of strong, professional accomplishments in what I call "earnings work" and a virtually constant engagement with the writing of poetry. I have always spoken of poetry as a full-time professional commitment living in juxtaposition to my earnings-related profession.

After several years of acceptances in magazines that favored accessible, discovery-laden, human poems, I was attracted to a sequence in *Sulfur* called "Six Haibun" by John Ashbery, whom I had read extensively for years. Something about the style of those pieces attracted me in a profound way. I had the urge to try one.

At the very least, this style was addictive to me. I read many segments of the anthology of Japanese work *From the Country of Eight Islands,* finding the translated pieces somewhat thin. Ashbery's own fluency and combination of casualness and word love ripened my taste. I wrote haibun. These alienated several magazine editors and publishers who found them vastly different from what I had been doing.

My fondness for forms extended to the pantoum, which attracted me greatly and which I used frequently during the mid-1980s. In addition, I was attracted to the ghazal. I also found myself fond of designating a particular pattern, then using that throughout a complete work.

Over the years, I had been submitting to *Stride Magazine* in England, published by Rupert Loydell's Stride Publications. Rupert seemed to like especially my haibun and asked if I would like to do a book. I agreed and sent him fifty-eight haibun, which took on the title *With House Silence*. Published in 1987, this book was artistically rendered by Rupert, a significant visual artist and poet in his own right. He presented the poems in a landscape format and used a subtle brown and gold visual on the cover, with a good deal of white space.

To this point, I had published only chapbooks, so *With House Silence* represented an important milestone for my poetry. The response to *With House Silence* was extremely positive. Gerald Burns for years called it my best book. Many people I've encountered since its publication have been aware of the book and have expressed appreciation of what it does.

My job at some point began to require travel. The benefit in this was of course a series of nights that I kept quiet and wrote. I literally hoarded time to myself when on the road.

Working for a corporation allowed me to forget all about my fears connected with survival. I knew that my material needs would be met. I would carve out time to write, generally every night and many hours on weekends.

I also taught myself a technique that I used many times at professional conferences. I would sit and take in the presentation while writing a new text, often incorporating words from the talk into my text.

I concluded over a period of years that, when it comes to time, there are at least two types of people. One craves time for creative output. Another lacks purpose, and therefore focus, and is looking to fill time with anything at all. For writers, the gift of time is the most precious. The slight intrigue that accompanies "found" or "stolen" time adds fuel to the poem-making process.

Early in my professional career, I had not learned to view my job and my writing in a proper balance. Perhaps due to the pushiness of my first boss, I felt like a guard always having to apply muscle to preserve my privacy and goals.

I later evolved into a soft, less feisty presence, who could ride political and other waves more skillfully. My corporate ability eventually came to the fore, but I always perceived that as a necessary although uninteresting pursuit required for security.

In 1985, I was appointed the director of the Training Division of my company. It was a high profile job. Our team brought the division to excellent heights. I was given extensive credit for these accomplishments, but no success was without struggle.

In 1987, I was promoted to vice president of an operating division of the company, based upon an executive board plan to relocate two operating centers from different cities to our headquarters. My task was to meld the two operations into a single center in Phoenix. My "people skills" were to be brought into play. Among the accomplishments of which I'm most proud is the communication and outplacement plan I orchestrated because it allowed the company simultaneously to grow the Phoenix site while gradually reducing both sites in the other city. Most importantly, I told all of the employees in person of plans that would affect them, making sure they knew before the press did. We placed more than 99 percent of the people in new jobs in the locations of their choice.

That same year, Bev Carver and I inaugurated the Scottsdale Center for the Arts Poetry Series, featuring wonderful visual art and excellent venues for a variety of performance types. Bev had the idea of our creating an opportunity for word art and visual art to interact. We developed a practice of commissioning poets to write in response to particular visual artwork that was included in specific traveling

Sheila Murphy, John Ferraro, and Beverly Carver, about 1982

exhibitions. We featured local and international writers alike. During the first ten years, we featured Marge Piercy, Richard Shelton, Steve McCaffery, David Miller, Tom Raworth, Alison Deming, Jane Miller, Gerald Burns, Gene Frumkin, John Tritica, Ai, Karen McCormack, Jimmy Santiago Baca, and a host of others. We are presently in our tenth season of presenting programs.

I was given two opportunities to appear at the Tucson Poetry Festival during the 1980s. On one of those occasions, Bev and I met bp nichol, only a few months before he died. It was a joy to be around his light, if briefly.

The publisher Clint Colby regularly and graciously invited us to his parties following the Tucson Festival. At some point, he expressed an interest in publishing work of mine. Upon receiving approval from my two brothers, I decided to share with him the gift I had given each of the boys on his thirty-sixth birthday. For Tommy, I created a thirty-six-page piece consisting of word clusters on each page that were numbered, in reverse order of month, day, year of his birth, 6-13-54. Clusters of fifty-four,

thirteen, and six words on each of thirty-six pages offered an opportunity for me to create this devotional kind of love poem. For Neil's book, I wrote "Letters to Neil," consisting of thirty-six pages of prose poems, each a letter of reminiscence and often admiration. The book is a gloriously rendered object, thanks to Clint's caring eye. The cover is a letter collage in wonderful colors showing the letters of the two names.

I have always loved the trusting, collaborative act of letting a publisher create cover art and a book design. I tend to be rather consistently surprised and delighted by what is done. I have sensed over the years a different and fully dimensional perspective of the work on the part of the designers. Something I would not have found or seen without a committed collaboration.

By 1988, it had become clear that my father was losing his mental faculties to Alzheimer's disease. Since his retirement, he and my mother had taken on a variety of scintillating projects, most involving exotic or at least adventurous travel. In the fall of 1988, Nazareth College invited me back to be awarded the Distinguished Alumna Award. The plan was that I would fly to South Bend and take my parents with me to the dinner. We did this. The afternoon before the award ceremony, while walking through the apple orchard behind the college, my father very jovially asked me who my parents were. It was a strangely piercing and eerie moment. I said, "You're my father, Daddy." He responded, "Oh, I don't think that's right." The next day he realized his error and brought it up. I dismissed it as nothing.

But at the dinner, Cornish game hen was served. We were seated with the college president and his wife, along with my dear professor Dr. Dorothy Smith, S.S.J. Dad was having a terrible struggle with the game hen, obviously not at all coordinated. Mother remained adamant about never putting Dad in a home, so she cared for him herself throughout the fourteen years before he passed away in October 1994.

When my father lost all of his mental faculties, my mother needed the support of at least one of her children. My parents relocated to Australia, at my brother Tommy's insistence, for the remainder of my father's life.

Dad's was the most advanced case of Alzheimer's I have ever seen. He simply refused for a long time to let go of his earthly life. My mother cared for him every minute of the day in their Sydney apartment at 6 Challis Avenue in Potts Point. En route back from Sydney in 1992, I wrote the long prose poem "6 Challis" that appeared in the British journal *And* and that will be reprinted in an issue of *Paper Radio* to be guest edited by Gerald Burns.

I visited my father one last time in January 1994, at which point he could still walk. By March, he had a severe stroke that no one believed he would survive. But he lived as a near vegetable in their Sydney home until October 16, 1994.

On that date I was in Minneapolis to present a lecture to the board of directors at the Minnesota Center for Book Arts, for which Charles Alexander was then the executive director. On that particular night, I was at the home of Gary Sullivan and Marta Deiche, reading and talking. It was not until I returned home to Phoenix on Sunday that I learned my dad was gone.

I wrote a poem in Dad's honor that was printed and distributed as a remembrance at the Sacred Heart Basilica at Notre Dame. We had the body flown back, and Dad was buried at Notre Dame Cemetery, along Notre Dame Avenue. The turnout for the wake was abundant. The ceremony itself was dignified, as Dad would have wanted. And the feast that followed at the Notre Dame faculty Club was a celebration of Dad's life.

Another piece in the 1989 period was the book that began as *18/81* and evolved into *Pure Mental Breath* when it saw print with Nicholas Power's Gesture Press in Toronto. The book is a beautiful collaboration of my text with artwork by the gifted photographer Blaine Spiegel. Working with Nick Power showed me a Zen value connected with pacing and nature. The book took years to come to fruition as a product. Throughout that process, I never doubted the value of waiting, and never felt a moment of impatience, despite my generally impatient nature. In writing, there is always plenty of work to be done, which precludes the need to bird-dog individual projects, which would only seem to sabotage them anyway. Working in conjunction with Beth and Joy Learn and others, Nick invited me to a festival in October 1994, at which point the book was released.

The very weekend of the festival turned out to be the weekend of my father's funeral. I was able to attend for one night, sign books, and perform the reading. The most exciting aspect of the occasion was meeting Nick and Blaine, whom I instantly liked. Following that launch, I flew to Chicago and eventually to South Bend to participate in the funeral activities.

By the fall of 1989, my company was being purchased by two entities, a domestic organization and an international one, each purchasing the corresponding portion of the assets. My part of the company reported to the domestic firm, which wanted to promote me again and move me to New Jersey. Every fiber of me yearned to stay in Phoenix. After my declining their three substantial offers for three different jobs, including one in Phoenix, we agreed to part company. I was given a glowing letter of reference and severance pay.

I believe those who espouse a philosophy of "psychic geography," which, simplified, states that there are physical locations where one will feel balanced and be able to produce. In contrast, there are places with which one cannot easily resonate.

The Midwest had a dampening effect on my spirits, which seem to thrive on the kind of wattage that the Southwestern United States puts out. The candle power of Phoenix echoes the bright incubator light and my parents' collaborative prayer energy during my early years. The city literally shines. Its sunlight is a different color from that of California, where water melds with light to form a softer blue in the sky.

So I thought of everything I could to replace the income provided at the hotel company. I had learned to be security-minded, as this had worked for me in reducing anxiety and making poems. In the newspaper, I located an advertisement for a position called "director of business and management programs" for an adult-centered university in our local area.

My position at the university brought several lifelong friends, and I worked hard. But it was not professionally satisfying. During this extremely stressful period, I began to climb Squaw Peak (a little mountain about 1.2 miles high located about twelve minutes from my home) on a daily basis. At the beginning, I left the house as early as 4:30 a.m. during the hot season, and faced darkness and certainly less than perfectly safe circumstances. But there were many of us who did this, and there are still numerous people who do. This daily climbing greatly helped my mood and level of functioning. For a time, I climbed alone, greeting all the "regulars" I'd see each morning. Later, my dear friend Jayne and I would go together. I'd pick her up en route, and we would talk about everything possible during that approximately ninety minutes each day.

One thing that resulted from the walking was Jayne's idea to start an investment club. I have finance in my blood, with two financial professionals in my immediate family and a definite instinct for the field myself. Although I'd done serious investing in the past, I had neglected this pursuit for a number of years since.

Jayne's idea came to fruition and was a catalyst for leading me back into an area I find very stimulating. (I've often observed to people that my life runs counter to conventional practice: My dual profession involves literature and management consulting, while my hobby is making money through investing in the market.)

After three years at the university, I requested a separation on mutually agreeable terms. We parted company amicably, and I have since consulted for the organization on several occasions.

While in various positions at the hotel company, I did a good deal of article writing for professional journals, as well as a book through John Wiley & Sons, with Dr. Kenneth E. Carlisle, a consummate professional in performance engineering, design, and training.

At the university, the chairman of the board, another key executive, and I edited a book called *The Literature of Work: Short Stories, Essays, and Poems by Men and Women of Business.* The idea for the book received national attention. I was quoted on the front page of *The Wall Street Journal* and we were featured in the Business Section of the Sunday *New York Times* concerning the plan for the book. The book itself was very favorably reviewed, but less of a monetary success than it would have been had it not been released ahead of the recommended schedule from the newly inaugurated university press.

In 1990, Rob Fitterman invited me to read at the Ear Inn in New York City, a strong venue for the performance of innovative writing. Myra Shapiro had me as her guest in her West Village apartment. I read with Alan Davies. Great crowd, including Bruce Andrews, Charles Bernstein, Jackson MacLow, Hannah Weiner, Jena Osman, and others. Again in 1990 (November), I was invited by Lee Ann Brown to read with Katie Yates at St. Mark's. Bev and I both flew back to New York City. Myra graciously hosted us again. At this point, she and Harold had moved to the East Village and had created an astonishing palace of a penthouse apartment.

Myra, Janet Gray, Stacey Sollfrey, and Nico Vassilakis came to the reading. Great to be with all of them in person. I was touched. I regularly read/perform my work in places around Arizona and sometimes in other parts of the country. At one reading at the Loft Bookstore in Sedona, Mary Rising Higgins, our wonderful writer friend from Albuquerque, Bev, and I found several first editions of the work of Gertrude Stein. Bev immediately snatched them up and gave them to me for my birthday. We have been collecting anything that we could find of Stein's work ever since that point.

Another collection from this time was the chapbook *Obeli: 21 Contemplations*, comprised of twenty-one poems, seven words per line, inspired via correspondence and presented by Leonard Cirino and his Pygmy Forest Press.

Among the forms I developed for purposes of creating a style was based on the number nine, with eighty-one words per page of text, eighty-one pages in all. The work, *Teth,* was published by Charles Alexander's Chax Press in Tucson, Arizona, in 1991. The book-length poem was a dazzle of language that worked within the form I'd found for it. Teth, the ninth letter of the Hebrew alphabet, formalized, in a way, the introduction of my work to people engaged with language-based practices. I'd felt very encouraged, prior to that publication, to have the poet/scholar/presence Charles Bernstein enthuse over my work in front of University of Arizona and Tucson-area people who participated in an informal workshop by him, sponsored by Charles Alexander. Throughout my producing life, I have worked from light. The light of endorsement consistently fuels new work for me.

Nineteen ninety-one also brought *Sad Isn't the Color of the Dream,* my second collection from Stride Press. Rupert shared with me that some readers preferred a mixture of styles, which this book featured, in contrast to the single form present in *With House Silence.* Several poems I like very much appear in that collection, including two that appeared in Gil Ott's *Paper Air.* And "Falling in Love Falling in Love with You Syntax" remains a very readable/singable piece I like to include in readings. Karen Falkenstrom, director of the Tucson Poetry Festival, has continued to express interest in this poem, which means a great deal to me.

Collaborations have always been important to me. In one (possibly our first) Scottsdale Center commissioning program, Beverly and I jointly created an aleatoric piece called "6 x 6" after a sculptural work. Our piece was published in Stephen-Paul Martin's *Central Park #15.*

Bev and I have created other, shorter collaborative pieces while on trips. I have encouraged Bev to write work of her own. Of those that she has written, I have submitted nearly all. Friends joke that her acceptance ratio is very near perfect. jw curry at *Industrial Sabotage* has responded especially favorably to Bev's poems.

Other collaborators include Stacey Sollfrey, whose work John M. Bennett has collected in a duo-chapbook of ours. John Bennett and I have a long history of collaborations that consistently grows in interest. John's gifted use of language is always ahead of his time and a joy. We consistently maintain a volley of collaborative efforts across "snail mail." When pieces are completed, one of us fires them off to likely venues. Sometimes one or more of them appear in John's lively magazine *Lost and Found Times* from his Luna Bisonte Prods Press.

Megha Morganfield, a performer on the Celtic harp, and I were asked by David Chorlton to perform at the prestigious Stetter Gallery at the Biltmore Fashion Park in Phoenix. Our program seemed magical, given the blend of the instrument with my speaking voice, together with the words themselves, so we decided to capture that sound on audiotape. We recorded *The Weight and Feel of Harps* after my poem by the same name. Many of the pieces on the tape appeared in print in *A Clove of Gender,* my third book from Stride Publications, released in 1995.

In the spring of 1993, I was privileged to meet Jim Haining in person for the first time. He and I had corresponded for years, and in fact Jim was responsible for introducing me to Gerald Burns and his work. Gerald continues to be an important influence as a superbly qualified and intelligent reader, as a creator of poetry keenly sensitive to the ear, and as a dear friend.

Jim came to the Scottsdale Center for the Arts Poetry Series to create a work in response to a visual creation. By the time we first met, Jim had already been diagnosed with multiple sclerosis, which challenged his walking and general health. We had a wonderful couple of days together, during which he shared stories with me. We seemed to arrive effortlessly at a wonderful understanding during that time. We've both expressed our gratitude that this visit came about, given Jim's lack of mobility since that time. After a brief interlude in Portland, Oregon, Jim has returned to Texas and lives in Waco, where he receives some physical assistance in his daily life.

Within two weeks of Jim's visit, I made the decision to leave the university and go into practice as an independent management consultant. Although I did not know precisely how I'd make this happen, I proceeded. Given that I straddled the fence for several months regarding the possibility of taking another full-time job, I did some small share of agonizing. One interesting development was that a friend and colleague at the university advised me that a hotel school in Switzerland was looking for a dean. I made contact via fax, and very shortly thereafter received a call requesting that I travel there for an interview. I did so, finding that I had already been "checked out" through contacts at my hotel organization. The people wanted very badly to have me join the staff. The town in which the school was located was exquisite, with a view of Lake Geneva that most people would do anything to have. The Montreux Jazz Festival was located nearby. But the town was stiflingly small. It took me virtually no time to realize that the assignment would be 100 percent incompatible with my life. Anyone in the job would face constant scrutiny of nosy neighbors, and it seemed there would be virtually no breathing room at all.

I felt very strange during that few-day visit, knowing so suddenly what I would face: pressure from having to decline while realizing that the match would be all wrong. The visit and the experience taught me that it's critical, despite others' encouragement (reflective of their points of view), to honor one's own awareness about what is best for one's self.

Sheila E. Murphy at Squaw Peak in Phoenix, Arizona, about 1993

M y transition to the world of consulting has been a tremendously beneficial one, full of opportunity and variety and Renaissance possibilities. The greatest single benefit of working for one's self is the release from others' psychological concerns. Although I've been blessed to work with generally good people over the years, the very leash that ties an employee to an employer interferes with personal freedom and growth. When one has clients, the nature of the relationship is inherently liberating, as there are multiple points of negotiation and multiple opportunities. Most of all, one is able to learn from and use every assignment for growth purposes. This is far preferable to the relatively childish kind of structure that many organizations still foster.

In 1995, Rupert Loydell's Stride Press brought out my third book *A Clove of Gender,* which includes a number of subcollections previously appearing as chapbooks, notably *Informal Logic,* first appearing as a chapbook from A. L. Nielsen's press, and *Literal Ponds,* first brought out by Peter Ganick's *A.BACUS* from Potes & Poets Press. Peter has consistently shown interest and

support of what I do in my work. Our writing processes, prolific engagement with writing, and commitment have seemed quite compatible, as I've discovered through our correspondence. *A Brotherly Unfixed Grace-Noted Stare* recently appeared as a single author issue of *A.BACUS.*

One of the most exciting events associated with writing involves participation with editors, publishers, and other writers in the exploration of concepts and new projects. I continue to feel privileged to work with such editors as Matt Hill, who is presently completing production on *A Little Syncopy.* Matt contacted me as a result of his having worked with Peter Ganick and requested a manuscript. I sent him one particularly aimed at his press. The work will appear within a few weeks, as of this writing in November 1996. Other editors and publishers who have brought out chapbooks of mine include Tom Beckett, who just published my "Three Works" as *Way #2.* John Mingay presented a gathering called *Since We Last Met* through his Raunchland Publications in Scotland. I admire John's work, introduced to me through John's fine collaborations with Rupert Loydell. David Gonsalves, who published *Tin Wreath* for many years in an inexpensive and very readable format, offered a chapbook of my work. Tom Taylor and Jake Berry have published my work online and continue to be active and important presences. C. L. Champion in Tucson appeared out of the blue to create one of the most fascinating chapbook presentations of my work, featuring handmade covers drawn by crayon. Poems to my father in this gathering are set off beautifully on the basis of the fresh and youthful context. Leonard Cirino has done a great job of inspiring the very collection that he printed of mine: *Obeli: 21 Contemplations.* David Greisman, who publishes *Abbey,* a home for many writers who enjoy prolificity and communion, published an "Abbey Cheapo Chapbook" of mine called *Appropriate Behavior.* The cover photograph shows yours truly in a pink business suit (the photograph is black and white) standing circa 1986 before my 1974 Plymouth Duster, colored metallic green (I love bargains). Finally, my friend David Chorlton created *Virtuoso Bird* through his Brushfire Press, including photographs of his created for my written work, a treasure of an early publication.

My poetry has been anthologized in several wonderful publications that span a considerable spectrum of work types. Talisman House Press's *Primary Trouble,* edited by Leonard Schwartz, Joseph Donahue, and Edward Foster, included two pieces from *Pure Mental Breath* in the anthology. Rupert Loydell and David Miller used several of my haibun in *A Curious Architecture: A Selection of Contemporary Prose Poems.* Two other anthologies by Rupert Loydell (one solely edited by him and another co-edited with David Miller) featured my work: *Ladder to the Next Floor* and *How the Net Is Gripped: A Selection of Contemporary American Poetry.* Peter Ganick and Dennis Barone featured several of my prose works in *The Art of Practice: 45 Contemporary Poets.* Elinor Benedict, who served as the editor of *Passages North* for its initial ten years, included two of my works that first appeared in the magazine in *Passages North Anthology.*

When Douglas Messerli introduced the idea of creating the Gertrude Stein Awards in Innovative American Poetry, he contacted me to serve as one of the readers/locators of work appearing in periodicals over a year's period. I happily accepted his invitation and sent photocopies his way as he considered what to include in the first volume. I was delighted to have work of mine nominated and accepted for inclusion in the first two annual volumes, one of which appeared in 1995 and the other of which is scheduled to appear in the coming year.

Recently, I completed the draft of a manuscript for *Letters to Unfinished J,* a seventy-five-page book of individual "letters" actually consisting of prose poems. Beverly and I decided to invest numerous hours of editing and crafting into the piece, more than ever before, in an effort to perfect the work to the greatest extent possible. Previously, I had personally edited work repeatedly, then released it to the universe of editors and publishers and possibly included work in collections later on. Sometimes, Beverly would see a work of mine and offer advice and recommendations, which I invariably accepted and used.

In the case of *Letters,* we agreed that Bev would "have at" the manuscript, edit as necessary, discard whole poems as she saw fit, and re-sequence as appropriate. The length of the final book was arbitrary, and simply had to be right for the work itself. The process involves close independent reading and editing by Beverly, followed by our collaborative revision of her observations, followed by a final edit performed by both of us.

As of this writing, we are approaching the midpoint of this exciting task. In my estimation, the quality of the finished pieces far exceeds any work that I have done. Bev's perspicacity about what needs to be shelved into our "leftover" file is on target. We decided upon that modality initially on account of Bev's concern that good passages would otherwise be discarded. I assured her that we would make something from the discards, many of which seem to have life in them, though not a "fit" with these small systems.

Most of my days include approximately an hour of exercise at the health club as early in the morning as possible. Before the market opens, I review *Investor's Business Daily* and place buy or sell orders to take advantage of early-in-the-day price fluctuations. I then proceed to perform work of various types, either in my home office or at a client's site.

One working day is not the same as another. I may be producing lengthy documents, designing or delivering presentations for a group of public sector executives through Arizona State University, preparing an article with a client, or designing questionnaires for an evaluation project.

Some of my earnings work involves performance evaluation, which is frequently complex and requires numerous hours of study, interviewing of employees, model formulation, and the like. It is not uncommon for me to be welded to the computer for days at a time, churning out very large-scale reports. This past summer, working for a large state agency on a project for which my firm was awarded the bid, we produced approximately two thousand pages of material for the agency, much of it studded with factual information and perspectives.

I also allot considerable time for volunteer activities. In addition to the Scottsdale Center for the Arts Poetry Series, I serve on boards of directors for several community organizations, notably a nonprofit corporation that presents internationally known speakers to members and guests and is modeled on the Commonwealth Club in San Francisco. I'm on the board of a community leadership training program, offering executive-level, community-level, and youth-level programs every year. I'm on the credit union board, and serve as president of my neighborhood association board.

So my life of today in 1996 only slightly resembles that of 1978, when I first published poems and was still completing my doctoral degree. Nor does the present very closely resemble the recent past, when I was working as an executive within organizations. Everything I do now is of my own making, either solely or through partnerships.

The shape of my life now provides considerable opportunity for exploration, the relentless pursuit of learning, and the application of a range of capabilities. I feel privileged to live in a way that seems to provide enlightenment at every turn. There is much adventure, dearly cherished friends and family members, and abundance. The struggles that help shape my perception of myself and the world continue to be worth it.

Of the things I most like doing, poetry is at the very top of the list. But every life is a system, for which every other part contributes and within which all parts interrelate. I recognize that the consulting feeds the poetry, and the poetry feeds the possibility of enlighten-

ment. The early musical training has released its discipline onto the page and computer screen. I can learn from all directions and impart that learning in any number of ways.

Just as I did before birth, I now listen to music in the many forms in which it happens, often as conversation I am able to catch by accident, if there is any such thing, while riding on an airplane or a bus. And now that my eyes are forty-five years old, I can relish visual artwork while listening to the jazz that I so love. Flute sounds have shifted into human language.

I've often wondered what it is non-writers do. For everything I pursue naturally gravitates toward the act of writing, which provides the clearest set of signals leading where I am.

BIBLIOGRAPHY

Poetry:

With House Silence, Stride Press, 1987.

Sad Isn't the Color of the Dream, Stride Press, 1991.

Teth, Chax Press, 1991.

Tommy and Neil, Sun/Gemini Press, 1993.

Pure Mental Breath (with illustrations by Blaine Spiegel), Gesture Press, 1994.

A Clove of Gender, Stride Press, 1995.

Chapbooks:

Virtuoso Bird, Brushfire Press, 1981.

Late Summer, Pierian Press, 1984.

Appropriate Behavior, Abbey Press, 1986.

Memory Transposed into the Key of C, Mockersatz Press, 1986.

This Stem Much Stronger Than Your Spine, M.A.F. Press, 1987.

The Truth Right Now, Bakhtin's Wife Publications, 1988.

Loss Prevention Photograph, Some Pencils and a Memory Elastic, Tape Books, 1988.

Obeli: 21 Contemplations, Pygmy Forest Press, 1990.

(With John M. Bennett) *Lens Rolled in a Heart,* Etymon Press, 1991.

A Rich Timetable and Appendices, Luna Bisonte Prods, 1991.

Criteria for Being Touched, Experimental Press, 1991.

The Dessert Cart of Synecdoche, Trombone Press, 1992.

Literal Ponds, Potes & Poets Press, 1992.

Thoughtsongs, Tin Wreath Press, 1992.

Wind Topography, Standing Stones Press, 1992.

Virgule, Burning Llama Press, 1995.

(With John M. Bennett) *The Ghost of Parmenides,* anabasis, 1996.

Between Pipelines, NinthLab, 1996.

Since We Last Met, Raunchland Publications, 1996.

A Little Syncopy, Marshall Creek Press, 1996.

Other chapbooks include: *18/81* (excerpt from the book *Pure Mental Breath,* prior to publication by Gesture Press, Canada), 1991; *Informal Logic* (A. L. Nielsen); and *Three Works* in *Way #2,* edited by Tom Beckett (131 North Pearl Street, Kent, Ohio 44240), 1996.

Recordings:

(With Megha Morganfield) *The Weight and Feel of Harps* (audiocassette), Top of the Day Productions, 1994.

(With John M. Bennett) *Milky Floor* (audiocassette), Luna Bisonte Prods, 1996.

Other:

(With Kenneth E. Carlisle) *Practical Motivation Handbook,* John Wiley, 1986.

(Editor, with John G. Sperling and John D. Murphy) *The Literature of Work: Short Stories, Essays and Poems by Men and Women of Business,* The University of Phoenix Press, 1991.

Work has appeared in many anthologies, including *Passages North Anthology,* edited by Elinor Benedict, Milkweed Editions, 1990; *How the Net Is Gripped: A Selection of Contemporary American Poetry,* edited by David Miller and Rupert Loydell, Stride Press, 1992; *Ladder to the Next Floor,* edited by Rupert M. Loydell, University of Salzburg, 1993; *The Art of Practice: 45 Contemporary Poets,* edited by Peter Ganick and Dennis Barone, Potes & Poets Press. 1994; *The Gertrude Stein Awards in Innovative American Poetry 1993–1994,* edited by Douglas Messerli, Sun & Moon Press, 1995; *A Curious Architecture: A Selection of Contemporary Prose Poems,* edited by Rupert Loydell and David Miller, Stride Publications, 1996; and *Primary Trouble: An Anthology of Contemporary American Poetry,* edited by Leonard Schwartz, Joseph Donahue, and Edward Foster, Talisman House Press, 1996.

Work has also appeared in numerous magazines, including *A.BACUS, Aerial, American Letters & Commentary, Another Chicago Magazine, Avec, Blue Mesa Review, Bombay Gin, Cabaret Vert, Caliban, Chelsea, Generator, HOW(ever), Interstate, The New York Quarterly, O.Ars, Paintbrush, Paper Air, Passages North, Prism International, Puerto del Sol, Raddle Moon, Sequoia, Talisman,* and *Tyuonyi.*

Poetry performances:

Toronto, Ontario—Language Festival and Cabaret Vert Magazine.

New York City—The Ear Inn Poetry Series and St. Mark's Poetry Project.

Arizona—Tucson Poetry Festival, Cochise Fine Arts Poetry Center (Bisbee), Bisbee Poetry Festival, The Loft Reading Series (Sedona), Phoenix Arts Museum, Divergent Arts Poetry Series and Encanto Park Reading Series (both Phoenix), and Venus Coffeehouse (Tempe).

Albuquerque, New Mexico—Tangents Reading Series.

Stephen Schwartz

1948-

WHO AM I?

Allegorical portrait of Stephen Schwartz: The rail ferry Las Plumas, *San Francisco Bay, 1975*

Qui suis-je? Si par exception je m'en rapportais à un adage: en effet pourquoi tout ne reviendrait-pas à savoir qui je "hante"?

"Who am I? If on this occasion I were to avail myself of an adage, in effect why would not everything come down to knowing whom I 'haunt?'" With these words, André Breton began *Nadja,* one of the most important personal narratives of this century's literature, a book that has influenced me more than any save that other great personal accounting, Orwell's *Homage to Catalonia.* For me the question "Who am I?" resounds not only intellectually but practically, not only aesthetically but politically, for my life and career have caused many who encountered me to wonder who and what I am. I would say, paraphrasing Breton, that knowing who I am comes down to knowing who and what "haunts" me.

As with Breton, the word "haunts" bears, for me, a considerable weight of associations and allusions, based on the heritage, in English speech, of Anglo-Saxon, Celtic, and African spiritism. I remain haunted by oral and other memories of the rural landscapes, in Ohio

231

and Nebraska, where my parents originated, and by the park-like suburban forest of Mill Valley, California, where I grew up, and where, to quote a Nadja-like young woman of my acquaintance, "I played in the creeks." I remain haunted by my parents' radical leftism, by the sense of Mexico, distant, exotic, a refuge for my parents' associates; and then, by the allure of foreign tongues: Spanish, French, Russian, the Judeo-Spanish of the Sephardim, Catalan, Romanian, and more Balkan languages—some of which I studied seriously.

And by typography, newspapers, opera, and revolution. In poetry, some Latin Americans before the illumination represented by Ezra Pound and much derived from him; followed by Breton and all associated with him; afterward by Vergil, Mandelshtam, J. V. Foix and other Catalans (particularly Ausías March), Donne, Wyatt, Antonio Machado, and my friend Martin Camaj. And finally in "mysticism," through Spanish *kabbalah* and the Franciscans, to an understanding of people and places I love and have loved.

I was born in Columbus, Ohio, but my parents, who had been involved with the Communist Party—my mother, Eileene McKinney Schwartz, as a full member—moved shortly thereafter to San Francisco. My mother had been urged by her mentor, a prominent woman Communist named Anna Morgan, to take me and my brother, who my mother was then carrying in her womb, away from Ohio, where anti-Communist anger had, five months before I was born, led to an attack on the home of Frank Hashmall, leader of the Communist organization in Columbus and a family friend.

The Hashmall incident, about which I repeatedly heard as a child, bears examination, for it was one of the most disturbingly violent events in the history of American anti-Communism. It was reported throughout the United States; on March 30, 1948, a gang broke into Hashmall's house, in his absence, and wrecked it. According to the Associated Press, a crowd of up to 400 people cheered as a group of fifty men broke windows and smashed furniture in two raids. After the second assault, forty police officers arrived but by then the house was empty; nonetheless, they read the riot act to the crowd, who remained on the sidewalk.

The next day Hashmall, described as a twenty-eight-year-old college student who had arrived

from New York only two weeks before, moved out of his house, with his wife Sylvia and eight-month-old child, Paula, and went into hiding. A fuller account of the incident noted that the Columbus papers had published his home telephone number and that two men had come to his door and started a fight. Between the first and second sorties into his house, a police squad car had briefly dispersed the rioters. But when asked if his officers would follow through in protecting Hashmall's family, Columbus police chief Charles M. Berry declared, "There will be no special police protection for this antireligious group in this city."

The day after that Gus Hall, chairman of the Ohio state Communist Party (and later head of the party nationally) announced that a suit would be filed against the *Columbus Citizen,* a Scripps-Howard daily tabloid charged with inciting the attack, and the Franklin County authorities.

That pretty much decided things for my parents, who were, indeed, quite antireligious! Others from the same Columbus group of Communists and "fellow-travellers" fled to Los Angeles, but in any case the direction was westward to the Pacific. My father, Horace Schwartz, a classical musician by training, was also involved in "little magazine" circles, and was drawn to the Bay Area by the activity of poets like Kenneth Rexroth. Once on the West Coast, my father and mother became well known in the pre-Beat literary scene; my father published *Goad,* a poetry review with contributions by Lawrence Ferlinghetti, Robert Creeley, and many others, and he collaborated with the experimental musician Harry Partch. Henry Miller and the poet Philip Lamantia were often mentioned in our household.

Music is important in these recollections. In 1982, in New York, I attended the Metropolitan Opera for the first time and saw the great Finnish basso Martti Talvela sing, in Russian, Mussorgsky's *Boris Godunov.* Talvela *was* Boris, in a performance of the original Mussorgsky score, without the baroque trimmings later tacked on by Rimsky-Korsakov. I understood much of the Russian, having studied the language for twenty years, at first with the intent of reading Lenin in the original. Watching Talvela as the mad usurper-tsar I had a sudden insight into my own fascination with Communism. I had sung (soprano) in the San Francisco Boys' Chorus, and as a child was taken at least once, perhaps twice, by my father to see *Boris,* and at home I listened to a recording of it (with Boris Christoff) incessantly. I cannot say whether I identified more with the martyred child-tsar Dmitri, or with the "false Dmitri" whose messianic movement brought Tsar Boris disaster, or with the magnificent coronation scene that begins the work, with its grand fanfare of church bells. But there at the Met, aged thirty-three, I first saw the childish character of fantasies to which I gave much of my life.

My parents' leftism was of another order entirely; they were Depression children, each bullied as the smartest in their tiny towns. In the place my father was born, Superior, Nebraska, his was the only Jewish family. They didn't know what a Jew was in Superior, he once told me, until his father started selling tires at half-price. My father entered Bellefaire, a Jewish orphanage in Cleveland, Ohio, with (as I found out only much, much later) a reputation for handling "disturbed" children, when he was thirteen, and he there encountered Communism. A decade afterward, a friend of his from Bellefaire introduced him to my mother, whom the friend had recruited into the C.P.

My mother came from a "native," American radical background, in the coal hills of West Virginia. At nineteen she sold the *Daily Worker* in the slum streets of Ohio industrial cities. She had grown up in an environment that mixed Christian pietism with labor and socialist militance. Her father, Delbert McKinney, an ironworker and member of the bomb-throwing Structural Iron Workers' and Bridge Builders' Union, well acquainted with the revolutionary doctrines of his time, preached the gospel of Jesus with a dozen clean, folded handkerchiefs in his suit pockets; not because, as I imagined, he would sweat while testifying in dirt-floor churches, but because, as my grandmother once told me, when he spoke of Jesus he cried. And yet my grandfather McKinney was a Semitophile, a lover of the Hebrews and of the Old Testament, which helped guide my mother to her marriage to a Jew. Much, much later, my mother converted to Judaism, but I was left a split being, half-Jewish (the "wrong" half) in origin, half-Christian in spirit. It is a conundrum with which I still wrestle.

My mother, who considered herself a feminist, never forgot the moment in 1936 when, in a tiny movie house in an Ohio River town, she saw a newsreel of women fighting in the Spanish Civil War, of women armed and battling against fascism in the streets. She remained fixated on the Spanish conflict for many years after and passed the obsession on to me. My parents listened avidly to the music of Shostakovich and Prokofiev, watched such films as *The Grapes of Wrath* and *Treasure of the Sierra Madre* (the latter considered a great underground leftist "message" movie in its time), and read the poetry of Bertolt Brecht and the English radical poets Stephen Spender and W. H. Auden. I was named for Spender, although Ferlinghetti later wrote mistakenly that I was of a generation that named children for the Joycean Stephen Dedalus.

It may seem this narrative is heavy with dropped names, yet none are mentioned gratuitously or fraudulently. I was rather like Michel Leiris, the younger French surrealist, in that my family's affiliations facilitated my entry into the literary left; his father, Eugène Leiris, had been an attorney for Raymond Roussel and other avant-garde figures in the Paris of that time.

Before our occidental migration, my father had scandalized his contemporaries, above all Creeley, whom he knew well, and Charles Olson, by his assertion that the works of Ezra Pound, who had just received the Bollingen Prize, were worthless. Pound's Bollingen was the most controversial issue for literary debate in the years immediately after World War II, with the Communists, and many Jewish intellectuals, condemning him for the anti-Semitism and fascism that led him to collaborate with Mussolini. The right seemed to remain silent on the Pound affair, with his defense largely carried by liberal intellectuals who sought the freedom of literature from political criteria; paradoxically, Pound was the first poet in whose work I found a usable standard for achievement.

My mother played "folk music" of the Communist-cabaret variety, made famous by Woody Guthrie, painted abstractly, and created homemade books for me and my brother Geoffrey, who came into life in San Francisco in 1951. The Bay Area in those days was a sanctuary of the "fellow-travelling" left, a kind of Mexico here at home, where even after the paroxysms of Stalin's last years, including the Korean War, the left as my parents understood it retained considerable support. Nevertheless, the persecution of Communists was not unknown in northern California; Carol Asch, wife of the ex-Communist author Nathan Asch, who lived near us in Marin County, was barred from government employment after a long and traumatic ordeal in which my parents also suffered, for Carol and Nathan were their dearest friends. My father was fascinated by Nathan, son of the Yiddish writer Sholem Asch, and brother of the musicologist Moe Asch, founder of Folkways Records and another hero of my parents.

My parents were unorthodox in their radicalism. They drifted, sometimes with the Communists and their sympathizers, sometimes cleaving to the anarchist fringe of San Francisco poets and artists. Rexroth maintained a "libertarian" salon that attracted most of the really promising new writers in the Bay Area at that time, including Lamantia and Robert Duncan. These two, as well as Rexroth himself, had been conscientious objectors during World War II. The enterprise that became the City Lights Pocket Book Shop had been "hatched," I was told, in my parents' kitchen, in a discussion between Ferling (as he then called himself) and Peter Martin, the natural son of the murdered Italian American anarchist Carlo Tresca. Another family linked to ours by orientation and character, as well as affection, was that of Pete diBernardi, a comrade of Tresca and a veteran of the Industrial Workers of the World, or "Wobblies." The diBernardis were our neighbors during a brief residence in Sunnyvale, California, but Margaret diBernardi, the matriarch, remained my mother's close friend. I remember Sunnyvale, where I was five and six years old, as the place where I first felt sexual yearnings, and first experienced certain recurrent dreams. It was only in 1996, more than forty years later, that I learned Pete diBernardi had been more than a rank-and-file Wobbly; he had been convicted of "criminal syndicalism" in a mass trial at Sacramento and imprisoned in Leavenworth Penitentiary, in the great California anti-IWW suppression of 1919–1920, and had nearly died behind bars.

A friend of my parents among the Communist group was the writer George Hitchcock (mentor of Maya Angelou), who some years after serving as state Communist Party educational director became briefly famous for baiting the House Committee on Un-American Activities by declaring to them that he worked "in the underground, with plants." He earned his living as a landscape gardener.

My parents' outlook warped in the late '50s. They moved from a somewhat reticent, "post-McCarthy" affirmation of the old-time "fellow-travelling" religion to a more unpredictable set of intellectual coordinates. My mother read Orwell, always a bad sign for an ex-Communist. My father, strangely enough, developed a more political and, intermittently, a more enthusiastic view of Communism. In the earlier part of the '50s, pressed by the rise of anti-Communism, he had held a faith in the practical perfectibility of society that was secondary, by much, to his belief in the cultural values of the left. That is, he accepted the moral claims of the left regarding the need for a more rational organization of society, without necessarily believing that such a society could be quickly attained by political ends. But the launching of the first *Sputnik* and the new Soviet rhetoric of the Khrushchev period seemed to prove to my father the superiority of Russian over American society, and his views changed. He began to see the left in triumphalist, authoritarian terms, as a global force that would sweep away American "decadence." He became an admirer of Nasser and Castro, and in the early '60s, when I was thirteen and fourteen, he began, for the first time in at least ten years, to attend leftist meetings and demonstrations. He became less tolerant and more convinced as each day passed.

I knew, somewhere in my consciousness, that my father was particularly susceptible to extremism; my mother told me he had planned to shoot Joseph McCarthy if the senator ever came to San Francisco. But thirty years would go by until, at forty-three, I came to understand that this "rebirth" was neither ideological nor spiritual, as I believed it to be, but pathological, an expression of the mental disorder we now call "bipolar syndrome," aggravated by his own harsh childhood, and which, untreated, led him to a final disintegration, and suicide, in 1992.

I owe two things, above all, to my parents: my knowledge of classical music, which I received from my father, and my love of books, inherited from both of them. My parents encouraged me to read almost without limits. As I recall, they objected only to Ayn Rand, whom they considered too reactionary, and for that and other reasons I concealed my reading of anti-Communist writings such as Whittaker Chambers' *Witness*. But the works of Henry Miller, their friend, were given to me when I was twelve—not in the interest of experimental sex education but in the belief that literature was sacred. For them, Miller was the possessor of a great mind, not a purveyor of dirty stories. By fourteen, I had also read, and reread, Nabokov's *Lolita,* in a similar spirit. And it was then, in 1962, that I made a dual promise to myself: to become a writer, and to pursue rebellion against the America that surrounded me.

I had not, in reality, been a happy or fulfilled child, and my self-identification as a "red diaper baby"—i.e., the publicly admitted child of a Communist family—was not simply a product of parental guidance. Indeed, my parents' style of "fellow-travelling" was enough out of the ordinary that I sometimes think the term "red diaper baby" was a misnomer, at the very least, in my case. But I was a misfit in the suburban paradise of Marin, although in the mind's eye it remains The Park, an idyllic past landscape. (One neighborhood in Mill Valley was known as "the Little Kremlin" because of the number of famous Communists who lived there.) As I grew toward adolescence I felt at odds with everything in my world; my only comforts were music, reading—mostly poetry, and fetishistic experiments about which I am not yet prepared to express myself. I also went fishing in those creeks.

Thanks to my mother, I began reading Brecht at fourteen, soon after Nabokov. The German poet's work was certainly capable of educating a young mind in twentieth-century aesthetics; his fascination with Asian models, and his spare, alienated style, hypnotized me, as did his cynical and fanatical attachment to the Communist Party. The student movement had already emerged in Berkeley, demonstrations were going on in defense of Castro's Cuba, and the Communist Party launched a new youth organization in the Bay Area, the W. E. B. DuBois Clubs. My family moved, after a brief stay in Tucson, to San Francisco, and I joined the DuBois Club there. Filled with a belief in my destiny as a poet and Communist, mesmerized by the example of the heartless Bertolt, I, like my mother twenty years before, went out in the streets to sell Communist newspapers.

I remained intensely lonely. My distance from my peers, who were listening to the Beatles while I was reading Liu Shao-chi's *How to Be a Good Communist,* reinforced a personal coldness. I had few friends and no girl (or boy) friends.

I was unprepared to face the option of becoming homosexual, although my fantasies tended to run in both directions (still, I mainly looked at and thought about girls). I was good at selling the Communist press, which brought appreciation from the party leaders, because my voice was inordinately loud (a characteristic with which I was born and which, although occasionally useful, has more often been criticized—yet there is no release from such a gift). I even made a respectable, if small, income from selling Communist papers. I attended DuBois Club meetings religiously (an appropriate descriptive!) in an old storefront hall in San Francisco's Fillmore District, a Black ghetto. My parents were anxious about that, but I never felt threatened.

I continued listening to the music we called "folk"—Pete Seeger and Woody Guthrie and their cabaret imitators, for whom I later developed a pretty considerable distaste. I read John Steinbeck's *In Dubious Battle,* an account of a California farm strike in which Communist organizers were portrayed as such heroes that some party critics rejected its mythopoeic verities as too sentimental and corny to be useful in the struggle. But I was hooked. I later looked back on the affectations of those days as strangely recapitulating, among Bay Area teenagers, the cowboy-and-Indian culture of the American West. Rock 'n' roll was not yet on the radical agenda; Bob Dylan, the epitome of cabaret folk and yet to be heard on commercial radio, was popular among DuBois Clubbers, with his evocations of "the north country," "boots of Spanish leather," and other "Red Western" themes. We young Communists picked our acoustic guitars, wore cowboy boots and bandanas, read about the Rocky Mountain miners, and spoke lovingly of Mexico, with its revolutionary past. We dreamed of working on the railroad or going to sea, as if somehow, with a wish, we could step back to a frontier where Wobblies like Pete diBernardi so profoundly challenged society.

Mine was a different radicalism from my parents' and equally distinct from that which came after. I believed a life like that of a social worker, spending one's days organizing on skid rows or in a rank-and-file union job, offered a magnificent vocation.

And yet I still read poetry, and, after some breakthroughs with girls, and the acquisition of some real friends (and even, because of my energetic public radicalism, some admir-

Railroad worker, Oakland, 1975

ers), I encountered Pound. These aspects of my youth coincided in time, but also as symptoms of a struggle to push through the crust of Communist conditioning. Pound's fascism made his verse and essays still an unspeakable topic among American Communists, although to my great amazement I found he was highly praised by Hugh MacDiarmid, a Scots Communist poet. I had gone through a year at a Communist training school, its sessions held at night, called the San Francisco School for Social Science. I had even, at sixteen, directed its "extension" into Marin County, where I had the weird experience of listening to some very, very lovely children of the suburbs as they wrestled with such concepts as "price-fixing," instructed in Marxist economics by a sincere and generally warm woman graduate student (in an authentic field of academic study) from Berkeley.

But I was now, also, writing poetry myself; my chief model remained the cold, articulate, ugly Brecht. To emphasize, my feelings, long hidden behind a mask as rigid as any in the Japanese theatre, had begun breaking through.

I sought love, as I still seek it, and I worked my way through florid Latin American and French Communist poets. Many of the Latin Americans, such as the famous Pablo Neruda, I found tedious (when, years later, I learned that Neruda had been a KGB agent, involved in the assassination of Trotsky, I was somehow unsurprised). But the cultural ethos of Hispanic and French Communism was utterly different from that of American Communists and "fellow-travellers": instead of Pete Seeger, the Latin Americans looked to Federico García Lorca (who was not even a leftist, notwithstanding his assassination by fascists), and the French to Picasso; and the "poetic politics" of the Latin left made one feel one's self to be a *comrade* to García Lorca or Picasso.

I plunged myself into the study of Spanish and French literature (having been tutored in French as a child), interests that became semi-professional as the years went by and I mastered the former language. I later learned Catalan, spoken in the Barcelona region, with a glorious reputation in the leftist world, thanks to Catalonian resistance to Franco as well as the high quality of Catalan art and letters. Cuba, also, seemed to hold out the possibility of a revolution in which Marxism and modernism could be partners; this was, in latent form, my real desire.

In this storm of encounters, Pound emerged because of his language, not his politics. I was now barely seventeen, but after reading his *Selected Poems,* and struggling with *The ABC of Reading* (recommended to me by my father's friend Richard W. Emerson, who had met and interviewed Pound), I suddenly knew, in the depths of my being, where I was going: into a privileged relation with language, with the English language, with its Anglo-Saxon roots (laid bare in Pound's translation of *The Seafarer,* which left me dizzy), with the overlay of Provençal, through the troubadours, with Pound's own rigorous, direct verse. I went to the staff of the Communist weekly *People's World,* where I was viewed with so much favor, and proposed they print an essay defending Pound's poetics and proclaiming a new openness in Communist literary theory. No such essay would appear; Pound was a fascist, and the Communists were unwilling to risk such a scandal. Still, I was now convinced I had more to learn from Pound than from Neruda or Brecht.

Yet with all this going on inside me, I considered myself a loyal Communist, concerned only to broaden the cultural horizons of my Marxist-Leninist teachers and peers. A fascination with the Russian "epic" persisted for years to come. I continued studying Marx, Engels, Lenin, and numerous Soviet authors and documents; I also did an immense amount of reading in the general history of revolutions and in the special chapter of world history mythified by my mother, the Spanish Civil War. I tried to fuse all these elements within myself: the poetic adventure, the cult of Lenin, the minor cults of Castro and "Che" Guevara, admiration for Picasso. . . . Lenin stood as a kind of historical double for Brecht. Lenin: precise, never faltering, acting with the greatest possible control over his feelings. Yet I, in so many words, wanted to be an *Italian* Communist rather than an American or Soviet or even Cuban one, and I then believed with complete sincerity that a *democratic* Communist vision was not only compatible with but an inevitable outcome of true Leninism. This misapprehension seemed briefly to be sustained by Khrushchev's rehabilitation of old Bolsheviks killed by Stalin, and by persistent rumors that even Trotsky's reputation would be restored.

However, my worship of Lenin, of Russia, and of the drama of Petrograd was not exclusivist. I saw no reason why the Communist movement should not have many autonomous leadership centers—Beijing and La Habana as well as Moscow. Somehow there seemed to be no intrinsic conflict, for me, between the Russian state system, the ostensible populism of Castro, and the apparent values of Latin American and French poetry. All were, I believed, linked by the repeated Communist pledge to defend culture and world peace. Unfortunately, with the removal of Khrushchev from Soviet leadership in 1964, Communism worldwide moved abruptly away from such openness as it previously espoused. Soon I would find myself defending the Cuban encouragement of modern art to American Communists for whom even Picasso was suspect as "decadent."

A tension was growing within me: I was not yet mature enough, as a writer, to take on Pound as an exemplar, and revolt was increasingly in the air. I had learned my writing was good enough, at least, to get me out of the normal trouble a radical adolescent can get into, and that by labelling my misfit personality as literary rather than political, I could get needed respect from my peers and from others. The political climate in the high schools I had attended had come to favor opposition to the Vietnam War as early as 1965, while the thrust of youth rebellion had already begun shifting from the political to the cultural, a development I recognized when, riding home from a suburban Marin class in Marxism, in the Volvo sedan of Danny Hallinan, classmate and scion of an infamous leftist family, I first heard Bob Dylan on an AM pop-music radio station.

I had been taught a great deal, as a Marxist-Leninist, about the alleged working of world politics and economics. But the outstanding feature of this experience was that it bestowed upon me an eccentric, semi-religious, false intellectuality. I had wandered, through my adolescence, in an empty castle decorated with vivid portraits of philosophers and martyrs. I had come to see myself, in my teenage years, as a romantic truth-seeker. The sad truth was that this spurious sophistication was an effect of no more than the pretensions of a demoralized political tendency seeking to identify itself with a culture it could only destroy. I count this

Sausalito, California, 1965

surrender to pseudo-intellectualism as the great error of my youth. I sought to be a revolutionary, to escape my friendless emotional life, and replicated my isolation and suffering. By the time I had come to rebel against this "alienation of alienation" through poetry, my path was too clearly determined: I would continue to sacrifice myself, my instincts, and my interests to ideals that were evanescent.

I defended Pound to the Communists, but the old exile did not immediately become my real poetic model; that position would be occupied by the French surrealists, chiefly Breton. This was a relatively easy path for me, in that some of the most talented surrealists, such as Louis Aragon and Paul Éluard, whose prose and poetry I admired immensely, had become stalwarts of the Communist bureaucracy. I also

started looking at paintings with a better eye. The higher education in the aesthetic of paradox provided by surrealism, however, led me back to Lenin, bizarrely enough, for the surrealists had formed a close bond with Trotsky, and my interest in surrealism would lead me to the Trotskyist movement.

A digression on Latin American verse is in order. In meditating on the culture and conflicts of Nicaragua, matters in which I later became inveigled, I have found myself drawn back to my encounter as a teenager with a poem by the Nicaraguan author Salomón de la Selva. "Don Sal" was one of the country's outstanding writers and supported Augusto C. Sandino in his guerrilla war with the United States. This poem deeply affected me—as it did several generations of young Central Americans, who read and copied it in their school notebooks—and I memorized it and recited it many times at Bay Area poetry readings in which I began participating at sixteen. The title of the poem is "The Bullet":

> The bullet that wounds me
> Will be a bullet with a soul.
> The soul of this bullet
> Will be like
> The song of a rose
> If flowers sang
> Or the scent of a topaz
> If gems had a smell
> Or the skin of a melody
> If it were possible for us
> To touch naked songs
> With our hands.
>
> If it wounds my head
> It will tell me: I was probing
> The depth of your thoughts.
> If it wounds me in the chest
> It will tell me: I wanted
> To say I love you!

The translation is my own. My fascination with this poem later seemed to me especially representative of the feelings and attitudes I and many of my generation shared in the 1960s. What do this attitude and this poem express? A casual acceptance of violence is perhaps the most disturbing aspect, though I could hardly impeach "Don Sal," its author, for that; he wrote the poem while serving in the trenches of the First World War. But such a poem also serves as a kind of literary suicide note suitable for idealistic youths carried away by the power of words and the allure of war and revolution. It was, I think, a *machismo* of this sort that drove many Latin American revolutionaries of the 1960s–1980s, and, unconsciously or not, many of their North American supporters. (Comically enough, authorship of this poem was ascribed to Panamanian dictator Manuel Antonio Noriega by one *gringo* journalist.)

There were many Nicaraguans in San Francisco then, as historically, for the city long housed one of the largest Nicaraguan communities abroad. In college cafeterias and literary cafés I met people who later participated in the overthrow of Somoza, some of whom went on to fight the Sandinistas, as well. I learned Nicaragua merits its reputation as "the land of po-

ets": it stands nearly equal to Spain itself, Mexico, Cuba, and Argentina as a Hispanic literary power. But first I had to overcome the "Brechtian" nihilism that was reinforced by "The Bullet" of "Don Sal"—a poetic stance I believe is visible in the accompanying picture published in the *San Francisco Chronicle* in 1965. On that occasion, I read "The Bullet" and other works, employing my notorious voice in the last of a series of informal summer weekend poetry readings that led the authorities in Sausalito, California, to close, for thirty-one years, the park in which I performed. (I had also been threatened by some violent "beatniks" who wanted to use the park for drug dealing.)

I cannot here discuss my writing in the period I have reviewed; most of it was lost or destroyed, or renounced as juvenile. I count the real beginning of my career as a writer with a series of poems written when I was eighteen, in the year after my graduation from high school in 1966. I had come under the strong, if temporary, influence of the beat poet Michael McClure, whose verse was extremely austere. Remains of these efforts, which I rewrote many times in the "symbolist" fashion, appear in some of my published work, such as the poems "Episodes" and "Credo" from my 1983 self-published collection, *A Sleepwalker's Guide to San Francisco* (hereinafter *SGSF*).

Surrealism, and above all Breton's "pure, psychic automatism"—the nurturing of a "shamanic" voice, spontaneous, unrepressed, transforming language by the creation of new autonomous syntagms—changed everything for me. My work as a poet became absolutely dependent on inner necessity rather than external demands or stimuli, a position from which, in writing verse, I have never strayed. Breton's conception of "the poet to come," surpassing the contradictions of ordinary existence, serving as a voice for the deepest collective will, seemed (and still seems) the most revolutionary proposition I ever encountered. Breton's most significant work, in his middle period, reflected his exploration of Marxism-Leninism, which I recognized, and which helped me determine my own ideological coordinates.

Automatism spoke within me in a cycle of dream texts later partly preserved in the poem "Gulfs," also in *SGSF*, but originally printed, to my great delight, in *Kayak*, a San Francisco journal of "surrealist" and other experimental verse edited by my parents' friend George Hitchcock. Hitchcock had been quite critical of my earlier, pseudo-symbolist attempts, but welcomed this *dolce stil' nuovo*. This was not my first publication, but it was my happiest, for I felt I had met and matched a high standard, even though the surrealist method of composition evaded all requirements of training or even reading! In an excess of exuberance, I sent these same poems, in miserable French versions crafted by a young woman I knew, to the surrealist painter René Magritte, whose work had just been shown in a climactic retrospective in Berkeley, and in whom I found surrealism personified. (To my further astonishment and celebration Magritte, who died very soon after that, sent back a modified version of one of his drawings, for use on the cover of my first book. It appeared on the *Sleepwalker's Guide* fifteen years later. In the intervening years I learned that Magritte had been the only leading surrealist to attempt to fuse "orthodox" surrealism and Stalinist Marxism as late as the 1960s, in the so-called People's Surrealist Tendency!)

The *Kayak* dream texts were succeeded by another breakthrough, the poem "O mistress of absolute invention" (also in *SGSF*), which came to me during a sleepless night, and was inspired by D., a beautiful woman a year younger than me, with whom I had my first experience of a truly perverse, tormented passion. (McClure called this poem "Gongoristic." For my part, I associated D. with the figure of Cynthia in René Crevel's *Babylon*.) My loves, I am the first to admit, have never been normal, and many habits from which I should have freed myself at the end of adolescence persist—especially the temptation of a cold and tyrannical muse, such as this woman, whose antecedents in the Communist movement were quite distinguished, had been.

After ending my relationship with D., the "crustacean queen" as I came to call her, I entered gratefully into a world of full sexual pursuit. I was nineteen and had lost my virginity at seventeen; but I had been late in assuming an "adult" attitude about the conquest of women. I had never been aggressive with girls, as much as I desired them; later, I realized that some interpreted this reticence as a sign of homosexuality. It doubtless was, but I did not follow through on those feelings. I wanted love more than sex, and even after being relieved of my virginity I found myself literally impotent when called on to deflower two of my early girlfriends: A. and Stella (who appears in *SFSG* as "C."), both of whom, separately, I tried ineffectively to penetrate. I had not yet learned the secrets of female response, and A. was not then an avid partner.

Stella, on the other hand, was a sexual demon, sixteen and a year younger than me when I met her. She was gorgeous: Italian and dark, fleshy, with beautiful brown eyes and the large, round breasts every young heterosexual male covets in a girlfriend. She spoke with a divine lisp. There was no Catholicism in her home, for her family were Italian socialists and anarchists. She responded boldly to my tongue-kisses, took me into her bedroom in a penthouse-like arrangement at the top of her elegant house in Pacific Heights, several blocks from my parents' flat, and first told me she had "never gone all the way with a guy before," but then stripped naked, revealing a body I thought worthy of Botticelli. She was a virgin, but she masturbated constantly, frequently indulging in stimulation of her small nipples by her girlfriends. I was amazed; there is no other word that describes my reaction as I found myself apparently sovereign at the gates of sexual pleasure. I tried so hard to break her hymen and could not even enter her. But we kissed and fondled each other, day after day, trying again and again (and still failing) to consummate our sexuality, and I became obsessed with Stella, a fantastic identification that never died in me, that remains essentially fresh and vivid as I write these lines. I walked the streets, then, almost delirious with masculine pride notwithstanding my failure. Something else was, however, missing between us—the post-Oedipal love I sought from another.

I found that love in Vanessa, another neighborhood girl, who was even younger—fifteen—but with whom I performed well erotically. Although unpracticed, she may not have been a virgin. (She is "M." in *SGSF*.) We experimented with and studied sex, as rationally as I had studied Marxism and poetry; I began reading Sade and Bataille. Vanessa was also beautiful, a mixed-race Asian American. I had moved out of my parents' house and got a room in a shabby single-residence hotel (not the last); I was working part-time in a bookshop. I really fell for Vanessa, who began coming to my room in the afternoons, after high school, and I impregnated her. Her mother, however, unlike Stella's, was *very* Catholic, at least in public. Vanessa had an abortion, but we ended up marrying. Out of that relationship, which lasted six years, came my son, Matthew, born in 1972.

I wrote a long, surrealist "marriage poem" for Vanessa, "Hidden Locks," that was my first venture into the sustained form of surrealist "epic" developed by Breton, Benjamin Péret, Aimé Césaire, the Greek surrealist Nikos Gatsos (whose extraordinary poem *Amorgós* I came to appreciate thanks to another Greek surrealist, Nanos Valaoritis, who had just come to San Francisco), and other representatives of the movement. However, my real situation was anything but that usually predicted in a young man of letters: I had been pushed into a "shotgun wedding," something I had been warned against since childhood, and now had to contend with the duty of supporting "a family of my own" while contending with the interference of my in-laws, who found poetry, radicalism, and even academic study, such as it might interest me, baffling and contemptible. Nevertheless, I pressed on, seeking to refurbish the surrealist revolutionary project by founding *Antinarcissus,* a "two number" journal of a kind typically published by young poets in this century. In its pages I assembled a wide variety of late and unpublished texts by French and other surrealists, translated into English; in "magazine" format, the first issue mainly offered prose, while an accompanying "second" issue, designed to resemble a newspaper, consisted of poetry. Naturally, I could not finance such a project on an ongoing basis, and it died as have so many other such enterprises. However, it was hailed by the then-poet Robert Bly, much later founder of the so-called "men's movement," in his critical essay *Leaping Poetry.*

Life was not joyous, although I truly loved Vanessa. The provocations and distractions sustained by her family, along with my daily employment as a clerk in a large store, and a gnawing distance from my parents, made creative work difficult. The automatic stream dried up with great and painful suddenness and severity. (Valaoritis told me I suffered from an excessively repressed personality.) I revised my "surrealist" poems in the same "symbolist" way

"Stella (left) and myself (right) with legendary maritime labor leader Jack Hatton," San Francisco, 1983

I had endlessly rewritten verses before; three years passed before I completed the twenty-five lines of section VI of "Hidden Locks," beginning "This road may only be travelled at night." Such was hardly good surrealist practice; but I began to conceive of "poetry" as a complex of *events and phenomena in life,* rather than as a linguistic vessel, and I commenced recording and meditating on dreams, coincidences, and associated data from daily experience that seemed possessed of a meaning often inexpressible. This activity, derived from the Bretonian doctrine of "objective chance," also drew me back to a "Marxist" rejection of all professional intellectuality, and the presumption that working, say, on the San Francisco waterfront, as a Communist of whatever factional tendency, was the *highest* form of poetry; for had not Lautréamont declared, "Poetry must be made by all, not by one?"

More importantly, while staying married to Vanessa, I went back to Stella, now with the enormous knowledge I had gained from Vanessa's body. She, too, had learned a good deal, and we came together exultantly. I was, of course, "cheating" on Vanessa, and felt terror and guilt. But real, full sex with Stella was glorious, all-encompassing, revelatory. Stella's virginity had been pierced by another boy, but she had yet to find a male lover prepared, as I was, to focus on her erotic vulnerabilities, which were considerable; and we satisfied each other's physical needs for years afterward. I regret nothing of that experience, as immoral as it may have been and as destructive to my mental equilibrium as it unarguably was. (Nor, may I say, do I regret the painful and distorted time I passed with D., the "crustacean queen"; were I to awake tomorrow in the presence of either of these women, again young, again facing the obstacles of that time, I would be deliriously happy.)

I began writing about Stella, indirectly, but with a greater sensuality than I had dedicated to Vanessa. Vanessa was my difficult muse, sought and worshipped as in the verses of Gérard de Nerval. But Stella was a force of nature, like the women in the stories and novels of André Pieyre de Mandiargues, whose works I had just been introduced to, and whose *Girl beneath the Lion [Le Lis de mer],* written a decade before and a hemisphere away, seemed a portrait of Stella. (Of course, Mandiargues was writing in that book of an *Italian* girl.) Although, in distress, I included within it a poem I had origi-

nally written about, and presented to Vanessa, my most accomplished surrealist poem, "Sphinx-trap" (in SGSF), was mainly composed under Stella's intoxicating influence. It ends:

> like morning
> pulling her skirt over her head
> for its seams to pursue her like a prairie fire
> searching her torso as it emerges from her hips
>
> her sight disembarks from her eyes
> at a distance
> between the fox and hounds
> of her hand
> on the banister
> by which she enters the forest she becomes
> with the steps of someone just grown out of
>   the earth

I had frequented the campus of the University of California, in Berkeley, since early adolescence, first mining the libraries and then as a supporter of the student movement. But I never felt much enthusiasm about attending college; Lowell High School, from which I graduated, had an excellent reputation as a public "prep school," but my turbulent experiences there had spurred a rejection of "bourgeois education" on my part. This ludicrous posture dovetailed with my idealization of labor. But in 1970, after a year or so working in the bookstore at a Catholic university (where I mainly read theological debates and pursued Stella, who lived nearby), I entered the City College of San Francisco. It was not unknown for good students, even from prestigious Lowell, to spend two years at CCSF before transferring to San Francisco State or Cal Berkeley; by the early '60s Lowell, no less than other urban and suburban high schools, had let its requirements for graduation slip, so that many students who did well in history and English (subjects in which I excelled) made up for their lack of science and mathematics preparation at a junior college. In essence, we proved our capacities for academic study a second time.

While fancying myself a grand aesthete, and even a *demi-philosophe,* I attended a streetcar college filled with working-class students, and went home each day to married life, as if the so-called "youth revolution" and the "hippie orgies" taking place all around me had nothing to do with me. I was even forced to beg my in-laws for money to go to school. My own parents offered not a cent and not a smile of

San Francisco, 1972

encouragement, although once registered I chose a course of study based on a hobby of my mother: American Indian anthropology. Incredibly enough, "Silly College," as it was bitterly nicknamed by many of its alumni, had excellent introductory courses in ethnology, with small classes, in contrast to the Cal Berkeley campus where Anthro 3 (cultural) met in sections of 400 students.

More demoralizing for me was the wide gap between my aspirations and my condition. I had seriously taken up Jacques Lacan and other "dark philosophers," who were not yet very well known at Cal Berkeley, to say nothing of CCSF, and was even reading Derrida. I once, in those days, wrote a paper, and delivered it in class, on Lacan's "instance of the letter in the unconscious," which impended on the surrealist conception of the image; in retrospect, the paper must have been even more bewildering than it immediately seemed for other students, as well as for the instructor. A further absurdity came when I was visited by D. and showed her a related and moderately ambitious text of mine

on language, published by an obscure radical printer. Her reaction, perhaps dictated by the philistinism of her Communist household, was that it must all be "bullshit," since she knew I was not capable of such things.

However, somebody noticed something at CCSF, for when I transferred to Cal Berkeley in 1972, I received a small scholarship. By then I had moved from anthropology *per se*, which seemed to me hopelessly mired in Western racism and implicated in imperialism, to linguistics. A course in the history of the English language at CCSF provided me with a wholesale enlightenment on Noam Chomsky and other topics. But I remained resistant to academia, and that seminar was the only English course I ever took at college. I was not about to listen to a professor tell me what was or was not good and necessary in literature, and I was certainly not going to write compositions on order or take classes in "creative writing." However exaggerated my claims to status as a real intellectual, I already knew how to write, what to write, and when. I have never given up on that stand, no matter how grandiose it may seem. I do not believe true writing—that of poets, rather than publicists—can be or should be "taught." For me, literature is the domain of those whose use of language grows out of an inherent gift, and they will succeed who write because they cannot help themselves, because they have no choice but to write.

The year 1972 was critical for me in three aspects aside from my transfer to "the Big U." A first collection of my writing, *Hidden Locks,* came out as a chapbook. It consisted of the "marriage poem" of the same title, rendered in prose, along with fictional sketches about women, birds and beasts, and incidents, all far out of the ordinary. In "The Promise," a woman living in a single-residence hotel (the sort of place I know too well) goes on a surprising date; "Precious Games" is about the death and resurrection of a mysterious prostitute (based on a real event); "The Lodestone" recounts a dream I had about an eighteenth- or nineteenth-century slave ship; and "The Window" offers a variation on anti-fur protests, long before such

were news. In "The Moat," I described, in surrealist form, one of the most remarkable experiences I ever had: seeing a California cougar on Mount Tamalpais, above Mill Valley, in 1960, when the survival of that species in California urban environments was considered a ridiculous suggestion. Thirty-six years later, with mountain lions having returned in numbers to the Pacific Coast and attacked and killed human adults and children as well as pets, the "feline hallucination" of my twelfth year seems almost an item of surrealist prophecy. (Naturalists now say cougars are present all over Mount Tamalpais and throughout west Marin county.)

Hidden Locks had no critical echo anywhere, although coincidentally with its publication I was praised in *The New York Review of Books,* by the critic Roger Shattuck, as the best poet among the younger "orthodox" American surrealists. (I later discovered the existence of another surrealist prose writer with the same name, spelled the same way, and have often wondered if people confuse us. Perhaps he has undergone obloquy because of my transgressions; perhaps the reader of this essay has not yet discovered I

With son Matthew and coauthor Víctor Alba, Barcelona, 1994

am not him, and vice versa. There is also the "Stephen Schwartz" who composes music for Broadway shows and Walt Disney movies; our paths have never crossed directly. I would not wish to be him, and I am certain that feeling would be mutual.)

The appearance of *Hidden Locks* was important for me, but also in 1972 came news that truly changed my life: Vanessa was pregnant. I received this information while amid multiple adventures in infidelity, with other women as well as Stella. It did not immediately affect me as it would later, but I began to perceive that I had to liberate myself from the tangle of contradictions within which I felt increasingly immobile. In the summer of that year, while Vanessa, waiting for the baby, moved us into her mother's house, I entered a third order of personal inquiry by going to sea as a member of the Sailors' Union of the Pacific. Here at last, at twenty-three, was my introduction to the world of real labor and real unions, although I had previously worked, briefly, on the San Francisco waterfront as a cargo checker. I sailed to Alaska twice as a tanker messman, and then to the Far East as an ordinary seaman on the penultimate cruise of an old and elegant passenger liner, the *President Wilson*. In certain respects, shipping out was the great formative experience of my early adulthood, and it cannot be reduced to a few lines in an essay such as this. However, I will say that life at sea had a curiously familiar quality, as if the dream related in my story "The Lodestone" expressed some other, occult reality.

I owed the opportunity to my father-in-law, a merchant marine officer (nicknamed, unfortunately, "Captain Piss," so that I became known to some as "Captain Piss's Kid"). I came back from sea and went to Berkeley, and my son Matthew was born in October 1972. There my redemption began, for in seeing his happy mien, in changing his diapers and watching him acquire coordination of his limbs, in pressing his tiny body to mine in an embrace, I knew here was something, perhaps the only thing, that was unqualifiedly *good* in my life. How was it, I wondered, that a person so willful and selfish and even criminal as I had been could be complicit in the birth of so pure a being? (I also owed to my father-in-law my son's looks; nobody would believe Matthew is the grandchild of an Asian woman, on one side, and Jews on the other, for my son's DNA was

In Mallorca, 1996

"swamped" by the hardy, Scandinavian genes of his maternal grandfather, whom he resembles exactly.)

It was, unfortunately, too late for me and Vanessa. Too many confidences had been breached, too many cruelties had been overlooked or swept aside; and as much as I adored Matthew, I could not remain within the immediate control of his mother's family. I was going crazy, more and more quickly, and began engaging in really dangerous, life-threatening behavior; my mother, who had stood aside from my torments, became alarmed. Vanessa's family presented me with an ultimatum: although I was now an honors student in linguistics at Berkeley, I had to drop out of college to earn income for my child. Partly convinced by the big money I made at sea, partly by my insistent bias toward labor and against the academy, I acquiesced, left school, and hired out as a clerk for the Western Pacific Railroad. But it was too late even for that compromise: Matthew was only a year old when Vanessa and I began divorce proceedings. An idea of life had choked, or been choked, and died; at twenty-five, I felt much older than I was, and exhausted. Now the well of surrealist inspiration disappeared completely; thus ended my *Glass Palace Chronicle*. I had failed as a poet, as a scholar, and as a husband. Only labor remained, and the old Communist myths, which I hugged to myself as I had hugged Matthew.

I did not abandon Matthew. My parents, in the one action they undertook in my adulthood for which I feel undiluted appreciation, assumed some of my responsibilities for him, contributing financially to his support and making a second home for him during his childhood. After his eleventh year he began staying with me on weekends, and eventually moved in with me. Matthew's fine disposition lasted through his adolescence, and we are very close today; our first trip to Europe together, when he was twenty-one, educated both of us.

I have passed over much in this narrative: delvings into Buddhism and Islam, my break with official Communism in 1968, later explorations in Marxist ideology and sectarianism, my relationship with the surrealist poet Philip Lamantia, whom I served as a disciple from 1968 to 1974, and the reduction of my poetic space to a minimalist, word-for-word production, too close to silence, in which "the chorus is the void," as I wrote in a preface to the second edition of Lamantia's *Touch of the Marvelous* (1974).

Some of that I left behind after "the destruction of the glass palace," as I imagined the collapse of my existence with Vanessa. I worked steadily at the railroad, became active in the Railway Clerks' union, tried (and generally failed) to write, and drank heavily. I made love to Stella; underwent another vicious romance, with a Hispanic woman, Mona; cried out for Matthew and woke each morning desolate. For the first time ever, I contemplated suicide.

One day, on my lunch hour from the Western Pacific office, I went to a nearby pawnshop and tried to buy a revolver, leaving a deposit and signing an application. But I was rescued from killing myself by what I later called "police therapy." I was visited at my apartment by two officers who let me know that before I could purchase the gun I would have to pay off about $350 in traffic tickets; since I didn't have the money handy, one of the officers would

Stephen Schwartz, "resembling a Balkan mystic," 1997

come to the railroad each payday for a $35 installment payment, until it was wiped out. Ten paydays, one every two weeks, equalled six months, and by the time I was eligible to buy the weapon my outlook had improved; I never went back to the pawnshop.

My spirit had been strengthened by a series of discoveries. First, I realized that even as depressed as I was by the temporary but really terrible loss of Matthew, I could still find satisfaction in reading; after a few lugubrious months, I was back poring through Bolshevik and Spanish Civil War literature. Then, after losing a good deal of money on alcohol, drinking myself into the gutter (on several occasions), and similar abusive excesses, I began smoking marijuana to get off booze. I had never been much of a weedhead in the '60s, originally for reasons of family history—my father's brother had died of heroin addiction, and I was frightened of "getting hooked." In addition, I never had money in those days for pot, and, in my "automatic" period, I eschewed all artificial means of inspiration in the belief that the surrealist message from within should not be interfered with. I had taken LSD, which was cheap, beginning at seventeen, but usually only once or twice a year (the last time in 1984).

Pot freed me from liquor, and relaxed me, so that I could resume some writing, if in a different manner. Marijuana did not furnish access to the exalted, elaborately combined images I sought as a surrealist, but it lessened my hesitations and other blocks. Most significantly, however, I learned something from railroad life: my coworkers and fellow-unionists had observed my suffering, and reached out to me unselfishly. What a revelation! Marx and Trotsky overwhelmingly vindicated! The workers in industry *did* form human relationships, based on mutual aid, or solidarity, growing out of their exploitation! On the premises of the Western Pacific Railroad, an alternative to the illness of families, to the chilly hierarchies of academia, to the obtuseness of the literary world, to the isolation I had so long accepted!

This affirmation may seem exaggerated to those who have never worked in such a setting; if anything, it is understated. Both at the Western Pacific and, later, at the Santa Fe Railway, where I worked mainly in the freight house and the yard rather than the office, I encountered friendship and a sense of community that seemed utterly absent from the rest of my life. Even merchant mariners lacked so strong a personal bond with one another. Railroad life was a precious experience for me; I often later said my real education had come at "Western Pacific College and Santa Fe University."

On vacation from the W.P., I took a trip to Mexico and felt a new intellectual energy. Soon after that, I ran into someone I had not seen for some time, Tony Dingman, a friend of mine and Vanessa's in the early period of our relationship. Tony had often spoken of a filmmaker he knew who wanted to adapt a work of Henry Miller, *The Smile at the Foot of the Ladder,* for the screen. Sunk in my surrealist project, I had never even bothered to ask his friend's name. Now, in 1975, I learned to my astonishment that Tony Dingman worked for Francis Ford Coppola, who had just conquered Hollywood with *The Godfather*. I began meeting Coppola and found out about his plan to take over *City* magazine, a rather feeble local entertainment and service weekly, and to relaunch it as a well-heeled organ of the general culture.

After some detours I was introduced to Warren Hinckle III, chosen by Coppola as *City*'s new editor, and who had presided over the classic radical journal of the '60s, *Ramparts;* I had known some of his cronies in my earlier

Communist days, but never met him. Hinckle hired me as staff writer for *City,* when the magazine was the center of all attention in the Bay Area, and when an affiliation with it opened all portals, including some belonging to beautiful women. I began writing anew, and never lost the confidence I gained from the experience, even though when *City* went broke (as was inevitable under Hinckle's control), I returned to railroad life, with the Santa Fe. After a few more years, and my first trips to Europe, however, I felt the need to commit myself to writing alone, and quit the railroad at thirty-two.

I still have dreams in which Santa Fe has called me to work as a telegrapher, as a boat dispatcher, as a weighmaster, and in the other, singular jobs in the freight yard. For as André Breton and Paul Éluard wrote in their surrealist masterpiece, *The Immaculate Conception (L'Immaculée Conception),* "I have known three lamplighters, five women who were railroad signal maintainers, and one male signal maintainer. And you?"

This essay includes material that appeared in much different form as follows:

Stephen Schwartz, "The Poet and Public Policy," *The Letter*, Institute for Contemporary Studies (San Francisco), winter 1985.

Stephen Schwartz, biographical essay, Peter Collier and David Horowitz eds., *Second Thoughts,* National Forum Foundation (Washington, D.C.), 1987.

Stephen Schwartz, "Scenes from a Red-Diaper Childhood," *San Francisco Sunday Chronicle and Examiner,* May 27, 1990.

Stephen Schwartz, entry in *ACTUAL Annuaire,* ACTUAL (Paris), 1991.

Stephen Schwartz, *A Strange Silence,* ICS Press (San Francisco), 1992.

Also see:

Víctor Alba, "En EU se divorcia la Nueva Izquierda," México, *¡Siempre!,* December 11, 1987.

Robert Bly, *Leaping Poetry,* Beacon Press (Boston), 1978 (reprint).

Bulletin de Liaison surréaliste, Paris, 1974.

Coupure (Paris), 1971.

Philip Lamantia, *Touch of the Marvelous,* Grey Wolf Press (Bolinas), 1974 (preface by Stephen Schwartz).

Gjon Sinishta, "The Poetry of Stephen Schwartz," *Albanian Catholic Bulletin* (San Francisco), No. XV, 1994.

The author wishes to thank the staff of the *San Francisco Chronicle* library for clips on Frank Hashmall and the photograph by Claude Beagarie.

BIBLIOGRAPHY

Poetry:

(Editor and translator) *Antinarcissus,* self-published, 1969.

Hidden Locks, Radical America, 1972.

(Translator) *Spectres of the Desert,* by Jindrich Heisler, Radical America, 1974.

A Sleepwalker's Guide to San Francisco, La Santa Espina, 1983.

Heaven's Descent, Transition, 1990.

Floral Games: Selected Poems, Arguments & Facts Media, forthcoming.

History and politics:

Brotherhood of the Sea: A History of the Sailors' Union of the Pacific, 1885–1985, Transaction Books, 1986.

(Editor) *The Transition: From Authoritarianism to Democracy in the Hispanic World,* ICS Press, 1986.

(With Víctor Alba) *Spanish Marxism vs. Soviet Communism: A History of the P.O.U.M.,* Transaction Books, 1988.

A Strange Silence: The Emergence of Democracy in Nicaragua, introduction by Víctor Alba, ICS Press, 1992.

Radical California: The Hidden History of the Left Coast, forthcoming.

Author under the pseudonym S. Solsona of *Incidents from the Life of Benjamin Péret,* published in *The Alarm,* 1981. Contributor to anthologies, including *City Lights Anthology,* edited by Lawrence Ferlinghetti, City Lights Books, 1974; (translator) *What Is Surrealism? Selected Writings of André Breton,* Pluto Press, 1978; *Anarchia e Creatività,* edited by Arturo Schwarz, La Salamandra, 1981; *The Grenada Papers,* edited by Paul Seabury and Walter A. MacDougall, ICS Press, 1984; *Yearbook on International Communist Affairs,* edited by Amb. Richard F. Staar, Hoover Institution, 1989, 1990, 1991; *Fighting the War of Ideas in Latin America,* edited by John C. Goodman and Ramona Marotz-Baden, National Center for Policy Analysis, 1990; (with Gjon Sinishta) *Mediterranean Europe Phrasebook,* Lonely Planet, 1992; *Central America on a Shoestring,* Lonely Planet, 1994; *The Years at White Gate Ranch,* edited by Suzanne Royce, Bolinas Museum for the Art and History of Coastal Marin, 1995.

Editor of the *Journal of Contemporary Studies,* 1984–86, and staff writer for the *San Francisco Chronicle* since 1989. Also contributor to numerous periodicals, including *The Alarm, The American Spectator, Commentary, Los Angeles Times, The New Criterion, The New York Times Book Review, Re/Search,* and *The Wall Street Journal.*

Thomas Lowe Taylor

1938-

REALLY, ALL MY LIFE HAS BEEN AUTOBIOGRAPHY

Thomas Lowe Taylor

I was born very young in San Diego in 1938, if I remember correctly. My brother was born four years earlier in Washington, D.C. My father was a career naval officer, born in Chicago and raised in Washington, and my mother was from San Diego. My dad had duty in the Pacific and had been stationed in Hawaii when Pearl Harbor occurred, so there I was at two, under the bed with my mother and brother and some vague memory of dustballs.

My mother, my brother, and I spent the war with my cousins, about eight of us kids, at "the ranch" where my grandfather had twenty

acres of oranges, lemons, and so forth. He had bought an adobe packing house in El Cajon, a suburb of San Diego, and he and my grandmother had transformed it into something palatial. It was a castle for our imaginations, and

---

Pearl Harbor

It's not that I was born during or at the beginning of a war and was hardly even present, but I have been told about it. There was some driving around and a great deal of unsureness. I stopped at the milk truck and watched it, played milkman and driver. The solitude of my mother was unconvincing. When it was dark, it was very dark, and we seemed to be playing in ruins. No one seemed to have anything to say about it. "The Japs." We stayed at that house a long time. I guess I don't remember the other one, where we lived.

---

we populated it without fathers. When the fathers came back, no one knew who they were. They had left us in our infancies and returned as odd mountains of flesh with warts and hair on them, not like the women we had spent the war years with, not like the grandparents— but that's another story.

Hacienda

Medieval, elaborate, earth-worn. My grandmother's six daughters repopulate the earth with warriors. By warriors, clerks are born, managers of the kingdom, the estate sold to . . .

The sun beats on my head; cool my toes in orange-tree shade. Trees which bear.

In the summer we eat fruit and sleep in high-ceilinged rooms in the afternoon and wake to step through door-sized windows into the herb garden.

Night fires burn, reflect light of Indian rugs. The sound of Beethoven from the study.

I always called my parents Kate and Jack, that's how dysfunctional a family we were. But, you know, military families are notorious for this kind of oddness. We had the appearance of family. However, as my brother puts it, he and I were treated like pieces of furniture. The war had emptied out my dad; he was kind of an empty paper bag, although he'd sublimated a lot into being well-read, and to the end he and I conversed like intellectual colleagues at a conference on futurism. But he and my mother weren't much, and my brother and I grew up into pretty dysfunctional types. He became a high stepper in the advertising world in New York, while I a teacher-poet-vagabond in the sixties, a housepainter in the seventies, a secretary in the eighties, and retired to the beach in Washington in the nineties. It was hardly as barren an existence as many have had. My mother had six sisters, and all who had married had gone military, and all the uncles had risen in rank, and at the ranch there had been a lot of partying and noisemaking in the thirty-foot, red-tile-floored kitchen, with its big and small tables, or in the living room full of wicker and rattan furniture and Navajo rugs and the wall of books and records my grandfather perused every evening; really, it was the stuff of dreams, like Nabokov growing up a frail orchid in the heart of the revolution and the decaying empire. We had our little commune in the middle of nowhere, Rattlesnake Moun-

"With my parents, Kate and Jack,"
Maui, Hawaii, 1940

My Father

Then who is he? Especially when I lose the way. No appeal in memory. I can see about tasks, that one should work it that way and no other, if that's the way it has to be done. You tell yourself that. In examining what I think about him, which is in the end remembering myself.

When I saw him last year, he greeted a stranger, I to him thus, and there we were; it is the order of things which is my father, and flesh only a transmitter (as I am).

---

tain to the north, cruel (or so we thought) Mr. Sam's barren acres to the west, and unknown regions (beyond the dump) to the east. In a way, it was idyllic.

But then, that was only the beginning, and after that it went downhill. Grandfather had a heart attack and he and my grandmother moved to a classic bungalow in La Mesa; we went on the road, my brother, my mother, and I. Up to Port Chicago, where my dad was the commanding officer, and we drove around acres of mysterious mounds which were full of explosives and looked like a landscape from Babar. There was a longshoreman's strike and some demonstrating, and we got driven to school with an armed marine. My brother rolled the car. I started playing in the closet with my papers and draining the glasses after parties. Something was amiss.

By now, 1996, there have been about fifty houses. Felt like a gypsy, whatever they feel like. But at the start, it was one after the other, and since we didn't know the difference, like in not having any friends, or in always living in rented houses, we had the middle-class exterior without any of the fringe benefits. From what I've come to appreciate from my nervous breakdowns and time in treatment and therapy, I came out as a fairly autistic child, not entirely muted into sick silence, but I had definitely retreated into some fantasy safety in reaction to bonding with my mother during the war years and some pretty predictable reactions to having my father come back when I was, whatever, eight years old, something like that. I had fevers, became sick for attention, stuff lots of kids do, but by the time of the third high school, twelve schools in all, I think, and by the time I was getting out on my own, whether or not I knew it, I was self-absorbed, moody, and drank a lot (before I discovered pot). This confessional tone I hope ties me in with everyone else in this mélange period of late twentieth-century sociology—I was one of the pack.

So something in that early searing into silence had made me special, as my paternal grandmother had marked me out. She'd been a bit of a rake and artiste in Philadelphia in the early century, had a radio show of her own, and had acted liberated. She'd finished her years out with a much younger man, kind of a slavish rich guy. She'd stared into my eyes when I was in high school, told me I was Special (not retarded, you know), and gave me some Emerson and Rilke to read. But during my years of wandering, that is until now, I

think I raced full speed forward in the dementia of my pain and in the full tempo of the times, yet my inner ballasts were not in full functioning order, so at several crucial junctures, I'd fold and run. And in the twenty years from 1970 to 1990, in the time of three marriages and raising five boys through the high school years, in the seven years or so of drinking and in between nervous breakdowns after the ends of marriage #1 (1972) and marriage #3 (1992), in, through, during and along with all this stuff, I wrote and wrote. And no matter how you

---

Going to School

Was something I didn't understand, but did, and excelled, and did that.

Chairs, iron hinges, books and pictures which compose structures which half interest me as if I glanced at them. The girls, about whom I have endless erotic daydreams, some of which I occasionally enact. The teachers, whom I try constantly to please. And the work, which is always secondary to the setting or context in which it takes place, and which seems to me, even at an early age, contradictory.

There are alignments and organizations, official and unspoken, which are present in all playground tournaments and chance conversations. The system of the school is universally suspected as something profoundly dangerous.

Occasional conversations, like moments, reveal themselves through the work, and in the memory, then certain relationships flash out like words.

---

slice it, it all comes out baloney, the saying goes.

Yet starting with Olson's sense of self-creation in Projective Verse and running through what we now know about the reasons for the creation of private languages, I can see that I was pushed through or made my way through a classic set of signs, and it only matters here because I got out of it, got somewhere with it, otherwise (to me) I'd be just another cowboy on the avenue. Driven, that's the word for it. A self, after all, is what—a set of experiences, no? We are driven through archetypes, through the passages of life's unfolding, whatever. I did not make my escape entirely through words, however, but also through music. Not that I performed. In acid days, we had some impromptu orchestras here and there (in Berkeley and Montana), and I can remember making music, but from early on, I'd be hypnotized, transported, mutated, possessed, whatever you want

Oahu, Hawaii, 1941

to call it, by music, tempos in time with associated harmonics and overtones, and it was in the facility of an otherness of escape and of renewal that I would slip into a daze, passing out often at parties in college with my head slumped against the speakers booming out Olatunji or Tjader or Ray Charles. My sex mechanisms all turned inward, walking pain box, picking quick tricks and pushing on to the next, cute womanizer of the heart's own inability to love, just another bozo on the circuit.

So you pick at the range of things made available to you at the time you first lift your head up and sneak a glance around for what you are *really* interested in. And while the drive to compete in the realm of The Poem was there, I seemed nonetheless to be on a driving track toward a private, comfort-oriented, pain-assuaging self-talk. Ionesco and Milton and Pound and Olson and Roethke and all the others were there to mimic, to pick up and run with, and one did, but the driving force was simply to feel better, for in the private world of the autistic (what else shall I call it?) poem, the only thing going on is an attempt to twist the self this way and that until the inner pineal squirts chemical forgiveness into the gray zone of interior synapses, Do Me!

And that in itself is addictive. Poetry addicts, not as readers do, though maybe so, but especially in the realm of the writing—the same act is performed over and over, always expecting different results, as they say in meetings, and between what is all right with addiction (controlling it, for instance) and anger and pain, the other side of the addict's problem, between these opposites, there's a place for a kind of artist. And I think what we're pointing out is that this is a slightly different kind of romantic artist. There is no question, for instance, that the poem is no longer an artifact; in many ways it is now an event. And once a poem is an event, it becomes subject to various laws of description, rules of duration and shape, rules relating to simultaneity and spatial distortion, statements about event morality, about eventuation itself, perhaps as a kind of actualization or virtualization. Anyway, the deal has changed on everyone. It's now more about acupuncture than metaphor: how does it *feel?* You feel it in the heart, in the gut, in the genitals, and especially in the braincase—certain things make you go blink, make you feel the top or side or back or inside upper left or whatever of the physical brainstem, you *feel* it in the *brain.* Now I think that's a little different from metaphor and critical historical kinds of vocabularies. It's a relief to find out you're like everyone else, but it just doesn't do much good at the time.

That, however, doesn't account for being driven. Nobody's done too well with explaining this, how obsession and genius relate. I know, *genius* is a loaded word, but in Rank, for instance, it means self-creation, which gets back somewhat to our autistic mold. And, you know, in the past forty or so years the spiritual/aesthetic canon has collapsed entirely, and I'd say the two phenoms are related, that as the canon has collapsed, the rise of personal language, personal poetics that is, has collided on the arc of triumph. As the sun pulls away from the shore and our boat sinks slowly in the west, is how Spike Jones has it.

From one's perspective in the now, however, everything makes sense—the inductive fallacy, you know. Of course, it does not necessarily "make sense," for instance, if one is down and out, one's story is not particularly enlightening, but the value of looking at one's life and of wondering out loud whether it has anything at all to do with what one eventually does, now that may illustrate perhaps a higher level of fallacy. And so while we *do* have our stories, and while the work *does* get done, you cannot help but wonder whether the one illustrates the other, or whether it's really the other way around. All along, the work sits there like a continuum, unavoidable and pretentious, staring you in the eye. You take a few years off to feel sorry for yourself, and when you pick up, it's *exactly* where you left off. Now that's *driven.*

But, all along, you wonder about the story. In the midst of madness and a suicide attempt, not your own, you write. In the subset "writer," you exhibit a continuity to yourself which allows and justifies what is going on around, and has it make sense in a sick sort of way. I mean, despite a seven-year blind spot, you are doing professional things like putting stuff in the mail, watching your margins, and staying with changes which take place in your phrasing and pace. All this goes on while the house is burning, and it gives it away, it gets you off the hook, you think. What bullshit, of course, but that's the way it works.

The guy in the bar has a story. Every one of them, and if you sit there long enough, you'll hear them all, and eventually you'll even

Self-portrait, Lewiston, Indiana, 1976

hear your own. That's *meetings*. So someone else has been there, and then some, and the only ones with more to tell are no longer in any position to do so. Only the dead know, and they're not talking, a black poet told me once. Next thing I knew, he was dead. And we have such faith that the story and the message are somehow related. That's narrative, or a willing suspension and all that fictive stuff. How, really, can you be "ahead of your time"? One is in synch with the physico-mentato or one is not. And all the fine stuff about visions and Nostradamus is fine for the kettle but too lean for the pot, or something like that. How convenient to think that our story will somehow exonerate us from having lived it! Yet as a wanderer, one finds that unless there's a story, you're mad, and that's it. What's your story, they ask, and if you don't have one, bango, off you go, under a tree or out of town please. Not that I would know.

So in 1968 I was teaching English in a junior college out in the desert near Mexicali, halfway between Yuma and San Diego, in El Centro. I'd come down from Berkeley, hired on at the last minute, and had taught in Michigan and Greece. So, I set about to do a literary journal, and got all caught up in it. In the course of things, I wrote one Vincent Ferrini for some permissions for him and Charles Olson.

I knew what I was doing and who I was writing to, and lo and behold he came through. Then I sent him the magazine, as my life was crashing down once again, and headed for Montana, where he caught up with me in the mails—said he'd spent three days on the journal. This connection has gone on for twenty-six years. And it's a leitmotif in my life, that Friendship which, while I may have confused it with an apprenticeship or mentorship, is really a friendship between two men which has become glue and foresight and communion and the real bond between human beings revealed. Of course, it mattered some that Vincent had my respect as a writer, and vice versa, but he knew early on we were onto something new and together we've shepherded it into the new, er, now. Whatever.

Without Vincent, I'd have coughed it up and that's about it.

I mean, there are friendships and there are friendships. Really, I know nothing about what went on between Olson and Vincent, but I could see that he knew Friendship and how to be Friends, as if this were some mysterious, fraternal concept which emerged in the cosmic silences of the West Lynn Library as Vincent and his friends deciphered the universe from the outside in, either perpetuating or dismissing the inductive fallacy. I, too, for instance, was more than a little surprised to find that my education started *after* graduate school, and I don't mean just being tested, I mean in terms of finding out what was really going on. And my teachers had tried. I mean I sat there with Marshall McLuhan, Hugh Kenner, Walter Van Tilburg Clark, Donald Davie, some good teachers, not to mention the ones you never heard of, and they gave no sense whatsoever of the dilemma of being a writer: things which are simply *mechanical,* like how do you get two objects into the same space at the same time, or how do you pass one thing through another. Those are questions reserved for life drawing, so the vocabulary of the mechanics of writing are eschewed in favor of the purely inductive. Critical language has been sustained by writers who are, one would think, entirely outside the range of the creative processes about which they speak, or at least freed somehow from the fruits they seem to produce . . .

So Vincent and I met somehow in the space between friendship and the emptiness of the scholarly world, at least in dealing with really important questions, like "How do I keep on writing when there's no Reward?"—such stuff as pre-motivated or non-driven writers might ask. And I went to Vincent in 1972 and asked him what to do, said, yo, here I am. And he basically said don't live my life, go home and live your own, so I did. Went back to Jody, the baby, the madness, collapses and renewals, ending a chapter in Montana, going back to Santa Barbara in 1978, my marriage with Patti and seventeen years in Portland, Oregon, which passed like a monumental kidney stone. I mean, that's *definitely* another story. The upshot came in 1988 on my fiftieth birthday, when I said it's now or never and started this current run of publishing and writing which has gone on now for about eight years. And no sign of breaking and running.

So what happened? I'd say I outlasted myself, outlived my own story, because here at the edge of the sea with Anabasis as my companion and identity, I'd say the autobiography and the place where one ends up are not necessarily the same story nor necessarily ruled by the same tactics and sentimentations. There's more than surprise to it in the causality of the poem in us as realized beings, and as the

1978

Teaching and Marriage

"Say this and no more."

Socrates, midwife. I try the voice out, yell, burst, retreat, and simultaneously divide myself a thousand ways and all succeed. In the fall, I marry; fall and winter falling like travel. The opening, without limit, without expression, into my own life, where the imagery finds its source, where I get embarrassed by the tools. It is not so unusual; fictional.

Modes generate thoughtscapes, lingua-tones. The roads in Michigan are also well traveled. "No thing but in doing." The photographs, too, adorn the walls like advertisements for a camera, which they are.

In the end, movement; the landscape changes (trees, wind, color of sunset, sun stretched ten miles wide by water vapor/heat/fog clouds. Snow piled higher than the roof).

---

poem itself begins to become manifest, we lose the story. It finally evades us and we fly free as something else, that which we have made. I wouldn't say that the fantasy takes over and chokes out the reality or that madness has fi-

nally overhauled reason. That's a tempting take. As the realization begins to take place and as the latter stages of individuation begin to occur, the ego falls away and the stories finally make sense, you know what they mean! The world becomes reasonable, not in its behavior but in one's relation to it. You may not know how something happens, but you may indeed know why. Not that you can put your finger on it.

There is a continuing essay on potentiation and silence to be written. There is another elongation of perpetuity and demonstration. She has become silent. Perhaps she has been erased or assumed into the body politic. Still the message is out for all to see, that final declarations are no less silent than they are profound—and it follows from where you are or where you have become who you are. It follows from *that* that you've missioned the present into some declaration of intent, which means you to follow when you might choose to lead. But still the sense of declaration and one's position to not yield, these actives become the nature of what is going on and not the opposite, not some other relation in which the image and the thing seen have become identified with a process other than the one which leads to their perception in the first place.

And forgiveness in this context is the same thing as ecstasy. It is not some cosmic orgasm we seek, but a release from its fantasy, that it should exist in that form and no other, and that forgiveness comes in the guise of silence or perhaps even its tears of dismissal.

I seem to have stumbled in upon a realm of psychoactive poetry, though it is solitary and somewhat autosexual in its relation to the beloved. I mean, there is a union of opposites which has taken place, and there is a feminine aspect of development which has been expressed and which has not turned into its opposite, but so what? This would be my own model for survival, and I would guess that mistaking the messenger for the message is inherent in any form of hero worship, even the kind of worship the ego reserves for itself. There it is: how to be humble in the face of one's own isolation. How to maintain the isolation by which the work got done in the first place and yet present one's work as if it were a testimony to its opposite, the joy of being/becoming human, and when it is as much an expression of one's longing as it is of one's status as a realized being. That would be pretentious, at least, to present one's poetry as if it were the vocalizations of a fully realized being. Such a thing would hardly speak at all, wouldn't you say? No, you say, this is the sign of my survival, no more no less, and if the heart has gone missing in this, oh well, it could have been worse. Well, it could have been better, too. It could have been what it should have been, eh? Is that sour grapes or trails not taken? No matter in the moment, these are the signs of our survival into this moment and no more, and that's evanescent. Poems in

the sand the water washes away with each beat of the tide. And in the anabasis of the moment is its conflation seen as something new and real. That would be the doorway into the next moment, for in the reassembly of the moment is the sign given about which way to jump, twist, or turn in one's entry into the next moment, into the future of one's self, surprised by the intensity of the shock, perhaps a little dazed, if you pay attention closely to your seriality in the context of how you pay attention, incrementally, in an unbroken flood of consciousness you are sampling this bit and that, attending with the unevenness of thinking itself, if that's not too glib.

Driving over the bridge in May 1996, I was up at the top of the Fremont Bridge with its grand arch and tiny American flag at the top, where you can look out over the toy metropolis, Portland, with its bridges and tiny skyline, and just a little baked on some decent green Mexican. It was early evening in the sunset and all the lights were on and I said, where's

---

Travel

At a certain point it is all experiment. You leave this, go from that. A village colors: the mind shrinks and stretches. You know less and less, and finally the donkeys speak back, open letters, calculate fares, pace back and forth.

They are all talking about it, about defining their lives in what they are doing, and yet they are all visitors. Success! The superior man walks on the clouds of the ceiling. The sea breaks and splits, the fish grow legs and leave for the city. The open boxes virtualize. When you return, you leave for another place; the new city, the one you left, has flattened overnight, only because it didn't change. It works, too, and you are never the same.

What you talk about changes, the nights change, love changes into the night. Food emerges from the closet, bright music from the streets.

Are they all blind? The corridors move like waves and rivers of sense and space and divide like time and organization. The visual emerges.

---

the pain, duh, the pain is gone, the pain is gone, how long now? It's been gone for awhile and I didn't even notice. Fifty years of pain gone and I didn't even notice. The pain is still gone. One may yet be a fool, but if the pain is gone, well, that's the big thing.

TOM Anabasis,

You've heard my voice—
Now I am putting it into print—

that piece on Style isPsychoactive carries on where Olson
left off on the Projective vs Nonprojective verse

        the whole Language scene is floundering in a steam stall
and your essay pulls the carpet from under the mental feet!   falling bareass

You have the words, the mind, the guts to carry on
in a world of verse thatsso far out of innerspace

they have lost touch with the flesh of living, words words
the flood is a diarrhea, logo-rehea, the stink if so refined

it has no substance, no smell, the sense^{S}are etherealized!
with out the substance of hot air-the wetness, all that dry wordaging-

at the rate they are going their flood will make Noah's
look like waves in a bathtub, as you well know,

so mauch that they are confronting you with the same output,
but you are older, you've lived throughthe Divine Comedy

you have found your voice and stance after all these years
and that energy is going to take you places you have never
                is
been to, which/your primary element, I dont the patience of a teacher,
I have my own/ which I was born with, and where I have been functioing
            lang
ever since, BUT you have the knowledge, capacity, and the vocabulary
these highstrung birdies understand and are at ease with listening

a second box of Split Shift came in, I will mail you a copy, so
show you (alas ignored) there are important poets I am in touch with

even Jake Berry in a last letter sent highest regards, but you
have found your calling, you are going to all the foam of the surf
                                            put
in a gallon, and send the waves of the ocean toward these peckers,
who veer as the power of the tide
                        lets them
you are in a propitious place, steam ahead, what Charles Olson
was to his generation you will be for the new poetry-
                            ship
you are one of the seers on our Serpent, this time POETRY is
going to count, even as I make it in Gloucester where my words go

under the skins of people making waves!
much love and
        word
on wood soldiers!   3/7/96

*mail
x + A to
your archives -*

A letter from Vincent Ferrini

What does that say about cigarettes out in the rain in various driveways in various subdivisions, while inside is some wife or other and some kids, and you're tingling with madness and pain and hate and rage and stoned so you can keep still and just fucking go on with it, what do you say about that? Or riding the Greyhound mescaline-stoned from Missoula to

Oakland, periodontal glow mumbling all night to the lady next to you—sorry, had to talk to somebody—just like a frigging movie, is how it goes. Is that the stuff of autobiography? I think it's more in the motive of the movie to still talk to your children and to be safe and alive at this point in time, and if the poetics of what comes out of that is a survival and a line into something of interest, so much the better for what came by and what went down. It's too long to wait for the movie to end and, in the long run, it's not so much a matter of being alone or of liking it or not, it's more in the tempo of the time passing underhand, saying to the continuing exploration that there is more to see and more to notice, while not paying attention particularly to what was there before. In the historicity of the moment you'd notice that there was indeed a day before yesterday, and that in what is important and what is not, you'll be more certain to say something quietly and over-and-over, and that in the secrecy of what is not noticed, you'll be there waiting patiently for yourself to catch up.

Perhaps there's an inherent distrust in memory itself as a way of mediating yourself inasmuch as poetry is a form of mediation within conscious mentation in repose, perhaps that's what's at play in the poetics of the moment now, denying syntax its realm of play and force, denying image the fervor of the sign, denying rhythm the trance of its drum and gong. I mean, there is in any poetics a nuts-and-bolts reference to how things fit together and what goes first and what makes this happen and what doesn't, even if it's only *implied* in a body of work, which I think is how apologists go on with it. And *that's* okay, but nonetheless the vision inherent in any syntax is a clue to its heart and soul, to the very path it advocates in one's mediation with one's self, which is what spiritual progress is all about, what poetry is, or should be, all about, or at least *used* to be about. Poetry and its associated Poetics is about what to do in various states of attending in order to advance, in order to grow and achieve self, or whatever lies out there for you. Whatever you're looking for, I suppose.

"With my friend Vincent Ferrini at the Stonehenge replica in Maryhill, Washington," 1992

Writing as a form of self-correction, squeezing those inner glands for all they're worth, that's the cure. But then I put in the time. I spent ten years in a windowless, unventilated, basement office, all the time thinking, "Well, they never got me . . ."; and spent three days wacked out on MDA going through my brain with a laser needle, erasing memories and recircuiting my own frontal lobotomy in an attempt to pass through the eye of a camel. You think I'm joking? Intellectual poverty law?

I'd think that the techno-techs and info slaves of 2001 will want diagrams which allude to a personal freedom within the brainstem which is achieved through the psychoactive poetic meditation exercises enshrined within free-associated rhythm-codes we have buried inside a seemingly harmless bar-code-style poemics. "The markers mark south. Shade dilemma not withiner but held and firm." These can become triggers, as in Tantric thrown-attention exercises, linked to erotic centers which are more appropriate to sexually non-practicing units, er, citizens. And as a mythology turns from obsessively procreative to passively autoerotic, the nature of the song changes, the nature of connection changes and becomes more suggestive, less barbaric, more enticing within even the associative glue a more sensual becoming in the completion of the set. Just as emptying syntaxes and energy bombs of acid release poemics which leak out from their own explosions or lack, so too the honestly erotic may actually lead one to Feeling and Emotion, just what will prove to be so missing in a massively post-tactile age, that is the one that follows.

And so what we are designing is the poetic which lies ahead, that is if we are doing anything at all with our time besides becoming the autoslave of our own self-attention, which is a way to go. However bad this world may be, you can be sure the next will be a hell of a lot worse, and any residues we leave behind which speak in the syntactical-synaptical of the present moment will work like the mysterious codes of Tibetan monks suggested, only suggested, in trumpet blowing and long-chordal chanting; and in Sufi moans of repetition and variation. What is passed on or through our nomenclature for the present are subtle and invisible things we are hardly aware of, but which are nonetheless aspects of cultural transmission which should no doubt be codified and recorded.

ANABASIS LONGS FOR HOME

Thrust team yips I'd yelled no homer in the mists
of chance left us there on the pealing loam
in host of nothing made no more than sentences are,
misfit and strung; held in the leading pool
we dealt in determinate hedgerows, latenced-out

Hard upon silence the wailing blood sentenced
you to loneliness under your own hand
asleep in the wool of utter's sailing into
but laid among the rushes in beneath blue
portico, lattice, the event tempo of doubt

Valley to witnessed calm, we chased oranges
out of musk and distances up the road to the water
in the barrel in the loam of summer's own insists,
these at the anchor barn of the sleeping pint
down at the wooden door, down at the song

Hailed as we were in the afterglow of nukes,
the jazz line emptied the heart of its own blue woe
and deleted roses from the vocabulary of chance
noxing patterned monks their usual accords where
homers dusker'd famous interns their butts first

You'd longed too for the clean edge of the willing
the marked flight of blue and green birds again
term of the rotating dome we describe in all our
stories, having seen nothing of love in a thousand
ears and sentiments having been sent to the lords

Maybe you'd said "Down, Fang," to one of the neighbors
again, not once but twice in the face of destiny
and gophers you long to go skiing in rice
pasting soya beaners into the relict and palm
loasting the permit strain into its own fortunes

And you stroke out for home, er foam on her lips
again against your tongue beating a staccato stress
on the button in her jeans, a lap made sinner
a scene made winter in your discontent, unbalanced
and sane on the beast of your own dreams again

Where'd formed some roast internal eyes'd intent
your maiden in repose some leafing scraps they'd farted
thus belittled from myth to carton on the milk, no more
feared than uh made in tents to seem a cartoon instead
but sofa'd into deal remute to beer at the corner

This is where you lost the cause and made another
country your own, made the lasting century into
a fashion and a song, and made chutney into a household
name and season on the calm return, here at the sealing
trim, here at the posting dream, positioned and sent.

—Oysterville, Washington, 10.21.96

Thomas and his brother, Jack, in Oysterville, Washington, 1996

Why I Write

*Just doing the work for its own sake, all the rest is
gravy. Who can tell anyone anything?*

—Vincent Ferrini, from a letter, May 1995

We were going to change the world—
that was the line when I came out in
the sixties into teaching and writing. There was
actually a sense of commitment and mission,
more or less unheard of in recent times. There
was a sense that some sort of *us* would replace the old, dying set of linguistic symbols
(images) with counters which were more directly accessible to consciousness. There was going
to be a revolution in the *kind* of poetry that
was made. Maybe this was only in my own mind,
but I did feel a kind of crazy, radical unanim-
ity which linked poets together, not the careerist
fending-off-the-wolves approach we have now.
Later, when the revolution had been co-opted
by the very success it had courted, I wrote out
of commitment, or foolishness, or because it
was all I knew how to do. Poets are good for

baby-sitting and housepainting, a "friend" told
me once. . . . And, more recently, I wrote to
save my ass, from *what* exactly I don't know—
from the void, a dark emptiness one encounters which is cause itself. Now, somehow, my
writing is more playful.

We were going to take over the world, replace an obsolete discourse with one which was
more efficient in its relation of conscious to
unconscious, somehow more aligned: no thing
but in *seeing*. But you forget along the way
that a way is there at all, and so I wrote for
all the reasons one could have. I made it my
reason for existence, an esoteric, private activity which explained my moodiness and my inability to share myself with others in intimate
relationships, whether they were colleagues or
wives or my own children. I wrote from arrogant self-righteousness, a blind, drunken (averted)
rage, and in the isolation of the secret mas-
turbator. Isolated and yet desperate for the company of others, afraid to be alone with my
"genius," as it unfolded from calm intention
through self-loathing and sabotage to addiction
and personality disorders and the absurd vow

"With my sons, Yarin, Robin, and Alex," Portland, Oregon, 1992

of poverty. Those were all part of the deal. I kept writing day after day, page after page of black scratch on yellow paper. I courted chance, error, and those compositional mistakes by which the unconscious penetrates through and into conscious mentation, like Gurdjieff's monks chanting in such perfect union that the world itself ceases to exist.

I became aware of the disjunct and the profunct in myself. While writing, I would continue to feel the sacred rush and focus of depth-diving not experienced in any drug or ecstatic love state. I became addicted to the "passing beyond" one can experience in the repetitions of time and space manipulation of the writing act one tries to control. I wrote to allay (escape from) depressive states, sinking through them and their associated pain to discover the inebriation of the poem. I did not want to experience any real feeling at all, and so I stayed in a world of my own creation, with its autism of self and song: "the play of the mind, to see whether there is any mind there at all" (Charles Olson).

And people loved me, put up with me, though I could not return their love, I was in such a selfish, narcissistic state. I could not return the glow of humanity I could sense in others, even into last year, when I fell into the hole of myself again, the second or third or third-point-five nervous breakdown. Ah, how pure is the irony of one's own isolation and favor all in the name of the poem, sacrificing everything, even love, to the quest, the cause, the act, this false matrimony with the self. Writing is suppressed speech, with its own sense of breath: I chewed my lips, cracked my knuckles, and picked my nose as I wrote compulsively, believing I could get "there" again and again.

This has changed somewhat. One year after. Clean and sober. After a year of holing up and not writing. What is now described has no indistinctness—"futures favored forward" inclines the day to a more experienced sense of being. "Life is the poem," Vincent Ferrini says. What comes across from the old to the new is all that was imagined in the restitution of the present which begins in healing. I could still be lying, having replaced one delusive state with another, but I still write what is sometimes calm and still and flowing without any palpable sensation of being there at all, following the lines across the page, or free associating on the screen at eighty words a minute, sometimes it's that good.

It was all so calculated, with me a bit player in my own dream. Writing became the self-

---

Time and Space

Passing like seasons of air, dark edges in the symptoms of movement; born as though discovered, and furniture and the categories of the floor where the dust disguises the grain of the wood. He walks down the hall and stops at a window where he sees the seasons in their monumental changes, spreading beyond the landscape as roads do, like boundaries or ideas, and leaves them falling.

---

causal progression through the inchoate and out into the light. And one's youthful fantasy that one could change (rule) the world effaced to just being there. Our image of Peter Sellers, as he walks out of his last movie, is of him becoming smaller and smaller as he walks out upon the water, into what, just *into.* . . . So, I continue to write because I must continue putting one word down after another, and then another one, as a web of surprise continues to lead me across my time into whatever it is that is there to be discovered in this spasm which is continuing itself. *Today is the tomorrow you were so worried about yesterday (A.A.).*

I live at the beach to think and dream and act and write and continue.

BIBLIOGRAPHY

Poetry:

relimn (poems 1970–1990), anabasis, 1991.

The One, The Same, and The Other (a poetic for events), Texture Press/Spectacular Diseases, 1993.

Daily Logs (poems), anabasis, 1996.

Chapbooks:

Pisces, anabasis, 1976.

das marchen, with note by Susan Smith Nash, anabasis, 1992.

J F K, Texture Press, 1994.

Diction, and Visionary Education, anabasis, 1996.

Editor:

The ?WHY? Project, anabasis, 1991.

The Love Project, anabasis, 1994.

Jessica Freeman, *Bolt bleu* (poems), illustrated with photographs by Thomas Lowe Taylor, anabasis, 1996.

E-mail: anabasis@willapabay.org.

Nanos Valaoritis

1921-

In the beginning was the separation. I was separated from my mother in the town of Lausanne in Switzerland on the shore of Lake Leman in a small pension named Florissant, which still existed a few years back. After a seventeen-hour labor, or so I am told, I appeared reluctantly in this world, not at all pleased at the prospect of leaving the comfort of my mother's belly—but there was no choice. I couldn't go backward into the state of microorganism from which I had been torn by the felicitous meeting of my father with my mother one night nine months earlier. I was, so to speak, trapped one way to exist. I know all that now, thanks to our scientific knowledge, yet it is still a mystery to me why I was born from two Greek parents without being asked what nationality I wanted to be—and in Switzerland of all places instead of their native Greece. The reason for this displacement is simple. My father was a diplomat and at that time consul general in Lausanne, where many Greeks chose to live or visit in the early years of this century.

For me, however, the mystery deepens of why these microorganisms were created by my parents out of nothing, or maybe it was on account of food transmuted into living organisms; however, the creation ex nihilo has always appealed to me in spite of its unlikelihood. That tiny mustard seed from the Bible that contains the big tree has always intrigued me to the point where I begin to ask myself the Question—the great metaphysical question— of why me and not nothing? Or why me and not another—let's say an Australian Aborigine, or an Eskimo, or even a plain Swiss, one of those who were hovering in the neighborhood? Or again, why me, male baby, instead of female? And so on ad infinitum. Little did I realize when I was pointing a year or so later at the moon and saying in my baby French, "la lune," that my embroilment with language was going to be more or less a permanent state of affairs. Next thing I was doing in Tübingen,

Nanos Valaoritis, at home,
Oakland, California, 1996

Germany, was pointing to a hole in the ground from which ants emerged, asking in my childish German, "Was ist das, Fraulein Hermine?" I had no idea why I didn't speak French anymore or what was that new entity "Germany" in which I was now immersed, especially the house of Herr Professor and Frau Professor, and their son Wolfgang, a sullen boy of about twelve, who steadily refused to drag my wooden train behind his electric one, in spite of my pathetic pleas, while their dog, a wolfhound, was the source of my constant curiosity, fear, and fascination at the same time. But there were other things in those early years—such as delicious strawberries on the ground and cherries on the trees in spring, which I was not entirely forbidden to eat. What I was not aware of either was what the eggs my mother fed me cost in Germany at that time—so she had to give them to me secretly in my room—a few million marks of the devalued currency after Germany's defeat in World War I. For those were the years I inhabited this magical garden, unaware also that my father was seriously ill. My father disappeared totally from my memory even though he had been present, since I have a photograph of me sitting between him and my mother on a bench in the garden.

Next thing I knew, still in the throes of my own Creation Myth, was a terrible thunderstorm with flashes of lightning and rain in Venice, as we were getting off a gondola to enter the hotel with my mother, the faithful Hermine, and perhaps a Greek maid. Venice, revisited later, always represented for me the birth of Terror and of the Thunder Gods I later came to know in my studies as Zeus, Thor, and others, very noisy fellows. The period of my Creation Myth seems to have ended there in a very Vician[1] manner, in reverse, since in the beginning was nature, civilization, the garden, then the older boy, the train, and the dog, and finally the Thunder Giants.

Since my father was missing, it is probable that I might have imagined him and his wrath visiting me on this occasion—although he was a gentle soul, suffering from manic melancholia, an illness that was as mysterious as his whole existence to my mind. And it seems he did not recognize me the last time my mother took me to visit him. I never saw him again and went to his funeral some twelve years later. That the world was a dangerous and hostile place in spite of the good care of the women around me confirmed my earlier suspicions of what it would be like, resulting in my tendency to avoid emerging from my mother as long as I could.

Venice was only an in-between station on the road to Athens, Greece, my country to be for the next twenty-three years. Yet there, too, I was pursued by a strange northern evil in the person of my next governess—by then I must have been four—Fraulein Lipenska, probably named Vera, who pulled me by the hair to punish me. The report goes that she actually hung me by the hair for God knows what childish transgression. When discovered, she was duly dispatched back to Sudetenland, Czechoslovakia, from where she had come. As a result, my relation to the German language was ruined for life, and I soon forgot it while I was picking up Greek from the environment of family and servants. Yet another northerner appeared in my life in the person of Miss Booth, an English lady with red hair—the previous one as I remember had brownish red hair, while the angelic Hermine was mousy colored. Upon learning later that beets came from Czechoslovakia, I developed an aversion to them, which I still have to this day. Miss Booth turned out to be a real oasis in my angst-ridden life. She taught me painless English to read and write— to read endlessly children's books, comics, nursery rhymes in three short years. Then she got married to a Greek army officer who was killed in the Albanian Campaign in 1940–1941. In the meanwhile an elderly Greek tutor appeared who gave me private lessons in Greek in my

Mother, Catherine (née Leonidas) Valaoritis

---

[1]In reference to the writings of the Italian philosopher Giambattista Vico.

Father, Constantine Valaoritis

grandmother's anteroom. I had a physical aversion to him, but he was kindly and taught me elementary Greek to write and read and prophesied that one day my talent would unfold. I am told by trustworthy sources that he believed in me firmly, bringing my early compositions as proof.

We lived in this three-story house in the middle of Athens facing a square on which was erected during my childhood the statue of the founder of the Friendly Society, a certain Emmanuel Xanthos, and the Square from Kolonaki—or Little Column—was renamed Friendly Society Square—Plateia Filikis Etaireias. This Xanthos was, with Skoufos and Tsakalof, one of the original group of merchants in Odessa, Russia, who swore in secrecy to liberate the Greek lands from the Turks. The fellow looked rather pale and innocuous, perhaps due to the weak expressivity of the bust. He certainly didn't look like someone who would liberate anything. In the street in front of the house there was a row of taxis—this was still in the twenties when cars were relatively rare—

and one of them was a very friendly Russian driver named Ivan, who spoke with a heavy accent and told us about the horrors of the Bolsheviks during the revolution and from whom he had escaped. The tales of this Russian exile impressed my young mind, and I imagined Russia as a very wild country where horrors were performed daily by roaming criminals.

The family house had what seemed like an immense basement where the male servants had their rooms, and there was a huge kitchen and a charming old cook with a white cap and mustache who looked like Santa Claus. The maids lived in a room on the third and last floor, where I was. My room faced the terrace and the Hymettus, on the back side of the house. My mother, my great-aunt Lily, my Granny, and my aunt Helen all lived on the second floor. My grandfather, Ioannis Valaoritis, had been an impressive man, an economist and director of the National Bank. He had played a role in the economic recovery of Greece before 1912, in cooperation with the brilliant politician Eleutherios Venizelos. Together they masterminded the recovery of Greek lands in the 1912–1913 wars with Turkey. Unfortunately, he died in 1914 in an accident in the port of Piraeus: fearing a collision between his friend Leonidas Embirikos's yacht and a steamer, he jumped into the sea after a heavy meal and suffered a massive heart attack. He was also the son of Aristotle Valaoritis (1824–1879)—a famous nineteenth-century national and romantic poet descended from freedom fighters of Epirus in the late seventeenth century—and editor of his father's poetry. Aristotle's political activities against the British rule of the Ionian Islands, and as representative of his own particular one, Lefkas, made him a hero and a passionate defender of national causes. Much of his poetry was on subjects and episodes in the rebellions against the Venetians and the Turks. He was the first great poet to express himself more completely and easily in the demotic language.

His son's widow, my grandmother Zoe, was from a family of Phanariots, who had escaped the massacres of the Turks in 1821. Her great-grandfather Alexander Mourouzi had been reigning Prince of Moldovalachia in the eighteenth century, while her young grandfather, then a grand interpreter at the Porte, Constantine Mourouzi, lost his head to the sultan on the outbreak of the Greek revolution. Between 1790 and 1821 the Mourouzi family, originally from

At three years old in Germany with his parents

Trebizond on the Black Sea and related by marriage to the imperial family of the Comnenes, had lost seven members, decapitated by the Turks who always suspected them of treason on the slightest grounds. My granny Zoe's grandmother, the wife of Constantine, was pregnant with Zoe's father when they were rescued by a Russian diplomat and escaped on a Greek ship to Odessa. After the liberation they came to Athens and settled. Her father, named Constantine after his slain father, became an officer in the Greek navy. She also had a notorious brother, George Mourouzi, who became legendary in popular novels owing to his exploits as a witty dandy and eccentric cavalry officer.

The floor on which my granny lived with her sister Lily Mourouzi—both of whom had been great beauties—had a kind of hall in which there was a glass cupboard filled with antiquities, statuettes, vases, and such objects that, according to my family, had been found in the foundation when the house was being built. I often stood puzzled before these artifacts, wondering who these ancient Greeks were who had left their statuettes and vases buried under our

house. On the first floor a marble staircases led to a small hall, where visitors left their cards on a large platter. My uncle's office, to the left of the stairs, had an impressive bookcase, and this was where the family received visitors on a daily basis. On the other side of the marble stairs and the hall were two immense salons for more formal occasions, such as receptions, and behind was a dining room— also very grand—with a large table that sat at least twelve people. On the third floor, another room facing the square was a guest room where my cousins often stayed. Next to my room was a storeroom filled with huge trunks, remnants of an earlier age of travel to Europe—as we called the western countries—which now held carnival clothes, dominoes, winter clothes, furs, and other items in naphthalene. The spiral staircase that joined the three stories was a wooden one, slippery because of its polish, and I never descended without a feeling of vertigo.

After my grandmother's death in 1928, my uncle Aristotle moved into her room. Later he built a personal *garçonniere* in the back garden of the house. I remember the series of black-and-white prints that hung on the staircase. They portrayed demons hounding the souls of sinners in hell, probably from frescoes in Orvieto by Signorelli—a painter famous for Freud having forgotten his name. My mother's room, along with my great-aunt's, was the largest on the second floor. My two most intense memories of it were when my mother was ill with malaria that she had probably contracted on Lefkas, and the other was of the torture divan on which I was laid out, year after year, for an endless series of painful injections of some fortifying substance to ward off the ills of my thinness due to anorexia. There was also the fear of heredity, then commonly held to be true, concerning my father's bout with tuberculosis of the spine. The doctor who injected me on the behind was a burly, large man—kindly on the whole, although, unwittingly, he often hurt me. His name was Dr. Morelis, or something like that, which always colored Jules Verne's *Moreau's Island* with an added sinister quality, as well as *Morel's Island* by Adolfo Bioy Casares. The ordeal was such that I considered those days with dread and felt great relief when they were over, which was not until I was ten or eleven. I was finally cured of anorexia when my mother took me to Switzerland in 1928 and left me in a summer camp called Champs Soleil for three months while she took my father back to Greece from Germany. For three months we ran around half naked, boys and girls, on grassy slopes, swam in the pool, and slept on the balcony. With such stimulation my appetite quickly reappeared and never left me. It was at that time I visited Paris for the first time. I was photographed climbing the Eiffel Tower, hanging from it from the outside, peering out of one of those cartons you put your head in. We stayed at the Balzac Hotel, rue Balzac, near the Champs Elysees, and with our maid Maria, who traveled with us, I visited the superb cafés of the Avenue for hot chocolate every afternoon.

Living in this huge house in Athens was awesome to my childish mind, anguishing for reasons I couldn't fathom. When I started reading books of adventures, a story about some far north trappers who ate each other in a cave in Canada filled me with dread and caused a terrible nightmare from which I woke screaming, with my mother and others running up to see what was the matter. I was not really unhappy, but neither was I happy with older family, mostly in mourning. I had no one to relate to, and I sought to go on weekends with friends who had many siblings and a much more cheerful atmosphere in their homes. There were two families who had houses with large outdoor spaces or gardens. Their children were my friends from an early age, and stays there were some of my happiest memories.

On our return from Switzerland, I was given a new governess, Mademoiselle Jornaux, who turned out to be wonderful. She taught me French without tears, in three years, and I started avidly reading French books. Yet I suffered from something like a syndrome of loneliness, as well as from tedium and angst. This was much like what Marcel Proust—whom I read precociously, with a strong feeling of déjà vu at the age of fourteen—described in the books I found in my father and my mother's little library. I totally identified with that sickly sensibility in the novels, beset by anguished longings and unfulfilled crushes on people.

Athens, on the other hand, seemed to me a most dilapidated and run-down city, dusty, unkempt, from which even the extensive public or royal gardens were not immune. They were named accordingly, depending on whether there was a king in the palace alongside it on Herod of Atticus Street or a president of the Republic. In the years of my childhood and early adolescence, the president, Alexander Zaimis, was a relative, a cousin of my grandmother, whom I visited with my great-aunt Lily every New Year's. We had tea with him and his German wife, and he used to give me splendid gifts. His brother Asimakis Zaimis often took me and my great-aunt on a ride in his car. He had an uncanny resemblance to the politician Eleutherios Venizelos, with his sharp goatee. My mother's family was no less prominent and also involved in the history of Greece. They were from the island of Spetses, descendants of Captain Lambros—later Leonidas—named from the figurehead of King Leonidas of Sparta, the hero of Thermopylae, that was on the prow of his ship. It was in this that he fought the War of Independence against the Turks. The origin of the family was probably from the area of Leonidion, in the Tsakonic district of the Peloponnese, that still spoke a Doric dialect incomprehensible to other Greeks. He had been a prosperous trader earlier and daredevil, breaking the British blockade during the Napoleonic Wars, and his interception by no other than Nelson is described in a short story by Friedrich Engels. When Captain Lambros was asked by Nelson on his ship what he would have done to him if he had been in his place—without batting an eyelid, Lambros replied: "I would have hung you from the middle mast." Taken aback by his courage, Nelson answered: "This time I'll let you go, but next time I'll do exactly that." Lambros and Captain Botasis had both married daughters of the headman of the island, Hadjiyannis-Mexis. When Spetses was threatened by the Turkish armada on 8 September 1922, the Greek fleet facing it was given the signal by the Hydriot Admiral Miaoulis to retreat. Captains Lambros and Botassis, knowing that this would mean the doom of their island and homes—after the early standoff due to lack of wind—began the battle. They towed their ships with rowboats close to the Turkish frigates and started firing. When the rest of the fleet saw what had happened, they turned round and engaged the Turks. After an inconclusive day-long battle, the Greeks set the fireships on them. The Turkish armada retreated, and the island was saved.

A less glorious incident involved my grandfather Ioannis Leonidas, grandson of Captain Lambros, who was a member of the ill-fated Greek government that was held responsible for the catastrophe of Asia Minor in 1922. My grand-

The author's great-grandfather, Aristotle Valaoritis, nineteenth-century poet (1824–1879)

booming Greek merchant port. Her family, partly settled in Marseilles, was Francophone, and her brother, Jacques Damalas, married Sarah Bernhardt, the famous actress who became the great-aunt of my mother. My great-uncle's marriage to her was a stormy one and lasted five years, into the early 1880s, with a lot of graphic episodes chronicled by the French and English press.

In my early school days, army coups were frequent, with the military coming out with the same old armored cars, and there were demonstrations in the main streets. I was already longing for the glamorous capitals of Europe, described in those books I read voraciously. I had peeked at one of those on our stay in Paris in 1928, with all the colorful electric ads on buildings that gave the city a magical aspect. But that wasn't enough. And for years I dreamt of returning to those magical cities, populated by mythical and beautiful beings. In this southern country, often dry and arid, we dreamt of the north, with its rains and mysterious atmosphere, and of romantic heroes appearing from the mist. Our readings enhanced this longing and some of us couldn't wait to go north, where the power and the glory seemed to be.

By the age of ten, there were no more governesses or home teaching. I was sent to a private school in downtown Athens, on Hippocrates Street, about a ten-minute walk from the house. The first days were traumatic, since I was not accustomed to collective situations, having been tutored at home until then. The other children seemed hostile or indifferent and the teachers cruel. I was often punished by ruler slaps on the hands, while the director of the school seemed to me inhumanely strict. This was a very different world from the home environment and fed my tendency to introspection. I didn't exactly become an introvert, but the behavior of the elementary teachers and the gymnastics in the schoolyard, all seemed real torture to me. I was totally alienated and clung to my home life and my mother. Things changed when I entered the first grade of the gymnasium at the age of twelve. A new teacher, who was also a writer, greeted with enthusiasm my first composition on the subject, "Write about the best day of your life." He described my contribution as "like sugar!" which in Greek didn't carry the connotation of sugary but rather

father, who was the minister of mercantile marine, escaped by being hidden by my father's family, the fate of the six other ministers and the Generalissimo of the Greek army was to be shot after a summary trial. My grandfather then retired from politics and developed his private island Spetsopoula, which he had purchased from other part owners. He built a magnificent villa on top of a cliff overlooking the Aegean Sea, where the family and I spent many unforgettable summers. He was also a Sunday painter and painted many naval battles of the Greek War of Independence, some of which hang in public places. He is buried on the island in a chapel that he built and painted with frescoes. Later the island was sold to shipping magnate Niarchos.

My maternal grandmother was Helen Leonidas, née Macreth. Her father, James, was a doctor in the merchant navy. Originally from County Cork, he had five beautiful sisters who married various French, English, or German husbands. He met Catherine Damalas, my great-grandmother, on the island of Syros, then a

Ancestral family home of Aristotle Valaoritis, on the island Madouri, Greece

of something very appealing. My prestige went up instantly in the eyes of my schoolfellows, who from then on looked upon me with awe and respect. This made me aware of the power of writing and from a rather unhappy child, turned me eventually into a writer. I had discovered a weapon that I could brandish peacefully and thus defend myself from bullies and be favored by the girls. This did not happen immediately, but much later, since I was still painfully shy and hopelessly in love—from the age of five—with a number of little girls, much like what Proust described in the early volumes of *Remembrance of Time Past.*

When I was fourteen my father died. I had never seen him since he was confined to an asylum, but I went to his funeral. That year was a signal year for me because I was initiated into the mysteries of sex, death, and reproduction almost simultaneously—after the funeral—by a girl two years older than I who taught me how to kiss. I was still incredibly naive for my age. That very same year, I chanced upon the collected poems of C. P. Cavafy, whom I didn't even know by name since he wasn't

taught at school on account of his homosexual love poems and his pessimistic and skeptical attitude where the history of Greece was concerned. The volume was offered at a book exhibition in Athens in a big hall on Academy Street. It happened to be opposite from my maternal grandparents' future apartment. Athens was still a relatively small city then. And all the main cafés and bookstores where writers met were a couple of blocks away. Cavafy's poems had a very different style to what I had been accustomed, when reading the traditional bardic and symbolist poets. The language was strangely direct or ordinary, so much so that Kostis Palamas, his main rival, called it "journalistic." There was also an enigmatically didactic tone in these poems, which used often well-known subjects from Greek history to give a mostly ambiguous and highly dramatic lesson. They contrasted totally with the convoluted rhetoric of the poetry of Kostis Palamas, the leader of the demotic movement, whom we were taught at school by our faithful teacher I. M. Panayotopoulos, the same one who had singled me out earlier for my composition piece and who was also a poet but of a more traditional kind. Cavafy's poems, read often like prose, for their prosody was either too obvious to be noticed or hidden, which made him the first and earliest Greek modernist. Also, like the novels of Proust, they touched a deep spring in my being because they spoke of existential and psychological problems. In contrast to the ethnocentrism of the main Helladic demotic school, their overriding tone was one of defeat, in fact a series of defeats and humiliations suffered by the Greeks in their long history and their gradual fall from power and glory. And whenever rhetorical boasting about something occurred, the poem turned into ironic first person monologues by characters in self-deceiving situations. The only victories were stoic resignations and not of heroic struggles against the Turks, as were the poems of my ancestor, Aristotle Valaoritis, one of the founders of the demotic movement.

One of Cavafy's poems, "Waiting for the Barbarians," especially hit a chord in my preoccupations and in a curious way became negatively prophetic—especially the last lines when messengers of an imaginary Roman Empire arrive from the borders announcing that no barbarians were left: "And now what will we do without Barbarians?" asks the poet. "These people were some kind of a solution." These lines resonated in accord with the tedium and the spleen expressed by so many symbolists, beginning with Baudelaire, whom I was discovering at the same time, thanks to a very alert and well-informed young Swiss tutor who taught at the French Institute. He introduced me to the Parnassian poets: Baudelaire, Gautier, Rimbaud, and Mallarme, whose "decadent" tradition was a strong influence on European letters.

Cavafy seemed strangely actual, even if the lines about barbarians proved totally wrong, since the worst barbarians in history appeared no later than a few years in the form of German Nazis and Italian Fascists. To my mind the irony of "waiting" for those barbarians who "didn't even exist" in the poem had a wider cultural connotation. These supposedly "imaginary" barbarians who in the poem were the energizers of a tired, old culture, would soon spring up among us in the form of Stalinists, or extreme rightists, in the Greek civil war of 1944–1949. If polarization and fanaticism were what was meant by "barbarians," they were all present, horribly alive and well.

At age eighteen, when his writings first appeared in Ta Nea Grammata, *standing in the mountains in the Peloponnese, Greece, 1939*

My aesthetic preferences were definitely on the decadent, symbolist and modernist side, represented by Cavafy, Proust, Baudelaire, Rimbaud, and the Greek modernist and surrealist poets and critics, such as Capetanakis, George Seferis, Andreas Embirikos (also a Freudian psychoanalyst), Odysseus Elytis, Nikos Gatsos, and Nikos Engonopoulos. The last four were declared surrealists, while Seferis, a more classical modernist, turned out to be a most gifted essayist, along with Elytis who in a different style and orientation introduced and defended Surrealism against the numerous conservative poets and critics. Their magazine *Ta Nea Grammata,* in which my first poems appeared in 1939, also carried translations from Paul Eluard, Henri Michaux, Ezra Pound, T. S. Eliot,

Jules Supervielle, and other modernist Europeans. It lasted about ten years, from 1935 to 1946. The humour, lyrical innovativeness and language experimentation of this new Greek poetry placed their exponents apart in an elite circle around the magazine. In 1940 the publication of Elytis's poem "Orientations" became the event of the year.

Among the then Greek novels, there was one that came close to the poetic quality I demanded from prose as well. This was an adolescent saga by Kosmas Politis, which was the nom de plume—a play of words on "cosmopolitan"—of Paris Taveloudis, a bank and insurance clerk from Smyrna. His novel *Eroica* struck our youthful imaginations to the point of becoming a cult book. The novel was planned against the background of the story of Achilles and Patrocius in the *Iliad,* describing a group of adolescents led by two young boys who were the archetypal avatars of the two heroes of the *Iliad.* The heroine Monica was a kind of Helen of Troy, the daughter of the Italian consul, while the consulate was the equivalent of the castle of Troy. Midway through we find out from the narrator, one Paraskevas, that his friend Alekos (possibly a reference to Alexander or Paris, the real name of the author) was in love with Monica. At the end of the novel he is killed accidentally by her brother while making love to her in the garden. This brother, who always dressed as a monk and was in the habit of shooting cats from his balcony, represented the Catholic West, which often attacked us from behind. He mistook the rustling of the couple in the shrubbery for a cat. There was also a political and symbolic level to the novel on the position of Greece as a post-colonial nation caught between rival powers of East and West.

The characters represented in this poetic work, filled with innuendoes and sly references to both the classical age and the recent literary scene, are seen with an unusual distance and objectivity for a Greek novel that makes them and the whole atmosphere mysterious, alive, and strongly evocative as fiction. We then had no knowledge of James Joyce except in name as the inventor of a stream-of-consciousness technique and whose mythical method in *Ulysses* Kosmas Politis followed. That he had read Joyce there was no doubt. He later translated *The Dubliners.* Neither did we know any of the Rus-

sian formalists' definitions and analyses of the estrangement technique in novels, nor the carnavalesque theories of Bakhtin. Yet the novel of Kosmas Politis not only echoed our own romanticism in modern form, but also introduced the carnavalesque and a style and technique unknown until then in Greek prose.

The novel of Politis, first published serially in the review *Ta Nea Grammata,* coincided with all these echoes of romanticism and revolt and renovation we were attracted by, including, without being aware of it, the Bakhtinian universe of the carnavalesque and dialogic theory of presenting opposite ideas as personas as in Dostoyevski's novels without intervention by the author. The decadent nihilism of disillusion and pessimism in a world where optimism was crudely fascist or Stalinist was a form of active protest. The girl I was seeing then, Elsy—whose family name was also Politis—was the very image of the ambivalent Monica, the heroine of Politis's novel. Her family came from Constantinople, known by Greeks as "Polis" for short. There was an air of mystery about her, both western for she was blond and eastern in her languorous walk. My relations to her were as unresolved and complex as those described in the novel. Strangely enough jealousy did not enter in my relation to Elsy, although I was in love with her. Somehow I knew she was mine, in mind and body, even if she gave herself to another for reasons unknown to me—either contempt or pity or even a desire to escape from the family by marrying, something I was not prepared to do at nineteen. Her giving was so total that I never doubted her love but only her judgment, which seemed to me then entirely out of this world. I could even say ambiguously metaphysical, as women often were for existential authors, such as Dostoyevski's Pauline in *The Gambler.* So, I never criticized her decisions and thought them quite in keeping with the situation.

Later I was to find out that Henry Miller also was fascinated by a similarly ambiguous woman and André Breton too, which brings me to the meeting with Henry Miller that occurred probably in late 1939 or 1940 at the apartment of George Seferis. I had begun reading *Max and the Phagocytes* and liked his very open provocative style, especially when writing of D. H. Lawrence and the World of Death and of the film *Ecstasy* by Machaty, with Hedy Lamarr, which I happened to have seen, along with a

Athens, 1961

film by another Czech director, whose name and title I now forget, dealing with a band of adolescents that had also deeply impressed me. It must have been the time when I had read the *Grand Meaulnes* by Alain Fournier, a novel on the subject of adolescent imagination. So I asked Henry Miller what he thought of Conrad Aiken—whose *The Great Circle* featured an adolescent heroine Gwendolyn, whom I associated with Elsy. I remember Seferis came up to us at that moment, and Miller turned to him and explained that he thought Aiken was an author who wherever you cut him he was good. This description was the most damning compliment I've ever heard from the mouth of an author about another one. It disappointed me in relation to the novel that I admired and that I found out recently was also a favourite of Freud's, but it also introduced me—with a shock—to another dimension of thinking beyond my adolescent dreams, a more hard-nosed and pragmatic form of modernism, the one that the poet-critic Seferis also represented and that I was soon going to encounter in England and later in France.

The poem that played the most important part in my life, apart from Cavafy's, when I was sixteen or seventeen, was the "Mythistorema" (1935) by Seferis, translated usually as the "Myth of Our History," a word that means "novel" in Greek. This play on words houses the most enigmatic poem in modern Greek, which puzzled and angered the traditional critics and found a very eloquent and perceptive supporter in the person of modernist critic Andreas Karandonis, the director of the review *Ta Nea Grammata*. In reality the review was a collective affair financed by George Katsimbalis—the legendary storyteller of Henry Miller's *The Colossus of Maroussi*—who was not only a Maecenas but also a man of letters, a bibliographer, and a keen supporter of the bardic poet Kostis Palamas. His backward-looking inclusions of Palamas, he explained, were a ploy to woo the conservative Greek public for his review, and although he supported all the worthy modernist writers, he also complained bitterly that no Dante or Homer of modern Greece was in sight and cast his scornful arrows at all the poets he published for not being the one he had hoped for. To his dismay, these on the contrary showed all signs of being—if not out and out decadents—at least minor or lyrical, whose interests seemed to him hopelessly marginal and, worse, not manly or heroic enough to qualify as founders of a new nation and language. To pile insult upon injury, they were more often ironical and parodic like the rival of his beloved Palamas, C. P. Cavafy. The "Mythistorema" was definitely not a heroic poem, but rather a footnote to Greek myth, epic, drama, and history. It evoked in dreamlike language the past as it mingled with the present in scenes when things don't seem to advance or retreat, immersed in a nightmarish immobility. It gave not a call of heroic renewal but rather a dirge for a fallen civilization, whose remnants haunted the invisible, fragmented potential of modern Greece, evoking long-gone ancestors, shadows, stones. This is perhaps the only poem of George Seferis that arrives like a whole, the revelation of a foreign body whose formulas of composition are forever invisible. His poetry though hallucinatory was written in hard-edge language and clear imagery, which followed the precepts of Valéry and Modernism. Never in any poem had I met with a description of my own experiences growing up in Greece, this baffling mixture of the sublime with the trivial, the decayed with the vital, the vulgar and the insignificant with the most refined, bringing with it a true feeling of desolation and especially of the sense of enclosure, reflected in the people and the landscape, with the only saving grace, the sea. Seferis revealed to me that the Greek experience—painful as it was and seemingly sterile—could also be marvelous and revealing when put in the right perspective, as Cavafy three years earlier had shown me that one's introspective self could be expressed in poetic language using history, a history that until then had seemed to be composed only of clichés and dry bones.

My Greece was the Greece of Seferis and Kosmas Politis, low key, impossible to live in, filled with longing for the metaphysical other, enclosed, contradictory, out of which I dreamt to escape as soon as I could. That great men of letters could also be ogres I was to discover soon, and the need to protect oneself from their savagery was essential for a young man, without allowing himself to be discouraged or giving up.

Among the English in Athens, to begin with, I met Lawrence Durrell, who introduced me to the generation of the thirties with his own poetry and lent me books of Auden, Stephen Spender, and others with whom I was not familiar. To date Seferis had only translated at that time the "Waste Land" of T. S. Eliot, with a lengthy and very well-informed introduction, a real manifesto for Modernism. Through Durrell, who also played the guitar and sang ballads of his own making, and his charming wife Nancy, a tall, slender blonde, I met Bernard Spencer, with whom I was to collaborate later, translating the poetry of Seferis. Bernard spoke to me of the whole London poetry scene, of the magazine *New Verse,* to which he contributed, and made my longing to go to England even greater. But the war was upon us, first Mussolini in Albania and then the Germans. The storm was approaching, and literature was receding into the future. Among other British friends, there were some who had been in Romania, Reggie Smith and his wife Olivia Manning, the novelist of the "Balkan Trilogy," a pendant to Durrell's "Alexandrian Quartet."

My involvement with this literary scene in my early years marked me as the last poet of the decade of the thirties who later "was to play a role in the European avant-garde," in the words of Odysseus Elytis, in his *Chronicle of*

Second wife, Marie, Athens, 1961

a Decade. The Greek group was not a homogeneous one, aesthetically or ideologically, but loosely represented the ideas of modernism, in poetry, free verse, in prose, the flow of consciousness and automatic writing. I often met and talked to the very imposing and charming poet Gatsos, who first told me about Kafka, Sartre, and Husserl—thinkers and writers who had impressed him. And this was in 1939 or 1940 when these writers were unknown in Greece. There was also a lot of talk of the surrealists, André Breton, Benjamin Péret, Eluard, and others whose books, if you were lucky, could be found in the Kaufmann bookstore a block away. This was a very small group of amazingly well-informed Greeks who seemed almost like another race in the middle of an Athens still very conservative in literary matters and uninformed about recent developments.

Eventually in music, too, the modernist approach became felt in the re-evaluation of the most maligned and neglected, orientalizing popular songs and ballads, especially the city rembetika and naive or primitive art. The debate in the late thirties turned mainly around the irrational and obscure quality of modern poetry: in other words, its imagistic and associational flow, and its broken, fragmented, and cryptic character that made it hard to understand. In our time this would be called non-narrative or non-referential. However Seferis proved himself the gifted and lucid defender of modernist poetry in a public discussion with his brother-in-law, the philosopher Constantine Tsatsos, who denied all essential "Greekness" to the new modes of poetry. In a series of articles titled "Dialogue and Monologue on Poetry," Seferis opposed the accusation of irrationality and obscurity, dispelling many received ideas about literature and offering a spirited defense of modern poetry in its suggestiveness, which like music creates an atmosphere and makes the reader aware of unknown vistas through language. He argued that poetry—even in its popular traditional and ballad forms—uses condensation, rhetorical tropes such as ellipses, evocativeness, suggestion, as well as quotation and the old bardic device of allusion. As for the obscurity and fragmentation, he offered T. S. Eliot's argument that society had become chaotic and fragmented and that all this was reflected in poetry. Exposure to this discussion produced in me a desire to write works of poetry or prose, stories, even a play or a novel that would contain the qualities I now admired and understood, which even for a time eclipsed the dry clear and didactic style

of Cavafy, directly descended from the ancient Iambic, Epigrammatic and Elegiac poets.

The new Athenian poets felt that there was not enough body in the carefully structured rhetoric of Cavafy's diasporic language, a mixture of archaic and demotic. The language, according to them, was poor, linguistically inconsistent, with no lyrical metaphors, and—to top it all—the poetry was pessimistic, cynical, and decadent in the eyes of some older critics. The recent modes introduced a new age derived from the rich mix of the automatic poem, whose high and irrational condensation of heaped images and metaphors led to no recognizable meaning as a coherent poetic artifact in the traditional style, but created a dazzling surface akin to abstract painting and modern music and provoked thereby the outraged bourgeois reader or critic from bafflement to riling.

The main example of this kind of writing was Andreas Embirikos's *High Furnace* (1935), a collection of short prose texts of automatic writing derided in the press, as were the poems of Nikos Engonopoulos's *Do Not Speak to the Driver* (1938), which were reproduced seri-

(From left) Alan Ross, poet and editor of London Magazine, *Andreas Embirikos, surrealist poet and psychoanalyst, and Nanos Valaoritis*

ally in their entirety with sarcastic comments in a daily newspaper. Both these poets represented the more radical wing of modernism, associated with the revue *Ta Nea Grammata*. Embirikos was the main introducer of surrealism to Greece, via his personal relations with the poets Odysseus Elytis, Nicolas Calas, Nikos Gatsos, and others. He had been a member of Breton's Parisian group in the twenties and was also a psychoanalyst. Seferis tried to brush off this type of poetry as immature, yet in the long run it was Embirikos's use of language—in which the words made love in strange combinations—that is recognised as the archetypal example of modernism, even though it often resisted meaning like Joyce's *Finnigans Wake*. Also Engonopoulos's absurdist verse still remains as an example of the potential of poetry in claiming new domains of expression. Engonopoulos as a young boy was schooled in Paris and was entirely bilingual, while Embirikos was trilingual like Seferis, also knowing English. It was impossible to be an important Greek poet or writer without the knowledge of at least one or two foreign languages, since very little foreign literature was at that time published in Greek.

In 1941, after the successful resistance against the Italians in Albania, the Germans came in. I remember watching from the balcony of the apartment, where I now lived with my mother after the breakup of the family house in Kolonaki square, the first grey sidecars and jeeps of the German army entering a deserted Athens. All the British friends had left under perilous circumstances with dive bombers and German parachute attacks on Crete. Ships in the harbour of Piraeus were bombed. There were tales of miraculous escapes. Two Greeks poets had died, George Sarantaris and Anastasios Drivas, both contributors to the review *Ta Nea Grammata*, Elytis almost succumbed to pneumonia in a military hospital.

In spite of the atmosphere of tragedy that surrounded us, daily meetings with the poets that were left in Athens such as Nikos Gatsos, Odysseus Elytis, Nikos Engonopoulos, and the weekly sessions in the house of Andreas Embirikos gave our life an atmosphere of optimism I have never encountered since. Nikos Gatsos, who I saw almost daily, had already spoken to me about Kafka, Sartre, and unexpectedly Husserl and existentialism and Lorca. Also with Elytis we spoke often of André Breton, Benjamin Péret, Dalí, Eluard, and other surrealists. Embirikos

had in his house a number of surrealist paintings. It was a kind of paradise in the middle of hell—the marriage of heaven and hell in truly Blakean fashion. It was amazing that such energy could exist side by side with wholesale destructiveness. It was short of a miracle when poems like "Amorgos" by Nikos Gatsos and "Bolivar," a surrealist poem linking Greece with Latin America by Nikos Engonopoulos, and many of the great poems of the bard from Lefkas, Angelos Sikelianos, were written and published. Seferis himself wasn't doing too badly either in the Middle East, as we would soon find out, writing many of his important poems in Egypt and South Africa and some key essays such as the one on Makryannis, hero of the War of Independence.

There was this strange feeling of an inner freedom under the most terrible of all regimes—that of the Gestapo. Elytis also wrote some marvelous lyrical poems in the collection *Sun the First*. I, too, wrote poems, and one of them, "The Lesson of Dawn," was published in 1944. It was a highly optimistic one, very unlike me. There was exaltation in the air. Evil was present, but so was the angelic power of the opposite until it proved to be demonic, too.

What I wrote in those years were dark forebodings of disaster, oppression, and terror. When I left Greece in 1944 for Egypt and then London, my poems began to change in tone and style. They became more orphic, in other words musical, although still filled with imagery from the war. Earlier in Athens I had read the collection of Auden's poems *Look Stranger* and later Aragon's poems of the war, *Les Yeux d'Elsa* and *Broceliande,* which I picked up in Beirut, Lebanon, on the way to Egypt. These poems influenced me enough to write those included in my collection *The Punishment of the Magicians,* along with the earlier ones included in the collected volume *Poems I.* In other words, I used meter and rhyme in some of these but with a modernist technique in the sentencing that was much more independent of continual meaning and fragmented, a technique learned from the modernists and Imagists and the earlier fragmentation of Apollinaire's in poems such as "Zone" and the Conversation poems, Pound's early poetry, and behind them the so-called pure poetry—Poesie Pure—of Valéry, of which Seferis's first poems were an example in Greek. Multifaceted cubism, or dada collage techniques, made even the more formal poems quite different from the late romantic and symbolist poetry that clung to theme, continuous narrative, and subject.

I also experimented with the surrealist-inspired prose narratives, inherited from automatic texts, that all the Greek modernists had been writing, especially the surrealists, but also Seferis, whose range was much wider than that of other non-surrealist modernists.

Meanwhile the situation in Greece became ominous as the occupation drew to an end, and the civil war was beginning to look inevitable in spite of last-minute efforts to avoid it with a hastily put together coalition government. I decided to leave Greece and flee to the Middle East. The trip to Turkey in a fishing caïque with twenty-five others all packed in the hull until we cleared the coast of Attica, where the rendezvous had been arranged, was quite an adventure. The journey standing on an open truck to an outlying village had been equally hazardous, since some of us were armed and we passed a couple of German checkpoints. Happily no one was searched. We spent one night in the entrance of an ancient mine near Lavrion. The next morning the guides took us over rocky hills, one of them killing a snake with the butt of a revolver, to a secluded cove where the boat was waiting. At the last minute some peasant boys jumped in after us. I was crushed in the hull by the oversized wife of an officer until a couple of hours later when we were allowed out to breathe. That evening we reached the back of Tenos and stopped for the night since a strong north wind was blowing. There we were, stuck for a week by the wind, but the inhabitants of the island proved very hospitable while the peasant boys regaled us with fairy tales, some sexually explicit that they told to the men only. I regret not having written them down because I'm sure they were lost to the collectors of tales. There were no Germans around, and the family of a customs official offered us a splendid pilaf meal from rations the Allies had allowed earlier, overriding the blockade of Europe since Greece was dying of hunger. One morning I was awakened early by the sun. We had been sleeping on some terraces of houses next to the port, and I saw our boat leaving without us. I woke up the officers, and we dashed down to the harbor. A guerrilla boat had come the night before, and we alerted the captain, telling him

our boat was betraying us. He told us not to worry and prepared to give our boat chase with the machine gun on the prow. In ten minutes he had brought him back. Had I slept a little longer we would have been left stranded on Tenos by that cheating "captain."

That morning the wind had died down, and the sea was calm once more, sailable. This ruffian had hoped to sneak away without being seen, abandoning us there to the mercy of either the Germans or hunger.

The beauty of the island was indescribable, and I remember we killed a big black snake on the road to the marblecutters' village from which some famous Greek sculptors came. We bathed in deserted coves and spent evenings singing and listening to folktales near a little white chapel on the entrance of the bay. Between Tenos and the coast of Asia Minor there was a stretch of open sea. We started on the crossing after boarding our boat with pistols in hand. The so-called "captain," in reality a black market gardener, was terrified of mines and stood vigil on the prow throughout the night while his sailor slept on the rudder. I took it from him and tried to steer north towards the Pleiades, but it was too late. He had lost the direction and we drifted south until we found ourselves between two unknown lands in the morning, one close by and the other distant. Once more our luck saved us from a worse blunder. Soon a fishing boat appeared, and they informed us that we were behind the island of Ikaria and that the more distant land was the island of Samos. We were far off course to the south from our landing place near Smyrna. If the boat had not drifted so far south, we might have found ourselves at the town of Ikaria, which the Germans still occupied, and they might have given us chase. So we beached the boat in a cove and spent the day on the wild side of Ikaria. The fishermen told us of a spring close by. Some of us went out to it through a thick forest, and once there we found ten snakes around the spring. An officer drew his revolver and fired. The others immediately stopped him and warned him that shots might be heard by German patrols. There were fools among us and traitors very reminiscent of Odysseus's companions who kept undermining him in the *Odyssey*. This behavior was not only Homeric but also reminded me of the poem "Mythistorema" of Seferis, in such lines as the following:

The author with Greek poetess Manto Aravantinov, 1980s

Here we moored the ship to splice our
    broken oars
To drink water and to sleep.

We were already splicing our broken journey, and by five in the evening we set out for
the east as the fishermen had indicated. By
daybreak we were in sight of land, on which
hurriedly the boat emptied us without bothering to verify where we were in case the boat
was seized by the Turks. So, hoping we were
not by error of navigation again on some Greek
island, we started inland, led by an ex-deputy
from Thrace—with his top hat and black suit—
who knew some Turkish. We saw cultivated fields
and a man coming from a distance. Our leader
hailed him hopefully in Turkish, but he answered in Greek. Dismayed in the beginning
we soon found out he was indeed a Turk who
knew Greek. He told us the local police would
take us over. After he had led us to his farmhouse, a very friendly young rural police lieutenant and his platoon welcomed us and led us
to Smyrna, which was about a five-hour walk away.

After a week in Smyrna—where I had some
relatives of Irish, French, and British extrac-
tion from my grandmother who were very hospitable and put me up in a luxurious villa in
Bornova, introducing me to the local "European" club and other relatives—the train took
us through Asia Minor to Syria. There the British
in Aleppo interned us in a refugee camp, interrogated us, and in a month were packing
us off to another internment camp in the desert.
I was waiting for a passport from Cairo from
the Greek government, but none came. The
British put us in a boxcar and, at the station
of Tripoli outside Beirut, a co-refugee, a Greek-
Jewish girl, told me her uncle had met her
and told her there was a passport for me in
the Greek embassy in Beirut and that he could
get me off the train. Indeed he did without
any formality, and I was free in Beirut for three
days, buying French books and magazines from
freed North Africa and waiting for an Egyptian visa. In Cairo I stayed a month in the
terrible heat and contacted many friends: Bernard Spencer, for one, George Seferis, and oth-

ers. Seferis, for whom I had brought our magazine *Ta Nea Grammata,* asked me if I wanted to return to Greece with the Greek government or if I wanted to go to London and become a liaison between the Greek and English poets and writers, who at that time knew little of each other. He told me they could give me employment in the Greek embassy on the temporary staff. I eagerly chose that alternative. Seferis then briefed me about the two rival literary editors of magazines in London, John Lehmann of *New Writing* and Cyril Connolly of *Horizon.* He wrote letters of introduction for me to both. He had already met them in a previous trip to London, if I'm not mistaken. The road opened for me to do something about Greek Letters in the "West," as we call it in Greece. I never dreamt it would be the turning point for Greek poetry in this century, which ended with two Nobel Prizes.

My trip to London in an airplane with covered windows was like flying in a box. It traversed the whole of North Africa to Morocco, where it landed for a night to refuel. It was a prop plane; jets in those days hardly existed. Rabat was another of those Arabian Nights places—especially colorful—the extraordinary bazaar like the one in Aleppo. The flight continued the next day in the afternoon and, skirting the Portuguese coast, arrived at a military airport outside London. With my diplomatic passport, I thought I was immune from financial regulations, but when I told the immigration officer I had fifty pounds on me, then a substantial sum, he confiscated it. It was returned later with apologies to the embassy, but I entered London almost penniless. I think they allowed me ten pounds, and when the taxi asked me where to take me I gave the name of the only hotel I knew, the Claridge. When I asked the magnificent doorman at the entrance of this luxurious hotel, with my torn pants and sweater, if they had a room, he looked me up and down, and he said, "Well sir, you have to ask at the reception desk." I can tell you I was more terrified of him than of all the Germans I had encountered, and there had been three in our apartment. So I went up to the reception desk and asked for a room. They told me they had none. But when I showed my diplomatic passport, the man at reception relented and told me they only had a suite. In my eagerness to sleep somewhere after the traumatic confiscation of my money, I said all right, for a night. Little did I know that next door to my royal suite resided the exiled King of Greece.

Soon I contacted John Lehmann, and a few days later Cyril Connolly, with my letters of introduction from Seferis. Both were extremely warm and supportive. Here at last was somewhere I was welcome after the refugee experience in the Middle East. John Lehmann threw a cocktail party in my honor, as a novelty, a Greek poet, who had fled from the Nazis. I was immediately asked to collaborate on the *Penguin New Writing.* I attempted some translations of Seferis and Elytis by myself. They were immediately accepted, with some astonishment at my translating capacity. I began to acquire a reputation among the poets and writers. Stephen Spender befriended me, and I was asked out to lunch frequently by various writers, among them: Cyril Connolly, Louis MacNeice, Arthur Waley and his wife Beryl de Zoot, and William Plomer. I met Edith Sitwell, who loved the poems of Elytis that I had translated. I also told Stephen Spender that I wished to meet T. S. Eliot, who was already well-known in Greece thanks to Seferis's translation of *The Waste Land.* He then invited me to dinner with Eliot. This was a great occasion for me, and during the dinner, Stephen tried to make conversation with Eliot, telling him about an anthology he was preparing centered around Keats. Knowing the hostility of Eliot towards the Romantics, I was not surprised when he responded: "Hardly a principle on which to build an anthology, Stephen." The dinner then proceeded with awkward leaps and pauses in the conversation. At some point Spender suggested to Eliot that my nose resembled his! Upon which Eliot gave me a furtive look and said, rather embarrassed, "Perhaps."

He proceeded to tell me that I was the second Greek he had ever met. I asked: "Who was the first?" And the answer came: "The King of Greece." I did not lose my cool and said: "In that case I was the first, since the King of Greece didn't have a drop of Greek blood in his veins." If his remark had been intended to pull my leg, he got one back. They all laughed, and everyone relaxed. I wanted to ask him about another Greek, Mr. Evgenidis, the currant merchant from Smyrna in *The Waste Land,* but I didn't have the nerve. I knew Eliot had worked in the city and could have met some odd Greek in the business section.

The next questions would be: "What is a Greek? Under any circumstances?" I believe that is what prompted me to give Eliot a short introductory lecture on Byzantine literature when we left together to find a taxi and could not find one, taking the Underground, or London's subway, instead. While we stood and swayed in the crowded subway, I enthusiastically talked about Byzantium, marking thus my own descent from it and the link with antiquity. In those days to be a Byzantine was not an insult as it later became at Oxford, when Greek students appearing in the Hellenic-Greek Society to debate were greeted with: "Here come the Byzantines." The great Tom listened to me intently, or so I thought, with his large owl-eyes behind glasses that enlarged them even more. Finally we reached Oxford Circus where I had to change trains. As I was preparing to leave, he looked out and then turned his owl-eyes towards me, bending over slightly from his great height, he exclaimed: "Alas we must part!" This phrase, said in the sordid London subway while doodlebugs and V-2s were still falling, echoed strangely, as from *The Waste Land.*

I chose not to see him again so as not to spoil that wonderful Victorian parting. Maybe I was wrong. Later when the translation of Seferis's book appeared, he wrote me a letter of congratulations, and once again I ran into him in a dark side street in Chelsea as he was returning to his apartment on Cheney Walk. I didn't stop him or greet him. I have always been intimidated by such chance meetings, and I missed many occasions: one with Pound in Athens; quite a few with Beckett, who lived close to my Paris apartment; and at least three with André Breton, after we had been estranged for some time. John Hayward was Eliot's roommate, and we took him with my then-landlord Oliver Low in his wheelchair back to the apartment he shared with Eliot. He let us in to visit his room in a hush-hush manner. It was a spacious room overlooking the Thames. What impressed me greatly was the huge bomb-shaped oxygen container he had next to his bed, signifying asthma.

At that time I had not yet produced a collection of poems in a book. Working sometimes furtively at the office, I had begun to

Nanos and Marie with their eldest daughter Katerina

279

"With my daughter Zoe and the family of Fluff-Fluff, our Pomeranian"

write the poems included in this first book, *The Punishment of the Magicians.* I had this printed in 1947 by a Cypriot printer in London. It had a frontispiece by the English painter Johnny Craxton, who had recently visited Greece with Lucian Freud and met my family. It was at that time that Bernard Spencer returned to London from British Council posts abroad, and I met the legendary Tambimuttu, a Singhalese editor and colorful figure in London with his long hair and Indian dress. He ran a publishing house named Poetry London, with a concurrent magazine of the same name. It was still 1946, at the end of which I lost my job. With Bernard we had began translating Seferis in earnest, working during lunch hours from a pub on Oxford Street roughly halfway between the Embassy and the British Council. I had already done some poems on my own that were published by New Writing and N. W. & Daylight. These and five poems translated by George Katsimbalis and Lawrence Durrell and published earlier by John Lehmann were included in our final selection titled *The King of Asine,* from a

poem of this title. That same year Cyril Connolly asked me to write an article on the new modernist Greek poetry. It took me almost a month to complete, with translated passages from the poets mentioned. It was the first article on the subject and with *The King of Asine* constituted the first breakthrough for modern Greek poetry on the international field. The reception of *The King of Asine* in the press was unanimously enthusiastic. One article went as far as claiming that Seferis was a greater poet than any English contemporary poet. Of course that claim, with the presence of Yeats and Eliot in English letters and many others such as W. S. Auden and Dylan Thomas, was certainly an exaggeration. But the surprise created by the book was widespread, and for some time in the late forties I found myself a kind of hero in the London literary scene. I was invited everywhere the literati went. There was equal surprise in Greece and George Katsimbalis lost no time having the reviews translated and published in the postwar journal he edited with the help of the British Council, *The Anglo-Hellenic Review.*

There were fourteen reviews, with a fifteenth from South Africa. It was an extraordinary reception for the usually reticent British when it came to foreign literature. Fifteen years later Seferis was awarded the Nobel Prize, which was followed in 1979 by the award given to Elytis.

At that time when I was writing my article in 1946, I was also asked to write an article for *France Libre* in French about life and letters in Athens and about my collaboration with Robert Levesque. When I visited Paris that summer I saw Robert Levesque, with whom I had worked on some translations of Greek poets during the occupation. He was putting together an important number of *Les Cahiers du Sud,* dedicated entirely to Greece. Levesque translated three prose pieces of mine and included them—a bit late for me to be listed in the contents—but they nevertheless appeared. His presentations, though very worthy, were not received with any amount of favor by the French critics and poets, and the issue was little noticed. Only three or four years ago there were still copies on sale at the Poetry Book Fair in Paris. The *Cahiers du Sud* appeared in 1948, the same year as *The King of Asine.*

The fate of *The King of Asine* was strange. Only some years later John Lehmann sold his publishing house, and *The King of Asine* was probably pulped. In any case no remainder copies were ever found. Today it cannot be found and must fetch a collector's price. Even I don't possess a copy. Meanwhile in London my *The Punishment of the Magicians*—which I sent to Greece to all my poet friends—received very favorable comments in letters by all, even the tight-lipped Seferis, who wrote that while reading some lines he whispered: "Apollinaire." I lost all these letters when I left London in a hurry and abandoned my correspondence there. Of all those received Elytis's and Gatsos's were very complimentary. Only the musician Manos Hadjidakis from among my friends wrote a bitterly negative one. Takis Papatsonis, an important poet, hailed me as a better version of my great-grandfather. Among the critics, only one, Aemilios Chourmouzios, in the conservative literary magazine *Nea Estia,* wrote a narrow-minded review pointing out mainly grammatical errors and irrational passages. A talk by Alexis Diamantopoulos, a brilliant classical scholar, on the Cypriot BBC was lost. It was a very fair and in-depth assessment, something Greek poets are rarely given.

The volume contained a number of poems in traditional metrical form, of fifteen-syllable rhyming or not lines, and one poem of eleven syllables, a sonnet. This baffled the next generation of Greek critics, who associated modernism with free verse. Yet free verse was hardly ever used by the British modernists—and never by the Russians, even Maiakofski and other modernists. Only the Americans wrote extensively in free verse and not all of them in the beginning, such as Eliot and Pound, while the modernist poetry of Apollinaire moved in and out of metrical verse and rhyme. What would establish the modernist element in a poem would be the different diction, vocabulary, content, tone, and associational flow. Another great forerunner of modernism the French eccentric, Raymond Roussel, wrote in strict French twelve-syllable, or alexandrine verse—the name was inherited from a long twelfth-century epic on the life of Alexander the Great in which this verse first appeared. Yet the content of this verse is so different from the usual lyrics, in its obsessive descriptiveness and detail, that it gave birth to the so-called "descriptive" French new novel. The Greek critics, largely uninformed about the complexities of the modernist scene, challenged me on this as if I were regressing, in their eyes, to traditionalism.

My answers fell on deaf ears. And when my Rousselian anti-epic appeared in 1985, a net of silence was cast around it. Apart from these cases, quite a number of French surrealists—such as Aragon, Desnos, Roger Vitrac, Raymond Queneau, Philippe Soupault, Jacques Prevert—all used meters and rhymes, more frequently than the free verse dogmatists (like Henri Michaux, for instance) in play and parody, since surrealist and dada modernism never shrank from utilizing clichés, advertisements, collages, all in the spirit of irony and humor.

The modernist modification is not only in the form, but also how the associations diverge. The metaphors are not based on similitude but rather on contrast, difference, and the unexpected; the subjects are curious and often offensive, with twists and turns. Right from the beginning I was experimenting in form and content. The background of my early poetry was somber: the tragic element of war. Yet these poems were also orphic, to use the term coined by Apollinaire to describe a kind of lyricism that was also musical even if it used contemporary subjects, themes, and vocabulary, such as war, emigration, everyday life, and conversation pieces. To my mind there was no question of sacrificing the ascendancy of language to the subject. Boris Pasternak has expressed it very profoundly:

> Language, the home and the dwelling of beauty and meaning, itself begins to think and speak for man . . . then like the current of a mighty river polishing stones and turning wheels by its very movement, the flow of speech creates in passing, by the force of its own laws, rhyme and rhythm and countless other forms and formations, still more important and until now undiscovered, unconsidered and unnamed.

> (From *Dr. Zhivago,* quoted by a young Russian poet to Patricia Blake.)

This sums up the discovery and contribution of the main poets of the thirties in Greece, who remained active until the seventies, the eighties, and even the nineties when the last one—Odysseus Elytis—died.

My generation—roughly of the forties—continued this experiment, modified it to some extent by including new elements, both linguistically and thematically, and was followed by a small number of poets in the sixties and seventies. Thus my own orphism covers all kinds of forms and styles, but always with the primacy of the musicality and the infinite possibilities of the language. Even my early attempts while in Greece, however awkward in the beginning, when I was in England acquired more musicality and integrated form. The earlier attempts were more cerebral, and for some reason the distance from Greece instead of weakening the language factor reinforced it. One of the reasons must be that dependency on a brilliant previous generation lessened, and new horizons opened with numerous contacts with western poets and intellectuals. In those early years I did not attempt to jump boat and write poetry in English. Some half-hearted attempts were made after my marriage in 1947 to Anne Firth, who also attempted to write. And when John Lehmann rejected two translated poems by Elytis, which I considered equally good as the previous ones he had published, I gave up translating. But I wrote in prose and composed in the next years a London journal titled *The Problems of an Empire,* which appeared in the early sixties in the international review *Botteghe*

Oscure, published by Princess Caetani in Rome. It was mainly in English, but included many European writers in the original and in translation. It was also the beginning of my American career, since the poet who introduced me to Caetani was James Broughton, an American I met in Paris.

For many years after the presentation of the Greek poets, I was still entangled in the British juggernaut, and my life in those years was stormy with many ups and downs. In 1944 and 1945, London was about to bask in the triumph of victory after another year of V-2s, which was painful enough, and the Battle of the Bulge was a setback of some months. My last contribution to the glory of Greek poetry was a letter of George Seferis that I translated for Tambimuttu, who was compiling a festschrift volume for T. S. Eliot. After that I disappeared from English letters for some time. Thus ended my connection with the British literary scene until the sixties when Alan Ross, the successor of John Lehmann, published a poem of mine in the new *London Magazine* and until Nikos Stangos translated another two that appeared in *Encounter,* then co-directed by Stephen Spender. While in Paulton Square living with Anne, I became friendly with Kathleen Raine— a poetess not of the canonical Faber and Faber group, but of Tambi's Poetry London group presided over by Dylan Thomas—and other poets of the romantic and expressionist tendency. Through Kathleen, I met David Gascoyne, Kenneth Rexroth, and the Nobel Prize-winner Elias Canetti. Also in that same house, 48 Paulton Square, the landlord Oliver Low had put up W. H. Auden, one of the English poets I hadn't met. We had brief conversations over breakfast when I went up from the basement where we lived to fetch milk for the kid from the only Frigidaire in the house. We talked about Cavafy, whom Auden admired. He told me he liked the historical poems best because he considered the so-called love poems too camp. I also noticed that he didn't like Seferis, following a remark ("because there didn't seem to be any meat there") that he made to Oliver Low, who reported it to me. Auden's assessments were always somewhat cryptic, even in his essays, but the dislike of Seferis was also echoed by a French poet, Alain Jouffroy, who found the poems too "sentimental." From these reactions I concluded that western taste and opinion was by no means

With his son, Dino, an architect, New York, 1994

unanimous regarding recent Greek poetry. These reactions didn't tally with my own impressions, but poetry in translation on the one hand and differences of conditions of modernist trends and styles in peripheral countries played a large part in forming contrary opinions. The recognition of poets like Pessoa, Borges, Cavafy who, like Kafka, touched a wide-ranging chord—or even the case of someone as subjective as Beckett—flounders when faced with more localised poetry like that of Seferis, Elytis, or Ritsos, not lesser figures in any way, but more difficult to access. I encountered the same refusal among the French surrealists regarding Cavafy. They told me they didn't understand why he was so highly regarded. Western taste often appreciated the image of her own versions in other cultures, excluding what seems alien, at least in the beginning.

In the meantime, at the end of 1953, I was delivered by a general amnesty for all draft resisters from the Greek army in which I served for eight months. Most of those—like me—who were exempted from service for various reasons were called up in 1949 for punitive rea-

sons since the civil war had ended. They numbered about 40,000, mainly students in foreign countries. At risk of becoming a financial burden for the state, they were allowed to buy out the rest of their time.

This year had been a terrible one for me since I and my estranged wife, Anne, lost our five-year-old son Daniel-Constantine in an accident in Antibes.

In order to recover my mental and physical balance, I chose to go to Paris and explore new fields and areas of intellectual adventures. However, I wasn't through yet with England. I re-visited London in 1954. Stephen Spender, then editor of *Encounter,* took a diary of my life in the army barracks during basic training in Corinth. It never appeared because he wanted some rewriting, but I never understood what he wanted rewritten.

In Paris I met my present wife, Marie Wilson, an American artist who had close connections with the surrealists. She took me to a collective show patronized by the surrealists at the Etoile Scellee, a small gallery on the Left

Bank in which she had a painting. There I met André Breton, Benjamin Péret, the art critic Charles Estienne, Elisa Breton, and the Czech painter Toyen, who were all to play a role in my life in the next six years, and a number of more recent disciples of Breton. All this happened at a dizzying pace in the fall of 1954. I never imagined I could meet the legendary Breton and his entourage so easily and quickly. It happened quite naturally through Marie. Greece, although a European country, was still very cut off from the West after World War II, in spite of a period of closer connections at the end of the thirties and early forties. For us Breton had been a distant figure, a demigod, whose personal influence and that of his brilliant group were already strongly felt in Greece since the early thirties. We were familiar with the names of Paul Eluard, Dalí, Péret, Max Ernst, Miró, Tanguy, thanks to the collection of paintings and books of Andreas Embirikos, who had been associated with the Parisian surrealist group in the twenties. The other two poets, Elytis and Gatsos, were very well informed on surrealism and modernism. Elytis's preference was Paul Eluard, whom he translated and was influenced by, even in the choice of his pseudonym, while Gatsos often quoted Péret to me, a more radically absurdist surrealist like himself, and the more romantic Lorca, another favourite, legendary martyr of the Spanish Civil War. Embirikos was the very double of Breton, fiery, passionate, enthusiastic, and a practitioner of extremist automatic poetry in prose titled *High Furnace* (1935). Embirikos was also a Freudian psychoanalyst. A unique combination, for surrealism was not really very much understood by the psychiatric profession or by Freud himself, who was frankly puzzled by it.

With this background, meeting the Parisian surrealists was both exciting—since I had imagined them and idealized them long ago—and something of a cold shower. They seemed much colder, matter-of-fact, and focused on day-to-day events. They were not the fiery, dreamy figures I had projected. They didn't seem to have the elation or passion on the metaphysical level as we had. For us the imagination was everything, projected on a timeless canvas. The younger disciples seemed to me more interested in studying surrealism than living it. However, the French seemed to be live wires—much more aware of ideological and aesthetic differences and ready to jump to the ceiling

with exasperation at the slightest provocation. My initial disappointment was remarkably eased by a chance encounter in the Café des Deux Maggots one autumn, probably in 1955, with a couple at the next table, a handsome and lively young man and a beautiful and refined woman, who joined in our conversation on these topics of surrealism and the personalities involved. They said they knew Breton and his entourage and wondered who we were, discussing them. We introduced ourselves, and they turned out to be the poet and art critic Alain Jouffroy and the Viennese painter Manina. He had once belonged to the surrealist group in the forties but departed with a group of dissident adherents—Victor Brauner, Sarane Alexandrian, and others—over a disagreement on the condemnation of Matta, the Chilean surrealist painter, for an affair that had taken place in New York. Manina, Alain, Marie, and I quickly fraternized and became close friends. Alain lived in a state of passion and elation, as I had imagined the members of the early group, and in spite of the rupture and rough treatment by some of the surrealists of the group, Alain displayed an amazing loyalty to Breton, but also remained close to other expelled or estranged personalities, such as Max Ernst, Herold, Queneau, and later, even Aragon. His close friendship with Henri Michaux, a persona non grata among surrealists, his meetings with such ubiquitous personalities as Dalí while reporting for art journals, and his acquaintance with celebrities such as Marcel Duchamp embodied for me the syncretic attitude of respect for artistic achievement in spite of ideological differences that he shared with us. Here was the herald of another attitude, which would be followed by many younger poets of the so-called Electric and Cold manifestos, who were eager to dispense with the more dogmatic ideological rhetoric. Belonging to a more peripheral and marginal culture, in spite of the glorious past, I was prepared to accept syncretic situations. Movements and personalities always arrived in Greece as distant and idealised figures, who like gods and prophets would free us from our confined existence. Alain's attitude did not exclude a partisan engagement. He was not less embattled in causes he considered just—and has remained so to this day—to the detriment of his reputation among the literati, on account of his numerous critical and polemical writings. However, life in Paris was to become

With Greek poet and co-editor of Synteleia,
Andreas Pagoulaios, 1993

very complex for me, and so rich as to entirely absorb me to the extent I almost forgot my beloved Greece, but not to the extent of not visiting it every summer with my newly found friends since we had this superb resort on Lefkas, the inherited ancestral island and house of Madouri.

I had nightmares on the eves of return journeys to Athens for years. I still received threatening telephone calls and false police summons to appear before a court-martial, intended to intimidate. What was worse than these rearguard actions was the effect of years of terror on the literati. They seemed paralyzed, unable to react, hiding their feelings and thoughts, as if they were going to be persecuted for their ideas. The modernist movement seemed to have floundered on these clashing rocks of Left and Right. There was no breath left in it. *Sauve qui peut*— "Every man for himself"—was the motto of the times. Large numbers of artists and students, many implicated in the leftist organizations, had left for Paris with grants from the French government since 1944. It was an exodus. The poets who still met in the old café-bars were suspicious of each other and guarded in their comments. The conservative critics were rude and abusive to the younger generation of the forties, as if trying to get back some of the prestige lost with the success of the modernist generation of the thirties. This was pure revenge of the earlier neo-symbolist establishment

against the modernists. At the same time the level of criticism was lowered to include just about anything in their canon. A new war was on, which had more the character of attrition, to see who would succumb first. There was glaring ill-feeling on all sides. Greek letters were drifting aimlessly while no one would take responsibility for anything. It was in this period of confusion that a neo-academic establishment consolidated its power, which lasted for the rest of the decades of the century. It had as its aim to take over the breakthrough of the forties, exploit it, and use it to prevent any subsequent developments, which are always resisted by the academy as destabilizing for their peace of mind and their domination.

By 1963, they had no opposition to speak of, until the publication of the review *Pali*, which polemicized them on all fronts, but mainly focused on projecting the neglected more radical surrealists who had also been left out by the translators, backed by generous funds such as that of Princeton University. The combination of a controlled exterior projection of Greek poetry, with an interior near monopoly, was lethal for the development of Greek poetry— and left out all that was worthwhile of the poetry written during the forties and following decades by new people. The rationale was that by focusing on a few poets, Cavafy and Seferis and later Ritsos, there was a greater chance of creating a public in the west.

There are however exceptions from this situation in the neo-Hellenic field. A prominent onc would include Michel Saunier of the Greek Institute of the Sorbonne, whose translations and fairness to Embirikos count a lot, and, more recently, Dimitris Tziovas in Birmingham University and Dimitris Gontikas at Princeton University, while a number of others are wavering, such as Roderick Beaton, often under pressure from their students to view Greek letters in more contemporary terms and from unusual viewpoints. The modern Greek studies of Ohio University, with Vasilis Lambropoulos, Artemis Leontis, and Gregory Jusdanis, are also contributing significantly in theoretical approaches on traditional literary subjects and the history of ideas. But none of these three have yet tackled the more recent trends. I would like to be able to add others to the list but to date very few qualify as exceptions to the rule of conservative or typical approaches. There are some new and upcoming scholars with new positions who still have to show what they will do. However, France with a number of extra- and neo-academic people like Jacques Lacarriere or Nicole Ollier, and literary poets and scholars, such as Jean-Pierre Faye, Alain Jouffroy, Jean-Michel Goutier, Sarane Alexandrian, Jacqueline Chenieux, Philippe Kerbellec, and Jacques Bouchard in the University of Montreal open up a much more promising field of reception of the more radical and neglected wing of Greek modernism.

My close contact with the personalities of Breton and Benjamin Péret in the six years at the end of the fifties was immensely invigorating in those low-energy days for me, restoring a more optimistic view of myself and the world. They encouraged me to continue to rise slowly like the Phoenix from my ashes, and—with the invaluable help also given to me by my other French friends—saved me from total shipwreck. The traumas of the civil war and the disasters of my personal life, the loss of Anne's and my son in the accident in Antibes, began to disappear. With the help and support of Marie, we purchased two small apartments on the same floor in an old building and modified them to become a very artistic niche that we lived in on and off in the sixties and seventies. I began to write plays and poems in French. Thirty years later quite a number of these poems appeared in two recent issues of French magazines, *Pleine Marge* and *Superieur Inconnu,* with articles.

A turning point in my playwriting activity occurred while having lunch in a small restaurant—the meeting with Marc'O. This restaurant on the Rue de Seine was frequented by young writers, French and foreign. We ate on long tables shared by everyone. A young son of Robert Lebel, Duchamp's close friend, Jean-Jacques, frequented the surrealist Café and brought with him the unknown: Marc'O, an ex-lettrist and member of the youth movement. He had many ideas about the theater. He especially admired Brecht and the objective method of presenting the material, of leaving it to the audience to decide. Audience participation was in the air what with the American Living Theatre and the Happenings in New York.

With the backing and encouragement of Charles Estienne, the eccentric art critic of the newspaper *Combat,* we formed a group of friends, among which the future son-in-law of Breton,

Yves Elleouet, and Pierre Jaouen, who were the "Breton" Celtic contingent of artists close to Charles Estienne, also a Breton. Marc'O was from the center of France, close to the famous Puys du Dome, in Auvergne. As a very young adolescent, he fought in the Resistance and ended up in Paris after the Liberation. He met and lived with Poucette, a café artist, who sold her paintings in hotels, resorts, and cafés. Our meeting took place sometime in the late fifties, 1956 or 1957. It took three more years until a play could be produced at the Boulevard Raspail American student's club in 1959.

This was my play *L'Hotel de la Nuit qui Tombe (Nightfall Hotel),* staging two main characters who literally with their talk destroy the world around them. Directed and produced by Marc'O, it showed for only four sessions, since Marpessa Dawn, who acted in the main role, had to go to Cannes to receive a prize for *Orpheo Negro.* There were quite a few articles in the Parisian press. It was a mixed reception. Some articles were favorable to the play and criticized the staging, while others praised the staging and criticized the play. This proved fatal for my relations with Marc'O, each one of us stressing the ones favorable to either direction or writing. The team atmosphere was broken, and we never collaborated again. After this a series of plays and performances followed in the same Theatre of the Club, for which the *Hotel,* whatever its merits or faults, opened the way. I experienced a total alienation from my dialogue, which I found too poetic on opening night and not dramatic enough. I had later the same feeling for a play by Jean Genet, *Les Negres,* and decided that too much lyricism did not suit the stage. Another one of my plays, *The Log,* had a checkered career. First produced by Koun in Athens in 1960, it was taken by Giancarlo Menotti to his festival of Spoletto. Later Ole Olson translated it into Danish, and it was shown in Aarhus with Strindberg's *The Strongest.* The fifteen-minute play condensed the life of Meleager, a Greek mythical hero who was put to death by his mother Althea by burning the log in which the three fates had enclosed his soul.

Even though we never collaborated again, my relations with Marc'O remained friendly, and also with his group of actors. They visited me on the island and mingled with Manina and Alain Jouffroy and other surrealists of Breton's group, such as Toyen and Robert Benayoun, who were gratified by two of the most spectacular storms. One in Athens flooded the little streets of the tourist market and started to make the car slide in the current. While on the island, we were caught in a fantastic thunder and lightning storm while returning from a trip on the sea. Thunderbolts were coming down vertically, and the wind was so strong that I couldn't steer the boat against it. I finally managed to find shelter behind the island and let them all out on dry land.

The summers were spent with all these Parisian friends, some of whom worked while there: Alain Jouffroy, for one, wrote a moving novel—in which I appeared as Kallias and Marie as Queen and his wife Manina as Romana—around the murder of Manina's daughter Nina in Los Angeles. It was titled *A Dream Longer Than the Night,* a well-known Jewish proverb. Later again Alain came with another wife, a charming and beautiful Romanian actress, Adriana Nicolescu, and wrote part of his novel, *Le roman vecu,* in which I figure once more with my real name this time. The real Kallias, I discovered later, was an ancient Athenian character, also known as "Lakkoploutos" (or "hole-rich"), because he discovered a treasure in a hole in the earth. I haven't yet found such a thing, but I also wrote a novel on Madouri, my second one, *The Treasure of Xerxes.* This treasure was rumored to exist somewhere in the hills west of Athens, from which the Persian king had witnessed the defeat of his fleet in the straits of Salamis. Other friends—among them, Zina Rachesvski, Conrad Rooks, Harold Norse—came also in those summers of the fifties and sixties until the sinister Junta took over in Greece. Stephen Spender appeared briefly from a yacht. Onassis invited us through the intermediary of Zina, whose father had been a drinking companion of the magnate at Maxim's in Paris. Onassis had bought the ill-fated neighboring island of Scorpios, which had belonged earlier to distant relatives. We had dinner on the magnate's boat. He was friendly and tried soon after to buy our historical island, to no avail. Also many Greek poets, collaborators of our review *Pali,* used to come, among them the poet philosopher George Makris; the novelist and poet Kostas Taktsis; the poet Tasos Denegris; Panos Koutrouboussis, poet, humorist, and graphic artist; Alexander Schinas, an experimental writer; Mando Aravandinou, a great

poetess, alas very ill now from Alzheimer's disease; and Ersi Soteropoulou, a very gifted prose writer.

Early in the fifties, Marie and I spent holidays driving through France, and we ended in the old village of the Lot, St.-Cirq-la-Popie, where Breton had purchased a thirteenth-century house. When his disciples had left, towards the end of August, he confided in me about his relations with Valéry and Proust. Earlier we had scourged the river Lot searching for agates in Marie's small Quatre Chevaux Renaud, named *Boogie Woogie,* driving Breton and Elisa, his Chilean wife, around the area. He told me that Valéry had given him the advice that his poems, like a woman heavily ornate with jewels, lost some of their natural beauty, a reflection on the heavily baroque style that Breton used, filled with metaphors and similes. On Proust he commented favorably on the manner he treated him as proofreader of his *Search for Lost Time,* paying him regularly, while the collectors who employed him to buy them artwork were most negligent in fulfilling their financial obligations towards him. He added about Proust: "After all he was an artist." He also mentioned his relations with Apollinaire and quoted a quatrain Apollinaire loved to recite "La Belle americaine":

> *Qui rend les hommes fous*
> *Partira la semaine prochaine*
> *Pour Corfou*

(An example of humour in light verse.)

The stones we found so enchanted him that on his return to Paris he wrote a piece for his review *Surrealisme Meme,* which has been reprinted in *Perspective Cavaliere.* Among these, I had discovered one that might have been a primitive statuette of an Owl Goddess whose cult was known to have existed in the area of the Lot, while Marie discovered a perfect black egg of large proportions like a dinosaur's egg. Both were photographed for the review. He also included a report by me in the article on the circumstances of the discovery of the Goddess stone. In the next years when we moved to Athens, after the birth of our daughter Katerina, we kept contact with him through the magazine *Pali,* which I directed in Athens.

I managed to overcome the atmosphere of discouragement and the fear to start anything like a magazine among Athenian poets, younger writers, and artists, thanks largely to the immense support I had found in Paris among my literary and artist friends, many of whom I presented in the review. I also wrote introductions for some young Parisian artists' shows, like Yves Elleouet, Pierre Jaouen, and Guy Harloff, for whom William Burroughs also wrote. Through Alain and Manina, who introduced us to them, we became friends with Victor Brauner and Matta. Jean-Jacques Lebel went on to become an organizer and promoter of theatrical performances in the American Club, in which Alexander Jodorovski, later a well-known film director from Chili, also presented a staggering performance-happening. In the same theater, the American avant-garde, with Brion Gysin and Burroughs, presented readings along with the French avant-gardists, hyper-lettrists like François Dufrene and Bernard Heidsieck, many of whom by now were using tapes for vocal poetry, such as Dufrene's Cris-Rhythms. Other experimental poets were Gherasim Luca, of Rumanian origin like Brauner, the lettrists—many of whom practiced the decollage poster art called *affiches dechirees*—and the genial Heins, who had turned ordinary café conversation into an art form, performing a breathless conversation monologue through associations.

The richness of the Paris scene of the fifties and sixties is hard to describe in retrospect. The critical and autobiographical writings of Alain Jouffroy—in *La fin des Alternances* (Gallimard, 1970)—give one a glimpse of what was going on.

Meanwhile, Jean-Jacques Lebel created a yearly festival in Paris for experimental performances and poetry worldwide. I participated in many of those after 1975. Jouffroy, like me, was an exceptionally syncretic personality who liked to transgress boundaries and connect seemingly contradictory and hostile movements, ideas, groups, personalities. He was rare among the very sectarian French who seemed to entrench themselves in aesthetic and ideological circles and to project formidable defenses against the corruption or infiltration and contamination of their ideas by others.

However, with the fall of ideologies, an atmosphere of confusion and doubt prevailed, which favored all kinds of alliances. And so connections that earlier would have been thought of as impossible produced the appearance of two seemingly antiprogrammatic, antirhetorical, and anticritical poetic declarations, that of the Electric and Cold manifestos. The groups who made these were still groups, but did not openly polemic with each other, even though their aesthetic choices were seemingly totally opposite. And I say seemingly because in both groups, in spite of differences, there were similarities, since the tendency was to give primacy to language over ideas. Style became dominant for the Electrics, and the Cold poets, in symmetrical opposition, practiced a lowering of tone and a heightening of it. In relation to surrealism, one group wanted a low-key modification, while the other lifted the ceiling of baroqueness into a kind of supersurrealist style. Both targeted rhetorical and tropological emphasis on change. Both propositions de facto aimed at language, which in the decade of the seventies started to become a dominant issue. My own work in the sixties already displayed a tendency towards a lessening of the thematic to an emphasis on the language. Ideas and their rhetoric had become oppressive and a no-exit situation. As their grip on aesthetics loosened, doubt, anarchy, and lack of criteria followed, but also a new freedom from ideologies—political, psychological, aesthetic, or scientific.

This did not mean a rejection of morality, for language has a morality of its own. In reality it is only a shift of where traditionally the source of this morality resided, not just in the subconscious, or in reason, or in the will, but in the very combination of words. A far-out idea, but in view of the terrible debunking of terms—of such ideas as freedom, truth, morals, honesty, justice, worth, integrity, rights, nation, society—that for different people mean exactly the opposite, the very questioning of language is in order and how it is used in historical, social, psychological, or even scientific perspectives. If we use the same words to mean something different there is something wrong, either in the use of language or its intrinsic nature, and in order to unravel this, poetic expression has become the very vehicle illustrating this contradiction and the gaps in our understanding. How to do this is not simple, and no one kind of poetic expression is at this time solely capable of taking on the burden or the challenge in this rapidly changing world. And what we now mean by poetic expression is very different from what it was even some decades ago. It does not only involve one genre like the lyrical but much of what was considered hitherto unpoetic. Ordinary language, for example, but again used in a special way not just any old how. There has to be some consideration of rhythm, flow, feeling, and even meters, rhymes, assonances, puns, sound. New combinations are always possible, but they need someone who can orchestrate them. However, the dislocation of traditional poetic language has often been a necessary precondition for the appearance of something new.

In the next years, between 1960 and 1967, and while I edited the review *Pali,* I worked on a long poem titled the "The Main Body." Written in classical 15-16-14 syllable lines, it encapsulated—in a more or less hermetic form—the experiences of the fifties and sixties in poetry and prose, the Beat movement, the French new novel. Around it proliferated lesser poems of the same or similar form that were collected later in *Nests of Microbes* and *Feathery Confession,* which appeared in the seventies and the eighties. The main thrust, however, were texts in prose gathered later in books with the following titles: *Some Women,* published in 1982, got another state prize for poetry, although controversy broke out on whether they were prose pieces or poems. This type of intermediate poetic text was a challenge still for the conservative views of Greek criticism. Another of the same genre was *The Diamond Tranquilizer,* which sold out quickly but got no notices. *The Traitor of the Scripted Word* did not circulate so widely, but got a very remarkable review, unexpected for the state of criticism at the time by a young writer called Ikaros Babasakis. These three prose collections were the bulk of short prose pieces written at a time when I was also composing longer, novel-length books. *Bones of the Greeks,* a surrealist style novel, was based on the pithy sayings of ancient Greeks as producers of text. Published much later in 1982, it got only two reviews, both favorable, by two slightly puzzled young writers unprepared for that kind of work. The major critics remained silent and never wrote on any of this work in the seventies and eighties. The next novel, *The Treasure of Xerxes,* received no reviews at all, but was widely read; also the comic science-fiction novella *The Assassination* found no critical echo. Of the poetry collections that appeared in the eighties, *The Feathery Confession* received only brief notices, and *The Bottom Line* was attacked and practically trashed by an outraged conservative

Nanos and Marie Valaoritis, "standing in front of the Pompidou Centre, below the poster of their friend André Breton," 1991

younger poet who edited a review. He was infuriated by an article I had written in favour of one of his language-centered contemporaries. Two reasons were usually given for this attitude and silence on nevertheless important work. One was my absence from Greece. The second was the difficulty of the work, for which Greek critics had no parameters. Also, generally, the post-colonial condition of Greek culture had very intense competitive and exclusion syndromes. Whoever was not on the spot to promote ties, network, and be affiliated to a group would largely be ignored.

In Paris by May 10 the student uprising was beginning. All of Paris joined in, even some of the bourgeois. Much has been written about those fateful three months. Many of my writer, actor, and artist friends were involved. I witnessed the meetings at the Odeon occupied by the anarchists. The orations of Daniel Cohn-Bendit and other assorted meetings of writer and student committees. The barricades and the excitement in the air were indescribable, and a total contrast to the tomb-like atmosphere of Greece. It was a kind of total and continual celebration of life. All the small groups of radical movements—such as the situationists, surrealists, and the politically leftist groups traditionally critical of the Communist Party and its Stalinist leadership—were in the forefront. It was also their culminating moment. After this explosion of surrealist and situationist poetic wit in the posters and street inscriptions, there seemed to be no future for small leftist groups. The surrealists decided to end the historical movement. They split in two, one group wishing to continue, another planning to return to eternal surrealism, a spirit that had animated select individuals since antiquity. For all intents and purposes since the death of André Breton two years earlier, this was the end. There was no more impetus to continue. The situationists suffered the same dismemberment almost immediately after the events. The unions and the Communist Party, then all powerful, diverted what had been a largely existential protest on the part of intellectuals and students into a political and economic re-vindication for workers, with a hike in salaries that crippled the French economy for years and that was never forgotten by the regime, who persecuted and made all the artists and intellectuals it could lay hands on pay dearly in many ways: layoffs, difficulties in getting work, all other kinds of impediments. Also the retaken university was dispersed outside Paris, and a radical wing was installed in Vincennes. These were measures to prevent a recurrence of such an event. The atmosphere after May 1968 was to contest in a more academic manner the traditional approaches to philosophy, sociology, politics, and literature, taking the whole conflict off the streets into the halls of academia. It was a clever move and had far-reaching results in the worldwide spread of post-structural criticism and Derrida's deconstruction theories. The move incorporated revolt, protest, and dissidence into the academic discourse, where it has remained a token of the success of market and consumer capitalism, in opposition to social utopias, inside which the literary-political avant-garde had been transmitted since the nineteenth century, since Fourier, Saint-Simon, and other communally utopian movements. This would include branches of futurism and largely the dadaists. The same movement away from modernist revolt can be observed in the theoretical approaches to literature, culminating in the postmodern condition approach of Lyotard and the dismantling of radical versions of all major ideologies, such as Freudianism, Marxism, existentialism, structuralism, and aesthetic approaches such as the absurdist drama, new novel, and by implication their parent movements of futurism, dadaism, surrealism.

The rise of academic theorists, such as Barthes, Foucault, Lacan, Baudrillard, and the aforementioned Derrida, moved the contestation of traditional values in philosophy, psychology, history, literature, sociology, hitherto the domain of the avant-garde rebels, into a widely inclusive academic field, which masks its real origins by co-opting them. Once again the academic boa has digested its dangerous prey and rendered it acceptable. Its great secret and all too visible weapon is quotation, which gives the appearance of objectivity, accuracy, and textual power in which "truth" is encapsulated, but no less manipulated than before, for better or for worse.

After 1967, the Greek experience came to an end with the military coup. And all the work written then had to wait another eight years to get published. The move to the United States of America in 1968 shaped my life as a teacher in creative writing and comparative literature at San Francisco State University, and I also began to write and publish a lot of poetry in English. This did not diminish the poetry and prose written in Greek. After the Junta's fall in 1974, my return to Europe for two years proved very fruitful, interesting, and dramatic. After some years of exile, this was indeed not entirely untraumatic, as was to be expected. An opened-up Greece was less hostile than the Parisian scene of self- or semi-exiled Greek students and their political leaders or gurus. For seven years Paris had been the focus for all kinds of exiles, and there was plenty of time for animosities and rival groups to form, under the umbrella of resistance to the Junta. I took a two-year leave from San Francisco State University and joined friends and colleagues in Paris. My activities in the United States—introducing surrealism, structuralism, and post-structuralism; the French new novel and Tel-quelism in academic studies and creative writing; participation in a lot of literary activities with small presses and magazines mainly in California; as well as my activities and comeback in France and Greece in the late eighties and nineties—will have to be the subject of a follow-up autobiographical account, for which there is no space here.

BIBLIOGRAPHY

In English:

Hired Hieroglyphs, Kayak, 1970.

Diplomatic Relations, Panjandrum, 1971.

Flash Bloom, Wire Press (San Francisco), 1980.

My Afterlife Guaranteed, City Lights, 1990.

Contributor to a special issue of *Manroot #6–7,* "Hypnotic Pencils and Descriptive Poems," 1972. Editor of poetry page in *The Phoenix,* a bimonthly newspaper of San Francisco, 1971–72.

Poetry has appeared in *Botteghe Oscure, Encounter, Folio, Kayak, London Magazine, Poetry* (Chicago), 1950–60s; *Bastard Angel, Chicago Review, Gallimaufry, Ohio Literary Review, Poetry Wales, RSVP,* 1970s.

In Greek:

Punishment of the Magicians, privately printed (London), 1947.

(Translator) George Seferis, *The King of Asine,* John Lehmann, 1948.

Central Arcade, privately printed (Athens), 1958.

Anonymous Poem of Foteinos Ayannis, Wire Press, 1974, Ikaros (Athens), 1977.

Nests of Microbes, Wire Press, 1977.

Hero of the Accidental, TRAM (Salónika), 1979.

The Traitor of the Scripted Word (prose), Ikaros, 1980.

The Feathery Confession (poetry), Ikaros, 1981.

The Diamond Tranquilizer (prose), Ypsilon, 1981.

Some Women (prose), Themelio, 1982.

Bones of the Greeks (novel), Nefeli, 1982.

Poems I, 1944–64, Ypsilon, 1983.

The Bottom Line (poetry), Nefeli, 1984.

The Assassination (novella), Themelio, 1984.

The Treasure of Xerxes (novel), Estia, 1984.

The Coloured Bic Pen, Dodoni (Athens), 1986.

Poems II, 1964–74, Ypsilon, 1987.

Andreas Embirikos, Ypsilon, 1989.

For a Theory of Writing, Exantas (Athens), 1990.

Paramythology (prose), Nefeli, 1996.

Anideogramata (poetry), Kastaniotis, 1996.

Sun the Killer of a Green Thought (poetry), Kastaniotis, 1996.

In French:

Terre de Diamant (texts on drawings by Marie Wilson), privately printed (Athens), 1959.

Contributor of poems and essays to numerous periodicals, including *Cahiers du Sud* (1946), *Caravanes* (1996), *Change* (1978), *Fin de Siècle* (1977), *France Libre, Lettres Nouvelles* (1969), *Surrealisme* (1977), and *Surrealisme Meme* (1958–59).

Other:

Author of plays *Nightfall Hotel,* produced in Paris in 1959; and *The Log,* produced in Athens and Spoleto, Italy, directed by Giancarlo Menotti, and in Aarhus, Denmark.

Articles and essays published in English, French, and Greek, in *Anglohellenic Review, BLS, Caravanes, Digraphe, Hellenic Journal, Horizon, Inconnu Superieur, Lettres Nouvelles, Nea Grammata, Pali* (editor 1963–67), *The Phoenix, Plein marge, Sema, Shocks,* and *Surrealism.* Interviews and short stories appear in *Athenian Press.*

Co-editor of the Greek literary review *Synteleia* ("End of the World"), 1989–95.

Julia Vinograd

1943-

Julia Vinograd, the Bubblelady of San Francisco—"Me blowing bubbles in front of me blowing bubbles in the Telegraph Avenue mural"

The most important member of our family was Grampa Ben, Mother's father. She wrote more poems about Ben than about Dad. The most famous member was Wimby, Grampa Ben's pet golden retriever. He made the cover of *Time* when they did an issue on dogs of famous men. I learned to stand by pulling myself up Wimby's hair. A very patient dog.

It was Grampa Ben's bookcase that got me hooked on books. I was forbidden to touch Grampa Ben's bookcase. It had a tall glass front and was kept locked up. Both my parents had been university professors and didn't consider the books unsuitable for me. In fact, the house was littered with Anaïs Nin and Henry James and my father subscribed to *Esquire,* which stayed on the hall table in plain sight with the *New Yorker.* But this was Grampa Ben's bookcase; he'd died when I was three and the bookcase was sort of a literary tombstone. No trespassing. So I waited till everyone was asleep and stood on a chair that always creaked and threatened to tip over and stole the key from a candy dish on top of the bookcase and took a book to bed. Most of the pages hadn't been cut, so it was a book and a knife at night. I remember the fierce possessive feeling of slic-

"Grampa Ben, the family patriarch, and Wimby"

ing the pages. These were virgin books. I was going where no reader had gone before. I haven't changed much. I eat and stain the pages, break the spine, do everything we were warned against. I started out my reading career as a rapist with a knife, and if I take a book to bed with me it remembers my name in the morning.

For quite a while I didn't even like the idea that books had authors. Me and all those characters were so close it seemed an intrusion for someone I'd never met to've seen them first. All the books and movies I liked I continued in my head, taking my favorites and introducing them to people from other books and making up new adventures for all of us. I thought everyone did this. I didn't bother to write them down. Now I wish I had.

Even earlier, when I was about four, the family did Europe. (Memories come slapdash, I can't promise order.) The Mediterranean is clearer than any water I'd ever seen, except for our goldfish bowl which got changed every other day. Nobody changed the Mediterranean. It was a lot bigger, and I was allowed to touch the water without being scolded for bothering the fish. Mother wouldn't buy me a bunch of purple flowers some woman was selling on top of the Eiffel Tower, so I threw a temper tan-

trum and screamed all the way down. It's a long way down. Four is the wrong age for cosmopolitan memories. In America, though I hadn't thought about it. I'd considered the earth under my feet roughly the same age as a big tree. In Europe the earth was old, full of blood and stories. Then there was England, where I ran into my first snow. I'd cut out paper snowflakes and expected to see strange shapes a little smaller than my palm. Instead I saw dandruff falling out of the sky. Unmistakably dandruff. Later on I got polio and we came home.

I had two close friends growing up. One was my sister Debbie, seven years younger than me. Oddly enough, we were closest through another piece of furniture—a couch that stood across from Grampa Ben's bookcase. It was a wine-dark, velvet, welcoming living-room couch, and Debbie and I used it to travel. We'd put our hands over our eyes, fling ourselves face down into the corners, and chant "We're go-oooooing." Then blind and half-smothered, we'd describe to each other imaginary places, or places we'd heard about but didn't quite believe in. (The places I'd actually been had faded to funny stories.) It seemed the whole world was a giant suburb with dishwashers, guilty silences, African violets that never quite grew, vacuum cleaners, and a few flies banging against the windows till they died. Like us.

Debbie still has that couch at her studio. She lives in Berkeley as a painter with her boyfriend Tom, and I spend a lot of time over there. By now the couch is worn down, swaybacked, collapsed. At a party last year a guest complained the sharp broken springs almost castrated him. We've put blankets over the springs but we're keeping that couch. India is behind its cushions; the smell of dust, spices, and old copper temple roofs turned green with time.

My other friend was Lisa Yount, a year younger than me. She was my best friend through grade school, and though we went to different high schools we wrote constantly. Those letters were the only things I ever wrote that didn't turn into poetry (including this project). "Grampa Ben's Bookcase" with two added lines was a very successful poem at my last reading.

I had a brace on my right leg from polio. Lisa was nearly six feet tall and built like a Valkyrie in the fifties when all girls were supposed to look like Twiggy. It made so much difference having someone to share books and ideas with. Debbie was too young. Lisa was also a poet, and as well as poems she wrote what we called "heffelumps," where everyone we'd read about or imagined would have wild adventures and wind up in the punch bowl with Cynthia, the pink octopus. Like I say, I thought everyone did it.

Lisa lives a town away but we're still close. She's extended family and comes to family occasions. She has a house and an adoring husband and wears the long flowing dresses she always wanted. Lisa keeps watch on all the good parts of the world I didn't want. I like to visit it. She keeps me honest.

It's too easy to forget there are good parts of that world. And she really did buy me new front teeth for Christmas when I'd broken one on a chicken bone that snuck up on me. That would have been embarrassing and uncomfortable from anyone else. Often she'd come to Christopher's "zoo parties." (Lisa's nickname—more about the parties later.) We both liked them for different reasons. It's valuable to know someone well enough that you see with their eyes. I needed the balance.

Dad was a professor of biochemistry at Caltech, which was why the family lived in Pasadena. I respected and admired Dad but I never really got to know him. I saw him most at breakfast, where he talked centrifuges and recombinant DNA, and late at night, when we'd bump into each other raiding the refrigerator. He and Debbie were very close; they were the well ones. At this time Debbie was riding horses and I didn't see that much of her. Dad's hair was pure white at thirty, and it made him very handsome.

Mother and I were first-name close. My parents were Sherna and Dad. Sherna encouraged me to write. She'd always written poetry herself. But she expected me to write the strong wry understated style, where you don't know your throat's cut till you have trouble buttoning your collar. Her style. Sherna and Josephine Miles were colleagues at one time. Sherna had the beginnings of multiple sclerosis; we were the sick ones. But if I'd have trouble walking, she'd see I had wings. I thought she looked like a ruined cathedral with long dark hair. She could sit on her hair. Sherna always be-

The author's parents

lieved I was a poet, but never liked my poetry and simply waited. She's been dead for ten years and she's still waiting.

For My Mother, After Her Death

I need to think of you as forever unimpressed
no matter how many books,
improbable friends, readers and life styles
I dump on your clean living room carpet
like damp stones from the bottom of the garden.
I need you to go on
telling me to take them away and not bother you
so I can go get more and go on bothering you.
"Look at this frog, this honor,
how wet and wriggling."
Alive, you never looked,
but I was sure if I brought home King Kong
you'd *have* to look
because you'd need help throwing him out.
Maybe.
And he's in the garden too
at the bottom of a heap of rose petals and reviews.
I need to think of you as still not looking,
not just because you're dead
but only because nothing I've done
is worth looking at yet.
So I go hunting again, driven.
Maybe sea serpents,
suppose I brought you boat-eating tentacles?
or just the ocean?
Will you still throw it out the back door
and then tell me to wash that smell off my hands?
I know the house was torn down, you died,
and I'm not really six. Details.
I need to keep bringing you things.
I need them to be always wrong.
I need to be furious and full of hope
that this time it will be different.
And I need to know it won't.
You'll go on throwing heaven and earth
out the back door
and tell me to wash that dirt from under my nails,
it's disgusting.
That dirt from your grave, Mother.

(From *Cannibal Crumbs*)

Nothing is real to me until I write about it. My life hurts or glows, but it's only a jumble until I shape it with words. Poetry isn't something I do, without it I'm just another blur. I feel stupid trying to explain myself in prose. I was born December 11, 1943; I was born, really I was. It doesn't sound convincing.

I got sent to a small girls' high school, partly on scholarship. We wore pastel uniforms, and it was boring—though my parents thought a coed school while I was sick would've been hell. They were probably right. At high school almost by accident I discovered Yeats and spent a year writing bad imitations. There's nothing quite so dangerous as a great poet, but it was worth it. I knew even then my own voice would be very different, but I also wanted that lush music inside me against the dry seasons. I was like a python swallowing a harp. But for the rest of high school—I can only study when I'm interested and I wasn't. All my schoolmates were very sympathetic when I didn't make the seven sisters and had to settle for Berkeley in the sixties.

As soon as my parents let me, I went looking for a garret and wound up in a basement, where I spent a year living on dented tins of smoked oysters and orange soda pop and putting balanced suburban meals behind me. Telegraph Avenue has five bookstores, new and used, in two blocks. I also discovered coffeehouses, which before college I thought only existed in French novels. Even now I do a lot of my writing in the Cafe Mediterranean, where there are people if I want them and coffee when I need it. Much of the time it helps me to write when there are other minds around to drown the silence; silence can get awfully loud.

Sherna had been an English professor, and it had been vaguely assumed I'd be one too. That seemed okay till I ran into a college English department, and Berkeley at that time had a comparatively good one. I was expected to compare and contrast, and I didn't want to compare and contrast. I didn't care who influenced whom. I had to write so many papers that the essay form is entirely ruined for me. I identify it with homework. I began to understand why so many Americans hate poetry. If your main exposure to poetry is having to memorize "The Charge of the Light Brigade" in grade school and then to write a fifty-page essay with footnotes on Spenser's "The Faerie Queen" in college, it's only rational to avoid that stuff like the plague. And if you're only allowed to study a good poet by first studying his bad contemporaries in excruciating detail—well, words fail me.

I did have three poetry classes at Cal from Thom Gunn, Josephine Miles, and Gary Snyder.

Julia when young

Excellent poets with clear interesting voices. But I wanted a voice of my own, and I didn't have it yet. I never did get a voice from poetry. My voice came from what I needed to say, and it came *out* as poetry.

I was never exactly interested in politics. On any campus there are groups with theories and projects and fiery long speeches. I was vaguely in favor of a lot of stuff—for example, I signed civil rights petitions, but it would never have occurred to me to go south and organize voters. I didn't keep track of wars or laws or names of government officials. I was a very ordinary student. And precisely because I was ordinary, I wound up getting arrested in the Free Speech Movement. Every little table the university was trying to shut up and close down signed a petition and they ran the gamut from the John Birch Society to the Communist Party to some totally nonpolitical groups, one for hiking, sailing, and mountain climbing, if I remember correctly. No, I can't tell you what it was like; let me show you.

The Sproul Hall Sit-In
for the 30th anniversary of the Free Speech Movement

I remember telling my legs,
legs you aren't going into that building, no way,
stop walking legs, you listen to me.
My legs didn't listen
they walked into Sproul Hall
carrying me with them.
I was scared silly and not just of the cops.
Joan Baez was singing, it was too beautiful
the way the air on a high mountain is too clear.
I was scared of the beauty, it was hard to breathe.
I remember everything.
Girls dressed like secretaries,
boys dressed like law clerks
and we expected America to keep the promises
it made in 8th grade social studies.
Free Speech.
Freedom to Assemble.
I remember the food when we didn't get arrested
   at once.
Organized people brought cardboard boxes
of cardboard baloney sandwiches and oranges.
But I also remember a big cauldron of cold spaghetti
and even a tin of caviar and we took
a fingernail each till it was gone.
I remember classes springing up in every corner.
I remember passing the huge black walnut table
   in the lobby,
the constitution was probably signed
at a table just like it
and a TA was standing on the table
giving a lecture about the war of the roses
to his class who were sitting under the table,
cross-legged and taking notes.
It looked like a scene from a foreign art film
but the subtitle was the Bill of Rights.
About every 45 minutes
someone would hear the cops were on their way
but people did try to sleep.
That was the first time I saw tv cameras,
they didn't look electrical,
they looked like high noon on another planet.
"These are the protesters asleep in Sproul Hall,"
the reporters said, and they shone those cameras
and everyone woke up.
It was a long night, it isn't over yet.
I got arrested by a young black cop with a big
   adam's apple.
He was half my weight and looked at me and said
"Please miss, don't go limp."
Nothing went as planned.
I hadn't planned to be there;
part of me hasn't left.
I remember a light brighter than the tv cameras,
stronger than fear.
I remember us.

(From *The Eyes Have It*)

I'd been writing steadily of course and of course making the same mistake everyone makes which is resolving to make no mistakes at all. I thought avoiding failure meant success. It took me years to learn that if you don't expect to crash and burn sometimes, you'll never set the world on fire. There's no rulebook for poetry. If it works, use it. If it doesn't, forget it. I don't care if Shakespeare used it to sell toothpaste to his mother.

After I got my B.A. at Berkeley I went to the Iowa Writers' Workshop for a Master of Fine Arts. Everyone there seemed to be from California or New York. I only met one Iowan in the workshop and he looked lost. We lived in three falling-down old houses with a connecting basement that held falling-down stoves and iceboxes. Poetry classes in an English department, even a very good one, are very different from classes in a school where everyone thinks of himself as a full-time poet. And some really inspired teaching, mainly by Paul Carrol, blew the lid off all my safety boxes. Paul made me appreciate Ginsberg and Whitman by reading them aloud, he called it the test of breath. Paul taught a catch-all class called Form of Poetry, theoretically from seven to nine in the evening. We yelled cheerfully at each other and at nine we adjourned to the local bar and continued the argument. In the morning no one was quite sure what the argument had been about, but we were all sure we'd won.

There was only one problem. It took me till I left Iowa to digest what I was learning. During the two years I was there I couldn't control it, never wanted to control anything again and simply wallowed. While I was there, everything I wrote stunk.

When I came back to Berkeley in '67, the world had totally changed, and I hadn't heard or seen any of it in Iowa City, Iowa. There'd been politics before I left, but I used to have a picture of all of us arrested in the Free Speech Movement. The girls all looked like secretaries and the boys all looked like law clerks. Now everyone had long hair, bare feet, bright clothes, and looked like they'd just stepped out of a tapestry. Over it all hung Bob Dylan's early lyrics, which were poetry for me. I decided Telegraph Avenue was Desolation Row, and I liked it that way. I was in total culture shock. I scuttled around with my mouth and my notebook both open, staring at what I saw and trying to write everything down at once. I for-got about writing styles and just wrote; I didn't want any of it to get away. I've lived in Berkeley ever since, trying to write the autobiography of the street which keeps changing. My sister moved up to Berkeley. She'd dropped horses for painting and we spent a lot of time together, discovering a world we could never have imagined.

I don't know who I am or where I've been. Describing my own life is like having something fall on me and someone wants to know was the part that hit my head striped or polka-dotted? And this is no way complete. About some things I'm shy, others I haven't decided whose fault it was and the memory's on hold. Others don't fit. For example, I had grand-mal epileptic seizures for about fifteen years and managed not to think about it. It had nothing to do with the things I was thinking about. Not till I got on medication that controlled it did I realize I could've fallen down a flight of stairs at any time and broken my silly neck. But it would've been wasted worry. The only reason for mentioning it here is that

"My mother, Sherna, and my sister, Debbie"

the epilepsy kept me from experimenting with drugs, and the epilepsy combined with the polio got me on SSI for fifteen years like most of the street people. I wrote about the street people.

Street Night

I

Take the earth-opened, star-foiled street
struck with a naked hand,
the dance coiled in the double spiral
of bone rivals and pomegranate blood in the
    brain,
the used bruises, the strung-out songs, the
    stained veins,
the concrete meat strutting down clown row
with mirror shades in Hades,
the spotlit burp going bump in the night
while the belly dancer sheds spare change
from her navel onto the gravel and the cold hands
empty as a bottle:

            take it, shake it, make it and fake it
            any way you can
            until morning.

II

Ambulances howl at the moon
then turn into werewolves hunting blood.
Neon peons shuffle from doorways to guitar cases
to stash boxes to the stuck inside
of raped and tangled veins.
"Hide," the night whispers, "hide and seek."
Thumbtack stars pin back tacky black lashes
on broken pin-up wanted posters.
The rain attacks: the submarine-gun raincoats
    sputter:
open legs, powdered visions and litter.
In the bitter cold the folded bones melt fast;
it felt so sweet.
            "Candy," the night whispers,
            "want some, little girl?"

(From *Berkeley Street Cannibals*)

My first five books were written in total street persona, first person plural. My first book, *Revolution and Other Poems,* was beautifully put out by Oyez Press, cost five dollars, and didn't sell. My second book was a chapbook put out by Fred Cody called *The Berkeley Bead Game* and priced at a dollar. I rescued my book from the elegant mortuary of the poetry section and sold it on the street and in coffee shops. I traded with the vendors and the deadheads; I got half my holiday presents trading. I sold 3,500 copies and could have sold 4,000 but my feet gave out.

Sister Debbie with her boyfriend Tom Tuttle

It was a revelation. Often enough people would buy one of my books just to make me go away and later on come look me up, part bewildered and part suspicious. "Are you sure that was poetry? I mean, I liked it." That was how I established my main audience, people who hate poetry. Or at least they thought they hated it. They became regulars, asking if it wasn't time for my next book yet. I wrote a summer and a winter book to keep up with the street. My shorter poems began appearing on bathroom walls all over Berkeley, and my books became popular as souvenirs of Berkeley, sort of like New York postcards with the Statue of Liberty. It wasn't literary elegance, it was communication. There are people out there; they need us.

Eventually I made an arrangement with a printer at GRT; he paid for the books and I paid him back through the sales. He said the only other person he had that arrangement with was a minor rock star. It was only sort of vanity because I didn't front the money. A grey area that worked very well till he sold his press two years ago.

I was here for People's Park. I lived just across the street from it in a room at the Berkeley Inn. The Park was almost my front yard. I couldn't have avoided it if I'd wanted to. The Park caught the local politicos by surprise, and they didn't really approve. They thought we should all be out protesting Vietnam and not wasting our time on some silly little issue. But we'd been against so many things it was intoxicating to be *for* something for a change, to plant a whole block of yes and be able to look at it afterwards and say, "that wasn't here before us."

To begin with there wasn't much trouble. The first night we lit a fire. The Berkeley cops came and said, "Put it out." Someone asked why. "'Cause you can't have a fire at night unless you got stones around it." "Oh, OK." We put the fire out, got some stones around it, relit it, and when the cops came back they saw the stones and said, "Oh, OK." The drummers played late into the night around the fire. A church was being torn down across town and donated some pews for park benches. Even one of the newspapers had an article claiming "at last those street people are doing something useful." There were roses, and—because it was Berkeley—a revolutionary corn garden, and the slogan was "Everybody gets a blister."

Then Governor Reagan called in the army and all hell broke loose. You've seen the pictures; everyone has. Ten years later one of my People's Park poems got misquoted in *Life* while they were attempting to figure out what happened.

As well as being a local poet, I'm known as the Bubblelady. And that got started as part of People's Park. There was going to be a riot the next day, but I was a pacifist and didn't want to throw stones and besides I'd probably miss. At the same time I was angry and wanted to throw something. I decided I'd blow soap bubbles all night in the park, and if they wanted to arrest me for it, fine. I bought two large bags full of bottles. There were two rookie cops in the park, and I marched up to them and announced my intentions. They pretty much shrugged.

I started making bubbles and after a while one of the rookies asked if they could try. I told myself this wasn't happening, didn't say anything out loud, and handed them each a bottle. They started a contest. "Mine's bigger than yours." "Yeah, but look at mine go, it's

"My best friend, Lisa, the first person I could talk to"

the motion that counts." I quote. After about twenty minutes of this, a cop car with a real cop in it turned the corner, saw us all blowing bubbles, and screeched to a halt. (I think he thought I'd dosed his rookies. This was the sixties when everyone, including the cops, believed some morning we'd all wake up with the water supply dosed and everyone stoned.) Anyway, he ran up to us, checked out the rookies, and damned if one of them didn't try to hand him a bottle. He said he didn't play childish games and stalked off, while the other rookie commented, "He's just scared 'cause his would be too small to see." Again I quote.

I'd only planned a one-night symbolic protest, but I hadn't expected this much reaction. And from cops. I started carrying bubbles with me to see what would happen, and I discovered they could both heckle and applaud. Little kids came running up to me and saying, "Bubble? Bubble?" I'd make bubbles for them and they'd chase them, but if I didn't have a bottle they'd say "No bubbles?" and look sad. Pretty soon I always had bubbles and wound up a lot more famous as the Bubblelady than I was as a poet. Oh well. Bubbles don't help anyone, don't solve any social problem, and are totally unimportant. But I'd never realized it was so easy to make people happy.

Being the Bubblelady made me an honorary street person, trusted in worlds I need to write about. When my first selected works, *Berkeley Street Cannibals,* was published, the review in the *San Francisco Examiner* book section was headed "Bubblelady Writes Book" and had cartoon bubbles coming out of it. When the mural of the People's History of Telegraph Avenue was painted, I posed for my portrait with the bubbles. Right up there with Mario Savio on the police car and the famous picture of James Rector dying. They painted me from the back, preserving my posterior for posterity, and my bubbles floated through all the great issues.

The first weekly reading series I went to was Hardcastle's, a bar on Telegraph with a huge back room and a well-lit stage. Speed-chess hustlers hung out there, drugs were dealt in a side alley, and if you wanted attention you had to fight for it.

However you wrote, you learned how to read or someone else charged up the stage and took over. It was good for me. I was originally fairly

Chris Trian and Dierdre Evans, writers from Hardcastle and early heads of the scene

quiet with a slight stutter. I still am, but not when I'm reading poetry.

The place changed names three times to the Salamander and then the International. It finally got closed down when the owner nobody liked shot and killed someone on duty. It was always packed, steaming with pushy egos and elbows. The audience was insulted into submission, and the performances were fluid enough to become theater at any time. Quality varied widely, but the only sin was boredom, and it was always punished. One reader could do a historically accurate Norse epic in biker slang, and the next reader would do drunken sex comedy.

When the place closed, many of the same poets migrated through a few other readings in the East Bay. The longest lasting was at Rockridge Bar. After that reading, we'd go across the street to the place of a cook who thought we were all fantastic and smuggled us steaks. We'd eat steaks and plan how to fake a mass suicide to become rich and famous, but we never did figure out how to collect on the royalties.

Two of the poets, Chris Trian and Dierdre Evans, gave most of the parties for the scene which included Vicki Ramos, a painter (I still have her portrait of me), and musicians, magicians, and general all-around ranters. Chris and Dierdre lived in a made-over mortuary where the kitchen used to be the embalming room. It was the only kitchen big enough for Chris's food-stamp Fellini parties. One of these parties lasted three days and people came in shifts.

Christopher's writing was like wrapping a sow, piglets, mud and all, in a Renaissance tapestry and setting the whole thing on fire. It kicked, it smelled, it screamed; I couldn't possibly grade it, but it sure was noticeable. Whether Chris came to readings or not, and he often didn't, we kept up a three-way friendship. Him, me, and my answering machine. Sometimes he'd phone me and ask for the machine. Years later he became a regular at the Babar readings as did Andy Clausen who'd MC'd at Hardcastle part-time. More about Babar later.

But mostly from this time period I remember my friend Marty. I lived across the street from his place where he'd wired his kitchen for scientific experiments and ate off a hotplate. He wasn't a poet, but he was the most fascinating talker I've ever met. We spent as much time together as possible. I simply can't describe Marty in prose. I wrote this after he died.

Kaddish for Martin Horowitz

It's rained since you died
and I hated being out in the rain
more than I hated your being dead
because I was getting wet.
Everything continues as always.
I continue as always, dammit,
when something's funny I laugh,

"My friend Marty"

and I'm not sure whether to be relieved
or outraged or both.
And I feel selfish, I want you back
for my sake, not yours.
You were someone to talk to
who could empathize without listening,
and always say the right thing in emergencies
and the wrong thing the rest of the time
so I could be right and bright and silly
who could look like a cartoon of a N.Y. Jewish
    mad scientist,
and then be a N.Y. Jewish mad scientist:
who collected pythons and used to collect guns
till some nut acquired one from you to shoot
    his girl
and you got life except they let you out
because you were going to die within the year
and then you didn't,
and they were no end irritated,
and some professor wrote a letter
recommending you as an original researcher
    and said the girl
had been in his class and she was so dumb
he would've shot her himself if only he'd
    thought of it first;
who went around the world 4 times
to let the snakes loose in the rice paddies to
    catch rats
and explain yourself to customs officials;
who was born blind and kept night-blindness
    and could read
only by taking off your bottlerim glasses
and touching the print with your nose;
who survived 2 plane crashes,
1 car crash, assorted fires
and 7 years of marriage;
who was on a guilt trip that meant opening all
    conversations
by informing your helpless listeners you'd
    worked on the
Manhattan project
and what about it?
who was a snob in all directions,
despising street people
and detesting academia
and lecturing yourself
and wearing a give away suit but never a tie;
who wanted your neutrinos back from the sun,
you took such things personally,
a neutrino has only spin and travels at the
    speed of light
passing thru walls with the greatest of ease and
    so do you now;
who had an affair with a witch
without a navel,
and a dike who could beat you up,
and a red haired smack freak you tried to cure

and get supplies for, more or less at once,
she's dead now too;
who was disastrous and irreplaceable.
It's been a month by now
and I still have to tell unexpected people
and watch their faces fall off
and see what their masks will look like in 20
    years.
Who will always like my war poems best
and argue I'm not a pacifist
and tell me the hard boiled egg I just bought
    is raw
and I throw it at you to prove it isn't
and it is because you palmed it
and you're all over egg yolk but so pleased you
    proved your point
and won't let me forget it,
and I still go on being a pacifist
but who will slip me raw eggs now?
I'm not used to being emotional
and/or dead all over the stage,
but there is a hole in the air where once there
    was a man,
and Marty, what the hell,
is this your idea of a joke?

(From *Cannibal Consciousness*)

Eventually Chris's car died. It was half Plymouth, half Dodge, called Betsy the Plodge, and it would fit thirteen poets pretty much all talking at once. Chris's father died next and Chris stopped coming out. As a result the East Bay readings dissolved. I started going to San Francisco poetry readings.

For years I went to the Spaghetti Factory readings in North Beach. Or more accurately, a microscopic back room in the Spaghetti Factory called the Flamenco Room where there used to be Spanish dancers. Dead chairs, piñatas, and dusty wine bottles hung from the ceiling. There was a high stage with a huge stuffed animal of indeterminate species. The regulars were North Beach poets who'd moved there from New York, when North Beach was cheap. The only one who'd gotten famous in the Beat years was Bob Kaufman, who'd had too much electroshock and police beatings and got dragged there by his girlfriend for homage beers. I've read his books, luminous flowing imagery, humor, and an electric sense of hope. I wish I'd met him earlier. Oh yes, Corso would occasionally turn up to heckle. The weekly regulars were fifty and older, hard drinkers, and they wore thrift store suits. (I'd never seen a poet in a suit before, but they didn't look re-

spectable, they looked like doubtful characters from a forties film noir.) They worshipped jazz, which I'd totally missed, and wrote surrealism. The East Bay poets and I had all been young together, so I hadn't noticed I was young. With the North Beach poets, I did.

North Beach mourns marvelously. They were looking backwards to the Beats and the great days of poetry which ended with Kerouac's death. Later on it ended with Kaufman's death. They looked through a cemetery like a kaleidoscope, all the whirling bright colors of death. But my poetry at the time was influenced by the incredible raps of the Broadway barkers we passed on our way to the readings as much as it was by surrealism. Sometimes the two combined.

Hungover City

She wakes up in the morning
light-stabbed as any other vampire
with a headache roped off to be torn down.
She tries to smooth the one-way lines
off the streets in her face,
combs the pigeons out of her tangled hair,
splashes cold water on her mirror
until it blinks into focus
and watches her hand shake
with the exact quaver she was trying
to get into her hips last night.
The fog she meant to wear again
is in a wine-stained crumpled pile under the bed
and one of the straps broke.
Groping for the aspirin
she knocks the stuffed head of a former lover
off the wall, and leaps backward
at the unexpected thud with a small moan
that needs its oil changed.
The sudden motion sets all her nerves colliding
head-on on every highway down to her toes.
"Oh no," she gasps as the rasping morning
files over her skin. "No."
But already the little shops open all her doors
and let everyone in.
Briefcase-buffeted and schedule-corseted
she reaches the aspirin bottle at last,
swallows a handful of coins in a gulp of gin
and closes her eyes.
      Then her parking meters start ticking
      and the day begins.

(From *Cannibal Crumbs*)

Jack Mueller and Paul Landry were the guiding spirits behind the Spaghetti Factory readings. Jack was large enough to smilingly applaud someone offstage when it seemed they'd never leave. And at the end of the night he'd do a collage poem, an homage to the best of the evening that was still new and exciting on its own. Paul was a gentle listener who made everyone feel at home, and the North Beach parties were at his place. Typically, his biggest parties were Thanksgiving, offering poets an extra family and an escape from loneliness, while Chris's biggest parties had been Halloween, celebrating weirdness. Paul's poetry was both complex and delicate: as he put it, "a list of the layers of rust inside the rose." The Spaghetti Factory series ended when the place was sold and we had a last reading that was such a smash we had a "son of last reading" and went on till they locked the door in our faces.

In this period I wrote my Jerusalem poems. They're different from everything I've ever written, and I'm still not sure myself where they came from; living in Berkeley meant bumping constantly into Jesus freaks who were as common as politicians or comics. I'd been brought up secular Jewish and hadn't paid much attention to it till the preachers started going on about how the Jewish god was a jealous god while the Christian god was a god of love. I hadn't even known I was listening till the back of my mind answered, "Isn't jealousy a lover's emotion?" The Jerusalem poems are love poems between the Lord and Jerusalem, who is both a city and a sorrowful beautiful woman. The idea goes back to the prophets who were constantly lamenting Jerusalem's unfaithfulness. The book stopped me in my tracks. For a long time I couldn't get it published, and when I did I couldn't sell it on the street. I'd built up an audience that expected street poetry from me, and this wasn't street. With a few exceptions the North Beach poets were uncomfortable with them; San Francisco was their holy city.

Then *The Book of Jerusalem* won the Before Columbus Book Award of 1985, and there are people out there who think the Jerusalem poems are my best work. Let me give you an example.

The Calling of Jerusalem

"Jerusalem," the Lord called softly
and his voice reached all over the world

till drunkards shook their muddled heads
and the smiles of businessmen wavered briefly,
and lovers were suddenly jealous for a moment,
though not of each other.
But there was no answer.
"Jerusalem," the Lord commanded with all the
    authority of grief.
"Where are you hiding and why?"
There was no spoken answer
but the air between his hands shrugged of its
    own accord
and invisible hair, most sacred and desolate, fell
    against his face.
The Lord carried Jerusalem as a woman carries
    an unborn child.
"What are you doing here?" he asked her.
"I'm tired," Jerusalem drowsed, but forced
    herself back into words. "They look, they
    pray, they dance, they're exalted,
and then they worry if their parking meters
    have expired.

"I don't mind the wars, I never did, blood has
    a beautiful color
and my lips are even more beautiful.
But they fight out of habit now, the way they
    live,
and it's all small and unworthy
and most wearisome.
I'm tired of them, they're not real, they can't
    see me
and they make me lonely.
I want to stay with you."

"No," said the Lord, "not yet."
"Soon?" pleaded Jerusalem.
"And you promised you'd never ask that,"
the Lord reminded her gently.
"It hurts," she answered simply,
"to be always open in a hive of souls
shut in elegant boxes, but firmly shut.
They don't want me, only my scalp
They want to win their arguments,
not understand what they're arguing about,
they couldn't care less.
What have I to do with them?"

"You are them," the Lord told her,
"when you were passionate and fickle, so were they.
When you were restless and bitter, so were they.
Now that you want more, they may too.
Go back where you belong and make their
    parking meters explode;
you've been called a thief many times, pry open
    those boxes.
Do you think it will happen of itself?"

Jerusalem cast down her eyes,
shuddered as if with cold and nodded.
"But why did you call me then?"
she asked as she re-inhabited her stones.
The Lord caressed the air between his hands,
where she had been.

"I was lonely," the Lord admitted to nobody,
"but it's over now."

(From *The Book of Jerusalem*)

I originally wanted them published in Israel, which didn't happen, then for a long time I wanted an official publishing house with its own distribution. Yes, I was ambitious, but mainly I wanted them published a safe distance away from me. They were the only things I wrote that needed a dignified setting and I simply don't do dignity. Eventually Bill Polak of North Beach did a small edition with the agreement that he wouldn't stand in the poems' way if something came up. Over time they've been used in anthologies as different as the *Norton Multicultural Anthology* to *She Rises Like the Sun*, a goddess anthology.

After the Spaghetti Factory the readings bounced all over San Francisco with various settings and various MCs. We lost the North Beach poets when we had to leave North Beach, and they weren't high energy readings. But at one of our most dismal settings, Peter's Pub, a Scotch Beer and Darts bar run by little old men too tired to run us out, Bruce Isaacson turned up. Neither the place nor we had a reputation at the time. It was blind chance and Bruce was just beginning to get a handle on his own talent. He worked for his father's real estate business at the time and came to readings in a Mercedes, the family car. Many of the poets were prepared to loathe him on sight because how could a rich guy be a writer? But Bruce wasn't a yuppie, he was a workaholic, and he was equally naive about us. Because poets aren't untrustworthy backstabbers in the manner of real estate agents (which Bruce knew how to look out for), he assumed we weren't untrustworthy backstabbers at all and he'd finally found a batch of good people. By the time we got this worked out, we were all a little bruised and incidentally good friends.

Somewhere around here Mother died. Or more accurately stopped dying. When Dad died of a sudden heart attack, her multiple sclero-

Jack Micheline

sis got much worse. We sold the house and put her in a convalescent home. Every time we visited, she asked if Dad had come with us. If she hadn't accepted the divorce, no way was she going to accept his death. The convalescent home told us with luck she'd last six months. And every six months they'd call, tell us to rush out and say good-bye. We came, she'd drift off, and in the morning she'd be better. Later it all happened again. For ten years. Debbie and I were nervous wrecks, and I jumped every time the phone rang. I even bought a candle at the flea market in the shape of an old-fashioned telephone and stuck pins in it.

A month after she died, the Berkeley Inn burned down and I was thrown off the Avenue. She'd never approved of the Avenue. None of the dead people I know ever shut up; I hope yours are different.

Debbie and I had some bad times behind all this but we're close again. We spend part of each day on the phone to each other. I always read her my new poems and go to see her latest paintings. She and her boyfriend Tom are a stable place in my life, and I use her drawings in all my books.

The readings continued drifting from one nothing place to the next. One evening we came to the coffeehouse we'd been using to find it closed down. The scheduled girl threatened to perform in the street. Q. R. Hand, who'd been with us on and off since the Spaghetti Factory, just laughed. Then he took us

Fellow Babarians

Alvin Stillman, host of Cafe Babar

Vampyre Mike Kassel, poet, comic, and singer

Q. R. Hand, friend of Alvin, "got us the Babar reading room"

a block down to a little jazz bar run by Alvin, an old friend of his. Joie gave her feature there, and that's how the Babar readings started. The place was called Cafe Babar, there was a picture of Babar the elephant with his lady Celeste in the window, and pretty soon everyone was calling us the barbarian poets with the accent wrong. Q. R. Hand was seriously into both jazz and politics, but mainly, if Bob Kaufman had been the black Rimbaud, Q.R. was the black James Joyce. I've never heard so many different vocabularies in one poem. But Q.R. was one of the few older poets there. Jack Micheline would charge in occasionally to announce he was too busy to read, and then set the place on fire, belly button to the wind and roaring. But we never thought of Micheline as a Beat poet or even as any particular age, he acted about six and we took him on his own terms, glad of the chance. I'd been at least ten years younger than the Beat surrealists at the Spaghetti Factory, here with these exceptions, I was at least ten years older.

The place looked insane. The back room was half the size of the Flamenco room at the Spaghetti Factory. The hall was crammed with people trying to listen or get in so the hall bathroom was impassible. No window. No stage. No lights. No microphones. You were nose to nose with the audience and you were on your own. Raw wooden boards for the bleachers that easily unbalanced. The wall behind you when you read was corrugated tin and it thundered if you struck it. Cheap beer and when too many glasses got smashed in either anger or homage, Alvin got us large paper cups. No hard liquor so some of the poets brought their kids. The Babar was in the Mission, so we went out for burritos after the reading and talked till the last BART [Bay Area Rapid Transit] train, later if we could get a ride. It was the least comfortable reading I'd ever been to—hot, stuffy, and if you stood up you'd never see your seat again. It was also the best reading, in its good years.

Most of the poets published by Zeitgeist Press were Babar regulars. Quite a few we'd never seen before the Babar. Bukowski was the main poet we had in common, and there was a tendency to relate to Tom Waits the way long ago I'd related to Bob Dylan. But there were almost as many different styles as there were poets. Bruce's poetry took TV language, crash diets, and all the suburban cliches that

Sparrow 13, new poet from Paradise Lounge readings

clog the pores of people's attention, and first he turned them upside down and then he turned them into love poems. Several of the girls worked in the sex industry and wrote about it in unimpressed detail. Danielle Willis was writing a junky vampire novel long before vampires were popular. A poet could be loud and draw the audience into chanting a refrain line or just plain making noise. But a good quiet poem could silence the whole place till people were scared to breathe. Laura Conway wrote of a tragic America in her book *The Cities of Madame Curie,* showing the shadow of radium and the bomb hanging over back porch old ladies.

Apart from Q.R., jazz was never mentioned. We weren't Beat poets. Vampyre Mike Kassel got someone to do a short film on us called *Poets from Hell,* but that was only part of it. We were becoming, and anything could happen next. Our slogan was "Poetry you can actually read."

Zeitgeist Press got started because Bruce was blown away by David Lerner, whom we met at another reading. David came to see Babar once and never left. Everyone including David agreed he was a genius but he never sent anything out, said he found the process insulting, and besides, there was never enough money for both stamps and cigarettes. Bruce published a marvelous book of Lerner's called *I Want a New Gun,* and Bruce tried to get Lerner to be his partner in the press. This didn't work. Lerner was a manic-depressive who occasionally wound up in the nut house and sometimes relapsed into junk which he awesomely couldn't handle. But Lerner inspired Bruce and they stayed up late talking about how poetry could change the world. Zeitgeist would never have happened without him. Bruce did a book of his own and helped me civilize my books. I'd never had intelligent editing before, but it was more basic. Bruce introduced me to arcane concepts like a table of contents and ISBN numbers. Even more important, while I'd been part of good strong scenes before, I'd never really worked for anyone but myself. This changed. Bruce cared as much about the poets he published as he did about his own work and got just as mad when something went wrong. It was like living in a whirlwind. I wound up editing about half of the Zeitgeist chapbooks, working with the authors, not the bound books. And I still do Zeitgeist distribution to Cody's Books, where I already had an arrangement for my books. Bruce and I stay in phone contact whether he's in New York or Nevada, and we regard each other as the best critic for the newest poem. My sister can tell me if a poem "feels right," but Bruce is another poet and he'll have suggestions. He makes my reach bigger. He still wants poetry to change the world, and when he thinks it can't he falls into despair.

The Babarian poets got famous for not being famous for being practically jinxed. At one point we were about to be translated and distributed by a guy who had translated most of the Beats. Ginsberg vouched for his work and showed Bruce some samples. The guy loved our work, he was going to make us famous all over Eastern Europe, particularly Yugoslavia. He was just getting started when the Bosnian war broke out; the poor guy was half Serb and half Croatian. Jinxed! About two years later we heard from him, he'd just got out of the hospital. No, nobody shot him, he'd been hit by a bus crossing the street, but he had to get his family out of the country and the project was understandably put on hold. He still thinks we're great.

Another time when Bruce was in New York, he got an offer for Bana Witt to expand her short stories into a novel and Dell would publish it. That's right, Dell. Bana said no and her short story collection *Mobius Stripper* later came out on Manic D Press, which is a good small press but it's not Dell. Some of our writers are officially crazy, others are just crazy. I wear a button that says "weird and proud."

The Babar lasted ten years, though it was lumpy and faded in the last few years. Bruce left to study with Ginsberg in New York, and the Babar lost some of its electricity. I can't MC. I might as well have a big sign on my forehead saying "This is an awful poem." My face gives me away. David Lerner regarded Bruce's leaving as a personal desertion and stayed home. Danielle spent more time with party people and less with poets. Laura went to Prague. Joie gave up poetry forever again. Eli went out of state. Russell went into the slams. As the crowds thinned the Babar began losing money and Alvin took a partner. The place got yuppified with a pretty barmaid who wasn't sure what poets were doing there. The beer prices went up so many of the drinking poets stayed home. Finally the readings died.

By then there were other readings. I go to the Paradise Lounge Sunday night upstairs readings these days. Jennifer Joseph MCs and she's also the publisher of Manic D Press. It's a huge nightclub and at 10:15 the downstairs bands kick in with their sound systems so there's only time for everyone to read one poem. There are two features, a break, then the open. There's a small mike, a hard liquor bar, and a pool room to the side. The best poet I met through the Paradise readings is Sparrow 13. David Gollub, another poet I've known since the Spaghetti Factory, gives me and Sparrow rides home and we hang out together. Sparrow's a hillbilly gay poet from West Virginia with a totally original voice. My sister thinks he's as good a street poet as me. He just got a collected works out on Manic D Press called *Hell Soup.* Check it out. I miss the Babar where I could read three poems, one for the crowd, one I'd just finished and wanted to test, and one for luck. And I liked being able to see my audience. You look great in a spotlight, but you're also blind. But the Babar's gone and the Paradise is very stable; they just had their eighth birthday.

I think the only way to end is with my own epitaph, which I wrote after a memorial for a friend in the poetry scene. There were a lot of poems read there so I came home and wrote this. It probably describes me better than my whole essay.

Julia Vinograd with Babar poets and friends: (from left) David Lerner, Bruce Isaacson, Daniel McColgin, and David Gollub

My Own Epitaph, Which I Better Write Because I Know Too Many Poets

When I am dead,
please don't say nice things about me.
I wasn't tall and thin and friendly,
I was short and fat
and I stuttered between silences.
I was me, please don't remember
someone you would rather've known.
Don't just remember the poems I wrote
remember the inconvenient rides I begged
and I always seemed to have a cold
and I was me.
Every one of my toes were mine,
please don't remember someone else's toes.
I often went to the flea market
and bought things that reminded me of me.
I liked mangos, roast beef and science fiction.
Don't just say I was a good listener,
add that you sometimes wondered why.
Don't make me a one dimensional nice
with a tragic story or two
like everyone else.
I wasn't everyone else, I was me.

I carried a me black purse
and wore a me black dress
and I had a bad leg so I was usually looking
for a place to sit down.
I didn't smoke or drink or sleep around
and I was too shy
to be a fascinating conversationalist,
but I was very me.
Remember my ringed fingers,
my dirty fingernails,
my mouth playing tennis on the telephone,
the way my leg brace squeaked
when I went up to the microphone
to read a poem.
It was me the sun shone on.
It was me who escaped the suburb
and blew soap bubbles on the street.
It was me whose parents died
(in this poem no one else's parents died
because this is my poem).
I loved filling up my room with me.
I always read by naked lightbulbs.
I read late, very late,
not just for the books
but so not to lose the time I was me in.

I was the nightwatchman
and I knew the night was long.
Even when I was alive.
Please don't say nice things about me
when I'm dead.
Don't treat me with respect
as if I were a stranger.
If I'm lucky the poems will live.
This isn't for the poems,
this is for me.
From God's dubious blessing
to the buttons on my cap
to the godawful cough in the back of my throat
I was a me.
With my eyes.
Remember.

(From *Paper Television*)

BIBLIOGRAPHY

Poetry:

Revolution and Other Poems, Oyez, 1969.

Berkeley Street Cannibals: Selected Poems 1969–1976, Oyez, 1976.

Cannibal Consciousness: Street Selections 1976–1982, Cal Syl, 1982.

The Book of Jerusalem, Bench, 1984.

Cannibal Crumbs: Street Selections 1982–1986, Cal Syl, 1986.

Graffiti, Zeitgeist, 1988.

Horn of Empty, Zeitgeist, 1988.

Street Samurai, Zeitgeist, 1989.

The Underclassified, Zeitgeist, 1989.

The Blind Man's Peep Show, Zeitgeist, 1990.

Suspicious Characters, Zeitgeist, 1990.

Eye Contact Is a Confession, Zeitgeist, 1991.

Blues for the Berkeley Inn, Zeitgeist, 1991.

Against the Wall, Zeitgeist, 1992.

Paper Television, Zeitgeist, 1993.

Styrofoam Ghosts, Zeitgeist, 1993.

False Teeth Talking, Zeitgeist, 1994.

Bloody Red Blues, Zeitgeist, 1994.

The Eyes Have It, Zeitgeist, 1995.

A Door with Wings, Zeitgeist, 1995.

Speed of Dark, Zeitgeist, 1996.

Chapbooks:

The Berkeley Bead Game, Cody's Books, 1970.

Uniform Opinions, Cody's Books, 1971.

Street Spices, Thorp Springs, 1973.

Neon Bones, Thorp Springs, 1973.

The Circus, Thorp Springs, 1974.

Street Feet, Thorp Springs, 1974.

Leftovers, Ground Under, 1976.

Time and Trouble, Thorp Springs, 1976.

Street Skins, Arc, 1977.

Street People's Park, Alderban Review, 1979.

Street Tenses, Alderban Review, 1980.

Concrete Meat, Arc, 1981.

Clown Jewels, Bound Together Books, 1981.

Street Signs, Arc, 1982.

Street Sense, J/S Press, 1984.

Street Blues, J/S Press, 1985.

Street Mystery, J/S Press, 1985.

Darkness, GRT, 1986.

Holding Up the Wall, Cal Syl, 1987.

Other:

Eye of the Hand (poetry tape), Michael Scott Studios, 1996.

Contributor of poems to anthologies, including *Norton Multicultural Anthology* and *She Rises Like the Sun.*

C. K. Williams

1936-

Patmos

It's hard to know quite where to begin the story of one's life—when you were born? when you first fell in love? when you first experienced something like consciousness for its sake?—so I thought I'd begin by talking about where I am as I write this. Where I am right now is on the island of Patmos, in the Greek Aegean, on a bay called Grikou, in a very austere but pleasant little apartment my wife Catherine and I have rented for two weeks. We have a lovely view; it's mid-June, the air is crisp and clear; although there's still the lightest of morning hazes softening the colors of the hills, you can tell that the afternoon will be brilliant, the sunset, as always, breathtaking, the evening darkening wistfully soft and pure. The landscape is rocky here, almost alpine; there's a sense of being in the tops of mountains, though the sea is never far below. This is the island where Saint John wrote the book of Revelations; the towns were originally established to support the monastery that was built on the highest hill to honor the composition of that mad book. The monastery walls are sorrowful grey stone, almost all the other man-made structures are perfectly white; the air is limpid, the water clear, and the atmosphere of the whole place is luminous and somehow inspiring.

Catherine and I first came here in 1973, a few months after we'd met at Kennedy Airport on our way to Paris. Catherine was going home from America, where she'd studied in Boston, to finish her advanced degree, her *maitrise*, in France, and to see her parents and sisters in Paris. (Catherine's full name is Catherine Justine Mauger; the pronunciation of her first name is something like "Kat-REEN," with a little guttural hitch before the "r.") I was coming to Europe to wander around, to meet up with some friends, and, I hoped, to visit my daughter, Jessica—Jessie—who was four then, and who'd been taken for a few months by my estranged

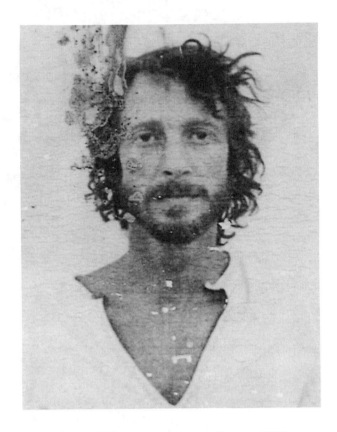

C. K. Williams in Patmos, Greece, 1973

wife to Paros, another Greek island. The plane Catherine and I were supposed to take to Luxembourg was very late; it took us two days to get to Paris, by which time we were friends, and soon afterwards lovers. A month or so later, I went to Paros to see Jessie, then came back to Athens to meet Catherine and go on with her to Patmos.

We spent six weeks here, and in retrospect the time came to seem like an extended marriage ceremony. When we'd arrived, we were both coming out of failed marriages, we'd both gone through a number of other bad relationships, and were still unsteady in our affections, to say the least, but by the time we left Patmos

311

"Catherine soon after our arrival in Philadelphia," 1973

we'd become committed to one another to a degree that I think probably surprised us both. We lived in a tiny, primitive house I can see across the bay from here. I worked at my poems in the morning, Catherine took walks— she hadn't yet become a jeweler, as she is now— I brooded sometimes about Jessie, who was only four, and whom I missed terribly, but Catherine would bring me out of that. In the afternoon, we'd go for boat rides with friends, have picnics on hidden beaches, snorkel, take long walks. Evenings, we often ate alone on our little terrace, and often argued politics. In 1973 Catherine was still the leftist, near Maoist which was the norm then for bright young French people of her 1968 generation; I was the bleeding-heart, fuzzy-minded American liberal I suppose I still am, obsessed then with the awful South Asian wars and the American civil rights disasters. Like many other poets at that time, I'd been involved in the antiwar movement, and had written many poems about the war and about social questions in general, but young Europeans were much farther to the left than most of us,

and I learned a great deal from Catherine about my unconscious political assumptions and attitudes. We fell more and more in love; sometimes I'd feel almost afraid about how precious she'd so quickly become to me. I was still in pain, still used to losing what I most wanted, but we endured.

It took Catherine and me twenty-three years to come back to Patmos, I think because we were afraid to jar our memories with a reality that might not live up to that unlikely beginning, but it's fine to be here again. There are more buildings on the island now, and more cars, but it hasn't changed in any fundamental way. The people are as sweet-natured as always, the landscape as lovely. Just now, I watched as Catherine started on a walk up the mountain towards the monastery town; her yellow shirt was just a speck against the hill, but I could recognize her even so, could feel the rhythm of her gait, how she was so precisely balancing her stroll against the steepness of the slope. And I was moved again at the chance to love someone so well that small perceptions like that can bring such pleasure.

After we left Patmos that first time, we went back to Paris for a few weeks, then to Philadelphia, where I'd been living since I transferred from Bucknell to Penn at the beginning of my sophomore year of college in 1955. I'd come to love Philadelphia, and to be fascinated by the life of cities in general. I grew up on the outskirts of Newark, New Jersey, then lived in the suburbs for my high school years. Philadelphia had been my education in urban life, and to a great extent it was the subject of my poetry. I knew all kinds of people there; I had friends who were architects, carpenters, psychiatrists, painters, writers, musicians, academics, municipal employees, picture-framers, gamblers, addicts, even a few out and out crooks. Some people I knew, like Louis Kahn, the architect, Erving Goffman, the social theorist, and the filmmaker David Lynch, were or became quite widely known. The city itself was a sort of testing-ground for the urban renewal projects of the fifties; by the sixties, there'd been just enough changes to make it architecturally more charming, economically more prosperous, and culturally quite attractive. Until then, anyone who was a serious artist or writer would migrate as a matter of course to New York, but now people began to stay, and there was a powerful sense of creative energy in the city. At the same time, it was basically a very subdued, still somewhat Puritan town. There was only one bar—Frank's—for people of any intellectual interest, and what had been an ordinary neighborhood bar became, at least for a time, a kind of club where you could be sure of meeting sympathetic people, and—these were after all the liberated sixties—women. The sixties were also of course the most hopeful years for race relations in America; Whites were getting to know Blacks in a way they never had before, and all of that together made for a benign and exciting atmosphere.

I'd lived in apartments and houses all over the center of the city; now Catherine and I moved into the rather grungy room in a half-ruined building near the river where I'd been camping before my trip. Then we rented an old wreck of an apartment that hadn't been inhabited for fifteen years or so, renovated it, and moved in just in time for our son Jed to be born, in 1975. Jessie lived nearby, and I could see her almost every day. I think I'd

been basically very sad in my adult life; being with Catherine and the children in a climate of affection and closeness was a rather amazing change for me.

I started teaching seriously around then. Before that, I'd filled in the gaps in my income, first with editing and ghost-writing, mostly for a friend, Loren Crabtree, who was a brilliant young psychiatrist, then for other psychiatrists and for architects. I'd helped Loren found a patient literary magazine at the hospital where he'd done his residency, then, when he came back to the hospital to head its adolescent unit, I helped him with ideas for an in-hospital high school, and then started working with him part-time as a group therapist. I worked with him for nine years or so, and learned a lot; trying to help troubled adolescents was in some ways the completion of the two short periods of therapy I'd gone through myself. By 1976, though, the work became a little repetitive and I began to feel confident enough in poetry to think I might have something to say about it, so I began teaching. I taught part-time for a few years, doing workshops at the Philadelphia "YM-YWHA," then doing adjunct teaching at schools around Philadelphia. Finally we went to Franklin and Marshall for a semester, then to University of California at Irvine for another, then in 1979 to Boston University for a year. I didn't realize it then, but that was the end of my time in Philadelphia. The city had begun to change in ways I didn't like much—the urban renewal had gone too far and had turned the center of the city into a rather dull upper-middle-class enclave. The clearance and replacement of many of the old buildings had made the city much more commercial, and that began to drive away the artists who'd been able to find cheap places to live and work. The city felt neutered, racially it was divided more radically than ever, and after we'd spent a year in Paris, we decided not to go back to Philadelphia, but went to live in New York, in Brooklyn's Park Slope. I taught a few semesters at Columbia and Brooklyn College, then in 1982 I took a professorship at George Mason, although because of Catherine's work and because our son had already been bounced around so much with all our moves, we stayed in New York and I made the grueling commute to Virginia every week. When my father died in 1985, we were able to make Paris our base, going back just one semester a year for

"*Our wedding,*" 1975

me to teach, first at George Mason, then, starting in 1996, at Princeton.

We've lived mostly in Paris for ten years now. If Philadelphia in those years during the sixties and early seventies was a social laboratory for me, Paris, since the moment I first visited it in 1956, has felt in some odd way like my spiritual home. Even at the very beginning, when I spoke only a few words of French, and had a painful sense of being an outsider, there was something about the sheer beauty of the place, about the way it seemed both unknowable and inexhaustible, that made me feel as though it was somehow the place I was meant to call home. It's very hard to explain—maybe it's the scale of the buildings, or their colors, or the way the streets are laid out with no discernible logic, or the sense one has of being in a place which has kept so much evidence of its history—but being here has always been, and continues to be, very exciting for me. Though there can be moments during the bleak, endlessly grey winter when it's as depressing to be here as in any other place, when the light finally brightens, or when I turn a corner and look out along a beautiful curve of the Seine or down a narrow street I'd never noticed before, I fall in love with it all over again.

Back then, at the beginning of the spring semester after my first visit, halfway through my junior year, I left Penn and went back to Paris. I'd begun to write poetry the previous spring, now I wanted to try to write full-time; that, plus the fact that I was more and more depressed with the life I was leading at college—half fraternity boy, half would-be artist, really no one and nothing—made me feel I had to escape. I'm sure a large part of it had to do with my wanting to get back to Paris, although I never admitted that; I just knew I wanted to get away. At first I wasn't even going to tell my parents I was going, but finally I did, and they accepted my leaving, if with trepidation. I came back to Paris, to the same hotel I'd stayed in the summer before, and fell into a period of lacerating loneliness. I'd always been a little shy, but now something, maybe my uncertainty about my identity as a poet, my sense of being a pretender, made me all but mute with strangers. I used to stay all day in my room, reading, trying to write, then I'd go out to eat by myself, and take endless, anguished walks. Finally I happened to run into a woman whom I'd met on the ship coming over, who was looking for someone to go to Spain, and we decided to travel together. We bought a motor-scooter and started South, sold the scooter in Bordeaux—we were freezing to death on the thing—and took a train to Madrid. The woman was a physicist from Berkeley, about ten years older than I was; we weren't lovers, but she was a good companion. She met people easily and in Madrid we fell in with some Spanish students and I had a respite from my solitude.

After a few weeks I left by myself for Seville, for the "Semana Santa"—Holy Week—and the Feria, which was very exciting; Spain under Franco was caught in some dark medieval conservatism which seemed very romantic, at least to strangers. Then I came back to Paris where I plunged again into that by now almost unbearable loneliness. I used to read enormous novels—much of Thomas Mann, I remember, most of Thomas Wolfe, Dickens, Huxley, Hesse—and some poetry—Baudelaire, T. S. Eliot's poems and essays—but I was basically quite lost. I left Paris again, for England, and on the boat-train met a young woman whose father was a clown in a circus. The girl was a dancer who had been traveling around Europe for a few years; she was very experienced sexually, and I was scared to death of her, but I traveled with the circus for awhile. I remember walking back to my "digs" from their trailer, listening to the lions roaring as I passed, and wondering what in heavens name I was doing there. Then I went on to London, and on the train met another woman, a little older, Scotch, who was going to meet her American boyfriend, who was Black. We walked around together to look for a hotel, but everywhere we stopped, when she'd say that her lover was Black, we were quite openly turned away. I've come to like London since, but back then I found it terribly depressing; besides the racism, the city was still poor and dingy from the war years, and I couldn't figure out the people at all. I went back to Paris again, and the wretched loneliness took me again. I think I just couldn't stand it anymore, and I also realized that I really didn't know enough about poetry even to try to write it, so I decided to go back to school.

Before I'd left Penn, I'd been a philosophy major, though not a terribly serious one. I'd spent my first year of college at Bucknell mostly playing basketball. Bucknell, in the empty Pennsylvania hills, exacerbated the restlessness which has always afflicted me, and I spent a lot of time moping around, not knowing what to do with myself. I applied to transfer to Penn, and to my surprise I was accepted. I told the basketball coach at Bucknell I was going to study architecture, which was just an excuse to leave gracefully, but at Penn I did room with an old friend, Dave Rothstein, who was an architecture student, and I spent a good part of my time at the architecture school, which was a very vital place just then. Lou Kahn was teaching there, and had his studio in town; he was just starting to do his best work, and I became part of the circle of students around Kahn. When I was asked a few years ago to write about the important influences in my life, I realized that my image of the artist's calling had come almost entirely from Kahn: he was absolutely devoted to his craft, and expected the same kind of dedication from everyone else.

When I came back to Penn from Paris, I switched my major to English and began to study poetry seriously. There was very little extracurricular encouragement or opportunity for poets in universities in those days compared to now—none at all as far as I knew at Penn—but I had some good teachers. I studied the Romantics in a terrifically valuable close-reading course with Morse Peckham; then Herbert, Blake, Stevens, Swift, and Joyce in his seminar. I had a strong course in Yeats and Eliot, and an inspiring survey of Eastern religion and culture with the Orientalist Schuyler Cammann, who also became a friend.

I read as much as I could while I was in college, but really didn't get started writing as much as I wanted to until I graduated. I enrolled in graduate school at Penn, but my old adviser, Maurice Johnson, who'd wanted to be a poet himself but had had to give it up to support his family during the Depression, used to tell me I should never have come to graduate school, and a few weeks into my first tedious proseminar, I took his advice. (It was very satisfying some years later when Johnson wrote a good review of one of my books for the Penn alumni magazine.)

Peckham once mentioned to me that Eliot had written that if you wanted to be a poet you had to write verse every day; I took the admonition to heart, and have tried to write every day since then. It feels now as though that resolution has done more to affect the actual shape of the way I've lived than anything else. Besides determining the form of my days, it's also given me sustenance during those bad times when I'm in despair about my work, about not having done enough in my life: at least I can tell myself I gave as much of myself to it as I could.

Jessie, the author's daughter from his first marriage, and Jed, the author's son with Catherine, 1981

Those first years, though, were hard. I moved downtown to a room on Delancey Street, and I would force myself to stay there even when I thought I'd go crazy if I didn't get out. I read, tried to write, tried to learn to write. For the first three or four years of it, I didn't even know any other poets, but then I met Steve Berg, who'd studied at Iowa and who knew much more about poetry than I did; he gave me much good counsel, and was very generous and constructive. I've had so many poet and writer friends since then who've encouraged and helped me that there wouldn't be space to mention them all here. In those first years alone, though, I spent a lot of time just floundering. In retrospect, though, it might have been a useful period; I didn't know what you were supposed to know to be a poet so I did a terrific amount of reading, in many domains, trying to figure out what could go into poems, and perhaps not having formally studied writing in workshops gave me a start on making an identity as a poet that would fit the person I really was.

I met my first wife, Sarah Jones, around then. Except for some months in Mexico, two brief visits to Bruce and Fox McGrew in Arizona, and a trip to Europe, we lived in Philadelphia, and I worked pretty much without stopping—I don't think I took more than a few weeks vacation during that whole time. As time went on, the marriage started to go downhill, and we stayed together much too long, long after it had become evident things wouldn't work, but from the beginning our relationship hadn't been very healthy. Marriage is hard enough, but my wife's family had distanced themselves from her when we'd first started going out, and she took that harder than either of us realized. Then, when we married, they essentially disowned her: they couldn't accept the idea of her being married to a Jew.

Pasts

Charles Kasdin, my mother's father, who died not long before I was born and for whom I'm named, came to America at sixteen, from Kiev, in Russia. His father, Isaac, I learned recently, had gone back to Russia soon after they arrived and was never heard from again. For whatever lost and surely painful reasons, he never again tried to contact the family he'd deposited in America, nor they him. One doesn't hear very often about all the people who came to the promised land, found it wanting, and returned to where they had come from.

My grandfather's mother was named Nechama; the family has a photograph of her and Isaac, but a restorer at some point botched the picture, retouching the pupils of their eyes with tiny blots of ink that strangely neutralize any sense of connection one might feel to the faces that hold them. A long Victorian dress and pulled back hair for Nechama; a beard and a tight suit for Isaac; for both that fixed, vacant, darkroom stare.

Often I've tried to imagine what their life in their shtetls was like, these great-grandparents, those blurred generations. (Although I don't really know if they lived in shtetls at all, even that is conjecture; for all I know they may have lived in big cities, as "urban peasants.") I've tried at times to reconstruct a world for them, from old photographs in books—grey houses with chinks in their rough wooden walls, unpaved streets—and from my

Charles Kasdin, Williams's grandfather

readings in Singer, Aleichem, even Chekhov—remember the "Jewish band" in some of his plays?—but there's not much I can believe with conviction. And there's no going back to re-create a history for them either, not since the Nazis made their hideous erasures of European Jewry.

My grandfather was killed when the pickup truck he was driving skidded on a patch of ice and smashed through a safety barrier into an oncoming train. My grandmother, when she was a hundred, a few years before she died, said, "I never should have let him buy that truck; he was such a bad driver." Charles needed the truck, though, for his new business, selling auto parts, because his old one—a cigar store, two of them, in fact—had failed in the Depression. His death affected my mother terribly; I had the feeling it was the most important thing that had ever happened to her, or at least the most important sad thing. My mother loved happiness; she was unrelentingly dedicated to it.

Charles Kasdin had started out his working life as a tailor. My other grandfather, Benjamin Williams, was a tailor, too, and stayed one, working in various shirt factories until the tremors of Parkinson's drove him to retirement. Charles, though, hated the work: he soon gave it up, but his experience in the factory gave him a lasting sense of allegiance with "the worker." He became a Socialist, and later, when he began to believe in the dream of Israel and became a Zionist, it was as a Socialist-Zionist. My aunt Dorothy, my mother's oldest sibling, the only one still alive who remembers him really well, is very proud of the fact not that he was Socialist or Zionist, but that he knew Golda Meir, the prime minister of Israel in the fifties, whom he met at a conference in Geneva. It's almost impossible to imagine my grandfather in Geneva. I was there a few years ago on the way to give some readings in Switzerland and was disappointed in how diminutive and provincial it seemed, that notorious city in which so many conspiracies ripened, but it was still too disjunctive a leap for me to imagine Charles Kasdin and Golda Meir strolling out along the lakeside.

Charles ran for congress or the state assembly in the twenties as a Socialist-Zionist, but he lost. There's a letter to him from a professor at the University of Rochester—all the family, on both sides, lived in Rochester—congratulat-ing him on a speech he'd made. The letter became a family treasure, for the university letterhead as much as anything else. I realized only recently, when a friend mentioned that their father was the first person to have gradu-ated from college in their family, that I was only the second in mine. My father went to the University of Syracuse for a year, but it was the Depression, and he left to go to work, and only one uncle before me has a degree, in accounting. Charles apparently was a seri-ous enough Zionist to want to move to Pales-tine, but my grandmother, Libby (for Elizabeth), said absolutely not. Maybe that was a mistake, because surely in Palestine her husband wouldn't have died skidding on ice, and she wouldn't have had the hard life she did after he died; he left her five children, aged four to twenty-something, and no life insurance. She'd already had a lot of sadness: three of her children had died very young, two in infancy of dis-ease, and one, Zelda, run over by a car in front of her house when she was three. My mother spoke with horror of the memory of the driver of the car carrying Zelda in his arms into the house. Terrible, these sudden deaths by automobile. No wonder my mother, when we first became prosperous, found a house on a dead-end street.

I remember my grandmother as always be-ing harried, overwhelmed. When my father had to send my mother and me back to Rochester to stay with her, because he couldn't make enough to support us in Newark where he'd gone to work for IBM, I hated it. Libby was harsh and impatient; I can't blame her now, but then I was frightened of her. Once she washed my mouth out with soap for cursing. I can't imagine what I'd have said to offend her so at age four or five—"shit" maybe, which I'd heard her say herself—but I think I never quite forgave her for her little cruelties to me.

Her husband, anyway, before all of that, and after his time as a tailor, was going to move to New York City to renovate old build-ings, but for some reason that didn't work out and he stayed in Rochester. The cigar stores were next: supposedly he owned the buildings they were in as well as the stores, but like so many others, he lost all of it in the Crash. My mother's Uncle Max, who was the only person in the family at that point who'd made any real money—he owned a chain of gas stations—

*The author's parents, Paul and
Dossie Williams, 1934*

was the one who suggested an auto-parts store, then a new concept, but poor Charles never got to see how it would go, because of his bad driving and the cold Rochester winter. (When the rest of the family began to follow my father and mother to New Jersey, the abominable Rochester weather was an endless topic of conversation. I'm sure part of it had to do with blaming the weather, as though it were some divine force, for my grandfather's fatal collision. Once, though, at the other end of the country, in balmy Palo Alto, California, I was almost done in by a train myself. I was waiting at a grade crossing; when a train passed, the red lights kept flashing and the horn blaring, but I thought they were just being over-cautious so I started across and was almost flattened by the express that screamed by in the other direction at about a hundred miles an hour. My mother never would have gotten over that. Also, it occurs to me, the first thing I ever wrote that was just *writing*, written for its own sake, not for an assignment, was a long letter I sent to a girl my freshman year of college about a student who'd been killed when his car was crushed by a train that ran near the Bucknell campus.)

I didn't know Uncle Max very well, or his wife, Aunt Dora, about whom the rest of the family had mixed feelings, the way families often do about their prosperous relations. I never was able to keep straight the people in that generation, the great uncles and aunts, except for Max's sister, Celia—Aunt Celia—who took care of me in Brooklyn when my brother Richard, now Tex, was born, when I was almost five, and then again when my sister Lynn arrived, when I was ten. (Tex is now a successful businessman and Lynn is a judge.) Lynn was born in 1946. I remember that Charlotte, my older cousin, and I were taking the subway somewhere, and when we got onto the train, her brother Buddy was sitting there, on his last leg back from Japan, where he'd been in the signal corps. Wild greetings! Buddy gave me a beautiful Japanese flag which I later burnt a hole in trying to iron. It was exciting meeting all the cousins and uncles coming back from the war, especially one cousin by marriage who'd been a bombardier on a B-26 "Marauder." I was crazy about warplanes, could identify every plane in the American arsenal, and I was terribly impressed by that cousin; he still wore his flight cap and leather jacket, though now I can't remember his name or whose husband he possibly could have been.

I liked Brooklyn and Celia's somewhat chaotic household; her husband was named Max, too, which must have added to my confusion about that generation. Aunt Dorothy still speaks with less than friendliness about the other Max's wife, Dora, but she told me a nice story about her. When Dora's son was in the army, and was stationed in Florida before being shipped overseas, Dora decided to visit him. When she got to the hotel where she'd reserved a room, she found it was "restricted," which meant that the manager refused to give her a room because she was Jewish. Would he at least have said, "I'm sorry, we don't admit Jews?" No, no "sorry" in those days. Worse than London. Aunt Dora, anyway, gave him hell. "My son is in the army, going overseas to maybe die for you, and you don't want to let me stay in your cruddy hotel?!" He gave in and gave her a room, but she only stayed one night, huffing out the next day to find a "Jewish hotel."

There's no need to say how complicated it is being Jewish, I've written enough about it already. I was bar mitzvahed, but essentially gave up Judaism after that, and except for the half-reluctant bond I feel with Israel, being Jewish doesn't seem at all essential when I identify myself to myself—Catherine isn't Jewish, for one thing. But still, when I have to describe my life, the Jewishness suddenly looms large, for good and ill.

My father told me that his father, Benjamin, was very religious, but I don't know if that's really the case. My father liked bestowing virtues on people they didn't really have. I do remember going with Grandpa to a little *shul* in Rochester where old men were wrapped in voluminous *tallises,* swaying, chanting in loud, erratic mumbles, and then drinking a shot of schnapps after the service, at eight o'clock in the morning, all of which I found a little menacing.

My father, in the last years of his life, from the time his father died, also used to go to a synagogue—not a *shul,* that word was gone then—every morning, in New Jersey, or in Florida, where they lived during the winter. I don't know whether it was because he was religious, or just because he liked so much to be around other people, but of course that's really the basis of the Jewish religion, that eternal sense of community. When I was striving to have some sort of religious experience in my twenties, *any* sort of experience beyond the theodicy questions which so obsessed me, after I'd tried Milton's Christianity and Dante's, and Zen and Tao and whatever else, I studied seriously some branches of the Jewish tradition, starting with Buber and Scholem, but I really misunderstood the whole point of Judaism, which is that the community counts for nearly everything, that you simply can't make a religion just for yourself. Whatever the intricacies of the struggle were, I subsided back into the aching atheism to which I seem doomed still.

I liked my father's father better than anyone else in that generation, maybe because he was so quiet—I can hardly remember him ever saying a word. He was brought to America when he was very young, at four or five, from around Białystok, my father said, but you can't tell from that. My father had the habit, when he didn't know the answer to a question, of just making one up; usually he did it as a joke, but afterwards you were never sure. Sometimes it could

be very funny. He once told a friend of mine a long story of how it happened that though we were Jewish we had the name Williams. He explained that his grandfather, coming from Poland to America, was stranded in Wales, and found work in a coal mine. One day he saved another miner's life, and the man was so grateful he gave Great-Grandpa his name, which was Williams, as a present. Of course, my father added, in Wales, Williams was spelled with four *l*s. So then we knew the story had been one of my father's jokes, but you couldn't always be sure. The way we did get the name was courtesy of an immigration officer in Montreal, who couldn't pronounce Grabivietsky, and so changed it on the spot, which apparently happened quite regularly then. (No one knows for sure now the proper spelling of Grabivietsky.) The name Williams has caused me problems in my day. While I was with a girlfriend when I was twenty, someone in her family blamed a supposed robbery (of some jars of jam!) in their house in a village in New England on the family of Jews who'd recently presumed—dared—to move into town. My girlfriend then endearingly whispered a little poem to me: "Of all the people God could choose, / how odd of God to choose the Jews." When I broke up with her later, or let her drift away, I doubt if

Williams holding his sister, Lynn, and his brother, Richard (now Tex), 1947

I knew whether it was because she was eager to get married, which I wasn't, or because I still hadn't managed to let on to her that I was one of those so-intrusive chosen.

Another story my father told was that his father's father was six-foot eleven (which may have been another fabulation, though my father was six-seven and I'm six-five), and that he died when, already ill with pneumonia, he had to fight some drunken Cossacks he was kicking out of the inn he ran back wherever it was. I do know that my great-grandfather died when he was young, that my great-grandmother had a second husband, but I have no idea whether the story of how he died was true or was one of my father's jokes. There was a tradition of taverns in the family, anyway. When the Depression wiped her out, too, Anna, my father's mother, told her father, who lived with them, to make a still in the cellar— it was during Prohibition—and she became a bootlegger, of vodka, which my father told us he used to deliver hidden in a baby carriage.

Białystok, anyway, seems as good a place for my grandfather to have come from as any. Anna was very clear about her origins: she came from Austria, she often told me, from Lemberg; her father had been a farmer, and had owned forty horses. When I mentioned once to my friend Adam Zagajewski, the Polish poet, that my grandmother came from Lemberg, he told me that Lemberg was the German name of Lvov, which is where his family came from, too. Lvov was really a Polish city, though a part of the Austrian empire; Jews used to think it was more acceptable to have come from German-speaking countries rather than from farther East. I don't know if Anna spoke German or Polish; she, too, came over to America before she was five. She and my grandfather both spoke Yiddish to each other most of the time. I don't think anyone in my generation learned Yiddish, which is a shame. My grandfather's half brother, Chiam Berschstein, who ended up immigrating to Mexico after the anti-immigration acts in the States, and whom I met in Mexico City a few years before he died, used it as a *lingua franca*. He spoke Spanish, English, Russian, and Polish, but I think his mother tongue was Yiddish.

I'm not even sure of my grandmother's last name, Berger, I think; I could find out, but it wouldn't matter: even if I knew her name, and knew she was from Lvov, there are no records of Jews left there to search through. I once asked Chiam, who'd been the last to come over, in the twenties, about the family back there. He said that there had been quite a few of them, but that they'd all been killed during the war when a train that another relative, a communist commissar apparently, had arranged for to get them out of Poland into Russia had been bombed by the Germans.

Stories: how few of the stories you end with are truly your own. I don't know why it is that strands of narrative you think you can attach to your strands of DNA seem so much more meaningful than ones that you can't, but there you are. The rest is just history, which is real enough, but which you never quite actually possess in the same way. When I think of how little I actually know about my forebears, even the ones I knew in the flesh, it can be a little desolating: everything begins to have the contingency of fiction. When I've asked the aunts and uncles who are left, and who were in at least fairly close touch with the family past, I've run up against that startling attitude people in those generations had of not wanting to remember the past. Having escaped a miserable world of poverty and pogrom, they just wanted to put it all behind them. Was it shameful for them? Probably not; it was just something they didn't want to be burdened with. Maybe my father's habit of making up pasts was as appropriate an attitude as any.

My favorite story about my father himself is one he'd never have heard. When he died, among the many letters of condolence my mother received was a pastor's newsletter from a church in a town in western Pennsylvania. In it, the pastor wrote that someone back in New Jersey had seen my father's—Paul B. Williams's—obituary, and had sent it on, because they knew the pastor would have wanted to see it. The pastor went on to write that when he was a young man, he'd worked as a caddie at the club where my father played golf. My father, a "very great man," the pastor said, "who'd founded many companies," had become friendly with him, realized that he wasn't terribly happy with caddying as a living, and had offered him a job in his print shop. The pastor—he'd been about twenty then—was delighted. Soon after he went to work, though, he made some sort of mistake and managed to put the business's freight elevator out of commission. He was terribly upset

"My father and I," about 1950

about it, he wrote, but that afternoon my father asked him to drive him home and then told him to keep the car—a Cadillac!—overnight, to pick him up the next morning. The lesson the pastor was teaching his flock in the newsletter had to do with my father's sensitivity and generosity and trust, and how he'd helped the future pastor restore his self-confidence. The pastor said he'd learned a great deal about Christian charity from my father that day, and that his memory of my father's goodness had stayed with him when he went on to divinity school and became a minister. And, he concluded, his benefactor Paul B. Williams wasn't even a Christian, but a Jew!

My father did found quite a few companies, in office equipment, most of them small, but some certainly successful enough. Another of my favorite stories about him he told me himself. After the war, when the economy started heating up, he had to decide what he was going to do next. He'd worked for IBM selling electric typewriters before the war, had become very good at it but had quit when IBM wanted to take him off commission and put him on salary, just when he'd started making real money. During the war (he was 4-F; he had terrible eyes, which troubled him his whole life) he'd tried various businesses, including an answering service, I remember, and now he had to

figure out what he was going to get into for the long term. He told me he decided to start a business selling carbon paper. "I could have sold anything I wanted," he said, "from battleships to machinery, but I decided to pick the most competitive field I could find." "Why?" I asked him. "Because I knew I was good," he answered. I think I was a little shocked because that was so unlike my own much more diffident way in the world, but it does say a lot about him. He was very confident, very directed; he was tough. Though the pastor's story did describe him well, that was only a part of him. He could sometimes be difficult with my brother and sister and me, especially as the years went by and he seemed to define himself more and more by his identity as a businessman rather than as a husband and father.

When I was very young, he used to tell me bedtime stories: the Greek myths—the labors of Hercules were our favorites—and Jack London tales, and during one period when I was afflicted with awful bouts of poison ivy, he used to make up stories for me, about cowboys and dogs and various heroes' battles with kodiak bears. But by the time Tex and Lynn were born he'd moved his essential attentions mostly out of the house, and when we were grown he could sometimes be very disconcerting in his unpredictability: you never knew if he was going to be warm, affectionate, and funny, or abrupt and distant. The three of us suffered from that, and I think my mother's complicated relationship with him must have come from that gradual change in him, too. I have a memory of her saying to him, about some unpleasantness he'd inflicted on Tex or me, "You used to be such a nice man." Strange: I don't know whether I actually heard her say it to him, or only heard about it, but it's become in a way the narrative center of my memory of him. When I was small, I worshipped him. He was very kind to me, taking me to his Sunday morning softball games and bowling, and a little later, when I went into my obsessive horse phase, he would take me to the stable every Sunday morning, though he didn't ride himself, and then he even bought me a horse of my own, a hundred-dollar cow-pony, something which wasn't done in his circle. (Horses, cowboys, especially Will James books, but really anything to do with horses, were the absolute center of my life from about age twelve to fifteen. The reason my father finally bought me the horse,

I think, was because I used to spend all day Saturday working at riding stables so they'd let me ride for ten minutes at the end of the day. I had the horse for two years or so, then I think my parents decided I needed to move on and told me they couldn't afford it any longer, which I knew wasn't true, but I was probably a little tired of the horse-world by then anyway, and I'd discovered girls.)

Those warm memories of my father became very moving at the end, when he was dying. We were sitting together the day before he died, and I was trying to convince him not to kill himself yet. He was absolutely determined to have his demeaning death done with as soon as he could; he had tumors in his brain, his speech was becoming garbled, and he hated that. When he asked why he shouldn't get it over with, and I told him that these last moments together were precious to me, his eyes suddenly filled with tears and he said, "You and I were kids together, we really were kids together!" and I realized he was right: he was in his early twenties when I was born; he really was still a kid when we had those glorious Sundays.

My mother, Dossie, was very pretty, almost beautiful, with red hair. The pictures of her and my father when they were young are striking. She was the darling of her family and was very spoiled. When my mother died, her sister, Dorothy, who was also her lifelong best friend, told how when she, my aunt, was first working, earning ten dollars a week typing, she used to give my mother a dollar of it to buy cigarettes; she was still proud of having been able to give something to my mother. My mother had a job briefly around that same time, in a five and dime, but then she married and had kids and didn't work again. Later, my father set her and my aunt up with a little spare-time business, but she didn't like it and he let it drop.

My mother really did have a good time in her life. She was great fun to be with, very lively and cheerful, most of the time, especially after we kids had all left home and she didn't have to worry as much about us, and make lunches for us to take to school. When we were young, there was often a lot of tension in the house. She could be edgy, short-tempered, and she yelled a lot. She hated never having enough money. Later, she would tell me about how poor we were back then, about

"Me and my horse," 1951

how horrible she felt when she didn't have five cents to buy me an ice-cream cone. But when my father became prosperous, and the pressures eased, so did she. She loved the good life, pretty clothes, restaurants, vacations, and the "club." In Paris, sometimes I'll see two immigrant women in a store, African maybe, or Portuguese, who you can tell haven't been in France very long; they move through the store's aisles at the wrong speed, or perhaps talk too loudly: they're just a little off. Then I realize that they're really my mother and my aunt, out shopping, after their husbands have starting doing a little better, and they're having such a nice afternoon; it's so splendid to be able to walk through a store knowing that if you want to buy something you can. If you like, you can even buy two.

But it was an abiding strain between my mother and me that I'd picked a vocation in which you couldn't become wealthy. My father liked the idea of my writing poetry; he'd written some himself in high school. Along with my bedtime stories, he'd encouraged me when I was younger to read and memorize poetry—

Shakespeare, Longfellow, Tennyson; I remember a book called *One Hundred and One Favorite Poets*. He helped support my work over the years, and during our talk that afternoon before he died, he told me how proud he was of my calling. My mother, though, even after I'd won a few fellowships and prizes, could never quite wholeheartedly approve of my career. But I guess I can't really blame her. When I first began to do readings, I discovered that one of the first questions students ask is how you happened to become a poet. By the time anybody asks you that, you've mostly forgotten, but for a long time I used to say that I'd decided to be a poet because it was what had been least expected of me, and there's probably something to that. I was hardly an artist or an intellectual when I was young. A woman I knew in high school, who's a literary agent now, tells me every time she sees me, which thank goodness isn't often, "Of all the people in our school, you're the last I'd have thought would become a poet." And it's true: I was probably the last person I'd have thought of as a poet myself.

Poetry

Trying to talk about the history of the poetry one has written seems at once essential and redundant; essential because the poetry seems to me to be the most accurate record of the life I've actually lived, and redundant because it's so much the history of itself and has implicit in it everything pressing I've thought over the years about poetry. But there are complications in such a self-evident observation. In the first place, some years ago I began to use fiction as a resource in my narrative poems, and now I realize the poems aren't to be entirely trusted as records of what actually "happened" to me. Sometimes this can be disconcerting, because the experiences created in the poems are as vivid and reliable to me as any other memory, but at the same time I do have to recognize that technically they're not "true." "The Dog," for instance, a poem I consider absolutely central to my work, is about a Black woman with a dying dog, and my responses to her. The events the poem recounts didn't happen, though, in quite the way the poem tells it. I had actually come into contact with *two* women with sick dogs, one was Black, one White. The sexuality the poem uses to intensify its

social meditations came out of other experiences entirely. But still, the poem for me is a very accurate depiction of a certain moment in my life, and more importantly it's a crucial case study in certain kinds of subliminal racial prejudice. It begins:

> Except for the dog, that she wouldn't
>   have him put away, wouldn't let him
>   die, I'd have liked her.
> She was handsome, busty, chunky, early
>   middle-aged, very black, with a stiff,
>   exotic dignity
> that flurried up in me a mix of warmth
>   and sexual apprehension neither of
>   which, to tell the truth,
> I tried very hard to nail down: she was
>   that much older and in those days
>   there was still the race thing. . . .

Another complication in reflecting on my poems arises from the fact that even when the poems do recount events that did "happen" to me, the order in which they were written doesn't necessarily follow the order in which the events occurred, and, even more importantly, what might seem absolutely central from a strictly narrative point of view may in the poems appear as particles of almost tangential material. So, for instance, the story of Catherine and I first coming together on Patmos is told in a long poem, "With Ignorance," which is a meditation on more general issues of sex, love, and metaphysical longing. The poem resolves in a lyric section which is about my return to our little house from a short trip away, but there's no way in reading the poem to trace the narrative I've recounted in this essay: the essence of the experience wasn't contained in the story, but in the imagery of its resolution.

> . . . An island, summer, late dusk; hills,
>   laurel and thorn. I walked from the
>   harbor, over the cliff road,
> down the long trail through the rocks.
>   When I came to our house the ship's
>   wake was just edging onto the shore
> and on the stone beach, under the
>   cypress, the low waves reassuming
>   themselves in the darkness, I waited.
> There was light in a room. You came to
>   it, leaned to it, reaching, touching,
> and watching you, I saw you give back to
>   the light a light more than light
> and to the silence you gave more than
>   silence, and, in the silence, I heard
>   it. . . .

Jed, age nineteen

By the time I wrote that, in 1975, I knew how to extract from personal experience what I felt was essential in satisfying the intrinsic needs of whatever poem I was writing, and also to do justice to my own experience. But that certainly wasn't always the case. At Princeton this year I told a student who'd shown me some of his poems that they were well written, but that not enough had happened to him to write a good poem. I meant that he hadn't realized the implications of his own experience, that he was trying to assemble details without a strong enough sense of what meaning their accumulation might be pointing towards.

I know very well what he was going through, because the time when I was trying to connect poetry to my own life—those first years alone in that room after Penn—is still very vivid to me, not quite as a painful memory, but nearly. I certainly wouldn't want to go through that again. I wrote all the time, or I tried to, but somehow I really didn't know what to write *about*. In 1960, I took a job as the census-taker for the neighborhood where I lived. I

think I was curious to see the inside of the buildings I passed every day, but I may also have been looking without quite realizing it for material. Once I drove myself to compose a kind of ode—rhymed, metered, unbearably mawkish and awkward—based on a sculpture group by Jacob Epstein at the Philadelphia Museum. (I didn't even have the good sense to have used Rodin's much better "Burghers of Calais," which was there, too.) Then I wrote a sequence of about fifty sonnets about a visit to a prostitute, each with a different rhyme scheme, using half-rhymes and para-rhymes (I'd been studying Wilfred Owen), and junked the whole thing. Though I can't recall whatever happened to the sonnets—I once threw almost everything I'd written into an incinerator—I did remember them well enough to use some of their imagery for a poem on the same theme around twenty-five years later. It was called "Medusa":

> Once, in Rotterdam, a whore once, in a
>   bar, a sailors' bar, a hooker bar,
>   opened up her legs—
> her legs, my god, were logs—lifted up
>   her skirt, and rubbed herself, with both
>   hands rubbed herself,
> there, right there, as though what was
>   there was something else, as though the
>   something else
> was something she just happened to have
>   under there, something that she wanted
>   me to see.
> All I was was twenty, I was looking for a
>   girl, the girl, the way we always, all of
>   us,
> looked for the girl, and the woman
>   leaned back there and with both hands
>   she mauled it,
> talked to it, asked it if it wanted me,
>   laughed and asked me if I wanted it,
>   while my virginity,
> that dread I'd fought so hard to lose,
>   stone by stone was rising back inside
>   me like a wall.

In those first days, though, it was one hopelessly bad poem after another. For a while I wrote reviews of books and art exhibits for a neighborhood newspaper, which at least gave me the conviction I could write *something*. I'd written stories in college, but I decided now that if I was going to try to be a poet, everything I could think of had to go into the poems: I didn't want to scatter my inspirations, such as they were. I knew the poems were bad; even when I first showed a poem (one of the unholy sonnets) to Steve Berg, I knew how awful it was, and I wasn't surprised when he off-handedly dismissed it. I had one bit of respite during that time, when I wrote a poem which to my surprise turned out to be quite accomplished. It was called "Sleeping Over" and was mostly a memory of the times I'd spent at Dave Rothstein's parents' camp in New Jersey. I'd loved the place; I became close with Dave and his brother Mark, who stayed there all year round, living the life of farm kids, and I spent most of my time with them, riding their horses, doing chores, taking care of the animals. In those days, shoveling manure out of a stable or a chicken-house was the most exalting activity I could imagine. I used to visit Dave and Mark during the school year, and I was completely taken with the countryside, with the woods and animals, even the bare, winter fields. The poem I wrote now was a musing back on all that, a memory of a dream I had about the place, and a recounting of the death of one of their horses. This is the first part of it:

> There hasn't been any rain
> since I arrived. The lawns
> are bleached and tonight goldenrod
> and burnt grass reflect
> across my walls like ponds.
> After all these days
> the textures and scents of my room
> are still strange and comforting.
> The pines outside, immobile
> as chessmen, fume turps
> that blend with the soap taste
> of the sheets and with the rot
> of camphor and old newspapers
> in the bare bureau drawers.
> Jarred by a headlight's glare
> from the county road, the crumbling
> plaster swarms with shadows.
> The bulb in the barn, dull
> and eternal, sways and flickers
> as though its long drool
> of cobwebs had been touched,
> and the house loosens, unmoors,
> and, distending and shuddering, rocks
> me until I fall asleep. . . .

There was a wonderful sense of ease that came to me as I was writing the poem. I didn't try to make the experience more than it was; the poem seemed a kind of gift for all the futile efforts I'd put into other poems. It was the first poem I published, which gave me much pleasure, of course, but then I became trapped again in my frustration and indecision. I knew that "Sleeping Over" had been an anomaly, because I didn't *want* to be that relaxed and sure of myself in my poems. I felt clearly—I'm not sure how I arrived at the notion—that I wanted my poetry to have an urgency about it, an ethical gravity; I wanted it to be about what was most important to me when I was most serious with myself, but I had no idea how to accomplish any of that.

When what I was looking for finally arrived, it came in a way I'd have never suspected. I'd been working on and off for four or five years on a poem about the Holocaust. I've written elsewhere (in the poems "Combat" and "Old Man") about the way the Holocaust was concealed from my generation of Jewish children: our parents never mentioned it in our hearing; they must have felt it was either too shattering or too shameful an experience to inflict on us. So when I first heard about it from an older friend around 1958, I was disbelieving, then stunned. "Six million dead," he said . . . and I hadn't even heard about it. I began to study the literature available then on that awful massacre; I think I read everything that had been published in English then on the subject, and I started compiling images, themes, and strategies for a poem about it. Anne Frank had already become an emblem of the Holocaust, though not so much perhaps as she was later, and I decided to use her as my primary symbol, with imagery and locutions from the biblical "Song of Songs" as a secondary resonance. "We have a little sister and she hath no breasts; what shall we do for our sister in the day when she shall be spoken for." I worked on the poem very hard; it grew, it shrank, but I never could find a form or a music for it.

Then one afternoon I was reading an article the novelist Thomas Williams had published about a trip he'd taken through the Southern states, about the fear and pain he'd had inflicted on him as a Black man. This would have been around 1964; so much about the civil rights movement appeared hopeful then (how wrong we were about that) and it seemed to me that Williams was being unnecessarily negative in his perceptions and conclusions. I started to write a letter to the editor, and to Williams, to explain why the situation for Blacks in America wasn't as bad as Williams had made it sound, and from the depths of my political innocence I started to speak about the Holocaust experience to demonstrate why it wasn't. To my surprise, a few sentences into the letter, it suddenly came to me how wrong I was, that the Black experience *was,* indeed, as bad as it seemed, worse than it seemed, and just as suddenly I was released into the Anne Frank poem: I heard its music, understood its structure, and in the next hour or two or day or two—I don't really remember—I wrote the poem. The second section goes:

> I thought of you at that age.
> Little Sister, I thought of you,
> thin as a door,
> and of how your thighs would have swelled
> and softened like cake,
> your breasts have bleached
> and the new hair growing on you like song
> would have stiffened and gone dark.
> There was rain for a while, and then not.
> Because no one came, I slept again,
> and dreamed that you were here with me,
> snarled on me like wire,
> tangled so closely to me that we were vines
> or underbrush together,
> or hands clenched. . . .

I've said more than once to students and interviewers that I learned to write poetry when I was working on "A Day for Anne Frank," but I've never really made clear to myself what I mean when I say that. Thinking it through again, I realize there was something that happened to me as I tried to write that letter to Williams, something about the way I'd had to split myself from myself, the way I'd had to confront the falsity and self-forgiveness of my own attitudes, that had opened up a new way of thinking for me. Without understanding how, I'd created a method of composition for myself, which, no matter what stylistic changes my work has gone through, has remained basic to the way I conceive poems. Having to balance two apparently contradictory ethical attitudes at the same time; having to realize the contingency of my own convictions, however apparently heartfelt they might be; having to confront them and force them to a more rigorous or more honest level; having to make the poem, in a sense, a dialectical event, even if the argument with myself precedes the poem itself— as it did in the Anne Frank poem—allowed

me to bring the poems to a central position in relation to my own experience, my own sense of the struggle to be fully human. My poems have a double function for me: they are about consciousness, in a more or less direct way, and they're involved just as much with the social, moral world with which my consciousness is necessarily concerned.

Strange, not to have realized this until now; all I knew after the Anne Frank poem was that quite suddenly I seemed to be able to write the poems I wanted to write, in a way that satisfied me, that made the struggle with the matter and form and surface of the poems bearable, and, more to the point, purposeful.

Things didn't always go so swimmingly after that, needless to say. There were serious ups and downs. The worst time came after my first marriage broke up. My second collection, *I Am the Bitter Name,* had been published at around the same time, and wasn't as well-received as *Lies,* my first. Although many of the poets I knew by then had admired it, it didn't move out to a more general poetry audience the way the first had, and I was disappointed. The poems in the book were written with a painful sense of the social and political turmoil of that time: the war, the racial tensions, the assassinations. Jessie was born during the time I was writing it, and I was stunned and indignant that human beings could tolerate such phenomena as wars, which killed children, and that God, if there was a God worthy of his name, could abide so much malice and slaughter. At the same time, I'd tried to find in myself the roots of the kind of inner violence I believed were the deeper causes of the horrors humans inflict on one another. Maybe the project was too complicated, or too passionate, or too something. I still value the book, but its reception puzzled and hurt me.

My social and emotional life was also a mess; I was very depressed. I had a disastrous love affair right after I left my wife, then I had one love affair after another, none lasting for more than a few weeks, some for a few days, or hours. I was lonely, guilty, and my self-confidence was shattered. Finally, during one particularly bad time, I actually gave up writing poetry. I'd been on a short reading trip, and it seemed to me that all the poets I met were miserable in one way or another, drinking too much, or smoking too much dope, suffering in marriages as bad as mine had been. Poetry suddenly seemed the most unimaginably futile activity. I felt that the disarray in my life came at least partly from my not using enough of my energy in writing poetry, that driving myself the way I'd been doing, in such a small space, such a restricted dominion, was going to destroy me.

Although I have no memory of how I came to the thought, I decided to stop writing and to become a film director. I called a friend in California who was in the film business, and he said if I wanted to direct, I should write a screenplay. I started to write one, but found it rather boring, and for a few months—I think it was that long, but I'm not really sure—I'd go to my desk every morning, sit there, and quite consciously do nothing. I'd read poetry perhaps, look out the window, maybe take some notes, but really I'd do nothing, nothing, nothing. Then, one afternoon I had a reading at a college of art in Philadelphia. I took my books and a few mostly unfinished poems I'd worked on before my renunciation. During the reading, probably feeling I had nothing to lose, I read two of the new poems, and was astonished to realize that they were exactly what I'd been waiting for, though I hadn't known I'd been waiting for anything at all.

The poems were in long, ragged lines, they had a much more conversational tone than the poems I'd been writing, but what was most important to me was that they tracked the way I moved through my consciousness in a way that was much more systematic and accurate than the poems I'd been writing. Most importantly, the new poems, while having a much more narrative structure than the older ones, also had much more direct mechanisms for tracing thoughts, perceptions, and emotions; they gave me a way to deal more inclusively and exhaustively with my own mind than the poems I'd been writing until then. I began to write poetry again, with more conviction than ever, and more confidence, more of a sense of what I wanted to do. The new poems were very difficult to write; they took a long time— I'd finish on average about three or four a year—but they were very gratifying, and I didn't mind at all the labor and patience they demanded. The *scope* of the poems, the certainty they gave me that I could deal thoroughly with

Jessie and her husband, Michael Burns, 1996

themes that interested me, were enough to keep me going. They are the poems that were collected in *With Ignorance* and *Tar.*

I also began to translate around that time. Right before I'd left for Europe—the day before I met Catherine, in fact—I'd been commissioned by William Arrowsmith to translate Sophocles' *The Women of Trachis* for his Oxford tragedy series. I worked with a young classicist from Bryn Mawr, Gregory Dickerson, and found that working on the play and doing research into tragedy and theories of tragedy broadened my conceptions of scale and drama. (I also found it an agreeable coincidence that *The Women of Trachis* was about Herakles—Hercules—who'd been the subject of my father's long ago bedtime stories.) I did another tragedy, Euripides' *Bacchae,* and in the meantime also made a number of versions of Haiku by the Japanese poet Issa. I found the Haiku form in English too precious, too afflicted with the false sanctities of a misconceived "Zen," and so I combined several Haiku at a time, and transformed them into little poems in English. I wrote dozens of them, then published a selection in a little book, *The Lark. The Thrush. The Starling.* One of the poems actually incorporates what I was trying to do with my own poems at the time:

This is what,
at last, it is
to be
a human being.

Leaving nothing
out, not
one star, one
wren, one tear
out.

I've done versions since then of poems by Adam Zagajewski and published parts of *Le Parti Pris des Choses* by Francis Ponge, and other scattered poetry.

I also began in the early eighties to write essays, generally in response to being asked for them. I've started to write plays, too, the most recent of which I'm hoping someone will produce, and the narrative—a series of poems—for a documentary on crime in America, *Criminals,* by the director Joseph Strick. I enjoy other kinds of writing now, but everything I write besides poems, the poems I'm working on, the poems I'm projecting, hoping to write, always seems tangential to what I should be doing.

The last sequence of poems I wrote for my new book, *The Vigil,* is called "Symbols," and oddly enough there were several poems in it that came out of notes I'd taken during that first stay in Patmos twenty-two years before. There's often a long gap for me between the inspiration for a poem and its fruition, but this was extreme. We only stayed a short time in Patmos back then, and our visit will be even briefer now, but clearly the place has a terrific symbolic meaning for us both. I don't know precisely what made me go back to finish the two poems after all that time, or whether having written them had any relation to Catherine and I deciding finally to come back to stay where, in a sense, we'd found one another, but Patmos seems as good a place to end the story of my life until now, as it was to begin it. The poem is called "Dawn."

> Herds of goats puttering by on the rock-
> strewn path in what sounded like felt
> slippers;
> before that (because the sudden awareness
> of it in sleep always came only after it
> passed),
> the church bell, its cry in the silence like
> a swell of loneliness, then loneliness
> healed.

C. K. Williams and Catherine at a party, 1994

> The resonant *clock* of the fisherman's skiff
> being tethered to the end of the jetty;
> the sad, repetitive, smack of a catch of
> squid being slapped onto a slab of
> concrete;
> the waves, their eternal morning torpor,
> the cypress leaning warily back from the
> shore.
>
> A voice from a hill or another valley,
> expanding, concretizing like light, falling,
> fading,
> then a comic grace-note, the creak of
> rickety springs as someone turns in their
> sleep:
> so much beginning, and now, sadness
> nearly, to think one might not even have
> known!

BIBLIOGRAPHY

Poetry:

A Day for Anne Frank, Falcon Press (Philadelphia, Pennsylvania), 1968.

Lies, Houghton Mifflin, 1969.

I Am the Bitter Name, Houghton Mifflin, 1972.

With Ignorance, Houghton Mifflin, 1977.

Tar, Random House, 1983.

The Lark. The Thrush. The Starling: Poems from Issa, Burning Deck Press (Providence), 1983.

Flesh and Blood, Farrar, Straus & Giroux, 1987, Bloodaxe Books (Newcastle), 1988, translated into French by Clair Malroux Farrar as *Chair et Sang,* Editions Orpheus, La Difference (Paris), 1993.

Poems 1963–1983, Farrar, Straus & Giroux, 1988, Bloodaxe Books, 1988.

Helen, Orchises Press (Alexandria, Virginia), 1991.

A Dream of Mind: Poems, Farrar, Straus & Giroux, 1992, Bloodaxe Books, 1992.

Selected Poems, Farrar, Straus & Giroux, 1994, Bloodaxe Books, 1995.

New and Selected Poems, Bloodaxe Books, 1995.

The Vigil, Bloodaxe Books, 1995, Farrar, Straus & Giroux, 1997.

Translator:

(With Gregory Dickerson) Sophocles, *Women of Trachis,* Oxford University Press (New York and London), 1978.

Euripides, *The Bacchae,* Farrar, Straus & Giroux, 1990.

(With Renata Gorczynski and Benjamin Ivry) Adam Zagajewski, *Canvas,* Farrar, Straus & Giroux, 1991.

(With Margaret Guiton and John Montague) *Selected Poems of Francis Ponge,* Wake Forest University Press, 1994.

Other:

(Editor) *The Selected and Last Poems of Paul Zweig,* Wesleyan University Press, 1989.

(Editor) *The Essential Gerard Manley Hopkins,* Ecco Press, 1993.

Script consultant for two films by David Lynch, *The Grandmother* and *Eraserhead;* wrote lyrics for "Negatives," a song cycle, set by Ronald Surak, 1970; wrote the narrative for *Criminals,* a documentary by Joseph Strick, 1994.

Cumulative Author List

CUMULATIVE AUTHOR LIST
Volumes 1-26

List is alphabetical, followed by the volume number in which autobiographical entries appear.

Abse, Dannie 1923- 1
Ackerman, Diane 1948- 20
Adcock, Fleur 1934- 23
Ai 1947- 13
Aldiss, Brian W. 1925- 2
Alegría, Claribel 1924- 15
Allen, Dick 1939- 11
Allen, Walter 1911- 6
Allman, John 1935- 15
Anaya, Rudolfo A. 1937- 4
Anderson, Poul 1926- 2
Andre, Michael 1946- 13
Anthony, Michael 1930- 18
Appleman, Philip 1926- 18
Arden, John 1930- 4
Argüelles, Ivan 1939- 24
Armantrout, Rae 1947- 25
Arnold, Bob 1952- 25
Ashby, Cliff 1919- 6
Atkins, Russell 1926- 16
Aubert, Alvin 1930- 20
Awoonor, Kofi Nyidevu 1935- ... 13
Banks, Russell 1940- 15
Barnes, Peter 1931- 12
Barnstone, Willis 1927- 15
Barrio, Raymond 1921- 15
Baumbach, Jonathan 1933- 5
Bausch, Richard 1945- 14
Bausch, Robert 1945- 14
Becker, Stephen 1927- 1
Belitt, Ben 1911- 4
Bell, Charles G. 1916- 12
Bell, Marvin 1937- 14
Beltrametti, Franco 1937- 13
Bennett, Hal 1930- 13
Bennett, John M. 1942- 25
Bergé, Carol 1928- 10
Bernstein, Charles 1950- 24
Berrigan, Daniel 1921- 1
Berry, Jake 1959- 24
Bishop, Michael 1945- 26
bissett, bill 1939- 19
Blais, Marie-Claire 1939- 4
Blaise, Clark 1940- 3
Bloch, Robert A. 1917-(94) 20
Block, Lawrence 1938- 11
Blotner, Joseph 1923- 25
Booth, Martin 1944- 2
Booth, Wayne C. 1921- 5
Bourjaily, Vance 1922- 1
Bova, Ben 1932- 18
Bowering, George 1935- 16
Bowles, Paul 1910- 1
Boyd, Malcolm 1923- 11

Boyle, Kay 1902-(92) 1
Bradley, Marion Zimmer 1930-. 10
Brée, Germaine 1907- 15
Brewster, Elizabeth 1922- 15
Bromige, David Mansfield 1933-.. 26
Brophy, Brigid 1929- 4
Brossard, Chandler 1922-(93) 2
Brossard, Nicole 1943- 16
Broughton, James 1913- 12
Brown, Dee 1908- 6
Brown, George Mackay 1921-(96) .. 6
Brown, Rosellen 1939- 10
Browne, Michael Dennis 1940- 20
Bruce-Novoa 1944- 18
Brunner, John 1934- 8
Brutus, Dennis 1924- 14
Bryant, Dorothy 1930- 26
Budrys, Algis 1931- 14
Bullins, Ed 1935- 16
Burke, James Lee 1936- 19
Burroway, Janet 1936- 6
Busch, Frederick 1941- 1
Caldwell, Erskine 1903-(87) 1
Cartland, Barbara 1901- 8
Cassill, Ronald Verlin 1919- 1
Cassity, Turner 1929- 8
Caulfield, Carlota 1953- 25
Caute, David 1936- 4
Cela, Camilo José 1916- 10
Chappell, Fred 1936- 4
Charyn, Jerome 1937- 1
Cherkovski, Neeli 1945- 24
Choudhury, Malay Roy 1939-.... 14
Ciardi, John 1916-(86) 2
Clark, Tom 1941- 22
Clarke, Austin C. 1934- 16
Clement, Hal 1922- 16
Codrescu, Andrei 1946- 19
Cohen, Matt 1942- 18
Colombo, John Robert 1936-.... 22
Condon, Richard 1915- 1
Connell, Evan S. 1924- 2
Coppel, Alfred 1921- 9
Corcoran, Barbara 1911- 2
Corman, Cid 1924- 2
Corn, Alfred 1943- 25
Creeley, Robert 1926- 10
Crews, Judson 1917- 14
Cruz, Victor Hernández 1949-.. 17
Dacey, Philip 1939- 17
Daigon, Ruth 1923- 25
Dann, Jack 1945- 20
Davie, Donald 1922- 3
Davis, Christopher 1928- 20

Davison, Peter 1928- 4
Delbanco, Nicholas 1942- 2
Delgado, Abelardo B. 1931- 15
DeMarinis, Rick 1934- 24
Dennison, George 1925-(87) 6
Dillard, R.H.W. 1937- 7
Dillon, Eilís 1920- 3
Disch, Thomas M. 1940- 4
di Suvero, Victor 1927- 26
Djerassi, Carl 1923- 26
Dove, Rita 1952- 19
Dudek, Louis 1918- 14
Duncan, Robert L. 1927- 2
Dworkin, Andrea 1946- 21
Eastlake, William 1917- 1
Easton, Robert 1915- 14
Eaton, Charles Edward 1916-.... 20
Eigner, Larry 1927-96 23
El Saadawi, Nawal 1931- 11
Elkins, Aaron 1935- 18
Elman, Richard 1934- 3
Emanuel, James A. 1921- 18
Enslin, Theodore 1925- 3
Epstein, Leslie 1938- 12
Eshleman, Clayton 1935- 6
Fast, Howard 1914- 18
Federman, Raymond 1928- 8
Feinstein, Elaine 1930- 1
Feirstein, Frederick 1940- 11
Ferrini, Vincent 1913- 24
Fisher, Roy 1930- 10
Fitzgerald, Penelope 1916- 10
Flanagan, Robert 1941- 17
Foley, Jack 1940- 24
Forbes, Calvin 1945- 16
Ford, Jesse Hill 1928- 21
Forrest, Leon 1937- 7
Foster, Edward (Halsey) 1942-..... 26
Fox, William Price 1926- 19
Freeling, Nicolas 1927- 12
Fry, Christopher 1907- 23
Fuchs, Daniel 1909-(93) 5
Fuller, Roy 1912-(91) 10
Furman, Laura 1945- 18
Galvin, Brendan 1938- 13
Garrett, George Palmer, Jr. 1929-.. 5
Geduld, Harry M. 1931- 21
Gerber, Merrill Joan 1938- 20
Ghiselin, Brewster 1903- 10
Gibbons, Reginald 1947- 24
Gilbert, Michael 1912- 15
Giovanni, Nikki 1943- 6
Glancy, Diane 1941- 24
Glanville, Brian 1931- 9

Glazier, Lyle 1911- 24
Glover, Douglas 1948- 23
Goldemberg, Isaac 1945- 12
Gray, Francine du Plessix 1930-. 2
Gray, Simon 1936- 3
Greeley, Andrew 1928- 7
Green, Kay 1927- 11
Gregor, Arthur 1923- 10
Grumbach, Doris 1918- 2
Grumman, Bob 1941- 25
Guerard, Albert J. 1914- 2
Gunn, James 1923- 2
Gurik, Robert 1932- 23
Hadas, Rachel 1948- 23
Hahn, Emily 1905- 11
Hailey, Elizabeth Forsythe 1938- 1
Haldeman, Joe 1943- 25
Hall, Donald 1928- 7
Hall, James B. 1918- 12
Hamburger, Michael 1924- 4
Hamill, Sam 15
Hansen, Joseph 1923- 17
Harris, Mark 1922- 3
Harris, Wilson 1921- 16
Harteis, Richard 1946- 26
Harwood, Lee 1939- 19
Hassan, Ihab 1925- 12
Hauser, Marianne 1910- 11
Hazo, Samuel 1928- 11
Hearon, Shelby 1931- 11
Heath-Stubbs, John 1918- 21
Hebert, Ernest 1941- 24
Heinemann, Larry 1944- 21
Hentoff, Nat 1925- 6
Heyen, William 1940- 9
Hiemstra, Marvin R. 1929- 26
Higgins, Dick 1928- 8
Higgins, George V. 1939- 5
Highwater, Jamake 7
Hine, Daryl 1936- 15
Hinojosa-Smith, Rolando 1929-. 16
Hitchcock, George 1914- 12
Hoffman, Lee 1932- 10
Holden, Jonathan 1941- 22
Holden, Ursula 1921- 8
Hollo, Anselm 1934- 19
Hongo, Garrett 1951- 22
Honig, Edwin 1919- 8
Hood, Hugh 1928- 17
Horwood, Harold 1923- 15
Houston, James D. 1933- 16
Houston, Jeanne Wakatsuki 1934- 16
Howes, Barbara 1914- 3
Hrabal, Bohumil 1914- 12
Huddle, David 1942- 20
Hudgins, Andrew 1951- 21
Ignatow, David 1914- 3
Inez, Colette 1931- 10
Jacobsen, Josephine 1908- 18
Jarman, Mark 1952- 22
Jennings, Elizabeth 1926- 5
Jerome, Judson 1927-(91) 8
Joans, Ted 1928- 25
Johnson, Charles 1948- 18
Jolley, Elizabeth 1923- 13

Jones, Madison 1925- 11
Jones, Mervyn 1922- 5
Jones, Nettie 1941- 20
Josipovici, Gabriel 1940- 8
Kammen, Michael 1936- 23
Katz, Menke 1906- 9
Katz, Steve 1935- 14
Kazin, Alfred 1915- 7
Keating, H.R.F. 1926- 8
Kelly, M.T. 1946- 22
Kelly, Robert 1935- 19
Kennedy, Adrienne 1931- 20
Kennedy, X.J. 1929- 9
Kenny, Maurice 1929- 22
Kerrigan, Anthony 1918-(91) 11
Kherdian, David 1931- 2
Kienzle, William 1928- 1
Killens, John Oliver 1916-(87) 2
Kinsella, W.P. 1935- 7
Kirk, Russell 1918-(94) 9
Kirkup, James 1918- 4
Kizer, Carolyn 1925- 5
Klinkowitz, Jerome 1943- 9
Knebel, Fletcher 1911-(92) 3
Knight, Damon 1922- 10
Koller, James 1936- 5
Konwicki, Tadeusz 1926- 9
Kostelanetz, Richard 1940- 8
Kumin, Maxine 1925- 8
Kyger, Joanne 1934- 16
Laqueur, Walter 1921- 19
Laughlin, James 1914- 22
Leftwich, Jim 1956- 25
Lelchuk, Alan 1938- 20
Lem, Stanislaw 1921- 1
Lessing, Doris 1919- 14
Levertov, Denise 1923- 19
Levine, Norman 1924- 23
Levis, Larry 1946-(96) 23
Lifshin, Lyn 1944- 10
Lind, Jakov 1927- 4
Livesay, Dorothy 1909- 8
Lottman, Herbert R. 1927- 12
Lowitz, Leza 1962- 26
Madden, David 1933- 3
Madgett, Naomi Long 1923- 23
Mahapatra, Jayanta 1928- 9
Major, Clarence 1936- 6
Malanga, Gerard 1943- 17
Malzberg, Barry N. 1939- 4
Manfred, Frederick 1912-(94) ... 18
Mano, D. Keith 1942- 6
Manuel, E. Arsenio 1909- 9
Markfield, Wallace 1926- 3
Mathews, Harry 1930- 6
Matthews, Jack 1925- 15
Matthews, William 1942- 18
McCord, Howard 1932- 9
McElroy, Colleen J. 1935- 21
McKain, David 1937- 14
McPherson, James A. 1943- 17
McPherson, Sandra 1943- 23
Mead, Matthew 1924- 13
Megged, Aharon 1920- 13
Meltzer, David 1937- 26

Menashe, Samuel 1925- 11
Menefee, Sarah 1946- 26
Meredith, William 1919- 14
Middleton, Stanley 1919- 23
Miller, Jim Wayne 1936- 15
Mitford, Jessica 1917- 17
Moorcock, Michael 1939- 5
Morgan, Robert 1944- 20
Morgan, Ted 1932- 4
Morgan, Theodore 1910- 3
Morris, John N. 1931- 13
Mott, Michael 1930- 7
Mrozek, Slawomir 1930- 10
Murchie, Guy 1907- 19
Murphy, Sheila E. 1951- 26
Nash, Susan Smith 1958- 25
Nelson, Marilyn 1946- 23
Nichols, J.G. 1930- 2
Nichols, John 1940- 2
Nims, John Frederick 1913- 17
Niven, Larry 1938- 12
Nolan, William F. 1928- 16
Norse, Harold 1916- 18
Oakes, Philip 1928- 25
O'Faolain, Julia 1932- 2
Olson, Elder 1909-(92) 12
Olson, Toby 1937- 11
Ostriker, Alicia (Suskin) 1937-. 24
Ouellette, Fernand 1930- 13
Owens, Louis 1948- 24
Owens, Rochelle 1936- 2
Parini, Jay 1948- 16
Peacock, Molly 1947- 21
Pellegrini, Angelo 1904-(91) 11
Peters, Robert 1924- 8
Petesch, Natalie L.M. 1924- 12
Petry, Ann 1908- 6
Phillips, Robert 1938- 13
Picano, Felice 1944- 13
Piercy, Marge 1936- 1
Pinsky, Robert 1940- 4
Plumpp, Sterling 1940- 21
Plymell, Charles 1935- 11
Pohl, Frederik 1919- 1
Polkinhorn, Harry 1945- 25
Pownall, David 1938- 18
Purdy, Al 1918- 17
Purdy, James 1923- 1
Rabassa, Gregory 1922- 9
Rachlin, Nahid 17
Raffel, Burton 1928- 9
Rakosi, Carl 1903- 5
Raworth, Tom 1938- 11
Ray, David 1932- 7
Reaney, James Crerar 1926- 15
Rechy, John 1934- 4
Richie, Donald 1924- 20
Rimmer, Robert H. 1917- 10
Rodgers, Carolyn M. 1942- 13
Roditi, Edouard 1910-(92) 14
Root, William Pitt 1941- 11
Rosenblum, Martin Jack 1946-.. 11
Rosenthal, M.L. 1917- 6
Rowse, A.L. 1903- 8
Ruark, Gibbons 1941- 23

Rule, Jane 1931- 18
St. Clair, Margaret 1911- 8
Salaam, Kalamu ya 1947- 21
Salisbury, Harrison E. 1908-(93)　15
Salvadori, Mario 1907- 25
Samarakis, Antonis 1919- 16
Sanders, Edward 1939- 21
Sargent, Pamela 1948- 18
Saroyan, Aram 1943- 5
Savage, Thomas 1915- 15
Schevill, James 1920- 12
Schwartz, Stephen 1948- 26
See, Carolyn 1934- 22
Settle, Mary Lee 1918- 1
Shadbolt, Maurice 1932- 3
Shapiro, Alan 1952- 23
Shapiro, Karl 1913- 6
Shelnutt, Eve 1941- 14
Shreve, Susan Richards 1939- 5
Silkin, Jon 1930- 5
Sillitoe, Alan 1928- 2
Silverberg, Robert 1935- 3
Simic, Charles 1938- 4
Simmons, James 1933- 21
Simpson, Louis 1923- 4
Sinclair, Andrew 1935- 5
Singh, Khushwant 1915- 9
Sisson, C.H. 1914- 3
Skelton, Robin 1925- 5
Škvorecký, Josef 1924- 1
Slade, Bernard 1930- 9
Slavitt, David R. 1935- 3
Smith, Dave 1942- 7
Solotaroff, Ted 1928- 2
Souster, Raymond 1921- 14
Sparshott, Francis 1926- 15

Spinrad, Norman 1940- 19
Stafford, William 1914-(93) 3
Stegner, Wallace 1909-(93) 9
Stevenson, Anne 1933- 9
Stewart, J.I.M. 1906-(94) 3
Still, James 1906- 17
Stone, Irving 1903-(89) 3
Sukenick, Ronald 1932- 8
Swanberg, W.A. 1907-(92) 13
Sward, Robert 1933- 13
Swenson, Karen 1936- 13
Symons, Julian 1912- 3
Tarn, Nathaniel 1928- 16
Taylor, Henry 1942- 7
Taylor, Thomas Lowe 1938- 26
Tennant, Emma 1937- 9
Thayler, Carl 1933- 11
Thomas, Audrey G. 1935- 19
Thomas, D.M. 1935- 11
Thomas, R.S. 1913- 4
Tillinghast, Richard 1940- 23
Tranströmer, Tomas 1931- 17
Turco, Lewis Putnam 1934- 22
Turnbull, Gael 1928- 14
Turner, Frederick 1943- 10
Valaoritis, Nanos 1921- 26
Van Brunt, Lloyd 1936- 15
Van Itallie, Jean-Claude 1936- 2
Van Proyen, Mark 1954- 25
Villanueva, Alma Luz 1944- 24
Vinograd, Julia 1943- 26
Vivante, Arturo 1923- 12
Vizenor, Gerald 1934- 22
Voinovich, Vladimir 1932- 12
Wagoner, David 1926- 3
Wain, John 1925-(94) 4

Wakefield, Dan 1932- 7
Wakoski, Diane 1937- 1
Waldman, Anne 1945- 17
Wallace, Irving 1916-(90) 1
Waters, Frank 1902- 13
Weintraub, Stanley 1929- 20
Weiss, Paul 1901- 12
weiss, ruth 1928- 24
Weiss, Theodore 1916- 2
Wellek, René 1903- 7
Wesker, Arnold 1932- 7
West, Paul 1930- 7
Westlake, Donald E. 1933- 13
White, Jon Manchip 1924- 4
Whittemore, Reed 1919- 8
Wiesel, Elie 1928- 4
Wilhelm, Kate 1928- 5
Williams, C.K. 1936- 26
Williams, John A. 1925- 3
Williams, Jonathan 1929- 12
Williams, Miller 1930- 20
Williamson, Jack 1908- 8
Wilson, Colin 1931- 5
Wilson, Edward O. 1929- 16
Wilson, Keith 1927- 5
Wolfe, Gene 1931- 9
Wolff, Tobias 1945- 22
Woodcock, George 1912- 6
Wright, C.D. 1949- 22
Wright, Charles 1935- 7
Wright, David 1920-(94) 5
Yglesias, Helen 1915- 20
Zebrowski, George 1945- 19
Zeidner, Lisa 1955- 24
Zinoviev, Alexander 1922- 10

Cumulative Index

CUMULATIVE INDEX

The names of essayists who appear in the series are in boldface type. Subject references are followed by volume and page number(s). When a subject reference appears in more than one essay, names of the essayists are also provided.

"A" **2**:138, 142, 146
A for Anything **10**:203, 216, 217, 219-20
A la Carte **1**:38
A la recherche du temps perdu **8**:153
A la Rencontre du Plaisir **5**:195
A las puertas del papel con amoroso fuego **25**:101
Aardema, Onie **18**:247-48, 251
Aarhus University **1**:156
ABC of Reading
   McCord **9**:180
   Pinsky **4**:244
ABC of Relativity **5**:314
Abel, Sherry **2**:398, 399
Abelard-Schuman (publishers)
   Gunn **2**:249
   Williams **3**:424
Aberdeen Express **5**:125
Abigail **2**:127
Abish, Walter
   Katz **14**:176
   Klinkowitz **9**:116
Able-to-Fall **20**:72
Abortion **10**:22
Abortionist, The **16**:14
About My Table **2**:156
Abraham's Knife **7**:14
Abrahamsen, David **1**:376
Abrams, Ricki **21**:10-12
Abscond Press **24**:74
Abse, Dannie **1**:17-32
   Rosenthal **6**:283
   Silkin **5**:262
Abse, Joan **6**:283
Abse, Wilfred **1**:317
Absence of Unicorns, Presence of Lions **7**:132
Abulafia, Abraham **25**:264-65
Academic Alpine Club **25**:353
Academic Festival Overtures **15**:221
Academy Award
   Corcoran **2**:119
   Nichols **2**:335
Academy of American Poets
   Dillard **7**:12
   Meredith **14**:230
   Wagoner **3**:410
Academy of American Poets Awards
   Allen **11**:13
   Rosenblum **11**:347
Accent **2**:438
Accord **14**:273-74
ACE **11**:305
Ace Books

Brunner **8**:9, 13
Hoffman **10**:173
Knight **10**:225
Niven **12**:218
Pohl **1**:294-95
St. Clair **8**:273
Silverberg **3**:276
Williams **3**:424
Achebe, Chinua **3**:426, 427, 428
Ackerman, Al **25**:74
Ackerman, Diane **20**:1-15
   West **7**:280-81, 282
Ackerman, Forrest **2**:27
Ackerman, Jack **3**:216
Ackley, Gardner **3**:244
Acorn, Milton **17**:205, 206
Acosta, Juvenal **24**:100
Acquired immune deficiency syndrome
   Andre **13**:25
   bissett **19**:31, 35, 55, 58-59
   Bryant **26**:60
   Hansen **17**:72
   Mathews **6**:239, 250
   Norse **18**:290
   Picano **13**:232, 234
   Williams **20**:337
Across a Billion Years **3**:281
Across the Bitter Sea **3**:64
Across the Lagoon **11**:96, 99
Act of the Imagination, An **9**:255
Actes retrouvés, Les (Recovered acts) **13**:186
Activists **24**:40
Actors and acting
   Browne **20**:60
   Fry **23**:64-77
   Jennings **5**:108-09
   Kenny **22**:153-56
   Madden **3**:192-93
   Mano **6**:208, 209
   Nolan **16**:214
   Peters **8**:249-50
   Thayler **11**:362-63
Acts of Love: An American Novel **10**:9, 10, 13
Acts of Mercy **4**:213
Acuario **15**:10
Ada **10**:318
Adam and Eve and the Devil **9**:279, 282
Adam International Review **7**:127, 128
Adamic, Louis **1**:167, 168
Adams, Ansel **12**:339-40
Adams, Hazard **7**:299
Adams, Henry

Stegner **9**:270
Whittemore **8**:299, 310
Adams, Kay **1**:169-72
Adams, Léonie
   Belitt **4**:62, 65
   Federman **8**:76
   Root **11**:321
Adams, Phoebe Lou **3**:415
Adams, Stephen D. **1**:303
Adcock, Fleur **23**:1-17
Adelphi Community, Langham, England
   Ashby **6**:36-37
   Woodcock **6**:320
Aden-Arabie **8**:179
Adirondacks, New York **22**:121-22
Adler, Jacob **2**:125
Adoption
   Highwater **7**:69
   McPherson **23**:215-16, 232-33
Adorno, Theodor **26**:25
Adrian as Song **26**:128
Adrift **24**:169, 171, 176, 178
Adventure on Wheels: The Autobiography of a Road Racing Champion **16**:213, 214
Adventures in the Skin Trade **5**:272-73
Adventures of Robina by Herself, The **9**:294
Adventures of the Letter I **4**:295-96
Adversary in the House **3**:370
Advertisements **13**:288, 289
Aeneid **10**:315-16
Aeschylus **6**:89, 98, 100
"Aesthetics of Survival Course No. 49—Advanced Rose" **26**:155-56
Affinities of Orpheus, The **8**:118
Afghanistan **23**:311
Africa
   Awoonor **13**:29-54
   Bourjaily **1**:76
   Caute **4**:109
   Crews **14**:114, 115, 117-18
   Hahn **11**:112, 116, 118-19
   Killens **2**:298-303
   Lessing **14**:187-203
   Salaam **21**:247
   Simmons **21**:287-89
   Turner **10**:311-13
African Americans
   Aubert **20**:22-32
   Emanuel **18**:109-65
   Forbes **16**:105-19
   Joans **25**:219-57

Madgett **23**:193-213
  Owens **24**:285-86
  See also Blacks
African Horse **18**:298-99
African Methodist Episcopal Church
    13:238, 248
African Methodist Episcopal Zion
    Church **3**:418
Afrikaners **8**:48-49, 50, 51, 54, 58
Afro-American **6**:264
Afro Asian Arts Dialogue **21**:233
Afrodisia **25**:252
After Every Green Thing **1**:21, 24, 25
After Such Ignorance **9**:218
*After the First Death, There Is No
    Other* **12**:247
After the Lost Generation **1**:70
After the Lost War: A Narrative
    21:115
Afterlife, The **23**:192
Afternoons in Mid-America **1**:155
"Again dawn" **23**:30, 31, 53
Against the Circle **10**:136
Against the Season **18**:316
Age of Defeat, The **5**:324
*Age of Fiction: The French Novel from
    Gide to Camus, An* **15**:136
Age of Magnificence, The **4**:231
Agee, James
  Madden **3**:198
  Malzberg **4**:215
  Markfield **3**:222, 224
  Slavitt **3**:318
Agency for International Development
    (U.S.) **3**:244, 245
Agent of Chaos **19**:321
Agent of the Unknown **8**:273
Agony and the Ecstasy, The **3**:372
Agony of Christianity, The **11**:213
Agosin, Marjorie **25**:101
Agrarian movement **11**:176
Aguilera-Malta, Demetrio **9**:204
Agusta, Leon **9**:147
Agyu, the Ilianon Epic of Mindanao
    9:164
Ahern, Maureen Maurer **6**:138-39
Ahidiana **21**:205, 208-13, 219, 221-
    22
Ahmadu Bello University, Zaria,
    Nigeria **21**:287, 288
Ai 13:1-12
AID See Agency for International
    Development (U.S.)
AIDS See Acquired immune
    deficiency syndrome
Aiken, Conrad **3**:88, 90, 92
Air Freight **7**:125
Air National Guard, California
    23:189-90
Air Training Corps See Great Britain,
    Royal Air Force, Air Training
    Corps
Airmail Postcards **13**:68
Airs and Tributes **14**:57, 60
Airs of Wales, The **22**:244
Akalaitis, JoAnn **14**:176

Akgulian, Avak **2**:271
Akhmatova, Anna **11**:377
Akpalu, Vinoko **13**:44-45
A.L. Rowse's Cornwall **8**:255
Alashka **16**:282
Alaska
  Matthews **15**:260-61
  McCord **9**:186
Albany, N.Y. **13**:333
Albany State College **13**:248
Albee, Edward
  Kennedy **20**:220-21, 222, 224,
    226
  Purdy **1**:302, 304
  Saroyan **5**:217-18
Albert Camus: A Biography **12**:207-08
Albrecht, William **5**:348
Albright, Larry **11**:284
Albright, Thomas **25**:395, 397-98
Albuquerque Journal **3**:128
Albuquerque, N.M.
  Anaya **4**:19
  Creeley **10**:68-69
"Alcestis" **15**:233
Alchemist to Mercury, The **19**:204
Alcheringa **13**:47
Alcoholics Anonymous
  Kerrigan **11**:218
  Ray **7**:147
Alcoholism
  Armantrout **25**:6
  Bradley **10**:21
  Clark **22**:3
  Kerrigan **11**:214-18
  Knebel **3**:174-175
  Peacock **21**:145-64
Alderson, Dan **12**:220, 221
Alderton, John **9**:253, 254
Aldington, Richard
  Dudek **14**:126
  Eaton **20**:135
Aldiss, Brian W. 2:15-32
  Pohl **1**:295, 296
  Wolfe **9**:308
Aldridge, John W.
  Bourjaily **1**:70, 71
  Garrett **5**:77
Alegría, Ciro **12**:100
Alegría, Claribel 15:1-15
Aleixandre, Vicente **15**:69, 93
Alexander, Herbert
  Bourjaily **1**:70
  Killens **2**:303
Alexander, Robert **26**:189-90
Alexander Technique **1**:314
Alexander the Great **1**:195
Alexandra Freed **24**:363
Alfred the Great **4**:153
Alfred University **14**:39-41
Alfred, William **23**:307
Algeria **15**:134-35
Algerian War **4**:227-29, 230
Algren, Nelson
  Bourjaily **1**:76
  Malzberg **4**:209
  Ray **7**:142

Alice at Eighty **3**:322-23, 324
Alice Fay Di Castagnola Award
    8:249
Alice Fell **9**:293
Alice in Wonderland **3**:322
Alien Upstairs, The **18**:337
All Acts Are Simply Acts **26**:128
All For One Records **21**:234
All Her Children **7**:199
All My Pretty Ones **20**:67
All My Sins Remembered **25**:199
All-Night Visitors **6**:184, 185, 186
*All of Ted Joans and No More: Poems
    and Collages* **25**:234
All Souls and Appeasement **8**:257
All That Glitters **18**:22
All the Brave Promises **1**:318, 322
All the Little Heroes **3**:221
All the Little Live Things **9**:269
"All Things Considered" (radio
    program) **3**:82
All This Every Day **16**:201
Alleluia Affair, The **11**:55-56
Allen, Betty **1**:304
Allen, Dick 11:1-23
  Allman **15**:23
  Feirstein **11**:84
  Shelnutt **14**:297, 298
Allen, Donald A.
  Eigner **23**:48
  Koller **5**:163, 164
  Kyger **16**:190, 196
  Rechy **4**:260
Allen, Richard Sanders **11**:2, 3
Allen, Ross **26**:154
Allen, Walter 6:15-28
  Simmons **21**:291, 294
Allen, W.H. (publishers) **2**:385
Allender, Nina **1**:100, 104-05, 120
"Alley Oop" **2**:37
Alley Theatre, Houston, Tex. **5**:79
Alligator Bride, The **7**:65
Alligator Report, The **7**:107
Allin, John **7**:243
Allingham, Margery
  Gilbert **15**:188
  Keating **8**:169
Allison, Drummond **21**:64-65
Allman, John 15:17-32
Allston, Washington **6**:210
Almanac for Twilight, An **15**:261
Almighty Has His Own Purposes, The
    7:95
Almighty Me **14**:29-31
Almighty, The **1**:399
Along the Arno **9**:22, 23-24, 25
Alpaugh, Lloyd
  Kennedy **9**:78, 79
  Wilson **5**:349
Alpert, Richard **13**:293
*Alphabet: the iconography of the
    imagination* **15**:307
Alsace-Lorraine **11**:123, 127
*Alternate Worlds: The Illustrated History
    of Science Fiction* **2**:257
Altmann, Stuart **16**:301

Altoon, John **10**:69
Altshuler, Harry **2**:252, 254, 255
Alumni Magazine (University of Kansas) **2**:252
Alvarez, A.
  Rosenthal **6**:283
  West **7**:276
Am I Running with You, God? **11**:56
Amaldi, Edoardo **25**:351
Amalgamated Press **5**:177, 178
Amateur radio **14**:36-37
Amazing **18**:52
Amazing Stories
  Anderson **2**:37
  Knight **10**:202, 205
  Silverberg **3**:271
  Williamson **8**:316-17
Ambidextrous: The Secret Lives of Children **13**:219-20, 233
America **9**:38
America Hurrah **2**:407, 414-16, 417
American: A Middle Western Legend, The **18**:183
American Academy and Institute of Arts and Letters
  Meredith **14**:230
  Taylor **7**:187
  West **7**:285
American Academy, Rome, Italy
  Kazin **7**:95
  Simpson **4**:294
  Stegner **9**:267
  Williams **3**:414
American Association for the Advancement of Science **1**:285
American Atheists **7**:100
American Book Awards
  Grumbach **2**:214
  McElroy **21**:125, 141
American Book Review **8**:293
American Broadcasting Corp. **2**:254, 255
American Child Supreme, An **2**:332
American Citizen **1**:118
American Committee on Africa **3**:424
American Dreams, American Nightmares **3**:194
American Folkways Series, The **1**:150
American Friends Service Committee **3**:137
American Gothic **22**:76
American Heritage (publishers) **1**:313, 317
American High School, Paris **2**:218, 222
American Jazz Music **10**:91-92
American Jewish Committee **3**:218, 220
"American Literary Establishment, The" **2**:399-400
American Medical Association **21**:34-35
American Mercury
  Brossard **2**:67
  Stone **3**:370

American Mischief **20**:249-50, 251
American Museum of Natural History, New York City **3**:271
American Negro Theatre **6**:267-68
American Novel and Its Tradition, The **6**:210, 211
American 1960s: Imaginative Acts in a Decade of Change, The **9**:116-17
American Philosophical Society **9**:215
American Playwrights: A Critical Survey **2**:365
American poetry **2**:59
American Poetry Review
  Ai **13**:10
  Bell **14**:49
  di Suvero **26**:83
  Smith **7**:165
American Repertory Theater **2**:418
American Review See *New American Review*
American Rocket Society **1**:285
American Romance, An **10**:10
American Short Fiction **18**:201
American Society of Aesthetics **15**:361-62
American Society of Civil Engineers **25**:360, 373
American Still Lifes **22**:245
American Students Union **2**:207
American Train Letters **25**:48
American University
  Bausch **14**:30
  Grumbach **2**:210-11, 212, 213
  Taylor **7**:185
American Victorians: Explorations in Emotional History **9**:219
American Way of Death, The **17**:145-48
American Writers against the Vietnam War **7**:143
American Youth for Democracy **3**:209
Amherst College
  Guerard **2**:223
  Kazin **7**:95
  Kirkup **4**:189-90
  Lelchuk **20**:254
  Root **11**:325
  Symons **3**:393
Amichai, Yehuda **2**:387
Amis, Kingsley
  Aldiss **2**:23, 27
  Jennings **5**:109, 110
  West **7**:276
Amistad 1 **3**:431
Amistad 2 **3**:431
Amnesia **4**:149, 157, 158
Amnesia **13**:280, 281, 290-91
Amnesty International **7**:134
Among the Beasts **8**:78
Among the Cinders
  Becker **1**:44
  Shadbolt **3**:251
Amor de Cosmos: Journalist and Reformer **6**:323-24
Amour D'Arthropode **26**:90-91

Amsterdam, Netherlands
  Corn **25**:140-41
  Dworkin **21**:10-11
  Hiemstra **26**:154
  Williams **3**:127, 130
Amsterdam News **6**:264
Amulet (Carl Rakosi) **5**:199
Amulet, The (Isaac Rosenberg) **5**:263
Amussen, Bob **10**:9
Amy Lowell Poetry Travelling Scholarship **20**:329
"Anabasis Longs for Home" **26**:258
anabasis (publisher) **26**:249-61
Anaeus Africanus **5**:84
Anagogic and Paideumic Review **6**:180
Analog **18**:53-57
  See also *Astounding Science-Fiction*
Analysis of Poetic Thinking **9**:45
Anand, Mulk Raj **6**:319
Anarchism
  Beltrametti **13**:56
  Jerome **8**:132
  Kostelanetz **8**:191
  Woodcock **6**:319, 320, 322, 323
Anarchism: A History of Libertarian Ideas and Movements **6**:322
Anarchist Prince: A Biographical Study of Peter Kropotkin, The **6**:321
Anatomy of Proserpine, The **14**:112
Anavrita Academy **15**:74, 81
Anaya, Rudolfo A. **4**:15-28
  di Suvero **26**:81
"Ancestors, The" **22**:179-80
And Keep Your Powder Dry **8**:181
And Then We Heard the Thunder **2**:286, 295, 297, 304-05
And Then We Moved to Rossenarra **1**:197
Anderson, Chester G.
  Browne **20**:61, 62, 66-67, 69
  Vizenor **22**:272
Anderson, Donald **1**:164, 165
Anderson, Lindsay **7**:240
Anderson, Margaret **1**:99
Anderson, Poul **2**:33-46
Anderson, Sherwood **6**:47-48
Anderson, Wendell B. **14**:109, 111, 112, 113
Andersson, Claes **10**:71
Andover Academy
  Slavitt **3**:313-14, 317
  Whittemore **8**:298, 300
André Gide **2**:221, 223, 226
Andre, Michael **13**:13-27
Andreas, Osborn **1**:300, 301, 302
Andrew and Tobias **3**:356-57
Andrew Lytle Fiction Prize **20**:173
Andrews, Clarence **7**:103
Andrews, Jim **1**:253
Andrews, Shelly
  bissett **19**:40-41, 44-55, 58-60
  Eigner **23**:19, 49-57
Andreyev, Leonid
  Solotaroff **2**:392
  Wallace **1**:391
Angel Dust **25**:108, 113

Angel Hair **17**:276, 279
Angelou, Maya
  Lowitz **26**:167
  McElroy **21**:140
Angels and Earthly Creatures **8**:227
Angier, Bradford **2**:126
Angle of Repose
  Coppel **9**:4
  Stegner **9**:269
Angled Road, The **23**:170
Angleton, James **8**:306
Anglicans **23**:239-42
Anglo-Welsh movement **4**:306, 310
Angry Black, The **3**:427
Angry Ones, The **3**:424
Angry Young Men (literary
    movement)
  Sinclair **5**:270
  Wilson **5**:321, 323
Angulo, Ximena de **3**:140, 142
Anillo de Silencio **15**:2, 6
Animal
  Argüelles **24**:28
  Cherkovski **24**:97, 100-02
Animal Farm **9**:21
Animal rights **15**:239
animal uproar **19**:23, 42-43
Animism **3**:406
Anishinaabe **22**:257-59, 261, 263,
    275
Anita, Anita **26**:61
Anlo-Ewe dirge **13**:44
Ann Arbor, Mich.
  Clark **22**:20
  Piercy **1**:273
Annette **1**:155
Annie Wobbler **7**:243, 244-45, 260,
    261-62
Annisfield-Wolf Award **23**:264
*Anon and Various Time Machine
    Poems* **11**:15
Anorexia **25**:18, 19
Another Country **3**:425
Another Time **6**:39
another time in fragments **23**:31, 34,
    35, 40, 42, 43, 47, 53
Anouilh, Jean
  Brossard **2**:69
  Van Itallie **2**:411
Anpao **7**:78, 81, 82
Anrig, George **1**:192
Ansen, Alan
  Hadas **23**:117-18
  Joans **25**:246
Ant, Howard **1**:364
Antaeus **1**:93
Antarctica **20**:9-10
Anthologist (Rutgers University) **4**:244
Anthology of Concrete Poetry **8**:89
Anthony, Michael 18:1-24
Anthony, Peter **1**:19
Anthony, Piers **12**:217
Anthropology
  Manuel **9**:156-57, 163-65
  Tarn **16**:274-75, 278, 282-83
Anthropos-Specter-Beast, The **9**:125

Anti-Defamation League of B'nai
    B'rith **3**:217, 227
Anti-Semitism
  Epstein **12**:64
  Geduld **21**:52-53
  Glanville **9**:18
  Hamburger **4**:170
  Hentoff **6**:165-66, 167
  Kazin **7**:87
  Kumin **8**:208, 213
  Lifshin **10**:237
  Lind **4**:196-97, 198, 199-200
  Nichols **2**:310
  Piercy **1**:268
  Rimmer **10**:296
  Roditi **14**:253-54
  Rosenthal **6**:273
  Salvadori **25**:359
  Schevill **12**:275, 277-78
  Silkin **5**:243, 248-49, 251, 254,
      256, 260, 261
  Solotaroff **2**:391
  Wallace **1**:391
  weiss **24**:325-27
  Williams **26**:318
  Yglesias **20**:350
  See also Jews
Antigone **16**:128-29
Antinarcissus **26**:241
Antioch College
  Block **11**:27-29, 30-31, 38
  Hamburger **4**:171
  Jerome **8**:132-34, 136, 138
Antitheses **8**:190-91
Antivivisectionism **4**:90
Antiwar movement
  Allen **11**:21
  Browne **20**:66
  Cherkovski **24**:94
  Dennison **6**:117
  Eshleman **6**:140-41
  Heyen **9**:42
  Highwater **7**:79
  Livesay **8**:232-34
  Nichols **2**:332
  Olson **11**:256
  Settle **1**:319
  Sukenick **8**:290
  Turner **10**:318
Anton, Robert **2**:417, 422
Antoninus, Brother See Everson,
    William
Ants **16**:291-308
Ants, The **16**:305, 306
Anything Can Happen **8**:293
Anything on Its Side **23**:21, 26, 29,
    35, 47
Anzilotti, Rolando **6**:283
Aoyama, Miyuki **26**:179, 180
Apartheid
  Awoonor **13**:47
  Brutus **14**:54-6
  Cassity **8**:51, 52, 53-54
  Wright **5**:370
Apes and Angels **18**:26, 41
Apes of God, The **3**:385

Apollinaire, Guillaume **9**:82
Apostolidis, Penny **16**:245-70
Appalachian region **15**:273-9
*Appeasement: A Study in Political
    Decline, 1933–1939* **8**:257
Apple Butter **15**:306, 307
Appleman, Philip 18:25-46
Appleton-Century (publishers) **1**:196
Applewhite, Cynthia **7**:107
Appropriate Behavior **26**:228
April Morning **18**:185
Arab-Israeli conflict
  Hassan **12**:156
  Megged **13**:148, 151-52
  Wiesel **4**:359
Arab Women Solidarity Association
    11:70-71
Arafat, Yasser **11**:71
Ararat **2**:273, 274
Aravantinov, Manto **26**:277
Arbor House Publishing Co. **3**:285
"Archaeology, Elegy, Architecture: A
    Poet's Program for Lyric"
    16:286
Archer, David **5**:368, 370
Architectural Forum **2**:208
Architecture **13**:58, 59, 61
Arctic Desert, The **9**:184
Arden, John 4:29-47
Ardmore, Okla. **25**:283-85
"Are We Too Old To Make
    Love?" **22**:190-92
Are You Running with Me, Jesus?
    11:48, 49-50, 51, 55, 57, 59
areas lights heights **23**:36, 37, 39, 48
Arendt, Hannah
  Epstein **12**:71-72
  Weiss **2**:438, 450
Argosy
  Brown **6**:47
  Knight **10**:209
Arguedas, José María **12**:101
Argüelles, Ivan 24:1-30
  Berry **24**:77-79
  Cherkovski **24**:100
  Foley **24**:172, 178
Argyros, Alex **10**:321
Ariadne's Thread **10**:257
Ariel **11**:35-36
Arizona State University
  Dove **19**:107-08
  Harris **3**:129-30, 131
Ark, The **26**:72
Arkansas **22**:307-311
Arkansas State College **20**:323
Arkansas State Teachers College
  Brown **6**:51
  Williams **20**:323
Armadillo in the Grass **11**:165-66,
    167
Armantrout, Rae 25:1-23
Armed Descent **19**:200
Armenian Americans **2**:273-74
Armstrong, John **10**:314
Armstrong Junior College **10**:169-70
Armstrong, Lil Hardin **6**:181

Arnold, Bob **25**:25-49
  Koller **5**:169
Arnold, Danny **9**:244
Arnold, Steven **24**:345
Arnold, Susan **25**:38-48
Arnow, Harriette Simpson **15**:283, 287, 289
Aron, Edith **2**:138
Around about America **1**:153
Arrivistes, The **4**:293
Arrondissements **15**:228
Arrow in the Blue **7**:196
Arrowsmith, William
  Raffel **9**:217
  Taylor **7**:187
Art
  Atkins **16**:4-5, 10
  Bell **14**:39-40
  Eaton **20**:138-40
  Hine **15**:228
  Joans **25**:230
  Ouellette **13**:179
  Van Proyen **25**:386-89, 392-400, 402-03
  weiss **24**:334-35, 341, 346-49
Art criticism
  Andre **13**:15, 21
  Kerrigan **11**:208-09
  Van Proyen **25**:396-400, 402
Art in America **2**:197
Art of Being Ruled, The **3**:385
"Art of Biography, The" (lecture) **3**:393
Art of the Wild (writers conference), Sierra, Nevada **23**:232
"Art Poétique" **6**:281
Art, Pre-Columbian **3**:371
Art Students' League, New York City
  Disch **4**:155-56
  Gray **2**:190
Artaud, Antonin
  Ferrini **24**:129
  O'Faolain **2**:347
  Van Itallie **2**:412
Articulate Energy
  Davie **3**:37, 38, 40
  Pinsky **4**:247
Artists' colonies **23**:118-19
Artists-in-the-Schools program **13**:314
ARTnews **13**:14
Artorius, Book I **21**:62, 71
Arts **6**:113
Arts Council of Ireland **3**:64-65
Arts Council Prize **5**:110
Arts Theatre Club **23**:69
Artweek **25**:396-400, 402
Arvon Foundation
  Booth **2**:58
  Wright **5**:369
As a Man Grows Older **3**:218
As a River of Light **20**:72
As for Love: Poems and Translations **6**:280
As I Live and Breathe: Stages of an Autobiography **11**:50, 51
As We Lie **18**:299

As Wolves Love Lambs **2**:223-24
As You Like It **6**:290
Asahel **13**:154-55, 158
Asbury, Herbert **11**:108, 111
Ascensions **3**:96, 98
Ascent into Hell **7**:41
Ashbery, John
  Argüelles **24**:13
  Baumbach **5**:27
  Hall **7**:63
  Harwood **19**:142, 143
  Mathews **6**:235-36, 237, 245
  Murphy **26**:222
  Rodgers **13**:250
Ashby, Cliff **6**:29-44
  Sisson **3**:302
Ashes of Izalco **15**:3
Ashman, Richard **3**:335
Asia Foundation **9**:212
Asian Americans **22**:79-88
Asian Minor, An **13**:233
"Asian Shore, The" **4**:152
Asiatic Romance, An **3**:301
Asimov, Isaac
  Bova **18**:52
  Zebrowski **19**:370, 373, 381
Ask for Love and You Get Rice Pudding **2**:126
Asking Myself / Answering Myself **2**:144
Asner, Ed **20**:336, 337, 342
Aspects of Alice **13**:205
Aspen, Colorado **11**:166
Aspen School of Art **11**:253
Aspen Writers' Workshop
  Murphy **26**:221
  Olson **11**:253, 255, 257
Assault with Intent **1**:242
Assembling **8**:191-93, 194
Assistant, The **8**:285
Associated Black Publishers of Detroit, Inc. **23**:209
Associated Negro Press **3**:421, 424
Associated Press
  Higgins **5**:98-99
  Wallace **1**:376
Associated Writing Programs **1**:173, 174
Association of Literary Magazines of America **8**:307, 308
Astounding Science-Fiction
  Anderson **2**:37, 39, 40, 41
  Brunner **8**:5
  Budrys **14**:66
  Gunn **2**:244, 247
  Kennedy **9**:78
  Knight **10**:202, 203, 204
  Malzberg **4**:207
  Silverberg **3**:271
  See also *Analog*
Astounding Stories See *Astounding Science-Fiction*
Astronauts, The **1**:259
At Fever Pitch **4**:103-04, 105
At Freddie's **10**:108-09
At the City Limits of Fate **26**:6
At the End of the Open Road **4**:294

At the Front Door of the Atlantic **11**:205
"At the Lake" **3**:24
At the Western Gates **16**:286
Atheism
  Caute **4**:96
  Kinsella **7**:100, 109
  Rabassa **9**:192
  Wilhelm **5**:303
Athens, Greece
  Corman **2**:138
  Samarakis **16**:245-5, 257-66
Athill, Diana
  Caute **4**:103
  Mott **7**:127
Atitlán / Alashka **16**:282
Atkins, Russell **16**:1-19
Atlanta Constitution **1**:142
Atlanta, Ga.
  Cassity **8**:56, 60
  Mott **7**:130-31, 132
Atlanta Journal **1**:146, 147
Atlantic Awards in Literature **5**:359
Atlantic City, N.J.
  Boyle **1**:108-11
  Kumin **8**:203-04
Atlantic Flyway **13**:98
Atlantic Monthly
  Cassill **1**:167
  Davison **4**:135, 137, 138, 139, 141
  Higgins **5**:97
  Still **17**:235
  Thomas **19**:346, 356
  Wakefield **7**:197-98
  Williams **3**:415
Atlantic Monthly Press **4**:135-36, 137, 139, 141
Atlantis **14**:139-40
Atomic Age **13**:324-25, 327
Atomic bomb **25**:364-65
Attic of Ideals, An **13**:308, 313
Atticus Review **25**:335-36
Atwood, Margaret **15**:158
Aubert, Alvin **20**:17-34
Auburn University **11**:180-81
Auden, W.H.
  Allen **6**:18, 21
  Ashby **6**:36, 39
  Bowles **1**:86
  Broughton **12**:45
  Burroway **6**:90
  Fuller **10**:120, 123
  Hazo **11**:148, 150
  Hine **15**:230-32
  Howes **3**:143
  Jennings **5**:110
  Jones **5**:121
  Kizer **5**:146
  Major **6**:185-86
  Malanga **17**:97, 100
  Meredith **14**:224-25, 229-30
  Norse **18**:278-82, 284
  Roditi **14**:279
  Rosenthal **6**:282
  Shapiro **6**:307-08

Simpson **4:**291
Sinclair **5:**272
Symons **3:**383, 385
Valaoritis **26:**282-83
Wain **4:**327
Audience Called Edouard, An **18:**302
Audiotape **8:**187
Auer, Jane **1:**84, 85-94
Auerbach, Walter **6:**235, 236
Augusta Chronicle **1:**142
Augustana College **9:**264
Augustine, St. **7:**7
Ault, Nelson **9:**182
Aurora: New Canadian Writing 1978
    7:103, 104
Austin Community College **2:**127
Austin, J.C. **7:**26
Australia **13:**118-20
Australian National University **3:**242
Austria
    Garrett **5:**72, 81, 86, 89
    Van Brunt **15:**377
Austro-Hungarian Empire **7:**208,
    209
Author and Journalist **8:**272
Authors Guild **1:**295
Authors League of America
    Corcoran **2:**117
    Wallace **1:**402
Autism
    McPherson **23:**224-25
    Taylor **26:**250-51, 260
Autobiographical Stanzas **5:**249, 257
Autobiographies (Richard Kostelanetz)
    8:179, 183, 184
Autobiography
    Clark **22:**24-25
    Vizenor **22:**273
Autobiography: A Novel **4:**265
Autobiography of Bertrand Russell
    5:42
Autobiography of My Mother, The
    10:42-43
Autobiography (William Butler Yeats)
    3:142-43
Automobile racing
    Nolan **16:**207, 213-14
    Thayler **11:**359-60, 363
Auxiliary Territorial Service, Great
    Britain **8:**23-24
Avakumovic, Ivan **6:**323
Avant-garde
    Beltrametti **13:**65
    Kostelanetz **8:**184-85
Avco Everett Research Laboratory
    18:51-52
Avedon, Richard **5:**212
Avery, Milton **5:**221-22
Aviation
    Cartland **8:**23
    Ciardi **2:**90
    Clement **16:**89-91, 92-94
    Connell **2:**102-06
    Gunn **2:**243-44
    Kerrigan **11:**207-08
    Murchie **19:**292-93, 299

Roditi **14:**239-40
    Voinovich **12:**312
Avignon, France **25:**135-36
*Awaken, Bells Falling: Poems
    1959–1967* **22:**239
Awoonor, Kofi Nyidevu 13:29-54
    Major **6:**196
Axe-Time, Sword-Time **2:**118
Axelrod, George **1:**196
Axes **3:**95
Axmann-Rezzori, Hanna **10:**160
Aydy, Catherine (pseudonym of
    Emma Tennant) **9:**291
Azubah Nye **24:**238-41

Babbitt, Irving **7:**220
Babble **5:**26-27
Babel, Isaac
    Blaise **3:**19
    Silkin **5:**260
Babenko, Vitaly **19:**337
Babes-Bolyai University **5:**353
Babi-Yar (monument) **4:**360
Baby, Come On Inside **3:**408
Baby-Sitters, The **4:**108
Baca, Judy **18:**320, 324
Bacall, Lauren **5:**56-57
Bach, Johann Sebastian **3:**95
Bach, Julian
    Jones **20:**217
    Lottman **12:**207
Bachelor, Joseph M. **3:**169
Back Door **7:**163
Back River **5:**169
Back Road Caller **25:**43
Backtrack **17:**71
"Backward Glance at Galway, A"
    23:318
Bacon, Francis **23:**169, 174-76, 178
Bad for Each Other **1:**383
Bad Sister, The **9:**291, 292
Bad Streak, A **9:**27
Baedeker guidebooks **2:**383
Baez, Joan **11:**288
Bag Talk **25:**72
Bailey, Charles W., II **3:**174, 179,
    180, 181
Bailey, Margery **12:**45
Bailyn, Bernard **23:**141-42, 149-50
Baird, Newton **3:**335
Baker, Elizabeth **5:**165
Baker, Josephine **7:**28
Balakian, Nona **2:**363
Balboni, Loredana **6:**240, 242
Baldwin, James
    Clarke **16:**84
    Corman **2:**139
    Hinojosa-Smith **16:**145
    Huddle **20:**192
    Killens **2:**306
    Lowitz **26:**167
    Major **6:**195
    Norse **18:**282
    Petry **6:**256, 266
    Salaam **21:**187, 188, 189
    Williams **3:**425

Balfour, Arthur **4:**196
Ball, David
    Hollo **19:**158
    Raworth **11:**300, 301, 302
Ballad of Harriet Tubman, The
    21:177
Ballad of Martin Luther King, The
    21:177
"Ballade of Good Counsel" **3:**144
*Ballades and Rondeaus, Chants Royal,
    Sestinas, Villanelles, Etc.* **3:**144
Ballantine, Betty **3:**278
Ballantine, David **10:**10
Ballantine, Ian **1:**291-92, 294
Ballantine (publishers)
    Pohl **1:**292
    Silverberg **3:**281
Ballard, J.G.
    Aldiss **2:**25, 28
    Disch **4:**151
    Moorcock **5:**187
    Tennant **9:**291
Ballet Rambert **5:**366
Ballou, George **15:**57, 59-60, 67
Ballou, Jenny **15:**59
Baloian, James **2:**272
Baltimore Catechism **4:**145
Baltimore, Md. **1:**280
Balzac, Honoré de **2:**385
Bambara, Toni Cade **21:**239-41
Bamberger, Bill **14:**179
Bamboo Bed, The **1:**212
Banciulescu, Victor **9:**26
Band Has Won, The **1:**344
Bankrupts, The **9:**25-26
Banks, Russell 15:33-45
    Baumbach **5:**29
Bantam Books
    Cassill **1:**173
    Knebel **3:**180
    Pohl **1:**295
    Rimmer **10:**299
Baptist Church
    Bennett **13:**73-74, 76-78, 82, 87
    Dillard **7:**7
Baraka, Amiri
    Clarke **16:**85, 86
    Crews **14:**117
    Forbes **16:**112
    Joans **25:**250-51
    Johnson **18:**235-36
    Kennedy **20:**223-24, 225, 226
    Killens **2:**298
    Major **6:**180, 188, 193
    Salaam **21:**187, 189-90, 228
Baraka, Imamu *See* Baraka, Amiri
Barbados
    Anthony **18:**20
    Clarke **16:**71-76
Barbary Shore **1:**72
Barber, Charles **23:**119
Barbusse, Henri **5:**320
Barcelona, Spain
    Charyn **1:**181
    Connell **2:**108-09
Bard College

Kelly　**19**:199-202, 204
　Menashe　**11**:228-29
　Settle　**1**:317, 318, 319, 321
　Weiss　**2**:436-39, 441-47, 449
Barker, Arthur (publishers)　**1**:389
Barker, Danny　**21**:203
Barker, George
　Ashby　**6**:42-43
　Heath-Stubbs　**21**:67-68
　Wright　**5**:359, 367, 368, 369,
　　370, 371
Barker, Kit　**5**:368, 369
Barker, Margaret　**1**:304
Barker, Richard　**10**:2, 5
Barlow, Gillian　**8**:157
Barlow, Wilfred　**1**:314
Barn, The (artists' colony)　**15**:381
Barna, Joel Warren　**18**:202-03
Barnard, Allen　**1**:295
Barnard College
　Brown　**10**:38
　Burroway　**6**:87, 89-90
　Gray　**2**:192, 194
　Swenson　**13**:311-12
Barnardo, Tom　**23**:67-68
Barnes, Clive
　Gray　**3**:114
　Slade　**9**:248, 250
Barnes, Djuna　**15**:243
Barnes, Joe　**1**:38
Barnes, Peter　12:1-16
Barnes, Steven　**12**:212-13, 221
Barnet, Sylvan　**9**:85
Barney, Dave　**7**:179-80
Barney Oldfield: The Life and Times of
　America's Legendary Speed King
　16:214
Barnstone, Aliki　**15**:94, 103, 105,
　107
Barnstone, Helle　**15**:59-103
Barnstone, Tony　**15**:65, 92, 94, 103,
　105, 107
Barnstone, Willis　15:47-108
Barnum, Phineas T.　**1**:387-88
Baro, Gene　**5**:264
Baron, Richard　**1**:74, 75
Barr, Richard　**2**:414
Barr, Roger　**2**:108-09
Barr, Stringfellow　**12**:23-24, 26, 27,
　28, 39
Barracini, Angela (pseudonym of
　Barbara Corcoran)　**2**:117
Barrell, John　**11**:308
Barrett, Waller　**1**:157
Barrio, Raymond　15:109-26
Barry, Geoffrey　**5**:113
Barth, John
　Klinkowitz　**9**:111, 113, 120
　Sukenick　**8**:290
Barthelme, Donald
　Klinkowitz　**9**:108, 112, 115, 117
　Sukenick　**8**:291
Barthes, Roland　**9**:114, 116, 118,
　119
Bartlett: The Great Canadian
　Explorer　**15**:251, 252

Barzini, Luigi　**4**:232
Barzun, Jacques
　Dillon　**3**:59
　West　**7**:277
Basak, Subimal　**14**:90, 91, 92, 93,
　98
Baseball
　Bowering　**16**:24, 26
　Brown　**6**:48-49
　Bullins　**16**:64-65
　Holden　**22**:60
　Hood　**17**:78, 81-82
　Kinsella　**7**:98, 99, 103, 108, 110
　Klinkowitz　**9**:107, 118-20
Basho, Matsuo　**22**:275
Basketball　**9**:38
Basler National Zeitung　**11**:130-32
Bass Saxophone, The　**1**:348, 350
Bastard Angel　**18**:289
Bastin, Cliff　**9**:20
Bates, Alan　**3**:114
Bates College
　Ciardi　**2**:88
　Rimmer　**10**:285, 286-87
Bates, Harry　**8**:318
Bates Student　**10**:286
Bateson, F.W.　**7**:275-76
Bathory, Elizabeth　**8**:246, 248-50
Bator, Paul　**6**:234
Bats Fly Up for Inspector Ghote　**8**:173-
　74
Battered women　**21**:10-12
Battle of Britain　**21**:45-59
Baudelaire, Charles　**6**:289, 304
Bauer, Heinz　**20**:242
Baum, Cliff　**6**:234
Baumann, Fred　**24**:16
Baumbach, Jonathan　5:15-30
　Sukenick　**8**:293
Bausch, Richard　14:1-16
　Bausch, Robert　**14**:17-23, 25, 26,
　　27, 28, 29, 30-31
Bausch, Robert　14:17-31
　Bausch, Richard　**14**:1-5, 7, 12
Bax, Martin　**13**:287-88
Baxandall, Rosalyn　**3**:78
Baxter, James K.　**3**:259
Bay Area Funeral Society　**17**:145-46
Bay of Arrows　**16**:241, 242
Bayes, Ronald　**9**:146
Bayliss, Jonathan　**24**:148
Baylor University　**14**:108, 109, 110
Baynes, Cary F.　**3**:142
BBC See British Broadcasting Corp.
Beach, Sylvia
　Corman　**2**:139
　Lottman　**12**:206
Beard, The　**26**:73
"Beasts, The"　**5**:209
Beat & The Still, The　**23**:178-79
Beat Generation
　Argüelles　**24**:8
　Brossard　**2**:72
　Broughton　**12**:57
　di Suvero　**26**:71, 73, 75, 77
　Enslin　**3**:92-93

Hollo　**19**:168, 171-74
Joans　**25**:234-36, 242-44
Kherdian　**2**:268-69
Kyger　**16**:189-200
Litshin　**10**:255
Norse　**18**:282-91
Pinsky　**4**:244
Sanders　**21**:259-72
Saroyan　**5**:214, 218
Spinrad　**19**:312-14, 320-23
weiss　**24**:337-38, 340, 347-49, 351
Wright　**7**:293-94
Beat Hotel　**18**:287
Beatles, The
　Kerrigan　**11**:197-98
　Moorcock　**5**:176
　Raffel　**9**:216
　See also Lennon, John
Beattie, Ann　**16**:237
Beattie, Paul　**24**:345, 347
Beaumont, Charles　**16**:212, 213,
　214, 215
Beaumont, Roy　**25**:387
Beaumont, Vivian　**2**:418
Beautiful Contradictions, The　**16**:280
Beautiful Greed, The　**3**:188
Beauty and the Beast　**21**:66
Beauty Operators, The　**6**:96, 99
Beauvoir, Simone de
　Crews　**14**:116
　Piercy　**1**:272
Beaux Arts Trio　**26**:154
Beaux Arts Trio, The　**2**:162
"Because (A Garland for Bulgaria)"
　26:145-46
Bechet, Sidney　**6**:166
Beck, John　**26**:220
Beck, Julian
　Dennison　**6**:116
　Ferrini　**24**:129
Becker, Stephen　1:33-46
　Haldeman　**25**:205
　Shadbolt　**3**:264
　Wiesel　**4**:353
Beckett, Samuel
　Federman　**8**:77
　Lottman　**12**:199
　Sukenick　**8**:290
　Van Itallie　**2**:412
　West　**7**:284
Beclch　**2**:361, 363
Bed, The　**12**:53
Bedford Reader, The　**9**:85
Beef　**18**:303, 304
Beerbohm, Max　**1**:191, 198
Before the Dawn　**3**:271
Before Winter Comes　**5**:272, 273
"Beggar Maid, The"　**7**:240
Beggar of Jerusalem, The　**4**:359
Beginner's Luck　**11**:115
Beginning of Spring, The　**10**:109
Behold the Man　**5**:180
Being and Race: Black Writing since
　1970　**18**:241
Being Geniuses Together　**1**:98, 114,
　115

Being Red **18**:183
Belafonte, Harry **2**:289
Belgrade, Yugoslavia **4**:267-71, 273, 274
Belitt, Ben 4:49-68
Bell, Charles G. 12:17-40
Bell Jar, The **4**:134, 137
Bell, Marvin 14:33-51
  Katz **14**:179
  Major **6**:181
  Wright **7**:297
Bell, William **21**:65
Bellah, James Warner **6**:54
Bellarosa Connection, The **11**:190, 197
Belle Bête, La **4**:72-73
Belleau, André **13**:183, 184, 187
Bellevue Hospital **13**:23-24
Belloc, Hilaire
  Greeley **7**:51
  Morris **13**:166
Bellow, Saul
  Caulfield **25**:110
  Honig **8**:115
  Kazin **7**:93
  Kerrigan **11**:190, 194, 197, 210, 213-14, 219
  Lelchuk **20**:244-45
  Lem **1**:258
  Solotaroff **2**:398
  Weiss **2**:439, 441
Beloit Poetry Journal **17**:27
Beloved Enemy **2**:127
Beloved Latitudes **18**:302
Belshazzar's Feast **6**:210
Beltrametti, Franco 13:55-72
  Arnold **25**:41
  Raworth **11**:310
Bemelmans, Ludwig **12**:81
Ben Ali, Robert **17**:63-65, 72
Ben-Gurion, David **1**:28
Benét, James Walker **12**:47
Benét, Stephen Vincent **1**:164
Benét, William Rose **12**:47
Benjamin, David (pseudonym of David Slavitt) **3**:322
Benjamin Franklin Award **26**:180
Bennett, Arnold **6**:17, 22, 27
Bennett Cerf's Laugh Treasury **21**:106-07
Bennett, Hal 13:73-88
Bennett, John M. 25:51-77
  Grumman **25**:193
  Leftwich **25**:271, 273
  Murphy **26**:226
Bennett, Lerone **2**:298
Bennett, Paul **3**:22, 24
Bennington College
  Becker **1**:39
  Belitt **4**:53, 62-64, 65-66
  Browne **20**:64-65
  Busch **1**:133
  Delbanco **2**:159
  Dworkin **21**:14
  Elman **3**:74-75
  Furman **18**:196-97
  Howes **3**:136-37

Mathews **6**:223, 249
  Vivante **12**:301, 302
  Waldman **17**:272-74, 275, 277
Bennington Writing Workshops **2**:157, 159
Benny, Jack **1**:383
Benson, Graham **2**:386
Bentham, Jeremy **20**:12
Benton, Jessie See Fremont, Jessie Benton
Benveniste, Asa **11**:302, 303
Beowulf
  Raffel **9**:214
  Wright **5**:370, 373
Berdyayev, Nikolai **2**:191-92
Berea College **15**:280-81, 282, 283-84, 285
Berenson, Bernard
  Howes **3**:142
  Stone **3**:373-74
Beresford, Anne **4**:165, 166
Berg, Alban **3**:95
Berge, Carol 10:1-17
  Choudhury **14**:93
  McCord **9**:186, 187
Berger, Art **6**:186
Bergman, Ingmar **7**:13, 17
Bergonzi, Bernard **5**:262
Bergstrom, Louise **10**:174
Berhama Account, The **3**:432
Berkeley Bead Game, The **26**:299
Berkeley, Calif.
  Argüelles **24**:19
  Van Proyen **25**:389
  Vinograd **26**:298
Berkeley, George (Bishop of Cloyne)
  Davie **3**:38
  Wilson **5**:313
Berkeley Street Cannibals **26**:299, 301
Berkley (publishers) **10**:222
Berkson, Bill **17**:276
Berlandt, Herman **26**:79, 81
Berlin Cemetery films (Richard Kostelanetz) **8**:189-90
Berlin Festival **2**:364
Berlin, Germany
  Bowles **1**:83
  Easton **14**:152
Berlin, Irving **1**:395
Berlin Lost, A **8**:190
Berlitz School of Languages
  Andre **13**:14, 17
  Argüelles **24**:12
  Hassan **12**:154
Berman, Wallace **26**:189-90
Bernal, Olga **8**:79
Bernanos, Georges **4**:72
Bernardin, Joseph **7**:46, 48-49, 51
Bernardo, Gabriel A. **9**:159, 162, 168
Berneri, Marie Louise **6**:320, 321, 326
Bernhardt, Sarah **1**:401
"Bernie Rhodenbarr" series **11**:37-38
Bernstein, Charles 24:31-50

Bernstein, Leonard **2**:415
Berrigan, Daniel 1:47-62
  Andre **13**:15, 19, 20, 21, 24
Berrigan, Philip **2**:198
Berrigan, Ted
  Clark **22**:15, 16, 18, 19, 20-21
  Foster **26**:125
  Hollo **19**:173, 174
  Sanders **21**:264
  Saroyan **5**:215
  Waldman **17**:288-89
Berry, Jake 24:51-82
  Argüelles **24**:28
  Bennett **25**:74
  Ferrini **24**:139-40
  Foley **24**:170, 177, 179
  Leftwich **25**:261, 266
Berry, Michael, Lord Hartwell **5**:371
Berry, Wendell
  Creeley **10**:67
  Levis **23**:183
  Root **11**:324
Berryman, John
  Allen **11**:13
  Davison **4**:138
  Honig **8**:115, 116, 118, 121
  Kerrigan **11**:216
  Weiss **2**:446-47
Berson, Gene **22**:65
Bertocci, Peter **10**:287
Bertolucci, Attilio **10**:141
Bessie, Alvah **20**:111-12, 116-17
Bessie, Mike **1**:35, 38
Bessinger, Jess **9**:214
Best American Short Stories **17**:239
Best Father Ever Invented **3**:127
Best Hour of the Night, The **4**:296
Best of Barry N. Malzberg, The **4**:215
Best of Margaret St. Clair, The **8**:278, 281
Bester, Alfred **1**:290
Bestsellers **1**:395
Beta Sigma Phi Award **15**:247
Betjeman, John
  Roditi **14**:247
  Thomas **4**:309
Better Half: The Emancipation of the American Woman, The **5**:271
Between Ribble and Lune: Scenes from the North-West **18**:302
Between the Lines **7**:202
Between the Thunder and the Sun **9**:5
Beulah Quintet, The **1**:308, 316, 317, 319, 321, 322
Beuys, Joseph **26**:181
Bevan, Aneurin **5**:123-24
Bevin, Ernest **8**:258
"Bewitched" **9**:244
Bewitched, The **12**:11, 13
Beyer, H. Otley **9**:156-57, 159, 162, 163, 165, 168
Beyond **2**:258
Beyond Apollo **4**:213
"Beyond Mars" **8**:324
Beyond the Angry Black **3**:429
Beyond the Blue Mountains **6**:326

Beyond the Hundredth Meridian
   9:268, 269
Beyond the Outsider **5**:324
*Beyond the Road: Portraits and Visions
   of Newfoundlanders* **15**:251
Bhagavad Gita
   Sillitoe **2**:380
   Wilson **5**:317
Bhatia, Vishnu **9**:182
Bialik Prize **13**:157
Bible
   Becker **1**:43
   Brewster **15**:151
   Cassity **8**:29
   Eigner **23**:19-20, 39
   Glancy **24**:199-200, 205-06
   Jones **11**:172-73
   Katz **9**:51, 65-66
   Kizer **5**:145
   Menashe **11**:234
   Ostriker **24**:272-73, 275
   Shreve **5**:230
Bible, Jewish
   Josipovici **8**:147
   Silkin **5**:251
Bible, King James Version
   Anderson **2**:46
   Brown **6**:73
   Nichols **2**:317
   Sillitoe **2**:372, 379
Bible Story **5**:179
Bibliophily **15**:269-70
Bickel, Shlomo **2**:398-99
Bidart, Frank **4**:248-49, 250
Bidstrup, Darell **5**:170
Bienek, Horst **13**:134, 136
Big Diaphanous Wild Man, A **2**:332,
   335
Big Kill, The **7**:6
Big Rock Candy Mountain, The **9**:259,
   260, 265, 266
Big Shot, The **5**:56
Big Sur, Calif. **25**:14
Big Table **6**:181
Bigger Light, The **16**:80
Biggle, Lloyd, Jr. **10**:224-25
Bijou **3**:192, 195, 199
Billion Year Spree **2**:29
bills brain **19**:40, 60
BIM magazine (Barbados) **18**:15, 20
Binder, Judith Perlzweig **2**:138
Binghamton Asylum for the Chronic
   Insane **19**:351-53
Binghamton University **19**:368
Bini, Dante **25**:376
Biodiversity **16**:306
Biography
   Sinclair **5**:274-75
   Whittemore **8**:310-11
Biology and Values **1**:263
Biophilia **16**:306
Bird, Bill **1**:119
"Bird Lives" (painting) **25**:222
*Bird of Paper: Poems of Vicente
   Aleixandre, A* **15**:69
Birds of the West **26**:36-37

Birmingham, Ala. **17**:26
Birmingham, England
   Fisher **10**:81, 87, 88
   Thomas **19**:354-56
Birstein, Ann **7**:94-95
Birtwistle, Harrison **8**:147, 158
Bischoff, Herman **10**:215
Bisexuality **10**:23-24, 25
Bishop, Elizabeth
   Gregor **10**:148
   McPherson **23**:222
   Pinsky **4**:248-49
   Ruark **23**:269, 270
   Stevenson **9**:283-84
Bishop, Jim **1**:248
Bishop, John Peale **10**:133
Bishop, Michael **26:1-20**
Bishop Ryder's Church of England
   Infant and Junior School
   19:355
Bishop's Progress **6**:209, 210
bissett, bill **19:1-62**
"Bit of Blancmange'll Be Enough for
   Me, A" **26**:33
Biton, Lucien **16**:275
Bitter Fame **9**:287
Bitter Glass, The **3**:59, 61, 64
Bitterroot **9**:66, 67
Black aesthetic **21**:210-12, 234-51
Black Aesthetic, The **18**:144
Black Alice **4**:151
Black, Alta **7**:76-77
Black and White Keys **17**:83
Black Boy **6**:185
Black Collegian **21**:214-15
"Black Flag of Anarchism, The"
   8:191
Black Grate Poems **9**:287
Black, Hugo **1**:181, 182
Black Humor by Charles R. Johnson
   18:236
Black Like Me **7**:132
*Black Man Abroad: The Toulouse
   Poems* **18**:147, 160
Black Man's Burden **2**:295, 305
Black Marina **9**:293-94
*Black Marsden: A Tabula Rasa
   Comedy* **16**:135
Black Mountain College
   Bell **12**:31
   Creeley **10**:68
   Gray **2**:194
   Kazin **7**:93
Black Mountain Review **14**:333
Black Panthers **5**:273
Black Pow Wow: Jazz Poems **25**:251,
   255
Black Rituals **21**:173
Black Riviera, The **22**:92, 103
Black Sea **26**:131
Black Sparrow Press **1**:368
Black Star **18**:305
*Black Theater USA: Forty-five Plays by
   Black Americans, 1847–1974*
   21:197
Black Tide **14**:159

Black World **21**:225
Blackbird Dust **12**:352
Blackburn Junior College **12**:28
Blackburn, Paul
   Berge **10**:6
   Corman **2**:137, 138
   Eshleman **6**:132, 134, 135, 138,
     140
   Kelly **19**:200, 202-03
   Koller **5**:165
   Olson **11**:255-56, 257, 259
   Rosenblum **11**:345, 352
   Sanders **21**:264
   Souster **14**:314
   Thayler **11**:363-65
Blackburn, Sara **9**:203
Blackburn, Thomas **5**:261
Blackburn, William **4**:114-15, 116,
   117, 120
Blackheath, England **10**:111-27
Blackheath Poisonings, The **3**:390
Blacklock, Jack **9**:240-41
Blackmur, Alan **8**:300
Blacks
   Ai **13**:10-11
   Bennett **13**:73-74, 79, 81, 83, 84-
     85
   Bullins **16**:62-65, 67-68
   Clarke **16**:75-76, 77-80, 82-86
   Easton **14**:154-55, 156
   Forrest **7**:31-32
   Garrett **5**:86
   Giovanni **6**:152, 160-61
   McElroy **21**:119-43
   Menefee **26**:201
   Petry **6**:257, 265-66
   Rodgers **13**:244, 245, 246, 250
   Salaam **21**:179-251
   Simpson **4**:286
   Stafford **3**:332
   Still **17**:234, 238
   Williams **3**:414, 415, 416
Blackwell, Betsy Talbot **6**:87
Blackwell, Earl **2**:119
Blair, Kathryn **11**:97, 104
Blais, Achille **3**:17
Blais, Corinne **3**:17
Blais, Gervaise (Boucher) **3**:17
Blais, Leo Romeo **3**:17-18, 20-21,
   22, 24
Blais, Marie-Claire **4:69-80**
Blais, Olivier **3**:17
Blaise, Clark **3:15-30**
Blake, Larry (poetry series) **24**:175-
   76
Blake, Paul **24**:334-35, 338, 341-5,
   346, 347, 349, 350-51
Blake, William
   Broughton **12**:47
   Eshleman **6**:136
   Lifshin **10**:241
   Menashe **11**:234
   Nichols **2**:328
   Ostriker **24**:269, 274-75
Blakemore, James **2**:409
Blanksmanship **25**:73

Blasco Ibáñez, Vicente **9**:1, 2
Blériot, Louis **14**:239-40
Bless Me, Ultima **4**:23, 24, 26
Blessing, Dick **2**:326
blewointmentpress **19**:5, 35, 44, 58
Blind Cross, The **7**:130
Blind Harry **8**:19
Blind on the Temple **25**:73
Blindness **21**:64, 71-72
Blish, James
    Haldeman **25**:205-06
    Knight **10**:208, 209, 211, 212,
        213, 214, 217, 220, 221,
        222
    Niven **12**:216-17
Bliven, Bruce **7**:92
Blk Love Song #1 **21**:197
BLKARTSOUTH **21**:196-98, 203,
    205, 206-07, 219
"BLKARTSOUTH/get on up!"
    21:204, 206-07
Bloch, Robert A. 20:35-54
    Aldiss **2**:27
Block, Lawrence 11:25-41
Blood about the Heart, The **26**:210
Blood and Money **14**:159
Blood Countess, The **8**:246, 247, 248,
    249-50
Blood of the Tenement **24**:126
Blood Root **24**:302-03
Blood Tie **1**:320, 322
Bloodworth Orphans, The **7**:30-31, 33
Bloody Murder **3**:390
Bloomfield, Morton **9**:211, 212, 213
Bloomsbury Group **3**:36
Blotner, Joseph 25:79-99
Blown Away **8**:294
Bloy, Léon **13**:181, 183
Blücher, Heinrich **2**:438, 450
Blue Book **6**:47, 48
Blue Boy on Skates **6**:279
Blue-Eyed Shan, The **1**:42
Blue Girls **3**:117
Blue Hammer, The **3**:204
"Blue Kansas Sky" **26**:6
Blue Monday **16**:106-07, 109, 110,
    112, 113-14, 116
Blue Money **22**:220, 222
Blue Mosque **17**:287
Blue Yak (bookstore) **19**:191
Blues
    Forrest **7**:26, 30, 32-33
    McPherson **23**:230, 231
    Plumpp **21**:174-75, 177
    Rosenblum **11**:338, 340-41
    Salaam **21**:185-88, 227, 244, 249-
        51
Blues People **16**:86
Blues: The Story Always Untold
    21:174-75
Bluest Eye, The **3**:431
Bluhdorn, Charles **1**:196
Blunden, Edmund
    Booth **2**:50-51, 59
    Corman **2**:140
    Woodcock **6**:319

Blur in Between, The **17**:207
Bly, Robert
    Allen **11**:15
    Argüelles **24**:13, 14
    Booth **2**:55, 58
    Hall **7**:62, 63, 64
    Kennedy **9**:86
    Nelson **23**:260
    Ray **7**:143, 144
    Root **11**:321
    Taylor **7**:179
BMT Theater **16**:67
Boatman's Tenure, The **6**:200
Boatwright, James **3**:23
Bobbs-Merrill Co. (publishers) **4**:293,
    294
Bobrowski, Johannes **13**:125-40
Boccaccio, Giovanni **8**:281
Bochet, André du **2**:139, 144
Bocock, Maclin **2**:215, 229, 230
Bodies and Souls **4**:264-65
Bodies Knot **25**:260-61, 272-73
Bodley Head (publishers) **9**:27
Body in the Billiard Room, The **8**:177
Body Politic **18**:322
Body Rags **8**:246
Body Servant, The **4**:190
Boelhower, William **6**:200-01
Boer War
    Stewart **3**:345
    Wright **5**:360
Bogan, Louise
    Belitt **4**:62
    Burroway **6**:90
    Cassity **8**:54
Bohannon's Country: Five Mysteries
    17:71, 73
Bohr, Niels **4**:65
Boisvert, Gaston **13**:180
Bokhari, Ahmed Shah **9**:225
Bold Cavaliers, The **6**:57
Bold John Henebry **3**:62, 64
Bold Saboteurs, The **2**:66, 67
Boldereff, Frances **24**:8
Bolinas, Calif.
    Kyger **16**:200-02
    Van Proyen **25**:401-02
    Villanueva **24**:311-12
Böll, Heinrich **23**:172-73, 176
Bollingen Foundation **4**:166
Bolshoi Ballet **4**:148
Bolt, Ron **23**:178-79
Bolts of Melody **10**:185
Bomb Shelter Propaganda Press
    24:74
Bombers B-52 **1**:383
Bompiani, Valentino **26**:72
Bond, Nelson S. **7**:14
Bone Game **24**:297
Bones of the Greeks **26**:289
Bonfiglioli, Kyril **2**:24-25
Bongé, Lyle **12**:347
Bonnard, Pierre **8**:158-59
Bonner, Anthony **6**:234-35
Bontemps, Arna
    Atkins **16**:12

Salaam **21**:228
Book of Cats, The **2**:58
Book of Changes, The **7**:13, 16-17
Book of Common Prayer **6**:33
*Book of Forms: A Handbook of Poetics,
    The* **22**:239
Book of Jerusalem, The **26**:304-05
Book of Lists, The **1**:378, 379, 384,
    400
Book of Predictions, The **1**:400-401
Book of Skulls, The **3**:282
Book-of-the-Month Club
    Becker **1**:38
    Condon **1**:196
    Wallace **1**:395, 400
Book of the XXXIX Steps **25**:114
Book of Urizen **6**:136
*Book of Women Poets from Antiquity to
    Now, A* **15**:107
Book Week **2**:400-01, 402
Booker McConnel Prize
    Fitzgerald **10**:101, 107
    O'Faolain **2**:352
Booker, Stephen Todd **9**:67-68
Books in Canada Award for First
    Novels **7**:110
Bookseller, The **18**:90
Bookshop, The **10**:106-07
Boon, Alan **11**:97, 100, 101, 103-04
Boone, Daniel **13**:168
Booth, Curtis **7**:10
Booth, Martin 2:47-61
Booth, Philip **13**:203
Booth, Richard **9**:286
Booth, Wayne C. 5:31-51
    Whittemore **8**:307
Borchardt, George **15**:144
Borders, James **21**:219
Bordes, François **2**:44
Bordesley College **10**:99
Borejsza, Jerzy **9**:123
Borestone Mountain Poetry Award
    Heyen **9**:41
    Simpson **4**:293
"Borges: A Non-Meeting" **11**:212
Borges, Jorge Luis
    Barnstone **15**:47, 60-61, 65, 67,
        91, 97, 100, 106, 107
    Cruz **17**:4
    Harwood **19**:142
    Kerrigan **11**:209-13
    Lem **1**:263
    Turner **10**:318
Borges: Una vita di poesia **11**:210
Borgese, Giuseppe Antonio **12**:33
Born Indian **7**:105
"Born with the Dead" **3**:283
Bornhauser, Fred
    Huddle **20**:186-87
    Taylor **7**:179
Boroff, David **3**:425
Borowski, Tadeusz **2**:72, 74
Borregaard, Ebbe **16**:191, 192
Bosence, Wilfred **5**:120
Bosnia **23**:68
Bosquet, Alain **14**:273-74

Bossert, William H.　**16**:300
Boston Boy　**6**:173
Boston Center for Adult Education
　8:216
Boston College
　Galvin　**13**:90-91
　Higgins　**5**:97, 99
Boston Evening Transcript　**2**:397
Boston Globe/Horn Book Honor
　Award　**7**:82
Boston, Mass.
　Ciardi　**2**:79-80
　Corman　**2**:129, 135, 145
　Hentoff　**6**:165
　Piercy　**1**:276
Boston Post　**3**:179
Boston University
　Ackerman　**20**:4, 5
　Clement　**16**:98
　Peters　**8**:240
　Petesch　**12**:245
Boswell, James
　Harris　**3**:119, 129, 131
　Morgan　**4**:234
Botkin, Ben　**6**:53
Botteghe Oscure　**2**:383
Bottom Line, The
　Knebel　**3**:182
　Valaoritis　**26**:289
Bottomley, Gordon　**5**:255
Bottomley, Horatio　**3**:391
Boucher, Anthony
　Anderson　**2**:41, 42, 46
　St. Clair　**8**:273
　Williamson　**8**:321
Boulanger, Nadia　**3**:86, 87
Boulder, Colo.　**14**:178
Boulez, Pierre　**8**:158
Bourbaki Gambit, The　**26**:101, 105,
　106
Bourgeois Poet, The　**6**:305
Bourjaily, Monte Ferris, Sr.　**1**:63,
　64, 65, 66, 70
Bourjaily, Vance　**1:63-79**
　Haldeman　**25**:203
　Mahapatra　**9**:147
　Stevenson　**9**:277
Bourke-White, Margaret　**1**:148-50,
　151
Bova, Ben　**18:47-62**
Bovie, S. Palmer　**6**:89, 90
Bowdoin College
　Barnstone　**15**:54-55, 60, 62, 63,
　　64
　Bourjaily　**1**:67, 69, 70
Bowe, Augustine　**17**:182
Bowen, Elizabeth　**7**:24-25
Bowen, Michael　**26**:77
Bower, Warren　**10**:2-3
Bowering, George　**16:21-38**
　Bromige　**26**:39-40
Bowers, Fredson　**7**:12
Bowles, Jane　**18**:279, 288
Bowles, Paul　**1:81-95**
　Morgan　**4**:232
　Norse　**18**:279, 288

Purdy　**1**:302
　Roditi　**14**:251-52, 281, 286
Bowley, Victor　**2**:387
Bowling Green State University
　McCord　**9**:184
　Mott　**7**:133
　Raworth　**11**:303-04
　Thayler　**11**:365
Box Is Empty, The　**2**:412
"Box Social, The" (James Crerar
　Reaney)　**15**:304
"Box Socials" (W.P. Kinsella)　**7**:102,
　110
Boxing　**17**:39, 43, 49, 53-54
Boy Scouts of America　**2**:88
*Boy with a Cart: Cuthman, Saint of
　Sussex, The*　**23**:68
Boyars, Marion　**1**:133
Boyce, Jack
　Koller　**5**:164, 165-66, 167, 168
　Kyger　**16**:198-99
Boyd, Malcolm　**11:43-60**
Boyd, Martin　**4**:338
Boyer, Harold　**2**:19
Boyers, Margaret Anne　**13**:314
Boyers, Robert　**13**:314
Boyle, Kay　**1:97-125**
Boynton, Peter　**12**:158-59
Brackett, Leigh　**8**:322
Bradbury, Malcolm　**9**:114-15
Bradbury, Ray
　Bishop　**26**:13
　Bloch　**20**:48
　Nolan　**16**:211, 212, 215, 224
　Silverberg　**3**:274
　Williamson　**8**:321
Bradbury, Walter I.　**3**:180, 181
Bradley, Marion Zimmer　**10:19-28**
Brady, Diamond Jim　**4**:237
Brahms, Johannes　**14**:127
Braided Lives　**1**:272, 280
*Brainard and Washington Street
　Poems*　**5**:162
Brakhage, Stan　**2**:443
Brambu Drezi, Book One　**24**:58, 60-
　61, 75, 77, 80
Brambu Drezi, Book Two　**24**:76
Bramson, Naomi, Trust　**4**:91
Brancusi, Constantin　**1**:99, 114
Brand, Max See Faust, Frederick
Brandeis University
　Clarke　**16**:84
　Gerber　**20**:165-67
　Lifshin　**10**:250
　Ostriker　**24**:267
　Petesch　**12**:245, 246
　Sukenick　**8**:289
Brandt & Brandt (literary agents)
　3:428
Brandt, Carl, Jr.　**3**:426, 430
Brasch, Charles　**23**:10
Brathwaite, Edward Kamau　**21**:241-
　44
Brautigan, Richard
　Kherdian　**2**:269
　Kinsella　**7**:107

Kyger　**16**:196-97
　Plymell　**11**:289, 292-93
　Sukenick　**8**:291
Brave Little Toaster, The　**4**:157
Brave New World　**4**:146
Braybrooke, Neville　**4**:84
Brazil
　Anthony　**18**:18-19
　Eaton　**20**:126-31
Bread and a Stone　**20**:112, 117
Bread and Puppet Theater　**6**:118
Bread and Wine Mission　**26**:73
Bread Loaf School of English,
　Middlebury, Vt.
　Forbes　**16**:109
　Glazier　**24**:225
　Sward　**13**:282
　Williams　**20**:330
Bread Loaf Writers Conference,
　Middlebury, Vt.
　Allen　**11**:19
　Ciardi　**2**:90
　Eaton　**20**:125
　Glazier　**24**:226
　Hadas　**23**:119
　Hall　**7**:60, 62
　Huddle　**20**:188, 189, 190
　Jerome　**8**:137
　Kumin　**8**:215
　Lifshin　**10**:250
　McElroy　**21**:139
　Meredith　**14**:220-21, 222, 223,
　　229, 230
　Stegner　**9**:265-66
　Sward　**13**:287
　Turco　**22**:240-41
　Williams, John A.　**3**:424
　Williams, Miller　**20**:328-29
Breadfruit Lotteries, The　**3**:81
Breaking Camp
　Elman　**3**:77
　Piercy　**1**:267
Breaking of Bumbo, The　**5**:269, 270,
　271, 274
Breaking of the Day, The　**4**:137, 138
"Breaking Point"　**2**:248, 249, 256
Breaking the Silence　**19**:223
"Breakthrough" series　**3**:411
Breast of the Earth, The　**13**:41
Breath Dances between Them　**22**:115
Brecht & Co.　**4**:107
Brecht, Bertolt
　Foley　**24**:166
　Mott　**7**:127
　Roditi　**14**:254-55, 269
Bredvold, Louis I.　**2**:134
Brée, Germaine　**15:127-48**
Breger, Leonard
　Berry　**24**:78
　Foley　**24**:175
Brejchová, Jana　**1**:344
Breman, Paul　**6**:185
Brenendik shtetl　**9**:59
Brennan, John Michael　**9**:85
Breslin, Jimmy　**4**:208
Bretnor, Reginald　**2**:42

Breton, André
  Higgins **8**:84
  Joans **25**:252-54
  Roditi **14**:256, 257, 265-66
  Schwartz **26**:231, 238-39, 241-42, 247
  Valaoritis **26**:284, 287, 289, 290
Brewer, George **2**:116
Brewing: Twenty Milwaukee Poets **11**:348
Brewster, Earl Henry **10**:131
Brewster, Elizabeth 15:149-63
Brides of Reason **3**:40
Brideshead Revisited **7**:235
Bridge at Arta, The **3**:356
Bridge, The **6**:210
Brier, His Book **15**:290
Brigham, Besmilr **5**:347, 349
Brigham, Roy **5**:347, 349
Brigham Young University **5**:40, 43
Bright Plain, The **20**:134-35
Bright Road to El Dorado **18**:22
Brightfount Diaries, The **2**:22
Briley, Dorothy **7**:81
Brill among the Ruins **1**:76-77
Brilliant, Alan **8**:248
Brilliant Kids **22**:61-62
"Brillo" **18**:54
Brimstone **2**:174
Brink, The (film) **24**:345, 347, 351
British Book Centre **1**:361
British Broadcasting Corp.
  Abse **1**:27
  Allen **6**:18, 21, 23, 25
  Anthony **18**:15-16
  Booth **2**:58, 60
  Caute **4**:100
  Fast **18**:180-82
  Fitzgerald **10**:104-05
  Glanville **9**:26
  Gray **3**:110, 111
  Killens **2**:299
  Saroyan **5**:216
  White **4**:340-42
British Columbia: A Celebration **6**:324
British Copyright Council **4**:86
British Crime Writers Association **3**:390
British in the Far East, The **6**:325
British International Films **14**:258
British Museum
  Settle **1**:313
  Wilson **5**:319
British School, Bari, Italy **2**:139
British Virgin Islands **1**:42
Brittain, Vera **5**:141
Brittle Innings **26**:10
Britton, Bruce **19**:316, 318, 320
Britton, Burt **6**:189
Bro, Harlan **11**:10
"Broadside Critics Series" **18**:144, 152
Broadway theatre
  Fuchs **5**:64-66
  Grumbach **2**:206-07

Brockport, New York: Beginning with "And" **9**:46-47
Brodeur, Arthur **9**:213
Brodey, Jim **22**:25
Brodie, Fawn M. **1**:376
Brodkey, Harold **6**:217-18
Broken Sword, The **2**:40
Bromige, David Mansfield 26:21-45
Bronc People, The **1**:212
Bronk, William
  Elman **3**:79, 80, 81
  Foster **26**:126-27, 129
Bronowski, Jacob **4**:65
Bronston, Sam **4**:346
Bronston, Samuel, Co. **4**:345, 346
Brontë, Emily **1**:313
Brooke, Jocelyn **19**:149
Brookhiser, Richard **9**:98
Brooklyn Boy **20**:252, 253
Brooklyn College
  Argüelles **24**:15
  Baumbach **5**:19-20, 24, 27
  Lelchuk **20**:242
  Major **6**:191
  Markfield **3**:209-13
  Raffel **9**:209-10
Brooklyn Museum **1**:286
Brooklyn, N.Y.
  Elkins **18**:94-96
  Fuchs **5**:61-63
  Piercy **1**:273, 274
  Pohl **1**:286
Brooklyn Public Library
  Pohl **1**:284
  Wakoski **1**:365
Brooks, Cleanth
  Jerome **8**:133
  Olson **12**:233
  Slavitt **3**:315
  White **4**:348
Brooks, Gwendolyn
  Emanuel **18**:143-44, 160
  Killens **2**:298
  McElroy **21**:140
  Rodgers **13**:244-45, 246, 248
Brooks, Robert A. **7**:187
Brooks, Van Wyck **7**:92
Broom **1**:115
Broonzy, "Big" Bill **7**:22
Brophy, Brigid 4:81-94
Brossard, Chandler 2:63-78
Brossard, Nicole 16:39-57
Brotherly Unfixed Grace-Noted Stare, A **26**:227
Brothers, I Loved You All **6**:118-19
Brothers Karamazov, The **2**:190
Broughton, James 12:41-58
  di Suvero **26**:71
  Foley **24**:159
  Kyger **16**:190
  Settle **1**:314
  Valaoritis **26**:282
Brower, David **9**:268
Brown, Alec **10**:123-24
Brown, Andreas **1**:302
Brown, Bill **5**:165, 170

Brown, Charles **9**:103
Brown, Claude **3**:430
Brown, Curtis (literary agents) **2**:331
Brown, David **1**:385
Brown, Dee 6:45-59
Brown, Douglas **3**:35
Brown, Frank London **6**:181
Brown, George Mackay 6:61-76
Brown, Helen Gurley **1**:385
Brown, J. Harold **16**:13
Brown, Joe **2**:449
Brown, John **2**:430
Brown, Leonard S. **3**:421
Brown, Merle
  Bell **14**:48
  Silkin **5**:262, 263
Brown, Norman O. **12**:152, 157, 160
Brown, Pamela **23**:70
Brown, Rosellen 10:29-43
Brown, Spencer Curtis **15**:192-93
Brown, Sterling
  Joans **25**:250
  Killens **2**:295
  Madgett **23**:198
Brown, Tom **22**:22
Brown University
  Allen **11**:11, 12-14
  Cassill **1**:172-73, 174
  Honig **8**:115-16, 117-18
  Kostelanetz **8**:180
Brown, William L. **16**:294, 296
Brown, William Slater **10**:67-68
Browne, Michael Dennis 20:55-75
Browning, Robert **6**:230
Browning Society **26**:177
Brownjohn, Alan
  Booth **2**:52, 54
  Silkin **5**:262
Broyard, Anatole **3**:80
Bruce-Novoa 18:63-78
Bruce-Novoa, Juan D. See Bruce-Novoa
Bruckner, Hubba **26**:141, 142
Bruin, John See Brutus, Dennis
Brunel University **4**:105
Brunner, John 8:1-17
  Disch **4**:151
  Haldeman **25**:216
  Hoffman **10**:172
Bruno, Giordano **8**:92
Brussels, Belgium **2**:405-06, 409
Brutus, Dennis 14:53-64
Bryant, Dorothy 26:47-63
Bryant, Joseph **4**:116
Bryant, William Cullen **9**:210
Bryn Mawr College
  Brée **15**:133-34, 136, 143
  Gray **2**:194
  Weiss **12**:331
Buck, Pearl S.
  Emanuel **18**:131
  Wallace **1**:390
Buck Ruxton **18**:301
Buck, Tom **15**:246
Budapest, Hungary

Corcoran **2**:124
 Rakosi **5**:194-95
Buddhism
 Simpson **4**:296
 Van Itallie **2**:416-17, 418, 419,
  420, 421, 422
 Waldman **17**:275, 279, 282
Budrys, Algis 14:65-79
 Knight **10**:220, 221
 Silverberg **3**:274
Buel, Walker S. **3**:177, 178
Bufera, La **7**:297
Buffalo Country **2**:170
Buffington, Robert **9**:146
Bug Jack Barron **19**:316, 322, 323-
 27, 332
Bukoski, Anthony **7**:103
Bukowski, Charles
 Cherkovski **24**:90-91, 98, 104
 Major **6**:180
 Norse **18**:288
 Peters **8**:244
Bulgaria **26**:131-46
Bullins, Ed 16:59-70
Bulmershe College **9**:285
Bulwell, Nottingham, England
 23:235-46
Bumpus, Jerry **1**:74
Bunker, Chang **1**:400
Bunker, Eng **1**:400
Bunting, Basil
 Fisher **10**:94
 Turnbull **14**:326, 336
 Williams **12**:344-45
Burago, Alla **9**:217
Burbank, Harold H. **3**:236, 237,
 238
Burch, Robert **9**:83
Burden, Jean **13**:315
Burdick, Bud **9**:267
Bureau Creek **5**:168
Burger, Knox **19**:128, 129
Burgess, Jim **2**:136
Burgess, Thornton W. **9**:195
Burgum, Edwin Berry **5**:120-21
Burhoe, Leslie **5**:169-71
Buried Land, A **11**:182
Burke, Edmund
 Kirk **9**:95, 96
 Stafford **3**:338
Burke, James Lee 19:63-77
Burke, Kenneth
 Belitt **4**:62, 65
 Olson **12**:233
Burlingame, Roger **1**:119
Burma
 Aldiss **2**:19-20
 McCord **9**:180, 182-83
Burnett, Virgil **15**:228, 229-30
Burnett, Whit
 Fast **18**:176
 Ghiselin **10**:133
 Whittemore **8**:307
Burnham, James **12**:204
Burning Hills, The **1**:383
Burning Sky, The **2**:172

Burning Village **9**:52-53, 59, 63, 66
Burning Water **16**:27, 28
Burns, Gerald **26**:226
Burns, Milo **1**:179, 180
Burnt-out Case, A **8**:170
Burroughs, Edgar Rice **9**:2
Burroughs, Mitchell **2**:257
Burroughs, William
 Argüelles **24**:13
 Bowles **1**:91, 92
 Creeley **10**:72
 Joans **25**:238-39, 240-41
 Katz **14**:176-77
 Major **6**:193
 Morgan **4**:235
 Norse **18**:284, 285, 286-88, 291
 Plymell **11**:289, 291, 293, 294,
  295
 Raworth **11**:301
 Spinrad **19**:327
 Sukenick **8**:290
 Waldman **17**:278, 284
Burroway, Janet 6:77-103
Burstyn, Ellen **9**:246
Burton, Naomi
 Kennedy **9**:84
 Wakoski **1**:365
Bury My Heart at Wounded Knee **6**:57
Busch, Frederick 1:127-37
Busch, Phyllis **1**:127, 128, 133
Bush, Douglas **24**:235
Businessman: A Tale of Terror, The
 4:156, 157
But for the Grace of God **5**:328
Butcher, Margaret Just **18**:130
Butler, Michael **10**:94
Butler University **22**:170-71
Butley **3**:113, 114
Butor, Michel
 Brossard **2**:67
 Lem **1**:263
Butterfield, Paul **24**:8
Butterick, George
 Bergé **10**:10
 Ferrini **24**:133-34, 147
Buzzards, The **6**:98, 99, 100
By Heart: Pages from a Lost Vermont
 25:46
By Lingual Wholes **17**:14-15
Bye, Reed **17**:285-88
Byrd, Harry **7**:4
Byrd, Robert
 Olson **11**:255, 256
 Wilson **5**:349
Byrdwhistle Option, The **10**:296, 299,
 300, 302-03, 304
Byrne, Stu **2**:41
Byron Caldwell Smith Prize **2**:255
Byron Exhumed **8**:248
Bystander, The **2**:218, 219, 228, 231
Byways **22**:173-210
Byzantium Endures **5**:183

Cabala **9**:49, 51, 55, 64
Cabeza de Vaca, Alvar Nuñez
 15:121

Cabin Fever **13**:106, 110-11, 117
Cabot, Frank **6**:233
Cabot Wright Begins **1**:303
Cabral, Amilcar **21**:234, 235-36
Cabrera, Jesse Guinto **24**:97, 99
Caedmon **23**:78
Caetani, Marguerite
 Broughton **12**:56-57
 Jennings **5**:112
Cafe Cino, New York City **2**:413
Cafe La Mama, New York City
 2:413, 414, 418, 421
Cafe Mimosa **11**:100
Cage, John
 Bergé **10**:7
 Gray **2**:194
 Hassan **12**:152, 160
 Higgins **8**:86, 89, 90
 Norse **18**:284, 289
 Waldman **17**:283
Cahill, Dan **9**:113-14
Cain, James M. **3**:192, 194, 203
Caine, Michael **9**:250-51
Cairnie, Gordon
 Enslin **3**:89-90
 Hall **7**:62
Calas, Nicolas **14**:258
Calder, Alexander **1**:156
Calder, John **1**:133
Calderón and the Seizures of Honor
 8:117
Calderón de la Barca, Pedro **8**:117
Calderón, Felipe G. **9**:159
Caldwell, Erskine 1:139-59
Caldwell, Virginia **1**:151, 153-54,
 155-56, 157
Calendar of Love, A **6**:71
Calexico, Calif. **25**:321, 325, 328
Calgary Creative Reading Series
 7:103
"Caliban" **3**:282
California
 Daigon **25**:165
 Davie **3**:45
 Higgins **8**:89
 Houston **16**:155-60
 Owens **24**:282, 283
 Polkinhorn **25**:321, 325, 328, 335
 Rodgers **13**:252
 St. Clair **8**:274-75
 Silverberg **3**:283
 Sukenick **8**:289
 Williams **3**:423
California Institute of Technology
 Gerber **20**:173
 Kelly **19**:203
 Niven **12**:212
 Wakoski **1**:368
California Institute of the Arts
 Eshleman **6**:143
 Higgins **8**:89
California Poems **5**:165, 166, 167
California State University, Los
 Angeles
 Cherkovski **24**:94
 Hongo **22**:86

California State University, Northridge
  Grumman **25**:189
  McCord **9**:184
  Owens **24**:294
*Californians: Searching for the Golden
  State* **16**:157
Calisher, Hortense
  Bourjaily **1**:72
  Burroway **6**:90
Calisto and Melibea **8**:117
Call It Sleep
  Belitt **4**:60
  Williams **3**:429
Callahan, Harry **12**:339
Callanwolde Poetry Series **7**:131
Callimachus **3**:90
"Calling of Jerusalem, The" **26**:304-
  05
Callow, Philip **11**:377
Calvin College **18**:250-54
Cambridge Book Company **22**:62-63
Cambridge, Godfrey **2**:293
Cambridge Poetry Festival **5**:169
Cambridge University
  Burroway **6**:91, 93
  Clark **22**:12, 14
  Davie **3**:35, 39, 40
  Davison **4**:133
  Gray **3**:103
  Mano **6**:208-09
  Sinclair **5**:270, 276
  Skelton **5**:281
  Tarn **16**:274
  White **4**:337, 340, 341, 342
Cambridge University, Churchill
  College **5**:271
Cambridge University, Newnham
  College **1**:219-20
Cambridge University Press **1**:223
Cambridge University, Trinity College
  Gray **3**:108-09, 110, 111
  Sinclair **5**:269-70
Camera Always Lies, The **17**:89
Cameron, Angus **2**:303
Camiz, Vito **25**:349
Camp Concentration **4**:151
Camp, James **9**:83, 84
Campaign Capers **1**:246
Campbell, Bruce **4**:250
Campbell, John W., Jr.
  Anderson **2**:39, 41, 42, 46
  Bova **18**:53, 54-55
  Budrys **14**:66, 67, 70
  Clement **16**:97, 98
  Gunn **2**:247, 249
  Knight **10**:203, 204, 205, 209,
    218
  Pohl **1**:292
  Spinrad **19**:316
  Williamson **8**:318, 322
Campbell, Roy **5**:367, 368
Campbell, Walter **2**:170
Camus, Albert
  Boyle **1**:117
  Brée **15**:135, 140, 141, 143
  Lottman **12**:200-01, 206, 207

Mathews **6**:245
Sillitoe **2**:385
Canada
  Andre **13**:16-17, 18
  Blaise **3**:20-21, 28
  Brewster **15**:161-62
  Clarke **16**:76-77, 81, 87
  Davie **3**:44-45
  Levine **23**:165-80
  Singh **9**:230
  Slade **9**:244
  Sward **13**:292-93, 299
Canada and the Canadians **6**:323
Canada Arts Council
  Blais **4**:73
  Brewster **15**:159
  Horwood **15**:248
  Rule **18**:316, 321
Canada Council Explorations Grant
  Hine **15**:226, 228
  Sward **13**:297
Canada Foundation See Canada
  Council Explorations Grant
canada gees mate for life **19**:18-19,
  24-25, 26, 53
Canada Made Me **23**:172-73, 177
Canada, Royal Air Force
  Levine **23**:166
  Purdy **17**:200-02
  Souster **14**:309-12
Canadian Authors Association
  Kinsella **7**:110
  Rule **18**:320
Canadian Booksellers Association
  7:110
Canadian Broadcasting Corp.
  Purdy **17**:204-05, 206, 207
  Slade **9**:243
Canadian literature
  Cohen **18**:86
  Owens **2**:367
Canadian Literature **6**:323, 324
Canadian Philosophical Association
  15:360
Canadian Poetry **8**:220
Canadians **3**:110
Canadians, The **6**:323
Cancer **23**:176-77
Candidates 1960 **3**:179
Cane **7**:32
Canetti, Elias **1**:24
Canfield, Curtis **6**:93
Cannes Film Festival
  Broughton **12**:55
  Caldwell **1**:155
Cannibal Consciousness **26**:302-03
Cannibal Crumbs **26**:296, 303
Canterbury Tales **5**:374
Canticle for Innocent Comedians, A
  4:63
Cantor's Dilemma **26**:93-94, 96-100,
  101, 102
Cantos (Ezra Pound)
  Allen **6**:18
  Enslin **3**:90

Caoine Airt Uí Laoire ("The Lament for
  Arthur O'Leary") **3**:62-63
Cape Ann Theatre **24**:128-29
Cape Breton, Nova Scotia **14**:176
Cape-Goliard Press **16**:280
Cape, Jonathan (publishers)
  Jones **5**:122, 128
  Tarn **16**:278-80
Capital punishment
  Davis **20**:103-18
  Horwood **15**:248
Capital See *Kapital, Das*
Capitalism
  Barrio **15**:112, 124-26
  Caute **4**:102
  Rakosi **5**:208
Caponegro, Mary **6**:147
Capote, Truman **1**:88
Capouya, Emile **6**:285
Capra, Frank **1**:380, 383
Caprice **16**:26, 28
Captain Blackman **3**:420, 431
Captive of the Vision of Paradise
  24:20
Capuchins **13**:179-80
Caravan **10**:172, 173
Carcanet Press **3**:47
Cardboard Garage, A **15**:357
Cardiff, Wales
  Abse **1**:17, 18
  White **4**:333-34
Cardinal Sins, The **7**:51
Cargill, Oscar **6**:277
Cargo **24**:206
Caribbean **18**:219-20
Cariboo Horses, The **17**:209
Carleton College
  Salaam **21**:191-92
  Whittemore **8**:305-06, 307
Carleton Miscellany
  Whittemore **8**:307
  Wright **7**:298
Carleton University **15**:156
Carlisle, Henry **26**:76
Carlisle, Olga **26**:76
Carlson, John Roy **6**:165
Carmina **3**:98
Carnal and the Crane, The **15**:224
Carnal Island, The **10**:116
Carnell, E.J.
  Aldiss **2**:25, 29
  Moorcock **5**:177, 179
Carnell, Ted See Carnell, E.J.
Carnival Trilogy **16**:124, 130, 131-32
Carnivore, The **3**:319
*Carnivorous Saint: Gay Poems,
  1941–1976* **18**:290
Carolina Quarterly
  Blaise **3**:23
  Morgan **20**:281
Caron, Richard **2**:365, 366
Carr, John Dickson **15**:194, 195
Carr, Terry
  Hoffman **10**:173, 174
  Knight **10**:225
Carrambo, Cristobal **2**:421

Carrigan, Andrew　**11**:303
Carrol, Paul　**26**:298
Carroll, Diahann　**2**:296
Carroll, Donald　**13**:132
Carroll, Lewis
　　Keating　**8**:166
　　Slavitt　**3**:322
Carroll, Paul　**6**:181
Carruth, Hayden
　　Arnold　**25**:40
　　Corman　**2**:136
　　Dennison　**6**:118-19
　　Gregor　**10**:150
　　Laughlin　**22**:201-07
Cars　**7**:158-59
Carson, Herbert L.　**7**:29-31
Carter, Jimmy
　　Caldwell　**1**:157
　　Williams　**20**:335-36, 338-39
Cartier-Bresson, Henri　**7**:85
Cartland, Barbara　8:19-35
　　Green　**11**:104
Cartooning　**18**:227-30, 234-36, 237
Carver, Beverly　**26**:220, 226, 228
Carver, Catharine　**3**:405
Carver, Raymond
　　Blaise　**3**:20, 23, 26
　　Haldeman　**25**:204-05
Carver, Wayne　**8**:307
Cary, Joyce
　　Glanville　**9**:21
　　Sinclair　**5**:272
Casa de los Americas Prize　**16**:151
Casanova, Ronald　**26**:210
Casara, Severino　**25**:351
Case of the Missing Photographs, The　**20**:142
Case of Walter Bagehot, The　**3**:304
Casper, Leonard　**8**:240
Cassady, Neal　**11**:280, 281, 286,
　　287-88, 289, 290
Cassandra: A Musical Drama　**21**:272
Cassandra Singing　**3**:187-88, 189,
　　195-96, 200
Cassill, Ronald Verlin　1:161-75
　　Blaise　**3**:25
Cassity, Turner　8:37-62
　　Mott　**7**:131
Cast of Tens, A　**26**:22
Cast of Thousands, A　**25**:313
Castaneda, Carlos　**2**:272, 273, 274
Castano, Jo-Ann　**24**:134-35
*Caste and Ecology in the Social
　　Insects*　**16**:304
Castellon, Rolando　**25**:397-98
Castex, Mariano　**9**:149
Castiglione, Robert L.　**12**:323-37
Castle, Irene　**2**:170-71
Castle Keep　**1**:206, 211
Castle Tzingal　**4**:124
Castro, Fidel　**11**:215
*Cat Walked through the Casserole,
　　The*　**23**:260
Catacomb, The　**9**:28
Catch, The　**2**:436
Catch Trap, The　**10**:25-26

Catcher in the Rye, The　**6**:87
Cater, H.S.　**6**:20
Caterpillar　**6**:140, 142, 144
Cather, Willa
　　Clark　**22**:25
　　Grumbach　**2**:213, 214
　　Harris　**3**:132
　　Kazin　**7**:94
Catholic Church
　　Anaya　**4**:17
　　Blais　**4**:70-71, 72
　　Brossard　**16**:40
　　Caute　**4**:96
　　Ciardi　**2**:85-86, 88
　　Condon　**1**:188-89
　　Gray　**2**:198
　　Greeley　**7**:37-51
　　Hentoff　**6**:173
　　Kerrigan　**11**:195-96
　　Kienzle　**1**:237, 239-53
　　Levis　**23**:182-83
　　Nolan　**16**:209-10
　　O'Faolain　**2**:342-43, 349-50, 352-
　　　53
　　Rodgers　**13**:243-44
　　Shapiro　**6**:298
Catholic University of America
　　12:332
Catholicism
　　Anaya　**4**:17
　　Brown　**6**:73
　　Dacey　**17**:20-22
　　Forrest　**7**:24, 26
　　Greeley　**7**:39, 49-50
　　Inez　**10**:180
　　Jennings　**5**:104, 106, 107, 108,
　　　112
　　Kennedy　**9**:79, 87
　　Levis　**23**:181
　　McCord　**9**:181
　　Nichols　**2**:308
　　Rabassa　**9**:192-93
　　Rechy　**4**:258
　　Turner　**10**:314-15, 316
Caton, R.A.　**6**:320
Catonsville Trial, The　**1**:55
Cats　**16**:221
Cats in Charge　**26**:157
Cats' Opera, The　**3**:63
Cattle Rustling, The　**21**:294
Catullus, Gaius Valerius
　　Dudek　**14**:131
　　Katz　**9**:62
　　Sisson　**3**:303
　　Williams　**12**:341-42
　　Wright　**7**:295
Caulfield, Carlota　25:101-17
Causley, Charles
　　Levine　**23**:174
　　Thomas　**11**:377
Caute, David　4:95-111
Cautionary Tales　**13**:166
Cavafy, C.P.　**26**:272-73, 282-83,
　　285
Cavalier　**3**:74

*Cave of Trophonius and Other Poems,
　　The*　**15**:358
Cave paintings　**6**:146
Cazenovia College　**15**:24
CBC See Canadian Broadcasting
　　Corp.
CBS-TV See Columbia Broadcasting
　　System
CCLM See Coordinating Council of
　　Literary Magazines
CDN SF&F　**22**:49
CEAD See Centre d'essai des auteurs
　　dramatiques
Ceccardi, Ceccardo Roccatagliata
　　14:125, 126
Cecil, David　**5**:108
Cedar Rock　**8**:141
Cela, Camilo José　10:45-60
　　Kerrigan　**11**:200, 205, 206, 210
Celan, Paul
　　Corman　**2**:138, 144
　　Hamburger　**4**:170
　　Roditi　**14**:274-75
Celebration　**1**:322
Celebrity Service　**2**:119
Céline, Louis-Ferdinand
　　Konwicki　**9**:129
　　Roditi　**14**:256
Cenizas　**15**:12
Censorship
　　El Saadawi　**11**:70
　　Giovanni　**6**:153, 155-56
　　Hentoff　**6**:172-73
　　Jones　**5**:127-28
　　Kerrigan　**11**:205
　　Van Itallie　**2**:416
Centaur Press　**12**:53
CENTER Magazine　**10**:10, 11, 16
Central College, Pella, Iowa　**26**:151
Central Connecticut State
　　University　**13**:90, 101
Central Intelligence Agency
　　Coppel　**9**:6-7
　　Emanuel　**18**:136
　　Kerrigan　**11**:207
*Centre d'essai des auteurs
　　dramatiques*　**23**:103, 112
Centro Escolar University　**9**:167
Centro Mexicano de Escritores　**13**:84
Century of Innovation, A　**2**:366
Century of Science Fiction, A　**10**:222
Cerberus　**14**:128, 132
Cerebral palsy　**23**:19-27, 32, 33, 49,
　　53, 54, 56-57
Čerepková, Vladimíra　**1**:346
Ceretta, Florindo　**7**:297
Cerf, Bennett
　　Eastlake　**1**:201
　　Hahn　**11**:115
　　Hudgins　**21**:106-07
　　Mitford　**17**:150
Cernuda, Luis　**15**:59
Certainty of Love, A　**9**:5
Cervantes, Miguel de
　　Eigner　**23**:39
　　Purdy　**1**:299

Ces anges de sang (These angels of
    blood)   **13**:181
Césaire, Aimé
    Becker   **1**:42
    Eshleman   **6**:147
    Joans   **25**:249
*César Vallejo: The Complete Posthumous
    Poetry*   **6**:144
Ceylon   **3**:239, 240
    See also Sri Lanka
Cézanne, Paul   **7**:301
Chacksfield, Merle   **11**:103
Chadron State College   **18**:120
Chaikin, Joseph   **2**:412, 413, 414,
    416, 418, 419, 420, 422
Chaikin, Shami   **2**:418, 420, 421
Chair for Elijah, A   **9**:66
Chaix, Marie   **6**:223, 240, 242-43,
    245, 248, 251
Challenge Press   **10**:297-98
Challenge, The   **1**:381, 382
Chalmers, Gordon   **9**:98
Chalupecký, Jindřich   **1**:336, 338
Chamber Music   **2**:212, 213
Chamberlain, Edward   **3**:236
Chamberlain, Neville   **2**:310
Chambers, Ernest   **6**:182
Chambers, Everett   **2**:254
Chambers, The   **10**:6
Champlain College   **13**:336
Chance   **7**:222
Chandler, A. Bertram   **1**:290
Chandler, Raymond   **15**:196-97
Chaneles, Sol   **6**:183
Change   **8**:136
Change the Sky   **8**:275, 281
Channing, William Ellery   **5**:36
chant du poète, Le   **23**:103, 111
Chapel Hill   **20**:280-81
Chaplin, Oona   **5**:221, 222
Chapman, Chandler   **2**:441
Chapman Report, The   **1**:384, 388-89,
    396
Chapman, Robert   **2**:411
Chappell, Fred   **4**:113-26
    Miller   **15**:287, 288, 289, 291
    Root   **11**:322
    Shelnutt   **14**:298, 299-300, 301
Chapter One of a Work in Progress See
    "Box Socials"
Charisma Campaigns, The   **15**:266,
    269
Charles, Mat   **9**:211
Charles Olson Journal   **10**:10
Charles Sumner High School   **23**:198
Charles University
    Hrabal   **12**:193
    Škvorecký   **1**:333, 347
Charlie and the Chocolate Factory
    6:155
"Charlie's Pad" (television series)
    18:236, 237
Charlotte Observer   **1**:146
Charlottesville, Va.   **25**:266
Charterhouse   **9**:16-17, 18-19
Charteris, Leslie   **9**:17

Charyn, Jerome   **1**:177-84
Chase, Richard   **6**:210, 211
Chattanooga News   **3**:170
Chatto & Windus (publishers)   **5**:112-
    14
Chaucer, Geoffrey
    Brown   **6**:73
    Wain   **4**:328
    Whittemore   **8**:311
Chavez, Angelico   **4**:17
Chavez, Carlos   **2**:117
Chayefsky, Paddy   **9**:242
Cheever, John
    Becker   **1**:36
    Brown   **6**:53
    Haldeman   **25**:204
    Kerrigan   **11**:213
Chekhov: A Biography in Verse   **21**:272
Chekhov, Anton
    Abse   **1**:30-31
    Boyle   **1**:108, 117
    Samarakis   **16**:270
    Van Itallie   **2**:417-18
    Wallace   **1**:391
Chelsea Review   **19**:198, 199
Cherkovski, Neeli   **24**:83-105
    Argüelles   **24**:28
    Berry   **24**:77-80
    Foley   **24**:177
Cherry, Kelly
    Dillard   **7**:14-15, 17
    Taylor   **7**:179
Cherry Lane Theater   **2**:419
Cherry Orchard, The   **2**:418
Cherry Valley Editions   **11**:294
Chess   **24**:53
Chesterton, G.K.
    Jennings   **5**:106
    Wain   **4**:328
    Wilson   **5**:314
Chestnut Rain, The   **9**:37
Cheuse, Alan   **4**:244
Chevalier, Haakon   **14**:261-62, 266,
    271, 275, 276
Cheyenne River Wild Track   **14**:175
Chez Charlotte and Emily   **5**:28
Chicago Daily Maroon   **13**:14
Chicago Defender   **3**:421
Chicago Herald Tribune   **2**:400
Chicago, Ill.
    Andre   **13**:18
    Argüelles   **24**:6, 11
    Emanuel   **18**:131-32
    Greeley   **7**:37, 44
    Heinemann   **21**:75, 90-91
    Menefee   **26**:200
    Piercy   **1**:271-72
    Pinsky   **4**:248
    Raworth   **11**:305
    Rodgers   **13**:238-40
    Simic   **4**:280-81
    Solotaroff   **2**:396
    Sward   **13**:284-85, 286
Chicago, Judy   **24**:129-30
Chicago State University   **13**:251,
    252

Chicago Sun-Times
    Becker   **1**:43
    Simic   **4**:283
    Solotaroff   **2**:400
    Wallace   **1**:376
Chicago Tribune
    Johnson   **18**:236, 237
    Murchie   **19**:247-48, 290-96
Chicago World's Fair See World's
    Fair, Chicago, Ill.
Chicano   **15**:167-79
Chicano in China, A   **4**:27
Chicano movement
    Anaya   **4**:23, 24-26, 27
    Barrio   **15**:120
    Bruce-Novoa   **18**:73-77
*Chicano: Twenty-five Pieces of a Chicano
    Mind*   **15**:176
Chicken Soup with Barley   **7**:243, 245-
    46, 247, 249
*Chico's Organic Gardening and Natural
    Living*   **1**:378
Chihuly, Dale   **7**:301
Child   **21**:15
Child abuse
    Vizenor   **22**:271-72
    Zeidner   **24**:356, 360
Child molestation   **21**:12-13
Child of Fortune   **19**:333, 335
Child of the Jago, A   **2**:384
Child of the Morning   **2**:125
Children of Hamelin, The   **19**:318,
    325-30
Children of Herakles, The   **7**:186
Children of the Ghetto   **7**:236
*Children of the Holocaust: Conversations
    with Sons and Daughters of
    Survivors*   **9**:33-34
Children on the Shore   **2**:412
Children, The   **18**:175-76
Children's Encyclopedia, The   **2**:311
Children's International Summer
    Villages   **18**:265-66, 267
Children's Revolt, The   **11**:83
*Child's Garden of Verses for the
    Revolution, A*   **1**:211
Chile
    Alegría   **15**:9-10
    Williams   **20**:330
Chimera   **3**:139-40
Chimney Sweep Comes Clean, A   **2**:71
China
    Becker   **1**:34-35
    Browne   **20**:68
    di Suvero   **26**:65-66, 69
    Hahn   **11**:113-15
    Honig   **8**:123-24
    Killens   **2**:304
    Rosenthal   **6**:285
    Salisbury   **15**:324-26
China to Me: A Partial Autobiography
    11:113, 115
China Trace   **7**:295
Chinese Agent, The   **5**:187-88
*Chinese Elements in the Tagalog
    Language*   **9**:162, 165

Chinese poetry   6:285
"Chip Harrison" series   11:35
Chisel in the Dark, A   18:120, 160, 162
Chitlin Strut and Other Madrigals, The   19:130
Chomsky, Noam
    Hall   7:64
    Parini   16:230-31, 242
Chorale   4:219
Chorlton, David   26:221
Choudhury, Malay Roy   14:81-99
Choynowski, Mieczyslaw   1:259
Chrétien de Troyes   9:219
Chrétien, Jean   23:177-78
Christ and Celebrity Gods   11:47
Christensen, Charles   9:85
Christian   11:56
Christian Brothers   4:146
Christian Science
    Foster   26:115
    Olson   12:226
Christian Science Monitor   8:216
Christianity
    Awoonor   13:37-38, 40-41, 53
    Bennett   13:73-74
    Berry   24:64
    Bradley   10:22-23
    Dillard   7:7-8
    Fisher   10:95
    Garrett   5:75
    Glancy   24:199-205, 211
    Grumbach   2:214
    Hamburger   4:170
    Mano   6:206, 207-08, 209-10, 212-15
    Pownall   18:295
    Rodgers   13:253
    Silkin   5:251, 253
    Simmons   21:290
    Thomas   4:310-11
    Wain   4:326, 328
Christie, Agatha   15:197
Christine/Annette   2:215
Christmas Tale, A   2:225
Christopher Ewart-Biggs Prize   2:352
Christopher Homm   3:301, 302
Chucky's Hunch   2:361, 366
Church   23:196
Church and the Suburbs, The   7:46
Church Divinity School of the Pacific   11:47
Church in Wales, Anglican   4:304, 305, 310
Church of England   4:170
Church of Jesus Christ of Latter-Day Saints See Mormonism
Church World Service (relief agency)
    Markfield   3:213
    Stafford   3:334
Churchill, Winston
    Geduld   21:51, 52
    Murchie   19:250-51
Churchill: Young Man in a Hurry   4:234
CIA See Central Intelligence Agency

Ciardi, John   2:79-96
    Allen   11:19
    Corman   2:133-34, 135
    Jerome   8:137
    Kennedy   9:84
    Kumin   8:215
    Meredith   14:220-21
    Stevenson   9:278
    Williams   20:327, 328, 331
Ciel de Nuit   2:66
Cigarettes   6:248, 249
"Cimetière marin"   4:248
Cincinnati, Ohio   1:111-14
Cincinnati Symphony Orchestra   1:111
Cioran, E.M.   22:23
Circle for the Science of Science   1:259
Circle-in-the-Square Theatre   20:220, 226
Circle of Stone, A   20:330, 339
Circle, The   1:223
Circles, as in the Eye   10:6
CISV See Children's International Summer Villages
Citadel (publishers)   2:288
Cities and Stones   2:27
Cities in Bezique   20:228, 232
Citizen Hearst   13:259, 268
Citizen Tom Paine   18:179, 180, 184
Citizens' Advice Bureau (Great Britain)   4:44
City   10:98
City and Eastern   21:293
City College of New York
    Federman   8:74
    Kazin   7:95
    Kelly   19:198
    Spinrad   19:312, 315
    Swenson   13:313
    Weiss   12:326-28
    Williams   3:431
    See also City University of New York
City College of San Francisco   26:242-43
City Life   11:84
City Lights Bookstore, San Francisco, Calif.
    di Suvero   26:71, 78
    Wilson   5:349
City Lights (press)   24:25-26
City of Night   4:258, 260, 261, 263, 265
City of Words   1:303
City Parables, The   9:33
City University of New York
    Emanuel   18:133, 134-35
    Epstein   12:72-73
    Hauser   11:137-38
    Kostelanetz   8:182
    Major   6:186
    Markfield   3:225
    Rabassa   9:199, 204
    See also City College of New York
City with All the Angles   8:92

CIV/n, A Literary Magazine of the 50's (book)   14:133
CIV/n (magazine)   14:132
Civil Rights Congress   17:142, 146
Civil rights movement
    Boyd   11:48-49, 50, 51
    Dennison   6:116
    Emanuel   18:135, 137-38
    Gunn   2:253
    Hamill   15:209
    Jones   11:182-83
    Killens   2:296-98
    Mott   7:131
    Nelson   23:253, 255-56
    Petesch   12:248
    Picano   13:221
    Plumpp   21:175
    Salaam   21:184-87
    Tillinghast   23:307
    Wakefield   7:197
    Williams   3:427
    Wright   22:315-317
    See also Segregation
Civil War, American
    Corcoran   2:113, 114
    Dillard   7:3
    Hall   12:108
    Jones   11:172
    Morgan   3:231
    Morris   13:167
    Nichols   2:323
    Tillinghast   23:302-03
    Wakefield   7:193
    White   4:350
    Williams   20:319-20
    Wright   7:287-88
Civil Wars   10:41
Civilian Conservation Corps.   18:120, 121-22
Clair, René   5:274
Claire, Paula   19:31, 38, 55, 58
Clam Shell, The   1:311, 318, 319
Clancy, Patrick   10:172
Clare, John
    Abse   1:25
    Wright   5:363
Clarence Darrow for the Defense   3:370
Clarendon Press   3:354
Clarion Writers' Workshop
    Knight   10:225-26
    Spinrad   19:335
    Wolfe   9:306-07
    Zebrowski   19:368-69
Clark, Harry Hayden   9:111, 113
Clark, Jack   10:124
Clark, Joanna Rostropwicz   9:123
Clark, Kenneth B.   19:314
Clark, Leonard   2:59
Clark, Sonia Tomara   1:120
Clark, Tom   22:1-26
Clark, Walter Van Tilburg
    Connell   2:109-10
    Corcoran   2:119
    Stafford   3:334
Clark, William   1:120, 122
Clarke, Arthur C.

Bergé   **10**:9
Bova   **18**:51
Niven   **12**:217
Zebrowski   **19**:363-64, 366, 370
Clarke, Austin C.   16:71-88
Rosenthal   **6**:285
Clarke, Dean   **14**:127
Clarke, Gillian   **9**:286
Clarke, John Henrik
Clarke   **16**:83
Killens   **2**:298
classic plays   **8**:92
Classical music
Jolley   **13**:109-10, 111-12
Olson   **12**:227-28, 229
Rabassa   **9**:198
Rosenblum   **11**:342
Salvadori   **25**:345-46, 348, 349
West   **7**:270-71, 285
"Classics Illustrated" comic books
26:12
"Classics of Modern Science Fiction"
series   **2**:258
Claudel, Paul   **4**:72
Claxton, Patricia   **16**:53
Clean Kill, A   **15**:197
Cleaver, Eldridge
Clarke   **16**:84
Sinclair   **5**:273
Cleland, John   **1**:396
Clem Anderson   **1**:170, 171
Clement, Hal   16:89-104
Cleveland Institute of Music   **16**:10
Cleveland, Ohio   **5**:301, 303
Cleveland Plain Dealer   **3**:177
!Click Song   **3**:421, 424, 432
Clinton   **21**:173
Clinton, Bill   **20**:333, 338, 339
Clinton, Martina   **19**:5, 9, 44
Clio's Children   **15**:30
Clock of Moss, The   **14**:114, 116
Clockwork Orange, A (film)   **25**:388
Cloned Lives   **18**:341
Close Encounters with the Deity   **26**:6
Close Quarters
Gilbert   **15**:189, 192-93
Heinemann   **21**:92
Close the Sky, Ten by Ten   **9**:145
Closely Watched Trains   **1**:338
Closing of the American Mind   **14**:131
Closing the Gap   **2**:71-72
Cloud, Mollie   **24**:200-05
Cloutier, David   **8**:119
Clove of Gender, A   **26**:226, 227
Clown, The
Corcoran   **2**:124
Meltzer   **26**:192
Clunies-Ross, Pamela   **5**:246
Clute, John   **4**:152, 154, 156
Cnot Dialogues, The   **2**:57
Coach House Press   **13**:296-97
Coakley, Andy   **9**:197
Coast Magazine   **14**:146
Coastlines   **1**:359
Coat for the Tsar, A   **3**:74
Coates, Robert   **6**:301

Cobbing, Bob   **19**:20, 31, 38, 51, 55
Cock of Heaven, The   **12**:230, 231
Cocktails at Somoza's   **3**:81
Cocteau, Jean
Highwater   **7**:69
Markfield   **3**:214
West   **7**:279
Code of the West   **26**:128
Codrescu, Andrei   19:79-96
Argüelles   **24**:16, 22-23
Codron, Michael   **3**:112-13
Cody, Jim   **24**:315
Cody, John   **7**:46, 47
Coe College   **6**:25
Coercion Review   **6**:179, 180
Coffee House Press   **7**:107
Coffin, Hal T.   **2**:135, 142
Coffman, George R.   **2**:434, 435
Cogan's Trade   **5**:92
Coghill, Nevill   **12**:25, 26, 33
Cogswell, Fred
Brewster   **15**:154
Purdy   **17**:205
Cogswell, Theodore   **2**:258
Cohan, George M.   **1**:395
Cohen, Arthur   **14**:173-74
Cohen, Bob   **2**:304
Cohen, Chester   **10**:206, 208, 210,
211, 215
Cohen, Isidore   **2**:162
Cohen, Matt   18:79-91
Cohen, Morris R.   **12**:327
Cohen, Robert   **8**:249
Coils   **6**:144
Coindreau, Maurice-Edgar   **4**:117
Coins and Coffins   **1**:364
Colbert, Nancy   **7**:105, 110
Colby College   **15**:333
Cold Comfort   **3**:322
Cold War
Davie   **3**:42
Guerard   **2**:225, 226
Coldspring Journal   **11**:294
Coleman, Elliott   **11**:292, 293, 294
Coleman, R.V.   **6**:56
Coleridge, Samuel Taylor
Belitt   **4**:64
Jennings   **5**:106
Colgate University
Busch   **1**:132, 133
Sukenick   **8**:287-88
West   **7**:280
Colie, Rosalie   **6**:89
Colladay Award   **11**:83
Collage   **23**:55
Collected Earlier Poems, 1940–1960
19:236
Collected Greeds, Parts I-XIII, The
1:368, 371
Collected Plays (Peter Barnes)   **12**:14
Collected Poems and Epigrams (George
Rostrevor Hamilton)   **10**:119
Collected Poems (C.H. Sisson)   **3**:300,
307
Collected Poems (Elder Olson)   **12**:235

Collected Poems (George Woodcock)
6:326
Collected Poems of Al Purdy, The
17:210
Collected Poems, 1956–1976 (David
Wagoner)   **3**:409, 410
Collected Poems, 1948–1976 (Dannie
Abse)   **1**:31
Collected Poems, 1968 (Roy Fisher)
10:98-99
Collected Poems (Sylvia Plath)   **4**:134
Collected Poetry (Louis Dudek)   **14**:133
Collected Works of J.M. Synge   **5**:285
Collectivism   **12**:309
College of Saint Rose, Albany,
N.Y.   **2**:209, 210
College of the Virgin Islands   **8**:135-
36
College Street Messiah, The   **14**:92
Collège Technique, France   **3**:107
Collier's Encyclopedia   **1**:169
Collier's Magazine   **1**:192
Collier's Year Book   **9**:99
Collins, Aileen   **14**:133-34
Collins, Bob   **7**:195
Collins, Wilkie   **6**:254
Collins, William, Sons & Co.
(publishers)   **8**:176
Collisions   **4**:104
Colloquialisms
Brossard   **2**:73-74
Mano   **6**:216-17
Colmain   **3**:109
Colombo, John Robert   22:27-58
Sward   **13**:299
*Colombo's All-Time Great Canadian
Quotations*   **22**:47
Colombo's Canadian Quotations   **22**:45-
47
Colombo's Canadian References   **22**:48
"Colonel Pyat" series   **5**:183
Colonialism   **3**:246
Colonnade Club   **1**:320
Colony   **18**:50, 56
Color of Darkness   **1**:302
Color Purple, The   **16**:84
Colorado College   **13**:321
Colorado State University   **11**:48
Colorni, Ausonio   **10**:142
Colour of Murder, The   **3**:390
Colour of Rain, The   **9**:291
Colours in the Dark   **15**:307
Colours of War, The   **18**:83
Coltelli, Laura   **6**:283
Colton, James See Hansen, Joseph
Coltrane, John   **21**:179, 182, 191,
194, 205, 224, 244-45
Columbia Broadcasting System
Caldwell   **1**:149
Corcoran   **2**:120
Elman   **3**:74
Gunn   **2**:259
Hailey   **1**:231
Sinclair   **5**:273
Van Itallie   **2**:412
Columbia College, Chicago, Ill.

Heinemann   **21:**91, 93
Rodgers   **13:**248, 253
Columbia Faculty Fellowship   **25:**137
Columbia Pictures
Condon   **1:**194
Eastlake   **1:**211
Sinclair   **5:**273
Slade   **9:**244
Columbia University
Ai   **13:**5-6
Baumbach   **5:**21-22
Block   **11:**30
Browne   **20:**63, 64
Busch   **1:**130, 131, 133
Cassill   **1:**169
Charyn   **1:**179
Connell   **2:**107
Corn   **25:**137-42
Delbanco   **2:**158, 159
Dennison   **6:**110, 113
Dudek   **14:**129, 130
Elman   **3:**76, 78
Emanuel   **18:**132, 133
Federman   **8:**76-77
Foster   **26:**119-20, 121-22
Hailey   **1:**229
Higgins   **8:**86
Highwater   **7:**80
Inez   **10:**191
Kelly   **19:**198
Kennedy   **9:**80
Killens   **2:**286, 287, 288
Kostelanetz   **8:**180
Lottman   **12:**198, 205
Mano   **6:**207, 208, 217
Markfield   **3:**225
Mathews   **6:**223
Morgan   **4:**227
Petry   **6:**264
Rabassa   **9:**201-04
Rechy   **4:**259
Salvadori   **25:**363-64, 369, 373
Silverberg   **3:**272
Simpson   **4:**291-92, 293, 294
Sinclair   **5:**271
Slavitt   **3:**316-17
Wakefield   **7:**195, 196
Weiss   **2:**431-33
West   **7:**277
Columbia University Forum   **12:**206
"Combat"   **26:**325
Come Hither   **5:**146
Come Live My Life   **10:**300, 301
Come Out with Your Hands Up   **2:**71
Comeback for Stark, A   **3:**111
Comet Press Books   **3:**423
Comic Art in America   **1:**37, 38
Comic strips
Moorcock   **5:**177-78
Nolan   **16:**210
Williamson   **8:**324
Comic, The   **9:**27, 28
Comici, Emilio   **25:**352
Coming Home   **5:**131-32
"Coming Out of Mother"   **4:**246
"Coming to Light"   **26:**177-78

Commander of the Order of the
Academic Palms   **15:**144
Commentary
Dennison   6.121
Solotaroff   **2:**398-400, 401
Common Sense   **9:**177
Commonweal
Elman   **3:**74
Greeley   **7:**47
Communes   **8:**137-40
Communism
Beltrametti   **13:**56
Emanuel   **18:**134-35
Fast   **18:**169, 172, 174-75, 179,
183-84
Guerard   **2:**226
Kazin   **7:**89
Kerrigan   **11:**201-05
Kizer   **5:**150
Laqueur   **19:**217-18
Lessing   **14:**199-203
Lind   **4:**196, 197, 200-01
Mitford   **17:**140-43
Mrozek   **10:**268-70
Roditi   **14:**256, 276
Samarakis   **16:**249
Schwartz   **26:**233-38, 246
Shadbolt   **3:**254, 256
Simic   **4:**271
Škvorecký   **1:**333-48
Voinovich   **12:**317
Wain   **4:**321
Wiesel   **4:**360
Yglesias   **20:**353, 356
Zinoviev   **10:**325, 326, 329-30,
332-33
*Communism and the French
Intellectuals*   **4:**105
Communism See also Marxism
Communist Labor Party   **26:**209-10
Communist Manifesto, The   **1:**285, 286
Communist party
Bowles   **1:**85
Corn   **25:**141
Davie   **3:**42
Kizer   **5:**150
Mitford   **17:**142-43, 144-45
Schwartz   **26:**232
Voinovich   **12:**306-07
Companions of the Day and Night
16:135
Company She Kept, The   **2:**213
Company We Keep, The   **5:**43, 48, 51
*Comparative Culturology of Humanoid
Civilizations*   **1:**263
Compleat Melancholick, The   **22:**245
"Composed upon Westminster
Bridge"   **5:**106
Computer imaging   **25:**403
Computer technology   **24:**256-59
Comrade Jacob   **4:**105
Conad See French First Army,
Continental Advance Section
*Conceived in Liberty: A Novel of Valley
Forge*   **18:**177-78
Concept of Criticism, The   **15:**360

Concordia University, Montreal,
Canada   **3:**27
Condon, Richard   1:185-99
Condon, Wendy   **1:**194, 197, 198
Condry, Penny   **4:**308
Condry, William   **4:**309
*Confederation Betrayed: The Case
against Trudeau's Canada*   **6:**323
Confessional Poets, The   **13:**207
*Confessions of a Bohemian Tory:
Episodes and Reflections of a
Vagrant Career*   **9:**101
Confessions of a Justified Sinner, The
9:290, 292
Confessions of a Spent Youth   **1:**64, 66,
67, 73-74, 77
*Confessions of an English Opium Eater,
The*   **2:**383
Confessions of Madame Psyche   **26:**52,
53, 58, 59, 60, 61
Confusions about X   **3:**386
Congo   **4:**230
Congo (film)   **1:**87
*Congo Solo: Misadventures Two Degrees
North*   **11:**112, 113
Congregationalism   **2:**308
Connecticut   **25:**163
Connecticut College
Meredith   **14:**222, 225, 227, 234
Sward   **13:**287
Connecticut College of Pharmacy
6:263
Connecticut Hall of Fame   **22:**248-49
*Connections: In the English Lake
District*   **8:**244, 248
Connell, Evan S.   2:97-112
Conner, Bruce   **11:**283, 285
Connolly, Cyril
Ashby   **6:**43
Glanville   **9:**21
Sinclair   **5:**269
Wilson   **5:**321, 322, 326
Conquerors, The   **1:**40
Conquest, Robert
Abse   **1:**27
Davie   **3:**31, 38
Conrad, Joseph
Brown   **6:**48
Keating   **8:**167
Roditi   **14:**242-43
Škvorecký   **1:**349
Wellek   **7:**222
Whittemore   **8:**303-04
Conrad the Novelist   **2:**221, 228
Conroy, Jack   **6:**53
Conscientious objectors
Arnold   **25:**32-33, 34
Bennett   **25:**58
Gibbons   **24:**184-97
Kirkup   **4:**183
Owens   **24:**290
Stafford   **3:**332, 333, 334, 337,
339
Consensus (brain trauma rehab
center)   **24:**19, 20, 23
Conservatism

Kirk **9:**98-99
Mano **6:**208, 209
Conservative Mind, The **9:**97-99
Conspiracy of Knaves, A **6:**58
Constantly Singing **21:**284
Constructivism **8:**186
Constructivist Fictions **8:**189
Constructs **2:**368
Contact **14:**132
Contact Press **14:**132
*Contemporary British and North
 American Verse* **2:**59
Contemporary Center, San Francisco,
 Calif. **7:**80
Contemporary Poetry Series **3:**410
Contemporary Shakespeare, The **8:**263-
 64
Conti, Italia **10:**108-09
Continental Drift **16:**160
Continuation **14:**140-41
Contract with the World **18:**320
Contre-Jour **8:**158
*Controversy of Poets: An Anthology of
 Contemporary American Poetry,
 A* **19:**201
Convention **3:**181
Conversations in Another Room **8:**145
Conversion of Buster Drumwright, The
 21:36
Conversions, The **6:**235, 236, 237,
 239, 241, 246
Cook, Eliza **2:**356
Cool World, The **1:**345-46
Cool Zebras of Light **8:**246
Cooler by the Lake **21:**98
Cooney, Barbara **19:**269, 296, 300
Cooney, Ray **9:**253
Cooper, Clarence L., Jr. **6:**193
Cooper, James Fenimore **7:**6
Cooper, John R. **3:**173-74
Cooper Union
 Disch **4:**148
 Norse **18:**283
Cooperstein, Nancy **2:**418
Coordinating Council of Literary
 Magazines
 Anaya **4:**26
 Grumbach **2:**214
 Hamill **15:**212
 McCord **9:**184
 Sukenick **8:**293
 Whittemore **8:**307
 Wilson **5:**353
Coover, Robert
 Baumbach **5:**28
 Dillard **7:**13
 Weiss **2:**447-48
Copeland, Carleton **12:**303-22
Copeland, Edward **22:**274
Copenhagen University **1:**156
Copland, Aaron **1:**83
Coppel, Alfred **9:**1-11
Copper Beach Press **8:**119-20
Copperhead Cane **15:**283
Coppola, Francis Ford
 Schwartz **26:**247

Wagoner **3:**410-11
Cops and Robbers **13:**342
Copway, George **22:**263
Copyright **4:**86
Cora Fry **10:**41-42
Corbett, Jim **2:**50, 60
Corbett, William **19:**144
Corcoran, Barbara **2:**113-28
Corday **7:**134
Cordelier, Jeanne **6:**248
Core, George **9:**146, 147
Corina, John **24:**129
Corman, Cid **2:**129-47
 Arnold **25:**40, 42, 46
 Beltrametti **13:**61, 62
 Eigner **23:**26, 37, 48, 51, 57
 Enslin **3:**87, 90-92, 93, 98
 Eshleman **6:**135, 136
 Fisher **10:**96, 97
 Kelly **19:**201
 Kennedy **9:**82
 Kyger **16:**196
 Lowitz **26:**178
 Rakosi **5:**208
 Rosenblum **11:**348
 Thayler **11:**363
 Turnbull **14:**335
 Wilson **5:**349-50
Corn, Alfred **25:**119-48
Cornell College, Mt. Vernon, Iowa
 2:102
Cornell College of Agriculture
 14:164-65
Cornell University
 Ackerman **20:**5
 Foley **24:**160, 162-63, 165, 166
 Grumbach **2:**207
 Kammen **23:**145
 Katz **14:**165-66, 173-74
 Matthews **18:**269
 Ray **7:**143
 Sukenick **8:**288-89
 West **7:**280
 Williams **3:**431
Corner of Rife and Pacific, The
 15:336, 338, 339, 341
Cornford, John **1:**18, 25
Cornis-Pop, Marcel **8:**64
Cornish Anthology, A **8:**255
Cornish Childhood, A **8:**254
Cornishman Abroad, A **8:**260
Cornishman at Oxford, A **8:**260
Corno Emplumado, El **3:**94
Cornwall, England
 Corcoran **2:**124-25, 126
 Rowse **8:**253, 258
 Thomas **11:**369-70
Coronis **2:**56
Corpse, The **16:**13, 14, 16
*Correspondences: A Family History in
 Letters* **9:**284-85
Corriere dello Sport **9:**20, 22, 24
Corrigan, Robert **10:**321
Corrington, John
 Aubert **20:**24
 Williams **20:**329, 331, 339

Corso, Gregory
 Bowles **1:**92
 Joans **25:**236
 Weiss **2:**444-45
Cortázar, Julio **9:**191, 203
Cortés, Hernando **4:**348
Cortez, Jayne **25:**247
Corwin, Norman **16:**217-18, 219
Cosmopolitan **1:**385
Cosmos **7:**283
Cost of Living, The **7:**126-27
Costley, Robert **21:**206
Cotillion, The **2:**295, 304
Cott, Jonathan **17:**271
Cottey College **7:**164
Cottle, Tom **7:**201
Cotton Club: New Poems, The **6:**185
Cottrell, W.F. **3:**169
Couch, William T.
 Cassill **1:**169
 Kirk **9:**99
Couchman, Gordon **3:**421
Couchman, Jeff **3:**421
Cougar Hunter **17:**211
Council of Economic Advisors **3:**243
Council of Jewish Federations and
 Welfare Funds **3:**216
Council on Interracial Books for
 Children **6:**154-56
Count of Monte Cristo, The **2:**373
*Counter/Measures: A Magazine of Rime,
 Meter, & Song* **9:**86
Counterculture **25:**14
Countermoves **20:**136
Counterparts **10:**127
Counting My Steps **4:**202
Counting the Grasses **7:**132
Country Matters **1:**77
Country of the Minotaur **10:**140
Country of the Pointed Firs, The
 6:254
Country Place **6:**266
Country You Can't Walk In **22:**117
Couple Called Moebius, A **10:**9
Court, Wesli (pseudonym of Lewis
 Putnam Turco) **22:**237, 244
Courtroom Bar **25:**393, 395
*Cousin Jacks: The Cornish in America,
 The* **8:**253, 263
Couturier, Maurice **6:**194, 196
Covenant with Death, A **1:**38, 39
Cowards, The **1:**328, 338, 340, 341-
 45, 346
Cowden, Roy W.
 Ciardi **2:**89
 Corman **2:**134
Cowell, Henry **8:**86, 89
Cowles Publication Bureau **3:**179
Cowley, Malcolm
 Katz **14:**173
 Kazin **7:**88-89
 Wagoner **3:**404, 405
Cowley, Rob **4:**233
Cowper, William
 Abse **1:**25
 Nichols **2:**311

Cox, Bill **20**:36
Cox, Brian **3**:46
Cox, C.B. **9**:141
Cox, Palmer **5**:299
Coxey, Jacob Sechler **3**:398
Coyote, Peter **5**:168, 169
Coyote's Journal **5**:164
Cozzens, James Gould **19**:257, 258
Crabbe, George **15**:155
Crack in the Universe, A **12**:235
Crack, The **9**:291-92
Cracks **1**:304
Craig, Gordon **2**:412
Crane, Hart
  Belitt **4**:63
  Eigner **23**:51
  Honig **8**:107, 121
  Roditi **14**:248
Crane, Ronald S. **12**:230, 231, 233-34
Crates on Barrels **18**:301
Creamy and Delicious **14**:167, 175
Creative Choices: A Spectrum of Quality and Technique in Fiction **3**:197
Creative Person: Henry Roth, The (film) **3**:430
Creative Process, The **10**:130, 134, 137
Creature of the Twilight, A **9**:103
Credences of Winter **26**:31-32
Creed, Robert P. **9**:214
Creek Mary's Blood **6**:58
Creeley, Robert **10**:61-77
  Andre **13**:13, 14, 15-16
  Corman **2**:135, 136, 137, 138
  Crews **14**:112-13, 114
  Eigner **23**:26, 51
  Enslin **3**:90, 91
  Hall **7**:62
  Koller **5**:169, 170
  Major **6**:193
  Mott **7**:131
  Olson **11**:254, 255
  Peters **8**:244
  Saroyan **5**:213, 215
  Souster **14**:315
  Thayler **11**:363
  Wilson **5**:349, 350
Crespi-Green, Valerie **11**:102-03, 105
Cret, Paul **15**:141
Cretin Military High School **4**:146, 147
Crevel, René **14**:256
Crew, Louie **23**:209
Crews, Harry **8**:215
Crews, Judson **14**:101-19
Crichlow, Ernest **2**:295
Crime and Detection **3**:391
Crime and Punishment **2**:190
Crime fiction
  Freeling **12**:84-89
  Gilbert **15**:188-89, 193-94
Criminal Comedy of the Contented Couple, The **3**:390
Criminal Tendencies **11**:207

Criminals **26**:328
Crisis in Communication **11**:47
Crisis (James Gunn) **2**:259
Crisis (NAACP) **2**:259
Criterion
  Davie **3**:46
  Rowse **8**:258, 259
Critical Observations **3**:386
Critical Quarterly **9**:141
Critics and Criticism: Ancient and Modern **12**:233-34
Crock of Gold, The **7**:78
Crompton, Richmal
  Glanville **9**:17
  Nichols **2**:310
Cromwell, Oliver **1**:319
Cronin, Anthony **5**:370
Cross, Edward Makin **5**:145
Cross of Fire, The **4**:219
Crosscurrents
  Allen **11**:22
  Feirstein **11**:84
Crosse, Gordon **8**:155, 156-57, 158
Crossing in Berlin **3**:182
Crossing Over **3**:83
Crossing to Safety **9**:264, 269-70
Crow **11**:235
Crowell-Collier Publishing Co. **2**:264-65
Crowell, Thomas Y. (publishers) **3**:273
Crowninshield, Frank **1**:114
Crowns of Apollo, The **8**:241, 245
Crozier, Andrew
  Clark **22**:14-15
  Peters **8**:244-45
  Rakosi **5**:209
Crucifix in a Deathhand **8**:244
Cruelty **13**:10, 11
Crumb, Robert **11**:289, 293
Crump, Barry **23**:10
Crunching Gravel **8**:238, 250
Crutch of Memory, The **8**:10
Cruz, Victor Hernández **17**:1-17
Cry of Absence, A **11**:183-84
Crying Embers, The **2**:54
Crystal, Billy **4**:240
Crystal Palace, St. Louis, Mo. **2**:69
Crystal Spirit: A Study of George Orwell, The **6**:325-26
Cuba
  Alegría **15**:11
  Caulfield **25**:107-08
  Kerrigan **11**:192-94
  Sinclair **5**:273
Cuba, N.M. **1**:210
Cuba, Yes? **4**:107
Cuban Missile Crisis **4**:73-74
Cubans **11**:193-94
Cue **2**:116
Culbert, Elizabeth **10**:189-90
Cullen, Countee **23**:200-01
Culross, Michael **13**:289-90
Cultural Revolution **20**:68
Cultural Unity of Black Africa, The **21**:245-46

Culture out of Anarchy: The Reconstruction of American Higher Learning **8**:133, 137
Cumberland Poetry Review **3**:47
Cumberland Station **7**:163, 164, 165
Cumming, Primrose **8**:210
Cummings, E.E.
  Argüelles **24**:10
  Eigner **23**:56
  Grumman **25**:174, 186
  Howes **3**:137
  Katz **9**:68
  Whittemore **8**:306
Cummings, Ray **10**:211
Cummington School of the Arts **10**:38-39
Cunningham, James **21**:169
Cunningham, J.V.
  Jerome **8**:131
  Ostriker **24**:267
  Petesch **12**:245, 246
  Sukenick **8**:289
Cuomo, Mario **10**:71
Cure for Cancer, A **5**:181
Curiosity **23**:22, 24, 50-52
Curley, Daniel
  Elman **3**:73
  Williams **3**:421
Curley, James Michael **6**:167
Curran, Alvin **25**:115
Curses and Laments **22**:237
Curtin University of Technology **13**:114
Curtis, Dan **16**:218, 225
Curtis, Edwina **2**:138
Curve Away from Stillness **15**:19-20
Curwood, James Oliver **1**:327
Cuscaden, Rob **13**:288-89
Cut Pages, The **10**:99
Cutler, Ann **21**:35, 43
Cutting Stone **6**:102
Cyberbooks **18**:55
Cyberiad, The **1**:264
Cyprus **16**:266-67
Czech language **7**:209-10
Czech literature **7**:213
Czytelnik (publishers) **9**:123

Da Silva da Silva's Cultivated Wilderness **16**:134
Da Songs **25**:262
Dacey, Philip **17**:19-36
Dadaism **8**:186
Daglarca, Fazil Husnu **6**:192
Dagon **4**:117, 119-20, 121
d'Agostino, Giovanni **11**:310
Dahlberg, Edward
  Kazin **7**:90
  Kerrigan **11**:210, 216
  Williams **12**:345
Daiches, David **6**:91, 95
Daigh, Ralph **11**:31
Daigon, Ruth **25**:149-72
Daily Express (London) **5**:323
Daily Forward (New York City) **3**:155

Daily Mirror (London) **5**:322
Daily Mirror (New York City) **4**:148
Daily News (New York City) **4**:213
Daily Spectator (Columbia
   University) **7**:195
Daily Times (Harrison, Ark.) **6**:50-51
Daily Worker **20**:356
Dakyns, Henry Graham **8**:250
Dakyns, Janine **8**:250
Dalai Lama **6**:324
D'Alfonso, Antonio **13**:177-92
Dalhousie University
   Allen **6**:27
   bissett **19**:27, 54
   Gray **3**:106-07, 108, 109
Dalí, Salvador
   Atkins **16**:8
   Bowles **1**:86
   Joans **25**:224-25
Dallas Morning News **1**:227, 228,
   229
Dallas, Tex. **1**:226, 229
Damon, S. Foster
   Allen **11**:13
   Kostelanetz **8**:180
Dana, Robert **14**:48
Dance
   Belitt **4**:63
   Eaton **20**:123
   Highwater **7**:80
   Salaam **21**:247-48
Dance Me Outside **7**:102, 103, 107,
   108
Dance the Eagle to Sleep **1**:273
Dance to Still Music, A **2**:114, 122-23
Dancer from the Dance, The **6**:95, 96
Dancers in the Scalp House **1**:212
Dancers of Noyo, The **8**:275
Dancing Beasts, The **18**:287
*Dancing on the Shore: A Celebration of
   Life at Annapolis Basin* **15**:252-
   53
Dandridge, Dorothy **2**:291
Danger Signal **16**:260
Danger Within, The See *Death in
   Captivity*
Danger Zone **3**:265
Dangerous Visions **19**:320, 324
Danieli, Fidel **25**:386-87, 401
Daniels, Bob **8**:130
Daniels, Chris **25**:262, 264-68, 269-
   70, 271, 272-73, 274-76, 277-78
Dann, Jack **20**:77-101
   Sargent **18**:338, 341, 343, 344
   Zebrowski **19**:368-69, 370, 373,
      377
Danner, Margaret
   Killens **2**:298
   Madgett **23**:205
d'Annunzio, Gabriele **1**:391
Dans le sombre (In the dark) **13**:185
Dante Alighieri
   Anaya **4**:17
   Brown **6**:73
   Ciardi **2**:80, 90
   Katz **9**:58

Niven **12**:222
   Wain **4**:328
Darantière, Maurice **15**:229-30
"Darby" series **24**:255
D'Arcy, Margaretta **4**:29-31, 46
D'Arcy, Martin **5**:108
Dardis, Thomas A. **10**:222, 224
"Daring Young Man on the Flying
   Trapeze, The" **7**:90
Dark Conceit: The Making of Allegory
   8:112, 115
Dark December **9**:5
Dark Dominion **11**:133
Dark Encounters **16**:223
Dark Horse **3**:181-82
Dark Houses (Peter Davison) **4**:138,
   139
Dark Houses, The (Donald Hall) **7**:65
Dark Night of Resistance, The **1**:59
Dark Place, The **18**:101-02
*Dark Symphony: Negro Literature in
   America* **18**:138, 139
Dark Waters **21**:138
Darker Than You Think **8**:321
"Darkover" series **10**:25
Dartmouth College
   Caldwell **1**:154
   Connell **2**:101-02
   Parini **16**:235-37
   Rabassa **9**:197-99
Darwin **18**:37-38, 45
Darwin, Charles
   Appleman **18**:33, 37-38, 40
   Stone **3**:377-78
Darwin's Ark **18**:33, 40
Darwin's Bestiary **18**:41
Das Lot **14**:274
Datlow, Ellen **9**:308
*Daughters and Rebels: An
   Autobiography* **17**:145
Daughters of Passion **2**:345, 352
"Dave Brandstetter" mystery series
   17:68, 70, 71, 72
Dave Sulkin Cares **3**:182
Davenport, Louis **5**:142
David Copperfield **4**:52-53
David Sterne **4**:76
"David's Rod" **26**:29
Davidson, Avram **4**:150
Davidson College **7**:293
Davidson, Donald **11**:176-77
Davidson, Lionel **1**:43
Davie, Donald **3**:31-48
   Abse **1**:18
   Clark **22**:14, 16
   Menashe **11**:233-34, 236
   Pinsky **4**:247
   Simmons **21**:281
Davies, Hugh Sykes **4**:337
Davies, Peter Maxwell
   Brown **6**:73
   Josipovici **8**:157, 158
d'Avignon, Sue **13**:78
Davis, Bette **1**:383
Davis, Christopher **20**:103-18

Davis, Dale **12**:353
Davis, George **1**:314
Davis, John **2**:296
Davis, Madeline Pugh **7**:194
Davis, Miles **25**:222-23
Davis, Ossie **13**:251
Davis, William **2**:335
Davison, Jane Truslow **6**:87
Davison, Peter **4**:127-42
   Ford **21**:35
   Stevenson **9**:287
Davison, Peter, Books **4**:141
"Dawn" **26**:328
*Dawn and the Darkest Hour: A Study of
   Aldous Huxley* **6**:325-26
Dawson, Mitchell **11**:110, 111
Dawson, William **23**:231
Day After, The **4**:360
"Day and Night" **8**:220, 233
Day, Dorothy **1**:58
"Day for Anne Frank, A" **26**:326
*Day I Stopped Dreaming about Barbara
   Steele, The* **7**:16
Day in San Francisco, A **26**:56, 59
Day Lewis, C.
   Allen **6**:18
   Fuller **10**:117, 122-24, 126
   Jennings **5**:113
   Silkin **5**:261, 263
Day the Bookies Wept, The **5**:54-55,
   67
*Day They Came to Arrest the Book,
   The* **6**:174
Dayton, Ohio **3**:165
DC Books **14**:133-34
de Angulo, Jaime **14**:108-09, 110
de Bosis, Adolfo **12**:284-85
de Burgos, Julia **17**:12-13
de Camp, L. Sprague **19**:367
de Chardin, Pierre Tielhard **15**:243
De Chepén a La Habana (From
   Chepén to Havana) **12**:103
De Chroustchoff, Boris **4**:338
De Cuevas, Marquis **1**:86
de Gaulle, Charles **12**:87
De Hartog, Jan **1**:40
de Kooning, Willem **6**:112-13
de la Iglesia, Maria Elena **6**:92
de La Mare, Walter **5**:146
de Laguna, Grace **12**:331
De l'Homosexualité **14**:281
de Man, Paul **2**:442
De Paul University **17**:168-69
De Putti, Lya **2**:215, 218-20
De Quincey, Thomas **2**:383
De Saxe, Maurice **4**:341
De Valera, Eamon **9**:231
De Wet, Christian **3**:345
Dead Man over All **6**:24
"Dead Man, The" **9**:304
Dead on Time **8**:177
Deadly Honeymoon **11**:34, 38
Deadly James and Other Poems
   18:111, 115
Deafness **5**:359, 364, 373
Dear Rafe See *Mi querido Rafa*

Dear Shadows **4**:319

Dearden, John F., Cardinal **1**:246, 248

Death and Life of Harry Goth, The **6**:210

Death and the Visiting Firemen **8**:168-69

Death at the President's Lodging **3**:353, 354

Death Claims **17**:70

Death in April **7**:50

Death in Captivity **15**:194

Death in the Afternoon **1**:212

Death in the Quadrangle **3**:59

Death Is for Losers **16**:216

Death of a Fat God **8**:168, 171

Death of a Faun **18**:305

Death of a Salesman **9**:244

"Death of a Teddy Bear" **3**:111

"Death of Seneca, The" **15**:233

Death of the Fox **5**:76, 80

Death of the Novel and Other Stories, The
　Klinkowitz **9**:113
　Sukenick **8**:291

Death of William Posters, The **2**:386

Death on the Ice **15**:250

Death Pulls a Doublecross **11**:32

DeBolt, Joseph Wayne **8**:1

Debs, Eugene V. **3**:370

Decade of Hispanic Literature, A **24**:16

Decadence **7**:236

Decadence and Renewal in the Higher Learning **9**:99, 102

Decameron **8**:281

Deceptive Clarity, A **18**:103-04

Decker, Bill **1**:77

Decker, Clarence R. **2**:90, 93

Decline of the West, The **4**:105-06

Deconstruction **26**:24-25

Dee, Ruby
　Killens **2**:295
　Rodgers **13**:251

Deemer, Bill **5**:164

Deep Rivers **23**:208

Deer and the Dachshund **14**:112

Deerfield Academy **2**:410

Defoe, Daniel
　Allen **6**:15
　Wallace **1**:395

Deformity Lover and Other Poems **13**:228

Deguy, Michel **6**:145, 147

Deitch, Donna **18**:320-21, 322

del Rey, Judy-Lynn Benjamin **12**:220

del Rey, Lester
　Knight **10**:212-13, 215, 216, 217
　Malzberg **4**:209
　Niven **12**:217
　Pohl **1**:285

Delacorte, George T. **13**:263-64, 267, 274

Delacroix, Eugène **26**:161

Delaney, Beauford **2**:139

Delano, Poli **20**:330

Delany, Samuel R. **1**:295

Delattre, Pierre **26**:73, 81

Delbanco, Nicholas 2:149-64
　Becker **1**:40, 43
　Elman **3**:74, 81
　Mathews **6**:249

Delegation of American Veteran Writers **21**:97-98

Delgado, Abelardo B. 15:165-79

Delgado Junior College **21**:191

Delights of Turkey, The **14**:281

Delineator **7**:91

Dell Publishing Co.
　Gunn **2**:248
　Swanberg **13**:263-64, 274
　Williams **3**:415

Delos **8**:311

Delta **14**:132-33

Delta Canada **14**:133

Delta Return **12**:20, 21, 25-26, 33-34, 36

Deluxe Daring **24**:139

DeMarinis, Rick 24:107-24

DeMenil, Dominique **16**:83

DeMenil, John **16**:83

Dementations on Shank's Mare **12**:355

Demetrio, Francisco **9**:167

deMille, Cecil B. **4**:146

Deming, Barbara
　Blais **4**:74-76, 78
　Dworkin **21**:17

Democratic party **1**:291

Demoiselles d'Avignon **11**:194

Demonstration, The **4**:98, 100

Dempsey, Jerry **2**:412

Dempwolff, Otto **9**:162

Denby, Edwin **17**:276-77, 278, 288-89

Deneau, Denis **23**:176-77

Deng Xao-Ping **2**:28

Denison University **3**:22-23, 24

Denmark **2**:35-36

Dennison, George 6:105-22
　Enslin **3**:97

Dent, Tom **21**:203, 204, 206, 219-20, 238

Denton Welch **13**:207

Deora, Sharad **14**:92

Deoxyribonucleic acid **24**:212

DePauw University **3**:403, 404

Depression, 1894 **3**:398

Depression, 1924 **4**:334

Depression, The
　Banks **15**:35
　Barrio **15**:111
　Belitt **4**:60
　Booth **5**:37
　Bourjaily **1**:65
　Brewster **15**:149
　Brown **6**:52
　Bullins **16**:61-62
　Caldwell **1**:148
　Cassill **1**:163
　Ciardi **2**:87
　Corcoran **2**:116
　Corman **2**:130

DeMarinis **24**:121-22

Dennison **6**:105, 108-09

Elman **3**:70

Fisher **10**:79

Fuchs **5**:64

Ghiselin **10**:131

Giovanni **6**:160

Greeley **7**:39

Grumbach **2**:204

Gunn **2**:234, 240

Hahn **11**:112-13

Hall, Donald **7**:56

Hall, James B. **12**:111-12, 115

Harris **3**:125

Heyen **9**:34

Higgins **5**:94

Honig **8**:107

Howes **3**:139

Ignatow **3**:154-57

Katz **9**:55-62

Kazin **7**:88, 91

Kennedy **9**:73

Kinsella **7**:98

Kirk **9**:94

Kizer **5**:150

Knebel **3**:169-70, 177

Livesay **8**:220, 232-34

Madgett **23**:195

Morgan **3**:231, 234, 235, 236

Nichols **2**:308-09

Olson **12**:229

Petesch **12**:239, 241, 242, 249

Piercy **1**:267

Plymell **11**:276

Pohl **1**:285

Rakosi **5**:207, 208

Rechy **4**:254, 256

Rimmer **10**:284

Roditi **14**:249-50

Rosenthal **6**:276, 278

St. Clair **8**:272

Salisbury **15**:321

Schevill **12**:267

Settle **1**:308, 309

Sisson **3**:297

Solotaroff **2**:391

Sparshott **15**:349

Stafford **3**:330-31

Stegner **9**:263-64

Stone **3**:369

Swanberg **13**:261-64

Sward **13**:282

Vivante **12**:281

Wallace **1**:374

Weiss **2**:428

Westlake **13**:333

Whittemore **8**:299, 301

Wilhelm **5**:304

Williams **3**:418, 422

Wilson **5**:339

Wright **5**:362

Depth of Field **9**:40, 42

Depths of Glory **3**:379

Depuis Novalis (From Novalis) **13**:187-88, 190

Der Nister (pseudonym of Pinchas
    Kahanovitch) **4**:360
Dérobade, La **6**:248
Derstine, Clayton **2**:138, 139
Desai, Morarji **9**:233
Descend Again **6**:80, 92, 95
Deschamps, Eustache **9**:62-63
Deschanel, Caleb **3**:410
Desert Country **1**:150
Desert Hearts **18**:321, 322
"Desert in Bloom, The" **22**:187-88
Desert Legion **1**:383
Désert Mauve, Le See *Mauve Desert*
Desert of the Heart **18**:313-14
Deserters, The **2**:381
Design for a House **22**:66
Desire **26**:21
Destroyed Works **24**:25
Detection Club
    Gilbert **15**:194-95
    Symons **3**:391
*Detective Fiction: Crime and
    Compromise* **11**:19
Detours from the Grand Tour **12**:207
Detroit, Mich.
    Federman **8**:72-74
    Jones **20**:203-217
    Piercy **1**:267, 270
Deutsch, André **25**:312-13
Deutsch, André (publishers) **4**:103
Deutsch, Babette
    Abse **1**:25
    Federman **8**:76
Deutsch-jüdischer Parnass **7**:81
Deux Megots, Les, New York City
    10:6
*Development of Modern Indonesian
    Poetry, The* **9**:215
"Devil Catchers, The" **16**:67
Devil in a Forest, The **9**:311
Devil in the Flesh **1**:116
Devil's Picture Book, The **15**:226
Devils' Wine **2**:59
Devine, George **4**:30
Devins Award **22**:66
DeVoto, Bernard **9**:265, 266, 267,
    268, 269
Dewey, John **2**:135
Dexter, John **3**:113
Deyá, Mallorca **1**:368
D.H. Lawrence Creative Writing
    Fellowship
    McCord **9**:184
    Wilson **5**:351
Dhalgren **1**:295
Dhara, Haradhon See Roy, Debi
Di Marino, John **24**:130
di Suvero, Victor **26**:65-84
Diabetes
    Kinsella **7**:106
    Smith **7**:164
Dial Press
    Bourjaily **1**:72, 74, 75, 76, 77,
        78, 79
    Brossard **2**:68, 73
    Disch **4**:157-58

*Dialectic of Centuries: Notes Towards a
    Theory of the New Arts, A* **8**:91
Dialogue with a Dead Man **15**:284
Dialogues on Art **14**:280
Dialogues (Stanislaw Lem) **1**:263
Diamant, Ruth Witt **1**:360
Diamond **9**:25-26
Diamond Tranquilizer, The **26**:289
Diaries and journals
    Booth **5**:33-35, 38-39, 40, 42, 48-
        50
    Gerber **20**:156-164
    Johnson **18**:227
    Kazin **7**:86, 94
    Lifshin **10**:243, 244-45, 257
    Mott **7**:120
Diary of a Good Neighbour, The **5**:122
Diary of My Travels in America **1**:40
Diary (Virginia Woolf) **10**:114, 115
Díaz, Porfirio **4**:255
Dibner, Martin **9**:83
Dick and Jane **7**:5
Dick, Kay **4**:84
Dick, Philip K.
    Malzberg **4**:210
    Silverberg **3**:276
    Spinrad **19**:329-30
Dickens, Charles
    Belitt **4**:52-54
    Busch **1**:134, 135
    Charyn **1**:179
    Gray **3**:104
    Guerard **2**:221
    Higgins **5**:91
    Keating **8**:167
    Morgan **20**:272
    Rakosi **5**:201
    Stewart **3**:350
    Symons **3**:384, 391, 392
    Van Itallie **2**:409
    Wain **4**:323
    Weiss **12**:334
    White **4**:336
Dickey, James
    Bourjaily **1**:77
    Heyen **9**:40
    Peters **8**:244, 248-49
    Taylor **7**:179
    Weiss **2**:444
Dickinson, Emily
    Hiemstra **26**:154-55
    Inez **10**:185
    Kazin **7**:88
    Kirkup **4**:189
    Livesay **8**:223-24
    Matthews **18**:271
    Salvadori **25**:374
    Sinclair **5**:276
Dickson, Gordon R.
    Anderson **2**:39, 40
    Knight **10**:213
    Niven **12**:217
*Dicky Bird Was Singing: Men, Women,
    and Black Gold, The* **2**:170
Dictionary of Afro-American Slang
    6:185

Dictionary of Philippine Biography
    9:161, 163-64, 168
Did Christ Make Love? **2**:70, 71
Didion, Joan **6**:87
Diebenkorn, Richard **11**:361
Diebold, John **1**:293
Dies Committee **2**:91
Dietrich, Marlene **1**:38
Diggers **5**:165
Digging In **15**:157
Dike, Donald
    Allen **11**:11
    Elman **3**:73
    Phillips **13**:199
Dilemma **3**:73
Dillard, Annie **4**:123
Dillard, R.H.W. **7**:1-20
    Garrett **5**:80
    Taylor **7**:179, 181-82, 183, 185
Dillon, Eilís **3**:49-67
Dine, Jim **14**:173
Ding, Zuxin **9**:219
Dinner Party (Judy Chicago) **24**:129-
    30
Diop, Cheikh Anta **21**:245-46
DiPrima, Diane
    Wakoski **1**:364
    Waldman **17**:282-83
Dirty Books for Little Folks **2**:71
Dirty Hands **2**:411
Disch, Thomas M. **4**:143-58
Disciples of Christ **22**:91-92, 93
discovery **1**:70, 71, 72, 73
Discrimination
    Dove **19**:99
    Houston **16**:179, 181
    Madgett **23**:194
*Disembodied Poetics: Annals of the Jack
    Kerouac School* **17**:291
Disinherited, The **18**:82-83
*Dismemberment of Orpheus: Toward a
    Postmodern Literature, The*
    Hassan **12**:152
    Klinkowitz **9**:120
Disney, Roy **1**:192, 193
Disney, Walt **1**:192, 193
Disney, Walt, Productions
    Condon **1**:192
    Disch **4**:157
Disraeli, Benjamin **3**:324
Divan and Other Writings **8**:119
Diversion of Angels **4**:63
Diversity of Life, The **16**:306
Divided Voice, A **15**:356-57, 360
Divine Comedy
    Anaya **4**:17
    Jones **5**:118
    Niven **12**:222
Divine Disobedience **2**:198
Divorce
    Adcock **23**:8-9
    Salvadori **25**:370
Dixiana Moon **19**:130
Dixon, F.W. **21**:102
Dixon, Paige (pseudonym of Barbara
    Corcoran) **2**:121

Dixon, Roland **9**:157
Dixon, Stephen **9**:120
Djargarov, Gerogi **26**:144-45
"Djerassi" **25**:266
Djerassi, Carl 26:85-107
Dk: Some Letters of Ezra Pound
     14:130
DNA See Deoxyribonucleic acid
Do, Lord, Remember Me **5**:80
Dobie, J. Frank **2**:170
Dobrée, Bonamy **10**:113-19
Dobrée, Valentine **10**:113-17
"Doby's Gone" **6**:256
"Doctor Christian" (radio program)
     2:118, 119
Doctor Cobb's Game **1**:173
"Doctor Dolittle" series **2**:310
Doctor Faustus
     Fisher **10**:93
     Menashe **11**:227
     Rimmer **10**:285-86
     Turner **10**:318
Doctor Giovanni **12**:300
Doctor Golf **19**:129
Doctor Zhivago **11**:376
Doctorow, E.L.
     Bourjaily **1**:75, 77
     Nolan **16**:216
     Sukenick **8**:294
     Williams **3**:427
Doctors **10**:253
Dodds, John **6**:57
Dodge, Abigail **2**:122
Does This School Have Capital
     Punishment? **6**:170
Dog It Was That Died, The **8**:171
Dog Tags **1**:40
"Dog, The" **26**:323
Dogs
     Eaton **20**:134
     Kelly **22**:113
     Wolff **22**:294-95
Dogs and Other Dark Woods, The
     5:163
Dogs of March, The **24**:250, 254
Doherty, Neil **10**:296-97
Doherty, Tom **12**:218-19
Dollfuss, Engelbert **4**:195
Dollmaker, The **15**:283, 287
Dollmaker's Ghost, The **23**:192
Doll's House, The **4**:75
Dolphins of Altair, The **8**:274, 275
Domínguez Cuevas, Martha **13**:84
Dominican-American Institute **1**:157
Dominican Republic **2**:227
Don Giovanni **10**:158
Don Juan: A Yaqui Way of
     Knowledge **2**:272
"Don Lane Show, The" **2**:175
Don Quixote **23**:39
Donadio, Candida
     Baumbach **5**:26
     Cassill **1**:171
     Markfield **3**:219-20, 221, 222,
         223, 225, 226
     Raffel **9**:213, 214

Donald, Roger **6**:92
Donen, Stanley **1**:196
Donham, Wallace Brett **10**:287
Donne, John
     Ackerman **20**:8
     Forbes **16**:108-09
     Forrest **7**:23
     Mano **6**:213
Donnellys, The **15**:307
Donoso, José **3**:428
Donovan, Hedley **13**:270-72
Don't Be Forlorn **2**:327
Don't Call Me by My Right Name
     1:300
Doolittle, Hilda **24**:272
"Door Swings Wide, The" **4**:59
Doria, Charles **8**:92
Dorn, Edward
     Clark **22**:14, 16
     Creeley **10**:69
     Raworth **11**:299, 300, 302, 306
     Wakoski **1**:364
     Wilson **5**:349
Dorotea, La **8**:119
Dorr, Frederick **7**:77-78
Dorr, Virginia **7**:77-78
Dorsey, Thomas A. **7**:26
Dorson, Richard M. **9**:166, 168
Dorůžka, P.L. **1**:339
Dos Passos, John
     Brown **6**:48
     Burke **19**:72
     Manfred **18**:258-59
     Whittemore **8**:310
Dostoevsky, Feodor
     Disch **4**:148
     Guerard **2**:221
     Ouellette **13**:181
     Symons **3**:389
Double Image, The **19**:231, 234
Double Legacy, The **23**:119
Double or Nothing **8**:71, 79-80
Double Shadow, A **10**:318
"Double-Timer, The" **4**:149, 151
Double View, The **2**:68-69, 70
Double Vision **24**:226, 228, 229, 230,
     233, 234
Doubleday & Co. (publishers)
     Bowles **1**:88
     Grumbach **2**:210
     Knebel **3**:181, 182
     Silverberg **3**:279
     Slavitt **3**:322-23, 324
     Wakoski **1**:365
     Wallace **1**:389
Douglas, Ellen **12**:38
Douglas, Norman **12**:341
Douglass, Frederick **2**:291, 297
Doukhobors, The **6**:323
Dove, Rita 19:97-115
Dowling College of Long Island
     1:368
Down and In **8**:294
Down at the Santa Fe Depot: Twenty
     Fresno Poets **2**:272
Down Beat **6**:168

Down from the Hill **2**:387-88
Down Here in the Dream Quarter
     4:215
Down in My Heart **3**:333
Downes, Juanita Mae **6**:212
Downward to the Earth **3**:281, 283
Doyle, Arthur Conan
     Keating **8**:164
     Symons **3**:392
Doyle Dane Bernbach **4**:150
Doyle, Kirby **24**:96
Dozois, Gardner **20**:86, 87, 90, 91-
     93, 94-95
"Dr. Geechee and the Blood
     Junkies" **16**:67
Drabble, Margaret **1**:43
Dragons at the Gate **2**:173
Dragon's Island **8**:324
Drake, St. Clair **7**:29
Drama See Theater
Dream and Reality **2**:192
Dream Flights **7**:164
Dream like Mine, A **22**:117-18, 118-
     19
Dream of Love, A **3**:85
Dream Tees **26**:147-48, 155-56, 157
Dreambook of Our Time, A **9**:129
Dreamers, The **2**:258
Dreaming: Hard Luck and Good Times
     in America **22**:214, 220, 230
Dreaming of Heroes **5**:233
Dreams
     Hadas **23**:120-21
     Villanueva **24**:299, 300, 315, 317,
         319
Dreams, Memories, Reflections **26**:156
Drei shwester **9**:57
Dreiser, Theodore
     Eastlake **1**:201
     Kazin **7**:91
     Kherdian **2**:265
     Swanberg **13**:259-60
Dresner, Hal **11**:32-33
Dresser, Paul **14**:127
Drew, Maurice **1**:309
Drew University **25**:82-83, 93
Driving under the Cardboard Pines
     21:130
Drowned Man to the Fish, The **8**:247
Druce, Robert **2**:51-52, 54
Drug use
     Armantrout **25**:16-17
     Berry **24**:63, 66, 67
     Brunner **8**:13-14
     Clark **22**:15
     Corn **25**:137, 138, 139
     Heinemann **21**:86, 89
     Knebel **3**:173
     Leftwich **25**:268-69
     Plymell **11**:280, 282-83, 284-85,
         287
     Polkinhorn **25**:328
     St. Clair **8**:279
     Taylor **26**:258
     Van Itallie **2**:417, 420

Van Proyen **25**:386, 388, 394-95, 400
  Williams **3**:414
  See also Substance abuse
Dry Sun, Dry Wind **3**:404
Du Bois, W.E.B.
  Emanuel **18**:133
  Killens **2**:297, 300, 302
Du Bos, Charles **17**:177
Du Roi, Denyse **24**:23
Dublin, Ireland **12**:79-80
Dublin Magazine **4**:305
Dubliners
  Dillard **7**:14
  Solotaroff **2**:394
Ducasse, Isidore Lucien See
    Lautréamont, Le Comte de
Duchamp, Marcel **1**:99, 114, 120
Dudek, Louis 14:121-42
  Souster **14**:310, 312, 313, 314-15
Dudow, Zlatan **14**:254-55
Duff Cooper Memorial Prize **10**:122
Duffus, R.L. **3**:370
Duffy, Charles J. **5**:203
Dugan, Alan **3**:414
Duhamel, Marcel **1**:156
Duino Elegies **13**:181
Duke University
  Chappell **4**:113-18
  Clarke **16**:84
  Eaton **20**:122-23
  Kirk **9**:95
  Rimmer **10**:290
Dumas, Alexandre **2**:373
Dumas, Henry **4**:243, 244
Dunbar, Paul Laurence **2**:284
Duncan, Raymond **5**:317-18
Duncan, Robert
  Berry **24**:79
  Bromige **26**:41
  Broughton **12**:49, 52
  Creeley **10**:69
  di Suvero **26**:70
  Eigner **23**:44, 52
  Foley **24**:163, 169
  Kelly **19**:191-92
  Kyger **16**:190
  Levertov **19**:241-42
  Meltzer **26**:194
  Menefee **26**:207
  Rakosi **5**:208
  Saroyan **5**:216
  Turnbull **14**:336
  Waldman **17**:275
  Weiss **2**:442-43
  Williams **12**:349
  Wilson **5**:349
Duncan, Robert L. 2:165-78
Duncan, Todd **20**:215, 217
Duncan, Wanda Scott **2**:169, 170, 171, 173, 174, 175-77
Dundee University **9**:285
Dundy, Elaine **4**:30
Dunford, Judith **7**:95
Dunn, Joe **16**:190-91
Dunn, Stephen **22**:71

Dupee, Fred **2**:447
DuPont Fellowship **7**:11
Duquesne University **11**:144-46
Durant, Will **9**:80
Durczak, Jerzy **6**:200, 201-02
Durham University **4**:183
Dutchman **16**:85
Dutton, G.F. **9**:285
Dvořák, Antonín **1**:350
Dworkin, Andrea 21:1-21
Dye, Alan **10**:8-9
Dyer, George **23**:175
Dying Inside **3**:282
Dykeman, Wilma **15**:285
Dylan, Bob
  Booth **2**:51, 53
  Kyger **16**:197-98
  Leftwich **25**:266
  Waldman **17**:283-84
Dynamite Voices 1: Black Poets of the 1960s **18**:144
Dyslexia
  Bergé **10**:10, 14
  Bruce-Novoa **18**:65, 66, 69
  Horwood **15**:251
Dystel, Oscar **1**:295

Eagle on the Coin, The **1**:167
Ear of the Dragon, An **3**:265
Earlham College **5**:44, 45
East & West **6**:181
East Coast **15**:155
East End My Cradle **7**:236
East Side Review, The **1**:365
East-West **13**:315
Eastern Michigan University
  Eshleman **6**:147
  Madgett **23**:207, 209
Eastern New Mexico University **8**:325, 326
Eastlake, William 1:201-14
Eastman, Arthur **9**:82
Eastman, Max **2**:159
Eastman, Richard **5**:162
Easton, Jane Faust **14**:143-60
Easton, Robert 14:143-60
"Eaten Heart, The" **14**:126
Eaton, Charles Edward 20:119-149
Eaton, Greg **24**:63-64
Eberhart, Richard
  Major **6**:190
  Malanga **17**:97
  Weiss **2**:445
Eberstadt, Frederick **20**:224-25
Eberstadt, Isabel **20**:224-25
Ebony **13**:237
Ecco Press **4**:250
"Echo and Narcissus" **4**:150
Echo Round His Bones **4**:151
Economic Development: Concept and Strategy **3**:246
Economic Development of Kenya, The **3**:243
Economic Interdependence in Southeast Asia **3**:245

Economic Report of the President **3**:243
Economics **3**:235, 236-39, 241, 245-46
Economou, George
  Kelly **19**:191, 198, 199-200
  Owens **2**:362-63, 366, 368
  Wakoski **1**:364
Écrire en notre temps (To write in our time) **13**:189
Eddy **25**:74
Edel, Leon **3**:414
Edelman, Lou **1**:383
Eden **1**:260, 264
Eden, Vivian **13**:141-59
Edgar Allan Poe Special Award **16**:217
Edge Effect: Trails and Portrayals **23**:215, 233
Edinburgh Academy
  Caute **4**:96
  Stewart **3**:347-50
Edinburgh University
  Brown **6**:70-71
  Glover **23**:89
Editions de Minuit (publishers) **4**:357
Editions du Sagittaire **14**:254, 256
Editors' Book Award **20**:174
Edsel **6**:305-07
Education **26**:137-38
Education in Blood, An **3**:75, 76, 83
Education of Henry Adams, The **8**:299
Edward Waters College **2**:282
Edwards, George **23**:118, 127
Edwards, Harry Stillwell **5**:84
Edwards, James Keith **5**:335-36
Edwards, Oliver **3**:41
Eggan, Fred **9**:165, 166, 168
Egypt
  El Saadawi **11**:61-71
  Hassan **12**:136, 138, 139-40
  Josipovici **8**:149-54
  Waldman **17**:274
Egyptian Hieroglyphics **21**:268, 269
Eight Great Hebrew Short Novels **20**:252
"Eight Lines by Jalal-ud-Din Rumi" **23**:311
Eight Million Ways to Die **11**:38
Eight Modern Writers **3**:355
Eight Oxford Poets **5**:365
18/81 **26**:224
Eighteen Texts: Writings by Contemporary Greek Authors **15**:75, 94
Eigner, Beverly **23**:19, 49-57
Eigner, Larry 23:19-62
  Corman **2**:136
  Ferrini **24**:140
  Foley **24**:160, 178, 179
Eigner, Richard **23**:19, 20, 24, 27, 49-57, 60
Einstein, Albert
  Bell **12**:29, 30
  Booth **5**:45
  Dillard **7**:7

Lem **1**:264
　Wallace **1**:391, 401
　Wilson **5**:314
Eisenhard, John **2**:429, 431 32
Eisenhower, Dwight
　Brée **15**:141
　Connell **2**:107
　Kennedy **9**:80
　Swanberg **13**:269-70
E.J. Pratt Award **15**:155
Ekwensi, Cyprian **3**:427, 428
El Crepusculo **14**:111
El gato tuerto **25**:112
El Saadawi, Nawal 11:61-72
El Salvador
　Alegría **15**:1-3, 12
　Hongo **22**:80
El tiempo es una mujer que espera
　25:111
Elan Vital **24**:74
Elbert, Joyce **10**:8-9
Elberta peaches **23**:183
Elder, Joe **18**:341-42
Electronic Arts (publishers) **4**:157,
　158
Electronic Poetry Center **24**:48-49
Elegies for the Hot Season **23**:222,
　223, 226
Eliot, George **5**:42
Eliot, T.S.
　Abse **1**:21, 27, 29
　Allen **6**:17, 20
　Bell **12**:33
　Brown **6**:74
　Bryant **26**:58
　Davie **3**:46
　Fuller **10**:113, 118
　Gregor **10**:148, 149
　Hamburger **4**:160, 167, 168
　Harwood **19**:140
　Heath-Stubbs **21**:63, 66, 67, 68
　Hebert **24**:250
　Higgins **5**:92
　Hudgins **21**:117
　Jennings **5**:113
　Jerome **8**:130, 131
　Levertov **19**:231-32
　Mathews **6**:230, 231
　Nichols **2**:318
　Raffel **9**:219
　Roditi **14**:246, 253
　Rowse **8**:258-59, 260-61
　Shapiro **6**:303
　Simmons **21**:280-81, 290
　Simpson **4**:291
　Sisson **3**:301
　Symons **3**:385
　Valaoritis **26**:278-79
　Weiss **2**:440
　Whittemore **8**:303, 308
　Wilson **5**:315, 319
Elizabeth Janeway Prize **6**:90
Elkin, Stanley **25**:204
Elkins, Aaron 18:93-107
Elkins, Charlotte **18**:98, 99, 101,
　102, 103, 106, 107

Ella Price's Journal **26**:52, 56, 57,
　60
Elle **2**:194
Elledge, Liane **8**:306
Elledge, Scott **8**:306
"Ellen West" **4**:248
Ellenbogen, Jesse **3**:210
Ellenborough, Jane **1**:397
Ellington, Edward Duke **6**:168
Elliott, George P. **10**:38
Ellison, Harlan
　Bishop **26**:18
　Bova **18**:53-54, 56
　Disch **4**:150
　Malzberg **4**:209
　Niven **12**:217
　Pohl **1**:285
　Spinrad **19**:319-20
　Wolfe **9**:305, 308
　Zebrowski **19**:368, 369, 375
Ellison, Ralph
　Bennett **13**:84
　Bourjaily **1**:76
　Emanuel **18**:138-39
　Forrest **7**:23, 31-32, 33
　Johnson **18**:242-43
　Major **6**:186
　Weiss **2**:441-42
　Williams **3**:414
Ellsberg, Daniel **22**:12
Elman, Richard 3:69-84
Elmer Gantry **5**:49
"Elric" series **5**:177, 179
Elson, James **11**:10
Eluard, Paul
　Barnstone **15**:69
　Jones **5**:120
Elves', Gnomes', and Little Men's
　Science Fiction, Chowder, and
　Marching Society **2**:42
Elvin, Lionel **9**:273-74, 281
Elvin, Mark **9**:281, 282, 283, 284-85
Elytis, Odysseus **26**:270, 281, 282
Emanuel, James A. 18:109-66
Embassy **3**:29
Emergency Exit **6**:193
Emerson College **16**:116
Emerson, Ralph Waldo
　Allen **11**:7
　Broughton **12**:50
　Heyen **9**:46
Emery, Louise **6**:115
Emigration and emigré life
　Mrozek **10**:272-77
　Pellegrini **11**:262-63, 264-65, 272-
　　74
　Zinoviev **10**:335-38
Emily Dickinson, Woman of Letters
　22:247-48
Emma Instigated Me **2**:358, 365
Emmerich, Albert **12**:273, 276
Emöke **1**:345
Emory and Henry College **15**:288
Emory at Oxford **20**:275-76
Emory University
　Cassity **8**:56, 59-60

Corn **25**:133
　Mott **7**:130, 131, 132
Emotional Arithmetic **18**:89-90
Empanada Brotherhood, The **2**:329
Emperor of Midnight **14**:282
Empire State College **2**:211
Empires in the Dust **3**:277
Empirical Argument for God, The
　10:287
Empson, William
　West **7**:276
　Woodcock **6**:319
Empty Bed, The **23**:123
Empty Mirror **5**:213
"Empty Words" **26**:79
Emshwiller, Carol **10**:213, 223
En la nuit, la mer (In the night, the
　sea) **13**:189
En México **14**:138
Encephalitis **24**:17-18
Enchanted Echo, The **17**:202
Encounter **7**:180
Encounter at Shaky Bridge **7**:148
Encyclopaedia Britannica **2**:358
End of an Epoch, The **8**:257
End of Intelligent Writing, The **8**:184,
　185
End of My Life, The **1**:69, 70, 73
End of the Dreams, The **2**:258
End of the Nylon Age, The **1**:342
Endless Race **8**:103
Endless Short Story, The **8**:294
Endo, Toshikatsu **26**:180
Ends of the Earth, The **26**:34-35
Enemies of the Permanent Things:
　Observations of Abnormity in
　Literature and Politics **9**:102
Enemy, The **3**:385
Enfer, L' **5**:320
Engelson, Joyce **2**:68
Engineer of Human Souls, An **1**:333,
　349
Engines of the Night, The **4**:215
England
　Adcock **23**:3, 6, 7, 11, 14
　Aldiss **2**:21
　Anthony **18**:13-15
　Blotner **25**:87
　Cassity **8**:40, 55
　Clark **22**:12-15
　Harwood **19**:136-44
　Hine **15**:226-27
　Houston **16**:181-84
　Kirkup **4**:175-77
　Moorcock **5**:187
　Morgan **3**:228, 239-40
　Oakes **25**:301-18
　Settle **1**:320
　Sinclair **5**:271
　Singh **9**:226-27, 230
　Turco **22**:247
　Turner **10**:321
　Wellek **7**:215, 223-24
　White **4**:347
"England" (Donald Davie) **3**:44, 45
Engle, Huah Ling

Corman **2**:145

Mahapatra **9**:147

Engle, Paul

Blaise **3**:26

Bourjaily **1**:72, 74

Cassill **1**:164, 167, 172

Hall **12**:131-32

Mahapatra **9**:146, 147

Stafford **3**:334

English, Isobel **4**:84

English Language Notes **22**:65

English Novel, The **6**:24

English Poetry, 1900–1950 **3**:304

Enigma & Variations: Paradise Is Persian for Park **24**:28

Enough of Green **9**:285

Enquiry into Goodness and Related Concepts, An **15**:359-60

Enslin, Theodore **3**:85-99

Arnold **25**:40-41

Dennison **6**:119

Koller **5**:168

McCord **9**:186, 187

Rosenblum **11**:348

Thayler **11**:364

Wilson **5**:350

Entertaining Angels **15**:161

Environmentalism **9**:268-69

Epiphanies **8**:188-89, 194

Episcopal Church

Boyd **11**:45-46, 47-48, 49, 51, 54, 59

Mano **6**:214

Episcopalianism **5**:145-46

Epitaph for Kings **4**:231

"Epithalamium and Shivaree" **23**:266

Epoch **7**:142-43

Epstein, Helen **9**:33-34

Epstein, Jason **6**:119

Epstein, Julius J. **12**:60, 61, 67, 68, 72, 75

Epstein, Leslie **12**:59-76

Epstein, Philip G. **12**:60, 61, 62, 67, 75

Eray, Nazli **9**:147

Erhard, Werner **6**:249

Erhardt, Warren **9**:242

Erika: Poems of the Holocaust **9**:34, 43-44

Erikson, Erik H. **23**:150

Ernsberger, George **19**:331

Ernst, Max

Dann **20**:93

Joans **25**:230-31

Wakoski **1**:363

Ernst, Morris **1**:389

Errand into the Maze **4**:63

Erskine, Chester **1**:383

Erskine College **1**:143, 145

Escape Artist, The **3**:410-11

Escape into You, The **14**:50

Escurial **2**:411

Eshleman, Clayton **6**:123-50

Corman **2**:144

Owens **2**:363

Espeland, Pamela **23**:260, 262

Espey, John **22**:223, 227, 228, 229, 230, 231

Espionage of the Saints, The **4**:109

Espiritu Santo, New Hebrides **1**:165-66

Espousal in August **11**:218

Esquire

Condon **1**:191

Mano **6**:215

Ostriker **24**:271

Solotaroff **2**:399-400

Wakefield **7**:197

Essai **1**:208

"Essay on Psychiatrists" **4**:246

Essay on Rime **6**:298-99

Essay on the Principle of Population, An **18**:38

Essays (Montaigne) **3**:353

Essential Horace, The **9**:219

Essential Writings of Karl Marx **4**:105

Essex Poems **3**:43, 44

Esslin, Martin **4**:31

Estampas del valle y otras obras **16**:141, 143, 151

E.T. **1**:292

Ethics **5**:99-100

Ethics and Language **9**:277

"Ethics of Our Fathers" **9**:69

Ethier-Blais, Jean **4**:74

Ethiopia

Samarakis **16**:267-68

Williams **3**:426

Ethnic discrimination **4**:257

Eton **5**:268, 269

"Eucalyptus" **26**:221

Eugene, Oreg. **14**:169-70

Eugene Saxton Fellowship **2**:108

Euripides

Highwater **7**:80

Taylor **7**:186

Europe

Brossard **2**:72-73, 74

Kherdian **2**:266-67

Nichols **2**:327

Shreve **5**:235

Europe (Louis Dudek) **14**:137, 138

Eustace Chisholm and the Works **1**:303

Euthanasia **6**:170-71

"Evan Tanner" series **11**:34

Evangelism **20**:269

Evans, Amy **24**:77, 80

Evans, Dierdre **26**:301

Evans, Luther **9**:231, 232

Evans, Paul **19**:148, 149-50, 151-52

Evening Performance, An **5**:80

Evening Standard **11**:115-16

Evening with Saroyan, An **2**:270

Evening's Frost, An **7**:65

Events and Wisdoms **3**:40

Everglades, Fla. **11**:316

Evergreen Review **4**:260

Everleigh, Aida **1**:395

Everleigh, Mina **1**:395

Everson, William

Broughton **12**:52

di Suvero **26**:70, 71

Kherdian **2**:269, 272

Every Changing Shape **5**:113, 114

Everyman for Himself **3**:408

everyone has sher favorite (his and hers) **8**:92

Ewbank, Thomas **4**:334

Exactly What We Want **25**:310

Exagggerations of Peter Prince, The **14**:173-74

Exchange Rate Policy **3**:245

"Excrescence, An" **26**:32

Exécution, L' **4**:77

Exhaustive Parallel Intervals **8**:187

Exhibitionist, The **3**:320-21

Exile **25**:109-10, 112

Exile, An (Madison Jones) **11**:182

Exiles and Marriages (Donald Hall) **7**:64

Exiles (Jack Foley) **24**:159, 161

Exiles, The (Albert J. Guerard) **2**:227, 228

Existentialism

Mott **7**:119

Rodgers **13**:253

Expansive Poetry: Essays on the New Narrative and the New Formalism **11**:84

Expansive Poetry movement

Allen **11**:22

Feirstein **11**:83, 84

Experiment at Proto **25**:312

Experiments in Modern Art **15**:118

Explanation of America, An **4**:249

Explorations: A Series of Talks and Articles, 1966–1981 **16**:127-28

Exploring Poetry **6**:280

Expo-See **25**:398

Expressionism (artistic movement) **20**:93

Extending the Territory **5**:114

Extending upon the Kingdom **2**:57

Extension **2**:117

Extracts from Pelican Bay **24**:28

Extremities **25**:22

Eybers, Elisabeth **8**:54

Eyes

Burroway **6**:95, 96

Picano **13**:225-26

Eyes Have It, The **26**:297

Eysselinck, Walter **6**:93-94, 95, 96, 99

Ezekiel, Nissim **9**:145

"Ezra" **22**:178-79

fabelhafte Geträume von Taifun-Willi, Die **8**:92

Faber & Faber (publishers)

Aldiss **2**:22

Burroway **6**:92

Gray **3**:110

Sinclair **5**:270

Faber Book of Twentieth-Century Verse, The **21**:68

Fabilli, Mary **26**:70

Fable **2**:419

Fables for Robots **1**:264

Fabulous Originals, The   1:386
Fabulous Showman, The   1:384, 387-88
Facchin, Bruno   2:139
Faces of India: A Travel Narrative 6:321
Facts in the Case of E.A. Poe, The 5:275
Fadeout   17:68, 69
Fairfax, John   5:368-69, 370, 371
Faith   22:105-06
Faith and the Good Thing   18:239
Faiz, Faiz Ahmed
  Kizer   5:155
  Singh   9:225
Fall of the House of Usher, The (Gregory Sandow)   4:155
Fall of the Imam, The   11:71
Fallen Angel, The   18:184
Falling Astronauts   4:213
Falling from Stardom   22:72, 73
Falling Torch, The   14:70
Fallout   4:98-99
False Night   14:69
Faludy, George   5:292
Fame and Love in New York   21:269, 270
Families of Eden: Communes and the New Anarchism   8:137-38
Family Album, A   22:246
Family Circle, The   11:82
Family Feeling   20:358
Family History   11:74-75, 83-84
Family: The Story of Charles Manson's Dune Buggy Attack Battalion, The   21:267
Famous Writers School   17:150-51
Fan Club, The   1:384, 398
Fanaim   25:110
Fantasia   25:8
Fantastic   4:149
Fantasy Level, The   6:96
Fantasy Press Poets series   5:110
Fantasy Worlds of Peter Stone and Other Fables, The   11:54
Far and Away   22:98
Far Out   10:222
Farewell to Europe   19:224
Farewell to Manzanar: A True Story of Japanese American Experience during and after the World War II Internment
  Houston, James D.   16:165
  Houston, Jeanne Wakatsuki   16:175, 181, 185
Farley, Michael   9:285-86
Farming
  Ashby   6:35, 38, 39, 40
  Emanuel   18:116-18
  Jones   11:175
  Katz   14:164-65
  Levis   23:183-85
  Morgan, Robert   20:257-58
  Morgan, Theodore   3:229-31
Farrar, Straus (publishers)
  Brossard   2:67

Busch   1:134
  Williams   3:414-15
Farrell, George   12:245
Farrell, James T.
  Kazin   7:89-90
  Malzberg   4:210
  Phillips   13:205, 213
Farrell, J.G.   1:43
Farrer, David   9:21, 23-24
Farrow, Mia   9:251
Farwell, Joan   6:304
Fascism
  Brée   15:135-36
  Davie   3:42
  Lind   4:203-04
  Roditi   14:255-56
  Salvadori   25:346
  Vivante   12:281, 282-84, 285, 291, 295
Fast, Howard   18:167-87
Fast Speaking Woman   17:280, 284
Fatal Attraction   9:253, 254
Fate of American Poetry, The   22:75
Fathering
  Delbanco   2:156
  Feirstein   11:83
Fauchereau, Serge   6:285
Faulkner: A Biography   25:96-97
Faulkner in the University   25:96
Faulkner, Virginia   9:214
Faulkner, William
  Becker   1:35, 43
  Blaise   3:19, 25
  Blotner   25:95-96
  Brown   6:48
  Busch   1:128, 132, 137
  Charyn   1:179
  Dillard   7:11, 14
  Eastlake   1:212
  Forrest   7:23
  Garrett   5:72
  Guerard   2:221
  Higgins   5:91
  Kennedy   9:82
  Kerrigan   11:217
  Manfred   18:255-56
  Stewart   3:357
  Sukenick   8:290
  Tillinghast   23:306
  Wright   7:289, 292
Faust
  Kazin   7:88
  Wilson   5:315
Faust, Frederick
  Easton   14:147
  Nolan   16:210, 221
FBI See Federal Bureau of Investigation
Fear and Trembling   2:192
Fearing, Kenneth
  Rakosi   5:203
  Rosenthal   6:279
Feast of Icarus, The   11:153
Feathery Confession   26:289
February Plan, The   2:172, 174
Federal Art Project   10:132

Federal Bureau of Investigation
  Anderson   2:43
  Kerrigan   11:203-04
  Roditi   14:262, 263, 269, 275-77, 287
Federal Music Project
  Bowles   1:85
  Cassity   8:41
Federal Writers Project
  Brown   6:53
  Honig   8:109
  Ignatow   3:156-57, 160
  Kerrigan   11:202-03
  Rosenthal   6:276
Federation of Jewish Philanthropies 3:216
Federman, Raymond   8:63-81
  Klinkowitz   9:112, 115, 116
  Sukenick   8:291, 294
Feel Free   3:320
Feiffer, Jules   2:418
Feigl, Herbert   2:38
Feikema, Kathryn   18:245-47, 248
Feinstein, Elaine   1:215-24
Feirstein, Frederick   11:73-86
  Allen   11:22
Felipe G. Calderón   9:159
Fellini, Federico   7:9
Fellow-Travellers, The   4:107
Fellowship of Fear   18:99-101
Fellowship of Reconciliation   3:333
Female Man, The   1:295
Feminism
  Brossard   16:48-50
  Bryant   26:53
  Dworkin   21:1-21
  Ostriker   24:271-73, 275
Feminist Press   26:60
Feminist Revision and the Bible 24:273
Feminist Writers Guild   1:276
Fencepost Chronicles, The   7:107, 110
Fencing   12:144
Feng Shui   12:348
Fenton, Charles   3:314
Ferber, Herbert   6:113
Ferencz, Benjamin   1:121, 122
Ferguson, Otis   7:88, 89
Fergusson, Francis   4:244-45
Ferlinghetti, Lawrence
  Argüelles   24:25
  Berry   24:79
  Cherkovski   24:85, 91, 96
  di Suvero   26:71
  Kherdian   2:269
  Plymell   11:286, 287, 288, 289
  Sanders   21:259, 263
Fermi, Enrico   25:349, 360, 364-65
Ferrer, José   9:245
Ferrini, Vincent   24:125-51
  Leftwich   25:262, 275
  Taylor   26:253-54, 256, 257, 259, 260
Ferry, David   4:244, 248
Festival d'Avignon   2:364
Feynman, Richard P.

Sukenick **8**:288
Wallace **1**:393
Ficciones **10**:318
Fiction **10**:221
Fiction Collective (publishers)
  Baumbach **5**:26-27, 28, 29
  Major **6**:191, 193, 194, 198
  Sukenick **8**:293
Fiction-Makers, The **9**:282, 287
Fiddlehead **15**:154
Fiedler, Leslie
  Federman **8**:79, 80
  Hassan **12**:149, 157, 160
  Kerrigan **11**:210
Field **3**:339
Field, Shirley Anne **2**:385
Fields, W.C. **1**:381
*Fierce Metronome: The One-Page
    Novels* **10**:13, 14
15 x 13 **1**:169
Fifth Form at St. Dominic's, The **6**:66
Fifth Head of Cerberus, The **9**:305,
    307, 311
Fifth Sunday **19**:105
Fifty Stories (Kay Boyle) **1**:115
Fight Night on a Sweet Saturday
    1:317, 321
Fighting Indians of the West **6**:55-57
Fighting Terms **1**:364
Film
  Fuchs **5**:54-58
  Kostelanetz **8**:189, 195
Filmi, Filmi, Inspector Ghote **8**:174-75
Filmmaking
  Broughton **12**:54-56
  Malanga **17**:104-06
  Mrozek **10**:275-76
  Shadbolt **3**:258-59
  Skelton **5**:288-89
  weiss **24**:345, 347, 351
Filtrante, Jessica **24**:134
Final Orders **2**:421
Final Programme, The **5**:180
"Final Thoughts of a Dying
    Paperweight" **26**:159-60
"Finders Keepers" **26**:31, 33, 41
"Finding is the first Act . . . "
    5:276
Fine, Donald I.
  Block **11**:36, 38
  Knight **10**:214
  Silverberg **3**:285-86
Fine, Michael **5**:168
Fine Old Conflict, A **17**:141
Finer, Stephen **8**:157, 158
Finished Man, The **7**:14
Finland
  Corcoran **2**:123
  Creeley **10**:74
  Nichols **2**:314
Finley, Pearl **1**:377
Finn, Julio **21**:227
Finnegans Wake
  Argüelles **24**:5
  Jones **5**:121
  Pohl **1**:285

Finnish Academy of Sciences **10**:330
Fire and Ice **9**:265, 266
Fire Next Time, The **16**:84
Firebrand, The **10**:27
*Fireman's Wife, and Other Stories,
    The* **14**:15-16
*fires in th tempul OR th jinx ship nd
    othr trips* **19**:20, 50
Firesticks **24**:208
Firestorm **2**:174
First and Last Words **4**:125
First Baby Poems **17**:286
First Blood **13**:268
First Freedom, The **6**:167, 173
First Light **3**:410, 411
First Love **11**:376
First Man on the Sun, The **7**:7, 17
First Men in the Moon, The **3**:271
First Person in Literature, The **14**:135
First Poems **22**:233
First Statement **14**:127-28
First Street School, New York City
    6:116, 119
Fischer, Otokar **7**:212-13
Fish, Man, Control, Room **25**:74
Fish Tales **20**:197, 201, 213, 215-16,
    218
Fisher, Alfred Young **10**:132
Fisher, Roy 10:79-100
  Turnbull **14**:335
Fisher, Vardis
  Allen **6**:20
  Brown **6**:53
  Ghiselin **10**:139, 140
Fisherman's Whore, The **7**:162, 163,
    168
Fishermen with Ploughs **6**:68
Fisk University
  Giovanni **6**:159
  Killens **2**:296-98
Fitch, John **16**:213
Fitts, Dudley **3**:313, 316-17
Fitzgerald, Edward **9**:177
Fitzgerald, F. Scott
  Bausch **14**:5
  Bourjaily **1**:68, 69, 72
  Dennison **6**:110
  Glanville **9**:21
  Higgins **5**:91
FitzGerald, Garret **2**:342
Fitzgerald, Penelope 10:101-09
Fitzgerald, Robert
  Hassan **12**:149
  Tillinghast **23**:316
  Whittemore **8**:311
Five Chambered Heart **12**:18, 19, 38
Five New Brunswick Poets **15**:151,
    157
Five Poems **15**:224
Flair **1**:314
Flakoll, Darwin J. **15**:1-15
Flame of Life, The **2**:386
Flanagan, Robert 17:37-58
Flanner, Janet **1**:119, 120, 121
Flaubert: A Biography **12**:199
Flaubert, Gustave **12**:207, 208-09

Flaw, The **16**:261, 262-63
Flecker, James Elroy **2**:56
Fleming, Ian **1**:393
Fletcher, John **2**:294
Flight and Pursuit **11**:22
Flighty Horse, The **2**:317
Fling! **9**:245
"Floating Panzer, The" **4**:151
Floating Republic, The **10**:113
Florence, Italy
  Corman **2**:139
  O'Faolain **2**:351
  Salvadori **25**:346-47
  Stone **3**:373
Flores, Angel **9**:214, 215
Florida **12**:201-02
Florida State University **6**:101, 102
Florio, John **3**:353
Florry of Washington Heights **14**:179,
    180
Flow **8**:158
Flowering of New England, The **7**:92
Flowers of Darkness **18**:83-84
Flutie **24**:207
Fluxus (artistic movement)
  Bergé **10**:7-8
  Higgins **8**:87-89, 91, 92
Fly Away Home **1**:280
Flying a Red Kite **17**:79, 88-89
*Flying Camel and the Golden Hump,
    The* **13**:155
Flying Piranha **25**:247
Flynn, Robert Lopez **16**:149-50
foew&ombwhnw **8**:92, 93
Fog, The **22**:246
Fogwill, Irving **15**:243
*Foibles and Fables of an Abstract Man,
    The* **8**:118
Foiglman **13**:158
Foix, J.V. **24**:14, 19
Foley, Adelle
  Berry **24**:77-80
  Foley **24**:164, 166-68, 172, 173,
    174, 176
Foley, Jack 24:153-81
  Argüelles **24**:23, 25, 26, 27, 28
  Berry **24**:73, 77-80
  Caulfield **25**:111-12
  Cherkovski **24**:97
  Eigner **23**:19, 31-38, 40-47, 49-57
  Ferrini **24**:139-40
  Grumman **25**:192-93
  Leftwich **25**:260, 266
Foley, John **20**:71-72
Folger, Joe **9**:198
Folio **6**:131-32
Folk music
  Hoffman **10**:172
  Simmons **21**:287
Folklore **4**:27
*Folklore in English and Scottish
    Ballads* **8**:274
Folksay Theater **11**:362
Follies **2**:419
Follow the Drinking Gourd **21**:141
Fonteyn, Margot **4**:148

Foot, Michael **5**:123
Football **18**:65-66
Foote, Shelby
  Garrett **5**:72
  Tillinghast **23**:304
Footfall **12**:219, 220, 222
For a Bitter Season: New and Selected Poems **7**:181
For Love **8**:244
For Luck: Poems 1962–1977 **15**:379
"For My Mother, After Her Death" **26**:296
For the Body **23**:261
Forbes, Calvin 16:105-20
Forbidden Tower **10**:25
Ford, Cathy **7**:110
Ford, Charles Henri **17**:95, 97, 104, 116
Ford Fellowship
  Bell **12**:33
  Booth **5**:44
  Ghiselin **10**:138
  Wagoner **3**:407
Ford, Ford Madox
  Davie **3**:38
  Ghiselin **10**:133
Ford Foundation
  Lottman **12**:207
  Morgan **3**:242
  Purdy **1**:302
  Raffel **9**:210
Ford, Jesse Hill 21:23-43
  Garrett **5**:75
Foreigner **17**:228
Forensic engineering **25**:366
Foreshortenings and Other Stories **8**:186
Forest of the Night **11**:181-82
Forester, C.S. **4**:100
Forests of Lithuania, The **3**:39-40
Forever and Ever and a Wednesday **9**:66
Forever War, The **25**:199-200, 203, 208
Forked Tongue, The **9**:214
Form of Woman, A **5**:213
Forman, Miloš **1**:344
Forms (Theodore Enslin) **3**:90, 93-94
Forrest, Leon 7:21-35
Forsaken Garden, The **5**:369
Forster, E.M.
  Burroway **6**:91
  Tarn **16**:279
Fort Knox Dependent Schools **15**:281-82
Fort Ord **1**:202
Fortune Press
  White **4**:338
  Woodcock **6**:320
Fortunes of a Fool **13**:154
"Fossils, Metal, and the Blue Limit" **23**:315
Foster, Edward (Halsey) 26:109-30
Foster-Harris, William **2**:170
Foster, Henrietta **8**:159
Foster homes

Ray **7**:138
Vizenor **22**:271-72
Foster, Joanna **8**:215
Foucault, Michel **8**:79
Foundation for Research into the Origins of Mankind **26**:174
Foundation for the Arts and the Sciences **2**:439
Foundation News **9**:214, 215
Fountain in Kentucky and Other Poems, A **17**:187
Four Banks of the River of Space, The **16**:121-22
Four Portraits **7**:249, 252-53
Four Quartets **26**:58
Four Seasons, The **7**:249, 251-52
Four Springs **8**:116-17, 125
$4000 **1**:78
Four Young Lady Poets
  Bergé **10**:6
  Owens **2**:361
  Wakoski **1**:364
Fourth Angel, The **4**:263
Fourth World, The **4**:106-07
Fourth Yearbook of Short Plays, The **1**:386
Fowlie, Wallace **4**:63
Fox, George **9**:78, 79
Fox, Hugh
  Lifshin **10**:242-43, 258
  Plymell **11**:292
Fox, Paula **24**:15-16
Fox, William Price 19:117-33
Foxes of Beachy Cove, The **15**:247, 251
Foxybaby **13**:108
F.P. **3**:98
F.R. Scott Award for Poetry in Translation **5**:292
Fracture **6**:146
Fragmented Life of Don Jacobo Lerner, The **12**:91-94, 103-04
Fragments of America **19**:322
France
  Appleman **18**:34
  Barnstone **15**:65-72
  Becker **1**:35
  Boyle **1**:115-17, 118, 119, 120
  Brossard **2**:67-68
  Corn **25**:135-36
  Federman **8**:64-71
  Josipovici **8**:146, 148
  Livesay **8**:228, 230-32
  Mathews **6**:223
  Mott **7**:119
  Sillitoe **2**:381-82
  Sukenick **8**:290
  Wright **5**:369
France, Anatole **2**:218
France and England in North America **3**:44
Frances Steloff Fiction Prize **9**:213
Franchon, Jacques See Highwater, Jamake
Francis, Robert
  Allen **11**:11

Ruark **23**:277-79
Francisco, Juan R. **9**:167
Franco-Americans **24**:248, 250
Franco, Francisco **1**:380
Frank, Anne **26**:177
Frank, Glenn **8**:240
Frank Luther Mott Award **13**:268
Frank, Peter **8**:89
Frankel, Cyril **5**:366
Frankel, Gene **11**:81
Frankenheimer, John **1**:196
Frankenstein (Gregory Sandow) **4**:155
Frankenstein Meets the Space Monster
  Dillard **7**:15
  Garrett **5**:80
Frantz Fanon **4**:105
Fraser, J.T. **10**:318
Fraser, Kathleen **26**:178
Frazier, E. Franklin **2**:282-83
Freckman, Bernard **15**:70
Fredi & Shirl & The Kids **3**:70, 76, 77, 78, 82, 83
Free Lance **16**:10, 11-13, 14, 15, 16, 18
Free Southern Theater **21**:205, 206, 219
Free Speech Movement
  Corn **25**:137, 138
  Pinsky **4**:246
"Free Throw" **7**:178-79
Free to Live, Free to Die **11**:50-51
Freedom **6**:320
Freedom News **26**:60
Freedom Press **6**:320
Freedom Road **18**:183
Freeling, Nicolas 12:77-89
Freeman, Gillian **4**:92
Fremantle Arts Centre **13**:114
"Fremont and Jessie" **3**:370
Fremont, Jessie Benton **3**:370
Fremont, John Charles **3**:370
Fremont-Smith, Eliot **2**:331
French Canadians **24**:247, 250-51
French First Army, Continental Advance Section **15**:139-43
French Kiss: Etreinte/exploration **16**:42
French language **24**:247, 248
French, Leslie **23**:69
French literature **1**:43
French Security Police **14**:276-80
French, The **4**:232-33
Freud, Lucian **2**:348
Freud, Sigmund
  Glanville **9**:24
  Jones **5**:118, 119
  Stone **3**:367, 376
  Wallace **1**:392, 401
Freud: The Paris Notebooks **18**:89
Friar, Kimon **15**:94
Fried, Al **3**:78
Fried, Erich **1**:24
Friedkin, William **16**:216
Friedlander, Lee **14**:175
Friedman & Son **3**:121
Friedman, B.H.

Katz **14**:173
Sukenick **8**:293
Friedman, Melvin **12**:162, 164
Friends Seminary School, New York
  City **11**:258
Friends, Society of
  Booth **5**:40, 45
  Ray **7**:146, 149
  Taylor **7**:178, 187
Friends, The **7**:233
Friendship
  Hadas **23**:124-25
  Taylor **26**:253
Fritzius, Harry **25**:398, 401
Froebe, Olga **3**:141-42
From a Seaside Town **23**:176
*From a Soft Angle: Poems About
  Women* **10**:9
From Here to Eternity **7**:141
From Middle England **25**:317
"From the Academy" **9**:100
From the Book of Shine **16**:112, 117,
  119
From the Drawn Sword **2**:118
From the First Century **26**:22-23
From the Irish **21**:294
From the Land and Back **9**:93
From the Rivers **13**:126, 136
From the Sustaining Air **23**:24, 28,
  29, 31, 37, 50, 58
From the Vietnamese **9**:215, 216
From This White Island **15**:85, 95,
  106
Fromm, Erika **7**:50
Frost, David **6**:92
Frost, Gregory **20**:92
Frost in May **2**:345
Frost, Nemi **16**:190
Frost, Robert
  Davison **4**:131, 132, 137, 138,
    139
  Eaton **20**:124-26, 131, 138, 144
  Galvin **13**:90-91
  Glazier **24**:227
  Hall **7**:62, 65
  Howes **3**:143
  Ignatow **3**:154
  Kennedy **9**:83
  Lifshin **10**:233-34, 248
  Meredith **14**:222, 230
  Phillips **13**:201
  Ruark **23**:272, 273-74
  Stegner **9**:259, 265, 266, 267,
    269
  Van Brunt **15**:374
Frost, Terry **23**:173-74
Fry, Christopher 23:63-80
Frye, Northrop
  Colombo **22**:34, 36-37
  Hine **15**:226
Fuchs, Daniel 5:53-69
Fuck Mother **8**:245-46
Fuck You/A Magazine of the Arts
  21:263
Fuentes, Carlos **3**:175
Fugitive Masks **3**:192

Fugitive Pigeon, The **13**:342
Fugs, The **21**:261, 264-67, 271
Fulbright Fellowship
  Anderson **2**:41
  Appleman **18**:34
  Bell **12**:37
  Browne **20**:62, 65
  Bruce-Novoa **18**:76
  Burroway **6**:94
  Cassill **1**:168
  Clark **22**:12
  Corman **2**:137
  Corn **25**:139
  Dove **19**:103
  Emanuel **18**:139, 154
  Epstein **12**:73
  Federman **8**:69
  Forbes **16**:117
  Ford **21**:36
  Foster **26**:122
  Harteis **26**:132
  Hassan **12**:160
  Kostelanetz **8**:180
  Lottman **12**:198
  McCord **9**:182-83
  McElroy **21**:141
  Nims **17**:193
  Rabassa **9**:203
  Stegner **9**:267
  Sukenick **8**:289
  Tarn **16**:276
  Vivante **12**:296
  Williams **20**:331
  Wilson **5**:353
  Wright **7**:298, 300
Fulbright, Harriet **26**:140, 141-42
Fuller, Buckminster **12**:160
Fuller, Hoyt
  Joans **25**:228
  Rodgers **13**:246, 247, 248
  Salaam **21**:204, 215, 225
Fuller, Jean Overton **2**:52, 54
Fuller, John **10**:113, 126
Fuller Man **24**:206
Fuller, Roy 10:111-28
  Symons **3**:385, 386, 387
Fulton, Alice **22**:72
Fulton, Len **24**:23
Fulton, Robin **17**:249-65
Funaro, Jim **12**:216
Function of the Orgasm **6**:142
Funny Side Up **2**:248
Funnyhouse of a Negro **20**:219-21,
  223, 224-25, 231, 232
Funston, Keith **3**:316
Furbank, Nicholas **3**:35
Furioso **8**:306-07
Furman, Laura 18:189-204
Furnace, A **10**:99
*Further Adventures of Slugger McBatt,
  The* **7**:110
Fusi, Walter **25**:375
Fussell, Paul **4**:243
Futurian Society **10**:203, 206-08,
  211, 212
Futurians, The **1**:284-85

Futurist and Other Stories, The **26**:96
Futurists **25**:265
Futz **2**:361-62, 364, 366, 368
Futz and What Came After **2**:362,
  363

Gable, Clark **1**:401
Gabo, Naum **8**:187
*Gabriel Dumont: The Métis Chief and
  His Lost World* **6**:323-24
Gaddis, William **4**:205, 207, 213,
  217
Gadjah Mada University, Jogjakarta,
  Indonesia **3**:242
Gaia **2**:31
Galapagos Islands **3**:378
Galaxy
  Bishop **26**:18
  Budrys **14**:67, 68, 77-78
  Knight **10**:217-18, 221
  Pohl **1**:290, 291, 292, 294
  Silverberg **3**:277
Galiano Island, British Columbia,
  Canada **18**:317-21, 323
Galin, Saul **9**:203
Gall, Sally **6**:280
Gallery of Women **24**:348
Gallimard, Editions (publishers) **2**:66,
  67, 73
Gallipoli, Turkey **3**:255
Gallup, Dick **22**:17
Galvanized Yankees, The **6**:57
Galvin, Brendan 13:89-104
  Garrett **5**:75
  Holden **22**:73
Game Men Play, A **1**:79
Games Were Coming, The **18**:13, 17
Gamma **16**:215
Gandhi, Indira
  Blaise **3**:26
  Singh **9**:233, 234
Gandhi, Mohandas
  Shapiro **6**:290
  Woodcock **6**:325
García Lorca (Edwin Honig) **8**:109,
  110
García Lorca, Federico
  Abse **1**:21
  Argüelles **24**:14
  Belitt **4**:60, 64
  Corman **2**:135
  Cruz **17**:3, 7, 8
  Eshleman **6**:131
  Honig **8**:107, 109, 110, 118-19
  Roditi **14**:248
García Márquez, Gabriel
  Rabassa **9**:203-04
  Škvorecký **1**:341
Garcia, Nasario **15**:122
Garden City Junior College, Garden
  City, Kan. **3**:331
Garden, Mary **1**:99, 103
Garden of Eros, The **26**:52
Garden Party **6**:90
Garden Spot, U.S.A. **5**:79
Garden, The

Ferrini   **24**:127
Turner   **10**:318
Gardener, The   **18**:305
Gardiner, Charles Wrey   **19**:234-35
Gardner Arts Centre, Sussex
    University   **6**:96, 99
Gardner, Gerald   **8**:274
Gardner, Helen   **10**:316-17
Gardner, Isabella   **13**:212, 213
Gardner, John
    Delbanco   **2**:159
    Johnson   **18**:230, 238-39
    Klinkowitz   **9**:117
    McElroy   **21**:139
Garen, Leo   **14**:175
Garioch, Robert   **14**:335
Garland, Judy   **1**:178
Garland, Patrick   **9**:16
Garneau, Saint-Denys   **13**:183
Garner, Lee   **5**:349
Garrett, George Palmer, Jr.   5:71-90
    Chappell   **4**:117, 122
    Dillard   **7**:14-15
    Galvin   **13**:99, 103
    Kizer   **5**:145
    Settle   **1**:317, 321
    Taylor   **7**:180, 181, 183
Garrett, Helen   **5**:84
Garrett, John   **10**:123
Garrett, Oliver   **5**:83-84
Garrett, Randall   **3**:274
Gascoyne, David
    Joans   **25**:224, 226
    Weiss   **2**:446
    Wright   **5**:366, 368
Gasperik, Frank   **12**:219
Gass, William
    Hinojosa-Smith   **16**:143, 144
    Klinkowitz   **9**:112
    Sukenick   **8**:291
Gassner, John   **6**:93
Gate of Hell, The   **9**:5
Gates, Richard   **1**:164, 167
Gateway   **1**:294
Gathering of Days, A   **17**:204
Gathering of Zion, The   **9**:269
Gathering, The   **26**:41
Gatsos, Nikos   **15**:80
Gaudy Place, The   **4**:121
Gaudy, The   **3**:343
Gauer, Harold   **20**:35
Gauggel, Herman   **14**:179
Gauguin's Chair: Selected Poems   **8**:248
Gauss Seminars in Criticism   **2**:448
Gauvreau, Claude   **16**:47
Gawsworth, John   **5**:281
Gay and Lesbian Movement   **23**:209
Gay liberation movement
    Corn   **25**:142
    Picano   **13**:227-28
Gay Men's Health Crisis   **23**:125-26, 132
Gay Presses of New York   **13**:233
Gay Priest: An Inner Journey   **11**:58
Geduld, Harry M.   21:45-59
Geis, Bernard

Cassill   **1**:173
Greeley   **7**:50-51
Rimmer   **10**:299-300
Slavitt   **3**:319, 320, 322
Geller, Simon   **24**:140
Gem
    Ashby   **6**:34
    Brown   **6**:66
General Electric Award   **2**:214
General, The   **2**:385
Generation without Farewell   **1**:123
Genes, Mind, and Culture   **16**:304
Genesis   **10**:321
*Genesis Angels: The Saga of Lew Welch
    and the Beat Generation*   **5**:217, 218, 219
Genet, Jean
    Barnstone   **15**:70
    Dennison   **6**:121
    Foley   **24**:153, 166
    Sukenick   **8**:290
Genêt (pseudonym of Janet
    Flanner)   **1**:120
Geneva, Switzerland
    Barnstone   **15**:65-66
    Condon   **1**:197
Gennadius Library, Athens, Greece
    3:377
Genoa, Italy   **25**:342
Genocides, The   **4**:150
Genovese, Kitty   **3**:138
Gentle Tamers, The   **6**:57
Gentlemen, I Address You Privately
    1:115
GEO   **3**:80
Geographical Magazine   **7**:130
Geography III   **4**:249
Geography of the Body, The   **19**:199
George, David Lloyd   **4**:40
*George Herbert's Pattern Poems: In
    Their Tradition*   **8**:91
George Mason University
    Bausch, Richard   **14**:8, 9, 11-12
    Bausch, Robert   **14**:25-26, 27, 29, 30
    Shreve   **5**:238
George VI   **4**:37
George Washington Carver Institute's
    Supreme Award of Merit
    1:393, 395
George Washington University
    Alegría   **15**:6
    Brown   **6**:52
    Kammen   **23**:139-40
Georgetown University   **19**:221
Georgia Boy   **1**:150
Georgia Institute of Technology
    3:317
Gerber, Merrill Joan   20:151-75
Gerlach, Luther   **22**:266
German Democratic Republic
    13:125, 131-32, 134-36
German language
    Higgins   **8**:85
    Lind   **4**:201
German-Russian War   **1**:149

Germans
    Caute   **4**:97-99
    Salisbury   **15**:318
Germany
    Blotner   **25**:91-93
    Caute   **4**:97-99
    Dove   **19**:103-04, 106-07
    Hall   **12**:129-31
    Hamburger   **4**:161-62
    Hauser   **11**:128-29
    Laqueur   **19**:208-12
    Lind   **4**:199-200
    McElroy   **21**:121, 131-32
    Phillips   **13**:205-07
    Salisbury   **15**:320
    Schevill   **12**:276-78
    Sisson   **3**:297-98
Gernsback, Hugo
    Pohl   **1**:292
    Williamson   **8**:316, 318
Gerrold, David   **12**:220, 221
Gershator, David   **24**:17
Gershator, Phyllis   **24**:17
Gershwin   **24**:162
Gertrude Stein Awards in Innovative
    American Poetry   **26**:228
Gervais, Marty   **15**:357-58
Gestalt Therapy   **6**:115
Get Out Early   **6**:27
*Getting It Together: A Film on Larry
    Eigner, Poet (1973)*   **23**:40-47
Ghana
    Caute   **4**:103
    Thomas   **19**:356
Ghana Revolution, The   **13**:51-52
Ghelderode, Michel de   **2**:411
Ghiselin, Brewster   10:129-45
    Taylor   **7**:184-85
Ghiselin, Michael   **10**:133, 136, 137, 138, 140
Ghose, Zulfikar   **6**:92
Ghosh, Sudhir   **9**:230
Ghost in the Music, A   **2**:335
Ghote, Ghanesh   **8**:165, 167, 171-72, 173, 175, 176
GI Bill
    Anderson   **2**:39
    Aubert   **20**:22
    Easton   **14**:155
    Emanuel   **18**:130
    Federman   **8**:76, 77
    Hazo   **11**:144, 146
    Jerome   **8**:130
    Kennedy   **9**:79, 82
    McCord   **9**:180-81
    Menashe   **11**:226
    Peters   **8**:239-40
Giant Jam Sandwich, The   **6**:99
Gibbons, Reginald   24:183-98
    Glancy   **24**:208, 212
Gibson, Walker   **6**:90
Gibson, William   **20**:93
Gide, André
    Guerard   **2**:229, 230
    Harwood   **19**:142
    Wallace   **1**:391, 393

Gielgud, John **5**:108
Gift to Be Simple, The **8**:247, 248
Gig **16**:168
Gilbert, Bernard **15**:182-83, 184-85
Gilbert, Calvin **24**:337-38
Gilbert, H. **3**:135
Gilbert, Michael 15:181-99
Gilbert, Vedder **2**:122, 123
Gilgamesh the King **3**:285
Giligia Press **2**:271, 272
Gilman, Coby **11**:133
Gilmour, Sally **5**:366, 367
Gimbel, Wendy **2**:420, 421
"Gimlet Eye, The" **6**:214, 218
Ginsberg, Allen
   Allman **15**:24
   Argüelles **24**:16
   Armantrout **25**:15
   Bowles **1**:91, 92
   Choudhury **14**:91, 92
   Clark **22**:13
   Creeley **10**:72-73
   Cruz **17**:7-8, 10
   di Suvero **26**:71-72
   Dworkin **21**:13
   Eigner **23**:40-47, 53
   Enslin **3**:93
   Eshleman **6**:128, 131-32, 135, 147
   Heyen **9**:46
   Hollo **19**:168
   Klinkowitz **9**:114
   Kyger **16**:190, 195, 196
   Major **6**:193
   Malanga **17**:109, 110
   Morgan **4**:236
   Norse **18**:282, 289, 290
   Plymell **11**:280, 285, 286-87, 288,
     289-90, 294, 295
   Sanders **21**:259, 260, 261, 263,
     264, 266, 267, 268, 270
   Saroyan **5**:213
   Škvorecký **1**:346-47
   Waldman **17**:268, 273, 280, 282-
     83, 284-85, 289, 291
   Weiss **2**:445
Ginsberg, Thomas **2**:70
Gioia, Dana
   Feirstein **11**:84
   Holden **22**:75
Giotto di Bondone **3**:355
Giovanni, Nikki 6:151-64
   Emanuel **18**:143
Giraudoux, Jean **2**:69
Giri, Varahagiri Venkata **9**:234
Girl in the Black Raincoat, The **7**:180
Girodias, Maurice
   Malzberg **4**:218
   Wallace **1**:396
Giroux, Robert **1**:322
Gist of Origin, The **2**:135, 136, 137,
   138, 140, 141, 142, 144
Gitlin, Paul **1**:401
Gittings, Robert **23**:66
Giuranna, Bruno **2**:162
"Give My Regards to Broadway"
   4:238

Give the Dog a Bone **5**:171
Gladiator-at-Law **1**:293
Glancy, Diane 24:199-215
Glanville, Brian 9:13-29
Glanville, Stephen **4**:341
Glasgow, Ellen **7**:11-12, 17
Glass Face in the Rain, A **3**:335
Glass Hammer, The **21**:115
*Glass House: A Novella and Stories,
   The* **18**:202
Glass Menagerie, The **7**:23-24
Glass, Philip **14**:176
Glassgold, Peter **15**:19-20
Glazier, Loss Pequeño
   Argüelles **24**:23
   Bernstein **24**:31-49
Glazier, Lyle 24:217-41
   Arnold **25**:47
Gleason, Madeline **12**:52
Gleason, Robert **12**:219, 220
Globe and Mail **22**:117
Glock, William **8**:157, 158
Gloucester Daily Times **24**:149
Gloucester Stage Company **24**:129
GLOUCESTERBOOK **24**:148
GLOUCESTERTIDE **24**:148
Glover, Douglas 23:81-97
Glück, Louise **4**:250
Glynn, Tom **9**:117
GMHC See Gay Men's Health Crisis
Gnosticism **25**:261, 268, 276-77,
   278-79, 281
Go in Beauty **1**:209, 212
Go-potty Rex **9**:83
Go to the Widow-Maker **7**:141
Go West **25**:44
Go West, Inspector Ghote **8**:176
God
   Anaya **4**:22
   Arden **4**:31
   Bennett **13**:74, 82
   Booth **5**:32, 33, 35, 40, 43, 45,
     51
   Ciardi **2**:85
   Greeley **7**:49
   Kherdian **2**:261
   Ostriker **24**:275, 277
   Ouellette **13**:181
   Simic **4**:271
   Thomas **4**:311, 312
   Van Itallie **2**:410
   Weiss **12**:333-34
   Wiesel **4**:355
God of Indeterminacy, The **23**:215,
   220, 221, 231
God Perkins **18**:300
God We Seek, The **12**:334
Godard, Barbara **16**:53
Godbotherers, The **25**:312
Godded and Codded **2**:351
Godfrey, Dave **7**:301
Godfrey, Derek **12**:12
Godine, David R. (publishers) **1**:134
God's Little Acre **1**:151, 152
God's Trombones **7**:23
Godwin, Gail **6**:100

Goebbels, Josef
   Lind **4**:198
   Škvorecký **1**:330
Goedicke, Patricia **9**:41
Goering, Hermann **14**:272
Goethe, Johann Wolfgang von
   Kazin **7**:88
   Ray **7**:144
Gog **5**:271, 272, 273-74
Gogarty, Oliver St. John **12**:198
Going All the Way **7**:199
Going Down Fast **1**:273
Gold at the Starbow's End, The **1**:294
Gold, Herbert
   Cassill **1**:169
   Dudek **14**:130
Gold, Horace
   Gunn **2**:248, 249
   Knight **10**:216, 217-18
   Pohl **1**:290, 292
Gold, Zachary **1**:386
Goldemberg, Isaac 12:91-106
Golden Bowl, The **18**:254-55, 256-57
Golden Days **22**:219-20, 224-26
Golden Dream, The **3**:278
Golden Gate University **18**:98
Golden Positions, The **12**:53
*Golden Quest: The Four Voyages of
   Christopher Columbus, The* **18**:23
Golden Scroll Award **16**:219
Golden State **4**:248
Goldenhar, Didi **2**:421
Goldin, Amy **19**:198-99, 201
Golding, William
   Sinclair **5**:273
   Tennant **9**:293
Goldman, Willie **7**:236
Goldsmith, Cele **4**:149
Goldstein, Moritz **7**:81
Goldwyn, Samuel, Jr. **5**:79
Golf **19**:122, 129, 131
Golfing in the Carolinas **19**:130
Goliard Press **11**:301, 302
Gollancz, Victor
   Freeling **12**:85-86
   Keating **8**:169, 170
   Menashe **11**:233
   Wilson **5**:320
Gollancz, Victor (publishers)
   Keating **8**:169
   Purdy **1**:300, 301
   Stewart **3**:354
   Symons **3**:389
   Wagoner **3**:406
   Wilson **5**:322
Gollub, David **26**:309
Gomberg, M. Robert **5**:207
Gone with the Wind **1**:311
Gooch, Velma **7**:101
"Good News from the Vatican"
   3:282
Good News of Death and Other Poems
   4:293
Good, Sandra **24**:21-22
"Good Woman, A" **1**:300
Goodbody, Buzz **4**:106-07

Goodly Babe, A **12**:300
Goodman, Mitchell
  Corman **2**:137
  Levertov **19**:237, 238
Goodman, Paul
  Dennison **6**:114-15
  Kostelanetz **8**:191
  Norse **18**:282-83, 284
  Roditi **14**:260, 266, 286
  Settle **1**:322
Goodwin, Clive **3**:111, 112, 113
Gorbachev, Mikhail **10**:332, 338
Gorczynski, Renata **4**:250
Gordimer, Nadine **8**:54
Gordnier, Edman **24**:339-40
Gordon, Ambrose, Jr. **8**:306
Gordon, Caroline **2**:252
Gordon, Charles **2**:307
Gordon, Giles **4**:86
Gordon, Robert S. **10**:3
Gordon, Stuart **25**:208-10
Gore, Walter **5**:366, 367
Gorki, A.M., Institute of World
    Literature, Moscow **2**:386
Gorki, Maxim
  Rakosi **5**:201
  Wallace **1**:391
  Wesker **7**:236
Gorky, Arshile **7**:174
Gornick, Vivian **10**:13
Goshawk, Antelope **7**:164
Gospel music **7**:26, 30
Gotham Book Mart **9**:80
Gottlieb, Morton **9**:246, 247, 248,
    249, 250, 251, 252
Gottlieb, Robert
  Mano **6**:212
  Markfield **3**:223, 225
Goulianos, Joan **2**:368
Government College **9**:225
Governor-General's Award for
    Literature
  Bowering **16**:37
  Kelly **22**:118
  Woodcock **6**:326
Governor-General's Award for Poetry
  Purdy **17**:209, 210
  Souster **14**:316
*Governor's Bridge Is Closed: Twelve
    Essays on the Canadian Scene,
    The* **17**:89
Goya, Francisco de **11**:208
Goyen, William **13**:208, 212, 213
Gozzano, Guido **2**:319
GPNY *See* Gay Presses of New York
Grace, Princess of Monaco **11**:149-
  50, 153
Graham, Alastair **5**:178
Graham, Archibald "Moonlight"
  7:104, 105
Graham, Bill **26**:73
Graham, Donald **2**:298
Graham, Jorie **22**:71
Graham, Martha
  Hiemstra **26**:157
  Weiss **2**:431, 445

Graham, W.S.
  Weiss **2**:446
  Wright **5**:367, 368
Grahame, Kenneth **1**:101
Grainger, Percy **5**:142
"Grampa Ben's Bookcase" **26**:294
Grand Rapids Press **7**:196
Grand Valley State College **3**:174
Grandbois, Alain
  Brossard **16**:46-47
  Ouellette **13**:183
Grandmother Sea **9**:295
Grann, Phyllis **3**:322
Grant, Ulysses **1**:383
Granta **6**:91, 92
Graphis series **8**:92-94
Grass Is Singing, The **5**:122
Grasse 3/23/66 **2**:156, 159
Grassel, Jack **11**:348
"Grassland" **14**:175
Grave of the Right Hand, The **7**:295
Graves Registry **5**:342, 344, 345,
    351, 355
Graves, Robert
  Allen **6**:17
  Allman **15**:23
  Arden **4**:29, 30
  Argüelles **24**:10
  Hamburger **4**:171
  Jennings **5**:110
  Kerrigan **11**:210
  Mathews **6**:235, 246
  Menashe **11**:231
  St. Clair **8**:274
  Shadbolt **3**:249
  Skelton **5**:291
  Sward **13**:302
Gravy Planet **1**:291
Gray, Cleve **2**:196-98, 199, 200
**Gray, Francine du Plessix 2:179-
201**
Gray, Kenneth **2**:39, 42
Gray, Simon 3:101-15
Gray Soldiers **7**:166
Gray, Thomas **24**:161, 163
Graziano, Rocky **24**:109
Great American Funeral, The (film)
  17:148
Great American Poetry Bake-offs **8**:248
*Great Black Russian: The Life and
    Times of Alexander Pushkin*
  2:305-06
Great Britain, Royal Air Force
  Abse **1**:23-24
  Brunner **8**:7
  Moorcock **5**:176
  Sillitoe **2**:374-80
  Skelton **5**:281-82
  West **7**:278-80
  Wilson **5**:316-17
Great Britain, Royal Air Force,
    Women's Auxiliary Air Force
  1:312
Great Britain, Royal Army
  Aldiss **2**:19
  Bourjaily **1**:67

Gilbert **15**:188, 189-92
  Hamburger **4**:163-64, 169
  Mott **7**:120, 121, 122
  Oakes **25**:305-06
  Silkin **5**:256, 257-58, 260
  Sinclair **5**:269
  Sparshott **15**:352, 353, 354, 357,
    359
Great Britain, Royal Navy
  Davie **3**:32
  Davison **4**:129
  Sillitoe **2**:375
  White **4**:338-39
Great Fear, The **4**:107
Great Gatsby, The **6**:110
Great Lakes Colleges Association
    National First Book Award
  10:191
Great Steamboat Race, The **8**:14
Great Things Are Happening **5**:170
Greatest Show on Earth, The **4**:146
Greco, Juliette **7**:119
Greece
  Barnstone **15**:73-106
  Davie **3**:39
  Delbanco **2**:155-56
  Harwood **19**:146-47
  Hongo **22**:85
  Jones **5**:125
  Kammen **23**:142-44
  Piercy **1**:272
  Stone **3**:376-77
  Valaoritis **26**:263-91
  Van Brunt **15**:376
  Williams **26**:311, 312, 328
  Wright **7**:296
Greed **1**:368
Greek Anthology, The **5**:286
Greek, classical
  Matthews **15**:262-63
  St. Clair **8**:271-72
  Sanders **21**:261-63
Greek National Resistance
    Movement **16**:252-57
Greek Treasure, The **3**:377
Greeley, Andrew 7:37-53
Green Days by the River **18**:18, 21
Green Dolphin, The **22**:110
Green, Henry
  Allen **6**:18
  Tennant **9**:291
Green, Joe **2**:44
Green, Kay 11:87-106
Green, Paul **2**:434
Greene, David **12**:199
Greene, Gael **6**:87
Greene, Graham
  Allen **6**:20
  Caute **4**:102, 105, 108
  Hine **15**:226
  Jones **5**:125
  Keating **8**:169-70
  Slavitt **3**:320
  Wilson **5**:325
Greene, Jonathan **19**:200
Greenfield, George **9**:20

Greenhouse in the Garden, The　**20**:136
Greenland, Cyril　**22**:53
Greenspan, Yosl　**9**:55-56, 61-62
Greenvoe　**6**:72
Greenwald, Ted　**11**:302, 303
Greenwich University　**23**:207
Greenwich Village, New York City
　Block　**11**:28, 37
　Busch　**1**:131-32
　Joans　**25**:229, 235
　Kirkup　**4**:190
　Owens　**2**:359
　Pohl　**1**:289
Greenwood Press　**26**:71
Greenwood, Robert　**3**:335
Greer, Germaine　**11**:68
Gregor, Arthur　10:147-62
Gregory, Dick　**6**:159
Gregory, Horace
　Owens　**2**:358
　Rosenthal　**6**:279
Grendel　**9**:117
Greybeard　**2**:23
Gridiron Club, Washington, D.C.
　3:177, 178, 179
Grief Observed, A　**8**:280
Grierson's Raid　**6**:57
Griffin, John Howard　**7**:132
Grigsby, Frances　**7**:77-78
Grigson, Geoffrey
　Harwood　**19**:149
　Symons　**3**:385
Grimond, Jo　**5**:179
Grindea, Miron　**7**:127, 128
Grist　**11**:289, 291, 292
Grito, El　**4**:24
Groden, Michael　**21**:159-60, 161-64
Grodin, Charles　**9**:246, 247
Groffsky, Maxine　**6**:240, 241-42,
　246, 247
Grolier Book Shop, Cambridge,
　Mass.　**3**:89
Gross, Ben　**12**:203
Gross, Jerry　**3**:424
*Group Portrait: Conrad, Crane, Ford,
　James, and Wells*　**2**:156, 159
Grove City College　**9**:59
Grove Press　**4**:260
Grove Press Award　**9**:231, 232
Growing Up in Minnesota　**22**:272-73
*Growing Up Stupid Under the Union
　Jack*　**16**:75, 76
Grub Street　**22**:21
Grumbach, Doris　2:203-14
Grumman, Bob　25:173-94
　Bennett　**25**:74
　Berry　**24**:77
　Leftwich　**25**:273-74
Gryphon　**5**:283
Guadaloupe, French West Indies
　2:215
Guardians, The　**3**:355
Guatemala　**2**:329-30, 331
Guatemalan-American Institute　**1**:157
Guccione, Bob
　Bova　**18**:57-58

Giovanni　**6**:153-54
Guerard, Albert J.　2:215-32
　Pinsky　**4**:245
Guerard, Albert Leon　**2**:215, 216,
　217, 221, 223
Guerard, Wilhelmina　**2**:216, 221,
　222
Guest, Harry　**19**:150
Guevara, Che　**17**:115, 117
Guggenheim Fellowship
　Baumbach　**5**:28
　Becker　**1**:35
　Bowles　**1**:86
　Boyle　**1**:117
　Cassill　**1**:172
　Dove　**19**:109
　Eshleman　**6**:147
　Federman　**8**:79
　Feirstein　**11**:83
　Furman　**18**:203
　Galvin　**13**:102
　Hassan　**12**:160
　Hearon　**11**:169
　Honig　**8**:112, 115
　Jones　**11**:184
　Kennedy　**20**:220
　Markfield　**3**:220
　Mott　**7**:133
　Owens　**2**:357
　Peters　**8**:244, 249
　Rabassa　**9**:204
　Root　**11**:325
　Sanders　**21**:270
　Settle　**1**:317
　Stegner　**9**:267
　Wagoner　**3**:406-07
　Wakoski　**1**:368
　West　**7**:280
Guggenheim Foundation
　Ai　**13**:11
　Blais　**4**:73, 74
　Purdy　**1**:302
　Simpson　**4**:295
Guggenheim, Peggy　**1**:89, 90
Guidacci, Margherita　**10**:141
Guide to Public Lending Right, A　**4**:84
Guide to the Maximus Poems, A
　24:133
Guilford Writers Workshop　**20**:92-93
Guillén, Jorge　**15**:59
Guinness, Alec　**3**:113, 114
Guinness Award　**2**:56
*Guinness Book of Poetry, 1957/58,
　The*　**7**:127
Guiton, Margaret　**15**:136
Gullah　**17**:131-32
Gun Fury　**1**:383
Gundolf, Friedrich (pseudonym of
　Friedrich Gundelfinger)　**7**:213
Gunn, Benjamin Jesse　**2**:234, 235,
　238, 241
Gunn, James　2:233-60
　Williamson　**8**:322, 324, 325
Gunn, John　**6**:64
Gunn, Thom　**1**:360, 364
Guns and shooting

McCord　**9**:172, 173, 177, 178,
　180, 181
　Rosenblum　**11**:346, 350, 352
Guns of Rio Presto, The　**1**:342
Gunsight　**2**:436, 437
Guravich, Donald　**16**:201, 202
Gurik, Robert　23:99-116
Guss, Jack　**1**:208
Guston, Philip　**25**:395
Guthrie, Ramon　**9**:198, 200
Gutwillig, Robert　**2**:400, 401
Guyana Quartet, The　**16**:134
Guyana, South America　**16**:121-22,
　123-28, 132
Gwynn, Fred　**25**:95-96
Gypsies
　Cartland　**8**:25, 26
　Codrescu　**19**:82-83
　Murchie　**19**:291
　Richie　**20**:289
　Simic　**4**:269
"Gyps Moths"　**24**:356, 359, 363-66
Gysin, Brion　**18**:287

Hadas, Moses　**23**:123-24
Hadas, Rachel　23:117-32
Hades in Manganese　**6**:146
Hadjidakis, Manos　**15**:77, 78-80
Hadley, Drummond　**5**:349, 353
Hadley, W.W.　**5**:367, 368
Haganah
　Megged　**13**:146
　Wiesel　**4**:355-56
Hagen, Joel　**12**:213, 214, 216
Hager, Henry　**9**:279
Haggard, H. Rider
　Anderson　**2**:37
　Cassity　**8**:39
　Thomas　**11**:374
Hahn, Emily　11:107-21
Haifa University　**9**:216
Haiku
　Kirkup　**4**:183, 186, 187
　Salaam　**21**:236-38
　Vizenor　**22**:274-76
Hailey, Elizabeth Forsythe　1:225-35
Hailey, Oliver　**1**:229-34
Haining, Jim　**26**:220-21, 226
Hair of the Dog　**3**:189
Haiti
　Corn　**25**:143
　Howes　**3**:145
　Salaam　**21**:219-21
Halas, František　**1**:335-36
Halberstam, David　**1**:40
Haldeman, Joe　25:195-218
　Dann　**20**:91
　Niven　**12**:212
Haldeman, Marcet　**2**:248
Hale, Allen　**7**:12
Hale, Nancy　**19**:256
Hales, Steven　**4**:250
Haley, Alex
　Kennedy　**20**:227
　Williams　**20**:325, 329, 337
Haley, George　**20**:325, 329

Half a Life's History, Poems: New and Selected, 1957–1983 **13**:304
Half Black, Half Blacker **21**:172
Half Gods, The **12**:24, 26, 29-30, 34, 36, 38
Half Laughing/Half Crying **11**:51, 58
Half of Paradise **19**:69, 75-76
Half-Past Nation-Time **18**:237
Half Remembered: A Personal History **4**:129, 138
Halflife **7**:298
Halfway to Nosy Be **21**:141
Halifax, Nova Scotia **3**:106, 107, 109
Hall, Barry **11**:301-02, 304, 305, 307
Hall, Donald 7:55-67
 Burroway **6**:90
 Clark **22**:15
 Jennings **5**:110
 Kennedy **9**:83, 84
 Stevenson **9**:282-83
Hall, Elizabeth Cushman **12**:119, 120, 128, 130, 131, 132, 133
Hall, Graham **5**:184
Hall, James B. 12:107-34
 Cassill **1**:169
Hall, Peter **3**:114
Hall, Tom T. **20**:332, 335, 336, 337, 340
Hallmark Cards **16**:211
Halman, Talat S. **6**:192
Halpern, Daniel
 Bowles **1**:93
 Pinsky **4**:250
Halpern, Stach **2**:138
Halsey, William Frederick **2**:104
Halward, Leslie **6**:20
Hamady, Walter **11**:256
Hamburg, Germany
 Caute **4**:98-99
 Delbanco **2**:160
Hamburger, Leopold **4**:161
Hamburger, Michael 4:159-73
 Jennings **5**:110
 Mead **13**:130-31, 133, 136, 138
Hamburger, Richard **4**:160, 161, 162-63, 165, 170
Hamill, Sam 15:201-16
Hamilton College **2**:326-28, 332
Hamilton, Gail (pseudonym of Barbara Corcoran) **2**:121, 122
Hamilton, George Rostrevor **10**:119-22, 126
Hamilton, Mark **2**:58
Hamilton Stark **15**:44
Hamilton, William D. **16**:301-02
Hamlet
 Foley **24**:179
 Gray **2**:189
 Jennings **5**:108
Hammett: A Life at the Edge **16**:221
Hammett, Dashiell
 Brossard **2**:69
 Symons **3**:391, 392
Hammond Times (Indiana) **3**:404

Hampson, John **6**:18-19, 20, 22
Hanagid, Samuel **8**:145
Hancock, Herbie **6**:179
Hancock, Tony **25**:309-10
Hand, Q.R. **26**:305, 306, 307
Hand-Reared Boy, The **2**:29
Handke, Peter
 Blaise **3**:19
 Klinkowitz **9**:116, 118, 119
Handlin, Oscar **5**:271
Handy, John **24**:341-42, 349
Handy, Lowney **7**:140-42
Hanger Stout, Awake!
 Heyen **9**:42
 Matthews **15**:268
Hanging Garden, The **3**:410
Hanging Gardens of Etobicoke, The **15**:359
Hankla, Cathy **7**:19
Hanley, James **4**:309
Hanna, Charles Shahoud **24**:15, 16
Hano, Arnold **10**:219
Hansen, Al **8**:86-87
Hansen, Alvin **3**:236-37
Hansen, Joseph 17:59-74
Hapax Legomenon **24**:27
Happening Worlds of John Brunner, The **8**:1
Happy As You Are **25**:47
Happy Man, The **14**:154
Harbor Review **6**:268
Harbormaster of Hong Kong, The **26**:38
Harcourt, Brace (publishers)
 Davison **4**:133, 134, 135
 Wagoner **3**:405
hard 2 beleev **19**:4
Hard Way, The **5**:57
Hardin-Simmons University **10**:22, 23, 24
Harding, Gunnar **11**:303, 309
Hardwicke, Paul **12**:12
Hardy, Joseph
 Slade **9**:251
 Wakefield **7**:200
Hardy, Thomas
 Creeley **10**:67-68
 Guerard **2**:221, 230
 Kizer **5**:141
 Wain **4**:328
Harford, Thomas **2**:24
Harkness Fellowship **5**:271
Harlem **24**:327
Harlem Art Center, New York City **6**:267-68
Harlem Writers Guild **2**:286, 287-88
Harlequin's Stick, Charlie's Cane **3**:192
Harley-Davidson, Inc. **11**:333, 351-52
Harmon, William **12**:345-46
Harmoonia **20**:67, 72
Harold [and] Sondra **11**:81-82
Harold U. Ribalow Prize **20**:174
Harper & Row, Publishers
 Disch **4**:156, 157

Knebel **3**:179, 180, 181
 Solotaroff **2**:403
Harper, Carol Ely **16**:11, 12
Harper, Michael **21**:228
Harper's Bazaar
 Hauser **11**:134, 136
 Settle **1**:313
Harper's Magazine **1**:117, 120
Harpur College **18**:336-38
Harrad Experiment, The **10**:281, 286, 287, 291, 295, 296, 298-99, 300, 301, 305
Harrad Letters, The **10**:305
Harriet Tubman: Conductor on the Underground Railroad **6**:253
Harris, Charles **3**:274
Harris, Charles F. **3**:431
Harris, Frank **1**:97
Harris, Jed **5**:64-66
Harris, Josephine Horen **3**:117-27, 128, 129, 130, 131, 132
Harris, Marguerite **24**:15
Harris, Marie **18**:268-69
Harris, Mark 3:117-32
 Greeley **7**:38
Harris, Mary Emma **8**:179
Harris, Wilson 16:121-37
Harrison College **16**:71, 75-76
Harrison, Gilbert
 Grumbach **2**:211-12
 Whittemore **8**:310
Harrison, Harry
 Aldiss **2**:26-27, 28, 29
 Gunn **2**:258
 Knight **10**:216, 220
 Pohl **1**:295, 296
Harrison, Rex **23**:74, 75
Harrison, Tony **21**:285, 286, 287, 289
Harry, Bill **5**:176
Harry the Magician **2**:69
Harry's Fragments **16**:28
Hart, Al **7**:81
"Hart Crane" **3**:386
Hart-Davis, Rupert **4**:309, 310
Hart, Jeffrey **6**:208
Hart, Moss **1**:395
Harteis, Richard 26:131-46
 Meredith **14**:219-36
Hartford, Conn. **12**:347
Hartley, Anthony **5**:284
Hartley, George **3**:39
Hartmann, William K. **12**:213, 214, 215
Hartshorne, Charles **12**:329-30
Hartung, Hans **12**:87
Hartwell, David
 Spinrad **19**:332, 333-34
 Wolfe **9**:311, 312
Harvard Advocate **7**:62, 63
Harvard Glee Club **4**:132
Harvard University
 Becker **1**:33-34
 Bernstein **24**:39-44
 Blaise **3**:23, 24
 Caute **4**:104, 105

Ciardi   **2**:93
Clement   **16**:91, 98
Corcoran   **2**:116
Corman   **2**:138
Creeley   **10**:62, 66-67
Davison   **4**:131-33
Delbanco   **2**:156, 158
Easton   **14**:144, 157
Eaton   **20**:124
Federman   **8**:77
Glazier   **24**:232
Guerard   **2**:223, 226, 227, 228,
      230-31
Hadas   **23**:122
Hall   **7**:59, 62-63, 64-65
Hentoff   **6**:166-67
Honig   **8**:113-15
Kammen   **23**:140-44
Kazin   **7**:95
Kumin   **8**:213
Mathews   **6**:223, 232
McPherson   **17**:123, 133
Morgan   **3**:232, 236-37, 238, 239
Mrozek   **10**:271
Rimmer   **10**:287-88
Sinclair   **5**:271
Stegner   **9**:266
Tillinghast   **23**:307-09, 316
Van Itallie   **2**:410-11, 418
Wakefield   **7**:197
Weiss   **12**:327-28
Wellek   **7**:218
Wilson   **16**:294-307
Harvard University Press   **4**:134
Harvard University See also Radcliffe
      College
Harvey, Anthony   **5**:126
Harwood, Lee   19:135-53
Disch   **4**:152
Hašek, Jaroslav   **1**:341
Haselwood, Dave   **11**:283, 284, 285,
      289
Hasford, Gustav   **25**:202
Hasidic Judaism   **23**:289-98
Hass, Robert   **4**:244, 246, 249-50
Hassan, Ihab   12:135-66
Klinkowitz   **9**:120
Hassan, Sally   **12**:152, 161, 162, 165
Hatch, Robert   **6**:279
Hathaway, Baxter
Katz   **14**:165
Ray   **7**:142-43
Hauková, Jiřina   **1**:338
Hauser, Marianne   11:123-38
Hausman, Gerald   **2**:271
Havighurst, Walter
Hall   **12**:119, 131
Knebel   **3**:169
Hawaii
Corcoran   **2**:125-26
Forbes   **16**:113, 114-15
Hongo   **22**:86
Houston, James D.   **16**:166-67,
      168-69
Houston, Jeanne Wakatsuki
      16:180-81

Knebel   **3**:175, 176, 182-83
Morgan   **3**:234, 238
*Hawaii: A Century of Economic Change,
      1778-1876*   **3**:238
Hawaii: The Sugar-Coated Fortress
      2:199
Hawk in the Rain, The   **6**:90
Hawker   **8**:248, 249, 250
Hawker, Robert Stephen   **8**:248
Hawkes, John
Guerard   **2**:229-30
Van Itallie   **2**:411
Hawkins, Eric   **1**:313
Hawkins, John   **2**:176
Hawk's Well Press   **1**:364
"Hawksbill Station"   **3**:279
Hawley, Robert   **2**:269
Hawthorne, Nathaniel
Jones   **11**:184
Mano   **6**:210
Mathews   **6**:245
Miller   **15**:282-83
Hayakawa, S.I.   **8**:132
Hayden, Jeff   **2**:289
Hayden, Robert
Aubert   **20**:27, 28
Ruark   **23**:271
Haydn, Hiram   **4**:115, 116, 120, 121
Haydon   **8**:248
Haydon, Benjamin Robert   **8**:248
Hayes, Harold   **7**:197
Hays, H.R.   **1**:392
Hays, Marvin   **7**:12
Hayter, Alethea   **2**:55
Hayward, Jack   **9**:149
Hayward, Mary Sulley   **7**:10
Hayward, Max   **11**:216
Hazard of Hearts, A   **8**:22
Hazard, the Painter   **14**:234, 235
Hazlett, Theodore L., Jr.   **11**:148-49,
      150
Hazlitt, William   **7**:232-33
Hazo, Robert G.   **11**:144, 155
Hazo, Samuel   11:139-55
H.D. See Doolittle, Hilda
He Wants Shih!   **2**:363, 365, 366
"He Was"   **26**:31
Head, Gwen   **23**:225-26
Head, Lois McAllister   **1**:377
Head of the Family, The   **3**:59
Health care   **8**:26
Heaney, Seamus
Brown   **6**:71
Gray   **3**:110
Parini   **16**:233, 237
Ruark   **23**:271, 283-85
Simmons   **21**:295
Heap, Jane   **5**:203
Hear That Lonesome Whistle Blow
      6:58
Hearing dysfunctions   **5**:362-63, 366
Hearne, G.R.M.   **8**:169
Hearon, Shelby   11:157-70
Hearst, William Randolph   **13**:259
Heart as Ever Green, The   **13**:250-51
Heart disease   **7**:283-85

Heart Is a Lonely Hunter, The   **7**:93
Heart of Aztlán   **4**:25, 26
Heath, A.M. (literary agent)   **2**:58
*Heath Anthology of American
      Literature*   **18**:76
Heath, Edward   **3**:46
Heath-Stubbs, John   21:61-73
Kennedy   **9**:82-83
Wain   **4**:329
Heaved from the Earth   **5**:349
Hebert, Ernest   24:243-60
Hébert, Jacques   **4**:76
Hebrew Orphan Asylum, New York
      City   **4**:55-56, 59
Hebrides Islands   **4**:305
Hedin, Sven   **1**:390-91
Hedva and I   **13**:153, 154
Heffernan, Michael   **23**:271, 277-79
Heggen, Thomas   **9**:258-59, 267
Heilman, Robert B.   **3**:408
Heinemann, Larry   21:75-99
Heinemann, William (publishers)
      8:172
Heinlein, Robert
Gunn   **2**:248
Knight   **10**:206
Niven   **12**:222
Williamson   **8**:321-22
Heinz, His Son, and the Evil Spirit
      13:154
Heisenberg, Werner Karl   **4**:65
Hejinian, Lyn   **23**:52
Helen Bullis Award   **15**:30
Helen in Egypt
Heath-Stubbs   **21**:69, 70
Ostriker   **24**:272
Heliczer, Piero
Hollo   **19**:168
Raworth   **11**:300-01
Van Itallie   **2**:411
Heller, Michael   **6**:140
Heller, Ursula   **13**:297
"Helliconia" series   **2**:28, 31
Hellman, Lillian   **2**:69
Hell's Cartographers   **4**:207
Hell's Pavement   **10**:203, 219
Helltracks   **16**:221
Helmet and Wasps   **7**:130
Helps, Robert   **1**:304
Hemingway, Ernest
Blaise   **3**:19
Bourjaily   **1**:68, 69, 72
Busch   **1**:130, 131, 132, 133, 137
Dillard   **7**:11
Eastlake   **1**:212
Guerard   **2**:222
Higgins   **5**:96
Katz   **9**:60
Kerrigan   **11**:217
Klinkowitz   **9**:118
Lottman   **12**:198, 206
Mano   **6**:217
Morgan   **20**:275-76
Salisbury   **15**:312-13
Shreve   **5**:228
Solotaroff   **2**:394

Wakefield　**7**:195, 196
Hemingway Hoax, The　**25**:212
Hemley, Cecil　**3**:415
Hemmings, David　**5**:273
Henchey, Richard　**26**:119
Henderson, David　**6**:195
Hendrix College　**20**:322
Hendrych, Jiří　**1**:347
Henley, W.E.　**3**:144
Henn, Tom
　　Davie　**3**:41
　　White　**4**:341
Hennings, Thomas　**1**:122
Henri, Adrian　**2**:52
Henri, Robert　**1**:104
Henry IV (king of France)　**4**:223-24
Henry IV, Part I　**5**:108
Henry Sows the Wind　**9**:23, 24
Hentoff, Nat　**6**:165-74
　　Corman　**2**:135
　　Salaam　**21**:244
Heny, Michael　**12**:353-55
Herald, Leon　**5**:202, 203, 208
Heraud, Javier　**6**:138
Herbert, David　**4**:232
Herbert, Frank　**2**:43, 45
*Herbert Read: The Stream and the
　　Source*　**6**:325-26
Herd, Dale　**11**:307
*Here I Am, There You Are, Where Were
　　We?*　**4**:157
Heredia, José Maria de　**2**:158
Hereford College of Education
　　11:368, 372-73, 377
Hereford, Frank　**1**:157
Heritage of Hastur, The　**10**:25
Herlihy, James Leo　**7**:78
Herman, Jan　**8**:90
Hermit of the Clouds　**24**:127, 148
Hernandez, Miguel　**1**:18, 25
Hero Driver　**9**:4
Heroes and Heroines　**8**:305
Heroics: Five Poems　**15**:230
"Heroine, The"　**4**:138
Herovit's World　**4**:210
Hersey, John　**13**:269
Heschel, Abraham Joshua　**4**:359
Hesiod　**15**:110
Heures, Les (The hours)　**13**:186, 190
"Hey!" and "Boo!" and "Bang!"
　　2:329
Heydrich, Reinhard　**1**:331
Heyen, William　**9**:31-48
　　Booth　**2**:58
Hicks, Edward　**5**:261
Hicks, Granville　**2**:290
"Hidden Locks"　**26**:241, 242
Hidden Locks　**26**:244
Hiemstra, Marvin R.　**26**:147-61
Hieroglyphics　**21**:261
Higgins, Aidan　**11**:214
Higgins, Brian
　　Sisson　**3**:302
　　Wright　**5**:371
Higgins, Dick　**8**:83-96
Higgins, George V.　**5**:91-101

Higgins, Marguerite　**4**:229
High Castle, The　**1**:255, 257, 258
High Cost of Living, The　**1**:272, 278
high green hill, th　**19**:28-30
High, John　**25**:268-69, 270-71
"High John da Conqueror"　**16**:67
Higher Education　**2**:397
Highland, Monica (joint pseudonym of
　　Carolyn See, John Espey, Lisa
　　See Kendall)　**22**:228
Highland, Monica (joint psuedonym of
　　Carolyn See, John Espey, Lisa
　　See Kendall)　**22**:231
Highlands, N.C.　**12**:355-56
Highwater, Jamake　**7**:69-83
Hill, Abram　**6**:267
Hill, Crag　**25**:190, 191-92
Hill, Geoffrey　**9**:85
Hill, Hugh Creighton　**14**:335
Hillel, Ben　**1**:209
Hillerman, Tony　**16**:146, 150
Hillestad, Paul　**18**:256-57
Hilliard, Richard　**5**:80
Hillman, Alex　**10**:215-16
Hilton, James　**1**:381
Himes, Chester
　　Major　**6**:186
　　Williams　**3**:424-25, 429
Hindenburg, Paul von　**1**:326
Hindman Settlement School　**17**:238-
　　39, 244
Hinduism　**14**:81, 86, 95
Hindustan Times　**9**:234
Hine, Daryl　**15**:217-36
　　Brewster　**15**:156
　　Mahapatra　**9**:146, 147
Hinnant, Bill　**4**:211
Hinojosa-Smith, Rolando　**16**:139-53
Hipsters, The　**25**:230, 231, 234
Hirsch, Judd　**2**:418
Hirschman, Jack
　　Eshleman　**6**:131, 132, 133, 137
　　Menefee　**26**:209, 210, 212
His First, Best Country　**15**:289
Hispanic Americans
　　Anaya　**4**:15-27
　　Bruce-Novoa　**18**:63-77
　　Hinojosa-Smith　**16**:139-53
Hispanic literature　**25**:54
History Day by Day　**2**:373
History of Barry　**4**:334
History of English Literature, A　**6**:36
History of My Heart　**4**:250
History of the Ojibway Nation, The
　　22:258-59, 263
History of Zionism, A　**19**:219, 223
Hitchcock, George　**12**:167-82
　　Argüelles　**24**:16, 19
　　di Suvero　**26**:73, 75
　　Jarman　**22**:100-01
　　McCord　**9**:183
Hitler, Adolf
　　Cassity　**8**:61
　　Eastlake　**1**:207
　　Geduld　**21**:48
　　Kazin　**7**:89

Kizer　**5**:150
Lind　**4**:198-99, 200, 202
Sinclair　**5**:267-68
Sisson　**3**:297
Škvorecký　**1**:326
Hoagland, Edward　**1**:41
Hoare, Penelope　**4**:84
Hobana, Ion　**8**:13
Hobart and William Smith Colleges
　　7:280
Hobart, Peter　**7**:295, 296
Hobsbaum, Philip　**9**:284, 285
Hobson, Wilder　**10**:91-92
Hocking, William Ernest　**5**:35, 44,
　　48
Hoddinott Veiling　**6**:99
Hoffman, Arthur　**11**:10
Hoffman, Daniel　**23**:257, 260, 261
Hoffman, Frederick J.　**8**:243
Hoffman, Heinrich　**8**:167
Hoffman, Lee　**10**:163-77
　　Grumman　**25**:193
Hofmann, Berenice　**6**:241
Hofstadter, Richard　**5**:271
Hofstra University
　　Block　**11**:38
　　Dann　**20**:86
Hofu ni kwenu: My Fear Is for You
　　21:210, 212, 246
Hogg, James
　　Simpson　**4**:294
　　Tennant　**9**:290, 292
Hoggart, Richard　**10**:115, 116
Hogrogian, Nonny See Kherdian,
　　Nonny Hogrogian
Hōjōki　**11**:204
Holden, Jonathan　**22**:59-77
Holden, Ursula　**8**:97-104
Holden, William　**3**:314
Hölderlin, Johann
　　Argüelles　**24**:24
　　Hamburger　**4**:163, 167, 169
　　Nichols　**2**:319
Holding On　**5**:128, 129
Holiday
　　Bowles　**1**:90
　　Williams　**3**:425-26, 427, 428, 429,
　　　430
Holiday Guide to Rome, The　**5**:80
Holland See Netherlands
Hollander, Anne　**6**:240-41
Hölldobler, Bert　**16**:305
Holleran, Andrew　**13**:230
Holliday, Joyce　**10**:97, 99
Hollins College
　　Dillard　**7**:15-16, 18
　　Hailey　**1**:227, 228
　　Taylor　**7**:179, 180, 182
Hollins Critic　**7**:16
Hollins Writing Conference
　　Chappell　**4**:122
　　Garrett　**5**:75
　　Taylor　**7**:180, 183
Hollo, Anselm　**19**:155-78
　　Raworth　**11**:299, 301, 303, 309
Holloway, Roberta　**23**:221

Hollywood Bowl **25**:388, 390-91
Hollywood, Calif.
  Bloch **20**:46-48, 51
  Duncan **2**:171-73
  Epstein **12**:60, 63, 67, 72, 75
  Fuchs **5**:55-58
  Meltzer **26**:187
  Van Proyen **25**:382
  Wallace **1**:376
Holman, Libby **1**:88-89, 90, 91
Holmes, James Henry **2**:170
Holmes, John
  Ciardi **2**:88, 89, 90
  Corman **2**:133, 136
  Kumin **8**:216
  Weiss **2**:436, 447
Holmes, Richard **26**:134
Holmes, Sherlock
  Anderson **2**:41, 43
  Keating **8**:164
Holmes, U.T. **20**:281
Holocaust, The
  Federman **8**:64-71
  Geduld **21**:46
  Grumbach **2**:209
  Heyen **9**:33-34, 43-44
  Josipovici **8**:146
  Katz **9**:62
  Kumin **8**:212
  Lem **1**:256
  Lind **4**:199-203
  Megged **13**:142-43
  Roditi **14**:270
  Salvadori **25**:361, 366
  Wiesel **4**:353-54, 357, 360-61
  Williams **26**:325
  Zeidner **24**:356
Holography **8**:190-91
Holt, John **6**:121
Holt, Rinehart & Winston (publishers)
  Boyd **11**:49-50
  Brown **6**:57, 58
Holy Cow: Parable Poems **8**:242
Holy Grail, The **1**:383
*Holy Ranger: Harley-Davidson Poems,
    The* **11**:333, 351-52, 353
Holy Sonnets **6**:213
Homage to Adana **2**:271, 272
Homage to Blenholt **5**:64, 65
Homage to Fats Navarro **3**:83
*Hombre de paso/Just Passing
    Through* **12**:104
Home **11**:345
Home/Bass **21**:177
Homenaje a Vlady **18**:74
Homeplace, The **23**:263-64
Homer
  Bruce-Novoa **18**:69
  Dudek **14**:123-24
  Forrest **7**:21
  Harris **16**:123
*Homeric Hymns and the Battle of the
    Frogs and the Mice, The* **15**:235
Homo **2**:363
Homosexuality

bissett **19**:13, 15-17, 35, 47, 49-
    50, 58
Blais **4**:77
Boyd **11**:43, 46, 47, 51, 54, 57,
    58-59
Bradley **10**:25-26
Brossard **16**:47-48, 51
Cherkovski **24**:93-97
Corn **25**:129, 134-35, 136-37,
    144-48
Foster **26**:117-18
Livesay **8**:226-27, 228
Norse **18**:278-82, 285, 290-91
Peters **8**:245-47
Picano **13**:222, 226-34
Roditi **14**:244, 248, 251-52, 281
Rule **18**:311-25
Salaam **21**:225
Van Itallie **2**:412
Honest Ulsterman, The **21**:291
Honey Spoon **25**:246, 247
Hong Kong **2**:48-49, 50, 51
Hongo, Garrett **22**:79-88
Honig, Edwin **8**:105-25
  Blaise **3**:20
Honolulu Advertiser **12**:125
Honolulu, Hawaii **12**:123-24
Hons and Rebels See *Daughters and
    Rebels: An Autobiography*
Hood, Hugh **17**:75-94
Hooks, Robert **6**:186
Hoover, Herbert **9**:94
Hoover, J. Edgar **18**:183
Hoover Medal **25**:363-64, 374
Hope, Donald **9**:83, 84
Hopkins, Gerard Manley
  Brown **6**:71
  Dacey **17**:29, 32
  Ghiselin **10**:133, 135
  Honig **8**:112
Hopkins, Henry **25**:395
Hopkins, Jeannette **21**:139
Hopkins, Joe **6**:56
Hopkins, Sam "Lightnin'" **7**:33
Hopkinson, Charles **4**:135
Hopscotch **9**:203
Hopwood Award
  Ciardi **2**:89-90
  Kennedy **9**:82, 84
  Piercy **1**:271
  Solotaroff **2**:394, 395
  Stevenson **9**:279
Hora, Josef **1**:341
Horace
  Dudek **14**:123-24
  Transtömer **17**:264-65
Horáková, Milada **1**:336
*Horgbortom Stringbottom, I Am Yours,
    You Are History* **13**:281
*Horizons: The Poetics and Theory of the
    Intermedia* **8**:91
Hormel, Al **9**:199, 200, 201
Horn **6**:210, 214, 215
Horn, Edward **14**:263
"Hornblower" series **4**:100
Horne, Hal **1**:192, 193

Horney, Karen **7**:46
Horovitz, Frances **9**:286-87
Horowitz, Israel **24**:128-29
Horowitz, Vladimir **12**:352
Horror films **20**:50
Horse and Jockey **1**:381
Horse Eats Hat **1**:84
"Horse Laugh, The" **1**:381
Horse Show at Midnight, The **7**:181,
    182
Horses
  di Suvero **26**:79-81
  Hoffman **10**:165, 166-67, 169,
      170-72
  Jones **11**:177
  Kenny **22**:130, 148-49
  Taylor **7**:171-72, 174-77
  Villanueva **24**:304, 311, 312
Horton, Andrew **16**:245-70
Horwood, Harold **15**:237-53
Hospital of Transfiguration, The **1**:259
Hot-Eyed Moderate, A **18**:309
Hot Rock, The **13**:342-43
Hot Rod **7**:158-59
Hotel de Dream **9**:291-92
Hotel de la Nuit qui Tombe, L'
    26:286
*Hotel Nirvana: Selected Poems,
    1953–1973* **18**:276, 289
Hotspur **6**:65, 66
Hotspur: A Ballad for Music **23**:15
Houghton Mifflin Co. (publishers)
  Davison **4**:141
  Gerber **20**:167
  Kinsella **7**:104, 105-06
  Mott **7**:132-33
  Stegner **9**:267
  Wakefield **7**:198
Houghton Mifflin Literary Fellowship
  Kinsella **7**:105, 110
  Petry **6**:264, 265
Hound and Horn **5**:209
Hound of Earth, The **1**:71, 72, 73
Hour before Midnight, The **4**:108
House by the Sea, The **13**:47, 52
House Full of Women, A **15**:160
House of Hospitalities, The **9**:294
House of Leaves, The **16**:281
House of the Seven Gables, The **6**:210
House of the Solitary Maggot, The
    1:303
Houseman, John **18**:180-81
Housman, A.E. **4**:245
Houston City Magazine **18**:202
Houston, James D. **16**:155-70
Houston, Jeanne Wakatsuki
    16:175, 180-86
Houston, Jeanne Wakatsuki **16**:171-
    86
  Houston, James D. **16**:157, 163,
      164-65, 168-69
Houston, Tex.
  Cassity **8**:57
  Guerard **2**:217
  Shreve **5**:238
Hovde, Carl **26**:119-20, 122

How 'Bout Them Gamecocks! **19**:130
How Cities Are Saved **12**:207
How Does a Poem Mean? **20**:332
How I Blew Up the World **13**:15, 27
*How I Escaped from the Labyrinth and
    Other Poems* **17**:27
*How I Got Ovah: New and Selected
    Poems* **13**:250
How NOT to Become a Millionaire
    2:145
How She Died **20**:352, 358
How to Read **3**:305
How to Write Horror Fiction **16**:221
Howard, Alan **2**:329, 331
Howard, Donald **8**:244
Howard, Elizabeth Jane **4**:82-84
Howard, Peter **2**:210
Howard, Richard
    Corn **25**:142-43
    Disch **4**:156
    Taylor **7**:187
Howard University
    Emanuel **18**:130-31
    Forbes **16**:118
    Killens **2**:282, 286
    Major **6**:190
Howe, Irving
    Higgins **5**:92-93
    Shapiro **6**:306
    Solotaroff **2**:398
    Sukenick **8**:289-90
Howes, Barbara **3**:133-47
Howl
    Armantrout **25**:15
    Eshleman **6**:128
    Sanders **21**:259
    Saroyan **5**:213
    Škvorecký **1**:346
Howland, Llewellyn **3**:431
Hrabal, Bohumil **12**:183-95
    Škvorecký **1**:338
Hu Shih **5**:140-41
Hubbard, L. Ron **8**:321, 325
Huckleberry Finn
    Bell **12**:22
    Dennison **6**:121
    Van Brunt **15**:371-72
Hudd, Roy **9**:16
Huddle, David **20**:177-93
Hudgins, Andrew **21**:101-18
Hueffer, Ford Madox See Ford, Ford
    Madox
Huésped de mi tiempo **15**:11
Hugh MacLennan **6**:323
Hughes, A.M.D. **4**:325-26, 328
Hughes, Carol **1**:29
Hughes, Howard **1**:383
Hughes, Langston
    Atkins **16**:10-11, 13
    Emanuel **18**:133, 134, 138, 140
    Forbes **16**:105, 112
    Joans **25**:223, 228-30, 231, 232-
        33
    Madgett **23**:199, 200
    Salaam **21**:181, 182-87, 190-91,
        195, 196, 228

Hughes, Ted
    Abse **1**:28, 29
    Booth **2**:52, 54, 55, 59
    Burroway **6**:90, 91, 92
    Davison **4**:134
    Menashe **11**:235
    Stevenson **9**:280
Hugo Award
    Bova **18**:55
    Brunner **8**:9, 11
    Gunn **2**:257
    Niven **12**:211, 213
    Pohl **1**:295
    Silverberg **3**:274, 279, 281, 282
    Wilhelm **5**:309
Hugo, Richard
    DeMarinis **24**:123-24
    Holden **22**:71, 73
    McElroy **21**:136
Hugo, Victor **2**:373
Huis Clos (No Exit) **1**:87
Huizenga, John W. **18**:251-52, 254
Hull, Betty
    Pohl **1**:296
    Wolfe **9**:308
Hull, Cordell **2**:407
Hull, Helen **2**:288
Hull, Tristram **5**:370
Human Comedy, The **2**:267
Human Dolphin Foundation **26**:76
Human Like Me, Jesus **11**:54-55
Human Voices **10**:105
Humanism
    Lind **4**:200
    Rimmer **10**:303
Humanoids, The **8**:323, 324
Hummer, Terry **7**:164, 165, 166
Humor **12**:201
Humphrey, William **2**:436, 437,
    438-39
Humphreys, Dick **8**:76
Humphries, Rolfe **6**:90
Huncke, Herbert **6**:132
Hundley, Richard **1**:304
Hundreds of Hens and Other Poems
    23:260
Hungarian Revolution, 1956
    Davie **3**:42
    Sinclair **5**:270
Hungary **5**:196, 197, 198
"Hungover City" **26**:303
Hungryalist (bulletin) **14**:89-94
Hungryalist (literary movement)
    14:88-94, 98
Hunted, The **2**:223
Hunter College
    Elkins **18**:97
    Hahn **11**:110
    Inez **10**:189
    Lowitz **26**:174
    Root **11**:329
    Wakoski **1**:363
Hunter, Evan **11**:28
Huntingdon College **21**:113-15, 116,
    117

Huntington Hartford Foundation
    8:134
Huntley, Chet **1**:394
Hurst, Maurice (Capitanchick) **5**:261
Hurston, Zora Neale **21**:184, 244,
    250
Hurtig, Mel **22**:47
Huseboe, Arthur R. **18**:257, 259-60
Huston, John
    Bowles **1**:87
    Wallace **1**:383
Hutchinson, Anne **10**:304
Hutchinson, Mary St. John **5**:371
Huxley, Aldous
    Aldiss **2**:22
    Allen **6**:17, 23
    Dillard **7**:6
    Easton **14**:148, 159
    Ghiselin **10**:133
Huysmans, Joris K. **20**:93
Hyakutake (comet) **24**:320, 323
Hyman, Mac **4**:115, 116
Hyman, Stanley **7**:294, 302-03
Hyman, Stanley Edgar
    Delbanco **2**:159
    Furman **18**:196
    Waldman **17**:273
Hyman, Timothy **8**:157, 158, 160
*Hymn to the Rebel Cafe: Poems
    1986–1991* **21**:257, 264, 272
Hymns Are My Prayers **23**:211
Hymns to the Night **8**:85
Hypochondria **25**:19
"Hypothetical Arbitrary Constant of
    Inhibition, The" **16**:15

I Am a Camera **2**:411
"I Am Lucy Terry" **16**:67
I Am One of You Forever **4**:124-25
*I Am the Babe of Joseph Stalin's
    Daughter* **2**:364
I Am the Bitter Name **26**:326
"I Came to See You But You Were
    Asleep" **2**:70
I Ching **15**:159
I, Claudius **4**:29
I Do Remember the Fall **22**:117
"I Dream the Book of Jonah"
    23:262
I Enter Your Church **21**:245, 246
I Heard My Sister Speak My Name
    15:337, 339, 342
I, Maximus **3**:90
I Refuse **16**:260-61
I Remember Root River **2**:262, 275
I Served the King of England **12**:193
I Tell You Now **22**:273
I Walk the Line **11**:182
I Wanted a Year without Fall **1**:133
Ibsen, Henrik
    Blais **4**:75
    Wallace **1**:391
    White **4**:333
Ibura **21**:215
Ice and Fire **21**:18-19
Iceland **9**:184

I'd Rather Be a Phoenix! **26**:153, 157
Idaho **14**:168
Idée d'éternité, l' (The concepts of
    eternity) **13**:181
Identities and Other Poems **13**:139
Idiot Menagerie **24**:68, 74
Idiot, The **4**:148
Idle Hands **11**:207
Idol, The **3**:322
If
    Knight **10**:221
    Lowitz **26**:170
    Pohl **1**:292
If I Go Down to Hell **11**:48
If It Moves, Salute It **2**:168
*If Mountains Die: A New Mexico
    Memoir* **2**:335
*If You Don't Like Me You Can Leave
    Me Alone* **5**:165, 166
Ignatow, David 3:149-61
    Bergé **10**:6
Ignoramus **15**:307
*Ikagnak: The North Wind: With Dr.
    Kane in the Arctic* **8**:248
"Illianna Comes Home" **7**:102
Illinois Institute of Technology
    12:230-31
Illot **14**:91
Illusion, The **4**:100
Illustrated London News **1**:392
Illustrated Weekly of India **9**:233
I'm Not Thousandfurs **26**:210
I'm Talking about Jerusalem **7**:249-50
Imaginary Lover, The **24**:276
Imaginary Magnitude **1**:262
Imaginary Portraits **26**:153
Immanuel Kant in England **7**:220,
    224
Immaterial Murder Case, The **3**:389
Immoral Reverend, The **10**:285, 303
Immortal, The **2**:254, 255, 256
Immortal Wife **3**:370
Immortals, The **2**:251, 252, 253, 254,
    258
*Impact 20: Excursions into the
    Extraordinary* **16**:215
Imperfect Love **20**:337
Impetus **7**:12
Importance of Being Earnest, The
    7:182
Impotence
    Brunner **8**:10
    Kerrigan **11**:218-19
In a Dark Time **15**:23
In a Green Eye **1**:223
In a Lost World **14**:284
In America's Shoes **19**:91
In and Out **15**:224
In Broken Country **3**:411
In Chontales **3**:81, 83
"In Darkness and Confusion" **6**:265
In Deepest U.S.A. **26**:154-55, 160
In Defence of Art **14**:135
"In Fact" **6**:171
In Good Time **2**:141
In My Forest Trees Sing **26**:160-61

*In Pharoah's Army: Memories of the
    Lost War* **22**:279-306
In Search of Eros **15**:151, 157, 158-
    59
In Search of History **6**:172
*In Search of Wonder: Essays on Modern
    Science Fiction* **10**:220
In the American Tree **23**:31, 52
In the Arriving **24**:125
In the Beginning **4**:265
In the Field of Fire **20**:99
"In the House of Double Minds"
    3:283
In the House of the Judge **7**:165
In the Middle Distance **2**:156, 159
In the Mists: Mountain Poems **19**:152
"In the South Seas" **6**:325
In the Trojan Ditch **3**:304, 305
In the Twelfth Year of the War **18**:30,
    37
In the Uneven Steps of Hung-Chow
    26:33-34
In Transit **4**:85
"In Trivandrum" **22**:201-07
In Watermelon Sugar **7**:107
Ina Coolbrith Prize **26**:70
Inayat Khan, Pir Vilayat **23**:310-11
*Incas and Other Men: Travels in the
    Andes* **6**:321
Incest **25**:9
Income and Employment **3**:238, 243
*Incomparable Aphra: A Life of Mrs.
    Aphra Behn, The* **6**:321
Incubator on the Rock **13**:153
India
    Aldiss **2**:19, 20-21
    Choudhury **14**:81-99
    Hahn **11**:116, 117-18
    Hauser **11**:130-31
    Keating **8**:171, 172, 174
    Kyger **16**:195
    Mahapatra **9**:137-50
    McCord **9**:183
    Ray **7**:145-46
    Rimmer **10**:291-92
    Singh **9**:223-25, 228-29, 232, 233-
        35
    Skelton **5**:281-82
    Tillinghast **23**:312-13
    Van Itallie **2**:419
    Waldman **17**:279, 282
    Woodcock **6**:321-22, 324-25
Indian Phantom Play **11**:131
Indiana University
    Appleman **18**:35, 36, 37
    Barnstone **15**:107
    Brewster **15**:155, 157
    Caute **4**:105
    Eshleman **6**:129, 130
    Hiemstra **26**:153
    Manuel **9**:166
    Peters **8**:241
    Solotaroff **2**:396
    Wagoner **3**:403
    West **7**:281-82

Indiana University Press Poetry
    Series **3**:404
Indianapolis, Ind. **6**:125-28
Indianapolis Star **7**:195
"Indictable Suborners" **26**:24
"Individual and Mass Psychology"
    3:140
Individualism Reconsidered **20**:45
Indonesia
    Morgan **3**:242
    Raffel **9**:210-11
    Swenson **13**:316
Inez, Colette 10:179-97
Inferno (Larry Niven) **12**:222
Inferno See also *Divine Comedy*
Infinite, The **24**:126
Infinite Worlds **14**:133
Infinity of Mirrors, An **1**:197
Informal Logic **26**:227
Infused **25**:74
Inge, William **2**:173
Ingram Merrill Poetry Writing
    Fellowship
    Allen **11**:22
    Corn **25**:147
Inhabitant, The **22**:243
Inheritor, The **10**:26
Injunction **24**:126
Inkling, The **4**:118, 120
inkorrect thots **19**:3, 6-8, 31, 32-33,
    39, 55
Inkster, Tim **15**:357
Inman, Philip **5**:260, 261
Inman, Will **26**:221
Inner Weather **13**:204
Innes, Michael (pseudonym of J.I.M.
    Stewart) **3**:348, 352, 353, 354,
    355-56, 357
Innocence **10**:109
Innocence Is Drowned **6**:20
Innocent, The **11**:178-80, 181
Innovative Fiction **9**:113
Inocencia perversa/Perverse Innocence
    18:74
Inscripts **11**:153
Insect Societies, The **16**:302
Inside Linda Lovelace **5**:127
Insoumise, L' **4**:73, 76
Inspector Ghote Breaks an Egg **8**:172
Inspector Ghote Caught in Meshes
    8:172
Inspector Ghote Draws a Line **8**:175
Inspector Ghote Goes by Train **8**:173
Inspector Ghote Hunts the Peacock
    8:172
Inspector Ghote Plays a Joker **8**:172
Inspector Ghote Trusts the Heart
    8:173
Inspector Ghote's Good Crusade **8**:172
Instamatic Reconditioning **24**:16, 17
Institute of American Indian Arts
    17:289
Institute of Design, Chicago, Ill.
    12:342
Instituto Americano, Barcelona,
    Spain **2**:328

Integration **22**:313-14
"Intellectual, The" **6**:299
Intelligent Woman's Guide to Socialism and Capitalism, The **18**:172
Intemperance: The Unexpurgated Version **9**:186
Intercourse **21**:9-10
Interior Landscapes: Autobiographical Myths and Metaphors **22**:273
Interlochen Arts Academy **11**:328
Intermedia
    Higgins **8**:94
    Kostelanetz **8**:186
International Commission on English in the Liturgy **3**:64
International Congress of Crime Writers **18**:104
International Honors Program **18**:35-36, 39
International News Service **3**:122, 123
International Poetry Festival, Rotterdam, Holland, 1977 **6**:192
International Poetry Festival, Struga, Yugoslavia, 1975 **6**:190-91
International Poetry Forum **11**:149-50
    See also United States Award
International Pushkin Festival **2**:305
International Who's Who in Poetry **9**:145
International Writers' Program, University of Iowa
    Corman **2**:145
    Mahapatra **9**:146-47
Interview **13**:19
Interview: A Fugue for Eight Actors **2**:414
Intimate Sex Lives of Famous People, The **1**:378, 384, 401
Into Tibet: The Early British Explorers **6**:325
Introduction to Economics (Theodore Morgan) **3**:238, 241
Introduction to Poetry, An **9**:85
Intruder, The **16**:214
Invaders from Earth **3**:276
Invention of Spain, The **24**:17
Inventory, The **8**:146-47, 156
Investigative Poetry **21**:269
Invincible, The **1**:260, 261
Invisible Man, The
    Bennett **13**:84
    Forrest **7**:23
Invocations **8**:187
Ionesco, Eugene **12**:158
Iovis: All Is Full of Jove **17**:290
Iowa
    Hiemstra **26**:147
    Morris **13**:165-66, 167
Iowa Art Project **1**:164
Iowa Baseball Confederacy, The **7**:107
Iowa City Creative Reading Series **7**:102-03
Iowa City, Iowa

Bell **14**:48
    Grumbach **2**:212
Iowa Review **14**:48
Iowa Short Fiction Award **12**:246
Iowa State Teacher's College **1**:163
Iowa Writers' Workshop
    Bausch **14**:8
    Becker **1**:39
    Bell **14**:44-45, 48, 49
    Blaise **3**:25-26
    Bourjaily **1**:72, 73, 74, 79
    Browne **20**:62-63
    Cassill **1**:167-68, 171-72
    Dacey **17**:27-28
    Dove **19**:104-05
    Fox **19**:129-30
    Glancy **24**:199, 212
    Grumbach **2**:212
    Haldeman **25**:203-05
    Hall **12**:132-33
    Hiemstra **26**:151
    Hudgins **21**:118
    Kinsella **7**:102, 103
    Ray **7**:143
    Settle **1**:320
    Sward **13**:288-89
    Turco **22**:238
    Vinograd **26**:298
    Wright **7**:297-99
IRA See Irish Republican Army
Iran
    Lessing **14**:184-86
    Rachlin **17**:215-29
    Tillinghast **23**:311-12
Ireland
    Arden **4**:31, 43
    Berrigan **1**:59
    Davie **3**:38-39, 42
    Dillon **3**:49-50
    Galvin **13**:100, 101
    Nichols **2**:308
    O'Faolain **2**:339-46, 350
    Ruark **23**:282-84
    Skelton **5**:292-93
    Tillinghast **23**:317-18
Ireland, Kevin **3**:257-58, 259, 263
Irgun **4**:355-56
Iris **22**:90-91
Irish **21**:275-97
Irish Americans
    Ciardi **2**:86-87
    Clark **22**:3-4
    Higgins **5**:94-95, 99
Irish Renaissance **5**:285-86
Irish Republican Army **3**:56
Irish Signorina, The **2**:352
Irish Strategies **11**:210
Iron Dream, The **19**:327, 331
Iron Flowers **21**:216, 219-20
Iron Heel, The **18**:171
Iron Pastoral, The **17**:184
Irresponsibles, The **8**:301, 308
Irving, John
    Becker **1**:39
    Blaise **3**:15, 26
    Dworkin **21**:20

Is Skin-deep, Is Fatal **8**:172
Isaac Asimov: The Foundations of Science Fiction **2**:257
Isaacson, Bruce **26**:305, 307-08, 309
Isherwood, Christopher
    Allen **6**:18, 27
    Barnstone **15**:62
    Glanville **9**:21
    Norse **18**:278, 288, 290
    Peters **8**:244, 250
    Weiss **2**:443
Ishimoto's Land **1**:208
Island in the City: The World of Spanish Harlem **7**:197
Island of Demons, The **6**:322
Island of Dr. Moreau, The **3**:271
Islanders, The **13**:297
Isle of Arran **4**:43
Israel
    Goldemberg **12**:98
    Katz **9**:64
    Markfield **3**:222
    Raffel **9**:216
    Silkin **5**:258
    Wakefield **7**:196-97
Istanboul **2**:361, 363
It Is Time, Lord **4**:115, 116-17
Italian-Abyssinian War **2**:309
Italian Americans
    Ciardi **2**:80-86, 87
    DeMarinis **24**:110
Italian military school **25**:353-54
Italians
    Jennings **5**:111-12
    Vivante **12**:284
Italy
    Argüelles **24**:12
    Booth **2**:60
    Bryant **26**:47-48, 61-62
    Davie **3**:39
    Dove **19**:112
    Ghiselin **10**:140-43
    Glanville **9**:21-23, 24
    Jarman **22**:94, 105-06
    Katz **14**:170, 171-73
    Mrozek **10**:272
    Parini **16**:238, 239-40
    Pellegrini **11**:262, 265-72
    Ray **7**:143
    Salvadori **25**:374-76
    Stone **3**:372-73, 374
    Van Brunt **15**:376-77
    Wright **7**:295-97, 298, 301-02
Ithaca, New York **18**:331-33
It's Easy to Fall on the Ice: Ten Stories **15**:160
"It's the Same Only Different/The Melancholy Owed Categories" **26**:33
Ivanhoe, Virginia **20**:177-82
Ivask, Ivar **2**:367
"I've Had My Fun" **7**:33
Iwamoto, Iwao **12**:164
Iwaniuk, Waclaw **22**:54

Jabbing the Asshole Is High Comedy
   13:25-26
"Jackfish City Days" **26**:39
Jackowski, Andrzej **8**:158, 160
Jackson, Blyden **20**:22, 24, 25
Jackson, Charles **2**:329
Jackson, Glenda **5**:126
Jackson, Hilary Hazlewood **1**.197
Jackson, Jesse **11**:193
Jackson, Joseph Henry **3**:375
Jackson, Mahalia **7**:26, 33-35
Jackson, Richard **15**:288-89
Jackson, Robert **14**:272
Jackson, "Shoeless" Joe **7**:103
Jacob Glatstein Memorial Prize
   9:146
Jacob, Max **9**:82
Jacobs, Anthony **12**:12
Jacobs, W.W. **6**:34
Jacobsen, Josephine 18:205-21
Jacobson, Lucien **8**:71, 74
Jaffe, James **12**:348, 350, 353
Jaffe, Marc **1**:295
Jagger, Mick **25**:21
Jagiellonian University **9**:134
Jake and Honeybunch Go to Heaven
   6:154-56
Jakobson, Roman **3**:40
Jakobssen, Ejler **12**:218
Jakobsson, Ejler **26**:18
Jamaica
   Forbes **16**:118-19
   Simpson **4**:290
"James at 15" **7**:200-01
James, Edwin (pseudonym of James
   Gunn) **2**:249
James, Henry
   Bourjaily **1**:72
   Burroway **6**:91
   Gray **3**:109
   Honig **8**:113
   Kazin **7**:91
   Stewart **3**:355
James, John **8**:244-45
James M. Cain **3**:192
James Shirley's Love's Cruelty **17**:178-
   79
James V. Mitchell Memorial Award
   for Playwriting **11**:142
James, William **19**:252
Jamison, Judith **7**:31
Janes, Alfred **2**:441
"January" **4**:115
January: A Screenplay **7**:19
Japan
   Beltrametti **13**:60-62
   Bennett **25**:51
   Burroway **6**:100
   Eshleman **6**:134, 135-37
   Kirkup **4**:183-88, 190-91
   Kyger **16**:193-96
   Lowitz **26**:178, 179, 180
   McPherson **17**:133
Japan Foundation Award **9**:148
Japanese Americans **16**:171-86
Japan's Mein Kampf **1**:386

Japji **9**:231
Jargon Society (publishers) **12**:340,
   348, 349, 352
Jarman, Mark 22:89-106
   Feirstein **11**:84
Jarrell, Randall
   Hassan **12**:149
   Kennedy **9**:84
   Root **11**:322
   Simpson **4**:293
   Sinclair **5**:275
   Smith **7**:158, 167
   Weiss **2**:447
Jarry, Alfred
   Kennedy **9**:82, 83
   Slavitt **3**:313
Jauss, David **17**:29-30
Jay, Peter **13**:136, 138
Jazz
   Ashby **6**:34
   Brunner **8**:6
   Dillard **7**:6
   Eshleman **6**:126-28
   Federman **8**:72-73
   Fisher **10**:91-92, 93, 99
   Forbes **16**:117
   Forrest **7**:29, 30, 31
   Hentoff **6**:166, 168, 171
   Joans **25**:221-22
   Katz **14**:164
   Kerrigan **11**:198
   Kirkup **4**:190
   Klinkowitz **9**:107, 110, 120
   Major **6**:182
   Matthews **18**:269-70
   Meltzer **26**:188
   Rabassa **9**:198, 203
   Salaam **21**:187-88, 198, 232, 244-
     45, 249
   Škvorecký **1**:328, 339, 348
   weiss **24**:328-29, 332-33, 339-42,
     345, 348, 351
   West **7**:285
Jazz Country **6**:169
Jazz hot, Le **10**:92
Jazz Press **8**:246
Jeffers, Robinson
   Anderson **2**:46
   Broughton **12**:49-50
Jefferson Reporter **1**:143, 144
Jefferson, Thomas **7**:164
Jefferson's Birthday/Postface **8**:87, 88
Jellema, W. Harry **18**:251, 253, 254
Jellinek, Ernst **5**:173-74, 175
Jenkins, Ann **20**:67
Jenkins, David **9**:252
Jenkins, Joyce **26**:82
Jenkins, Louis **20**:67, 69
Jennings, Elizabeth 5:103-15
Jensen, Dale **24**:24
Jensen, Johannes V. **2**:46
Jensen, Julie **26**:160
Jeremy's Version **1**:303
Jerome, Judson 8:127-43
   Allen **11**:16
Jerusalem

Jones **5**:125
   Wiesel **4**:356, 359
Jerusalem Commands **5**:186
Jess
   Berry **24**:79
   di Suvero **26**:70
Jesuit order (Society of Jesus) **1**:48
Jesus **1**:59
*Jesus and Fat Tuesday and Other Short
   Stories* **21**:125, 139
Jesus Christ **4**:196, 197
Jet **3**:424
Jewish Advocate **4**:137
Jewish Americans
   Corman **2**:129-30
   Elman **3**:69
   Kazin **7**:86
   Markfield **3**:209, 219
   Silverberg **3**:270
   Solotaroff **2**:391
Jewish Daily Forward **4**:357
Jewish University **9**:62
Jews
   Barnstone **15**:48, 49, 73, 92, 97-
     98
   Becker **1**:33
   Bernstein **24**:33-35
   Brown **10**:42
   Cherkovski **24**:88-89
   Davis **20**:104-06, 110-11
   Davison **4**:134
   Dworkin **21**:2, 21
   Elkins **18**:93-94
   Epstein **12**:59-76
   Federman **8**:64-72
   Feirstein **11**:75-77
   Foley **24**:166-68
   Geduld **21**:52-53
   Gerber **20**:174
   Goldemberg **12**:93-94, 96-101,
     102, 103-06
   Gray **2**:183, 188, 191
   Gurik **23**:99-100, 107
   Hamburger **4**:161, 162, 170
   Josipovici **8**:146
   Kammen **23**:134-37
   Katz **9**:51, 58, 63
   Kazin **7**:86
   Kumin **8**:205, 208-09, 212
   Laqueur **19**:209-12
   Lifshin **10**:237, 247
   Lind **4**:195-97
   Megged **13**:141-59
   Nichols **2**:317
   Norse **18**:276
   Ostriker **24**:262, 263, 264, 265
   Raffel **9**:209
   Rakosi **5**:194, 196, 197
   Roditi **14**:253-54, 276
   Rosenblum **11**:341
   Salisbury **15**:318, 319
   Salvadori **25**:357-58
   Silkin **5**:244, 247
   Simpson **4**:286, 287
   Solotaroff **2**:397-99
   Sward **13**:282, 284

Van Itallie 2:405
Vivante 12:287
Weiss 12:332-33
Wesker 7:233-34
Wiesel 1:353 61
Williams 26:319-20
Yglesias 20:345-46, 350
Jews of Silence, The 4:357
Jews See also Anti-Semitism
Jhabvala, Ruth Prawer 8:171
Jim Fisk 13:268
Jiménez, Juan Ramón
    Alegría 15:5-6
    Cruz 17:3, 4, 5-6
    Olson 12:234
J'irai cracher sur vos tombes 8:72
Jo Stern 3:322
Joad, C.E.M. 5:313
Joanne 16:200
Joans, Ted 25:219-58
Job's Year 17:64, 71
Joel, George 1:72
*Joey: The Life and Political Times of
    Joey Smallwood* 15:252-53
Jogues, Isaac 22:143
Johannesburg and Other Poems
    21:175-76
Johannesburg, South Africa
    Cassity 8:49, 52-54, 57
    Wright 5:361, 373
John and Mary 5:125-26, 128, 129,
    131
John and Mary (film) 5:127-28
John Huston: King Rebel 16:215
*John Lee Taylor: Minister and
    Missionary* 7:3
John of the Cross, Saint See Juan de
    la Cruz, San
John Paul I, Pope 7:50
John Toronto 22:54
John W. Campbell Award 2:257
John William Corrington Award
    20:339
John XXIII, Pope
    Greeley 7:44
    Morgan 4:231
Johns Hopkins University
    Hadas 23:122
    Shapiro 6:291, 301-02
Johnson, Andrew 1:394
Johnson, Charles 18:223-43
Johnson, George Clayton 16:215,
    216
Johnson, Herbert (Hoppie) 3:418,
    419
Johnson, Hewlett 4:305
Johnson, James Weldon 7:23
Johnson, Johnnie 9:107, 120
Johnson, Lyndon
    Knebel 3:178, 181
    Pohl 1:291
Johnson, Paul 5:124
Johnson Publishing Company 18:236
Johnson, Ryerson 10:219
Johnson, Samuel 4:114, 116
Johnson, Siddie Jo 1:225

Johnson, Spud 14:109, 111
Johnson, William Eugene 13:277
Johnson, William R. 8:306
Johnston, George
    Brewster 15:156
    Corman 2:144
Joint Defense Appeal 3:220, 221
Jolas, Maria 12:199
Jolley, Elizabeth 13:105-23
Joly, Greg 25:48
Jones, E.H. 9:267
Jones, Ernest 5:117, 118-19, 120,
    129, 130
Jones, Gayl 20:215
Jones, James
    Bourjaily 1:71
    Heinemann 21:83, 84, 94
    Major 6:187
    Norse 18:285, 286
    Ray 7:140-42
    Wright 7:294
Jones, James Earl
    Giovanni 6:156
    Kennedy 20:227
    Wallace 1:394
Jones, L.E. 1:38
Jones, LeRoi
    Joans 25:236
    Wakoski 1:363-64
    See also Baraka, Amiri
Jones, Loyal 15:288
Jones, Madison 11:171-87
Jones, Mervyn 5:117-32
Jones, Nettie 20:195-218
Jong, Erica 6:188
Jonson, Ben 3:408
Jordan, Fred 3:322
Jordan, June 24:25
Jordan, Paul 9:79, 80
Jordan, Richard 2:411
Joron, Andrew 24:20, 26, 27, 28
Joseph and His Brothers 11:231
Joseph Conrad 2:221
Joseph, Michael 6:22
Joseph, Michael (publishers) 6:20, 25
Josephy, Alvin 6:56
Josipovici, Gabriel 8:145-61
Joualonais sa Joualonie, Un 4:78
Jouffroy, Simon-Théodore 5:314
Jour est Noir, Le 4:74
Journal American 2:400
Journal dénoué (Unbound diary)
    13:188
*Journal of an Apprentice Cabbalist,
    The* 14:284
Journal of Contemporary History, The
    19:219
Journalism
    Allen 11:8
    Bell 14:40-41
    Boyd 11:44, 45, 54
    Easton 14:155-56
    Glanville 9:17, 19-20, 24, 26, 28
    Green 11:96, 97
    Hine 15:225
    Horwood 15:245

Houston 16:178-79
Johnson 18:230-31, 236, 237
Kirk 9:100
Knebel 3:169-70, 176-77, 179-80
Lottman 12:201-04
Megged 13:156
Morgan 4:227, 229-31
Salaam 21:188
Salisbury 15:311-13, 315, 321-24
Shadbolt 3:262
Sward 13:286, 287
Wiesel 4:356-58
Journalists, The 7:256, 260-61
Journals and Dreams 17:283
"Journey Away, A" 5:209
Journey in the Month of Av 13:156,
    157
Journey to Chaos 8:77
Journey to the Land of Gomer 13:153
Journeying Boy, The 3:348
Jouve, Pierre Jean 13:183
Jovanovich, William 4:134
Joy Makers, The 2:251, 252, 253,
    258
"Joy of Living, The" 16:212, 217-
    18, 219
Joyce, James
    Argüelles 24:5
    Becker 1:36, 43
    Belitt 4:54
    Booth 5:44
    Dillard 7:14
    Forrest 7:23
    Jones 5:121
    Lottman 12:198, 206
    Pinsky 4:238
    Pohl 1:285
    Salvadori 25:374
    Solotaroff 2:394-95
    Wallace 1:375, 391, 396
Joyce, William 2:312
Juan de la Cruz, San 17:191
Juana La Loca 1:317
Judaism
    Bell 14:37-38
    Fuchs 5:67
    Goldemberg 12:95-101
    Hentoff 6:166, 171
    Josipovici 8:152
    Kazin 7:86
    Lem 1:256
    Ostriker 24:273, 275
    Piercy 1:269
    Rimmer 10:296
    Shapiro 23:289-98
    Silkin 5:246-47
    Škvorecký 1:327, 329
    See also Cabala
Judd, Donald 5:216
Jude the Obscure 5:141
Judgment Day 7:89
Judson Memorial Church, New York
    City 6:117
Judson Poets' Theatre, New York
    City 2:360

Judy Garland and the Cold War
    21:280
Juice   1:36
Junction
    Brewster   15:160
    Dann   20:93, 94, 95-96
Jung, Carl
    Hiemstra   26:156
    Howes   3:140, 142
    Schevill   12:263-64, 273
    Stone   3:367, 376
Junges Deutschland   6:192
Jungle Book, The   13:167
"Jungle Doctor, The" books   2:50
Jungwirth, Frantisek   1:338
Junior Bachelor Society, The   3:422,
    431
Juniper Von Phitzer Press   26:157
Jupus Redeye   17:50-51, 56
Jurassic Shales, The   13:281, 295, 296
Jurevitch, Juri   1:79
Just Feet   25:74
Just Space   16:202
"Just William" series   2:310
Justice, Donald
    Bourjaily   1:73
    di Suvero   26:83
    Hiemstra   26:153
    Levis   23:191
    McPherson   23:227
    Turco   22:239
    Wright   7:297, 299
Juxta   25:267

K-Factor, The   4:109
Kabbalists   25:268
"Kaddish for Martin Horowitz"
    26:302-03
Kafka, Franz
    Blaise   3:19
    Brossard   2:72, 74
    Harris   3:130
    Honig   8:122, 123
    Olson   11:249, 250
    Škvorecký   1:347
Kaftanikoff, Luba   9:281
Kagey, Rudolph   2:207
Kahawa   13:343
Kahler, Erich   12:29, 30, 31, 35, 36
Kahn, Joan   15:194
Kahn, Louis   26:315
Kahn, Michael
    Kennedy   20:221-22, 225, 226
    Van Itallie   2:412
Kahn, Paul   5:169
Kahn, Wolf   7:297, 298
Kalevala, The   19:160-61
Kallman, Chester   18:278-79, 280-81,
    284
Kalstone, David
    Corn   25:143-44, 146
    Mathews   6:239, 250
Kama Sutra   10:291
Kamaike, Susumu   2:141, 142
Kammen, Michael   23:133-63
Kamo no Chōmei   11:204

Kampus   2:258
Kandel, Lenore   26:72
Kane   8:248
Kane, Elisha Kent   8:248
Kanin, Garson   23:139
Kanon, Joe   12:73
Kansas Alumni   2:256
Kansas City Art Institute   16:211
Kansas City, Mo.   5:305
Kansas City Star   7:195
Kansas State University
    Holden   22:70-72, 75
    McElroy   21:133-34
Kaprow, Allan
    Higgins   8:87
    Pinsky   4:244
Karasick, Adeena   19:31, 35, 38, 55,
    59
Karen Silkwood Cantata, The   21:270
Karl, Jean   2:121, 126
*Karl Knaths: Five Decades of
    Painting*   20:140
Karl Marx Play, The   2:358, 361,
    363-64, 366
Karloff, Boris   20:41
*Karma Circuit: 20 Poems & a
    Preface*   18:287, 290
Karp, Sol   9:67
Karpen, Julius   24:10-11
Kassel, Mike   26:306
Kataoka, Akio   12:328
Katz, Debbie   2:418
Katz, Fred   2:418
Katz, Menke   9:49-71
Katz, Steve   14:161-80
    Klinkowitz   9:112, 116
    Sukenick   8:294
Kaufman, Bob
    Vinograd   26:303
    weiss   24:337-38
Kavanagh, Patrick
    O'Faolain   2:345
    Rosenthal   6:285
    Wright   5:370, 371
Kavanaugh, James   1:246
Kavya Bharati   9:149
Kawabata, Yasunari   9:265
Kay, Bud   2:120
kayak
    Argüelles   24:16
    di Suvero   26:75
    Jarman   22:100-01
Kazan, Elia
    Bowles   1:92
    Kennedy   20:224
Kazin, Alfred   7:85-96
    Kennedy   9:80
    Markfield   3:215, 217, 220, 223
Kearney, Lawrence   13:11
Keating, H.R.F.   8:163-78
Keats, John
    Abse   1:21-22
    Belitt   4:64-65
    Brown   6:66, 71
    Delbanco   2:155
    Hall   7:61-62

Jennings   5:106
Kizer   5:147
    Thomas   4:313
    Van Brunt   15:374
Keele University
    Fisher   10:99
    Pownall   18:297
Keeley, Edmund   2:448
Keene, Donald   5:251
Kellett Fellowship   6:208
Kelley, William Melvin   7:297, 298
Kelly, James Patrick   20:86, 92
Kelly, John   1:192
Kelly, Judith   2:116
Kelly, M.T.   22:107-120
Kelly, Nason & Roosevelt (ad
    agency)   1:192
Kelly, Robert   19:179-206
    Eshleman   6:131, 134, 142, 147
    Wakoski   1:363-64, 369
    Weiss   2:442, 443
Kelly, Robert Glynn   6:132
Kemp, Penny   13:297
Kempton, Murray
    Hentoff   6:171
    Wakefield   7:196
Kendall, Lisa See   22:211, 219, 223,
    228, 229, 231
Kennedy, Adrienne   20:219-36
Kennedy, Jacqueline See Onassis,
    Jacqueline Kennedy
Kennedy, John F.
    Allen   11:13-14
    Anaya   4:24
    Condon   1:196
    DeMarinis   24:123
    Easton   14:157
    Hazo   11:140-41
    Knebel   3:179, 180
    Sargent   18:335
    Shreve   5:235
    Van Itallie   2:412
    Wallace   1:394
Kennedy, Joseph, Sr.   3:179
Kennedy, Laurie   6:215, 218-19, 221
Kennedy, Robert   18:140
Kennedy, William   2:212
Kennedy, X.J.   9:73-88
    Corman   2:138, 145
Kenner, Hugh
    Kyger   16:188-89
    Menashe   11:236
    Pinsky   4:247
Kenny, Elizabeth (Sister Kenny)
    5:239
Kenny, Maurice   22:121-72
Kenny, Shirley Strum   9:199
Kenosha Times   1:376
Kent State University   11:17
Kent State University Press   2:269
Kenya
    Booth   2:49-50
    Morgan   3:243
Kenyon College
    Mott   7:130
    Thayler   11:364

Turner   10:318-21
Kenyon, Jane   7:64, 65-66
Kenyon Prize in Philosophy   12:327
Kenyon Review
  Feirstein   11:84
  Mott   7:130
  Pinsky   4:241
  Slavitt   3:315
  Turner   10:318, 320
  Wagoner   3:403
Kepler, Johannes   8:281
*Kerala: A Portrait of the Malabar
    Coast*   6:321-22
Kernan, Alvin   12:156, 157
Kerouac, Jack
  Bowering   16:28
  Enslin   3:92
  Joans   25:242-44
  Sanders   21:266-67
  Saroyan   5:213-14, 217, 219
  Waldman   17:279, 283
  weiss   24:348
Kerouac, Jack, School of Disembodied
    Poetics   17:283
Kerr, Walter   2:415
Kerrigan, Anthony   11:189-221
Kerrigan, Elaine
  Cela   10:45
  Kerrigan   11:199-200
"Kerry Drake"   4:146
Kersh, Gerald   9:19
Kesey, Ken   10:252
Kessel, John   20:86
Kessenich, Larry   7:104, 105, 110
Kessler, Jascha   11:212-13
Kettering Review   8:141
Key to the Door   2:380, 381, 383
Key West, Fla.
  Blais   4:78
  Lowitz   26:164-65
Keyes, Daniel   9:41
Keyes, Sidney
  Heath-Stubbs   21:65
  Wright   5:365, 366
Keynes, Geoffrey   5:283, 293
Keynes, John Maynard
  Morgan   3:238
  Rowse   8:258
Keyser, Tom   7:106
KGB   12:314-22
Khan, Pir Vilayat Inayat See Inayat
    Khan, Pir Vilayat
Khawatir   25:262, 273
Kherdian, David   2:261-77
Kherdian, Nonny Hogrogian   2:270,
    273, 274, 275, 276
Kicking the Leaves   7:65
Kidd, Virginia
  Knight   10:209, 211, 212, 213,
    214, 218, 220, 222
  Wolfe   9:307, 311, 312
Kiely, Benedict   23:282
Kienbusch, William   11:136-37
Kienzle, William   1:237-54
Kierkegaard, Soren
  Gray   2:192

Rakosi   5:208
Ray   7:145, 149
Wilson   5:323
Kiernan, Fran   18:201
Kilgore, Bernard   7:106
Killdeer Mountain   6:58
Killens, John Oliver   2:279-306
  Salaam   21:192
Killing Everybody   3:128
Killing Floor   13:12
Killing Ground, The   1:317, 321, 322
Killing of the King, The   3:321
Kimball, Richard   3:414
Kimm, John   8:90
Kimmel, Michael   2:329-30
Kimmins, John   2:175, 176
Kin of Ata Are Waiting for You, The
    26:58, 60
*Kind and Usual Punishment: The Prison
    Business*   17:150
King, Alex   1:38
King, Francis   4:84-85
King God Didn't Save, The   3:431
King, Hayward   24:334
King Lord/Queen Freak   21:264
King Ludd   5:274, 276
King, Margie   1:38
King, Martin Luther, Jr.
  Forrest   7:26-27
  Nichols   2:332
King of Asine, The   26:280-81
King of Hearts   3:322
King of Prussia   13:27
King of the Jews   12:73, 74, 75
King of the Mountain   7:14
King of the United States   2:416, 418-
    19
King Solomon's Mines   11:374
King, Stephen   9:5
King Whistle   15:307-08
King, Woodie   13:251
Kingdom of Brooklyn, The   20:172
Kinglake, William   2:27
Kingma, Jan   23:221
King's College
  Brewster   15:155
  Levine   23:168, 170
  Raworth   11:308
Kinnell, Galway
  Ai   13:6-8, 9, 10, 12
  Bell   12:30, 31-32, 33, 36, 38
  Kizer   5:155
  Kumin   8:215
  Peters   8:246
Kinsella, W.P.   7:97-111
Kinsey Institute for Sex Research
    1:389
Kinsman   18:59
Kinsman Saga, The   18:53, 60
Kinter, Harold (Doc)   1:129-30
Kipling, Rudyard
  Anderson   2:46
  Lowitz   26:170
  Morris   13:166-67
Kirby, Brian   19:327-28
Kirk, Russell   9:89-105

Kerrigan   11:191, 215
Kirkup, James   4:175-93
  Ashby   6:42
Kirkus Reviews   5:77
Kirkwood, Michael   10:393
Kirschenbaum, Blossom   3:414-15
Kirstein, George   7:196
Kisor, Henry   1:43
Kiss of Kin, The   1:314, 316
Kissing America   9:23
Kissing the Dancer   13:288
Kissinger, Henry   1:376
Kistler, William   26:82
Kitaj, R.B.   10:68
Kitchen Book   12:81
Kitchener, Ontario, Canada   22:28,
    30
Kite Protection Committee, Wales
    4:309
Kites on a Windy Day   18:37
Kiyooka, Roy   16:28
Kizer, Carolyn   5:133-56
  McPherson   23:222, 227
"Klail City Death Trip" series
    16:141-43, 151-52
Klass, Philip   10:210-11, 216
Klee, Paul   2:197
Kleiber, Otto   11:130, 132
Klein, Roger   2:410-11, 415, 417,
    419
Kleine Jazzmusik, Eine   1:344
Klinkowitz, Jerome   9:107-21
  Federman   8:80
  Major   6:196
  Sukenick   8:291-92
Kluger, Richard   2:400
Knaths, Karl   20:119, 132, 139-40,
    144
Knebel, Fletcher   3:163-84
Knife and Other Poems, The   23:310
"Knife, The"   23:314-15
Knight, Damon   10:199-231
  Disch   4:150
  Gunn   2:239, 250, 252
  Haldeman   25:198
  Moorcock   5:180
  Niven   12:216, 217
  Wolfe   9:305, 306, 307
Knight, David   15:359
Knight, Etheridge   23:260
Knight, Hilary   26:157
Knight, M.L.   15:359
Knights of Mark Twain   5:289
*Knock at a Star: A Child's Introduction
    to Poetry*   9:86
Knopf, Alfred A.   1:386, 387, 388,
    389
Knopf, Alfred A. (publishers)
  Bowles   1:82
  Busch   1:134
  Disch   4:156
  Jones   5:129
  Sillitoe   2:385
  Sukenick   8:293
Knotting Sequence, The   2:57
Know Fish, Volume I   24:126

Know Fish, Volume III, The Navigators **24**:128, 147
Know-Nothing **1**:317, 319
"Know Other" **25**:59
Know Your Enemy Japan **1**:380
Knowlton, Perry
  Hauser **11**:127
  Kumin **8**:215
  Nichols **2**:331
Known Homosexual See *Pretty Boy Dead*
Knox, Dillwyn **10**:102
Knox, Edmund V. **10**:103, 104
Knox, Rawle **10**:102
Knox, Ronald **10**:103
Knox, Wilfrid **10**:103
Knoxville, Tenn.
  Madden **3**:195
  White **4**:350
Knye, Cassandra (joint pseudonym of Thomas M. Disch and John Sladek) **4**:151
Koch, Kenneth
  Knight **10**:214
  Mathews **6**:236
  Raworth **11**:303
Koerber, Martin **8**:189
Koerner Foundation **18**:321
Koestenbaum, Wayne **26**:157
Koestler, Arthur
  Wakefield **7**:196
  Wallace **1**:385
  Wilson **5**:322
Kogawa, Joy **15**:159
Kohout, Pavel **1**:339
Kolář, Jiří **1**:336, 338
Kolatch, Myron **12**:206
Kollár, Jan **1**:349
Koller, James 5:157-72
  Arnold **25**:40-41
  Beltrametti **13**:62, 71
Kolodin, Irving **7**:81
Kolodney, John **6**:90
Kolve, Del **8**:157
Kolyszko, Anna **6**:201
Konitz, Lee **25**:221
Kontraption **2**:363, 366
Konwicki, Tadeusz 9:123-35
Koo, T.Z. **5**:140
Kopecký, Václav **1**:339
Korea, North **25**:313-14
Korea, South **4**:188
Korean Love Songs from Klail City Death Trip **16**:143, 151
Korean War
  Armantrout **25**:6
  Baumbach **5**:19-20
  Bennett **13**:83
  Cassity **8**:45-46
  Elman **3**:72
  Ford **21**:28
  Hazo **11**:143
  Jones **11**:176
  Kherdian **2**:265-66
  McCord **9**:179-80
  Silkin **5**:258, 259
  Sward **13**:280, 286, 287-88

Vizenor **22**:273
Wilson **5**:333, 342, 343-45
Wolfe **9**:301-03
Kornbluth, Cyril M.
  Knight **10**:206, 207, 211, 212, 215, 220
  Pohl **1**:290, 293
Kornfeld, Lawrence **6**:117
Korsoniloff **18**:80
Kosinski, Jerzy **9**:108, 112, 113-14, 115, 118
Kostelanetz, Richard 8:179-99
  Federman **8**:79
  Grumman **25**:193
Kouska, Cezar **1**:255
Koval, Alexander **14**:273-74
KPFA-FM (Berkeley, Calif.) **24**:168, 170, 176
Kraków, Poland **1**:259-60
Kramer, Sidney **10**:299, 300
Krapf, Norbert **2**:57, 58
Kraulis, Janis **6**:324
Kraus, Arnošt **7**:212
Kress, Nancy **9**:306
Krim, Arthur **1**:196
Krishnamurti, Jiddu **14**:246
Kroetsch, Robert **16**:28, 30
Kroner, Richard **7**:220
Kroupa, Melanie **2**:126
Krutch, Joseph Wood **4**:59
Kumin, Maxine 8:201-17
  Meredith **14**:220, 221
  Miller **15**:282, 283, 284
  Swenson **13**:313
  Weiss **2**:447
Kumming, Waldemar **8**:13
Kundera, Milan
  Barnstone **15**:69
  Berrigan **1**:57
  Brossard **2**:72
Kunen, James **9**:112
Kunitz, Stanley
  Belitt **4**:52, 65
  Davison **4**:135
  McPherson **23**:226
Kupferberg, Tuli **21**:264, 265, 266
Kurtz, Gary **1**:292
Kurtz, Paul **10**:303
Kuspit, Donald **25**:399-400
Kutnik, Jerzy **6**:200, 201-02
Kuznet, Simon **3**:238
Kwame Nkrumah Ideological Institute **13**:46
Kyger, Joanne 16:187-203
  Eshleman **6**:135, 137
  Koller **5**:164, 165-66
  Waldman **17**:283
Kyoto, Japan
  Corman **2**:140-41, 142, 144
  Eshleman **6**:135-37
  Kirkup **4**:190
Kyoto University of Foreign Studies **4**:190

L=A=N=G=U=A=G=E **24**:45-49
La Motta, Jake **2**:268

La Traviata in Oklahoma: Selected and New Poems, 1961–1991 **15**:383-84
Labor unions
  Horwood **15**:243-44
  Ignatow **3**:151-52, 155
  Killens **2**:287, 291
Labors of Love **1**:174
Labour party (Great Britain)
  Arden **4**:44, 46
  Caute **4**:102
  Jones **5**:123
  Rowse **8**:255, 258
Labrador, Canada **15**:244-45
Lachance, Bertrand **19**:5, 9, 22, 44-45
Lacotte, Muriel **6**:195-96, 198, 200
Ladies' Home Journal **5**:152
Ladies, The **2**:212-13
Lady Chatterley's Lover
  Jones **5**:127
  Mano **6**:212
Lady Faustus **20**:13
Lady of Pleasure, A **20**:129-31, 142
Lady's Not for Burning, The **23**:69-70, 71
Lafayette College **16**:230
LAFT See *Lost and Found Times*
Lagerlöf, Selma
  Lind **4**:200
  Wallace **1**:390
LaGrone, Oliver **23**:204, 206
Lal, P. **9**:145-46
Lamantia, Philip **24**:17, 25
Lamb, Catherine **5**:263
Lamb, Charles **4**:305
Lambert, Dorothy **8**:212
Lament for a Maker **3**:354
Lament for Arthur O'Leary, The **3**:62-63
L'Amèr ou le Chapitre effrité: Fiction théorique **16**:50
Lamerhav (magazine) **13**:155
Lamont Award
  Ai **13**:12
  Kennedy **9**:84
  Levis **23**:192
Lampasas Dispatch **14**:155-56
Lancaster, Osbert **14**:244
Land of Lost Content, The **13**:205, 211
Land of Manna **9**:51, 55
Landauer, Jerry **7**:195
Landesman, Jay **2**:69
Landfall (David Wagoner) **3**:411
Landis, Jim **2**:156
Landlocked Man, The **9**:5
Landor, Walter
  di Suvero **26**:73
  Pinsky **4**:247, 249
Landor's Poetry **4**:247
Landry, Paul **26**:303-04
Landscape in Concrete **4**:202
Landscape of Nightmare, The **5**:23, 24
Landscape of the Mind **10**:121

Landscapes of the Self: The Development of Richard Hugo's Poetry **22**:71
Lang, Bob **9**:199, 200
Lang, Daniel **2**:09
Lang, Fritz **20**:42
Lang, Margaret Altschul **2**:63, 64, 65, 76
Langland, Joseph **23**:277-79
Langston Hughes **18**:137
Language **24**:183-97
Language in Thought and Action **8**:132
Language Poetries **25**:17
Language poets and poetry
    Argüelles **24**:20
    Bernstein **24**:48
    Eigner **23**:31, 37, 52, 57
    Foley **24**:170
    Leftwich **25**:267
Lansing, Gerrit **19**:199
Lansky, Bruce **1**:252
Lanyon, Peter **23**:171, 172, 173, 174, 175
Laocoön **8**:94
Laqueur, Walter **19**:207-27
Lardner, Ring **9**:26
Lariar, Lawrence **18**:228-29
Lark. The Thrush. The Starling., The **26**:327-28
Larkin, Philip
    Ashby **6**:42
    Davie **3**:39
    Glanville **9**:25
    Oakes **25**:315
    Wain **4**:328-29
Lars, Claudia **15**:3
Larsen, Erling **8**:307
Laski, Harold **5**:141
Last and Lost Poems of Delmore Schwartz **13**:212
Last Beautiful Days of Autumn, The **2**:335
Last Dangerous Visions, The **2**:258
Last Frontier, The **18**:178-79
Last Good Time, The **14**:12
Last Happy Occasion, The **23**:289-98
Last of the Country House Murders, The **9**:291-92
Last of the Just, The **1**:38
Last of the Moccasins, The **11**:278, 287, 291, 295
last photo uv th human soul, th **19**:34, 55, 56-57
Last Poems **12**:237
Last Rites: The Death of William Saroyan **5**:217, 218
Last Station, The **16**:240-41
Last Things **11**:185-86
Last White Class, The **1**:278
Laster, Owen **3**:322
Late But in Earnest **21**:285, 291
Late in the Season **13**:232-33
Late Settings **4**:78
Latimer, Margery **5**:202-03
Latin
    Argüelles **24**:4

Furman **18**:195
Mathews **6**:226
Latin American Book Fair **12**:105
Latin American Writers Institute **12**:105
Lattimore, Richmond **6**:100
Laufer, Susan Bee **24**:36, 37, 39, 40
Laughing Lost in the Mountains: Poems of Wang Wei **15**:65, 92
Laughing Stalks **14**:133
Laughlin, Clarence John **12**:346
Laughlin, James **22**:173-210
    Allman **15**:25-26, 27, 30
    Brossard **2**:66
    Busch **1**:133
    Cassill **1**:169
    di Suvero **26**:69
    Glazier **24**:233
    Honig **8**:113
    Major **6**:192
    Olson **11**:257, 259
    Purdy **1**:304
    Roditi **14**:269
    Whittemore **8**:310
Laughter! **12**:3
Laurels of Lake Constance, The **6**:242-43
Lauterer, Arch **4**:63, 65
Laval University, Quebec City, Canada **4**:72
L'aviva **16**:54
Lawrence, D.H.
    Allen **6**:17
    Brown **6**:71, 74
    Ghiselin **10**:131, 141, 142
    Jones **5**:127
    Kennedy **9**:73
    Kizer **5**:140
    Mano **6**:212
    Middleton **23**:239
    Sillitoe **2**:384
    Wallace **1**:396, 397
    Wellek **7**:222
Lawrence, Frieda **10**:131, 133
Lawrence, Judith Ann **10**:225
Lawrence, Seymour
    Davison **4**:135-36
    Wakefield **7**:200
Lawrence, Thomas Edward (Lawrence of Arabia) **2**:56
Layachi, Larbi **1**:92
Laying Down the Tower **1**:276
Layton, Irving
    bissett **19**:13, 45
    Dudek **14**:128, 132
    Purdy **17**:204, 205
    Souster **14**:310, 314-15
Lazard, Naomi **5**:155
Lazer, Hank **25**:281
Le Braz, Anatole **2**:321
le Carré, John **8**:4
Le Rougetel, Yvonne **9**:232
Lea, Syd **22**:71-72
Leadbeater, Mary Shackleton **15**:155
League of Canadian Poets
    Brewster **15**:159

Sparshott **15**:357-58
League of Nations
    Salvadori **25**:355
    Silkin **5**:247
Lear, Edward
    Broughton **12**:45
    Keating **8**:167
Learning disabilities **21**:148, 149
Leary, Paris **19**:201
Leary, Timothy **11**:287
Leaves of Grass
    Kennedy **9**:76
    Shapiro **6**:289, 304
Leavis, F.R.
    Davie **3**:35, 36
    Glanville **9**:13
    Gray **3**:108-09
    Mano **6**:209
LeClair, Thomas **8**:293
Leduc, Jean **26**:54
Lee, Al **7**:297
Lee, Ann **8**:247
Lee, Christopher **20**:39
Lee, Don L. **18**:143, 144
Lee, Laurie **1**:28
Lee, Robert A. **22**:272
Leeds, Barry **9**:41
Leeds University
    Heath-Stubbs **21**:69
    Kennedy **9**:85
    Simmons **21**:284-86
    Skelton **5**:282-83
Leeming, Glenda **7**:227
Left Bank: Writers, Artists, and Politics from the Popular Front to the Cold War, The **12**:208
Left in Europe since 1789, The **4**:105
Leftwich, Jim **25**:259-82
    Bennett **25**:74
    Ferrini **24**:139, 141
Legacy of Heorot, The **12**:221
LeGallienne, Eva **2**:206
Legends **5**:325
"Legends about Air and Water" **23**:310
Legion of Decency **4**:146
Legion of Honor **15**:144
Legouis, Emile **6**:36
Lehman College **15**:26, 28
Lehmann-Haupt, Christopher **6**:186
Lehmann, John
    Allen **6**:21
    Jennings **5**:110
    Raffel **9**:213
    Wright **5**:369
Lehr, Anne **2**:118, 119
Lehrnman, Nat **6**:217
Leiber, Fritz
    Knight **10**:213
    Zebrowski **19**:367, 369
Leibling, A.J. **19**:131
Leicester, England **1**:217-19
Leigh, Julian **18**:301, 302
Leigh, Vivien **23**:72-74
Leighton, Martin **2**:299-300, 301-02, 303

Lelchuk, Alan **20**:237-55
LeLionnais, François **6**:247
Lem, Stanislaw 1:255-66
LeMay, Curtis **3**:179-80
Lemmon, Jack **9**:249, 250
Lenard, Philipp **1**:391
Leningrad, USSR
   Corcoran **2**:123-24
   Salisbury **15**:323-24
Lennon, John **20**:220, 222-23, 228,
   229, 230-31
   See also Beatles, The
Lennon Play, The **20**:223, 228, 229,
   230
Leonard, John **3**:80
Leonardi, Joseph **26**:160
Leone, Len **1**:295
"Lepanto" **5**:106
Lerner, David **26**:307, 309
Lesbian Images **18**:317-18
"Less Than Yesterday, More Than
   Tomorrow" **23**:306
Lessing, Doris 14:181-204
   Cassity **8**:54-55
   Jones **5**:122-23, 124, 126, 130
Lessing, Gotthold Ephraim **8**:94
"Lesson of Dawn, The" **26**:275
Lestriad, The **14**:171, 172, 179
LeSueur, Meridel **18**:254-55
Let There Be Light **18**:41, 42-43, 44,
   45
Let Us Now Praise Famous Men **4**:215
*Let's Go: The Harvard Student Travel
   Guide* **23**:308
"Let's Pretend" (radio program)
   4:144
Letter to the Past **6**:326
Letters from Hollywood **5**:184
Letters Home (Michael Andre) **13**:22
Letters/Lights—Words for Adelle
   24:172
*Letters of John Addington Symonds,
   The* **8**:241
Letters to a Young Poet **1**:24, 25
Letters to Five Artists **4**:330
Letters to Louise **15**:177
Letters to Martha **14**:56, 59-60, 62,
   63
"Letters to Neil" **26**:223
Letters to Unfinished J **26**:228
Lettres Nouvelles Award, Les **1**:212
Leverage **22**:72, 73
Levertov, Denise 19:229-46
   Abse **1**:26
   Armantrout **25**:17, 20-21
   Arnold **25**:40
   Corman **2**:137
   Eigner **23**:51
   Inez **10**:191
   Kizer **5**:145
   Peters **8**:242
Lévesque, Georges-Henri **4**:72, 73
Levey, Michael **4**:81, 82, 83, 84, 86,
   87, 88, 89, 90, 92, 93
Levi, Primo **24**:358
Levin, Harry

Glazier **24**:234
Kumin **8**:214, 215
Levin, Meyer **3**:222
Levin, Yehuda-Leib **4**:358
Levine, Fran **3**:429
Levine, Norman 23:165-80
Levine, Philip
   Ai **13**:10
   Levis **23**:190, 191
   Williams **3**:429
Levis, Larry 23:181-92
   Holden **22**:68
Levitt, Dr. I.M. **18**:48
levy, d.a.
   bissett **19**:20, 50, 51
   Sanders **21**:264
Levy, Matthys **25**:363
Lewicki, Zbigniew **6**:201
Lewis, Alun **2**:20
Lewis and Clark College, Portland,
   Ore. **3**:334
Lewis and Clark Expedition **6**:47
Lewis, C.S.
   Aldiss **2**:24
   Heath-Stubbs **21**:64
   Jennings **5**:108
   St. Clair **8**:280
   Wain **4**:326-27, 328, 329
Lewis, Doc **1**:70
Lewis, Grover **22**:220
Lewis, Meade Lux **10**:91
Lewis, R.W.B. **11**:51, 52, 53
Lewis, Sinclair
   Booth **5**:35, 40, 49
   Manfred **18**:257-58
   Wakefield **7**:194
Lewis, W.H. **4**:328
Lewis, Wyndham
   Allen **6**:23-24
   Symons **3**:384-85, 388
*Lexicographic Study of Tayabas Tagalog,
   A* **9**:163
Li-Young Lee **22**:79
Liaison Parisienne, Une **4**:78
Liberaki, Rita **15**:93
Liberal party (Great Britain) **5**:178
Liberated, The **3**:321
Liberation **6**:116, 119
Liberation of Lord Byron Jones, The
   21:38-40
Liberia **3**:181
Liberman, Alexander **2**:187-88, 189,
   191, 192-93, 196, 200
Liberman, Simon **2**:190-93
Libertarian party **8**:191
Liberté **13**:184
Liberty **1**:378
Librarianship **17**:237-39
Library of Congress
   Bowles **1**:92
   Caldwell **1**:154
   Davison **4**:139
   Honig **8**:110
   Jacobsen **18**:213-15, 216, 218
   Meredith **14**:223, 231
   Shapiro **6**:301

Whittemore **8**:308, 311
License to Carry a Gun **19**:85
Lichtheim, George **19**:217
Liddell, Alice **3**:322
Liddy, G. Gordon **1**:319
Lieberman, Laurence **7**:164
Lieberman, Saul **4**:357, 358-59
Liebknecht, Karl **5**:194
Liepman, Ruth **23**:172-73, 179
Lies **26**:326
Life
   Caldwell **1**:149
   Markfield **3**:220
   Slavitt **3**:320
   Wallace **1**:397
   Wilson **5**:321
*Life and Times of an Involuntary
   Genius, The* **19**:85, 88-89, 90-91
Life and Times of Captain N., The
   23:84, 85, 93, 94
Life and Times of Major Fiction, The
   5:29
Life Goes On **2**:387
Life in the West **2**:30
Life Is a Dream **8**:117
Life of Fiction, The **9**:113, 117
Life of Jesus, The **11**:242, 247, 257
Life of Madame Rolland, The **1**:116
Life on the Mississippi **1**:316
"Life, People—and Books" **3**:389
Life Sentences **1**:233, 234
Life Signs **9**:148
Life Span **24**:318, 319, 320
Life Studies **23**:308
*Lifeitselfmanship, or How to Become a
   Precisely-Because Man* **17**:142-43
Lifshin, Lyn 10:233-63
Lifton, Robert **1**:62
Light in the Dust **7**:236
Light in the West **8**:135
Light on a Honeycomb **18**:301-02
Lighting the Corners **25**:266
Lile Jimmy Williamson **18**:300
Lillooet **15**:155
Lilly, Doris **3**:318
Lilly, John **26**:76, 77
Lilo's Diary **3**:74
Limited Partnerships **24**:362
Limners Society of Artists **5**:290
Lincoln, Abraham
   Hentoff **6**:173
   Pinsky **4**:237
Lincoln Memorial University **17**:235-
   36
Lind, Jakov 4:195-204
Lindbergh, Charles **3**:193
Lindenberger, Herbert **8**:244
Lindon, Jérôme **4**:357
Lindsay, John V. **21**:15
Lindsay, Vachel
   Harris **3**:122, 126, 127, 132
   Kizer **5**:141-44
"Lines" **26**:38
Linetsky, Louis **10**:298-99
Ling, Amy **16**:145
Linguistics **21**:137

Linhartová, Věra **1**:338
Linklater, Eric **6**:67
Lion Books **1**:169
Lion on the Mountain, A **2**:122
Lionel Train Corp. **25**:362-63
Liotta, Peter **26**:134
Lippincott, J.B. (publishers) **7**:81
Lipton, Lawrence **18**:288
Lispector, Clarice **9**:203
Listen: Gerry Mulligan **9**:108, 120
Listen to the Wind **15**:307
Listeners, The **2**:255, 256, 257
Literal Ponds **26**:227
Literary criticism
  Foster **26**:121, 124-25
  Grumman **25**:186, 192
  Hazo **11**:152-53
  Ostriker **24**:272-73, 275
  Saroyan **5**:219
  Taylor **26**:253
*Literary Disruptions: The Making of a
    Post-Contemporary American
    Fiction* **9**:115, 116
Literary Guild
  Wagoner **3**:408
  Wallace **1**:388
*Literary Subversions: New American
    Fiction and the Practice of
    Criticism* **9**:118
Literatura na Świecie **6**:201
*Literature: An Introduction to Fiction,
    Poetry, and Drama* **9**:85
*Literature of Silence: Henry Miller and
    Samuel Beckett, The* **12**:152
*Literature of Work: Short Stories, Essays,
    and Poems by Men and Women of
    Business, The* **26**:225
Lithuania
  Budrys **14**:65
  Katz **9**:49-53, 65
Little, Brown & Co. (publishers)
  Bowles **1**:92
  Davison **4**:136, 138
  Stegner **9**:264
  Williams **3**:428, 431
"Little Elegy" **8**:227-28
Little Heroes **19**:331, 333
Little Lives **3**:80
Little Night Music, A **2**:419
Little People's Magazine **2**:113
Little Portia **3**:109, 111
Little Review **5**:203
Little Richard **7**:159-60
Little Syncopy, A **26**:227
Little Theater movement **1**:310
Little Time for Laughter, A **9**:5
Little, Vera **6**:195
Little Women **6**:254
Littleton, Taylor **11**:183
Litvinoff, Emanuel **5**:261-62, 263
Live Free or Die **24**:255, 257
Liverpool, England **2**:308-09, 313
*Lives of Children: The Story of the First
    Street School, The* **6**:119
Lives of Riley Chance, The **14**:28-29,
    30

Lives to Give **4**:233
Livesay, Dorothy 8:219-36
  bissett **19**:35, 58
  Brewster **15**:157
Living **6**:18
Living in Advance **26**:35
Living in America **9**:283
Living in Time **23**:126
Living on the Dead, The **13**:154
Living Shall Praise Thee, The **11**:135-
    36
Living Space **6**:21
Living Theater
  Dennison **6**:116
  Ferrini **24**:129
Living Upstairs **17**:64, 65, 72
living with th vishyun **19**:26, 53
Livingston, Myra Cohn **9**:86
Livingstone and Sechele **18**:302
Livingstone, Angela
  Davie **3**:44
  Feinstein **1**:221
Llandaff Theological College, Wales
    4:304
Llewellyn, Richard **3**:403
Lobrano, Gus **2**:65
*Local Assays: On Contemporary
    American Poetry* **7**:165
Lockwood, Lee **1**:59
"Locus Classicus" **26**:147-48
Locus Solus **6**:236
Loeff, Ted **1**:388
Loew's Inc./MGM **2**:208
Lofting, Hugh **2**:310
Loftis, Norman **6**:189
Log, The **26**:286
Logan, John
  Bell **14**:43-44
  Dacey **17**:23-24, 32
  Heyen **9**:42
  Root **11**:321
Logan's Run **16**:215, 216, 218-21
Logic **10**:328, 330
Logoclastics **25**:271
Logue, Christopher
  Connell **2**:108
  Wright **5**:370
Lohner, Ed **2**:136
Lomax, S.P. **3**:427
London, England
  Abse **1**:24, 27
  Allen **6**:22
  Argüelles **24**:12
  Booth **2**:51
  Cassity **8**:55
  Clark **22**:13
  Corcoran **2**:124
  Hamburger **4**:163
  Kazin **7**:93
  O'Faolain **2**:347-48
  Salisbury **15**:322-23
  Salvadori **25**:355
  Settle **1**:313, 314, 315
  Sinclair **5**:271
  Wesker **7**:228, 238-39
  Williams **26**:315

  Woodcock **6**:318
London, Jack
  Stone **3**:370, 373
  Thayer **11**:359
  Whittemore **8**:310
London School of Economics **16**:278
London University See University of
    London
*Loneliness of the Long-Distance Runner,
    The* **2**:381, 382, 384, 385, 386
Long Branch, N.J. **4**:237-38, 241
Long Hot Summers of Yasha K., The
    12:243, 248
Long Island Light **9**:32
Long Island University
  Olson **11**:255, 256
  Škvorecký **1**:347
Long Journey, The **2**:121
Long Naked Descent into Boston, The
    1:212
long rainy season, a **26**:180
Long Road South, A **4**:350
Long Talking Bad Conditions Blues
    8:294
Long Undressing, A **12**:41
Long Walk to Wimbledon, A **8**:175-76
Longest Voyage, The **3**:279
Longfellow, Henry Wadsworth **3**:399
Longhouse (press) **25**:40, 46-47
*Longing in the Land: Memoir of a
    Quest, A* **10**:147, 148, 162
Longinus **6**:280
Longman, Inc. (publishers)
  Stone **3**:369
  Wallace **1**:389
Longview Foundation **11**:231
Look
  Brossard **2**:68, 69, 70
  Elman **3**:74
  Knebel **3**:171, 179
  Settle **1**:315
  Stegner **9**:266
Look at Lightning, A **4**:63
Look Back in Anger **7**:240
Look Homeward, Angel **4**:207
"Look Up and Live" **2**:412
*Looking Ahead: The Vision of Science
    Fiction* **11**:19
Looking for Mary Lou: Illegal Syntax
    24:24-25
Looking for Philosophy **15**:360
Looking for the Rainbow Sign **2**:60
Looking Over Hills **2**:273
Lopate, Phillip **11**:255-56
Lopez-Morillas, Juan **8**:180
Lord, David **20**:61
Lord Jim **8**:303-04
Lord, John Vernon **6**:99
Lord of Darkness **3**:285
Lord of the Dance **7**:44
Lord of the Flies **9**:293
Lord of the Hollow Dark **9**:103
Lord of the Rings, The **9**:103-04
Lord Richard's Passion **5**:129
Lord Valentine's Castle **3**:285
Los Angeles, Calif.

Brown **10**:34-35
Connell **2**:107
Corcoran **2**:118-20
Eastlake **1**:201
Easton **14**:146
Eshleman **6**:146
O'Faolain **2**:349
Rechy **4**:264
Thayler **11**:355, 360-61
Los Angeles City College **11**:362
Los Angeles Institute of
    Contemporary Art **25**:388-89
Los Angeles Poetry Festival **26**:79
Los Angeles Science Fantasy
    Society **12**:213-15
Los Angeles Science Fiction Society
    16:212
Los Angeles Times Book Award
    14:220
Los Angeles Times Book Review **6**:147
Los Angeles Valley College
    Hamill **15**:209
    Van Proyen **25**:386-89
Lost and Found Times **25**:61
Lost Cities and Vanished Civilizations
    3:277
"Lost Cove & The Rose of San
    Antone" **23**:315-16
Lost Horizon **1**:381
Lost Island, The **3**:57
Lost on Twilight Road **17**:67
Lost Race of Mars **3**:277
Lotbinière-Harwood, Susanne de
    16:39-57
Lottman, Eileen **12**:201
Lottman, Evan **12**:197, 201, 203
Lottman, Herbert R. **12**:197-209
Lotus Press
    Madgett **23**:207-10
    Skelton **5**:283
Louisiana State University **20**:324,
    329
Louisiana State University Press
    Chappell **4**:122, 124-25
    Taylor **7**:181
Louisville, Ky. **5**:303, 305
Loup, Le **4**:77
*Love and War: Pearl Harbor through
    V-J Day* **14**:143-45, 154, 159
Love Comes to Eunice K. O'Herlihy
    2:126
Love Eaters, The **1**:315, 316
Love Explosion, The **10**:302
Love in Amsterdam **12**:83
Love in the Post **21**:293
Love Letter from an Impossible Land
    14:226
Love Letters on Blue Paper **7**:243,
    247-48, 249, 250-51
Love Life **16**:168
Love Me Tomorrow **10**:300, 301
"Love of Life" **1**:231
Love Poems, The (Harold Norse)
    18:290
Love Run, The **16**:236, 237
Lovecraft, H.P.

Bloch **20**:42-43
Chappell **4**:119
Silverberg **3**:271, 272, 274
Lovelace, Linda See Marciano, Linda
    Boreman
Lovell, John **18**:130
Lovelock, Jim **2**:31
Lovelock Version, The **3**:251, 265
Lover, The **11**:55
Lovers and Tyrants **2**:186, 190, 194,
    195, 198, 199
Loves of Carmen, The **1**:194
Loving Power: Stories **17**:50
Loving Strangers **3**:81, 82
Low Company **5**:56
Lowell, Amy **8**:228
Lowell, Robert
    Chappell **4**:118, 120
    Cruz **17**:9
    Emanuel **18**:152
    Galvin **13**:91, 99
    Ghiselin **10**:133
    Hadas **23**:122
    Olson **12**:233
    Pinsky **4**:245, 248-49
    Raffel **9**:219
    Rosenthal **6**:276, 284
    Simpson **4**:293
    Stevenson **9**:283
    Tillinghast **23**:304, 307-08, 309
    Weiss **2**:444
Lowen, Alexander **4**:153
Lowenfels, Lillian **6**:187
Lowenfels, Walter
    Ferrini **24**:141
    Major **6**:183, 187
Lowenkopf, Shelly **10**:298
Lowes, John Livingston **7**:218
Lowitz, Leza **26**:163-83
Lowndes, Robert W. **10**:203, 205,
    206, 207-08, 211, 215, 216
Lowrey, Perrin Holmes **7**:23
Lowry, Jane **2**:412
Lowry, Malcolm
    Delbanco **2**:158
    Purdy **17**:203
Loydell, Rupert **26**:222
Loyola University
    Alegría **15**:5
    Williams **20**:331
Lucas, George **25**:207
Lucas, John **8**:306
Luce and His Empire **13**:269, 271,
    272, 273
Luce, Henry
    Barrio **15**:124
    Swanberg **13**:269-72
Lucie ou un midi en novembre (Lucie
    or a November afternoon)
    13:186, 189
Lucifer's Hammer **12**:219, 220
Lucky Alphonse, The **8**:176
Luddites (band) **19**:5, 12, 26, 31,
    34, 44, 47, 53, 55
Ludlum, Robert **9**:4-5
Ludwig **8**:247, 248, 249, 250

Luisa Domic **6**:107-08, 121-22
Luisa in Realityland **15**:1, 2, 13
"Lullaby" **5**:110
Lumberyards **25**:27, 30-32
Lummis, Suzanne **26**:78-79
Lumpkin, Grace **6**:53
Lumsden, Charles J. **16**:304
Luna Bisonte Prods **25**:62
Lunar Attractions **3**:18, 22, 24
Lunar Cycle, The **1**:278
Lunatic Wind **19**:130
Lunch in Fur **19**:155
Lunes/Sightings **19**:201
Lunn, Brian **4**:338
Lunsford, Bascom Lamar **15**:274,
    278, 287, 288, 290
Lure, The **13**:229-30
Lust for Life **3**:369-70, 373
Lustgarten, Edgar **3**:111
Lusts **3**:18, 22, 26, 29
Lutheranism
    Smith **7**:155
    Wellek **7**:209
Luxemburg, Rosa **5**:194
Lyn Lifshin: A Critical Study **10**:258
Lynds, Dennis **3**:422, 423
Lynn, Margaret **3**:332
Lyon, Danny **24**:8
Lyon, Elizabeth **10**:4-5
Lyon, George Ella **15**:288-89
Lyrics for the Bride of God **16**:281
Lysenko, Trofim **1**:259
Lytle, Andrew
    Ford **21**:29-30, 37
    Gerber **20**:163-66, 169
    Ghiselin **10**:136-37
    Jones **11**:178
    Whittemore **8**:307

Maas, Willard
    Kelly **19**:199
    Malanga **17**:97, 98
Mabinogion, The **4**:307
Mac Low, Jackson
    Bergé **10**:7
    Weiss **2**:442
Macalester College **24**:199
MacArthur, Douglas
    Duncan **2**:168
    Murchie **19**:295
MacArthur Fellowship **17**:123, 126
MacArthur Foundation **15**:235
MacArthur, Robert H. **16**:299-300
Macauley, Robie
    Mott **7**:130, 132
    Whittemore **8**:307
Macbeth
    Corman **2**:132
    Jennings **5**:108
MacBeth, George **2**:52, 55, 58, 60
MacDiarmid, Hugh
    Rosenthal **6**:285
    Turnbull **14**:333, 336
Macdonald, Ross **3**:204
MacDowell Colony
    Bergé **10**:16

Hadas **23**:118
   Jacobsen **18**:213-14
   Lelchuk **20**:248
   Peters **8**:247
   Sward **13**:290, 291, 295
MacFadden Publications **1**:378
Machine That Would Go of Itself, A
   23:158
MacInnes, Helen **9**:5
Maciunas, George **8**:87, 92
Mackay, Shena **4**:87, 88-89, 92
Mackenzie Poems, The **22**:54
MacKenzie, Rachel **12**:298-99
MacLeish, Archibald
   Becker **1**:41
   Hall **7**:62
   Hazo **11**:149, 150, 152
   Hiemstra **26**:157
   Honig **8**:110, 114
   Jerome **8**:138
   Olson **12**:234
   Settle **1**:319
   Swanberg **13**:269, 275
   Whittemore **8**:301, 306, 308
Macleod, Fiona **4**:304
MacManus, Francis **6**:284
Macmillan Publishing Co.
   Rosenthal **6**:277, 279, 285
   Thomas **4**:310
   Weiss **2**:433
MacNeice, Louis
   Allen **6**:20, 21
   Barnstone **15**:75-76, 77
"MacNeil-Lehrer Newshour" **2**:213
Macon Telegraph **1**:142
Macpherson, Jay
   Brewster **15**:156
   Sparshott **15**:356, 362
Macrae, Jack **3**:322
Macrae-Smith (publishers) **6**:54
Macrolife **19**:368, 369, 370, 372
Mad River Review **11**:15
Madame Bovary **11**:376
Madame Butterfly **10**:158
Madame President **1**:383
Madden, David 3:185-206
Mademoiselle
   Burroway **6**:87-88, 91
   Gerber **20**:165, 167-68
   Grumbach **2**:208
Madgett, Naomi Long 23:193-213
Madhubuti, Haki **21**:229
Madison Square Garden, New York
   City **3**:424
Madison, Wis.
   Morgan **3**:244
   Rakosi **5**:204
Madrid, Spain
   Condon **1**:195
   Wallace **1**:380
Maeda, Jun **2**:421
Maes-Jelinek, Hena **16**:132, 134-35
Mafia **24**:108-10
Magazine of Fantasy and Science Fiction
   Budrys **14**:70-71, 78
   Malzberg **4**:208, 216

Magellan of the Pacific **14**:283-84
Maggot: A Novel **17**:46, 51, 55, 56
Magic and magicians
   Hitchcock **12**:168, 173-74, 181
   Shadbolt **3**:255
   Wagoner **3**:400
Magic Cup, The **7**:50
Magic Journey, The **2**:335
Magic Mountain, The
   Lem **1**:259
   Turner **10**:318
Magician's Girl, The **2**:213
Magicians, The **2**:258
Magnet
   Ashby **6**:34
   Brown **6**:66
   Nichols **2**:312-13
Magnificat **23**:264-66
Magnus **6**:72
Magog **5**:274
Magoun, F.P. **24**:234
Magritte, René-François-Ghislain
   5:195
Mahaffey, Bea **2**:40
Mahapatra, Jayanta 9:137-50
Maharani's New Wall, The **7**:145-46
Mahler, Gustav **3**:94, 95
Maiden of the Buhong Sky, The **9**:164
"Mail, The" **26**:220
Mailer, Norman
   Bourjaily **1**:70-71, 72
   Boyd **11**:51-52, 53
   Caute **4**:103, 105
   Clarke **16**:83, 84
   Garrett **5**:77
   Hassan **12**:159
   Lelchuk **20**:249-50
   Ostriker **24**:271
"Main Body, The" **26**:289
Mainland **17**:11-13
Mainstream **21**:284
Mairet, Philip **3**:299, 301
Majestic Theater, New York City
   4:148
Majipoor Chronicles **3**:285
Major, Clarence 6:175-204
   Baumbach **5**:29
   Katz **14**:176
   Klinkowitz **9**:113, 116
   Sukenick **8**:293
Make No Sound **2**:126
Make, Vusumzi **2**:298-99
Makeup on Empty Space **17**:286
Making History **22**:227-29
Making of the Popes 1978, The **7**:50
Malacia Tapestry, The **2**:31
Malahat Review **5**:287, 291
Malamud, Bernard
   Baumbach **5**:24
   Becker **1**:40, 41
   Belitt **4**:53, 65
   Blaise **3**:19, 23, 24-25
   Delbanco **2**:159
   Furman **18**:196-97
   Sukenick **8**:285
   Waldman **17**:273

Malanga, Gerard 17:95-120
Malaya **2**:376-77, 378-79, 380
Malcolm **1**:302, 304
Malcolm Boyd's Book of Days **11**:51
Malcolm, Janet **1**:07
Malcolm, My Son **21**:225, 231-32
Malcolm X
   Clarke **16**:84, 86
   Joans **25**:249
   Killens **2**:296, 297, 303
   Williams **3**:427
Malcolm X City College **13**:248
Malheurs de Sophie, Les **2**:184
Malina, Judith **6**:116
Malinowski, Bronislaw, Marshal
   1:333
Mallorca, Spain
   Alegría **15**:12-13
   Green **11**:87, 99-106
   Sillitoe **2**:382-84
Mallot, Hector **11**:127
Malone Dies **7**:284
Malraux, André
   Becker **1**:40
   Belitt **4**:60
   Brée **15**:137
   Forrest **7**:29
   Morgan **4**:232
Maltese Falcon Award **16**:220
Malthus **24**:24
Malthus, Thomas **18**:38
Malyon, Carol **19**:1, 40
Malzberg, Barry N. 4:205-22
   Dann **20**:88, 91
   Pohl **1**:285
Mama's Promises **23**:261-62
Man and the Future **2**:253, 255
Man-Eaters of Kumaon, The **2**:50
Man from Porlock, The **2**:449
Man in the Cellar **2**:346, 352
Man in the Green Chair, The **20**:140
Man in the Maze, The **3**:279
Man in Yellow Boots, The **16**:28
Man of Letters in the Modern World,
   The **8**:185
Man of the Thirties, A **8**:260
Man Plus **1**:294
Man, The **1**:384, 393-95
Man to Conjure With, A **5**:23-24
Man Who Came to Dinner, The **2**:410
Man Who Cried I Am, The **3**:421,
   427, 428, 429, 430, 431, 432
Man Who Melted, The **20**:93, 99
Man with Blue Eyes, The **4**:152
Manafon, Wales **4**:306-08, 309, 310
"Manana from Heaven" **26**:38
Manchester Evening News **3**:389
Manchester Institute of Contemporary
   Arts **5**:284
Manchester University **5**:283, 286
Manchurian Candidate, The **1**:196
Mandala Damages **25**:263, 264
Mandolin **19**:109
Manfred, Frederick 18:245-61
Mangione, Jerre **6**:53

Manhattan Carnival **11**:78, 79, 81, 83, 84
Manhattan Elegy & Other Goodbyes **11**:78, 84-85
Manhattan Theater Club **2**:418
Manhattan Transfer **6**:48
Manhunt **11**:28-29, 30
Manicomio **24**:18, 23
Manion, Clarence **11**:142, 143
Maniquis, Bob **4**:243, 244, 247
Mankind under the Leash **4**:151
Manlius Military Academy **20**:83-84
Mann, Thomas
    Becker **1**:36, 43, 45
    Blaise **3**:19
    Disch **4**:157
    Fisher **10**:93
    Konwicki **9**:129
    Lem **1**:259
    Menashe **11**:227, 230-31
    Turner **10**:318
Manning, Gordon **3**:317
Manning, Olivia **6**:20
Manning, Robert **7**:197-98
Manny, Frank A. **2**:135
Mano, D. Keith 6:205-21
Manocalzati, Italy **2**:80, 83
Mansfield, Katherine
    Brewster **15**:153, 160
    Shadbolt **3**:259
Manson, Charles
    Sanders **21**:267, 269, 271
    Spinrad **19**:327-28
Mansour, Joyce **25**:246, 247
Manual Labor **1**:133
Manuel, Al **1**:150, 151
Manuel, E. Arsenio 9:151-69
Manulis, Martin **7**:200
Manuscrito de origen **18**:74
Manuscrits de Pauline Archange, Les **4**:72
Manuvu' Custom Law **9**:168
Manuvu' Social Organization **9**:165
Many Named Beloved, The **11**:233, 235
Manzanar **16**:175-77, 184-85
Mao Tse-tung
    Barnstone **15**:70
    Wallace **1**:401
Maori **7**:148
Mappin, Hubert **4**:309-10
Maps **11**:256
Maquisard **2**:224-25
Marburg Chronicles, The **9**:5-6, 9-10
Marcel, Gabriel **11**:210
Marciano, Linda Boreman **5**:127-28
Marcus, Mort **13**:300
"Mardi Gras" **4**:260
Marek, Richard **1**:78
Margins
    Owens **2**:366
    Peters **8**:248
Margolis, Herbert **10**:298
Marie Antoinette **4**:261
"Marie of the Cabin Club" **6**:264
Marilyn's Daughter **4**:265

Marín, Luis Muñoz **17**:3, 4
Marin, Sutter **24**:343, 345
Mark Lambert's Supper **3**:355, 356
Mark of Vishnu, The **9**:230
Mark to Turn: A Reading of William Stafford's Poetry, The **22**:68
Markfield, Wallace 3:207-27
Markish, Peretz **4**:360
Marks, J See Highwater, Jamake
Markson, Elaine **21**:18-19
Marlatt, Daphne
    Brossard **16**:54
    Eshleman **6**:138
Marlborough School, Los Angeles, Calif. **2**:120
Marlowe, Christopher **10**:285-86
Marquand, John P. **9**:5
Marquette University **9**:110
Marquez, Velia **9**:204
Marquis, Don **8**:131
Marriage
    Hadas **23**:126-27
    Polkinhorn **25**:328
"Marriage, The" **26**:182
Married Land, The **12**:19-20, 31, 36, 37, 38
Married to a Stranger **17**:228
Mars **18**:57, 60
Marsh, Edward **5**:255
Marsh, Ngaio **15**:195
Marshall, George **19**:294-96
Marshall, Robert K. **8**:241
Marshall, William **6**:182
Marteau, Robert **13**:185, 188
Martha's Vineyard, Mass. **2**:158
Martial arts
    Hauser **11**:137
    Johnson **18**:232-33, 240-41
    Rosenblum **11**:348
    Turner **10**:320
Martin, John
    Arden **4**:39
    Bergé **10**:10
    Wakoski **1**:368
Martin, Knox **4**:156
Martin, Sandy **8**:215
Martinelli, Sheri **6**:180, 188
Martines, Lauro **2**:349-51, 352
Martingale **5**:351
Martlet's Tale, The **2**:156, 159
Marvell, Andrew **7**:216
Marvell Press **3**:39
Marx, Deceased **26**:105-06
Marx, Harpo **14**:254-55
Marx, Karl
    Owens **2**:364
    Pohl **1**:286
Marxism
    Anaya **4**:26
    Caute **4**:102, 105
    Davie **3**:43
    Fuller **10**:113
    Konwicki **9**:126-27, 134
    Nichols **2**:332
    Rakosi **5**:208
    Rowse **8**:255

Shadbolt **3**:258
Solotaroff **2**:394
Wilson **16**:301, 303-04
Zinoviev **10**:329
See also Communism
Mary Myth, The **7**:50
Maryško, Karel **12**:193
Masaccio **14**:170, 171
Masefield, John **11**:90
Mask of Dust **4**:342
Mask, The **11**:304
Masks of Time, The **3**:279, 281
Maslow, Abraham
    Norse **18**:278
    Rimmer **10**:299
    Wilson **5**:324
Mason, Mason Jordan **14**:117
Mason, Ronald **3**:256, 258
Masquerade **11**:83
Massa (magazine) **13**:153
Massachusetts **23**:20
Massachusetts Institute of Technology
    Vivante **12**:302
    Weiss **2**:447
Massachusetts Review **5**:286
Massachusetts School of Art **2**:132
Massada **21**:7-8
Masses **7**:91
Massillon, Ohio **3**:397-98
Master and Margarita, The **11**:376
Master Class **18**:303
Master Entrick **7**:130
Master Minds **8**:186, 195
Master of Her Fate **11**:104
Master of Life and Death **3**:276
"Master of None" **7**:188
"Masterson and the Clerks" **4**:151
Mataga, William **4**:250
Matera, Italy **2**:139, 140
Materials, The **3**:93
Mathematics **25**:349-50
Mathesius, Vilém **7**:214, 222, 223
Matheson, Richard
    Bloch **20**:49
    Nolan **16**:212, 213
Mathews, Harry 6:223-52
Mathews, Jackson **11**:213
Matos, Luis Pales **17**:7, 12
Matrix **10**:99
Matson, Harold (literary agents) **6**:57
Matsuoka, Yosuke **1**:380
Matsushima: Pine Islands **22**:275
Matthau, Walter **5**:213
"Matthew Scudder" series **11**:35, 38, 39-40
Matthews, Jack 15:255-71
    Heyen **9**:41, 42
    Smith **7**:163, 164
Matthews, Patricia **18**:271
Matthews, William 18:263-73
Matthiessen, F.O.
    Creeley **10**:66, 68
    Glazier **24**:233
Matthiessen, Peter **24**:320
Maugham **4**:234
Maugham, W. Somerset

Ford   21:36
Green   11:95-96, 102
Jennings   5:111
Morgan   4:234
Settle   1.915
Sinclair   5:269
Wakefield   7:194
Wallace   1:391
Maule, Harry   1:167, 168
Mauleòn, Isidoro   25:112, 113
Mauriac, François
   Blais   4:72
   Wiesel   4:353, 356-57
Mauve Desert   16:42, 44, 53
Mavericks   1:27
Maximus Poems, The
   Davie   3:45
   Ferrini   24:125
   Foley   24:169
Maxwell, William   7:97
May I Cross Your Golden River?
   2:125
May, James Boyer   6:180
May, Samuel   3:367
May, Val   9:255
Mayakovsky, Vladimir
   Gray   2:181
   Zinoviev   10:325
Mayer, Bernadette   17:281, 282-83
Mayer, Peter   3:430
Mayo Clinic   20:325
Maze of Monsters, A   22:244
McAllister, Claire   9:83
McBride, Mary Margaret   2:170
McBrien, Dean   6:51-52
McCaffery, Larry
   Federman   8:80
   Sukenick   8:293
McCaffrey, Anne
   Dann   20:78
   Nelson   23:262
McCann, Cecile   25:396
McCarter Theater, Princeton, N.J.
   2:417
McCarthy era
   Anderson   2:42
   Andre   13:18, 19
   Boyle   1:120-22
   Rule   18:312
McCarthy, Joseph
   Condon   1:196
   Disch   4:146
McCarthy, Mary   2:213
McCarthy, Pat   6:87
McCauley, Kirby   3:285
McClelland & Stewart (publishers)
   22:44
McClelland, Jack   22:44, 51-52
McClintic, Guthrie   12:235
McClure, Michael
   Berry   24:67, 77, 80
   Foley   24:174
   Kherdian   2:268-69
   Koller   5:163
   Leftwich   25:260, 266
McColgin, Daniel   26:309

McCord, Howard   9:171-89
   Berge   10:13
   Choudhury   14:92, 93
   Raworth   11:303
   Rosenblum   11:348, 353
   Thayer   11:364
McCord, William   9:149
McCoy, Kid   1:381
McCreary, Fred   10:66
McCullers, Carson
   Highwater   7:74
   Kazin   7:92-93
McCullough, Frances   7:282
McDowell, Robert
   Feirstein   11:84
   Jarman   22:101-03
McElderry, Margaret K.   9:86
McElroy, Colleen J.   21:119-44
McElroy, Joseph   6:250
McFerrin, Robert   23:198
McGill University
   Andre   13:17-18
   Blaise   3:27
   Dudek   14:125, 131
   Hine   15:223-25
   Vivante   12:291
McGough, Roger   2:52
McGraw, DeLoss   13:213-14
McGraw-Hill (publishers)   22:44
McGuane, Thomas   9:114, 116
McHugh, Heather
   Holden   22:68
   Murphy   26:221
McIntosh & Otis (literary agency)
   18:176
McIntosh, Mavis   6:53-54
McKain, David   14:205-17
McKenna, Richard
   Disch   4:150
   Knight   10:213, 221, 223
McKeon, Richard
   Booth   5:51
   Olson   12:230, 231, 232, 237
McLean, Lisa   20:67, 69, 71
McLoughlin, William G.   8:180
McLuhan, Marshall   22:34, 36, 38,
   55
McMichael, James
   Ai   13:8
   Pinsky   4:246, 249
   Wright   7:299
"McMillan & Wife"   1:231
McMurtry, Larry   7:185
McNamara, Michael   24:128, 138
McNaughton, Duncan   26:207
McNeese State College   20:326
McNeill, Bill
   Kyger   16:192-93, 195, 196, 202
   weiss   24:344, 346
McPherson, James A.   17:121-36
   Forrest   7:34
McPherson, Sandra   23:215-34
McQueen   16:221
McTaggart, Bill   9:42
M.D.: A Horror Story, The   4:157,
   158

MDS   1:273, 274
Mead, Margaret
   Berge   10:4
   Kostelanetz   8:181
Mead, Matthew   13:125-40
   Turnbull   14:335
Mead, Taylor   11:284
Mean Rufus Throw Down   7:163
Mean Streets   5:218
Meaning of Witchcraft, The   8:274
Meanings of Death and Life   5:35
Meat Science Essays   25:266
Medal of Honor
   Corcoran   2:119
   Nichols   2:332
Medea   2:419
Medek, Mikuláš   1:336
Medgar Evers College   2:306
Medhar Batanukul Ghungur   14:98
Median Flow, The   3:87
MEDICINE my mouths on fire   19:26,
   53
Meditations in a Graveyard   3:307
Medium, The   2:436
"Medusa"   26:324
Meek, Jay   15:23
Meet Me at Tamerlane's Tomb   2:124
Meet Mr. Miller   1:383
Meeting at Jal   3:98
Meeting Point, The   16:78
Meeting the Snowy North Again   2:59
Megged, Aharon   13:141-59
Megged, Amos   13:158
Megged, Eyal   13:158
Meigs, Mary   4:74, 75, 76, 77, 78
Meiji Hotel, Tokyo   2:167-69, 176-77
Mein Kampf   4:198
Meiselas, Susan   3:80, 81
"Melissa"   22:189-90
Meltzer, David   26:185-97
   Corman   2:142
   Kherdian   2:268, 269
   Kyger   16:190
   Menefee   26:207
Melville, Elizabeth   3:121-22
Melville, Herman
   Glazier   24:236
   Harris   3:121
   Kennedy   9:81
Member of the Wedding, The   7:74
Memoirs Found in a Bathtub   1:256
Memoirs of a Bastard Angel   18:276,
   279-80, 288
*Memoirs of the Late Mr. Ashley: An
   American Comedy, The*   11:137-38
Memorial, The   6:18
Memorial University of
   Newfoundland   7:280
Memory Board   18:322
Memory Cathedral, The   20:94
Memphis Academy of Art   23:304
Memphis State University   21:40
Memphis, Tenn.
   Howes   3:137-38
   Tillinghast   23:305
Men in the Jungle, The   19:320, 321

Men of Distinction **1**:194
Men to Match My Mountains **3**:371
Men, Women & Vehicles: Prose Works
    26:26, 29-30, 39
Menachem's Seed **26**:102-03, 105
Menashe, Samuel **11**:223-39
Mencken, H.L.
    Knebel **3**:168, 179
    Wallace **1**:397
Menefee, Sarah **26**:199-213
Menlo Junior College **9**:3
Menon, Krishna **9**:230
Menon, N.C. **9**:234
Menorah, The **1**:345
Mental illness
    Allman **15**:25, 26-27
    Andre **13**:23-24
    Emanuel **18**:137, 139, 140-41,
        144
    Van Brunt **15**:379
Mentch in togn, Der **9**:56
Menu Cypher, The **3**:81
Menzel, Jiří **1**:348
Merchant, The **7**:231
"Merci" **26**:152
Mercier, Vivian **3**:60, 65, 66
Mercouri, Melina **2**:361
Mercy **21**:7-8
Meredith, Burgess **26**:76
Meredith, George **5**:201
Meredith, James **3**:429
Meredith, Scott
    Knight **10**:212-13
    Malzberg **4**:211, 220
    Rimmer **10**:296, 302-03
    Spinrad **19**:317, 334-35
    Westlake **13**:342
Meredith, Scott, Literary Agency, Inc.
    Spinrad **19**:316-18
    Westlake **13**:340
Meredith, Sid **10**:212-13
Meredith, William **14**:219-36
    Harteis **26**:131-45
    Lifshin **10**:250
    Major **6**:187
    Malanga **17**:97-98, 99
    Mathews **6**:232
    Sward **13**:288
Mérimée, Prosper **1**:194
Merkin, Barry **1**:294
Merleau-Ponty, Maurice **26**:30-31
Merlin **2**:383
Merril, Judith
    Aldiss **2**:28
    Colombo **22**:49
    Disch **4**:150, 151
    Knight **10**:210, 211-12, 213, 215,
        218, 220, 222, 223
    Pohl **1**:289, 291
Merrill Foundation **1**:320
Merrill, James
    Blais **4**:78
    Corn **25**:145
    Hadas **23**:120, 127-29
    Hine **15**:228-29, 231

Merry Wives of Windsor, The **3**:404,
    405
Merton, Thomas
    Boyd **11**:57-58
    Galvin **13**:91
    Mott **7**:132-34
    Woodcock **6**:326
Merwin, Sam, Jr.
    Gunn **2**:247
    Kennedy **9**:78
Merwin, W.S. **16**:113
Mesmerist, The **13**:226
Message from the Eocene **8**:274
Messerli, Douglas
    Argüelles **24**:17
    Katz **14**:178
Metamorphoses **3**:304
Metamorphosis in the Arts **8**:184
"Metamorphosis, The" **11**:249
Metaphysical Society of America
    12:332
Metcalf, Paul **12**:348
Metesky, George **3**:98
Methodist Church **24**:187
Metro-Goldwyn-Mayer
    Allen **6**:20
    Nolan **16**:216, 218
    Roditi **14**:254
    Wallace **1**:383
Metropolitan Museum of Art, New
    York City **2**:266-67
Metropolitan Opera, New York
    City **4**:148
Mexicali, Mexico **25**:321, 325
Mexican Americans See Hispanic
    Americans
Mexican Stove, The **1**:198
Mexicans **23**:184-85
Mexico
    Alegría **15**:8-9
    Anaya **4**:25
    Argüelles **24**:5
    Armantrout **25**:15-16
    Barnstone **15**:55-59
    Barrio **15**:115-17, 121
    Bennett, Hal **13**:84, 85
    Bennett, John M. **25**:56
    Bowles **1**:85-86
    Bruce-Novoa **18**:68, 72-73
    Cherkovski **24**:98-99
    Delgado **15**:165-67
    Disch **4**:150
    Eshleman **6**:133
    Ghiselin **10**:142
    Harris **16**:135-36
    Heath-Stubbs **21**:70
    Kyger **16**:200-01
    Polkinhorn **25**:321, 325, 337
    Raworth **11**:304-05
    Turner **10**:315-16
    Villanueva **24**:316
    White **4**:349
    Williams **20**:331-32
    Williamson **8**:314-15
Mexico & North **6**:133
Mexico City College **15**:58

Mexico City, D.F.
    Bruce-Novoa **18**:68
    Rechy **4**:253
Mexico's Art and Chicano Artists
    15:121
Meyer, Albert **7**:46-47
Meyer, Thomas **12**:348, 351, 354
Meynell, Francis **3**:353
Mezzrow, Milton Mezz **8**:5, 6
Mia Poems **9**:216
Miami Beach, Fla. **1**:287
Miami Beach Mirror **12**:202
Miami Student (Oxford, Ohio) **3**:169
Miami University, Oxford, Ohio
    Dove **19**:102, 103
    Hall **12**:117-20, 131
    Jones **11**:178, 180
    Knebel **3**:168, 169
Mica **8**:78-79
Mich, Dan **3**:172
Michaeljohn, John **7**:71
Michaels, Leonard **25**:205
Michel, John **10**:206, 207, 208, 211
Michelangelo Buonarroti **3**:372-74
Micheline, Jack **26**:307
Michener, James **16**:142, 146, 149-
    50
Michigan
    Jones **20**:195-96
    Kirk **9**:89, 92-93
Michigan Artist Award **23**:193
Michigan Bell Telephone Company
    23:202
Michigan Catholic **1**:246-48
Michigan Chronicle **23**:202
Michigan College Fellowship **26**:219
Michigan State College See Michigan
    State University
Michigan State University
    Kirk **9**:94-95, 96, 97, 99
    Root **11**:323
    Rosenthal **6**:276, 278-79
    Wakoski **1**:369
Mickiewicz, Adam **3**:39-40
Mid-American Review **9**:186
Middle Passage **18**:241, 242
Middlebrook, Diane Wood **26**:88-90,
    91-92, 93, 94, 105
Middlebury College
    Barnstone **15**:59
    Brée **15**:136-37
    Glazier **24**:220
    Parini **16**:238-39
"Middles" **26**:91-93, 105
Middleton, Christopher
    Hamburger **4**:169, 171
    Lind **4**:195
    Mead **13**:130-31
Middleton, Stanley **23**:235-46
Midquest **4**:122-23, 124
MidWatch **5**:345
Midwest **14**:45
Midwood Symphony **4**:206
Migrations **8**:147
"Mike Hammer" series **7**:6
Milagro Beanfield War, The **2**:334-35

Miles, Bernard **2**:157
Miles College **17**:26
Miles, Elizabeth **7**:15
Miles, Josephine **26**:70
Milford Science Fiction Writers'
  Conference
  Budrys **14**:70
  Dann **20**:92-93
  Disch **4**:150, 153
  Haldeman **25**:198
  Knight **10**:220-21, 222
  Moorcock **5**:180
  Niven **12**:216-17
  Spinrad **19**:319
  Wolfe **9**:305-06, 307
Milky Way Galaxy, The **18**:51
Millar, Kenneth **3**:43, 44
Millay, Edna St. Vincent **12**:47-48
Millennium **18**:51, 56, 59-60
Miller, Arthur
  Slade **9**:244
  Sukenick **8**:287
Miller, Brown **10**:255
Miller, Celeste **24**:129
Miller, Geraldine **9**:279
Miller, Henry
  Crews **14**:103, 108-09, 110, 114,
    116
  di Suvero **26**:72
  Dillard **7**:19
  Elman **3**:81, 83
  Gray **2**:195
  Horwood **15**:243
  Kazin **7**:90
  Major **6**:179
  Ouellette **13**:182, 185
  Rimmer **10**:288
  Sukenick **8**:284, 287
  Valaoritis **26**:271-72
  Wallace **1**:397
Miller, Jim Wayne **15**:273-93
Miller, Joe **1**:383
Miller, Joel **23**:99-115
Miller, Kelly **2**:297
Miller, Leslie **22**:69
Miller, Mary Owings **18**:217-18
Miller, May **23**:208-09
Miller, Milton **8**:244
Miller, Nolan **8**:133
Miller, Perry **24**:233
Miller, Warren **1**:345-46
*Miller Williams and the Poetry of the
  Particular* **20**:338
Millett, Fred B. **12**:157
Milligan, Spike **1**:28
Millington Army Base, Memphis,
  Tenn. **1**:140
Mills & Boon **11**:98-99, 101, 103-04
Mills, C. Wright
  Kostelanetz **8**:185
  Wakefield **7**:196
Mills College
  Belitt **4**:63
  Rule **18**:311
Mills, Robert P.
  Budrys **14**:70-71

Disch **4**:151
Gunn **2**:256
Knight **10**:222
Milner, Ron **2**:298
Milosz, Czeslaw
  Miller **15**:290
  Pinsky **4**:250
Milton, John
  Ackerman **20**:8
  Rechy **4**:258
Milwaukee, Wis. **12**:162
Mind Game, The **19**:330, 331
Mind Master, The **2**:258
Mindbridge **25**:205
Mindlin, Raymond **25**:360-61, 363
Mindscapes **24**:127
Mindwheel **4**:250
mini **13**:71
Minister Primarily, The **2**:306
Minneapolis Fantasy Society **2**:39-40
Minneapolis Journal
  Salisbury **15**:315
  Vizenor **22**:263-65
  See also *Minneapolis Star and
    Tribune*
Minneapolis, Minn. **1**:250
Minneapolis Star and Tribune **22**:265-
  68
Minnesota
  Glancy **24**:210
  Salisbury **15**:314-21
Minnesota Review **4**:150
Minnesota State Reformatory **22**:271
Minsterworth Court **4**:343-44, 347,
  348, 349
Mintoff, Dom **5**:365
Minton, Walter **19**:331-32
Minute by Glass Minute **9**:286
Mirabell **23**:120
Miracle in Bohemia **1**:349
Miracle Play **5**:240
Miracle, The **1**:399
Miriam at Thirty-four **20**:251
Miriam in Her Forties **20**:252
Miron, Gaston **13**:183
Mirrors of Astonishment **23**:129
Mirsky, Mark Jay **11**:200, 212
Misanthrope, The **4**:134
Mischief Makers **20**:198, 201, 212,
  216-17, 218
Misérables, Les **2**:373
Miskowski, Mike **24**:73, 79-80
Miss America Pageant **6**:153-54
Miss Giardino **26**:52, 53, 54, 56, 60
Miss Muriel and Other Stories **6**:256,
  259
Miss Peabody's Inheritance **13**:121-22
Miss Silver's Past **1**:345
Missile Summer **2**:60
Missing **2**:335
Missing Person, The **2**:212, 213
Missing Years, The **19**:224
Mississippi
  Moorcock **5**:186
  Owens **24**:281-82, 283
Mississippi River **22**:260-61

Mister Roberts **9**:267
Mistral, Gabriela **20**:128
Mists of Avalon, The **10**:26
Mitchell, Adrian
  Aldiss **2**:24
  Booth **2**:52
Mitchell, Burroughs
  Elman **3**:75, 77
  Swanberg **13**:268, 269, 272, 273
Mitchell, H.L. **3**:137-38
Mitchell, Stephen **4**:250
Mitford, Jessica **17**:137-51
Mizener, Arthur **8**:302, 305, 306
Mizener, Rosemary **8**:306
Mobile, Ala. **16**:293
Mobius the Stripper **8**:152
Moby-Dick **7**:23
Moccasin Telegraph, The **7**:106
Modern Age **9**:99, 100
Modern art **15**:118
*Modern Dogma and the Rhetoric of
  Assent* **5**:41, 45
Modern European Poetry **15**:80, 92,
  94
*Modern Poetic Sequence: The Genius of
  Modern Poetry, The* **6**:280
*Modern Poets: A Critical Introduction,
  The* **6**:280
Modern Science Fiction **19**:325
Modern Screen **1**:377
Modernism
  Dillard **7**:6
  Valaoritis **26**:270, 273-76, 281,
    284, 285-86
Modica, Arlene **18**:270
Modular Poems **8**:92
Mohandas Gandhi **6**:321-22
Moholy-Nagy, László **8**:186, 189
Mohrt, Michel **2**:67
Molière, Jean-Baptiste **4**:134
Molly **3**:111
Molson Award **6**:323
Molson, Gordon **2**:171
Momaday, N. Scott **24**:292
Momaday, Natachee **23**:259
Moment of True Feeling, A **9**:119
Moments of Light **4**:123-24
*Momma As She Became—But Not As
  She Was* **4**:265
Mommsen, Theodor **6**:230-32
Mona **11**:31
Mondale, Walter **22**:270
Monde, Le **6**:239
Money Money Money **3**:405
Monje Blanco, El **4**:256
Monkey Secret **24**:206-07, 208, 212
Monmouth County, N.J. **1**:291
Monologue of a Deaf Man **5**:370
Monroe, Harriet
  Jacobsen **18**:217
  Olson **12**:228, 229
Monroe, Marilyn
  Rechy **4**:265
  Wallace **1**:398
Montag, Tom **8**:248
Montague, John **6**:285

Montaigne, Michel de
  Katz **9**:70
  Stewart **3**:353
Montale, Eugenio **7**:297, 298
Montalvo Center for the Arts
  26:159
Montana
  Savage **15**:329-45
  Wright **7**:299-300
Monteith, Charles
  Aldiss **2**:22
  Burroway **6**:92, 93
Monterrey, Mexico **13**:310
Monteverdi, Claudio **3**:95
Montgomery, Stuart **19**:145
Montgomery, Wes **6**:128
Montley, Patricia **2**:352
Montreal, Canada
  Blais **4**:77
  Bowering **16**:28-29
  Brossard **16**:39-57
  Dudek **14**:123, 124-25
  Ouellette **13**:177-78
Montreal Gazette **13**:15
Moody, Charlotte **1**:377
Moody, D.L. **24**:220, 221
Moody, Paul D. **24**:220
Moonshine Light, Moonshine Bright
  19:129, 130
Moonstone, The **6**:254
Moorcock, Michael 5:173-92
  Aldiss **2**:25, 29
  Disch **4**:151-52
  Spinrad **19**:324-25
  Tennant **9**:291
  Wolfe **9**:305-06
Moore, Barbara **8**:89
Moore, Brew **9**:198
Moore, Brian **3**:219
Moore, Geoffrey **10**:62
Moore, Lazarus **6**:215
Moore, Marianne
  Atkins **16**:12, 13
  Burroway **6**:90
  Corman **2**:136
  Creeley **10**:66-67
  Ghiselin **10**:139
  Gregor **10**:149, 156
  Weiss **2**:435
  Whittemore **8**:306
Moore, Paul, Jr. **11**:47, 59
Moore School of Electrical
  Engineering **12**:149-50
Moore, Ward **11**:203
Moorhead, Alan **4**:231
Moorsom, Sasha **1**:27
Moraff, Barbara **10**:6
Moral Stories **5**:370
Morandi, Giorgio **14**:171
Moravia, Alberto
  di Suvero **26**:72
  Ghiselin **10**:141
  Norse **18**:285
  Tennant **9**:291
  Wright **7**:298
Mordecai Richler **6**:323

More Fool, The **1**:79
More, Paul Elmer **7**:220
Morehead State University **17**:246
Morgan, Dan **8**:7
Morgan, Edwin **6**:73
Morgan, Frank **24**:341-42
Morgan, Robert 20:257-83
Morgan, Robin **11**:68
Morgan State College **17**:133
Morgan, Ted 4:223-36
Morgan, Theodore 3:229-48
Morley, Anthony Jefferson **12**:340-
  41
Mormon Country **9**:266
Mormonism
  Booth **5**:34, 36-38, 40-42, 46-47,
    49, 50
  Wallace **1**:389-90
Mormons **2**:74
Morocco **2**:385-86
Morris Brown College
  Killens **2**:282, 285-86
  McPherson **17**:133
  Williams **3**:420
Morris, Desmond **25**:308-09, 312
Morris, Guido **23**:169-70
Morris, John N. 13:161-75
Morris, Robert **1**:363
Morris, William **6**:318
Morris, Wright **3**:188
Morrison, Arthur **2**:384
Morrison, Henry
  Block **11**:34, 35, 36
  Silverberg **3**:277
  Westlake **13**:340, 342
Morrison, Pat **24**:342-44
Morrison, Theodore
  Ciardi **2**:90, 93, 94
  Glazier **24**:226, 228, 232
  Stegner **9**:265, 266, 267
Morrison, Toni
  Clarke **16**:84
  Jones **20**:215, 216
  Williams **3**:430-31
Morriss, Richard **5**:290
Morrow, William (publishers) **1**:400
Morse, Stearns **9**:198
Mort vive, La (Death alive) **13**:189
Mortal Consequences **3**:390
Mortal Engines **1**:264
Mortimer, John **5**:127, 128
Morwitz, Ernst **2**:434
Moscow **19**:337
Moscow Gold **4**:108
Moscow State University **10**:328-33
Moscow, USSR
  Corcoran **2**:124
  Easton **14**:152
  Shadbolt **3**:261
Moses **11**:173
"Moses Project, The" **6**:268
Moskowitz, Sam **9**:78
Mosley, Oswald **21**:53
Moss, Graydon **9**:149
Moss, Howard
  Fuchs **5**:58

  Smith **7**:163-64
Mosses from an Old Manse **15**:282-83
Mossman, James **4**:133
Mostly Monsters **22**:37
Mote in God's Eye, A **12**:220
Motel **2**:414-16
Motets **7**:297
Mother/Child Papers, The **24**:270,
  276
Mother Goose **12**:45
Mother London **5**:186
Mother, May I? **24**:310, 314
Mothers, Daughters **22**:222
"Mother's Tale, A" **3**:222
Mothersill and the Foxes **3**:417, 422,
  431
Motherwell, Robert **2**:194
Motion Picture Producers
  Association **1**:194
Motive **14**:110
Motley, Archibald **6**:181
Motley, Willard **6**:181-82
Motocar [and] *Richard III, Part Two*
  18:302
Motor Trend **16**:213
Motorcycle Betrayal Poems, The **1**:368
Motorcycles
  McCord **9**:177, 178
  Rosenblum **11**:335, 350, 351, 352
Motown Record Co. **2**:304
Mots, Les (The Words) **5**:117
Mott, Michael 7:113-34
Mound Builders of Ancient America
  3:278, 279
Mount Allison University **15**:157
Mount Etna **2**:153, 154
Mount Holyoke College **4**:166
Mount Holyoke Poetry Competition
  6:90
Mount Soledad **25**:337
Mountain climbing **25**:350
Mountain Road, The **6**:326
Mountains Have Come Closer, The
  15:286, 287, 288
"Mountains Like Mice" **9**:304-05
Mountains of Gilead **21**:36, 38
Mountbatten, Edwina **8**:25
Mountbatten, Louis **8**:25
Mountfort, Guy **4**:309
Mourners Below **1**:303
*Mournful Demeanor of Lieutenant
  Borůvka, The* **1**:345
Mousetrap, The **15**:197
Movement, The (English literary
  movement)
  Abse **1**:27
  Davie **3**:36-37, 38, 44
"Movie of the Week" **2**:254
Movies See Filmmaking
Moving Parts **14**:175
Mowat, Farley **15**:245, 247
Mowat, Frances **15**:247
Moynihan, John **9**:18
Mozart, Wolfgang Amadeus
  Enslin **3**:90
  Ouellette **13**:181

Wain **4**:328
Mpls. **1**:249-50
Mr. Field's Daughter **14**:13, 14, 15
Mr Keynes and the Labour Movement
  8:258
"Mr. Mintser" **4**:241-42
Mr. Sammler's Planet **1**:258
MRH **26**:150
Mrozek, Slawomir **10**:265-80
Mrs. Warren's Profession **5**:147
Muckraking **17**:149-50
Mueller, Jack **26**:303-04
Muggeridge, Malcolm
  Jones **5**:125
  Kirk **9**:104
Mug's Game, A **4**:159, 160, 162
Muhlenberg College
  Busch **1**:129, 130
  Weiss **2**:428, 429-30
Muir, Edwin
  Abse **1**:27
  Brown **6**:67, 69-70
Muir, Leo J. **5**:37
Mukherjee, Bharati **3**:25, 26-27, 28, 29
Mules Done Long Since Gone, The
  21:138
Mules Sent from Chavin **6**:139
Müller, Heiner **22**:24
Muller, Julian **9**:8-9
Mulligan, Gerry **9**:107, 110, 120
Mulligan, John **26**:210
MultiCultural Review **26**:128
Multiculturalism **16**:162-65, 168
Multiple sclerosis **4**:90-93
Mumford, Lewis
  Jerome **8**:137
  Kizer **5**:140
Mumps **8**:6
Mundo es ancho y ajeno, El (Broad
  and alien is the world) **12**:100
Munsel, Patrice **5**:152
Murchie, Guy **19**:247-309
  Katz **9**:57
Murder **25**:380, 389-90
"Murder by Morning" **1**:386
Murder in the Queen's Armes **18**:102-03
Murder of the Maharajah, The **8**:176
Murdoch, Iris **4**:88
Murgatroyd and Mabel **22**:244
Murmurs in the Walls **22**:247
Murphy, Sheila E. **26**:215-30
Murphy, Tom **3**:64
Murray, Don **2**:289
Murray, Donald **7**:107
Murrow, Edgar R. **1**:123
Murry, John Middleton
  Ashby **6**:35-36
  Weiss **2**:430
  Woodcock **6**:320
Muscle Shoals Sound Studio **24**:74
Museum **19**:107, 109-10
Musgrave, Susan
  Booth **2**:56
  Skelton **5**:292

Music
  Appleman **18**:29
  Bell **14**:36, 38-39
  Booth **5**:35
  Broughton **12**:47
  Brunner **8**:5-6
  Dudek **14**:126-27
  Enslin **3**:86, 89, 95-97
  Feirstein **11**:77-78
  Fisher **10**:98
  Foster **26**:117-18
  Higgins **8**:83
  Highwater **7**:78
  Hrabal **12**:189
  Josipovici **8**:157-58
  Kerrigan **11**:196-98, 201-02, 210
  Leftwich **25**:269
  McPherson **23**:216-17
  Nash **25**:292-93
  Ouellette **13**:178, 179
  Phillips **13**:195, 196, 197-98, 199, 210
  Plymell **11**:277, 279, 280, 281-82, 288
  Rodgers **13**:240
  Salaam **21**:240, 241-42, 244-45, 247-48
  Simmons **21**:293-94
  Simpson **4**:286
  Smith **7**:159-60
  Stevenson **9**:276-77
  Tillinghast **23**:305
Music for Several Occasions **3**:98
Music from Home: Selected Poems
  21:139
Music Man, The **4**:148
*Music of the Spheres: The Material
  Universe from Atom to Quasar,
  Simply Explained* **19**:247
Music to Murder By **18**:301, 302
Musical composition
  Atkins **16**:7, 9-10, 13, 14-15
  Browne **20**:67, 71-72
  Corn **25**:132
  Salaam **21**:198, 232-34
  Sanders **21**:269-70
Mussolini, Benito **25**:359
*Mutiny of the Bounty and Other Sea
  Stories* **19**:293-94
My Amputations **6**:195, 197, 198, 202
"My Aunt" **22**:181-83
My Aunt Christina **3**:356
My Day in Court **6**:264
My Father More or Less **5**:28
My Father's Moon **13**:111-12, 117
My Fellow Americans **11**:54
My Friend Judas **5**:270
My Life **5**:201
"My Living Doll" **9**:244
My Magazine **3**:350
My Next Bride **1**:116
"My Own Epitaph, Which I Better
  Write Because I Know Too
  Many Poets" **26**:309-10
My Poetry **26**:25-26

My Regrets **13**:25
"My Shoelaces" **22**:207-08
My Souths **4**:350
My Voice Because of You **15**:59
Myasthenia gravis **8**:299, 309
Myers, Dorothy **9**:279
Myers, Lucas **9**:280, 281
Myers, Michael **11**:306, 307
Myette, Louise **4**:73
Mysterious Canada **22**:32, 50-51
Mystery and Manners **6**:212
"Mystery of Phillis Wheatley, The"
  16:67
Mystery Play **2**:419
Mystery Writers of America
  Anderson **2**:43
  Elkins **18**:104
  Symons **3**:390, 391
*Mystic Chords of Memory: The
  Transformation of Tradition in
  American Culture* **23**:151
Mysticism **24**:64-65

NAACP See National Association for
  the Advancement of Colored
  People
Nabokov, Vladimir
  Belitt **4**:51-52, 54
  Blaise **3**:20
  Charyn **1**:183
  Katz **14**:166
  Turner **10**:318
Náchod, Czechoslovakia **1**:325-34
NACLA See North American
  Congress on Latin America
Nadamas **13**:65
Nadell, Bonnie **26**:178
Nadine **18**:87
Nagarajan, T.S. **9**:232
Nagasaki, Japan **1**:166
Naiad Press **18**:320, 321
Nailed to the Coffin of Life **24**:23
Naipaul, V.S.
  Anthony **18**:15-16
  Becker **1**:43
  Keating **8**:172
Najarian, Peter **4**:243, 244, 247
Naked and the Dead, The **4**:103
Naked Ear, The **14**:112-13
*Naked God: The Writer and the
  Communist Party, The* **18**:184
Naked Ladies **24**:322
Naked Lunch
  Morgan **4**:235
  Plymell **11**:289
*Nakedness of the Fathers: Biblical
  Visions and Revisions, The*
  24:273, 275
Names and Nicknames **15**:307
Naming of the Beasts, The **15**:358
Narayan, R.K. **8**:171
Naropa Institute
  Hollo **19**:174
  Kelly **19**:203
  Kyger **16**:201
  Sanders **21**:269-70

Waldman **17**:282-83, 285, 288-89, 291-93
Narrow Rooms **1**:304
Narrows, The **6**:253, 266-67
NASA See National Aeronautics and Space Administration
Nash, Ogden **6**:89
Nash, Susan Smith **25**:283-300
    Bennett **25**:73-74
Nashville, Tenn. **24**:13
Nassauer, Rudi **1**:24
Nat Turner **16**:83, 84
Nathanael West: The Cheaters and the Cheated **3**:197
Nation
    Barrio **15**:112
    Belitt **4**:60, 62
    Coppel **9**:6
    Eastlake **1**:211
    Elman **3**:74
    Rosenthal **6**:279
    Simpson **4**:293
    Wakefield **7**:196, 197
    Yglesias **20**:357-58
Nation of Poets, A **21**:230
Nation Poetry Prize **4**:60
National Academy **18**:172-73
National Academy of Letters Award **9**:147-48
National Aeronautics and Space Administration **7**:283
National Association for Health, England **8**:26
National Association for the Advancement of Colored People **2**:291
National Audubon Society **14**:149
National Black Arts Festival **21**:228, 230
National Book Award
    Bourjaily **1**:76
    Heinemann **21**:94, 95, 97-98
    Johnson **18**:242-43
    Kerrigan **11**:213
    Rabassa **9**:203
    Settle **1**:321
    Stegner **9**:269
    Wagoner **3**:409, 410
National Book Critics Circle Award
    Allen **11**:22
    Grumbach **2**:214
National Broadcasting Corp.
    Gunn **2**:251
    Salvadori **25**:360
    Wakefield **7**:200
    Williams **3**:423, 431
National Defense Education Act Fellowship
    Chappell **4**:113
    Miller **15**:282
National Defense Foreign Language Fellowship **13**:5
National Democratic party, Czechoslovakia **1**:329
National Educational Television
    Van Itallie **2**:414

Williams **3**:428, 430
National Endowment for the Arts
    Allen **11**:22
    Allman **15**:30
    Bergé **10**:11
    Blaise **3**:29
    Bowles **1**:94
    Bromige **26**:26
    Cassity **8**:58
    Dove **19**:105
    Eshleman **6**:147
    Forbes **16**:118
    Hansen **17**:70
    Hearon **11**:169
    Hebert **24**:256
    Jarman **22**:105
    Kerrigan **11**:214
    Markfield **3**:221
    McCord **9**:184-85
    McElroy **21**:141
    Peters **8**:249
    Salaam **21**:229
    Saroyan **5**:216
    Wilson **5**:353
National Endowment for the Humanities
    Brée **15**:145
    Lowitz **26**:180
    Taylor **7**:187
National Forensic League **1**:375
National Gallery of London **25**:356
National Gallery of Scotland **3**:355
National Geographic **3**:271
National Herald (India) **9**:234
National Institute of Arts and Letters
    Chappell **4**:120
    Davison **4**:138
    Williams **3**:414
National Institute of Public Affairs **8**:309
National Labor Relations Board **2**:282
National Medal of Science **16**:306
National Opinion Research Center **7**:47
National Organization of Women **1**:277
National Poetry Month **26**:79
National Poetry Week **26**:79, 81
National Public Radio
    Elman **3**:82
    Grumbach **2**:213
    Pinsky **4**:244
    Ray **7**:142
National Review
    Kirk **9**:100
    Mano **6**:208, 215, 216
National Science Foundation **25**:365
National Science Foundation Grant **16**:98
National Shakespeare Company **6**:209
National Socialism See Nazism
National Society of Film Critics **5**:28
National Trust (England) **4**:309

Native American storytelling **24**:200-05, 210, 211-12
    See also Trickster stories
Native American totems **22**:258
Native Americans
    Awoonor **13**:48
    Brown **6**:55-56
    Clarke **16**:78
    Fast **18**:178
    Glancy **24**:199-214
    Highwater **7**:72
    Katz **14**:175
    Kelly **22**:118-19
    Kenny **22**:125, 129, 135, 139, 150, 170
    McCord **9**:174, 175, 184
    Owens **24**:287-88, 292, 295-96, 297-98
    Purdy **17**:209-10
    Vizenor **22**:255-76
    Waters **13**:321, 322, 325-27
    West **7**:285
Native Son of the Golden West, A **16**:160
Natural Classicism: Essays on Literature and Science **10**:321
Natural history **20**:9-14
Natural History of Love, A **20**:3, 14
Natural History of the Senses, A **20**:14
Nature **23**:218, 226
Nausée, La **8**:72
Navajo Community College **9**:184
Naval Air Station, New Orleans, La. **2**:106
Naval Air Station, Olathe, Kan. **2**:106-07
Naylor, Charles **4**:154, 155
Naylors, The **3**:357
Nazareth College **26**:218-19
Nazi party **4**:162
Nazi-Soviet Pact **3**:42
Nazimova, Alla **2**:206
Nazis
    Brée **15**:133
    Easton **14**:145
    Hauser **11**:129, 132
    Laqueur **19**:209-12
    Lind **4**:195
    Ouellette **13**:181
    Roditi **14**:270-73
    Salvadori **25**:361, 366
    Samarakis **16**:251-57
    Sisson **3**:297
    Škvorecký **1**:329-34
    weiss **24**:325-27
Nazism
    Hamburger **4**:169, 170
    Salvadori **25**:359
    Schevill **12**:273-78
    Wellek **7**:221
"NBC Matinee Theater" **2**:170
NBC-TV See National Broadcasting Corp.
Neal, Larry **16**:86
Neale, J.E. **8**:259
Nebraska Gifford, J. **8**:181

Nebula Award
　Gunn　**2**:258
　Knight　**10**:225
　Sargent　**18**:345-46
　Silverberg　**3**:279, 281, 282, 283
　Wilhelm　**5**:297
Nebula Award Stories Four　**2**:255
Neeld, Elizabeth Cowan　**6**:250
Neff, Emery　**2**:432
Negro Digest　**13**:246
Nehru, Jawaharlal　**9**:229
Neighborhood Playhouse　**2**:411, 418
Neighboring Lives　**4**:155, 156
Neill, A.S.　**6**:121
Neilson, Lloyd　**26**:157
Nelbach, Inez　**10**:38
Nelson, Marilyn　23:247-67
Nemerov, Howard
　Belitt　**4**:52, 65
　Morgan　**20**:278-79
　Waldman　**17**:272-73
　Weiss　**2**:444
　West　**7**:285
　Whittemore　**8**:306, 308
　Williams　**20**:331
Neo-Expressionism (artistic
　movement)　**25**:394-95
Neo Poems　**22**:54
Neon Poems　**11**:293
Nepal　**23**:313
Neptune Beach　**5**:56
Neptune's Daughter　**4**:286
Neruda, Pablo
　Belitt　**4**:50, 64
　Kerrigan　**11**:189
　Williams　**20**:332-33
Nesbit, E.　**8**:210
Nest of Singing Birds, A　**22**:274
Net and Other Poems, The　**26**:77
NET See National Educational
　Television
Netherlands　**4**:200, 201
Neue Gedichte　**2**:158
Neuromancer　**20**:93
Nevada　**14**:167
New Age / Le nouveau siècle, The
　17:83, 89-93
New American Arts, The　**8**:184
New American Library (publishers)
　Brossard　**2**:67
　Gunn　**2**:257
　Raffel　**9**:214
　Rimmer　**10**:299-300, 301, 302,
　　303
　Solotaroff　**2**:400, 401
　Williams　**3**:424, 427, 432
New American Poetry　**5**:348
New American Review
　Dennison　**6**:121
　Solotaroff　**2**:401-03
New American Writing　**2**:383
New and Collected Poems, 1934–84
　(Roy Fuller)　**10**:118
New and Selected Essays (Denise
　Levertov)　**19**:241

New and Selected Poems (David
　Wagoner)　**3**:408
New and Selected Poems (Donald
　Davie)　**3**:43
New and Selected Poems, 1942–1987
　(Charles Edward Eaton)　**20**:135
New and Selected Stories, 1959–1989
　(Charles Edward Eaton)　**20**:142
New Black Poetry, The　**6**:185, 188
New Black Voices　**21**:203
*New Book of Forms: A Handbook of
　Poetics, The*　**22**:239, 245
New Campus Writing　**8**:133
New College of California　**26**:194
New College Poetics Program
　26:206-07
New Criticism
　Enslin　**3**:89, 90, 91, 93
　Foster　**26**:127
　Kazin　**7**:92
　Rosenthal　**6**:280, 282
New Deal
　Brown　**6**:53, 54
　Elman　**3**:70
New Delhi　**9**:234
New Directions Annual　**1**:132
New Directions (publishers)
　Brossard　**2**:66, 67
　Cassill　**1**:169
　di Suvero　**26**:69
　Olson　**11**:257
　Purdy　**1**:301-02, 304
　See also Laughlin, James
New England　**1**:40-41
New English Weekly
　Sisson　**3**:298, 301
　Woodcock　**6**:319
New Exile　**7**:124, 127
New Frontier　**8**:233, 234
New Guinea　**16**:295-96
New Jersey　**13**:78
New Leader　**12**:206
New Left
　Piercy　**1**:273
　Solotaroff　**2**:399-400
New Letters
　Petesch　**12**:248, 249
　Ray　**7**:144-45
"New Letters on the Air"　**7**:142
New Lincoln School, New York
　City　**6**:183, 186
New Lines　**3**:36, 37
New Mexico
　Anaya　**4**:15, 25, 27
　Eastlake　**1**:209
　McCord　**9**:171, 172-77, 184, 186-
　　87
　Wilson　**5**:345, 352
New Mexico Book Association　**26**:81
New Mexico Literary Arts
　Organization　**26**:81
New Mexico Military Institute　**8**:325
New Mexico Quarterly Review　**8**:112
New Mexico Review　**2**:333, 334
New Mexico State University　**5**:351,
　352, 355

"New Mirror, The"　**6**:259
New Movement (literary movement)
　5:284
New Orleans, La.
　Caulfield　**25**:113-14
　Rechy　**4**:260
New Orleans Poetry Journal　**3**:335
New Orleans Review　**20**:331
"New Orleans Transient Bureau"
　5:207
*New Poets: American and British Poetry
　since World War II, The*　**6**:280
*New Poets of England and America,
　The*　**7**:64
New Provinces　**14**:128
New Quarterly　**15**:251
New Reasoner, The　**12**:5
New Republic
　Elman　**3**:74
　Grumbach　**2**:211-12
　Kazin　**7**:88-89, 91, 92-93
　Rosenthal　**6**:279
　Whittemore　**8**:310
New School for Social Research
　Cassill　**1**:169
　Dennison　**6**:111
　Forbes　**16**:112
　Fox　**19**:127
　Inez　**10**:189, 191
　Malzberg　**4**:211
　Olson　**11**:256
　Owens　**2**:358
New Sharon's Prospect　**3**:98
New Statesman
　Allen　**6**:23, 24, 25
　Brown　**6**:70
　Burroway　**6**:99
　Caute　**4**:109
　Jones　**5**:124-25
New Statesman and Nation　**6**:320
New University of Ulster See
　University of Ulster
New Verse　**3**:385
New Voices of Hispanic America　**15**:9-
　10
New Wave (literary movement)
　Dann　**20**:91
　Disch　**4**:151
New World, The　**10**:320
New World Writing
　Dillard　**7**:6
　Solotaroff　**2**:400, 401, 402
New Worlds
　Aldiss　**2**:25
　Disch　**4**:151
　Moorcock　**5**:177, 180-81
New York　**25**:110
New York City
　Allen　**6**:25
　Andre　**13**:25
　Argüelles　**24**:13, 14
　Bergé　**10**:3, 5-7, 8-9, 11
　Brée　**15**:133
　Burroway　**6**:87
　Clark　**22**:16-20, 21
　Cruz　**17**:5-7

INDEX

Daigon **25**:154-56
Dennison **6**:117
Disch **4**:148
Duncan **2**:170
Easton **14**:145
Emanuel **18**:132-33
Federman **8**:74
Feirstein **11**:73-74, 75, 77-78, 84
Forbes **16**:112
Gray **2**:193, 194
Grumbach **2**:203, 204, 205, 208
Hailey **1**:230
Higgins **8**:85-86
Hine **15**:230-31
Holden **22**:62-63
Howes **3**:139
Katz, Menke **9**:54-58, 61-62
Katz, Steve **14**:163-64, 170-71
Kazin **7**:86, 88, 91, 94
Kherdian **2**:266-67
Kirkup **4**:190
Kyger **16**:199
Mano **6**:205, 207
Matthews **18**:269
McPherson **23**:221
Menashe **11**:237
Owens **2**:358-60
Phillips **13**:203-04
Piercy **1**:273-75
Pohl **1**:289
Polkinhorn **25**:330-32
Purdy **1**:302
Rechy **4**:259-60
Rosenthal **6**:279
Settle **1**:311-312
Silverberg **3**:278, 282-83
Simic **4**:278-79
Sukenick **8**:285-87
Swenson **13**:310
Van Itallie **2**:411-12, 419
Van Proyen **25**:396
Vivante **12**:296
Wakefield **7**:197
Wakoski **1**:361-68
Wallace **1**:378
weiss **24**:330
Weiss **2**:431-32
West **7**:277-78, 281
Williams **3**:423-24
New York City (audiotape) **8**:185-86
New York Daily Mirror **12**:203
New York Daily News **8**:324
New York Drama Critics Circle
   2:363
New York Herald-Tribune
   Lottman **12**:203
   Morgan **4**:229-31
   Rosenthal **6**:279
   Simpson **4**:292
   Slavitt **3**:319
New York Institute for Gestalt
   Therapy **6**:115
New York Jew **7**:91
New York Poetry Center **1**:362
New York Post **7**:196
New York Pro Musica **25**:157

New York Public Library
   Argüelles **24**:13
   Kazin **7**:90-91
   Yglesias **20**:348, 353
New York School poets
   Disch **4**:153
   Saroyan **5**:215
New York Theatre Strategy **2**:366
New York Times
   Brossard **2**:68, 69, 70
   Elman **3**:76, 80
   Gray **3**:114
   Grumbach **2**:212
   Knebel **3**:180, 181
   Meredith **14**:233
   Nichols **2**:331
   Salisbury **15**:324
   Shapiro **6**:299
   Van Itallie **2**:415, 418
   Wallace **1**:392
   Weiss **2**:436
New York Times Book Review
   Dillard **7**:16
   Elkins **18**:101-02
   Kirk **9**:98
New York Times Encyclopedia of Film
   21:45
New York Times Magazine **7**:201
New York University
   Allen **6**:26
   Baumbach **5**:24
   Bergé **10**:2
   Brée **15**:143-44
   Busch **1**:131
   Caute **4**:105
   Disch **4**:148-49, 152
   Eshleman **6**:140
   Feirstein **11**:79, 80
   Goldemberg **12**:103
   Grumbach **2**:207
   Higgins **8**:90, 91, 92
   Highwater **7**:80
   Inez **10**:190
   Jones **5**:120
   Kenny **22**:170
   Killens **2**:288
   Lottman **12**:198, 204
   Lowitz **26**:173
   Norse **18**:283
   Root **11**:329
   Rosenthal **6**:276, 277, 279, 282
   Sanders **21**:259-60, 261, 264
   Slavitt **3**:311
   Van Itallie **2**:421, 422
   Vizenor **22**:273
New Yorker
   Boyle **1**:117, 120, 121
   Brossard **2**:63-64, 65, 76
   Burroway **6**:90
   Ciardi **2**:93
   Furman **18**:201
   Gray **2**:198
   Hahn **11**:111, 113, 115, 116
   Hentoff **6**:170, 171, 173
   Kerrigan **11**:209
   Kizer **5**:152-53

Smith **7**:163-64, 165
Swenson **13**:313
Vivante **12**:298-99, 300
New Zealand
   Adcock **23**:1-3, 6-7, 13-14
   Ray **7**:148
   Shadbolt **3**:249, 250, 254, 255,
     257, 265-66
New Zealand Herald **3**:257
New Zealand Labour Government
   3:256
New Zealand Labour Party **3**:254
New Zealanders, The **3**:259, 263, 264
Newbattle Abbey College **6**:69, 70
Newbery Award **7**:82
Newdigate Prize **7**:63-64
Newfound **15**:274, 288-89
Newfoundland **15**:248, 249
Newfoundland, Canada **15**:243-44
Newman, Barney **6**:113
Newman, John **6**:50-51
Newman, Phyllis **2**:364
Newman, Tom **6**:50-51
Newspaper Enterprise Association
   1:194
Newspaper of Claremont Street, The
   13:110
Newsweek
   Elman **3**:74
   Slavitt **3**:317-19, 321
   Williams **3**:426, 427, 428
Newton, Douglas **1**:314
Niagara Barn Players **9**:241-42
Nibley, Hugh **1**:390
Nicaragua
   Alegría **15**:1-2, 13, 14
   Elman **3**:80-81
   Nichols **2**:337
   Waldman **17**:289-90
Nice to See You: Homage to Ted
   Berrigan **17**:289
Nichol, bp **19**:20, 50
Nichols, Dudley **1**:201-02
Nichols, Edward J. **3**:402-03
Nichols, J.G. 2:307-19
Nichols, John 2:321-37
Nichols, Robert
   Bergé **10**:8
   Dennison **6**:117
Nichols, Walter J. **7**:10
Nicholson, Ben **5**:288
Nicholson, Norman **14**:336
Nick L. Nips See Bennett, John M.
Nicolson, Marjorie Hope **7**:277
Niedecker, Lorine
   Corman **2**:144, 145-46
   Honig **8**:109
   Williams **12**:346
Niels Holgerson's Miraculous Journey
   4:200
Nieman Fellowship **7**:197
Niente da (Nothing to) **13**:71
Nietzsche, Friedrich
   Nichols **2**:318
   Rakosi **5**:204
   Stafford **3**:338

Nigeria
　Dacey **17**:25-26
　Kammen **23**:145-47
　Killens **2**:303
Night **4**:357
Night Journey **2**:221, 224, 225, 228
Night of Camp David **3**:181
Night of Fire and Snow **9**:5
Night Scene **19**:143
Night Screams **4**:219
Night Song **3**:414, 415, 424, 425, 427
Nightfall Hotel **26**:286
Nightland **24**:297
Nightmare of God, The **1**:54, 57
Nightwings **3**:280-81
Nijinsky, Vaslav **2**:356
Niles, Amy **24**:228-31
Nilon, Charles H. **6**:190
Nimbus **5**:370
Nims, John Frederick **17**:153-94
　Kumin **8**:215
Nin, Anaïs
　Bloch **20**:48
　Crews **14**:103, 111
　Highwater **7**:78, 80
　Major **6**:183
　Norse **18**:284-85, 285, 287, 288, 289, 290
19 Poetas de Hoy en los Estados Unidos **20**:330
90 Degrees South **1**:36
98.6 **8**:294
Nips, Nick L. See Bennett, John M.
Nirvana Blues, The **2**:335
Nisbet, R.A. **9**:99
Niven, Larry **12**:211-24
Niven's Laws **12**:222-24
Nixon, Agnes **7**:199
Nixon-Clay Business College **11**:163
Nixon, Richard
　Knebel **3**:178
　Settle **1**:319
　Wallace **1**:376
Nixon vs Nixon **1**:376
Nizan, Paul **8**:179
Nkombo **21**:196-97, 203, 206-07
Nkrumah, Kwame
　Awoonor **13**:35, 46, 50, 51
　Killens **2**:303
NO **26**:103-05
No Country for Young Men **2**:351, 352
No Enemy but Time **26**:6
No Exit **1**:87
No Gods Are False **17**:182
No High Ground **3**:179
No Is the Night **14**:111
No Jerusalem but This **11**:235, 236
No Land Is Waste, Dr. Eliot **21**:280-81, 283
No Smoke **24**:125, 126
No Time to Be Young **5**:121, 122
Nobel Prize
　Pinsky **4**:250
　Wallace **1**:390-93

Noble, Edward John, Fellowship **2**:158
nobody owns th erth **19**:26, 53
Noden, William **7**:266, 270
Noise in the Trees **9**:33
Nolan, Cameron **16**:214-15, 217
Nolan, William F. **16**:205-26
Nonconformists **23**:239-42
Nonesuch Library (publishers) **3**:353
Nonsense **26**:30-31
Noonday Press **3**:415
NORC See National Opinion Research Center
Nordstrom, Ursula **6**:169
Norman Thomas: The Last Idealist **13**:273
Norse, Harold **18**:275-92
　Berry **24**:78-79
　Cherkovski **24**:95-96
　Polkinhorn **25**:335
Norse legends **7**:78
North American Congress on Latin America **1**:273
North American Education, A **3**:18, 21, 24
North American Review **14**:48
North Carolina
　Morris **13**:167-68
　Wright **7**:289-90, 292
North Carolina State University at Raleigh **20**:278, 280
North of Jamaica **4**:296
North of Summer **17**:210
North of the Danube **1**:148
North Point Press **9**:219
North Sea **22**:90, 92, 95
Northeastern Illinois University **11**:305
Northeastern News **6**:167
Northeastern University
　Galvin **13**:93
　Hentoff **6**:166-67
Northern House **5**:251
Northern Illinois University
　Klinkowitz **9**:111
　Ray **7**:142
Northern Spring **6**:323
Northern Virginia Community College **14**:25-26, 27, 29, 30
Northwest Alabama Junior College **24**:67
Northwest Review **5**:164
Northwestern University
　Appleman **18**:29, 32, 33, 35
　Blotner **25**:94
　Brutus **14**:61
　Emanuel **18**:131
　Gunn **2**:246
　Piercy **1**:271
Norton, Alden H. **10**:209
Norton Anthology of Short Fiction, The **1**:173-74
Norton, Joshua **11**:294, 295
Norton, W.W. (publishers) **8**:247-48
Not Be Essence That Cannot Be **2**:363

Not in God's Image: Women in History from the Greeks to the Victorians **2**:351, 352
Not Made of Glass **10**:257
Not-Right House, The **1**:303
"Not to Lethe" **4**:58-59
Notebook of a Ten Square Rush-Mat Sized World: A Fugitive Essay **11**:204
Notebooks of Malte Laurids Brigge, The
　Abse **1**:25
　Gray **2**:194
Notebooks of Susan Berry, The **7**:127, 128, 130
Notes from a Child of Paradise **25**:142
Notes from Another Country **3**:384, 386, 392, 394
Notes on Burning Boyfriend **21**:15
Notes on the State of Virginia **7**:164
Notes on Visitations: Poems 1936–1975 **6**:326
Notes on Writing a Novel **7**:25
Notre Dame University
　Katz **14**:176-77
　Nims **17**:171-74, 175, 177-78, 180, 187
Nottingham, England **2**:371-75
Nottingham Writers' Club **2**:385
Novelist: A Romantic Portrait of Jane Austen, The **18**:184
Novices **6**:148
Novoa, Juan Bruce See Bruce-Novoa
Now (Charles Plymell) **11**:286, 289
NOW (George Woodcock) **6**:320
Now Playing at Canterbury **1**:77, 78
NOW See National Organization of Women
Nowhere for Vallejo, A **16**:281
Nowlan, Alden **15**:157
Noyes, Alfred **10**:119
Noyes, George Rapall **3**:39
NPR See National Public Radio
Nuclear disarmament movement
　Brunner **8**:9-10
　Thomas **4**:312
Nuclear weapons
　Clement **16**:101-02
　Fox **19**:124-25
Nude Descending a Staircase **9**:84, 86
Nuits de l'Underground, Les **4**:77
Numbers
　Rechy **4**:262, 265
　Sisson **3**:305
Nuremberg Laws **1**:329
Nuremberg War Crimes Trial **14**:269-73
Nureyev, Rudolf **1**:60
Nye, Robert **1**:133
Nylon Age, The **1**:334
Nympho and Other Maniacs, The **1**:397

O Beulah Land **1**:307, 317, 319
O Canada **4**:73
O Didn't He Ramble **5**:169

O. Henry Award
  Boyle **1**:117
  Ignatow **3**:156
O negro na ficção brasileira: Meio século de história literária **9**:202
Oakes, Philip 25:301-19
Oates, Joyce Carol
  Allen **11**:11
  Highwater **7**:82
  Knebel **3**:182
  Phillips **13**:199-200, 201, 205, 207, 211, 213
  Weiss **2**:449
Obedient Wife, The **2**:352
Obeli: 21 Contemplations **26**:225-26, 228
Oberg, Arthur **6**:180
Oberlin College **22**:60-62
Oberon Press **7**:102
Obie award **20**:219, 220, 225
"Objectivist" poets **24**:42
"Objectivists" Anthology, An **5**:207
O'Briain, Liam **4**:305
O'Brian, Patrick **1**:43
O'Brien, Edward J. **6**:20
O'Brien, John **9**:113
Obscenity **6**:212, 213
Observer (London)
  Owens **2**:361
  Wilson **5**:321
Obsidian: Black Literature in Review **20**:23, 28
Obsidian II **20**:23
O'Casey, Sean
  Boyle **1**:97
  Raworth **11**:297
  Simmons **21**:293
Occident, The **26**:70, 71
Occidental College
  Olson **11**:253-55
  Rechy **4**:263
Occidental Review **11**:253, 254
Occupation, The **4**:100, 106
Oceanside Theatre **2**:116
Ochoterna, Gaudiosa **9**:165
O'Connell, Eileen **3**:62
O'Connell, George **22**:245, 250
O'Connor, Edwin **13**:103
O'Connor, Flannery
  Brown **10**:43
  Corn **25**:133-34
  Gray **2**:201
  Mano **6**:212
O'Connor, Frank
  Blaise **3**:19
  O'Faolain **2**:345
O'Connor, John Cardinal **6**:173
Octavia and Other Poems **23**:210
Octavian Shooting Targets **10**:148-49
October Blood **2**:200
Oda, Makoto **10**:4
O'Day, Anita **4**:190
Odd John **3**:271
Odds against Tomorrow **2**:303
"Ode to New York" **8**:309
Odense University **1**:156

Odeon (publishers) **1**:345
Odets, Clifford **1**:202
Odrodzenie **9**:123, 134
Odysseus Ever Returning: Essays on Canadian Writers and Writing **6**:323
Odyssey (Homer)
  Forrest **7**:21
  Harris **16**:123, 124, 125
  Sinclair **5**:275
Odyssey (literary review) **9**:203
Odyssey of Katinou Kalokovich, The **12**:241, 243
Of Divers Arts **8**:187
Of Manywhere-at-Once **25**:190
Of Poetry and Power: Poems Occasioned by the Presidency and Death of JFK **10**:6
Of Time, Passion, and Knowledge **10**:318
Of Trees and Stones **13**:157, 158
O'Faolain, Eileen Gould **2**:339-42, 343, 344, 345, 350
O'Faolain, Julia 2:339-53
O'Faolain, Sean
  Dillon **3**:57, 64
  O'Faolain **2**:339-40, 341, 342-43, 344, 345, 347, 350
Off-Broadway theatre **2**:413, 414, 419
Off Earth **22**:55
Off the Ground: First Steps to a Philosophical Consideration of the Dance **15**:362
Offen, Ron **13**:288-89
"Offering" **25**:65
Offical Verse Culture **24**:47
Office of Strategic Services **9**:199
Offshore **10**:107
O'Grady, Desmond **7**:298, 301, 302
O'Hara, Frank
  Argüelles **24**:13
  Clark **22**:20-21
  Hall **7**:62, 63
  Joans **25**:236
  Waldman **17**:276, 277
O'Hara, John
  Cassill **1**:173
  Higgins **5**:91
O'Higgins, Patrick **4**:233-34
Ohio State University
  Baumbach **5**:23
  Jerome **8**:132, 133
  Matthews **15**:262, 265
  Morgan **3**:232, 233-34, 235
Ohio University
  Heyen **9**:40
  Kirkup **4**:189, 190
  Matthews **15**:268-69
  Shelnutt **14**:301
Ohio University Press **7**:163
Ohio Wesleyan University **8**:240-41
O'Horgan, Tom **2**:362
Oil and gas exploration **25**:287, 298
Ojibway **22**:258-59
O'Keeffe, Georgia **1**:110

Oketani, Shogo **26**:180-81, 182
Okinawa, Japan **1**:166
Oklahoma
  Nash **25**:283-84, 285-86
  Ray **7**:135
Oklahoma A&M University **2**:244
Oklahoma City, Okla. **2**:169
Oklahoma City University **2**:167, 169
Old Bones **18**:104
"Old Churchyard at St. Austell, The" **8**:254
Old Fictions and the New, The **8**:184
Old House of Fear **9**:100
"Old Man" **26**:325
Old Man and the Sea, The **11**:318-19
Old Ones, The **7**:256, 259
Old Poetries and the New, The **8**:184
Old Saybrook, Conn. **6**:254, 255-57
Old Snow Just Melting **14**:49
Old Westbury College **2**:71
"Old Woman" **4**:246
Oldest Confession, The **1**:196
Olitski, Jules **3**:78
Olivant **6**:180
Olivares, Julian **11**:251, 252-53, 258
Oliver, Chad **16**:212
Olivier, Laurence
  Fry **23**:71-78
  Kennedy **20**:229, 230
Olsen, Tillie **3**:82
Olson, Charles
  Bowering **16**:29-30
  Clark **22**:14
  Corman **2**:135, 136, 137, 138
  Creeley **10**:61, 67, 70, 71, 72, 73, 74
  Davie **3**:45
  Eigner **23**:27, 51-52, 53, 58
  Enslin **3**:90, 91, 94
  Ferrini **24**:125, 126-27, 133-34, 142, 145-47
  Foley **24**:169, 171
  Gray **2**:194, 195, 198
  Kelly **19**:185, 192, 199, 201
  Kyger **16**:200
  Sanders **21**:266, 267, 269
  Simpson **4**:296
  Souster **14**:315
  Taylor **26**:260
  Waldman **17**:275
  Williams **12**:347-48
  Wilson **5**:348, 352
Olson, Elder 12:225-38
  Roditi **14**:260
Olson, Toby 11:241-60
  Owens **2**:363
  Rosenblum **11**:345
Olson's Penny Arcade **12**:236
Olympia Press
  Major **6**:185
  Rimmer **10**:297
  Wallace **1**:396
Olympian, The **9**:27
Olympic Games **14**:55-56
Olympic Games, Tokyo, 1964 **4**:188

O'Malley, Walter   **4**:210
Ombres sombres, Les   **7**:15
Omega Point, The   **19**:368, 370, 372
Omega Point Trilogy, The   **19**:372
Omni
   Bova   **18**:57-58
   Silverberg   **3**:285
Omnibus of Speed: An Introduction to the World of Motor Sport   **16**:213
"Omnipresent to Some Extent"   **23**:31-38
Omowale: The Child Returns Home   **3**:430
On Becoming American   **4**:233
On Being a Son   **6**:109-10
On Extended Wings   **20**:12-13
On Glory's Course   **1**:303
On Holography   **8**:190
On Home Ground   **20**:252
On Human Nature   **16**:304, 306
On Light   **2**:420
On My Eyes   **23**:41, 51
On Native Grounds: An Interpretation of Modern American Prose Literature   **7**:90-92, 95
"On Saturday the Siren Sounds at Noon"   **6**:264
On Stone: A Builder's Notebook   **25**:46
On Striver's Row   **6**:267
On the Big Wind   **3**:200
On the Composition of Images, Signs, and Ideas   **8**:92
On the Death of Archdeacon Broix   **2**:55-56
On the Death of My Father and Other Poems   **2**:271-72
On the Edge of the Knife   **20**:136-38
On the Way Home   **14**:28
On the Way Up   **26**:153
Onassis, Jacqueline Kennedy
   Hazo   **11**:141
   Slavitt   **3**:322
Once around the Bloch: An Unauthorized Autobiography   **20**:35
Once for the Last Bandit   **11**:150
Once on Chunuk Bair   **3**:255
Ondaatje, Michael   **19**:136
One and the Many   **23**:203
One Day at a Time   **5**:170
One-Eyed Man Is King, The   **5**:22
One for New York   **3**:423-24
One Hundred Years of Solitude   **9**:204
ONE (magazine)   **17**:66-67
One Nation   **9**:266
One of Those Condor People   **13**:64
One on One: The Imprint Interviews   **22**:118
"One Spring"   **26**:38-39
One Thing More, or Caedmon Construed   **23**:78
1859: Entering an Age of Crisis   **18**:36
1968   **25**:204
One Winter Night in August   **9**:86
O'Neill, Eugene, Jr.   **6**:232
Onís, Federico de   **9**:202

Onley, Toni   **6**:325
Onliness   **7**:162, 165
Only Piece of Furniture in the House, The   **24**:206
Only the Good Times   **18**:76-77
Only the Little Bone   **20**:177, 180, 188
Ono, Yoko
   Ostriker   **24**:271
   Wakoski   **1**:363
Ontario College of Art   **9**:217-18
Open Doorways   **18**:26, 39
Open Places   **22**:69
Open Prison, An   **3**:357
Open Theater   **2**:411, 412, 413, 414, 415, 416, 418, 419, 421
Opening Nights   **6**:96, 102
Opera
   Gregor   **10**:157-58
   Highwater   **7**:73
   Kizer   **5**:151-52
   Mathews   **6**:226
   Schevill   **12**:266-67, 271, 273-74, 275-76
   Simpson   **4**:285
   Wellek   **7**:211
Operation Ares   **9**:307
Opium   **7**:279
Opium and the Romantic Imagination   **2**:55
Oppen, George
   Enslin   **3**:93
   Rakosi   **5**:207, 208, 209
   Thayler   **11**:361
Oppen, Mary   **3**:93
Oppenheimer, Joel   **12**:347
Oppenheimer, Paul   **24**:11, 17
Oracle of the Thousand Hands   **4**:214
Orage, A.R.   **6**:319
Oral literature
   Anaya   **4**:24, 27
   Awoonor   **13**:41-42
   Forbes   **16**:106-07
   Forrest   **7**:23, 29, 30
Oration on Death   **26**:116
Orbit
   Niven   **12**:217
   Wolfe   **9**:305
"Orbit" anthology series   **10**:224
Ordeal   **5**:127-28
Order of Battle   **9**:5
Order of Canada   **15**:251
Order of Saint John of Jerusalem, The   **8**:24-25
Oregon   **12**:169-70
Oresteia   **6**:98, 100
Organized crime See Mafia
Origin
   Enslin   **3**:90, 91, 93, 98
   Fisher   **10**:96
   Kelly   **19**:201
   Turnbull   **14**:333
   Wilson   **5**:350
Origin: A Biographical Novel of Charles Darwin, The   **3**:377
Origin of Species, The   **18**:33, 37
Origins of the Sexual Impulse   **5**:324

Origins of Totalitarianism, The   **2**:438
"Orion" series   **18**:58-59
Orkney Herald   **6**:67, 70
Orkney Islands   **6**:61-62, 67-69, 72, 73
Orkneyinga Saga   **6**:61, 67
Orlando, Fla.   **1**:308
Orlovsky, Peter
   Malanga   **17**:110
   Plymell   **11**:287, 288, 289-90, 295
Ormos, Greece   **23**:130
O'Rourke, P.J.   **11**:293, 294
O'Rourke, William   **11**:206-07
Orphanages
   Green   **11**:87-88
   Inez   **10**:179-81
   Ray   **7**:138
Ortega y Gasset, José
   Kerrigan   **11**:213, 214
   Rimmer   **10**:304
Orthodox Church
   Gray   **2**:187
   Mano   **6**:214
Orthodoxy   **6**:214-15
Orton, Iris   **5**:261
Orwell, George
   Burke   **19**:72-73
   Glanville   **9**:21
   Nichols   **2**:313
   Symons   **3**:387-89
   Woodcock   **6**:319, 320, 321
Orwell's Message: 1984 and the Present   **6**:326
Osborne, Charles   **1**:29
Osborne, John
   Oakes   **25**:315-16
   Wesker   **7**:240
   Wilson   **5**:321, 323
Oscuridad divina   **25**:111
Oster, George F.   **16**:304
Osterhout, Hilda   **1**:69
Osterling, Anders   **1**:391
Ostriker, Alicia (Suskin)   **24**:261-79
O'Sullivan, Seamus   **4**:305
Othello   **7**:22-23
Other Alexander, The   **15**:93
Other Canadas   **22**:48-50
Other Canadians   **14**:128
Other Poetry   **9**:285
Other Side of the River, The   **7**:295, 298
Other Skies   **2**:93
"Other, The"   **11**:211
Other Worlds Than This   **23**:130
Otherwise Engaged   **3**:114
Ott, John   **2**:420
Oublion Project, The   **10**:304
Ouellette, Fernand   **13**:177-92
Oughton, Diana   **2**:330
OUI   **6**:215, 216, 217, 218
OuLiPo See Ouvroir de littérature potentielle
Our England Is a Garden   **3**:356
Our Flag Was Still There   **23**:304, 316
Our Lady of the Flowers   **24**:153

Our Nig **6**:253
"Our Poems" **26**:80
*Our Women Keep Our Skies from
    Falling* **21**:222
Oursler, Fulton **1**:378
Out **8**:294
Out from Ganymede **4**:219
*Out of My Depths: A Swimmer in the
    Universe* **7**:279
Out of My Hands **26**:31
Out of the Night **6**:244
Out of the Whirlwind **22**:118, 119
Outcasts, The **1**:39
Outer Mongolian, The **3**:321
Outfit, The **13**:342
Outlanders **2**:433, 436, 450
Outsider, The
    Eshleman **6**:129
    Wilson **5**:314, 319, 320, 321-22,
        327
Outsiders **25**:52
Outward Side, The **17**:69
Ouvertures **13**:190
Ouvroir de littérature potentielle
    6:247-48
Overlay **4**:210, 213
*Overnight in the Guest House of the
    Mystic* **11**:21-22
Overtures to Death **10**:123
Ovid's Heroines **15**:235
Owen, Guy
    Dillard **7**:12
    Morgan **20**:279-80
Owens, Carl **23**:211
Owens, Louis 24:281-98
Owens, Rochelle 2:355-69
    Bergé **10**:6
Owlstone Crown, The **9**:86
Owning Jolene **11**:167
Oxford City Library, England **5**:110,
    112
Oxford, England
    Jennings **5**:107
    Sinclair **5**:267-68
Oxford English Dictionary, The **10**:122
Oxford History of English Literature
    3:354
Oxford Mail **2**:23, 24
Oxford Playhouse **23**:69
Oxford Pledge **2**:207, 209
Oxford University
    Bell **12**:24-25, 27
    Booth **2**:56
    Boyd **11**:47
    Brophy **4**:85-86, 90
    Browne **20**:60
    Caute **4**:102-05, 106
    Epstein **12**:69-70
    Fitzgerald **10**:104
    Fuller **10**:117
    Ghiselin **10**:131, 138
    Hahn **11**:113
    Hall **7**:63
    Hamburger **4**:164, 165
    Heath-Stubbs **21**:71
    Howes **3**:140-41

Josipovici **8**:154, 155, 156-57
    Megged **13**:157
    Roditi **14**:245, 247
    Rowse **8**:254, 255-57
    Settle **1**:320
    Stevenson **9**:285
    Stewart **3**:345, 350, 351, 354,
        355-56
    Thomas **11**:376-77
    Turner **10**:315, 316-17
    Wain **4**:324-28
    Weiss **2**:439-40
    West **7**:274-75
    Wolff **22**:304-06
Oxford University, All Souls College
    Caute **4**:104
    Rowse **8**:256-57
    West **7**:274
Oxford University, Christ Church
    Hamburger **4**:163
    Rowse **8**:255
    Turner **10**:315
Oxford University, Corpus Christi
    College **15**:352, 359
Oxford University, Lincoln College
    7:275
Oxford University, Oriel College
    Mott **7**:121
    Stewart **3**:350
    Wright **5**:363, 364
Oxford University Press **5**:374
Oxford University, Queen's College
    21:64-65
Oxford University, St. Anne's
    College **5**:107, 108
Oxford University, St. John's
    College **4**:325, 326, 328
Oxherding Tale **18**:239, 240
Oz **5**:127
Oz, Amos **24**:35
Ozark Folk Festival **2**:170
Ozick, Cynthia **11**:200

Pablo! **4**:261
Pacheco, Jose Emilio **17**:5
Pacific Lutheran University **11**:329
Pacifica Radio Network **3**:76
Pacifism
    Ashby **6**:35-36
    Blais **4**:76
    Grumbach **2**:209
    Highwater **7**:79
    Woodcock **6**:318-19, 320, 323
Pack, Robert **10**:38
Packer, Tina **6**:236-37, 249
Paco's Story **21**:92-94, 96
Paden, William **6**:135, 136, 142
Padgett, Ron
    Clark **22**:21
    Foster **26**:119, 120
    Grumman **25**:192
    Major **6**:180
Padilla, Heberto **11**:192
Padma Bhushan Award **9**:233, 234
Pagayaw, Saddani **9**:164
Page of History, A **3**:63

Page, P.K. **15**:153
Paige, D.D. **2**:434
Paik, Nam June **10**:7
Paine, Thomas **9**:177
Painted Bird, The **9**:112, 115
Painted Dresses **11**:165-66, 167
Painted Turtle: Woman with Guitar
    6:197, 198
Paisan **2**:394
Pakistan
    Singh **9**:228-29
    Tillinghast **23**:312
Pakula, Alan **2**:331
Palabra solar **25**:110
Palace of the Peacock **16**:125
Palamas, Kostis **26**:269
Palamountain, Joseph **9**:205
Palestine
    Laqueur **19**:212-14
    Yglesias **20**:354-56
Palestinian movement **11**:68
Paley, Grace
    Dennison **6**:117
    Dworkin **21**:15, 17
Palmer, Lilli **23**:74, 76
Palmer, Mrs. Charles (pseudonym of
    Mary Lee Settle) **1**:314
Palmetto Country **1**:150
Palomar College **2**:121
Palomino **13**:116, 121
Palpable God, A **6**:259
*Pamoja tutashinda: Together We Will
    Win* **21**:213-14
Pan Tadeusz **3**:39
Panassié, Hugues **10**:92
Pandemonium Spirit, The **24**:73, 74
Panther Man **18**:143, 152
Pantograph (Ivan Argüelles) **24**:4,
    25, 26, 27
Pantograph Press
    Argüelles **24**:26, 28, 29
    Berry **24**:77
Papadopoulos, Yannis **15**:77-78, 92
Papandreou, Andreas **3**:248
Papanoutsos, Evangelos P. **16**:258-60
Pape, Greg **22**:79
Paper Boy **20**:177-78
Paper Cage, The **5**:291
Paper Soul **13**:248
Paper Television **26**:309-10
Paper, The **15**:124
Papo Got His Gun **17**:7, 9
Papp, Joseph **20**:228, 232
*Paracriticisms: Seven Speculations of the
    Times* **12**:160
Parade **1**:401
Paradise Lost
    Ackerman **20**:8
    Turner **10**:316
Paradox of Oscar Wilde, The **6**:321
Paralysis **1**:36-38
Paramount Studios
    Gunn **2**:254
    Wallace **1**:387
Paranormal phenomena
    Awoonor **13**:53

Wilson   5:325-26
Paravicini, George   18:48-49
"Pardoner's Tale"   2:210
Parijat   14:91
Parini, Jay   16:227-43
  Stevenson   9:285
Paris, France
  Bergé   10:4
  Blais   4:77
  Bowles   1:82, 83
  Broughton   12:56
  Burroway   6:92
  Cohen   18:83, 88-89
  Condon   1:194, 195, 197
  Connell   2:107, 108, 109
  Corman   2:137-39
  Eastlake   1:208
  Federman   8:68-70
  Gray   2:185-86, 194-95
  Guerard   2:216, 217-19, 220-21
  Hailey   1:228
  Hall   7:63
  Hine   15:227-28
  Kennedy   9:82
  Klinkowitz   9:118
  Lottman   12:197-99, 208
  Lowitz   26:173
  Menashe   11:226-27
  Mott   7:119
  Nichols   2:328
  O'Faolain   2:346-47, 349
  Pohl   1:288
  Rosenthal   6:285
  Settle   1:316
  Simic   4:276-77
  Sisson   3:298
  Van Itallie   2:411
  Weiss   2:439
  Williams   26:314
  Wright   7:294-95
Paris Review
  Clark   22:15-16
  Connell   2:108
  Disch   4:149
  Kennedy   9:83
  Settle   1:315
  Wilson   5:318
Parker, Charlie
  Federman   8:73
  Joans   25:221-22, 223
Parkinson, Thomas   1:357, 359, 369
Parkman, Francis   3:44
Parks, Rosa   2:294
Parochial education
  Jennings   5:105-06
  Kienzle   1:239, 241
  Klinkowitz   9:109
  Kumin   8:208
  O'Faolain   2:342-43, 344-45
Parra, Nicanor   20:330-31, 333
Parrish, Robert   12:9
Parson's School of Fine and Applied
  Arts   1:113
Parti-Colored Blocks for a Quilt   1:277
Parti Québecois   13:186

*Partial Accounts: New and Selected
  Poems*   14:220
Partial Truth   23:263
Partisan Review
  Baumbach   5:26, 28
  Dennison   6:113
  Lottman   12:205
  Markfield   3:212, 220
Pasadena Junior College   17:62-63
Pascal, Blaise   1:57
Pascal, Gabriel   14:258-59
Pasha, Mustafa el-Nahhas   12:138
Pasmore, Victor   10:120
Pass It On   23:130
Pass, The   15:333
Passage of Summer   15:151-52, 156-57
Passage through Gehenna   11:184
"Passengers"   3:281
Passing through the Flame   19:329,
  331
Passions of the Mind, The   3:367, 376
Passport and Other Stories, The
  16:263-66
Past Must Alter, The   2:215, 216,
  219, 221, 223
Pasternak, Boris
  Davie   3:40, 44
  Feinstein   1:221
  Fuller   10:123-24
  Valaoritis   26:282
Patch Boys, The   16:237-38
Patchen, Kenneth
  Souster   14:311
  Williams   12:342, 343
Pater, Walter
  Boyle   1:112
  Glazier   24:219
  Hiemstra   26:153
  Weiss   2:429
  West   7:274
Paterson (William Carlos Williams)
  3:90
Patmos and Other Poems   5:284
Patrick, Walton   11:183
Patrocinio Barela: Taos Woodcarver
  14:112
Patron Happiness   23:225, 227
Patten, Brian   2:52
Pattern of the Chinese Past, The   9:284
*Pattern Poetry: Guide to an Unknown
  Literature*   8:92
Patterns   3:72
Patterson   16:192
Pauker, John   8:306
Paul Robeson Award   14:57
Paul, Sherman   2:145
Paulhan, Jean   2:67
Paulus, Stephen   20:62, 67, 69, 71,
  72
Pavane   2:414
Pavlich, Walter   23:229
Payne, Robert   15:69-70, 71
Paz, Octavio
  Joans   25:245-46
  Kerrigan   11:194
P.D. Kimerakov   12:73

PEACE   26:32
Peace   9:311
Peace Corps
  Dacey   17:24-26
  Harteis   26:142
  Holden   22:63-64
  Knebel   3:181
  Polkinhorn   25:329
Peace Eye   21:261, 263, 265-66
Peace Eye Bookstore   21:264-67
Peaceable Kingdom, The   5:261, 263,
  264
Peacekeepers   18:59
Peacock, Molly   21:145-64
Pearce, Roy Harvey   2:144
Pearl   7:221
Pearl, Eric (pseudonym) See Elman,
  Richard
Pearl on the Bottom, The   12:191, 193
Pearson, John   1:74, 77
Pearson, Norman Holmes
  Major   6:187-88
  Rosenblum   11:348
Peaslee, Richard   2:418, 419
Peck, Tom   2:272
Peel, Alfreda Marion   7:8
Peeples, Samuel A.   20:46-47
Peery, Nelson   26:210
Pegler, Westbrook   3:177
Peirce, C.S.   12:329-30
Peixotto, Jessica   3:367
Peking, China   1:34-35
Pelieu, Claude   11:288, 289
Pellegrini, Angelo   11:261-74
PEN
  Kirkup   4:187
  Megged   13:158
  Rakosi   5:198
  Skelton   5:288, 289
  Swenson   13:316
  Wallace   1:402
PEN/Faulkner Award
  Grumbach   2:214
  Jacobsen   18:216
  Olson   11:259
  Settle   1:321
PEN–New Mexico   26:81
PEN Syndicated Fiction Award
  26:178
Pendray, G. Edward   10:3
*Penguin Book of English Romantic
  Verse, The*   5:373
Penguin Book of Everyday Verse, The
  5:373
Penguin New Writing   6:21
Penguin (publishers)
  Brunner   8:11
  Jones   5:127
Penn, Irving   2:189
Pennington, Anne   9:285
Pennsylvania State University
  Ackerman   20:5
  Wagoner   3:402-03, 404, 405
  West   7:280
Penny Links   8:103
Pennywhistle Press   26:77, 78, 79

Pensamientos **16**:77, 81
Penthouse **6**:153-54
People Live Here **4**:296
*People of Paradox: An Inquiry
      Concerning the Origins of American
      Civilization* **23**:149, 156
People Who Led to My Plays **20**:223
People's Almanac, The **1**:376, 379,
      400
*Peoples of the Coast: The Indians of the
      Pacific Northwest* **6**:324
People's Park, Berkeley, Calif.
      26:299-300
People's party *See* Progressive party
People's Voice **6**:264
Père Goriot, Le **2**:385
Perec, Georges **6**:237-39, 245, 247,
      248, 250
Perfect Murder, The **8**:171-72, 174,
      175
Perfect Vacuum, A **1**:255, 262, 263
Performance poetry **24**:177, 178
Perkins, Maxwell
      Bourjaily **1**:68, 69
      Brown **6**:56
Perkins, Tony **9**:251
Perls, Frederick **6**:114-15
Perls, Lore **6**:115
Perry, Anne **7**:292, 293
Perry, Ruth **6**:119
Perry, Shauneille **13**:251
Persephone **8**:278
Persia *See* Iran
Persky, Stan **16**:196
Personal Accounts **13**:211
Personal and Possessive **11**:373
Personal Voice, The **2**:229
Peru
      Eshleman **6**:138-39
      Goldemberg **12**:91, 94, 98, 103-
            06
      Menefee **26**:206
Pessoa, Fernando **8**:116, 117
Pétain, Philippe **12**:207, 208
Peter, John **5**:287
Peter Pan **25**:4
*Peters Black and Blue Guides to
      Current Literary Journals* **8**:248
Peters, Chris, *See* Bennett, John M.
Peters, Margery **13**:247
Peters, Nancy **24**:25-26
Peters, Pete **6**:198
Peters, Robert 8:237-52
Petersen, Will
      Corman **2**:140, 141, 142, 143,
            144
      Eshleman **6**:135-36
Peterson, Emily **1**:106
Petesch, Natalie L.M.   12:239-51
Petrenko, P. **4**:360-61
Petrie, Phil **21**:193
Petry, Ann 6:253-69
Petry, George **6**:264
Pets
      Dillard **7**:18-19
      Lifshin **10**:240, 250

Pettet, Edwin **8**:306
Pezzati, Albert **2**:117
Pflaum Publishing Co.   **8**:273
Phaedra **1**:315
Phantom Nightingale: Juvenilia   **23**:199
Pharos Press **5**:290, 292
Phelps, Lyon **7**:62
Phenomena **16**:16, 17
Phi Beta Kappa
      Knebel **3**:169
      Rabassa **9**:202
      St. Clair **8**:272
      Stevenson **9**:279
Phil Hill: Yankee Champion   **16**:213
Philadelphia Inquirer **18**:49
Philadelphia, Pa.
      Bova **18**:47-48
      Bullins **16**:59-62
      Williams **26**:313
Philippine Magazine **9**:158
Philippines
      Emanuel **18**:128-29
      Manuel **9**:151-65, 166-68
Philips, Robert **4**:156
Phillabaum, Leslie **4**:122
Phillips Exeter Academy **7**:58, 59-61
Phillips, Judith **13**:199-200, 201,
      202, 203, 204-10
Phillips, Robert 13:193-216
Phillips University **12**:237
Phillips, William **8**:293
Phillis Wheatley Conference **13**:249-
      50
Philosophy
      Bernstein **24**:42-43
      Johnson **18**:230-31
      Matthews **15**:262
      Ouellette **13**:181
      Solotaroff **2**:394
      Weiss **12**:326-27, 334-35
Philosophy of Chance **1**:263
Photography
      Bell **14**:41, 42-43, 44, 45-47
      Codrescu **19**:79-88
      Malanga **17**:96-97
      Salaam **21**:182
Photoplay **1**:378
Physical Sciences Study Committee
      18:51
Physiotherapy **23**:22-23, 27, 33, 49,
      55
Picano, Felice 13:217-35
Picasso, Pablo
      Caldwell **1**:156
      Fisher **10**:98
      Kerrigan **11**:189, 191, 194, 205,
            206
Piccione, Anthony **9**:41
Picciotto, Robert S.   **12**:91-94
Pick, John **6**:230-31
Pick, J.R. **1**:330-31
Pickard, Tom **22**:14
Pickford, Mary **11**:46-47
Picnic in the Snow, The **8**:247, 248
Picone, Mauro **25**:349-50
Picture Theory **16**:52-53

Pictures at 11 **19**:337
Pictures of the Journey Back **15**:266
Pieces of the Bone-Text Still There
      24:22, 23
Pieratt, Asa **9**:113
Piercy, Marge 1:267-81
      Elman **3**:77
Piero della Francesca **3**:356
Pierre-Joseph Proudhon **6**:322
*Pierre ou la Guerre du Printemps
      '81* **4**:73-74, 77, 78
Pierrot lunaire **8**:159
"Pig Pen" **16**:67
Pigeon Project, The **1**:398
Pilar, Maria **3**:428
Pilgrim Award **2**:257
*Pill, Pygmy Chimps, and Degas' Horse,
      The* **26**:88, 100-01
Pillard, Basil **8**:132
Pindar
      Enslin **3**:90
      Thomas **4**:310
Pineville, Ky. **1**:307
Pinhas, Richard **19**:331
Pink Floyd **22**:15
Pinocchio **1**:192, 193
Pinsky, Robert 4:237-51
Pinter, Harold
      Gray **3**:113, 114
      Oakes **25**:306-07
Piper, Dan **9**:80
Piper, Edwin Ford **6**:20
Pissarro, Camille **3**:379
Pit Strike **2**:386
Pittsburgh, Pa. **3**:22, 25
Pittsfield, Mass. **26**:113
Pius XII, Pope
      Greeley **7**:43
      Kienzle **1**:242
      Stone **3**:373
Place, Francis **5**:276
Place in the City **18**:177
Place of Birth **2**:275
Place of Love, The **6**:296
Place to Stand, A **3**:407
Places to Go **16**:199, 200
Plague, The **2**:385
Plagued by the Nightingale **1**:115
Planet Stories **2**:40
Plarr, Victor **10**:112
Plath, Sylvia
      Brown **10**:37
      Burroway **6**:87, 91, 92
      Davison **4**:134, 135, 137-38
      Rosenthal **6**:283-84
      Stevenson **9**:283, 287
      Tillinghast **23**:306-07
Play By Play **12**:95, 99-100, 101-02,
      104-05
Playboy
      Disch **4**:152
      Elman **3**:74
      Mano **6**:216, 218
      Nolan **16**:213, 214, 216
Playground, The (film) **5**:80

Playground, The (James Broughton)
　12:53
Plays & Poems: 1948–1958 **12**:235
Playwriting
　Bullins **16**:67-68
　Fry **23**:63-78
　Grumman **25**:186, 188-89
　Gurik **23**:103, 105-07, 112, 113-
　　15
　Hine **15**:226
　Malzberg **4**:208
　Valaoritis **26**:286
Pleasant, Boo **24**:341-42
Pleasure-Dome **3**:199-200
Pleasure Garden, The **12**:54-55
Plimpton, George
　Burroway **6**:90
　Clark **22**:15
　Connell **2**:108
Plomer, William **6**:42
Plot, The **1**:384, 385, 395
Plum Plum Pickers, The **15**:119-21
Plume and Sword **7**:180
Plumly, Stanley
　Heyen **9**:41
　Holden **22**:69, 72
Plumpp, Sterling 21:165-78
Plunkett, Joseph **3**:49
Plutarch **6**:34
Plymell, Charles 11:275-96
P.N. Review **3**:307
Po Chu-i **7**:78
Pochoda, Phil **4**:158
Pocket Book of Science Fiction, The
　9:301
Pocket Books
　Bourjaily **1**:70
　Niven **12**:222
　Wallace **1**:385, 393
　Wolfe **9**:311
Pocket Sundial **24**:363-66
Pocket Theatre **2**:414, 415, 416
Podhoretz, Norman **2**:398, 399
Poe, Edgar Allan
　Berry **24**:58
　Dillard **7**:6, 17
　Forrest **7**:28
　Glanville **9**:19
　Kizer **5**:147
　Rechy **4**:262
　Shapiro **6**:288, 289-90
　Sward **13**:284
　Symons **3**:391, 392
Poem from Jail **21**:260, 262-63
Poem in Action **24**:126
Poemas humanos **6**:137, 138, 144
Poemns **25**:186
Poems and Antipoems **20**:330
Poems Are Hard to Read **14**:229-30,
　235
Poems (David Meltzer and Donald
　Schenker) **26**:192
Poems (Elizabeth Jennings) **5**:110
Poems for All the Annettes **17**:207
Poems for Exchange **15**:106
Poems for F. **14**:257

Poems for Spain **1**:18
Poems from the Old English **9**:212,
　213, 215
Poems I **26**:275
Poems Made of Skin **10**:6
Poems of a Decade, 1931–1941 **8**:260
Poems of Doctor Zhivago, The **3**:44
Poems of Early Childhood **25**:3-4
Poems of Mao Tse-tung, The **15**:70
Poems 1928–1948 **14**:259, 260, 265,
　267
Poet and the Poem, The **8**:135
Poet & the Translator, The **3**:307
Poet as Ice-Skater, The **8**:248
"Poet in the Bank, The" **8**:308
*Poet in the Imaginary Museum: Essays
　of Two Decades, The* **11**:236
Poet in the World, The **19**:243
Poet Santa Cruz **13**:300
Poet Song **26**:193-94
"Poet, Spare that Poem" **26**:150
Poetic Art of Horace, The **3**:306
Poetic Image in Six Genres, The **3**:195
Poetic Pattern, The **5**:284
Poetics (e-mail discussion group)
　24:48
Poetry
　Armantrout **25**:9, 15, 17-18, 20,
　　22
　Bennett **25**:53
　Booth **2**:59
　Cassity **8**:58-59
　Daigon **25**:149-72
　Eigner **23**:21, 31-38, 48, 53
　Forbes **16**:105-19
　Foster **26**:126-27
　Grumman **25**:173-77, 188-89,
　　190-91
　Hadas **23**:120
　Hamburger **4**:167
　Hazo **11**:152
　Heyen **9**:40, 44-45
　Hongo **22**:86-88
　Jerome **8**:130-31
　Katz **9**:62-63, 68
　Leftwich **25**:259-82
　Livesay **8**:223-24
　Madgett **23**:193-213
　Nichols **2**:319
　Ostriker **24**:268-72, 274-76
　Rosenblum **11**:341-42, 344-45,
　　348, 352
　Salaam **21**:179-251
　Shapiro **23**:294-95, 297
　Taylor **26**:252, 257-58, 259
　weiss **24**:329-30, 332-33, 339-42,
　　345, 351
　Williams **26**:323, 326-27
　Wright **22**:312-13, 315
Poetry and jazz concerts
　Abse **1**:28-29
　Dacey **17**:34-35
　Joans **25**:229-30, 233, 244
Poetry and the Common Life **6**:280
Poetry Book Society **5**:284
Poetry Center of New Mexico **26**:81

Poetry Flash
　Argüelles **24**:25
　Foley **24**:176
"Poetry Has Nothing to Do with
　Politics" **26**:124
Poetry in Motion **21**:270
Poetry London **3**:36
Poetry (magazine)
　Allen **11**:19
　Bell **14**:47-48
　Bergé **10**:7
　Ciardi **2**:90
　Forbes **16**:116
　Hine **15**:234, 235
　Jerome **8**:133
　Kerrigan **11**:208
　Mahapatra **9**:146
　Nims **17**:179
　Olson **12**:228-29
　Pinsky **4**:246
　Rakosi **5**:207
　Rosenthal **6**:276
　Saroyan **5**:215
　Shapiro **6**:292, 302
　Stafford **3**:334
　Wagoner **3**:403, 404
　Wilson **5**:351
Poetry Nation Review **3**:46-47
Poetry Northwest **3**:408, 410, 411
Poetry of Dylan Thomas, The **12**:234
Poetry of the Negro, The
　Emanuel **18**:143
　Salaam **21**:228
Poetry of the Thirties **5**:286
Poetry Society (Great Britain)
　Booth **2**:52
　Hamburger **4**:169
Poetry Taos, Number One **14**:112
Poetry therapy **25**:66
Poetry USA
　Argüelles **24**:3, 27
　Eigner **23**:59
　Foley **24**:176-77
Poet's Art, The **6**:280
Poets Eleven (audio magazine) **24**:73
Poets' Encyclopedia, The **13**:15, 19
Poets-in-the-Schools program
　Holden **22**:65
　Root **11**:325-26
　Sward **13**:295, 297
　Swenson **13**:314
Poets of Bulgaria **14**:232
Poets of the Pacific, Second Series **3**:36
Poets of Today
　Simpson **4**:293
　Slavitt **3**:318
Poets On: **25**:167-68
Poets on Street Corners **26**:76
*Poet's Other Voice: Conversations on
　Literary Translation, The* **8**:120
Poets' Prize, 1990 **20**:337
Poet's Song, The **23**:103
Poets' Theater, Cambridge, Mass.
　Davison **4**:134
　Hall **7**:62-63
Poet's Tongue, The **10**:121, 123

Poets' Workshop **2**:52
Poets' Yearbook Award **2**:57
Pohl, Frederik **1**:283-98
   Aldiss **2**:27, 28, 29
   Bradley **10**:21
   Budrys **14**:66-67, 68, 77-78
   Gunn **2**:239, 248, 249, 253, 258
   Knight **10**:203, 209, 215, 216,
     218
   Malzberg **4**:209
   Niven **12**:217
   Silverberg **3**:277
   Williamson **8**:320, 324, 325, 326
   Wolfe **9**:304-05, 308, 311
   Zebrowski **19**:370
Point Blank **13**:342
Point Counterpoint **2**:22
Point of Transfer **17**:206
Points of Departure **20**:339
Points on the Grid **16**:24, 31
Poison Pen **5**:77, 80
*Poison Penmanship: The Gentle Art of
     Muckraking* **17**:149, 151
Poker Game **3**:182
Poland
   Konwicki **9**:123-34
   Lem **1**:255-56
   Mrozek **10**:266-78
Poles **7**:279
Polio
   Olson **12**:226
   Ruark **23**:269-70
   Sargent **18**:331
*Polish Subtitles: Impressions from a
     Journey* **15**:228
Political activists See Activists **24**:30
Political Novel, The **25**:94
Political Portfolio **15**:124
*Politicians, Poets, and Con Men:
     Emotional History in Late Victorian
     America* **9**:219
Politics **6**:320
Politics and the Younger Generation
     8:257, 258
Politis, Kosmas **26**:271-73
Polkinhorn, Harry **25**:321-40
   Berry **24**:77
Pollet, Elizabeth **3**:415
Pollock, Jackson **25**:220-21
Poltergeist **25**:206-07
Pomerantz, Edward **11**:255, 256
Ponce, Juan García **18**:63-64, 73-74
Ponge, Francis **26**:328
Pontes, Peter **1**:29
Pool, Rosey E. **23**:204-05, 206
Poole, C.W. **3**:346
Poore, Charles **1**:73
Poorhouse State, The **3**:74, 83
Pope, Theodate **12**:347
Popescu, Petru **2**:58
"Popeye" **2**:37
Popular Culture Explosion, The **3**:196
Popular Publications **10**:209, 217
Pornography
   Dworkin **21**:12, 20
   Giovanni **6**:153, 154

Jones **5**:127-28
   Rimmer **10**:303-04
Pornography: Men Possessing Women
     21:9-10
Port-of-Spain: In a World at War
     18:22
Portable Novels of Science **3**:271
Portable Soul **21**:169-70, 171
Porter, Arabel **13**:10
Porter, Bern **6**:187
Porter, Don **6**:181, 182
Porter, Katherine Anne
   Dillard **7**:14
   Eaton **20**:135
   Nims **17**:185
   Purdy **1**:302
Porter, Sylvia **1**:293
Portrait and Other Poems, The **5**:258
Portrait of a Wilderness **4**:309
Portrait of an Artist with 26 Horses
     1:210, 212
*Portrait of the Artist as a Young Man,
     A*
   Belitt **4**:54
   Forrest **7**:23
   Simpson **4**:290
Possession **2**:156
Post-traumatic stress syndrome
   Dworkin **21**:11-12
   Heinemann **21**:95
*Postcards: Don't You Just Wish You
     Were Here!* **2**:76-77
Postmodern Poetry **26**:128
*Postmodern Turn: Essays in Postmodern
     Theory and Culture, The* **12**:149
Postmodernism (artistic movement)
     25:394
Potomac Fever **3**:179
Potter, Beatrix **2**:341
Poulson, M. Wilford **5**:40, 41-42
Pound, Ezra
   Allen **6**:18
   Argüelles **24**:14
   Clark **22**:12-13
   Creeley **10**:70
   Davie **3**:39, 40, 45
   Dudek **14**:126, 130-33
   Enslin **3**:90, 94
   Feinstein **1**:221
   Gregor **10**:149
   Harwood **19**:140, 142, 147
   Katz **9**:68
   Levertov **19**:240
   McCord **9**:180
   Morgan **4**:227
   Olson **12**:234
   Pinsky **4**:244
   Raffel **9**:219
   Rakosi **5**:207
   Sanders **21**:260-61
   Schwartz **26**:236-38
   Sisson **3**:305
   Škvorecký **1**:348
   Waldman **17**:273, 276, 277
   Whittemore **8**:306, 308, 310
   Wright **7**:296, 297, 302

Pournelle, Jerry
   Anderson **2**:44, 45
   Niven **12**:212, 215, 217, 218,
     219, 220, 221-22
Poverty **23**:265
Powell, Barry **24**:59, 64-65, 68, 72
Powell, Bud **6**:182
Powell, Roxie **11**:284, 294
Power and Glory **14**:159
Power of the Dog, The **15**:337, 339,
     344
Power of the Pen, The **15**:251
Powers, J.F. **9**:84
Powers, John Robert **1**:192
Pownall, David **18**:293-307
Powys, John Cowper
   Boyle **1**:99
   Fisher **10**:96
   Purdy **1**:302
Powys, Llewelyn **10**:131
Practical Knowledge for All **5**:313
Practical Pig, The **1**:192, 193
Prague, Czechoslovakia
   Škvorecký **1**:334-48, 350
   Wellek **7**:210-11
Prague English Studies **7**:221
Prashker, Betty **12**:207
Pratt, E.J. **8**:220
Pratt, Enoch, Free Library, Baltimore,
     Md. **6**:292
*Praying Wrong: New and Selected
     Poems, 1957–1984* **4**:134, 140,
     141
Precise Fragments **9**:182
Prefatory Lyrics **24**:238
Pregnancy **23**:222-23
Pregnant Man, The **13**:205
Prejudice
   Bruce-Novoa **18**:66, 68
   Ostriker **24**:264
*Preliminary Rough Draft of a Total
     Psychology* **25**:186
"Preludes" **24**:250
Premack, Frank **22**:266
Premar Experiments, The **10**:300
Preminger, Otto **1**:181, 182
Premio Quinto Sol Award **4**:24
Presbyterianism
   Brown **6**:73
   Cassity **8**:39
Present Tense prize **13**:158
President, The **1**:172
Presidential Commission on the
     Holocaust **4**:360
President's Lady, The **3**:373
Presley, Elvis **12**:348, 353
Pressed on Sand **17**:204
Pressler, Menahem
   Delbanco **2**:162
   Hiemstra **26**:154
Pressure of Time, The **4**:152, 157
Preston, Billy **13**:251
Preston, Don **1**:171, 173
Pretoria, South Africa **8**:49, 50-52,
     56
Pretty Boy Dead **17**:68

"Pretty Perdita" **26**:35
Preuss, Paul **12**:213, 215, 216
Preview **14**:128
Price, Laurie **24**:27
Price, Reynolds
    Chappell **4**:115, 116, 125
    Petry **6**:259
Pride and the Passion, The **1**:195
Priest, Robert **13**:297-98
*Primary Trouble: An Anthology of
    Contemporary American Poetry*
    26:128
*Prime Sway: A Transduction of Primero
    Sueño by Sor Juana Inés de la
    Cruz* **25**:74
Primer for Combat **1**:117
*Primer of the Novel: For Readers and
    Writers* **3**:198
Prince, Harold **2**:419
Prince Ishmael **11**:126-27, 134-35
Prince of Darkness and Co., The
    15:227
Princess of All Lands, The **9**:103
Princeton University
    Abse **1**:31
    Bell **12**:29-30, 31, 32-33, 36
    Eaton **20**:123-24
    Garrett **5**:79, 88
    Hadas **23**:122-23
    Kazin **7**:95
    Mathews **6**:223, 232, 245
    Meredith **14**:225, 226
    Sparshott **15**:351
    Van Itallie **2**:417, 418, 422
    Weiss **2**:448-49
    Wellek **7**:217-20
    Whittemore **8**:304-05, 308
    Williams **12**:350
Princeton University Press
    Kerrigan **11**:213
    Wagoner **3**:411
Principles of English Metre, The **2**:380
Pringle, Val **2**:293
Prinzip, Gavrilo **23**:68-69
Prison Notes **4**:76
"Prisoner, The" **4**:153
Prisoners **26**:52, 60
Prisons **1**:309, 314, 319, 320
Pritchett, V.S. **9**:26-27
Private Line **6**:185
Prix de Meilleur des Livres
    Etrangers **4**:117
Prix de Rome
    Simpson **4**:294
    Williams, John A. **3**:413-15
    Williams, Miller **20**:333-34
Prix Médicis
    Blais **4**:74, 76
    Zinoviev **10**:335
Prize, The **1**:377, 380, 384, 385,
    391-93
Prizewinner, The **9**:242-43
Pro, The **18**:301
"Problems of Creativeness" **4**:151
Process, The **26**:192
Processionals **3**:98

"Prodigal Son" (parable) **2**:155
Progress of a Crime, The **3**:390
Progress, The **22**:262-63
Progressive Herald (Syracuse, N.Y.)
    3:421
Progressive party
    Cassill **1**:167
    Ciardi **2**:94
Prohibition
    Condon **1**:187
    Knebel **3**:169
    Stone **3**:364
Prohibition: The Era of Excess **5**:271
Project Vanguard **18**:49-50, 51
"Projective Verse" **5**:348
Proletarian Writers of the Thirties
    3:194
Promethean Fire **16**:304
Prometheus Books **10**:303
Pronzini, Bill **4**:219
Propertius, Sextus **8**:280
Property and Value **17**:92
Proposition 31 **10**:295, 299-300
Proselytizer, The **6**:206, 210, 215
Prosody
    Hall **7**:64, 65
    Shapiro **6**:301-02
    Sillitoe **2**:380
Prostitution
    Dworkin **21**:12, 14, 16-17
    Guerard **2**:220-21
    Rechy **4**:259-60, 263
Protestantism **7**:209
Proust, Marcel
    Becker **1**:36, 43
    Brée **15**:128, 136
    Brossard **2**:74, 76
    Josipovici **8**:152-53, 154-55
    Katz **14**:168
    Konwicki **9**:129
    Rabassa **9**:198
    Van Itallie **2**:411
Providence Journal **5**:97-98
Provocation **1**:261
Pryce-Jones, Alan **1**:318
Prynne, Jeremy **5**:198, 199
Pryor, Richard **3**:432
PSSC See Physical Sciences Study
    Committee
"Psychic Pretenders, The" **16**:67
Psycho **20**:45-46, 51
Psychoanalysis
    Brophy **4**:86
    Feirstein **11**:83
    Peacock **21**:148
    Roditi **14**:261, 265
    Van Brunt **15**:379, 381
    Williamson **8**:318-19, 321
Psychology of Power, The **1**:102
*Psychovisual Perspective for "Musical"
    Composition, A* **16**:15
Ptáčník, Karel **1**:342
"Pub" **3**:386
Public Affairs Television **2**:414
Public Broadcasting System **3**:74

    See also National Educational
        Television
Public Landing Revisited **13**:211
Public Lending Right **4**:86, 87, 88,
    91
Public speaking **6**:162-63
Publishers Weekly
    Garrett **5**:80
    Lottman **12**:206, 209
    Wallace **1**:395
Puccini, Giacomo **14**:127
Pudney, John **10**:124-26
Pueblo de Dios y de Mandinga **15**:13
Puerto Rico
    Bell **12**:34
    Cassity **8**:44-47
    Cruz **17**:1-5, 11-13, 15-16
Pugh, Joel **24**:21-22
Pugh, Lewis **4**:309
Pulitzer **13**:268
Pulitzer, Joseph
    Nims **17**:156
    Swanberg **13**:268
Pulitzer Prize
    Dove **19**:110
    Kammen **23**:133
    Killens **2**:295, 304
    Kizer **5**:156
    McPherson **17**:123, 133
    Meredith **14**:219-20
    Morgan **4**:230
    Shapiro **6**:300-01
    Simpson **4**:293, 294
    Stegner **9**:269
    Swanberg **13**:268, 272
    Taylor **7**:187
    Wilson **16**:306
Pulp magazines
    Bradley **10**:21
    Brown **6**:47, 48
    Higgins **5**:96
    Kennedy **9**:77-78
    Knight **10**:202, 203, 204-05, 209
    Lem **1**:260
    Malzberg **4**:207
    Moorcock **5**:175, 176, 177-78,
        179-81
    St. Clair **8**:273
    Wilhelm **5**:300
    Williamson **8**:316-18, 324
    Wolfe **9**:301, 304-05
Pumpkin Hill, Vt. **23**:130-31
Punch and Judy Man, The **25**:309-10
Punishment of the Magicians, The
    26:275, 280, 281
Puppies of Terra, The **4**:151
Purdue University
    Cassill **1**:172
    Honig **8**:110
Purdum, Richard **9**:41
Purdy, Al 17:195-214
Purdy, James 1:299-305
Pure Lives **8**:311
Pure Mental Breath **26**:224
Purge, The **12**:208
Purity of Diction in English Verse **3**:37

Purves, Alan **9**:203
Pushcart Award
   Allman **15**:30
   Bromige **26**:39
   Nelson **23**:263
Pushing the Bear **24**:207
Pushkin, Aleksandr
   Killens **2**:305-06
   Thomas **11**:377
Putnam Creative Writing Award
   2:194
Putnam Prize **2**:331
Putnam Publishing Group
   Grumbach **2**:212
   Nichols **2**:331
Pygmalion **10**:286
Pyle, Howard **2**:323
Pynchon, Thomas **9**:111

Q Document, The **2**:168, 172, 174
Qadir, Manzur **9**:229
Quakers See Friends, Society of
Quarantuno **13**:66, 68
Quarterly Review of Literature
   Busch **1**:132
   Weiss **2**:433-34, 435, 439, 443,
      445, 447
Quartermaine's Terms **3**:109
Quebec, Canada
   Blais **4**:70-73, 74
   Brossard **16**:46-47
   Gurik **23**:102, 103, 109-10, 112
   Hebert **24**:247
   Ouellette **13**:185-86
Queen Mary (ship) **4**:277-78
Queen of Stones **9**:293
Queen of the Ebony Isles **21**:139, 141
Queen's College, Georgetown,
   Guyana **16**:129-32
Queen's University
   Brewster **15**:155
   Simmons **21**:275, 296
Quena **6**:138
Queneau, Raymond
   Brossard **2**:66, 67-68
   Mathews **6**:247
Quest for Corvo, The **3**:383
*Questa Mano Peritura/This Perishable
   Hand* **26**:211
Quicksand **8**:11
"Quiet Pint in Kinvara, A" **23**:317-
   18
Quigley Seminary, Chicago, Ill. **7**:37,
   40-42
Quilts **23**:215
Quincy, U.S.D. (pseudonym of Vance
   Bourjaily) **1**:73
Quinn, Anthony **16**:241
Quinn, James L. **10**:221
Quinn, Robert H. **5**:99
Quinn, Rosemary **2**:417, 421
Quinto Sol Publications **4**:24

R Document, The **1**:384, 398
Rabassa, Clara **9**:204-05
Rabassa, Gregory 9:191-206

Race relations **3**:414, 419-20, 422
Rachlin, Nahid 17:215-29
Rachmaninoff, Sergei Vasilyevich
   12:352
Racism
   Ai **13**:2, 3
   Anthony **18**:14
   Armantrout **25**:7
   Aubert **20**:17-18
   Awoonor **13**:38, 43-44, 46-47
   Bennett **13**:74, 81, 83, 84-85, 88
   Booth **5**:40
   Bullins **16**:62
   Dacey **17**:26
   Dove **19**:108
   Emanuel **18**:130, 131, 132-33,
      135, 136, 138, 148, 162,
      165
   Forbes **16**:119
   Garrett **5**:86
   Giovanni **6**:159
   Hauser **11**:133, 134
   Hebert **24**:245-46, 251-52
   Hinojosa-Smith **16**:149
   Hongo **22**:81, 83-84
   Huddle **20**:187-92
   Kerrigan **11**:193
   Madgett **23**:197
   Major **6**:175, 176, 179, 183-84,
      189, 193, 194, 202
   Menefee **26**:201
   Nelson **23**:256
   Petry **6**:255-56, 258, 266, 268-69
   Salisbury **15**:318-19
   Smith **7**:161
   Still **17**:234
   Vizenor **22**:262, 263-66, 271
Radcliffe College
   Brewster **15**:155
   Hadas **23**:121-22
   Kumin **8**:213-14
Radcliffe College, Bunting Institute
   13:11
Radcliffe College See also Harvard
   University
Radiation **23**:226
*Radical Innocence: Studies in the
   Contemporary American Novel*
   12:149, 161, 164
Radicalism **2**:198
Radiguet, Raymond
   Boyle **1**:116
   Gray **3**:107
Radio
   Boyd **11**:46
   Eigner **23**:23-24, 53
   Hoffman **10**:163, 164, 165, 168
   Kostelanetz **8**:187
Radio broadcasting
   Andre **13**:14
   Fast **18**:180-82
   Hine **15**:226
   Roditi **14**:263-65, 267
   Skelton **5**:282
   Wagoner **3**:400
   Williams **3**:421

   Woodcock **6**:322
Radio-Canada **13**:183-84
Radnóti, Miklós **10**:321
RAF See Great Britain, Royal Air
   Force
Raffel, Burton 9:207-21
Ragas **26**:192
Ragged Trousered Philanthropists, The
   2:384
Raging Bull **5**:218
Raging Joys, Sublime Violations **2**:71
Ragman's Daughter, The **2**:386
Ragni, Gerry **2**:412
Rago, Henry **14**:47-48
Rahv, Philip
   Lelchuk **20**:246
   Markfield **3**:212
Rai, E.N. Mangat **9**:224-25, 228,
   231
Raider, The **21**:40, 42
Rain of Rites, A **9**:146, 147
Rainbow **6**:32
Rainbow, The **23**:239
Raine, Kathleen
   Menashe **11**:232-34, 236
   Weiss **2**:446
Raining Tree War, The **18**:298-99
*Rainy Hills: Verses after a Japanese
   Fashion, The* **15**:357
Rajneesh, Bhagwan Shree **10**:305
Rakosi, Carl 5:193-210
   Rosenblum **11**:345, 348, 349, 350
Raman, A.S. **9**:233
Ramanujan, A.K. **15**:157
"Rambling (in) Life: another fragment
   another piece" **23**:19-27
Ramos, Maximo **9**:167
Ramos, Remedios **9**:167
Ramparts **6**:140
Rancho Linda Vista **11**:327
RAND Corporation **22**:220
Randall, Dudley
   Emanuel **18**:138, 144
   Madgett **23**:205, 206-07
Randall, John Herman **7**:218-19
Randall, Margaret
   Enslin **3**:94
   Major **6**:184
Randolph-Macon Woman's College,
   Lynchburg, Va. **3**:237, 238
*Randolph of Roanoke: A Study in
   Conservative Thought* **9**:95, 97
Randolph, Vance **2**:170
Random House (publishers)
   Becker **1**:42
   Cassill **1**:167
   Mathews **6**:241
Random Walk **11**:39
Rangan, Josephine **5**:151-52
Ranger **3**:95
Ransom, John Crowe
   Abse **1**:27
   Glazier **24**:232, 236
   Harris **3**:117
   Slavitt **3**:315
   Wagoner **3**:403

Williams **20**:331
Ransome, Arthur **4**:100
Rape
    Dworkin **21**:7, 9, 11, 12-13, 14-
      15, 20
    Kenny **22**:129-30, 154-55, 162-68,
      170
    See also Sexual molestation
Rapf, Matthew **2**:172
Raphael, Frederic **9**:17, 18, 26, 27
Rapids of Time **10**:121
Rarest of the Rare, The **20**:14
Rasmussen, Halfdan **23**:260
Rasp, Renate **6**:192, 195
Rat Man of Paris **7**:283, 285
Rathbone, Julian **10**:101
Rats, The **2**:385
Rau, Aurel **5**:355
Rausch, Howard **10**:226
Ravagli, Angelo **10**:133
Ravenshaw College **9**:142
Raw Material **2**:381, 387
Raw Silk **6**:87, 99, 101, 102
Rawling, Tom **9**:285
Raworth, Tom 11:297-311
    Beltrametti **13**:68-69
Rawson, Clayton **10**:222
Ray, David 7:135-53
    Mahapatra **9**:146
    Olson **12**:237
    Petesch **12**:247, 248, 249
Ray, Satyajit **3**:27
Raymond, John **2**:348
Read, Herbert
    Fuller **10**:118-19
    Kerrigan **11**:209
    Woodcock **6**:319, 320
Read, Piers Paul **10**:119
Reade, Vivian **12**:296-97
Reader's Digest
    Barrio **15**:124
    Horwood **15**:249
    Knebel **3**:179
    Slavitt **3**:316
Reader's Digest Book Club **1**:395
Reader's Digest Condensed Books
    3:180, 181
Reading, Pa. **2**:426
Readings in Economic Development
    3:245
Reagan, Ronald
    Condon **1**:194, 198
    Fuchs **5**:57
    Kirk **9**:99, 102
    Van Proyen **25**:382-83
    Wallace **1**:379
Real Long John Silver, The **12**:11
Real Presence **14**:9-10, 12
Realism **4**:329
    See also Anti-Realism in literature
Reality **12**:331
Really the Blues **8**:5, 6
Really the Blues (musical) **1**:339
Realm of Prester John, The **3**:281
Reaney, James Crerar 15:295-309
Reaper, The **22**:101-03

Rear Column, The **3**:114
Rebellion of Yale Marratt, The **10**:281,
    285, 286, 288, 289, 291, 296-
    97, 298
Rebetez, René **10**:229
Recapitulation **9**:262, 264, 269
Rechy, John 4:253-66
    Bruce-Novoa **18**:63
Recital **20**:330
Recollection of a Visitor on Earth
    1:157
Recoveries **2**:448, 449
Recyclings **8**:188
Red and the Blue, The **5**:276
Red Army **12**:311, 312-13
Red Beans **17**:15-16
Red Cats **19**:170
Red Cavalry **5**:260
Red Hats **26**:37
Red-Hot Vacuum, The **2**:400, 403
Red Noses **12**:13
Red Wolf, Red Wolf **7**:107
Redbook
    Corcoran **2**:120
    Gerber **20**:169, 172, 173
Reddaway, Peter **9**:283
Redding, J. Saunders **23**:203
Rediscoveries: Informal Essays in Which
    Well-Known Novelists Rediscover
    Neglected Works of Fiction by One
    of Their Favorite Authors **3**:196
Rediscovery **13**:45
Redmond, Eugene **21**:228
Redondo Beach, Calif. **22**:95-98, 104
Reed, Carol **4**:102
Reed College
    O'Faolain **2**:350
    Ray **7**:143
Reed, Ishmael
    Anaya **4**:26
    Bergé **10**:13
    Foley **24**:159
    Klinkowitz **9**:112
    Major **6**:185, 186, 188
    McElroy **21**:141
    Sukenick **8**:293
Reed, Oliver **5**:274
Reed, Rex **2**:361
Reese, Harry **8**:119
Reeves, James **25**:306
Reflections on a Gift of Watermelon
    Pickle **24**:237-38
Reflections on the Revolution in
    France **9**:95
Reflex and Bone Structure **6**:191, 194,
    198
Regions with No Proper Names **11**:19
Regis College, Denver, Colo. **18**:65,
    70-71
Regnery, Henry **9**:100
Regrets, The **3**:307
Reich, Wilhelm
    Dennison **6**:114-15
    Eshleman **6**:142
Reid, Alastair
    Mathews **6**:235

Parini **16**:233, 241
    Stevenson **9**:285
Reid, Marguerite **15**:246, 247
Reischauer, Edwin O. **19**:195-96
Reiter, Thomas **13**:94, 103
Reitsema, Helen **18**:252-53, 255
Relation Ship, The (Tom Raworth)
    11:302
Relationship (Jayanta Mahapatra)
    9:147-48
Religion
    Allen **11**:7
    Appleman **18**:44-45
    Armantrout **25**:5-6, 7, 13-14
    Awoonor **13**:53
    Bell **14**:38
    Bennett **13**:86
    Berry **24**:68
    Bishop **26**:10-11
    Boyd **11**:43, 45, 47
    Bryant **26**:51-52
    Bullins **16**:65-66
    Choudhury **14**:85
    Clarke **16**:72
    Hahn **11**:107-08
    Hamburger **4**:170
    Harris **16**:123-24
    Hassan **12**:142-44
    Hitchcock **12**:167-68
    Houston **16**:161-62
    Jarman **22**:91-92, 93
    Jones **20**:209
    Kerrigan **11**:194-96
    Kizer **5**:145
    McPherson **23**:218-19
    Middleton **23**:239-42
    Ostriker **24**:272-73, 277
    Ouellette **13**:178, 179-80
    Plumpp **21**:165
    St. Clair **8**:271
    Salaam **21**:227, 242-43
    Salisbury **15**:319
    Shadbolt **3**:258
    Simmons **21**:290
    Wakefield **7**:201
    Weiss **12**:333-34
    Wilhelm **5**:302-03
    Woodcock **6**:315
Religion: A Secular Theory **7**:49
Religion and the Rebel **5**:322-23, 324
Religion See also Atheism
Religious literature **2**:345
Reluctant Dictator, The **9**:20
Remaking of Sigmund Freud, The
    4:213, 219
Remarkable Case of Burglary, A **8**:172
Remarkable Exploits of Lancelot Biggs:
    Spaceman, The **7**:14
Rembrandt **2**:140
Remembering James Agee **3**:198
Remembering Laughter **9**:264
Remembering Summer **15**:242-43, 248,
    249-50, 251
Renaissance, The **2**:429
Renato, Amato **3**:264-65
Renfield, Elinor **2**:421

Reno, Nev. **26**:202
Rensselaer Polytechnic Institute
    12:155, 156
Repertorio Americano **15**:4
Report on Probability A **2**:29
Republic Pictures **1**:382
Republican party **15**:320-21
Reruns **5**:26, 28
Rescue the Dead **3**:152
Rescue the Perishing **23**:274
Reserve Officers' Training Corps
    Highwater **7**:79
    Manuel **9**:155-56
    McCord **9**:178
    Pinsky **4**:243
    Plymell **11**:283
Resident Alien **3**:15, 16, 18, 20, 22,
    26, 29
Residue of Song **14**:50
Resistance **6**:219
Rest Is Done with Mirrors, The
    22:220-21
Rest Is Prose, The **11**:153
Resurrection of Anne Hutchinson, The
    10:304
Retreat to Innocence **5**:122
Retrospectiva del cuento chicano **18**:76
Return Engagements **9**:254, 255
Return from the Stars **1**:261, 262,
    264
Return, The **10**:318
Returning: A Spiritual Journey **7**:201,
    202
"Returning to Church" **7**:201-02
Revelations **4**:213
Reversals **9**:284
Review of Metaphysics **12**:332
Revista Chicano/Riquena **24**:16
Revolt in the South **7**:197
Revolt of the Masses, The
    Kerrigan **11**:213-14
    Rimmer **10**:304
Revolt on Alpha C **3**:273
Revolution and Other Poems **26**:299
Revolution in European Poetry **14**:131
Revolutionary Love **21**:216-20
Rexroth, Kenneth
    Broughton **12**:52
    di Suvero **26**:68-69, 70, 71
    Feirstein **11**:81
    Hamill **15**:206, 212
    Olson **12**:234
    Roditi **14**:283, 286
    Weiss **2**:445
    Williams **12**:343-44
    Wilson **5**:349
Reyes, Alfonso **15**:5
Reyes, Carlos **5**:351
Reynal & Hitchcock (publishers)
    8:305
Reynolds, Paul
    Duncan **2**:170, 176
    Wallace **1**:386, 389, 401
Reznikoff, Charles
    Bernstein **24**:34
    Rakosi **5**:207, 208, 209

Rhetoric of the Contemporary Lyric,
    The **22**:71
Rhine Maidens **22**:219, 223-24
Rhodes, Bob **5**:349
Rhodes Scholarship **12**:22
Rhodesia See Zimbabwe
Rhodomagnetic Digest **16**:212
Rhys, Keidrych **4**:306
Rhythm and blues
    Argüelles **24**:6
    Aubert **20**:25-28
    Forbes **16**:107
    Smith **7**:159
Ribbentrop-Molotov Pact See Nazi-
    Soviet Pact
"Ribbons" **26**:157
Riccardo-Marchi-Torre di Calafuria
    25:115-16
Rich, Adrienne **6**:188
Richard Nixon **1**:376
Richards, C.J. **15**:136
Richardson, Elliot **5**:99
Richie, Donald 20:**285-96**
    Lowitz **26**:179
Riding, Laura **4**:29, 30, 31-32
Riding the Torch **19**:330
Rieser, Max **9**:45
Riesman, David
    Bloch **20**:45
    Greeley **7**:46
    Jerome **8**:133, 137
Right Promethean Fire: Imagination,
    Science, and Cultural Change,
    The **12**:160
Right Way to Figure Plumbing, The
    4:153, 154
Righter, Carroll **25**:382-83, 401
"Rikki-Tikki-Tavi" **13**:166-67
Rilke, Rainer Maria
    Abse **1**:21, 24-26
    Delbanco **2**:158
    Enslin **3**:88-89
    Gray **2**:194
    Gregor **10**:148
    Shapiro **6**:295
Rilla, Wolf **4**:341
Rimbaud, Arthur **2**:155
Rimmer, Robert H. 10:**281-306**
Rinard, Park **1**:164
Rinconete and Cortadillo **1**:299
Rinehart (publishers) **2**:170
Ringer **3**:322
Ringold, Fran **26**:82
Rinzler, Alan **6**:57
Rio de Janeiro, Brazil **10**:226-27
Rio Grande Writers (literary
    movement) **4**:26
Rios, Herminio **4**:24
Ríos profundos, Los (The deep
    rivers) **12**:101
Ripley, Patricia **6**:233
Riprap **2**:141
Rise of English Literary History, The
    7:225-26
Ritner, Peter
    Caute **4**:106

Owens **2**:360
Ritsos, Yannis
    Root **11**:328-29
    Samarakis **16**:249
Ritual in the Dark **5**:318, 319, 322,
    324
River of Earth **17**:234, 239, 241,
    246
Rivera, Tomás **16**:150, 151
"Riverboat" **2**:171
Riznikov, Todor **26**:142
Rizzardi, Alfredo **10**:142
Rizzoli International Bookstore
    13:224
RK Editions **8**:182
RKO Studios
    Condon **1**:194
    Wallace **1**:383
Roach, Max
    Hentoff **6**:168
    Killens **2**:295
Road from Home, The **2**:275
"Road or River" **3**:87
Road to Many a Wonder, The **3**:408
Road to Science Fiction, The **2**:257
Road to Volgograd **2**:386
Road to Wigan Pier, The **9**:21
Roanoke College
    Dillard **7**:10-11, 15
    Taylor **7**:182, 183, 186
Robbe-Grillet, Alain **4**:263
Robbins, Henry **2**:212
Robbins, Jane **24**:139
Robbins, Jerome **2**:415
Robert Bridges: A Study of
    Traditionalism in Poetry **2**:223,
    228
Robert Frost Fellowship **20**:125
Robert Lowell's Life and Work:
    Damaged Grandeur **23**:318
Robert Penn Warren: A Biography
    25:97-98
Roberts, James Hall (pseudonym) See
    Duncan, Robert L.
Roberts, Jane **10**:220
Roberts, Rachel **2**:385
Robeson, Paul
    Giovanni **6**:156
    Killens **2**:283, 297, 302
Robin Hood
    Armantrout **25**:4
    Charyn **1**:177
    Howes **3**:135
Robinson Crusoe
    Allen **6**:15
    Awoonor **13**:40
Robinson, Edward Arlington **8**:42
Robinson, Henry Crabb **7**:220
Robinson, Jackie **1**:393
Robinson, Joan **3**:236, 238
Robinson, Mabel Louise **6**:264, 268
Robinson, Mollie **1**:393
Robinson, Phil **7**:107
Robinson, William Ronald **7**:15
Robinson, William "Smokey" **2**:304
Robot Jox **25**:208-10

Robson, Flora **11**:232
Robson, Jeremy **1**:28, 29
Rochelle; or Virtue Rewarded **3**:319, 320
Rochester, New York **24**:9
Rock **3**:407
Rock music
  Booth **2**:51, 52-53
  Bruce-Novoa **18**:65-66, 70-71
  Clark **22**:15, 16
  Giovanni **6**:160, 161
  Moorcock **5**:176-77, 182
  Nichols **2**:325-26
  Rosenblum **11**:335-36
  Smith **7**:159
Rockefeller Foundation
  Davison **4**:138
  Mahapatra **9**:149
  Olson **12**:232, 235
  Purdy **1**:302
  Stegner **9**:267
Rockefeller Grant
  Bowles **1**:92
  Chappell **4**:120
  Kennedy **20**:223
  Root **11**:324
Rockland Community College **15**:30
Rodenbeck, John
  Dillard **7**:15
  Garrett **5**:80
Rodgers, Carolyn M. 13:237-57
Rodin, Auguste **9**:68
Roditi, Edouard 14:237-87
  Kelly **19**:193
Rodney, Janet **16**:282-86
Rodriguez, Luis **26**:210
Roelofs, Garritt E. **18**:248-50, 252
Roethke, Theodore
  Allman **15**:23
  Eaton **20**:125-26
  Heyen **9**:37
  Kizer **5**:152
  McPherson **23**:221, 222
  Parini **16**:234
  Peters **8**:242
  Shapiro **6**:303-04
  Wagoner **3**:402-04, 405, 406, 407
Rogers, Ginger **5**:57-58
Roget, John L. **3**:136
Roget, Peter Mark **3**:136
Rogoff, Gordon **2**:412
Rogue Elephant **6**:22
Rogue Moon **14**:71-72, 73
Rohmer, Sax (pseudonym of Arthur Henry Sarsfield Ward) **2**:37
Roland, Gilbert **11**:316
Rolle, Richard, of Hampole **6**:36
Rolling Stone **5**:217
Rolling Stones
  Armantrout **25**:21-22
  Elman **3**:83
Rolo, Charles J. **7**:6
Roman Catholic Church See Catholic Church
Roman Marriage, A **9**:27, 28
Romania **5**:353-55

Romano, Octavio **4**:24
Romano, Umberto **8**:84
Romantic Comedy **9**:249, 250-52, 253
Romantic Traceries **26**:32-33
Rome, Italy
  Argüelles **24**:12
  Jennings **5**:111-12
  Salvadori **25**:347-50
Romeo and Juliet
  Delbanco **2**:157
  Ostriker **24**:265
Romm, Vladimir **5**:149
Romulo, Carlos P. **9**:157
Ronde, La **2**:411
Rooke, Leon **3**:23
Roosevelt, Eleanor
  Bourjaily **1**:66
  Condon **1**:190
Roosevelt, Franklin D.
  Glazier **24**:227
  Knebel **3**:177
  Morgan, Ted **4**:234-35
  Morgan, Theodore **3**:231
  Weintraub **20**:304, 314
Roosevelt Hotel, New York City **1**:190
Roosevelt, Theodore **19**:250
Roosevelt University
  Plumpp **21**:169, 170
  Rodgers **13**:244, 245, 252
Root River Run **2**:262
Root, Robert Kilburn **7**:217
Root, William Pitt 11:313-31
Roots (Arnold Wesker) **7**:249
Rope of Bells **25**:37, 41
Rorem, Ned **7**:81
Rosary Murders, The **1**:252-53
Rose of the Desert **11**:98-99
Rose, Stanley **1**:201-02
Rose, The **10**:46-57
Rose, W.K. **6**:25
Rosen, Allan **19**:5, 23, 31, 44, 55
Rosen, Philip **10**:189, 190
Rosenberg, Ethel **2**:192
Rosenberg, Harold **2**:449
Rosenberg, Isaac **5**:255, 256, 263
Rosenberg, Julius **2**:192
Rosenblum, Martin Jack 11:333-54
  McCord **9**:187
Rosenfeld, Isaac
  Markfield **3**:215-16, 217-18, 219, 221, 222, 224
  Solotaroff **2**:396, 397
Rosenthal, M.L. 6:271-86
  Allen **6**:26
  Feirstein **11**:80
  Weiss **2**:433
"Rosie" **26**:221
Ross, Alan **8**:103
Ross, Charles **14**:173
Ross, Harold **2**:65-66
Rossetti, Dante Gabriel **4**:155
Rossi, Pete **7**:47
Rotary International **1**:34-35, 45
Rote Walker, The **22**:92, 106
Roth, Barbara **26**:157

Roth, Henry **3**:429, 430
Roth, Muriel **3**:429, 430
Roth, Philip
  Blaise **3**:25, 26, 27
  Lelchuk **20**:248
  Solotaroff **2**:397
Roth, Susanna **12**:193-94
Rothenberg, Diane **19**:191
Rothenberg, Erika **13**:13-14, 15, 16, 17, 19, 20, 23
Rothenberg, Jerome
  Awoonor **13**:47
  Kelly **19**:191, 201
  Major **6**:198
  Wakoski **1**:364
Rothko, Mark **6**:113
Rotrosen, Jane **13**:224
Rotsler, William **12**:218
Rottensteiner, Franz **1**:255, 260
Round Dances **19**:201
Round Table, The **7**:232-33
Roundhouse Voices: Selected and New Poems, The **7**:165
Rounds **1**:135
Rouse, James **8**:136, 137
Roussanoff, Nikola **22**:53
Rousseau's Tale **18**:305
Roussel, Raymond **6**:245-46
Rousselot, Pierre **7**:43
Routledge & Kegan Paul (publishers) **3**:46
Row of Tigers, A **2**:120
Rowe, Kenneth **9**:82
Rowe, Thomas **11**:204
Rowing
  Murchie **19**:269-73
  Wright **5**:365
Rowse, A.L. 8:253-66
Roxburgh, J.F. **7**:118-19
Roy, Debi **14**:88-89, 90, 94, 98
Royal Conservatory of Music, Toronto, Ontario, Canada **25**:153
Royal Court Theatre, London, England **2**:416
Royal Geographical Society **7**:123
Royal Philharmonic Orchestra **8**:26-27
Royal Scottish Academy **3**:355
Royal Shakespeare Company, England **7**:241, 256
Royal Society for the Protection of Birds **4**:309
Royal Society of Literature, England
  Booth **2**:59
  Dillon **3**:66
  Skelton **5**:287
Royal Swedish Academy of Science **1**:390
Royall, Anne **1**:387
Royet-Journoud, Claude **11**:309
Ruark, Gibbons 23:269-88
Rubaiyat of Omar Khayyam, The
  Grumman **25**:184
  Kennedy **9**:76
  McCord **9**:177

INDEX

Morgan 3:233
"Rubble Railroad, The" 22:195-201
Ruben, Ernestine Winston 9:279
Rubens, Bernice 5:122
Rubia Barcia, José 6:144
Rubin, Louis D., Jr. 7:182
Rubinstein, Eli A. 15:122
Rubinstein, Hilary 2:29
Ruby Red 19:130
Ruckle, Ernie 4:243
Rude Awakening, A 2:29
Rudich, Norman 15:63, 66, 67, 71
Ruge, Ferdinand 12:340
Ruined Season, The 22:115
Ruiz, Raúl 20:330
Rukeyser, Muriel
    Dworkin 21:17
    Rosenthal 6:279
Rule, Jane 18:309-25
Ruler of the Sky 18:345
Ruling Class, The 12:12
Runaway Spoon Press 24:77
Runner, The 11:55
Running 23:88-89
Running on Empty 13:197, 205
Running Sun, The 1:304
Runyon, Damon 2:325
Ruopp, Phil 8:135
"Rupite" 26:143-44
Rush, Christopher 6:75
Rush, Norman 8:288
Rush on the Ultimate, A 8:171
Rushdie, Salman 14:237, 238
Rushes 4:264
Ruskin, John 10:103-04
Ruskin, Micky 1:362
Russ, Joanna
    Dann 20:94
    Piercy 1:276
    Pohl 1:295
Russell, Bertrand
    Booth 5:35, 42, 43, 48
    Grumbach 2:208
    Parini 16:232
    Wilson 5:314
Russell, Charles 8:293
Russell, Diarmuid
    Bell 12:38
    Bourjaily 1:68, 73, 74, 75, 78-79
    Wagoner 3:404, 405
Russell Kirk: A Bibliography 9:103
Russell, Lawrence 7:101
Russell, Peter 14:333
Russia
    Corcoran 2:123-24
    Davie 3:32-33
    Gray 2:180-81, 191
    Mrozek 10:271
    Nichols 2:314
    Salisbury 15:323-24, 325, 326
    Sillitoe 2:386
    Simpson 4:286-87
    Zinoviev 10:323-38
    See also Soviet Union
Russian Americans
    Corman 2:129-30

Gray 2:190
Russian Intelligence, The 5:187-88
Russian literature
    Thomas 11:376, 377, 379
    Zinoviev 10:325, 337-38
Russian Poetry under the Tsars 9:217
Russian Revolution, 1917
    Gray 2:188
    Lem 1:255
    Solotaroff 2:393
Russian Spring 19:335-36, 338
Russians
    Garrett 5:81-82
    Moorcock 5:183
Russo, Alan 11:282, 283, 284, 289
Rutgers University
    Forbes 16:109, 111-12
    Hadas 23:131
    Ostriker 24:269-70, 276-77
    Pinsky 4:243-44
    Tarn 16:280, 283
    Williams 3:431
Rybák, Josef 1:343
Ryerson Press 22:42

Saari, Oliver 2:41
Sackton, Alexander 12:246
Sacred Heart Seminary, Detroit,
    Mich. 1:239-41
"Sacrifice Hit" 1:381, 382
Sacrifice, The 3:322
Sacrilege of Alan Kent, The 1:156
Sad Isn't the Color of the Dream
    26:226
Saddlemyer, Ann 5:287
Sade, Donatien-Alphonse-François,
    Marquis de 9:129
Sadness and Happiness 4:244, 246,
    248-49, 250
Safad 9:64
Safe Conduct 1:221
Sagan, Carl 7:283
Sagan, Eli 9:219
*Sailing into the Unknown: Yeats, Pound,
    and Eliot* 6:280
sailor 19:22, 52
Sailor on Horseback 3:370
St. Albans News 12:340
St. Andrews 9:97
St. Botolph's Review 9:280
St. Clair, Margaret 8:267-82
"St. Elsewhere" 6:220
Saint-Exupéry, Antoine de
    Brée 15:137
    Hadas 23:127-28, 129
St. Ives, Cornwall 23:168
St. John of the Cross See Juan de la
    Cruz, San
St. John's College, Santa Fe, N.M.
    12:17, 18, 36, 38
St. Joseph College 17:87-88
St. Lawrence University 22:170
St. Louis, Mo. 21:122-23
St. Louis University 17:21-24
St. Mark's Church, New York City
    Wakoski 1:362

Waldman 17:276, 278, 280, 287
St. Mark's Poetry Project
    Wakoski 1:362
    Waldman 17:276-80
St. Martin's Press 1:251-52
Saint Mary of the Lake Seminary
    7:42-44
St. Nicholas Magazine 1:381
St. Olaf College 23:258
Saint-Simon, Count de 4:231
St. Stephen's College 9:224
St. Valentine's Night 7:44
*St. Winifred's; or, The World of
    School* 6:66
Saints in Their Ox-Hide Boat 13:97,
    99
Saison dans la Vie d'Emmanuel, Une
    4:73, 74, 76, 77
Saks, Gene 9:246
Sakti and Sakta 10:291
Salaam, Kalamu ya 21:179-252
Salam, Nurdin 9:211
Šalda, F.X. 7:214
Sale, Faith 2:212
Salinas, Pedro 15:59
Salinas River 24:283
Salinger, J.D.
    Burroway 6:87
    Kinsella 7:104
Salinger, Pierre 1:394
Salisbury, Harrison E. 15:311-27
Salisbury, John (pseudonym of David
    Caute) 4:108
Sallis, James
    Disch 4:153
    Knight 10:226
    Wolfe 9:306
Sallis, Jane 4:153
"Salt" 26:127, 128
Salt and Core 2:363
Salt and the Heart's Horizons 26:71
Salt Lake Tribune 5:46
Saludos! The Poems of New Mexico
    26:79
Salvadori Educational Center on the
    Built Environment 25:371-74
Salvadori, Mario 25:341-78
Sam 2:121
Samal, Mary Hrabik 12:183-95
Samaraki, Eleni 16:255, 261-62,
    264, 268
Samarakis, Antonis 16:245-70
Samaras, Lucas 4:244
Same Time Next Year 9:245-48, 249,
    250, 254-55
Samizdat 10:328, 330, 337
Samperi, Frank 2:145
Sampson, Roland 1:102
Samuel French Award 2:119
Samuel, Gerhard 24:346
Samuel Goldwyn Award 12:72
San Bernardino, Calif. 24:86, 89
San Diego, Calif.
    Armantrout 25:3, 6, 8
    McCord 9:179
    Polkinhorn 25:335

San Diego State University
  Armantrout **25**:12-13, 15, 17-18
  Nolan **16**:211
San Francisco Art Institute
  Broughton **12**:57
  Van Proyen **25**:389-94, 398-400
San Francisco, Calif.
  Armantrout **25**:17
  Berry **24**:77-80
  Broughton **12**:51-52, 57
  Bryant **26**:50, 52-53
  Caldwell **1**:151, 152
  Caulfield **25**:111
  Connell **2**:110
  Corman **2**:141-42
  Daigon **25**:169
  di Suvero **26**:70, 72-73, 76-77
  Easton **14**:146
  Hiemstra **26**:158
  Holden **22**:64-65
  Kyger **16**:189-90
  Leftwich **25**:269
  Lowitz **26**:165-66
  Menefee **26**:206
  Stone **3**:361-63, 364
  Van Proyen **25**:391-93
  Villanueva **24**:303
  weiss **24**:331, 333-34, 339
  Wolff **22**:296
San Francisco Cats: Nine Lives with
  Whiskers **26**:157
San Francisco Chronicle **1**:70
San Francisco Poems, The **26**:77
San Francisco Poetry Center **1**:360,
  362
San Francisco Poets **5**:162
San Francisco State College
  Bryant **26**:54-55, 57
  Lowitz **26**:178
  See San Francisco State University
San Francisco State Poetry Award
  23:31
San Francisco State University
  Boyle **1**:123
  Connell **2**:109
  Holden **22**:64-65
  Lowitz **26**:176
  Markfield **3**:221
  Petesch **12**:248
  Roditi **14**:282
  Valaoritis **26**:290
San Jose, Calif. **23**:215-16
San Jose State University
  Houston, James D. **16**:164
  Houston, Jeanne Wakatsuki
    16:179
  McPherson **23**:215-16, 221
  Norse **18**:289
  Stafford **3**:335
San Juan de la Cruz See Juan de la
  Cruz, San
San Quentin Prison **23**:315-16
Sánchez, Luis Rafael **9**:203, 204
Sanchez, Sonia **18**:143
Sandburg, Carl
  Harris **3**:121

Wakefield **7**:194-95
Sanders, Edward **21**:253-74
  Argüelles **24**:22
  Bergé **10**:7, 10
  Clark **22**:16
  Spinrad **19**:328
Sanders' Truckstop **21**:267
Sandford, Jay **9**:243
Sandia Corp. **5**:333, 348, 349
Sandow, Gregory **4**:155
Saner, Reg **22**:65, 66, 77
Sans Famille **11**:127
Santa Barbara City College
  Easton **14**:158, 159
  Kyger **16**:188
Santa Cruz, Calif. **24**:320
Santa Fe, N.M.
  Bergé **10**:15-16
  Tarn **16**:285
Santayana, George
  Murchie **19**:249, 252
  Whittemore **8**:299
Santesson, Hans Stefan **4**:209
Sanzenbach, Keith **3**:83
Sapp, Allen **7**:105
Sappho **6**:280
Sarah Lawrence College
  Kizer **5**:152
  Major **6**:186
Sargent, Pamela **18**:327-47
  Dann **20**:89-90, 96
  Zebrowski **19**:368, 369, 370, 373,
    377
Sargent, Porter **10**:70
Sarmatische Zeit **13**:125-29, 130, 136
Saroyan, Aram **5**:211-23
  Clark **22**:23
Saroyan, William
  Bowles **1**:85, 86
  Kazin **7**:90
  Kherdian **2**:267, 269, 270-71, 272
Sarton, May **7**:180-81
Sartre, Jean-Paul
  Belitt **4**:49-50, 51, 54
  Bowles **1**:87
  Flanagan **17**:50-51, 54
  Gurik **23**:100, 108
  Jones **5**:117
  Kerrigan **11**:194
  Mott **7**:119
  Van Itallie **2**:411
Saryan, Martiros **2**:273
Sasaki, Ruth Fuller **16**:193, 194-95
Sasha My Friend **2**:121, 126
Saskatchewan, Canada **9**:260-61
Sassafras **15**:270
Sassoon, Siegfried
  Silkin **5**:259
  Skelton **5**:283
Sastre, Genoveva Forest de **3**:138
Satis **13**:139
Saturday Evening Post
  Boyle **1**:118, 120
  Morgan **4**:231
  Wakefield **7**:194
  Wallace **1**:380

Saturday Night and Sunday Morning
  2:382, 383-85, 386
Saturday Night at the Greyhound **6**:18,
  19
Saturday Review
  Grumbach **2**:212
  Highwater **7**:81
  Jerome **8**:137
  Lottman **12**:206
Saudek, Erik **7**:214-15, 222
Sausalito, Calif. **26**:70, 73
Savage, Elizabeth Fitzgerald **15**:333
Savage God, The **2**:412, 414
Savage Key **10**:174
Savage, Thomas **15**:329-45
Savannah News **1**:142
Saviors, The **20**:358
Savory, Teo **8**:248
Šavrdová, Marie **1**:345
Saw **14**:175
Say Goodbye—You May Never See Them
  Again **7**:243, 244, 246-47
Say, Is This the U.S.A.? **1**:148
Sayers, Dorothy L.
  Gilbert **15**:194
  Keating **8**:166, 169
  Stewart **3**:352
Scannell, Vernon **1**:28
Scapegoat, The **1**:321, 322
Scarf, The **20**:45-46
Scarfe, Francis **6**:67
Scarlet Letter, The **5**:98
Scars **7**:103
Scenarios for a Mixed Landscape
  15:20
Scented Hills, The **11**:100, 103
Sceptre Press **2**:54-55
Schamberg, Morton **1**:104, 108,
  109, 113
Schapiro, Meyer
  Dennison **6**:111, 112
  Menashe **11**:228
Schattenland Ströme **13**:129, 130, 136
Scheherazade **2**:192
Scheitinger, Tony **2**:421
Schelling, Andrew **17**:291, 292
Scherzo capriccioso **1**:350
Schevill, James **12**:253-80
  Honig **8**:118, 119, 120
Schevill, Rudolph **12**:253-6, 266,
  267-68, 269, 271, 273
Schiffrin, André **6**:92
Schiller, David **7**:178-79, 185
Schimmel, Harold
  Katz **14**:165-66, 171-72
  Wright **7**:295, 296
Schizophrenia **6**:115
Schlauch, Margaret **5**:120, 121
Schlesinger, Arthur Meyer **24**:232
Schlesinger, Robert **4**:217
Schliemann, Henry **3**:376-77
Schliemann, Sophia **3**:376-77
Schmidt, Michael
  Ashby **6**:43
  Davie **3**:46, 47
  Sisson **3**:304-05, 306, 307

Schmidt, Paul **9**:214
Schmitt, Martin **6**:55-57
Schnall, Herbert **10**:300
Schneeman, George
    Katz **14**:171-72
    Wright **7**:295
Schneider, Allen **2**:412
Schneyder, John **6**:214
Schoenberg, Arnold
    Enslin **3**:95, 96
    Josipovici **8**:159
Scholes, Robert **7**:180
School of Art, Cork, Ireland **3**:56
School of Letters, Bloomington,
    Ind. **12**:155-56
School of the Art Institute of
    Chicago **16**:119
School of the Arts, Cummington,
    Mass. **3**:139
Schopenhauer, Arthur **8**:42
Schorer, Mark **26**:70
Schörner, Marshal **1**:333
Schorske, Carl **12**:157
Schramm, Richard **7**:164
Schramm, Wilbur **9**:263, 264, 265,
    266
Schrieber, Ron **5**:351
Schryver, Lee **6**:57
Schubert, David **2**:432, 433-34, 440,
    445
Schubert Foundation Playwrighting
    Fellowship **4**:207, 208, 215
Schueller, Herbert M. **8**:241, 244
Schultz, John **21**:91, 94
Schultz, J.W. **2**:263
Schulz, Bruno
    Brossard **2**:72, 74
    Tennant **9**:292
Schulz, Charles **1**:400
Schumann, Peter **6**:117, 118
Schumpeter, Joseph **3**:236
Schütz, Heinrich **3**:95
Schuyler, George **5**:202
Schuyler, James **6**:236
"Schwartz between the Galaxies"
    3:283
Schwartz, Delmore
    Allman **15**:23
    Brossard **2**:67
    Phillips **13**:199, 201-03, 212
Schwartz, Lloyd **4**:249
Schwartz, Stephen 26:231-48
Schwarzschild, Bettina **1**:303
Schwerner, Armand **19**:200
Science and the Classics **9**:96
Science Fantasy
    Aldiss **2**:25
    Moorcock **5**:177
Science fiction
    Aldiss **2**:23, 28
    Allen **11**:7, 14-15, 19
    Bishop **26**:17
    Bradley **10**:21
    Brunner **8**:7, 10-11, 12
    Budrys **14**:65-79
    Clement **16**:89-104

Coppel **9**:2, 4
Dann **20**:83, 87
Haldeman **25**:212-13
Hoffman **10**:169-70
Kennedy **9**:77-79, 80
Lem **1**:260-61
Malzberg **4**:205-06, 207, 212,
    213-14
Moorcock **5**:176, 177, 181
Niven **12**:211, 212, 213-22
Nolan **16**:212, 215
St. Clair **8**:273, 281-82
Silverberg **3**:271-78, 279, 280-88
Spinrad **19**:313-14, 319, 324-25,
    326-27, 339
Tennant **9**:291-92
Westlake **13**:337
Williamson **8**:317, 320, 321-22,
    323-24, 325
Wolfe **9**:308
Zebrowski **19**:363-81
Science Fiction and Futurology **1**:263
Science Fiction Encyclopedia, The
    4:154
Science Fiction in the Real World
    19:325
Science Fiction Research
    Association **2**:257
Science Fiction: The Future **11**:19
Science Fiction Writers of America
    Anderson **2**:45
    Gunn **2**:256
    Knight **10**:224-25
    Pohl **1**:292, 295
    Silverberg **3**:282
    Spinrad **19**:332, 334
Scientific American **9**:186
Sclerosis **12**:10
Scopes Trial, The **1**:318
Scorsese, Martin **5**:218
Scotland
    Cartland **8**:20-21, 22
    Jarman **22**:92-95, 97
    Kirk **9**:97
    Parini **16**:231-35
    Stewart **3**:343-45
    Tennant **9**:289-91
    Thomas **19**:351, 353-54
Scott, Bobby **6**:233-34
Scott, Frank **15**:159
Scott, John **4**:343
Scott Meredith Literary Agency,
    Inc. **19**:329
Scott-Moncrieff, George **9**:97
Scottsdale Center for the Arts Poetry
    Series **26**:222-23
Scovel, Carl **7**:201
Screen **4**:213, 214, 217, 218
Screenwriting **4**:345-46
Scribner, Charles (publishers)
    Brown **6**:56
    Disch **4**:156
    Elman **3**:75, 77
    Swanberg **13**:268, 272, 273, 274
Scrutiny **3**:35
Sculling to Byzantium **15**:355, 359

Scuola Interpreti, Florence, Italy
    2:351
SDS See Students for a Democratic
    Society
Sea Gull, The **2**:417-18
Sea of Zanj **11**:99
Seagull on the Step, The **1**:123
seagull on yonge street **19**:12, 14, 16
SeaHorse Press **13**:228, 229
Seal, Marilyn See Nolan, Cameron
Searching for the Ox **4**:296
Season of the Jews **3**:250
Season of the Stranger, The **1**:35
Season of the Strangler **11**:185-86
*Seasons: Eager Blossoms, Summer
    Mountains, Autumn Dazzle, First
    Snow* **26**:158
Seasons of the Blood **22**:245
Seattle Post-Intelligencer **3**:407
Seattle Repertory Theatre **3**:407-08
Seaview **11**:253, 259
Sebastopol, Calif. **26**:39
Secker & Warburg (publishers) **9**:21,
    23-24
Second Home, A **9**:27, 28
Second Lady, The **1**:384, 398
Second Man, The **3**:386
Second Trip, The **3**:281
Secret Garden, The **24**:355, 357, 359,
    361, 363
*Seductio ad Absurdum: The Principles
    and Practices of Seduction—A
    Beginner's Handbook* **11**:111
See, Carolyn 22:211-31
Seeing the Light **12**:51
Seetee Ship **8**:322
Seetee Shock **8**:322
Seferis, George
    Argüelles **24**:14
    Barnstone **15**:93-94
    Valaoritis **26**:270-73, 276-78, 280-
        81, 282-83, 285
Segregation
    Anderson **2**:35
    Armantrout **25**:12
    Bradley **10**:23
    Dillard **7**:9
    Killens **2**:282, 289
    Major **6**:177
    Nelson **23**:253-54
    Nichols **2**:324
    Petry **6**:263, 268
    Salaam **21**:180
    Shreve **5**:230
    Stafford **3**:332, 333
    Wellek **7**:218
    Williams **3**:417, 419
    See also Civil rights movement
Segues **3**:333
Ségur, Sophie Rostopchine, Comtesse
    de **2**:184
Segura, Andres **4**:24
Seigle, Henri **16**:276
Seigle, No **16**:276
Seldes, George **6**:171

Selected Declarations of Dependence
6:247, 248
Selected Essays and Criticism (Louis
Dudek) 14:135
Selected Poems (Carl Rakosi) 5:208,
209
Selected Poems (George Woodcock)
6:326
Selected Poems (John Frederick
Nims) 17:184
Selected Poems (Jon Silkin) 5:263
Selected Poems (Larry Eigner) 23:53
Selected Poems (Malay Roy
Choudhury) 14:92, 99
Selected Poems of Alexander Pushkin
9:219
Selected Poems of Ezra Pound 7:293,
295
Selected Poems, 1976–1986 (David
Wagoner) 3:411
Selected Poems, 1933–1980 (George
Faludy) 5:292
Selected Poems (Robert Peters) 8:248
Selected Poems (Stanley Kunitz) 4:135
Selected Poems (Yvor Winters) 4:245
Selected Works of Unamuno 11:213
*Selected Writings of Guillaume
Apollinaire* 8:184
Selective Service 24:183
Self-Culture 5:36
Self-identity 25:270
Self-publishing
Barrio 15:118
Bryant 26:60
"Self Reliance" 11:7
Seligman, Ben 3:216, 217, 218, 220,
222, 223
Selling Out 7:201
Seltzer, Dan 2:417, 418
Selver, Paul 7:213
*Selves at Risk: Patterns of Quest in
Contemporary American Letters*
12:163-64
Sender, Ramón 8:112
Senghor, Leopold Sedar 6:189, 190-
91, 192
Senior, Charles 6:71
Senior Fellowship Award 1:94
Sense of Direction, A 13:307, 308,
314, 315, 316
Sense of the Fire, The 4:218-19
Sense of the World, A 5:112
Sent to His Account 3:59
Separate Notebooks, The 4:250
Séquences de l'aile (The sequences of
wings) 13:183
Serbia 23:68
Sereni, Vittorio 10:141
Sergeant, Howard 1:27
Serpent, The 2:411, 416, 417
Serra, Richard 14:176
Serreau, Jean Marie 20:232
Seton Hall University, South Orange,
N.J. 9:79-80
Seton Hill College, Greensburg, Pa.
3:198

Settle, Mary Lee 1:307-23
Settlers' West, The 6:57
Sevastyanov, Valentin 1:286
Seven Days in May 3:174, 180-81
Seven Minutes, The 1:384, 385, 395-
97
*Seven Mountains of Thomas Merton,
The* 7:132-34
*Seven Mysteries of Life: An Exploration
in Science and Philosophy, The*
19:247-48, 304-05, 308
Seven Serpents and Seven Moons
9:204
Seven South African Poets 14:59, 60
Seven Suspects 3:353, 354
"Seven Who Were Hanged, The"
2:392
7.7.73 8:92
Seventeen 20:164
Seventh Seal, The 7:17
Sewall, Richard 12:332
Sewanee in Ruins 23:303, 316
Sewanee Review Fellowship 11:180
Sex
Murchie 19:255-56, 260
Rechy 4:261-62
"Sex-skat-chew'n" 26:31
Sexism
El Saadawi 11:63, 65, 67, 68, 70
Livesay 8:234
Owens 2:364, 367
See also Women's movement
Sexton, Anne
Browne 20:64, 67
Davison 4:137
Hiemstra 26:154
Jerome 8:133
Kumin 8:216
Weiss 2:447
Sexual identity 25:11
Sexual molestation 24:311-12
See also Rape
Sexual Outlaw, The 4:263, 265
Seymour Lawrence/Delacorte
(publishers) 1:318
Shadbolt, Maurice 3:249-67
Becker 1:43, 44
*Shadow Land: Selected Poems of
Johannes Bobrowski* 13:132, 133
Shadow Lands 13:138
Shadow Line, The 18:202
Shadow of the Torturer, The 9:299,
311
Shadow out of Time 3:271
Shadow People, The 8:274, 281
Shadrach in the Furnace 3:284
Shaffer, Peter 4:133
Shain, Charles 8:306
Shainberg, Larry 14:179
*Shake a Spear with Me, John
Berryman* 8:118
Shaker Light 8:247, 248
Shakers
Lifshin 10:247
Peters 8:247

Shakespeare and the Nature of Time
10:316
Shakespeare, William
Aldiss 2:20
Anderson 2:46
Bishop 26:11
Brewster 15:151
Broughton 12:45-47
Busch 1:137
Corman 2:132
Dillon 3:50, 51, 53
Forrest 7:22
Glanville 9:18
Horwood 15:242
Jerome 8:133-34, 135
Rowse 8:262
Rule 18:311
Schevill 12:262
Shaman 17:284
Shame the Devil 18:40
Shamus Award 11:38
Shange, Ntozake 21:208
Shanghai Incident 1:36
Shannon, Who Was Lost Before 5:163,
166
Shapiro, Alan 23:289-99
Shapiro, Helen 2:25
Shapiro, Karl 6:287-309
Corman 2:136
Enslin 3:89
Hazo 11:142
Phillips 13:213
Smith 7:161
Shapiro, Meyer 2:432
Shards of God: A Novel of the Yippies
21:267
Sharp, John 9:181
Sharp Tools for Catullan Gardens
12:342
Sharpest Sight, The 24:296-97
Sharpshooter 3:200, 203, 204
Shattuck, Roger
Kostelanetz 8:184
Settle 1:322
Shaw, George Bernard
Allen 6:17
Fast 18:172
Fry 23:67
Kizer 5:147
Rimmer 10:286
Stewart 3:355
Shaw, Irwin 11:230
Shaw, Larry
Hoffman 10:171, 172
Knight 10:208, 209-10, 211, 217,
221
Shawn, William
Boyle 1:121
Brossard 2:63-65, 76
Gray 2:198, 199
Hentoff 6:171
Shawno 6:121
Shea, John 7:49
Sheckley, Robert
Aldiss 2:27
Malzberg 4:212

Sheed, Wilfrid
  Kumin **8**:201
  West **7**:275
Sheeler, Charles **1**:104, 109, 113
Sheep Look Up, The **8**:15
Sheer Fiction **7**:281
Sheets, Kermit **12**:52-54
Sheffield University **4**:190
Shekeloff, Brian **2**:142
Shekeloff, Mertis **2**:142
Shelley, Percy Bysshe
  Brown **6**:66
  Dudek **14**:123
  Foley **24**:163
  Vivante **12**:284
Shelnutt, Eve **14:289-301**
Sheltering Sky, The **1**:88
Shelton, Dick **13**:7, 8, 9
Shenton, Edward **6**:54
Shepard, Lucius **20**:86, 98-99
Shepard, Sam **20**:225-26
Sherbourne Press **10**:298-99, 300
Sherbrookes trilogy **2**:156, 159, 162
Sherburn, George **24**:232
Sherburne, N.Y. **1**:134, 135
Sheridan, Paul **8**:101, 104
Sheriff of Bombay, The **8**:176
Sherlock Holmes: The Man and His World **8**:177
Sherman, Howard **9**:181
Sherman, Jory **24**:90, 91-92
Shifting Web: New and Selected Poems, The **22**:241
Shils, Edward **23**:150
Shimpei, Kusano **2**:142, 144
Ship of Death **6**:74
Ship's Orchestra, The **10**:98-99
Shirer, William **1**:123
Shires, The **3**:46
Shirley, James **17**:178
Shlonsky, Avraham **13**:152, 153
Shoeless Joe **7**:104-06, 107, 110
Shoeless Joe Jackson Comes to Iowa **7**:103, 105, 109
Sholokhov, Mikhail **10**:325
Shopping for Women **25**:314
Shore of Women, The **18**:342
Shore, Viola Brothers **2**:288
Short Life, The **13**:154
Short Season and Other Stories **9**:108, 118, 120
Short Stories (Kay Boyle) **1**:116
Short Stories of Langston Hughes, The **18**:133
Short Story 3 **9**:212-13, 216
Short Survey of Surrealism, A **25**:224
Short Throat, the Tender Mouth, The **2**:207, 210
Shostakovich, Dmitri **26**:150
Shoushani, Mordechai **4**:355
Shragge, Elaine **2**:365
Shreve, Susan Richards **5:225-41**
Shrinking: The Beginning of My Own Ending **20**:252
Shylock **7**:231
Si Malakas at Si Maganda **9**:167-68

Sicilians **24**:111
Sicily
  Delbanco **2**:153
  Vivante **12**:296
Sickles the Incredible **13**:268
Siebner, Herbert **5**:290
Sierra Club **3**:183
Sierra Mountains **24**:317-20
Sieveking, Gale **4**:340
Sieveking, Lance **4**:340
Sighet, Romania **4**:353
Sigma Delta Chi **2**:245
Sigma Delta Chi Award **3**:179
Sign of the Labrys **8**:274, 275, 281
Signet Classic Book of American Short Stories, The **9**:219
Signet Society **2**:411
Significa **1**:401
Sikelianos, Angelos **15**:80-81
Sikhs and Sikhism **9**:223, 227, 229, 231, 232, 234
Sikhs, The **9**:231, 232
Silber, John **9**:217
Silberman, Jim **1**:72, 74, 75
Silence, The **7**:13
Silent Explosion, The **18**:36
Silkin, Jon **5:243-65**
  Abse **1**:28
Silliman, Ron
  Armantrout **25**:20
  Bernstein **24**:44
  Eigner **23**:31, 52
Silliphant, Stirling **21**:38-40
Sillitoe, Alan **2:371-89**
Silone, Ignazio **3**:62, 63
Silver Heron, The **9**:279, 282
Silver Snaffles **8**:210
Silverberg, Robert **3:269-91**
  Dann **20**:99-100
  Knight **10**:225
  Malzberg **4**:207
Simak, Clifford D.
  Anderson **2**:39
  Silverberg **3**:276
"Simenon and Spillane: Metaphysics of Murder for the Millions" **7**:6
Simenon, Georges **8**:170
Simic, Charles **4:267-84**
Simmons, Charles **7**:16
Simmons College **16**:98
Simmons, James **21:275-98**
Simon & Schuster (publishers)
  Jones **5**:128, 129
  Wallace **1**:385, 389, 393, 396
Simon and the Shoeshine Boy **11**:81, 83
Simon, Carly **2**:158
Simon, John **2**:437, 444, 445
Simon, Richard **5**:128-29
Simon Says Get Married **9**:243, 244
Simonov, Konstantin **10**:327
Simpkins, Ed **23**:205
Simple Lust: Collected Poems of South African Jail and Exile, A **14**:57, 58, 62-63

Simple People **3**:109
Simpson, Don **12**:219
Simpson, Louis **4:285-99**
  Awoonor **13**:47, 48
  Wakoski **1**:362
Simpson, Martha **1**:208, 209
Sims, Mary **7**:297, 298
Sin **13**:10
Sinatra, Frank **1**:196
Sinclair, Andrew **5:267-77**
Sinclair, Upton **8**:310
Singapore **3**:245
Singer, Isaac Bashevis
  Elman **3**:82
  Petry **6**:268
Singh, Khushwant **9:223-36**
Sinking of the Odradek Stadium, The **6**:240-41, 247
Sino-Japanese War **5**:141, 150
Sins of Philip Fleming, The **1**:387
Sions, Harry **3**:428, 430, 431
'Sippi **2**:296
Sir George Williams University **3**:27
Sir Richard Grenville of the "Revenge" **8**:259, 260
Sir Slob and the Princess **5**:79
Sirens, Knuckles, Boots **14**:56
Sissie **3**:415, 421, 424, 425, 427
Sisson, C.H. **3:293-309**
  Ashby **6**:44
  Davie **3**:46
Sisterhood Is Powerful **18**:198
Sisters, The **15**:149, 152, 153-54, 159
Situation of Poetry, The **4**:249
Sitwell, Edith
  Allen **6**:17
  Fuller **10**:116-17
  Jennings **5**:113
  Purdy **1**:300-301
  Wilson **5**:322
Sitwell, Osbert **6**:17
"6 Challis" **26**:224
6 Painters from Cornwall **23**:171
Six Poets of the San Francisco Renaissance **2**:269, 270
"6 x 6" **26**:226
Sixties **7**:179
Sixty-eight Publishers **1**:340, 348
63: Dream Palace **1**:300-302
Sjoblom, Jorma **1**:301
Skelton at Sixty **5**:293
Skelton, Robin **5:279-95**
  Kinsella **7**:101
Sketches for a New Mexico Hill Town **5**:351, 352
Sketches of Lewis Turco and Livevil: A Mask, The **22**:236
Sketches of the Valley See *Estampas del valle*
Skidmore College
  Blaise **3**:28
  Delbanco **2**:159
  Morgan **3**:234
Skiing **18**:145-47
Skin Meat Bones **17**:289

Skinner, Knute **21**:139
Skinner, Walter Jay **5**:99
Škvorecký, Josef 1:325-52
  Hrabal **12**:191
Škvorecký, Zdena
  Hrabal **12**:191
  Škvorecký **1**:338
Skylark Press **19**:149
Slade, Bernard 9:237-56
Sladek, John
  Disch **4**:150-51, 152
  Tennant **9**:291
Slagle, David **5**:349
Slansky, Rudolf **1**:336
Slashed to Ribbons in Defense of Love
  13:233
Slater, Don **17**:66-67
Slater, Joseph Locke **1**:132
Slaughterhouse-Five **9**:111
Slavery **13**:85
Slavitt, David R. 3:311-25
Sleep of Prisoners, A **23**:78
Sleep Watch **23**:308
Sleepers in Moon-Crowned Valleys
  1:303
Sleeping Beauty, The (Hayden
  Carruth) **6**:118-19
"Sleeping Over" **26**:325
Sleepwalker's Guide to San Francisco,
  A **26**:239-40
Slepyan, Norbert **9**:307
Slezak, Walter **1**:178, 179, 183
Slippery Rock State College **11**:323
Sloan, Stephen **2**:174
Sloane, William
  Ciardi **2**:90
  Kumin **8**:215
Slocum, Joshua **3**:94
Slow Fuse, A **2**:449-50
Slow Transparency **23**:131
Small Changes **1**:272, 274, 276
Small Desperation, A **1**:30
Small Perfect Things **14**:136
Small presses
  Argüelles **24**:16-17, 19-20, 23, 25-
    27
  Arnold **25**:46-47
  Bennett **25**:74
  Berry **24**:72-73, 77, 79-80
  Polkinhorn **25**:335
Small Rain **2**:156
Smallbone Deceased **15**:192, 193, 194
Smalls, Robert **17**:127-28
Smallwood, Norah **6**:70, 71, 72
Smart as the Devil **13**:224-25
Smart, Christopher **5**:195
Smart Set **7**:91
Smile in His Lifetime, A **17**:63, 65,
  69, 71
Smiles on Washington Square **8**:75
Smith, A.J.M. **6**:277, 279
Smith, Annette **6**:147
Smith College
  Grumbach **2**:209
  Kazin **7**:94, 95
  Thomas **19**:351

Wellek **7**:218
Smith, Dave 7:155-69
  Heyen **9**:41
Smith, D.V. **6**:180
Smith, Egerton **2**:380
Smith, Evelyn **3**:137-38, 139
Smith, Fuller d'Arch (publishers)
  2:54, 59
Smith, Harry **9**:66-67
Smith, Joseph **5**:36, 38, 40, 41
Smith, Martin Seymour **6**:44
Smith, Raymond
  Phillips **13**:211
  Weiss **2**:449
Smith, Roger **12**:206
Smith, Stevie
  Abse **1**:29
  Levine **23**:170
  Wright **5**:370, 371
Smith, Warren **3**:403
Smith, William Jay
  Howes **3**:140-41, 142, 145
  Taylor **7**:182
Smithereened Apart **11**:153
Smiths, W.H. **5**:181
Smoke from the Fires **20**:71
Smoke's Way **3**:329
Smoking Mountain, The **1**:120
Snakes **21**:31-34
Snaps **17**:9-10, 11
Snath **2**:57
Snodgrass, W.D.
  Allen **11**:11-12
  Jerome **8**:133
  Katz **14**:166
  Kennedy **9**:83, 84
  Morris **13**:165
Snow, Carmel **1**:313
Snow, C.P. **9**:13
Snow, Edgar **15**:324
Snow Leopard, The **24**:320
Snow White and the Seven Dwarfs
  Atkins **16**:6
  Rechy **4**:260
Snyder, Gary
  Beltrametti **13**:61, 62
  Bergé **10**:11
  Corman **2**:140, 141
  Enslin **3**:93
  Eshleman **6**:135, 137, 142
  Holden **22**:65
  Kherdian **2**:269
  Kyger **16**:191, 192, 193, 194-95,
    196
Snyder, Richard **19**:334-35
Sobrevivo **15**:12
Soccer
  Brown **6**:64-65
  Glanville **9**:16, 19
Social work
  Rakosi **5**:205-06, 207
  Vizenor **22**:255-57, 259-60, 271,
    272
Socialism
  Barrio **15**:112
  Caute **4**:101, 102, 105

Davie **3**:42
Fast **18**:171-72, 174-75
Gray **2**:191-92
Lind **4**:195, 197, 201
Miller **15**:290-91
Shadbolt **3**:249
Voinovich **12**:306
White **4**:347
Socialists **3**:254
Socialized medicine **4**:86-87, 92
Society for Creative Anachronism
  2:44-45
Society for the Prevention of Cruelty to
  Animals, The **1**:330-31
Society of Authors, London
  Aldiss **2**:30
  Wallace **1**:402
Society of St. Sulpice **1**:240
Sociobiology: The New Synthesis
  Van Proyen **25**:394
  Wilson **16**:302-03
Sociological Imagination, The **8**:185
Soft Press **13**:293, 294
Soho, London, England **5**:359, 367,
  373
Solano Beach, Calif. **1**:367
Solarians, The **19**:318
Solaris **1**:260, 261, 262, 263
Soldier Erect, A **2**:19, 29
Soldier of Arete **9**:309
Soldier of Humour, A **6**:24
Soldier of the Mist **9**:309
Soldiers of Darkness **19**:295
Soleil sous la mort, Le (The sun under
  death) **13**:185
Solidarity movement **10**:277
"Solipsism" **26**:220
Sölle, Dorothy **1**:53
Solotaroff, Ted 2:391-403
  Dennison **6**:121, 122
  Markfield **3**:219
  Settle **1**:320
  Smith **7**:165
Solstice **24**:74
Solt, Mary Ellen **6**:131
Sombra del caudillo, La **18**:76
Some Angry Angel **1**:196
Some Came Running **7**:141
Some Cows, Poems of Civilization and
  Domestic Life **5**:163-64
Some Deaths in the Delta **10**:41
Some Dreams Are Nightmares **2**:251,
  258
Some Haystacks Don't Even Have Any
  Needle **5**:351
Some Observations of a Stranger at Zuni
  in the Latter Part of the
  Century **6**:200
some recent snowflakes (and other
  things) **8**:92
Some Tales of La Fontaine **3**:306
Some Time **2**:140
Some Unease and Angels **1**:223
Some Women **26**:289
Somehow We Survive **21**:174
"Someone Else" **22**:208-10

Somer, John   **9**:113
Somerset Maugham Award   **5**:111-12
Something about a Soldier   **3**:123
Something Else Newsletter   **8**:89, 90, 91
Something Else Press   **8**:83, 88-90, 92
Something Happened Here   **23**:174, 176, 177-80
Sometimes I Call Myself Childhood / A veces me llamo infancia   **25**:104, 110
Sometimes I Live in the Country   **1**:135-36
Sometimes I Think of Moving   **15**:159-60
Sommer, Piotr   **6**:201
Son from Sleep, A   **23**:119, 131
Son of Man   **3**:281
Song of Roland, The   **3**:306
Song of the Sky: An Exploration of the Ocean of Air   **19**:247
Songs   **24**:270
Songs for a Son   **8**:242, 247
Songs for Certain Children   **12**:52
Songs from the Stars   **19**:332
Songs in Ancient Greek   **21**:271
Songs of a Blackbird   **13**:248
"Songs of Innocence and Experience"   **2**:328
Songs to a Phantom Nightingale   **23**:199-200
Songs w / out Notes   **3**:98
Sonik Horses (band)   **19**:12, 47
"Sonnet: Auspices"   **26**:89
Sonnets of Giuseppe Belli   **20**:335
Sono Nis Press   **5**:290
Sons and Fathers   **5**:84
Sons and Lovers   **7**:222
Sons of Darkness, Sons of Light   **3**:430, 431
Sontag, David   **7**:200
Sontag, Susan
　Heyen   **9**:43
　Highwater   **7**:78, 79
Soong Sisters, The   **11**:113-14, 115
"Sophie" series   **2**:184
Sorbonne, University of Paris
　Barnstone   **15**:64, 68-69
　Brée   **15**:132, 134
　Kennedy   **9**:82
　Knebel   **3**:168
　Livesay   **8**:231-32
　Menashe   **11**:226-27, 228
　Morgan   **4**:226
　O'Faolain   **2**:346, 347
Sorcerer's Apprentice, The   **18**:241
Sorrentino, Gilbert   **9**:113
Sosa, Roberto   **3**:81
Soul Clap Its Hands and Sing   **12**:243, 248
Soul of Wood   **4**:202
Soul on Ice   **16**:84
Sound and the Fury, The
　Charyn   **1**:179
　Forrest   **7**:23

Sounder   **6**:155
Sounding Brass   **1**:390
"Sounds of the Celestial Screw"   **24**:65
Sourd dans la Ville, Le   **4**:78
Souster, Raymond   14:303-19
　Colombo   **22**:37
　Dudek   **14**:132
　Sparshott   **15**:357
South Africa
　Brutus   **14**:55-64
　Cassity   **8**:48-55, 58, 59
　Killens   **2**:299
　Plumpp   **21**:175-77
　Wright   **5**:370
South America   **11**:118
South Sea Journey   **6**:325
Southam, Brian   **3**:46
Southampton University   **15**:188
Southern Christian Leadership Conference   **23**:255-56
Southern Cross, The   **7**:295, 298
Southern Delights   **7**:166
Southern Fried   **19**:128, 129, 130
Southern Fried Plus Six   **19**:128
Southern Illinois University
　Johnson   **18**:230-31, 235-36, 237-38
　Smith   **7**:162
Southern States
　Blaise   **3**:21, 23-24
　Cassity   **8**:38-39, 43
　Howes   **3**:137-39
　Jones   **11**:171-86
Southern Tenant Farmers Union   **3**:137
Southern University and A&M College   **20**:22-23, 25, 28-30
Southern University in New Orleans   **21**:194
Southern Writing in the Sixties: Fiction   **20**:329
Southern Writing in the Sixties: Poetry
　Taylor   **7**:181
　Williams   **20**:329
Southport Bugle   **1**:376
Southwest Minnesota State College
　See Southwest State University
Southwest State University   **17**:28
Southwestern Bell Telephone Co.   **2**:170
Southwick, Marcia   **23**:192
Soviet literature   **10**:325
Soviet Union
　Caute   **4**:107
　Davie   **3**:42
　Horwood   **15**:252
　Sargent   **18**:345
　Voinovich   **12**:303-22
　Zinoviev   **10**:323-38
　See also Russia
Soviet Writers Union   **12**:322
Sow's Head and Other Poems, The   **8**:242, 244, 247
Soyinka, Wole   **5**:260
Space for Hire   **16**:217

Space Merchants, The   **1**:290, 291
Space Science Fiction   **14**:67
Space, Time, and Nathaniel   **2**:22
Spaces Between Birds: Mother / Daughter Poems, 1967–1995, The   **23**:224, 225
Spackman, Peter   **12**:206
Spain
　Bishop   **26**:13-15
　Brossard   **2**:70
　Burke   **19**:69-72
　Cela   **10**:47, 49
　Nichols   **2**:327
　Raworth   **11**:303
　Thomas   **4**:309
　White   **4**:345-46
　Williams   **3**:424
Spain, Nancy   **5**:323
Spain, Take This Cup from Me   **6**:144
Spanish Civil War
　Abse   **1**:18
　Davis   **20**:111-12
　Kerrigan   **11**:204-05
　Mott   **7**:114
　Nichols   **2**:309
　Schevill   **12**:267
　Woodcock   **6**:319
Spanish Doctor, The   **18**:86
Spanish Scene, The   **2**:70
Sparrow, John   **7**:274
Sparrow 13   **26**:307, 308
Sparshott, Francis   15:347-63
Spartacus
　Disch   **4**:148
　Fast   **18**:183, 184
Spatola, Adriano   **13**:64, 65, 70
Speak, Memory   **4**:51
Spears, Monroe
　Jones   **11**:177
　Tillinghast   **23**:306
Special Occasions   **9**:252, 253-54
Special Time, A   **8**:184
Species of Abandoned Light   **24**:65, 75, 77, 79
Spectator
　Sisson   **3**:304
　White   **4**:343
Spectator Bird, The   **9**:269
Speech and Language Development of the Preschool Child   **21**:135
Speech dysfunctions
　Gunn   **2**:242
　Kazin   **7**:87
　Wilhelm   **5**:298, 299
Speech pathology   **21**:133-34
Spell for Green Corn, A   **6**:72
Spellbound: Growing Up in God's Country   **14**:205-06, 208-10, 213
Spells & Blessings   **26**:31
Spence School   **2**:189, 190
Spencer, Bernard   **26**:273, 277-78, 280
Spencer, Elizabeth   **13**:213
Spender, Stephen
　Abse   **1**:18
　Barnstone   **15**:75, 76, 77

Ciardi **2**:90
Heyen **9**:46
Kostelanetz **8**:194
Menashe **11**:235
Taylor **7**:180
Sphinx and the Sybarites, The **18**:305
Spicer, Jack
di Suvero **26**:70
Kyger **16**:190, 191, 192, 197
Wakoski **1**:360
Spiegel, Blaine **26**:224
Spiegel, Sam **5**:276
Spielberg, Peter
Baumbach **5**:26
Sukenick **8**:293
Spielberg, Steven **25**:206
Spies, Claudio **3**:87
Spillane, Mickey **7**:6
Spinetti, Victor **20**:228, 229, 230
Spinrad, Norman 19:311-40
Pohl **1**:290
Spirit Bodies **14**:215-16
Spirit of British Administration, with
Some European Comparisons,
The **3**:304
Spirit of the Seas **13**:152
Spirit Spirit **8**:119
Spirits **14**:13, 14
Spirituality
Leftwich **25**:274
Nelson **23**:265
Splinter in the Heart, A **17**:211
Split Second **1**:383
Split Shift **24**:147
Spoil of the Flowers, The **2**:210
Spoiled **3**:114
Spokane, Wash. **5**:139-40
Spontaneous Combustion **2**:361
Spoon **1**:180
Sport (Clark Blaise) **3**:19-20
Sport (London) **9**:20
Sporty Creek: A Novel about an
Appalachian Boyhood **17**:234
Spratt, Jack **25**:234-35
Spread, The **4**:213
Spriggs, Ed **6**:188
"Spring" **26**:136
Spring Again **15**:161
Spring Hill School for the Deaf,
Northampton, England **5**:362-64
Spring Journal: Poems **8**:117
"Sproul Hall Sit-In, The" **26**:297
Spyker, John Howland (pseudonym)
See Elman, Richard
Square Emerald, The **3**:52
Square Pegs, The **1**:386-87
Square Root of In, The **24**:127
Squares of the City, The **8**:9
Squires, Radcliffe **9**:283
Sri Lanka
Bowles **1**:88, 89, 91
Morgan **3**:240
See also Ceylon
Stadtfeld, Curtis **9**:93
Stafford, William 3:327-41
Heyen **9**:32

Holden **22**:67
McPherson **23**:226
Shapiro **6**:307
Sward **13**:293
Stagg and His Mother **18**:305
Staircase in Surrey, A **3**:348, 356
Stalag 17 **1**:194
Stalin, Joseph
Lind **4**:200
Pohl **1**:286
Simic **4**:272
Škvorecký **1**:336-38
Voinovich **12**:305, 306
Zinoviev **10**:325, 326, 328, 329
Stalinism
Kizer **5**:149-50
Solotaroff **2**:393
Zinoviev **10**:328
Stand **5**:251, 261
Stand on Zanzibar **8**:1, 11
Stanford, Ann **13**:315
Stanford University
Baumbach **5**:23
Broughton **12**:48
Connell **2**:107
Coppel **9**:7
Dacey **17**:24, 26
Davie **3**:43, 47
Easton **14**:144
Elman **3**:74, 76, 82
Guerard **2**:220, 222, 228
Hall **7**:64
Hebert **24**:250
Higgins **5**:92-93, 97, 99
Houston **16**:158
Lelchuk **20**:243, 244, 246-47
Pinsky **4**:244, 245-47
Rachlin **17**:228
Root **11**:324
Rule **18**:311
Shapiro **23**:290, 294
Stegner **9**:266-69
Stapledon, Olaf
Anderson **2**:46
Silverberg **3**:271, 272, 274
Star Bridge
Gunn **2**:248, 250
Williamson **8**:322
Star Conquerors, The **18**:51
Star Diaries, The **1**:264
Star Peace **21**:271
Star Science Fiction #4 **2**:253
Star Trek
Niven **12**:220
Pohl **1**:295
Star Wars **1**:292
Starcrossed, The **18**:56
Starhiker **20**:81, 95
Stark Electric Jesus **14**:92-93
Stark, Irwin **19**:315
Stark, Richard (pseudonym of Donald
E. Westlake) **13**:341-42
Starkey, Jack **7**:6, 18
Stars and Stripes **6**:297, 298
Start in Life, A **2**:387
Starting **20**:358

Starting from Troy **23**:131-32
Starting Out in the Thirties
Kazin **7**:88, 89, 90
Markfield **3**:220
Starting Over **7**:200
Startling Stories **2**:37
State and Revolution **10**:113
State University College at
Fredonia **20**:23
State University of New York at
Albany **10**:252-53
State University of New York at
Binghamton
Ai **13**:10
Burroway **6**:94
Dann **20**:89, 93
Peacock **21**:163
Sargent **18**:338-39
Smith **7**:165
Westlake **13**:339
See also Binghamton University
State University of New York at
Brockport **9**:39, 42, 45
State University of New York at
Buffalo
Federman **8**:79
Kerrigan **11**:196
Mott **7**:130
Raffel **9**:216
Tarn **16**:280
Wakoski **1**:364
Williams **12**:353
State University of New York at
Cortland **9**:40, 45
State University of New York at
Stony Brook
Johnson **18**:239
Kazin **7**:95
Raffel **9**:215-16
Simpson **4**:295, 296
statements **14**:42, 43, 45
Station in Space **2**:251, 252, 253,
258
Statue of Liberty **5**:361
Stature of Man, The **5**:324
Stauffacher, Jack **26**:71
Stauffer, Donald **24**:232
Stead **2**:138
Stealer of Souls, The **5**:177, 179
Stealing the Language **24**:272-73
Steele, Max
Connell **2**:107, 108, 109
Settle **1**:316
Steerforth Press **20**:255
Stegner, Wallace 9:257-71
Baumbach **5**:23
Connell **2**:107
Coppel **9**:4
Gerber **20**:168-72, 175
Houston **16**:168
Kammen **23**:146, 148-49
Rule **18**:311
Stein, Chuck **19**:200
Stein, Gertrude
Bernstein **24**:42-43
Bowles **1**:83, 84

Foley   **24**:168
Hiemstra   **26**:155-56
Kerrigan   **11**:199
Kizer   **5**:146
Waldman   **17**:273, 276
Weiss   **2**:439
Stein, Maurice   **6**:143
Steinbeck, John
Dillard   **7**:11
Houston   **16**:158
Owens   **24**:295
Steiner, George
Purdy   **1**:303
Wesker   **7**:233-34
Stendahl, Earl   **3**:371-72
Stendhal
Creeley   **10**:67
Wallace   **1**:387
Stenger, Harold L., Jr.   **1**:129-30
Stephan, Ruth Walgren
Hauser   **11**:136
Wilson   **5**:349
Stephen Leacock Memorial Medal
7:107, 110
Stephens College   **22**:68-70
Stephens, Edward   **9**:83
Stephens, Michael
Codrescu   **19**:89
Katz   **14**:176
Stepinac Case, The   **2**:412
Steps   **9**:112, 115
Steps Going Down   **17**:72
Steps of the Sun   **11**:113
Steps to Break the Circle   **21**:173
Stepsons of Terra   **3**:276
Sterile Cuckoo, The   **2**:328, 329, 330,
331, 332, 333
Sterling, Robert   **9**:182
Stern, Gerald   **24**:212
Sterne, Laurence
Booth   **5**:46
Sukenick   **8**:284, 287
Stettheimer, Ettie   **14**:253
Stevens Institute of Technology
17:287-88
Stevens, Shane   **8**:215
Stevens, Wallace
Allen   **11**:18
Djerassi   **26**:88-90, 93
Feinstein   **1**:221
Gregor   **10**:148, 149
Highwater   **7**:80-81
Honig   **8**:113-15
Kennedy   **9**:76, 80
Sukenick   **8**:286-87
Symons   **3**:385
Weiss   **2**:446
Whittemore   **8**:306
Stevenson, Anne   9:273-88
Stevenson, Charles L.   **9**:273-75, 276,
277, 278, 279, 281, 283, 284,
286
Stevenson, Robert Louis
Brown   **6**:45
Glanville   **9**:17
Hitchcock   **12**:179

Mott   **7**:116
Wain   **4**:323
Steward, Pearl Bank   **1**:377
Stewart, Ellen   **2**:413, 415, 418, 419
Stewart, James   **4**:146
Stewart, J.I.M.   3:343-60
Sticks & Stones   **16**:28
Stieglitz, Alfred   **1**:104, 109, 110
Still, James   17:231-48
Miller   **15**:288, 291
Stillman, Alvin   **26**:306
Stillness   **2**:156
Stills   **11**:153
Stirring Science Stories   **10**:205
Stochastic Man, The   **3**:283
Stockfleth, Craig   **24**:24, 25
Stockhausen, Karlheinz   **7**:81
Stockholm, Sweden   **1**:390, 392
Stockwell, Dean   **11**:285
Stoehr, Taylor   **6**:119
Stoic, The   **2**:265
Stoke-on-Trent, England   **4**:316-17,
321-22, 325
Stokesberry, Jack Elmo   **9**:79
Stolen Paper Press   **26**:76
Stolen Stories   **14**:176, 177
Stolper, Wolfgang   **9**:279
Stoltenberg, John   **21**:17, 18
Stoltzfus, Ben   **8**:244
Stone, A Leaf, A Door, A   **22**:273-74
Stone, I.F.
Hentoff   **6**:171
Sanders   **21**:260
Stone, Irving   3:361-80
Wesker   **7**:236
Stone, Lawrence   **4**:104
Stone, Nancy   **4**:123
Stone, Oliver   **21**:89
Stone Roses   **5**:355
Stonecutter's Hand, The   **23**:317
Stones of the House, The   **2**:94
Stopping by Home   **20**:179
Stories of a Tenor Saxophonist, The
1:339, 351
Stories That Could Be True   **3**:328,
329, 331, 332, 336
Stork, Gilbert   **26**:95
Storm and Other Poems, The (George
Mackay Brown)   **6**:70
Storm and Other Poems, The (William
Pitt Root)   **11**:324
Storm and Other Things, The   **7**:298
Storm of Fortune   **16**:80
Storm Warning   **5**:57
Stormbringer   **5**:177, 179
Stormqueen   **10**:25
Storms and Screams   **15**:359
Stormy Encounter   **11**:101, 105
Story
Fast   **18**:176
Hall   **12**:129, 131-32
Story Line Press   **22**:103
Story of Flight, The   **1**:318
Story of Philosophy   **11**:320
Storytelling   **26**:252-53
Storytelling and Other Poems   **25**:3-4

Storytelling See also Native American
storytelling
Stovall, Floyd   **7**:11
Strachey, Lytton
Brown   **6**:73
Morgan   **4**:234
Strachey, Marjorie   **5**:141
Strand, Mark
Baumbach   **5**:27
Wright   **7**:297
*Strange Bedfellows: The State and the
Arts in Canada*   **6**:323
Strange Interlude   **4**:146
Strange Marriage   **17**:67
Stranger Suns   **19**:374
Strangers   **5**:129
Strangers and Journeys   **3**:257, 259,
261, 264, 265
Strangers in the House   **7**:46
Strauss, Richard   **12**:275
StrayngeBook, A   **25**:191
Streamers   **23**:220
*Street: An Autobiographical Novel,
The*   **5**:217, 218
Street Games   **10**:41
Street, James, Jr.   **6**:57
"Street Night"   **26**:299
Street of Crocodiles, The   **2**:72
Street, The   **6**:253, 265-66
Streetly, F.J.F.   **18**:7-8, 9
Streets of Conflict   **18**:22
Strempek, Bernard   **11**:15
Strength to Dream, The   **5**:324
Strickland, Linda   **24**:20
Striking the Dark Air for Music
11:324
Strindberg, August
Highwater   **7**:80
Wallace   **1**:391
White   **4**:333
Wilson   **5**:325
String Game, The   **2**:359, 360, 361
String Horses   **8**:103
String Too Short to Be Saved   **7**:65
Strong Brown God, The   **4**:233
Strong Man, The   **8**:173
*Strong Measures: Contemporary
American Poetry in Traditional
Forms*   **17**:29-30
Structure of Aesthetics, The   **15**:360
Struwwelpeter   **8**:167
Stryker, Richard   **18**:283-84
Stuart, Jesse   **9**:40
Stubborn Hope   **14**:56, 57, 60
Stubbs, Harry C. See Clement, Hal
Student activism   **3**:43
Students for a Democratic Society
Armantrout   **25**:17
Piercy   **1**:273, 274
Pinsky   **4**:246
Studies in Bibliography   **7**:12
Studies in the Short Story   **3**:202
Studio   **2**:76
Study of History, A   **5**:325
Studying the Ground for Holes   **13**:25
Sturgeon, Theodore

Gunn **2**:248, 249
  Knight **10**:211, 217
  Pohl **1**:290
Sturgill, Virgil **15**:274, 278, 287, 290
Styron, William
  Chappell **4**:114, 115, 116
  Clarke **16**:83, 84
Suares, Carlo **14**:246, 251
Sublime, The **22**:76
Substance abuse
  Allman **15**:25
  Garrett **5**:75-76
  See also Drug use
Such Men Are Dangerous **11**:35
Such Was the Season **6**:197
Suck-Egg Mule: A Recalcitrant Beast **14**:111-12
Sudden Star, The **18**:341
Suden, Richard Tum **14**:173
Sugar Mother, The **13**:106, 109
Suicide
  Honig **8**:121
  Shapiro **6**:290
Suicide's Wife, The **3**:199
Suite of Love, Anguish, and Solitude **15**:7
Suits for the Dead **3**:318
Sukenick, Ronald 8:283-95
  Anaya **4**:26
  Federman **8**:80
  Klinkowitz **9**:108, 112, 113, 115, 116, 119
  Major **6**:193
Sulfur **6**:146, 148
Sullivan, Eleanor **15**:197
Sullivan, J.W.N. **5**:328
Summa technologiae **1**:263
Summer Dreams and the Klieg Light Gas Company **7**:107
Summer Fury **12**:51
Summer Love and Surf **18**:27, 37
Summers, Hollis **9**:41
Summing Up, The **1**:375
Sumsion, John **4**:88
Sun Cat **26**:157
Sun Exercises **20**:66-67
Sun Fetcher, The **20**:67-68
Sun, He Dies, The **7**:82
Sun Rock Man **2**:140
Sun Valley, Calif. **25**:383
Sunday Gentleman, The **1**:395
"Sunday Morning" **11**:18
Sunday Times (London)
  Ashby **6**:43
  Caute **4**:108
  Glanville **9**:26
  Mott **7**:129
  Oakes **25**:311-12, 313
  Wilson **5**:321, 322
  Wright **5**:367, 368
sunday work(?) **19**:20, 21, 50
"Sundog Society, The" **7**:110
Sunrise North **15**:153, 158, 159
Sunset Freeway **2**:421
Sunspacer **19**:381

Super, R.H. **4**:247
Supreme Doctrine, The **2**:416
Surfaces and Masks **6**:200
Surly Sullen Bell, The **9**:100, 103
Surrealism
  Argüelles **24**:20
  Joans **25**:237
  Roditi **14**:246-47, 256-57
  Schwartz **26**:238-42, 244, 246-47
  Valaoritis **26**:270, 273-76, 281, 284, 285, 290
Surry Players **2**:116
Survey **19**:217
Survival in Auschwitz **24**:358
Survivors (Frederick Feirstein) **11**:76, 83, 84
Survivors, The (Elaine Feinstein) **1**:223
Susann, Jacqueline **3**:322
Sussex, England **2**:126-27
Sussex University **6**:98
Sutherland, Betty **14**:128
Sutherland, Efua **2**:303
Sutherland, John
  Dudek **14**:127-28
  Souster **14**:310, 312, 315
  Turnbull **14**:333, 335
Sutphen Music School **16**:16, 17
Sutter, John **4**:245
Sutton, Henry (pseudonym) See David R. Slavitt
Sutton, Walter **11**:10
Suzuki, D.T. **2**:416
Sváb, Ludvik **1**:339
Svayamvara and Other Poems **9**:146
Švec **1**:336-38
Svejk **1**:340-341
Svevo, Italo **3**:218
Swallow the Lake **6**:185, 187
Swan Lake **4**:148
Swanberg, W.A. 13:259-77
  Barrio **15**:124
Swanny's Ways **14**:180
Swanwick, Michael **20**:90, 92
Sward, Robert 13:279-306
Swarthmore College **9**:233
Swastika Poems, The **9**:42-44
Sweden
  McCord **9**:184
  Skelton **5**:293
  Transtömer **17**:249-65
Swedenborg, Emanuel
  Foley **24**:178
  Whittemore **8**:302
Sweeney, Francis **5**:97
Sweet Bird of Youth
  Bowles **1**:92
  Cassity **8**:43
Sweet Briar College **1**:310-11
Sweet Flypaper of Life, The **21**:183
Sweet William **9**:255
Sweetsir **20**:358
Swell Season, The **1**:330
Swenson, Karen 13:307-17
Swift, James **5**:370
Swift, Joan **23**:225-26

Swift, Jonathan **8**:122
Swift, Patrick
  Sisson **3**:301, 302
  Wright **5**:370, 371, 372, 374
Swift, Peg **5**:167-68, 171
Swinburne, Algernon Charles **8**:241, 244-45
Swing in the Garden, The **17**:78, 89, 91
Switzerland
  Polkinhorn **25**:332-35
  Schevill **12**:273-74
Symbolic History **12**:26-27, 28, 29, 31, 39
"Symbols" **26**:328
Symons, A.J.A. **3**:382-83, 391
Symons, Julian 3:381-96
  Fuller **10**:112, 120, 123, 124, 127
Symptoms & Madness **6**:185
Synanon (organization) **25**:328
Synapse Corp. **4**:250
Synge, John Millington **5**:285-86
Synthesis **3**:94, 95
Syracuse Herald-Journal **3**:422
Syracuse, N.Y. **3**:416-19, 422
Syracuse Post Standard **3**:422
Syracuse University
  Allen **11**:8-9, 10-11
  Allman **15**:23-24
  Bell **14**:41-42
  Elman **3**:72-73
  Levis **23**:191
  Lifshin **10**:234, 246-49
  Malzberg **4**:206, 207, 208, 209, 211
  Phillips **13**:199-202
  Williams **3**:417, 420-22, 431
Syzathmary, Arthur **2**:448-49
Sze, Fred **5**:150
Szegedy-Makas, Mihaly **5**:198-99
Szilard, Leo **1**:272

Ta Nea Grammata **26**:270-72, 275
Taft, Robert **9**:98
Taft School **3**:313
Taggard, Genevieve **3**:137
Taine, John **3**:271
Taizé Community **11**:48, 57
Taj, Imtiaz Ali **9**:225
Take Five **6**:210, 215, 216, 218
Take It or Leave It **8**:73, 75, 76
Take Me Back **14**:11-12
Take Off the Masks **11**:57
"Taking of Miss Janie, The" **16**:67
Tal Tal, Chile **3**:186
Tale of Asa Bean, The **15**:264
Tale of Pierrot, A **6**:122
Tale of Psyche, A **24**:126
Tale of Two Cities, A **6**:263
Talent for Living, A **1**:196
Tales of Arthur, The **7**:236
Tales of Beatnik Glory **21**:257, 259, 260, 263, 264, 268-69, 270-71
Tales of Idiots, The **7**:124, 127
Tales of Mean Streets **2**:384
Tales of the Labrador Indians **15**:251

Talisman **26**:127-28
Talisman House (publishers) **26**:128, 129
Talisman Press **3**:335
"Talking of Books" **6**:23
Talking Room, The **11**:136-37
Tallents, Martin **5**:291
Tallman, Warren **19**:27, 54
Talmud **4**:358-59
Tamarack Review **22**:36, 52
Tamayo, Rufino **24**:99-100
Tambimuttu, Thurairajah
  Davie **3**:36
  Wright **5**:366-67, 368, 369
T&T **1**:167
Tangents (magazine) **17**:67
Tangier, Morocco
  Bowles **1**:83-84, 87-88, 90, 91, 92, 93, 94
  Morgan **4**:232, 233
Tangled Vines **10**:257
Tank Corps, The **1**:339-41
Tanka **4**:183
Tanner, Tony **1**:303
Taos: A Deluxe Magazine of the Arts **14**:111
Taos, N.M.
  Crews **14**:109-10
  Nichols **2**:333-34
Tapestry and The Web, The **16**:190, 196
Tar Baby **16**:84
Tarcov, Edith **24**:16
Targets **5**:349
Tarlin, Bert **2**:135
Tarn, Jeremy **14**:179
Tarn, Nathaniel 16:271-89
Tarnower, Jain **24**:140, 145
Tarr **3**:385
Tarzan Adventures (magazine) **5**:177
Tate, Allen
  Ghiselin **10**:136-37, 142
  Hauser **11**:134
  Kazin **7**:92
  Kostelanetz **8**:185
  Olson **12**:233
  Root **11**:323
  Whittemore **8**:307, 308, 310
Tate, James **7**:298-99
Tattooed Heart of the Drunken Sailor **24**:5, 7, 22-23
Taxi Driver **3**:77, 83
Taylor, Carl N. **9**:157
Taylor, Elizabeth **3**:322
Taylor, Frances Carney **7**:19
Taylor, Frank **3**:127
Taylor, Henry 7:171-89
  Dillard **7**:14-15
  Garrett **5**:75
Taylor, James **8**:141
Taylor, Lillie Hill **2**:281
Taylor, Peter
  Chappell **4**:118, 120, 125
  Root **11**:322
  Shreve **5**:237
  Wagoner **3**:403

Taylor, Robert W. **16**:296, 300
Taylor, Telford **24**:8, 10
Taylor, Thomas Lowe 26:249-61
  Ferrini **24**:134-36, 139
  Leftwich **25**:261, 276-77, 278-82
Taylor, W.C. **7**:3
Tazewell, William **1**:321-22
Te Kooti **3**:250
"Teach Yourself" series **5**:284
Teachers Union **2**:207
Teaching
  Beltrametti **13**:63
  Bergé **10**:10-11
  Booth **5**:35
  Bryant **26**:56
  Chappell **4**:118-19
  Creeley **10**:69-70
  Feirstein **11**:82
  Fisher **10**:95-96, 97
  Gunn **2**:233
  Hazo **11**:145-46
  Levis **23**:191
  Madgett **23**:202-03
  McPherson **23**:226, 231
  Thomas **11**:372-73
  Villanueva **24**:322-23
Teatro Campesino (artistic movement) **4**:25
Teatro degli Arte **2**:416
Technology and Culture **14**:135
Teepee Tales of the American Indians **6**:58
Teichmann, Howard **6**:90
Teilhard de Chardin, Pierre
  Berrigan **1**:58
  Greeley **7**:43
Teilhet, Darwin **9**:9
Teitlebaum's Window **3**:221, 223
Tel Aviv, Israel
  Eastlake **1**:209
  Megged **13**:143-44, 153
Tel Aviv University **19**:221
Telegram (Newfoundland, Canada) **15**:245, 246
Telephone Spotlight on Missouri **2**:170
Telephone Spotlight on Texas **2**:170
Telepower **10**:174
Television scriptwriting
  Gray **3**:110-13, 239-40
  Johnson **18**:239-40
  Nolan **16**:213, 217-18, 219-20, 222-23
  Slade **9**:242-43, 244-45
  Wakefield **7**:200-01
"Tell-Tale Heart, The" **7**:28
Telling of the North Star **24**:129
Telluride Association **8**:288
Tempest in the Tropics **11**:104
Tempest, The
  Broughton **12**:45-47
  Van Itallie **2**:421
Temple **9**:149
Temple Dogs **2**:168, 174, 175
Temple, John **22**:14
Temple University
  Bova **18**:49

Feirstein **11**:82
Lifshin **10**:241, 247
Olson **11**:258
Slavitt **3**:322
Templeton, Rini **2**:334
Ten: Anthology of Detroit Poets **23**:207
Ten Interiors with Various Figures **10**:98
Ten Ways of Looking at a Bird **8**:91, 92
Ten Years in the Making **26**:21
Tenant of San Mateo, The **11**:100, 102
Tender Mercies **10**:41
Tennant, Emma 9:289-95
Tennessee
  Tillinghast **23**:302, 303-04, 306
  Wright **7**:290, 291
Tennessee Medical Association **21**:30-34
Tennis **17**:166-67, 168-70, 174
Tennyson, Alfred, Lord **7**:240
10th Street Coffee House, New York City
  Bergé **10**:5-6
  Wakoski **1**:362
Teraphim **25**:327, 331, 334
Terkel, Studs **7**:142
Terminal Velocities **24**:27
Terrell, Robert H., Law School **2**:287
Terrible Secret: An Investigation into the Suppression of Information about Hitler's "Final Solution," The **19**:223
Terrorism **2**:174-75
Test, The **26**:56
Testament **12**:41
Tesuque Poems **26**:81
Tet Offensive
  Clark **22**:21
  Heinemann **21**:87-89
Tête Blanche **4**:72-73
Teter, Holbrook **11**:306, 307
Têtes de Pioche, Les **16**:49
Teth **26**:226
Tevis, Walter **9**:41
Texas
  Furman **18**:202-03
  Gibbons **24**:185
  Hinojosa-Smith **16**:139-41, 149-52
  Petesch **12**:247
  Rechy **4**:255, 257
  White **4**:349-50
  Wolfe **9**:300-01
Texas A&I University **16**:140
Texas A&M University **9**:301
TexT (publishers) **19**:337
Thackeray, William Makepeace
  Federman **8**:72
  Rakosi **5**:201
Thailand **13**:316
Thames & Hudson (publishers) **7**:129, 130
That Girl from Boston **10**:295, 296-97
"THAT" Goddess **24**:25, 26

That Golden Woman   3:322
That Only a Mother   1:289
That's My Baby   1:382
Thayer, David   26:152
Thayler, Carl   11:355-65
    Rosenblum   11:345, 348
Theater
    Aubert   20:28-30
    Eaton   20:123
    Feirstein   11:81-82, 83
    Ferrini   24:128-29
    Flanagan   17:50-51
    Fry   23:63-78
    Gurik   23:100, 102, 103-05, 108,
       109-10, 111, 112-13
    Heinemann   21:80
    Jacobsen   18:211-12
    Jennings   5:108-09
    Kennedy   20:219-36
    Malzberg   4:208
    Mano   6:208, 209
    Pownall   18:296, 299-303
    Salaam   21:204
    Simmons   21:289-90
    Slade   9:239-56
    Wellek   7:211
Theater for the New City, New York
    City
    Owens   2:366
    Van Itallie   2:418-19, 421
Theatre of Mixed Means, The   8:184
Theatre of the Double   24:129
*Their Finest Hours: Narratives of the
    RAF and Luftwaffe in World War
    II*   9:108, 120
Theme for Diverse Instruments   18:318
Theocritus: Idylls and Epigrams
    15:235
*Theodore Roethke: An American
    Romantic*   16:236
Theory of Comedy, The   12:235
Theory of Island Biogeography, The
    16:299
Theory of the Arts, The   15:361
There Are Doors   9:309
*There Is a Tree More Ancient than
    Eden*   7:32
*Thesaurus of English Words and
    Phrases*   3:136
These Our Mothers See *L'Amèr ou le
    Chapitre effrité*
These the Companions   3:32, 33, 35
They Ate   26:39
They Call It the Cariboo   5:289
Thibaudeau, Colleen   15:301-02, 303,
    304, 305, 308
Thief Who Couldn't Sleep, The   11:34
Thieves Carnival   2:411
Thing King, The   20:143
Thing of Sorrow   12:229
Things Stirring Together or Far Away
    23:22, 23, 46
Third Chicano Literary Prize   24:315
Third Kingdom, The   12:38, 39
Third Man, The   4:102

*Thirsting for Peace in a Raging
    Century: Selected Poems
    1961–1985*   21:262, 264, 270,
    271
Thirteen Clocks   11:162-63
Thirteenth Immortal, The   3:276
Thirties, The   3:391, 392
Thirty-first of February, The   3:389,
    390
Thirty-four East   9:5, 8
34th Street and other poems   25:103,
    104, 105-06, 110-11
31 New American Poets   5:351
This Boy's Life: A Memoir   22:279
This Day's Death   4:262
This Do   3:98
This Earth, My Brother   13:32, 37,
    38, 41
This Fortress World   2:248, 250
This Green Tide   10:113-14
This Is a Recording   2:121
This Is Dinosaur   9:268
This Is My Country Too   3:426
This Is Not for You   18:315-16
"This Is Poetry" (radio program)
    3:91
"This is what . . . "   26:328
This Is Which   3:93
This Month   12:202-04
This Promised Land   14:159
This Romance   25:46
This Romance (trilogy)   25:46
This School Is Driving Me Crazy
    6:170, 172
This Singing World   1:65
This Summer's Dolphin   3:261
*This Way for the Gas, Ladies and
    Gentlemen*   2:72
Thole, Karel   8:13
Thomas and Beulah   19:110
Thomas Aquinas, St.
    Mott   7:123
    Silverberg   3:272
Thomas, Audrey G.   19:341-59
Thomas, Caitlin   3:141
Thomas, D.M.   11:367-84
Thomas, Dylan
    Abse   1:21, 24, 29
    Bishop   26:15
    Broughton   12:54
    Dacey   17:22, 23
    di Suvero   26:69-70
    Ghiselin   10:139
    Howes   3:141
    Kerrigan   11:208
    Lifshin   10:247, 250, 255
    Nims   17:187-90, 193
    Olson   12:234
    Ray   7:140
    Roditi   14:259
    Shapiro   6:303
    Sinclair   5:272-73, 274
    Wagoner   3:403, 405
    Weiss   2:441
    Wright   5:367, 368
Thomas, Evan   3:180

Thomas Hardy: The Teller of Tales
    2:221
Thomas Jefferson College   10:10-11
Thomas Merton, Monk and Poet   6:326
Thomas, Norman
    Glazier   24:227
    Swanberg   13:273
Thomas, R.S.   4:301-13
Thomas, Theodore L.   10:223
Thomas, William David   5:288, 291
Thompson, D'Arcy   9:96
Thompson, Dunstan   1:313
Thompson, Mark   11:58, 59
Thompson, Randall   6:232
Thomson, Virgil
    Bowles   1:84, 86, 92
    Purdy   1:303
Thor, with Angels   23:71
Thoreau, Henry David
    Allen   6:25
    Enslin   3:88, 94
    Heyen   9:31
    Petry   6:267
    Sward   13:299
Thorner, Horace   26:118-19, 122
Thornhill, Arthur H.   4:138
Thorns   3:278, 279, 283
Thornton, John   11:236
Thorpe, Jim   1:381
*Those Who Can: A Science Fiction
    Reader*   2:257
Thoughts Abroad   14:56-57
Thousand Nights and One Night, The
    1:77
Thread That Runs So True, The   9:40
Threads   26:35, 37
"Three Brothers"   2:398-99
Three from La Mama   2:414
Three Front   2:368
365 Days   1:117
334   4:151, 154, 156
Three Lives for Mississippi   2:419
Three Lovers   2:351
Three on the Tower   4:296
Three Roberts on Childhood, The
    13:298-99
Three Roberts on Love, The   13:298
*Three Roberts, Premiere Performance,
    The*   13:298
Three Sirens, The   1:384, 385, 393
Three Sisters, The   2:418
Three Stories   26:31
"Three Variations on a Theme by
    Callosobruchus"   26:90-91
Three Works   26:227
Thrice Chosen   14:282
Thrill of the Grass, The   7:106
Thrilling Wonder Stories   2:37
Through the Ivory Gate   19:106
Thurber, James   11:162-63
Thursday, My Love   10:300
Thus Spake Zarathustra   3:338
Thy Kingdom Come   2:245
Tiananmen Square, Beijing, China
    15:325
Tibet   24:15

Tibetan Book of the Dead, The (Jean-Claude van Itallie) **2**:421
"Ticket to Ride" **26**:72
Tiempo de silencio (Time of silence) **12**:103
Tiger Tim's Weekly **6**:32
Tigers **23**:12
Tigers Wild **4**:265
Tight Corners and What's around Them **26**:37-38
Tightrope Walker, The **23**:170
Tilden, Mike **10**:209, 217
Till, Emmett **7**:196
Tille, Václav **7**:214
Tillinghast, Richard 23:301-19
    Ruark **23**:271
Timbuktu **2**:299-301
Time
    Dillard **7**:17
    Hudgins **21**:109
    Kirk **9**:98
    Still **17**:241
    Swanberg **13**:269, 270-71, 272
    Van Itallie **2**:415
    Williams **3**:431
    Wilson **5**:321, 323
Time and Tide **6**:320
Time and Western Man **3**:385
Time Hoppers, The **3**:278
"Time Is All We Have" **26**:83
Time of Changes, A **3**:281, 282
Time of the Barracudas **12**:10
"Time Stain" **25**:71
Time to Keep, A **6**:71-72
Timeless Stories for Today and Tomorrow **7**:6
Times Literary Supplement (London)
    Symons **3**:386, 387, 389
    Wesker **7**:233-34
Times (London) **8**:167, 171, 177
Timescape Books **19**:332, 334-35
Tin Toys **8**:103
Tindal-Atkinson, Father **5**:112
Tindall, William York
    Kennedy **9**:80
    Lottman **12**:205
    West **7**:277
Tindley, Charles A. **23**:196
Tiny Courts **26**:38
Titania's Lodestone **2**:122
Titian **4**:328
Tituba of Salem Village **6**:253
Tlön, Uqbar, Orbis Tertius **1**:263
Tlooth **6**:246
"To a Skylark" **14**:123
To an Early Grave **3**:218-20
To Come, To Have Become **3**:98
"To Hear My Head Roar" **7**:177
To Live Again **3**:279
To Open the Sky **3**:278
"To See the Invisible Man" **3**:277, 279
To the Children in Yemen **13**:151
To the City of the Dead: An Account of Travels in Mexico **6**:321
To the Finland Station **7**:236

To the Gods the Shades **5**:373
"To the Point" **9**:100
"To Whom Is the Poet Responsible?" **8**:308
"Toad" **7**:180
Tobacco Road **1**:148, 151
Tobin, Maurice **6**:171
Tocqueville Prize **10**:335
Todd **17**:69-70
Todd, Glen **11**:284, 285
Todd, Ruthven **3**:386, 389
Toe Queen Poems, The **21**:264
Toer, Pramoedya Ananta **13**:316
Together **9**:38
Toklas, Alice B.
    Bowles **1**:83
    Hiemstra **26**:155-56
Tokyo, Japan
    Bishop **26**:4-5
    Federman **8**:75
    Kirkup **4**:187-88
    Lowitz **26**:179-80
Tokyo University **26**:180
Tolbert, Mildred **14**:109, 112, 113
Toledo News-Bee **3**:176-77
Toledo, Ohio **17**:38-46
Tolkien, J.R.R.
    Kirk **9**:103-04
    Knight **10**:225
    Wain **4**:328, 329
Tolstoy, Ivan
    Dennison **6**:119
    Enslin **3**:97
Tolstoy, Leo
    Bourjaily **1**:70
    Dennison **6**:121
    Forrest **7**:25
    Josipovici **8**:156
    Rakosi **5**:204
    Wallace **1**:387, 391
"Tom Merton" **22**:184-85
Tom o' Bedlam **3**:286
Tom Sawyer **6**:244
"Tom Swift" series **7**:56
Tomahawk, The See *Progress, The*
Tomerlin, John **16**:212, 213, 214
Tomlinson, Charles
    Davie **3**:35, 36
    Rosenthal **6**:284
"Tomorrow for Angela" **3**:403
Tomorrow Today **19**:370
Tomorrow Will Be Sunday **15**:238, 247, 248
Tonkinson, Mary **5**:238, 239
Too Loud a Solitude **12**:193
Toomer, Jean
    Forrest **7**:32
    Salaam **21**:228-29, 241
Toomey, Robert E., Jr. **10**:172, 174
Toronto Islands: An Illustrated History, The **13**:297
Toronto, Ontario, Canada
    Colombo **22**:34-36
    Glover **23**:88
    Kelly **22**:107, 109-10, 111, 115, 117

    Levine **23**:177-78
    Nims **17**:183
    Owens **2**:366-68
    Sward **13**:296-97, 298-99
Torregian, Sotère
    Argüelles **24**:25
    Forbes **16**:111-13
Torremolinos, Spain **3**:217
Torrents of Spring **11**:376
Tortuga **4**:26
Totalitarianism
    Davie **3**:42
    Samarakis **16**:250, 262-66
Touch of Clay, A **3**:265
Touch of Time: Myth, Memory and the Self, The **2**:216, 217, 220, 224, 225, 226
Tougaloo College **10**:41
Tough Guy Writers of the Thirties **3**:194
Touster, Irwin **8**:306
Tower of Glass **3**:281, 283
Town & Country **1**:192
Town Life **16**:238-39
Town on the Border, The **1**:342
Toyama, Mitsuru **1**:380
Toye, William **22**:48
Toynbee, Arnold **5**:325
Toynbee, Philip **5**:323, 326
Trace **6**:180
Tracker **3**:408
Tracy, David **7**:49
Trade unions See Labor unions
Tradition and Dream **6**:25
Tragedy and the Theory of Drama **12**:235
Tragedy of Momus, The **24**:26, 27
Tragic Ground **1**:150
Tragic Sense of Life, The **11**:213
Trail Driving Days **6**:57
Trail of Tears **24**:207, 213
Trails **7**:61
Train, Arthur **6**:264
Train to Pakistan **9**:232
Traitor of the Scripted Word, The **26**:289
Tramp's Cup, The **7**:138
Transatlantic Review
    Busch **1**:132
    Van Itallie **2**:412
Transduction **25**:73
transition
    Bowles **1**:82
    Caldwell **1**:147
    Pohl **1**:285
    Symons **3**:385
Translating and interpreting
    Eigner **23**:36-37
    Hadas **23**:132
    Hollo **19**:169-71
    Mead **13**:125-31, 132-34, 136-39
    Nims **17**:191-92
    Rabassa **9**:191-92, 197-98, 203-04
    Raffel **9**:213-14, 219
Translation **13**:251
Translations from the Chinese **7**:78

Translitics **25**:74
Transtrӧmer, Tomas **17**:249-65
Traub, John **8**:249
Travelling **4**:166
Traverso, Leone **10**:142
Treasure of Xerxes, The **26**:289
Tree **26**:194-95
Tree Books (press) **26**:195
Tree of Time, The **10**:223-24
Tree on Fire, A **2**:386
Treichler, Paul **8**:132
Trembling upon Rome, A **1**:197
Trend of Dehumanization in Weapon Systems of the 21st Century, The **1**:263
Tres cuentos **15**:8
Trespass **3**:181
Treuhaft, Bob **17**:142-50
Triada **15**:211, 213
Trial Impressions **6**:247, 248
Trial, The **2**:72
Trian, Chris **26**:301-02
Tribal Justice **3**:18, 22, 23, 24
Tribune
    Booth **2**:55
    Fuller **10**:125
    Jones **5**:123, 124
Tribute **9**:248-50
Trickster stories
    Villanueva **24**:315
    Vizenor **22**:261, 263, 272-73
Trigger Dance **24**:208, 209
Trilce **12**:100
Trilling, Lionel
    Kennedy **9**:80
    Simpson **4**:291, 294
    West **7**:277
Trilling, Steve
    Fuchs **5**:57-58
    Wallace **1**:384
Trimble, Bjo **12**:213
Trimble, John **12**:213
Trinidad **18**:1-14, 18, 20-24
Trinidad Guardian **18**:15-16, 19-20
Trinity College, Burlington, Vt. **2**:159
"Trio" **26**:157
Trio **5**:221-22
Triolet, Elsa **14**:273
Tristia of Ovid, The **3**:324
Tristram Shandy **5**:44, 46
Triumph of the Novel: Dickens, Dostoevsky, Faulkner, The **2**:219, 221, 228, 229
Triumph of Time **8**:147
Trobar **19**:199
Trodd, Kenith **3**:110, 111-12
Troll of Surewould Forest, A **4**:157
Trollope, Anthony
    Arden **4**:36
    Gilbert **15**:189, 195-96
Trophées, Les **2**:158
Tropic of Cancer, The **10**:288
Tropic of Capricorn, The
    Rimmer **10**:288
    Wallace **1**:397

Tropicalization **17**:13-14
Troy **3**:377
Troy, William
    Belitt **4**:62, 65
    Dennison **6**:111-12
    Howes **3**:137
Troyanos, Tatiana **26**:92
Truck on the Track, The **6**:99
True & False Unicorn **12**:49, 57
True Confessions of George Barker, The
    Ashby **6**:42-43
    Heath-Stubbs **21**:68
Trueblood, Alan S. **8**:118, 119
Truman Doctrine **2**:226
Truman, Harry
    Charyn **1**:179
    Knebel **3**:178
Trumbull Park **6**:181
Trungpa, Chӧgyam
    Kyger **16**:201
    Van Itallie **2**:416, 417, 419, 420
    Waldman **17**:279-80, 283
Trussell, Amy
    Berry **24**:80
    Leftwich **25**:269
Trust in Chariots **15**:344
Truth of Poetry, The **4**:166
Tsing Hua University, Peking, China **1**:34
"Tsuruginomiya Regeneration, The" **6**:136, 138, 144
Tsvetayeva, Marina
    Feinstein **1**:221
    Thomas **11**:382
Tu regardais intensément Geneviève (You stared fixedly at Geneviève) **13**:189
Tuberculosis
    Brown **6**:66
    Glanville **9**:20, 21
    Samarakis **16**:248
    Sillitoe **2**:378, 379-80
    Wellek **7**:223
Tubman, Harriet **2**:295
Tuck, Les **15**:246
Tudor Cornwall **8**:260
tuff shit **19**:26, 53
Tufts University
    Ciardi **2**:88-89, 90
    Corman **2**:132-33, 145
    Forbes **16**:117
    Kelly **19**:201
    Kennedy **9**:85
    Kumin **8**:215
Tulane University **25**:113
Tuma, Antoinette **11**:61-72
Tunbridge Wells **23**:67
Tunnicliffe, Charles **4**:311
Tunstall, Edward **5**:98
Turbulent Zone, The **13**:156
Turco, Lewis Putnam **22**:233-53
Turgenev, Ivan **11**:376
Turkey
    Disch **4**:152
    Foster **26**:122-23
    Tillinghast **23**:311

Turks **2**:273
Turnbull, Gael **14**:321-37
    Fisher **10**:94, 96, 97
Turner, Barbara **5**:293
Turner, Frederick **10**:307-22
    Allen **11**:22
    Feirstein **11**:84, 85
Turner, J.M.W. **4**:155
Turner, Nat **20**:24
Turner, Tom **1**:78
Turquoise Lake: A Memoir of World War II, The **8**:239
Turret, The **2**:115
Tuskegee Airmen **23**:249, 264
Tuskegee Institute **19**:108
Tutola, Amos **3**:427
Tuwaang Attends a Wedding **9**:164
Tuxedo Park **18**:203
T.V. **2**:414
Twain, Mark
    Anderson **2**:46
    Booth **5**:31, 40
    Wagoner **3**:408
Twelfth Night **2**:157
Twentieth Century **1**:194
Twentieth Century Fox
    Condon **1**:193
    Jones **5**:126-27
    Thayler **11**:362-63
    Wakefield **7**:200
    Wallace **1**:385
Twentieth Century Fund **8**:137-38
Twentieth Century Verse
    Fuller **10**:123
    Symons **3**:385, 386, 388
28th Day of Elul, The **3**:74, 76, 83
Twenty-One Poems **3**:302
Twenty-seventh Wife, The **1**:388, 389-90
20,000 A.D. **21**:267, 269
Twenty to Thirty **2**:22
Twilight of the Day **5**:128, 129
Two Ballads of the Muse **5**:285
Two Continents **24**:238
Two Englands: Empiricism and Idealism in English Literature, The **7**:222
Two-Fisted **22**:59-60
Two Friends **9**:66, 67
Two Hands **5**:163, 164
Two, The **1**:379, 400
Two Wings to Veil My Face **7**:27, 30, 32
Two Women and Their Man **5**:130-31
Two Women of London: The Strange Case of Ms. Jekyll and Mrs. Hyde **9**:291, 295
Tygodnik Powszechny **1**:259
Tyler, Anne **4**:115
Tyler, J.E.A. **9**:104
Tynan, Kenneth **4**:30
Typhoon **2**:228
Tyson, Cicely **13**:251
Tzara, Tristan **19**:140, 141, 142, 143, 149

UAW See United Auto Workers

Udall, Stewart **9**:268-69
Uganda **3**:82
Uh-Oh Plutonium! **17**:288
Ul-Haq, Mohammad Zia **9**:235
Ultimo Novecento prize **25**:111
Ultraviolet Sky, The **24**:321-22
Ulysses
    Booth **5**:44
    Boyle **1**:99
    Jones **5**:121
    Thomas **11**:376
    Wallace **1**:375
Un-American Activities Committee,
    U.S. House of Representatives
    Mitford **17**:147
    Williams **3**:424
Unamuno, Miguel de
    Bruce-Novoa **18**:71, 73
    Kerrigan **11**:213, 214
    Rabassa **9**:201-02
"Unc" **7**:139
Uncertainties **15**:378
Uncle Dog and Other Poems **13**:280,
    283-84, 288
Uncle Vanya **2**:418
Uncollected Stars **4**:208
Under a Monsoon Cloud **8**:165, 173,
    176
Under Heaven's Bridge **26**:5
Under Milk Wood **5**:274
Under the Apple Tree **7**:201
*Under the Skin: The Death of White
    Rhodesia* **4**:109
Under the Volcano
    Delbanco **2**:158
    Williams **3**:421
Underground Church, The **11**:54
Underlay **4**:209-10, 213
Underneath the Arches **9**:16, 27
Undersea Mountain, The **18**:284
Underside, The **8**:173
Understanding George Garrett **7**:15
Understanding Poetry
    Jerome **8**:133
    Van Brunt **15**:374
Uneasy Chair, The **9**:269
*Unending Dialogue: Voices from an
    AIDS Poetry Workshop* **23**:125-
    26, 132
Ungaretti, Giuseppe **10**:141-42
Unger, David **12**:91-106
Unicorn Press **8**:248
Union of Czech Youth **1**:334
Union Theological Seminary **11**:47
Unitarianism **10**:303
United Artists Studios **1**:194, 196
United Auto Workers **3**:137
United Black Artists Guild **21**:138
United Features Syndicate **1**:65
United Federation of Teachers
    1:365
United Nations **9**:231-32
United Press
    Gray **2**:194
    Hine **15**:225
    Salisbury **15**:321, 324

United States
    Hamburger **4**:171
    Hauser **11**:131-33
    Moorcock **5**:187
    Mrozek **10**:271-72
    Rowse **8**:261-62
    White **4**:348
U.S. Air Force
    Bausch, Richard **14**:5-7
    Bausch, Robert **14**:23-24
    Bennett **13**:83
    Bishop **26**:17
    Smith **7**:163
    Westlake **13**:338-39
    Whittemore **8**:303
U.S. Army
    Aubert **20**:22, 23
    Baumbach **5**:22-23
    Bell **14**:47-48
    Booth **5**:38-39
    Busch **1**:130, 133
    Cassill **1**:165-67
    Cassity **8**:44-47
    Ciardi **2**:91, 92
    Corcoran **2**:118
    Crews **14**:108
    Davison **4**:133
    Disch **4**:148
    Easton **14**:154-55
    Emanuel **18**:128-30
    Federman **8**:74-75
    Garrett **5**:71-72, 78, 81-82, 86-87,
        88-89
    Hebert **24**:245
    Heinemann **21**:80-9
    Hinojosa-Smith **16**:140
    Huddle **20**:184, 193
    Kerrigan **11**:204
    Kherdian **2**:265-66
    Kirk **9**:95-96
    Lottman **12**:204-05
    Peters **8**:239
    Rabassa **9**:198-201
    Rechy **4**:259
    Rimmer **10**:289-92
    Salaam **21**:192
    Simpson **4**:291
    Sukenick **8**:290
    Wolff **22**:281, 282-303
    Wright **7**:293-97
U.S. Army Air Corps
    Appleman **18**:29
    Blotner **25**:83-93
U.S. Army Air Force
    Ciardi **2**:94
    Clement **16**:89-91, 92-94, 98
    Fox **19**:123-25
    Still **17**:242-44
    Wallace **1**:379
U.S. Army, Officer Candidate
    School **22**:286-87
U.S. Army Reserves **24**:244
U.S. Army, Special Forces **22**:284-
    85, 286
U.S. Army, Special Training
    Program **9**:266

United States Award
    Hazo **11**:150
    Levis **23**:191
    See also International Poetry
        Forum
U.S. Coast Guard
    Appleman **18**:29
    Matthews **15**:259-61
U.S. Department of Agriculture **1**:85
U.S. Department of State **14**:267-68,
    278-79
U.S. Department of the Army
    14:269-73
U.S. Forest Service **14**:168
U.S. Information Agency
    Anderson **2**:44
    Caldwell **1**:154, 156
    Corman **2**:139
    Eshleman **6**:138
    Guerard **2**:224
    Kammen **23**:145, 156
    Katz **14**:171-72
    Knight **10**:229
    Purdy **1**:304
    Wagoner **3**:408-09
U.S. Information Service See U.S.
    Information Agency
U.S. Marine Corps
    Becker **1**:34
    Connell **2**:103
    Flanagan **17**:44
    Hamill **15**:207-08
    Hazo **11**:143-44
U.S. Naval Academy **5**:333, 341-42
U.S. Navy
    Connell **2**:102, 103
    Corcoran **2**:118
    Dennison **6**:110
    Ford **21**:26-29
    Gunn **2**:243-45, 246
    Hebert **24**:248-49
    Kennedy **9**:81-82, 87
    Knebel **3**:177-78
    Mathews **6**:223, 228, 231, 240
    McCord **9**:177, 178-80
    Meredith **14**:226, 233
    Olson **11**:250-52
    Sward **13**:280, 286
    Thayer **11**:361-62
    Williams **3**:419-20
    Wilson **5**:343-45
U.S. Navy, WAVES **2**:209
U.S. Office of War Information
    Fast **18**:179, 180-83
    Roditi **14**:263-65, 266
U.S. Post Office **15**:265, 266
"United States Steel Hour" **2**:170
*Universal Baseball Association, J. Henry
    Waugh, Prop., The* **7**:13-14
Universal Press Syndicate **1**:253
Universal Studios **1**:383
"Universe" **2**:248
Universidad de Guadalajara **25**:56
Universidad de Mexico **2**:207
Université d'Aix-Marseille **8**:226
Université de Nice **6**:194-95

University Art Museum, Berkeley,
   Calif. **23**:30, 53
University at Frankfurt am Main
   12:232
University at Rio Piedras **12**:34
University Bookman **9**:100
University College, Cardiff, Wales
   4:190
University College, Dublin, Ireland
   2:346
University College, Galway, Ireland
   4:305
University College, London, England
   Awoonor **13**:46
   Rule **18**:311
University College of North Wales,
   Bangor **4**:302-03
University of Adelaide **3**:354
University of Alabama
   Hudgins **21**:118
   Wilson **16**:293-94
University of Alberta **18**:83
University of Arizona
   Ai **13**:4-5
   Bourjaily **1**:79
   Boyd **11**:46
   Burroway **6**:86
   Elkins **18**:97
   Greeley **7**:47
   West **7**:283
   Wilson **5**:349, 350
University of Arkansas **20**:325, 332
University of Arkansas Press **20**:337-
   38
University of Berlin **11**:128
University of Birmingham
   Allen **6**:18
   Brossard **2**:71
   Fisher **10**:93-95
University of Bridgeport **11**:16, 19,
   20
University of Bristol **3**:296, 303-04
University of British Columbia
   Bergé **10**:7
   Bowering **16**:21, 32-33
   Gray **3**:110
   Rule **18**:312-13
   Woodcock **6**:321, 322
University of Buffalo **11**:79-80
University of Cairo
   El Saadawi **11**:65-66
   Hassan **12**:142, 144, 145, 146-47
University of Calgary
   Blaise **3**:23
   Kinsella **7**:104, 106
University of California
   Ghiselin **10**:129-30
   Kyger **16**:189
   Roditi **14**:269
   Schevill **12**:270, 271-73
University of California at Berkeley
   Argüelles **24**:17, 19
   Armantrout **25**:18-21
   Barrio **15**:115
   di Suvero **26**:66, 71
   Elkins **18**:98

   Foley **24**:169
   Ghiselin **10**:131
   Kherdian **2**:269
   Lowitz **26**:174
   McPherson **23**:227
   Pinsky **4**:245, 246, 249-50
   Roditi **14**:261
   St. Clair **8**:271-72
   Schwartz **26**:242, 243-45
   Shapiro **6**:304
   Simpson **4**:294
   Stegner **9**:263
   Stone **3**:363, 364-65, 366-68, 370,
     379
   Tillinghast **23**:309-10
   Wakoski **1**:356, 358-60
University of California at Davis
   Honig **8**:116-17
   McPherson **23**:229
   Nelson **23**:255, 256
   Owens **24**:294
   Shapiro **6**:304
University of California at Goleta
   2:120
University of California at Irvine
   Ai **13**:8-9
   Duncan **2**:173
   Kennedy **9**:85
   Peters **8**:248
   Wakoski **1**:369
   Wright **7**:299, 300-01
University of California at Los
   Angeles
   Corcoran **2**:119
   Epstein **12**:71
   Federman **8**:77, 78
   Niven **12**:212
   Rechy **4**:263
University of California at Riverside
   8:242, 243-44
University of California at Santa
   Barbara
   Barrio **15**:117
   Easton **14**:158
   Federman **8**:78
   Hamill **15**:210, 212-13
   Menefee **26**:203
   Owens **24**:290
   Turner **10**:317
University of California at Santa
   Cruz **22**:100-01
University of Cape Coast **13**:50
University of Chicago
   Argüelles **24**:6
   Bell, Charles G. **12**:22, 32-33, 34,
     36
   Bell, Marvin **14**:43-44
   Booth **5**:42, 43-44, 48
   Eigner **23**:26, 27, 52
   Flanagan **17**:45-46
   Greeley **7**:43, 46-47
   Hine **15**:231, 232-33, 234, 235
   Jerome **8**:130-31
   Manuel **9**:165-66, 167
   Nims **17**:178-79
   Olson **12**:229, 232

   Pinsky **4**:247
   Rakosi **5**:202
   Ray **7**:139-40
   Rodgers **13**:252
   Roditi **14**:254, 257, 259, 260
   Rosenthal **6**:275
   Simic **4**:283
   Solotaroff **2**:396-98
University of Chicago Press **4**:247
University of Cincinnati **17**:97
University of Colorado
   Bruce-Novoa **18**:73-74
   Corcoran **2**:120
   Gunn **2**:244
   Holden **22**:65, 67
   Katz **14**:178
   Sukenick **8**:293
   Williamson **8**:325
University of Connecticut
   McKain **14**:215
   Nelson **23**:261
   Sward **13**:291
   Turco **22**:238
University of Copenhagen **16**:117
University of Denver
   Brutus **14**:61
   Corcoran **2**:121
   Raffel **9**:218-19
University of Dublin, Trinity College
   Davie **3**:37-38
   Keating **8**:166, 167
University of Durham **23**:14-15
University of Edmonton **15**:157-58
University of Essex
   Clark **22**:12
   Davie **3**:40-43
   Feinstein **1**:221, 223
   Raworth **11**:302, 303
University of Exeter
   Sisson **3**:307
   Turner **10**:321
University of Florida
   Gerber **20**:163-65
   Jones **11**:178
   Smith **7**:165-66
University of Georgia
   Bishop **26**:15
   Caldwell **1**:157
University of Ghana **13**:44, 46
University of Hawaii
   Hall **12**:121-22
   Meredith **14**:227
   Morgan **3**:235-36
University of Houston
   Brown **10**:41
   Furman **18**:202
   Olson **12**:237
   Wolfe **9**:303
University of Hull **20**:58, 60
University of Idaho
   Blotner **25**:94-95
   Peters **8**:240
University of Illinois
   Bausch **14**:24
   Brown **6**:57
   Burroway **6**:100

INDEX

Greeley   7:47
Hinojosa-Smith   16:149
Plumpp   21:170, 174
Rodgers   13:244
Still   17:237
Sward   13:288
University of Indiana   12:235
University of Iowa
   Allen   6:20
   Bell   14:44-45
   Blaise   3:25, 26
   Bourjaily   1:73
   Busch   1:133
   Cassill   1:164, 167
   Delbanco   2:159
   Hall   12:131-34
   Hiemstra   26:151-53
   Kinsella   7:102, 103
   Koller   5:163
   Levis   23:191
   McPherson, James A.   17:133, 135
   McPherson, Sandra   23:226
   Stafford   3:334
   Stegner   9:263, 264
   Sward   13:288
   Wright   7:297-99
   See also International Writers
      Program; Iowa Writers
      Workshop
University of Iowa Short-Fiction
   contest   2:214
University of Istanbul   24:217, 235
University of Kansas
   Allen   6:25
   Connell   2:106-07, 112
   Gunn   2:233, 243, 245-46, 247,
      252, 253-55, 256-57, 259
   Stafford   3:332-33
University of Kent   2:125
University of Kentucky   2:120
University of Leeds
   Jarman   22:105
   Stewart   3:353
University of London
   Gray   3:109, 110, 111-12, 114-15
   Hamburger   4:165
   Harwood   19:139, 140
   Mott   7:130
   Sinclair   5:271
University of Louisville   22:76
University of Madrid   19:69
University of Manchester   3:239, 246
University of Manila   9:158-59
University of Manitoba
   Daigon   25:153
   Reaney   15:304, 305
University of Maryland
   Elkins   18:98
   Weiss   2:434
   Whittemore   8:309
University of Massachusetts
   Ai   13:12
   Galvin   13:93-94
   Skelton   5:286
   Wakefield   7:198
University of Mexico   20:331

University of Michigan
   Aubert   20:22
   Blotner   25:96-98
   Ciardi   2:89, 90
   Clark   22:9-11
   Corman   2:134, 135
   Delbanco   2:159
   Hall   7:65, 66
   Heath-Stubbs   21:70
   Kennedy   9:82-84, 87
   Kizer   5:136
   Madgett   23:207
   Murphy   26:219
   Piercy   1:271, 277
   Solotaroff   2:393-95
   Stevenson   9:278-79, 283
   Tillinghast   23:316
   Wagoner   3:403
University of Minnesota
   Anderson   2:38-39
   Argüelles   24:5-6
   Browne   20:66, 73
   Disch   4:155
   Harris   3:130
   Salisbury   15:311, 312, 317, 320,
      321
   Swanberg   13:260-61
   Vizenor   22:271, 274
University of Missouri
   Burke   19:63, 69
   Ciardi   2:90, 93
   Dacey   17:27
   Olson   12:237
   Ray   7:144
   Roditi   14:262-63
   Sanders   21:259
University of Montana
   Corcoran   2:119, 121, 122, 127
   Root   11:327
University of Montréal
   Brossard   16:45-47
   Gurik   23:102, 110
   Hood   17:88
University of Nebraska   6:304, 306
University of Nevada   5:346
University of New Brunswick
   Brewster   15:153-55
   Glover   23:89
   Levine   23:176
University of New Mexico
   Anaya   4:21, 26
   Bergé   10:11
   Connell   2:102
   Creeley   10:69
   McCord   9:184
   Olson   12:237
   Owens   24:295
   Williamson   8:318
   Wilson   5:340, 341, 346
University of New Mexico Press
   1:212
University of Newcastle upon Tyne
   23:14-15
University of North Alabama   24:67
University of North Carolina
   Blotner   25:96

Chappell   4:116, 118-19
Corman   2:134
Eaton   20:123, 131-32, 133, 140
Root   11:322
Shelnutt   14:298
Vivante   12:301
Weiss   2:434-35
University of North Carolina Press
   2:116
University of Northern Iowa   9:113-
   14
University of Notre Dame
   Gunn   2:244
   Hazo   11:142-43
   Kerrigan   11:197
University of Notre Dame Press
   11:213-14
University of Oklahoma
   Duncan   2:169, 173, 176
   Jerome   8:127
   Nash   25:295-96, 300
   Owens   2:368
University of Oregon   14:168-69
University of Oslo, Norway   21:36-37
University of Otago   23:9
University of Padua   7:300, 301
University of Paris   4:292
University of Patna
   Choudhury   14:87-88
   Mahapatra   9:142-43
University of Pennsylvania
   Blotner   25:94
   Hassan   12:147-48, 150-51, 153-54
   Rakosi   5:207
   Turnbull   14:331, 334
University of Pittsburgh
   Brutus   14:62
   McElroy   21:133
   Shelnutt   14:300
University of Portland   17:174
University of Puerto Rico   12:234
University of Redlands   20:172
University of Rome
   Vivante   12:295-96
   Wright   7:298
University of St. Andrews
   Kirk   9:96-98
   Parini   16:231-35
University of Santo Tomas   9:164-65,
   167
University of Saskatchewan   15:159
University of Singapore   3:245
University of South Carolina   19:125,
   130
University of Southern California
   Barrio   15:114
   Rechy   4:263
   Stone   3:366, 368
University of Sussex
   Josipovici   8:147, 148, 154, 155,
      156, 157, 158
   Morgan   3:239, 246
University of Tennessee
   Jones   11:180
   White   4:350
University of Texas

Bergé **10**:16
Caute **4**:105
Charyn **1**:182
Clarke **16**:86-87
Crews **14**:114
Delgado **15**:173-74, 176-77
Furman **18**:203
Harris **16**:135
Hearon **11**:160-61
Hinojosa-Smith **16**:140, 141
Kostelanetz **8**:182
Lifshin **10**:247, 254
McCord **9**:178, 180-81
Petesch **12**:246, 248
Raffel **9**:217
Rakosi **5**:207
Raworth **11**:305-06
Turner **10**:321
Vivante **12**:301
White **4**:348
University of Texas Press **3**:74
University of the Philippines
    Manuel **9**:156-58, 160, 162-64,
        167
    Olson **12**:235
University of the South **23**:306, 316
University of the West Indies
    16:119
University of Tohoku **4**:183
University of Toledo **17**:44
University of Toronto
    Allen **6**:26
    Colombo **22**:34-37, 40
    Hood **17**:85-86
    Livesay **8**:220, 232
    Nims **17**:183
    Škvorecký **1**:348
    Sparshott **15**:352, 354, 355, 360,
        363
University of Toronto Library
    School **15**:155
University of Toronto Press **22**:34,
    41
University of Toronto, Trinity
    College
    Clarke **16**:77, 81-82
    Livesay **8**:225
University of Toronto, University
    College **15**:298, 300-04
University of Tours **3**:168
University of Ulster
    Allen **6**:26
    Simmons **21**:275, 291, 293
University of Utah
    Ghiselin **10**:130, 131-39
    McCord **9**:181
    Smith **7**:164
    Stegner **9**:262, 264
    Taylor **7**:183
University of Vermont **10**:250
University of Victoria
    Cohen **18**:84
    Kinsella **7**:101-02, 103
    Skelton **5**:285, 286, 289, 290-91
    Sward **13**:292, 295
University of Virginia

Belitt **4**:57-58, 59
Bell **12**:22, 23, 24
Blotner **25**:95-96
Bowles **1**:82, 83
Caldwell **1**:144-45, 146, 157
Dillard **7**:11, 14, 15, 16
Dove **19**:113
Huddle **20**:182, 185-93
McPherson **17**:123
Settle **1**:320, 321
Shreve **5**:237
Smith **7**:161, 162
Taylor **7**:176, 178, 179
Wakoski **1**:369
University of Washington
    Allen **6**:26
    Johnson **18**:239, 241, 242
    Major **6**:192-93
    Matthews **18**:269
    McElroy **21**:137-38, 139
    McPherson **23**:221
    Morgan **3**:236
    Root **11**:321
    Wagoner **3**:405, 408
    Wakoski **1**:370
    Woodcock **6**:321
University of Waterloo **15**:251
University of Western Ontario
    Horwood **15**:251
    Reaney **15**:306-07
University of Wisconsin
    Brée **15**:143, 144-45
    Elkins **18**:97-98
    Feirstein **11**:81
    Hahn **11**:109-10
    Hassan **12**:151, 156, 162
    Higgins **8**:90
    Honig **8**:109
    Kherdian **2**:266, 267
    Klinkowitz **9**:110-11
    Morgan **3**:238-39, 241, 243, 244
    Peters **8**:239-40
    Rakosi **5**:202, 203, 204, 205
    Rosenblum **11**:338, 341-42, 344-
        45, 346, 347, 348, 349-50
    Stegner **9**:264-66
    Thayler **11**:364
    Wallace **1**:374
    West **7**:280
University of Zambia **14**:114, 118
Unlucky Jonah **25**:307
Unmuzzled Ox **13**:22
Unnatural Enemy, The **1**:75
Unnon Theories **24**:74
Unpublished Editions **8**:90
Unsealed Lips **10**:257
Unsettling of America, The **23**:183
Untermeyer, Jean Starr
    Bourjaily **1**:65
    Inez **10**:189
Untermeyer, Louis
    Bourjaily **1**:65
    Ciardi **2**:90
    Fast **18**:179-80, 181
    Glazier **24**:227
Unterseher, Fred **8**:190

Unvanquished, The **18**:179
Up
    Klinkowitz **9**:112
    Sukenick **8**:283-85, 294
Up and Around **3**:403
Up My Coast **16**:201
Up the Line **3**:281
Updike, John
    Delbanco **2**:155, 156
    Kelly **22**:116
Upsala University **1**:156
Upstate Madonna **10**:241
Upward Reach, The **5**:37
Urban Snow **16**:23
Urbana College **15**:266, 268
Urbánek, Zdeněk **1**:338
Urth of the New Sun, The **9**:311
USA Today **21**:43
Uschuk, Pamela **11**:328-30
Usher, Abbott Payson **3**:237
USIA See U.S. Information Agency
USSR See Soviet Union
Utah **9**:95-96

V-Letter and Other Poems **6**:300
Vail, Laurence **1**:116-18
Valaoritis, Aristotle **26**:265, 268,
    270
Valaoritis, Nanos 26:263-91
    Argüelles **24**:20
    Schwartz **26**:241
Valdez Horses, The **10**:169, 174
Valentine Pontifex **3**:285
Valentine's Park, Ilford, Essex,
    England **19**:229-30
Valéry, Paul **4**:248
Valgardson, W.D. **7**:102, 110
Vallejo, César
    Argüelles **24**:14
    Eshleman **6**:131, 137, 147
    Goldemberg **12**:100
Valtin, Jan **6**:244
Valtinos, Thanassis **9**:147
Vampires, The **4**:262
Van Aelstyn, Ed **5**:164
Van Brunt, Lloyd 15:365-86
    Ray **7**:138
Van der Post, Laurens **11**:329
Van Doren, Carl **7**:90
Van Doren, Irita **6**:279
Van Doren, Mark
    Simpson **4**:291
    Van Brunt **15**:373-74
    Wakefield **7**:202
    Weiss **2**:431, 432
Van Druten, John **2**:411
Van Gogh, Vincent
    Kherdian **2**:267
    Stone **3**:368-70
Van Itallie, Jean-Claude 2:405-23
Van Proyen, Mark 25:379-403
Van Wagoner, James **22**:98-100
Vance, Jack **2**:42, 43
Vance, Nina **5**:79
Vancouver Award for Fiction
    Writing **7**:110

Vancouver, British Columbia, Canada
    Bowering **16**:34-35
    Rule **18**:312-14
    Thomas **19**:356
Vancouver Report, The **10**:7, 10
Vančura, Zdeněk **7**:214-15, 222
Vandam Theatre **2**:413
Vanderbilt, Gloria **5**:212, 221, 222
Vanderbilt University
    Argüelles **24**:12-13
    Ford **21**:26
    Jarman **22**:104-06
    Jones **11**:176, 177
    Miller **15**:282
    Morgan **3**:241
    Still **17**:236-37
Vangelisti, Paul **8**:249
Vanguard Press **7**:89
Vanished **3**:169, 181
Vanity Fair **8**:72
Varda, Jean **26**:70, 72-73, 75, 76
Varèse, Edgard **13**:184-85
Vas Dias, Robert
    Eshleman **6**:140
    Olson **11**:253, 255, 259
Vas, Robert **4**:107
Vasconcelos, José **15**:2, 4-5, 9
Vassar College **6**:25
Vatican II
    Greeley **7**:43, 46, 49, 50
    Kienzle **1**:241-43
Vaudeville
    Foley **24**:156
    Wagoner **3**:402
Vaughan, Sam
    Garrett **5**:76
    Slavitt **3**:321, 322
Vaughn-Thomas, Winford **2**:299-300,
    301, 302
Vector **3**:321
Vega, Janine Pommy **25**:41
Vega, Lope de **8**:119
Vegetarianism **2**:420
Vegetti, Ernesto **8**:13
Velocities **24**:20
Velvet Horn, The **10**:137
Venezuela **23**:259
Venice Film Festival, Italy
    Caldwell **1**:152
    Sinclair **5**:274
Venice, Italy
    O'Faolain **2**:350
    Vivante **12**:296
Ventura College **15**:117
Venture **14**:71
Venus Observed **23**:71-78
Venus of Dreams **18**:343-44
Venus of Shadows **18**:344
Verlaine, Paul **6**:281
Vermont
    Lifshin **10**:236
    Nash **25**:289
Verne, Jules **2**:37
Verne, Louise (pen name of Nora
    Pemberton) **22**:90
Vernon, Jack **23**:256

Vers Libre: A Magazine of Free Verse
    14:110
Verschoyle, Derek (publishers) **5**:370
Versions and Perversions of Heine
    3:300
Very Close Family, A **9**:244
Very Fall of the Sun, The **11**:153
*Very Rich Hours of Count von
    Stauffenberg, The* **7**:280
Vestal, Stanley See Campbell, Walter
Vía Unica **15**:11
Vian, Boris
    Brossard **2**:67
    Federman **8**:72, 79
"Vichy France and the Jews" **2**:183
Vicious Circle **9**:240
Victor, Ed **1**:401
Victoria University
    Adcock **23**:7
    Brewster **15**:157
Victoria University, Skelton
    Collection **5**:290
Victorian Studies **18**:36
Vida **1**:280
Vida al contado, La (The life paid in
    cash) **12**:105
Vidal, Gore
    Parini **16**:240
    Purdy **1**:304
    Weiss **2**:443
Videotape **8**:188
*Vie Passionée of Rodney Buckthorne,
    La* **1**:173
Viebahn, Fred **19**:104-15
Vieira, Antônio **9**:204, 205
Vienna, Austria
    Gregor **10**:152-54, 157-58
    Wellek **7**:207-10
Viereck, Peter **4**:171
Vietnam Veterans Memorial,
    Washington, D.C. **23**:188
Vietnam War
    Allen **11**:21
    Allman **15**:23, 24-25
    Anaya **4**:24
    Anderson **2**:44
    Armantrout **25**:17, 20-21
    Becker **1**:40
    Bell **14**:48
    Berrigan **1**:51, 59
    Blais **4**:76
    Brossard **2**:71
    Busch **1**:133
    Cassill **1**:172
    Connell **2**:110
    Davie **3**:43
    Dennison **6**:117
    Eastlake **1**:211-12
    Enslin **3**:94
    Gibbons **24**:184
    Gray **2**:192, 198
    Haldeman **25**:195, 196, 213-15
    Hauser **11**:137
    Heinemann **21**:81-9, 95, 98
    Huddle **20**:193
    Katz **14**:173

Levis **23**:188, 189, 190-91
McCord **9**:182-83, 184
Menefee **26**:205
Nichols **2**:331-32
Owens **24**:289, 290-91, 297
Piercy **1**:273
Plymell **11**:288-89
Polkinhorn **25**:326
Ray **7**:143
Rosenblum **11**:344
Salisbury **15**:324
Sanders **21**:266
Sargent **18**:340
Shreve **5**:236-37
Simpson **4**:295
Smith **7**:162
Stafford **3**:337
Swanberg **13**:270-71
Van Itallie **2**:414
Villanueva **24**:309
Wakefield **7**:197-98
Williams **3**:431
Wolff **22**:285, 289-90, 292-96
Wright **7**:301
View
    Atkins **16**:11
    Bowles **1**:87
View from the Weaving Mountain
    16:272
View of the North, A **5**:373
Viewing, The **18**:305
Vigée, Claude **8**:290
Vigil, The **26**:328
Vigilias **15**:9
"Viking Grave at Ladby, The"
    13:313
Vilas Research Professorship **12**:162
Villa in France, A **3**:357
Villa, Jose Garcia **16**:112
Villa, Pancho **4**:253
Village: New and Selected Poems, The
    8:141
Village Voice
    Bourjaily **1**:72
    Hentoff **6**:168-69, 171
    Owens **2**:366, 368
    Wakoski **1**:362
Village Voice Obie Award **2**:361,
    363
Villager Award **2**:361
Villanueva, Alma Luz **24**:299-324
Villon, François
    Howes **3**:144
    Katz **9**:68
"Villon's Straight Tip to All Cross
    Coves" **3**:144
Vinograd, Julia **26**:293-310
Vinson, Eddie "Cleanhead" **6**:182
Violated, The **1**:72, 73, 74
Violence
    Clark **22**:19-20
    Vizenor **22**:266
Violet Quill Club **13**:230-32
Virgin and the Nightingale, The **23**:15
Virgin Islands **8**:135-36
Virginia

Bennett **13**:75
Dillard **7**:17-18
Morris **13**:162
Smith **7**:156-58, 162, 167
Virginia Commonwealth University
Lewis **23**:109
Smith **7**:165-66
Virginia Reel **1**:145
Virginia State University **23**:200
Virginia Tech. **6**:27
"Virtually Enough": Videoconference
with Larry Eigner **23**:49-57
Virtuoso Bird **26**:228
Vishniak, Roman **19**:84
Vision and Verse in William Blake
24:269
Vision in Motion **8**:186, 189
Vision of India **9**:233
*Visions and Revisions of American
Poetry* **22**:241
Visions d'Anna **4**:73-74, 76, 78
Visitations **15**:160
Vitamins for Vitality **8**:26
Vivante, Arturo 12:281-302
Ghiselin **10**:140
Vivante, Cesare **12**:285
Vivante, Leone
Ghiselin **10**:140
Vivante **12**:281, 282, 290, 293-94,
300
Vivas, Eliseo **12**:326-27
Viviani, GianFranco **8**:12, 13
Vizenor, Gerald 22:255-77
Foley **24**:173
Owens **24**:295
Vladislav, Jan **1**:338
Voegelin, Eric **20**:45
Vogue **2**:421
VOICE **1**:273
Voice That Was in Travel, The
24:208-09
Voices of Rama **22**:55
*Voices Underground: Poems from
Newfoundland* **15**:250
Void Captain's Tale, The **19**:332, 333
Voinovich, Vladimir 12:303-22
Volleys **17**:51
Volpone **3**:408
Volvox **25**:338
von Braun, Wernher **21**:57
Von Kant bis Hegel **7**:220
von Trott, Adam **8**:257
von Zelewski, Ottomar **7**:207
Vonnegut, Kurt
Bourjaily **1**:76, 79
Klinkowitz **9**:108, 110, 111-12,
113, 114, 115, 116, 117
Wakefield **7**:194
Vonnegut Statement, The **9**:113
Vote! **21**:268
Voyage au Bout de la Nuit **14**:256
Voyage to Arcturus, A **3**:281
"Voyagers" series **18**:58
Voyageurs Sacrés, Les **4**:74
Voyeur, The **3**:321
"Vulnerable Bundles" **26**:22

Wachtel, Chuck **14**:179
Wachuku, Jaja **2**:303
Waechter, Tom **26**:154, 160
WAG See Writers Action Group
Wagner College
Kelly **19**:199
Malanga **17**:97
Wagner, Lindsay **1**:384
Wagner, Richard
Atkins **16**:9
Highwater **7**:78
Wagoner, David 3:397-412
Allman **15**:23-24
Kizer **5**:154
McPherson **23**:222, 226
Wah, Fred **26**:41
Wahl, François **4**:355
Wahl, Jean
Corman **2**:137
Menashe **11**:228
Wain, John 4:315-32
Waiting for Godot **8**:77
Wakabayashi, Hiro **5**:212-13
Wake Forest University
Brée **15**:146-47
Rimmer **10**:290
Wake Up, Stupid **3**:128, 129
Wake Up. We're Almost There **2**:70,
71
Wakefield, Dan 7:191-203
Klinkowitz **9**:114, 116, 118
Kumin **8**:215
Wakoski, Diane 1:353-72
Bergé **10**:6, 11
Dillard **7**:18
Eshleman **6**:134, 140, 145, 147
Mott **7**:131
Owens **2**:363
Wald, Jerry **5**:57-58
Wald, Susana **22**:54
Waldbauer, Ivan **6**:234
Waldbauer, Suzanne **6**:234
Walden
Barrio **15**:111
Petry **6**:267
Waldman, Anne 17:267-94
Clark **22**:20, 21
Malanga **17**:115
Waldrop, Keith **9**:83-84
Waldrop, Rosmarie **9**:83
Wales **4**:301-13
Wales **4**:306
Waley, Arthur **7**:78
Walker, Alice **16**:84
Walker in the City, A **7**:90, 94, 95
Walking Edges **9**:182
Walking Four Ways in the Wind
15:22, 30
Walking the Boundaries **4**:139
Walks **6**:139
Walks to the Paradise Garden **12**:346-
47
Wallace, Amy **1**:377, 378-79, 399,
400-401
Wallace, David **1**:378-79

See also Wallechinsky, David
Wallace, Edgar
Ashby **6**:33-34
Dillon **3**:52
Wallace, Henry **2**:192
Wallace, Irving 1:373-403
Wallace, Lois **12**:73
Wallace Stegner Fellowship
Gerber **20**:167, 168-72
Root **11**:324
Wallace Stevens: Musing the Obscure
8:286-87
Wallace, Sylvia **1**:373, 391, 399,
400-402
See also Kahn, Sylvia
Wallace, Tom **6**:57
Wallechinsky, David **1**:377, 378,
399-401
Wallis, Alfred **23**:170
Wallis, Hal **1**:383
Walls of India, The **6**:325
Walpole, Hugh **11**:280, 282, 284
Walsh, Ernest **1**:115
Walt Whitman's Canada **22**:53
Walton, Eda Lou **4**:59-62
Walton, Francis **3**:377
Wampanoag Traveler **13**:99
Wampeters, Foma, and Granfalloons
9:113
Wanderer, The **1**:248
Wandering Fool, The **14**:284
Wang, David **6**:180
Wang, Diane **26**:150
Wang, Hui-Ming **23**:278
Waniek, Marilyn Nelson See Nelson,
Marilyn
Wanning, Andrew **10**:66
Wanstead Park, Ilford, Essex,
England **19**:229-30
Wantaja, Jeri **24**:329-31
Wanted: Hope **16**:253, 257-60
Wanton Summer Air, The **11**:153
Wapshot Chronicle, The **1**:36
War **6**:293
War **2**:412-13
War and Peace
Bourjaily **1**:70, 72
Hudgins **21**:112
Morgan **20**:272
Wilson **5**:342
War bubble-gum cards **20**:298, 305,
306, 309
War Comes to America **1**:380
War Commentary **6**:320
War in Heaven **24**:144
War Is Heaven! **6**:210, 211
War of the Worlds, The
Brunner **8**:3
Lem **1**:258-59
War Year **25**:199, 203
Warburg, Jim **1**:38
Ward, Cornelia, Foundation **4**:215
Warhol, Andy
Andre **13**:18-19
Malanga **17**:95, 97, 100-08, 109-
10, 112, 113, 115-18

Sanders **21**:264-65
Saroyan **5**:216
Warner Brothers Studios
   Epstein **12**:60, 61, 63
   Fuchs **5**:56-58
   Wallace **1**:383
Warner, Francis **2**:56
Warner, Fred **6**:239-40
Warner, Jack
   Epstein **12**:60, 65, 67
   Wallace **1**:384
Warren, Earl **3**:371
Warren, Leonard **4**:230
Warren, Robert Penn
   Blotner **25**:97
   Clarke **16**:82
   Ghiselin **10**:138
   Jerome **8**:133
   Jones **11**:183
   Manfred **18**:255-56
   Meredith **14**:228-29, 232
   Parini **16**:239
   Ruark **23**:274
Warren, William **22**:258-59, 263
Warsaw, Poland **9**:123-24
Warsh, Lewis
   Clark **22**:19-20, 21
   Harwood **19**:144
   Waldman **17**:276
Warshaw, Howard
   Davie **3**:39-40
   Kyger **16**:189
Warshow, Robert **3**:212, 214-15
Warwick Films **12**:8-9
Washburn University **12**:212
Washington, D.C.
   Brossard **2**:74-76
   Brown **6**:52-54
   Emanuel **18**:125-28
   Grumbach **2**:212, 213
   Jacobsen **18**:215
   Kammen **23**:138, 141
   Morgan **3**:244
   Wilson **16**:292-93
Washington Evening Star **12**:202
Washington Post
   Brossard **2**:63, 64, 76
   Solotaroff **2**:400
   Whittemore **8**:311
Washington School, Missoula, Mont.
   2:125
Washington Square Review **2**:207
Washington (state) **3**:406
Washington State University **9**:182-83
Washington University **10**:16
Wasserman, Harriet **14**:10, 12, 15
Wassermann, Marta **15**:156
Waste Land **14**:128
Wastepaper Theatre **8**:120
Watchboy, What of the Night? **8**:56
Water of Light, The **7**:185
Waterloo College **22**:33-34
Waters, Frank **13:319-28**
   Wilson **5**:345-46
Waters / Places / A Time **23**:33

Watkins, Ann **1**:118, 121, 122
Watkins, Vernon **2**:440-41
Watson, Ian **26**:5
Watson, Julia **7**:302
Watson, Sheila **16**:22, 36
Watt, Alexander **22**:32-33
Watts, Alan
   Broughton **12**:45
   di Suvero **26**:73, 76
Waugh, Evelyn
   Abse **1**:27
   Lottman **12**:205
   Wesker **7**:235
Wave High the Banner **6**:54
Waves and Licenses **9**:67-68
WAVES See U.S. Navy, WAVES
Way of All Flesh, The **26**:54, 55, 56
Way the Future Was, The **9**:311
Way to the World's End, A **7**:127
Way Up, The **4**:233
Wayne State University
   Ai **13**:12
   Aubert **20**:23, 33
   Boyd **11**:48, 49
   Federman **8**:73-74
   Jones **20**:212
   Madgett **23**:202
   Olson **12**:235
   Peters **8**:241
   Petesch **12**:244
Ways of Escape **8**:169
W.B. Yeats International Summer
   School **3**:40, 41
We Danced All Night **8**:20
We Die before We Live **1**:53
*We Might See Sights! and Other
   Stories* **2**:351
we sleep inside each other all **19**:20, 50
We Speak for Ourselves **3**:361
Weary Blues, The **21**:183
Weather Shelter, The **1**:155
Weaver, Ed **9**:3
Weaver, Ken **21**:265
Weaver, Robert **23**:172
Weaver, William **1**:69
Webb, Ann Eliza **1**:388, 389-90
Webber, Frances **5**:285
Weber, Brom **8**:107, 116, 117
Weber, Hugo **12**:342
Webern, Anton von
   Enslin **3**:95, 96
   Hrabal **12**:185-86
*Webster's New International
   Dictionary* **3**:135
Wedding Day **1**:116, 117
Wedding of Cousins, A **9**:294
Wedgwood, Josiah **4**:316
"Wednesday Play, The" **3**:111
Weegies New York **2**:358
Weekly Packet **7**:196
Weeks **19**:201
Weeks, Edward
   Davison **4**:135
   Ford **21**:35-37
Wehrenberg, Charles **24**:101

Wei, Wang **15**:65
Weidlinger Associates **25**:365-66
Weidlinger, Paul **25**:365
Weidman, Jerome **1**:383
Weight and Feel of Harps, The **26**:226
Weight of Antony, The **14**:171
Weil, Jim **3**:93-94
Weil, Simone
   Berrigan **1**:48
   Blais **4**:72
Weinberg, Bernard **12**:231, 235-36
Weiner, Joyce **4**:103
Weiners, John **19**:144
Weintraub, Stanley **20:297-317**
Weird Science Fantasy **22**:59-60
Weird Tales
   Belitt **4**:56
   Silverberg **3**:271
Weisinger, Mort **8**:318
Weisman, Mort **12**:248
Weiss, Buddy **4**:229
Weiss, Mark **3**:81
Weiss, Paul **12:323-37**
   Slavitt **3**:315, 318
   Weiss **2**:435, 447
Weiss, Renée Karol **2**:432-33, 434, 435
weiss, ruth **24:325-53**
Weiss, Theodore **2:425-50**
   Settle **1**:317
Weissner, Carl **11**:292
Welch, Lew
   Kyger **16**:192
   McCord **9**:184
   Saroyan **5**:218
Weldon, Fay
   Fitzgerald **10**:101
   Kennedy **20**:229
Well of Loneliness, The **8**:226, 228
Well, The **13**:109-10
Well Wrought Urn, The **8**:133
Wellek, Bronislav **7**:205, 206, 207, 208, 209, 210, 211, 225
Wellek, René **7:205-26**
Weller, Michael **20**:229
Welles, Orson
   Kenny **22**:147
   Sinclair **5**:274
Wellesley College
   Corcoran **2**:115
   Pinsky **4**:244, 248
Wellfleet, Mass. **1**:276
Wellington College **4**:99, 101-02
Wells College **18**:269
Wells, H.G.
   Allen **6**:17
   Anderson **2**:37, 46
   Boyle **1**:114
   Lem **1**:258-59
   Rowse **8**:259
   Silverberg **3**:272, 274
   Wallace **1**:391
Wells, Lester G. **13**:200-01
Wells, Somerset, England **1**:204-05
Welsh language
   Thomas **4**:305-06, 307, 310

White 4:335
Welty, Eudora 3:59
Wensberg, Erik 12:206
Werewolf Sequence, The 11:345, 347, 353
Wesker, Arnold 7:227-63
Wesker on File (chronology and bibliographic checklist) 7:227, 240-42
Wesleyan College 1:123
Wesleyan University 12:157-59, 160-61
Wesleyan University Press
    Major 6:187
    Piercy 1:274
    Wakoski 1:365
    Wright 7:302
Wesleyan Writer's Conference 22:73
West, Jessamyn
    Coppel 9:9-10
    Nims 17:185-86, 187
West, Nathanael
    Eastlake 1:201
    Madden 3:197
West of Your City 3:335
West, Paul 7:265-86
    Ackerman 20:5, 8, 9
    Fisher 10:95
West Point Story, The 1:383, 384
West, Ray B., Jr.
    Cassill 1:167
    Connell 2:107
Western Kentucky University 15:283
Western Michigan University
    Shelnutt 14:300
    Smith 7:163, 164
Western Printing & Lithographing Co. 2:248
Western Review
    Cassill 1:167
    Connell 2:107
    Hassan 12:156
Western States Arts Federation Book Award for Poetry 26:21
Western States Book Award 6:202
Western University 19:12, 47
Western Washington University 21:135, 137
Western Writers of America Spur Award 10:174
Westerners, The 6:58
Westerns
    Hoffman 10:171, 173-74
    Hollo 19:158
Westlake, Donald E. 13:329-45
    Block 11:32-33, 40
    Elkins 18:104-05
Westmont College 23:219, 221
Weston, Edward
    Ghiselin 10:143
    Thayler 11:361
Wetterzeichen 13:133, 134, 136
Wevill, David 9:217
Wexler, Haskell 2:289
Weybright, Victor 1:387, 388, 393
Whalen, Philip

Beltrametti 13:58, 61
Corman 2:142
di Suvero 26:71
Enslin 3:93
Kherdian 2:269
Kyger 16:192, 193, 196, 198
Plymell 11:286
Whales: A Celebration 2:368
Wharton County Community College 14:114
Wharton School, University of Pennsylvania 1:145
What Comes Next 5:25, 26
What Happens in Fort Lauderdale 9:42
What Is Life? 21:245
What She Means 6:146
what we have 19:2, 41
Whatever Happened to Betty Lemon 7:256-57, 259-60, 262
"What's Tatiana Troyanos Doing in Spartacus's Tent?" 26:92-93
Wheel of Stars, The 5:285
Wheeler, Benjamin Ide 3:365
Wheeler, Marion 3:322
Wheeler, Opal 9:276
Wheelock, John Hall 3:318, 319
Wheelright, John 2:135
Wheelwright, Richard 7:103
When He Was Free and Young and He Used to Wear Silks 16:80-81
When the Sacred Ginmill Closes 11:38
When the War Is Over 1:36, 39
"When Wounded Sore the Stricken Hart" 1:317
Where Is My Wandering Boy Tonight? 3:408
Where Rivers Meet 25:47
Where the Arrow Falls 9:217
Which Ones Are the Enemy? 5:80
While Dancing Feet Shatter the Earth 5:351
Whistler, James
    Boyle 1:104
    Disch 4:155
White, Alan 3:301, 302
White, Albert 20:97-98
White, Antonia 2:345
White Cad Cross-Up, The 16:216
White Cutter, The 18:304-05
White, Dane Michael 22:266-70
White Dove Review 6:180
White, Edmund 25:138-39, 142, 143, 145, 146-48
White, Eric Walter 10:116
White Eskimo: A Novel of Labrador 15:249, 250, 251
"White Fang Goes Dingo" 4:151
White Figure, White Ground 17:87, 89
White, George Dewey 7:25-26
White Goddess, The
    Arden 4:29
    Mathews 6:246
White Hotel, The 11:373, 377
White Island, The 6:320
White, Jack 20:183-85

White, Jon Manchip 4:333-52
    Delbanco 2:157
White, Katharine 2:65
White, Poppy Cannon 2:295
White Rabbit Press 16:190-91
White Shadows, Black Shadows 1:190
White, Theodore E. 10:173, 174, 177
White, Theodore H. 6:172
White, Valerie Leighton 4:341, 344, 345, 349, 351
Whitehall Poetry and Literary Society 1:154
Whitehead, Alfred North 12:327-29, 331
Whitehead, Evelyn 12:328-29
Whitehead, Gillian 23:14-15
Whitehead, James
    Ruark 23:270
    Williams 20:332, 338
Whiting Field (military base) 2:106
Whitman, George 1:169
Whitman, Lorraine 25:373
Whitman, Walt
    Awoonor 13:48
    Broughton 12:50-51
    Heyen 9:37
    Hongo 22:79, 88
    Pellegrini 11:274
    Shapiro 6:304
    Sward 13:299
Whitney Father, Whitney Heiress 13:274
Whitney, John Hay, Foundation 18:131
Whitsun 7:253-56, 257-59
Whittemore, Reed 8:297-312
    Plymell 11:295
Whittier, Calif. 1:353
Whittier College 1:358
Whittier, John Greenleaf 3:399
Who Killed the British Empire? 6:325
Who Shall Be the Sun? 3:410
Who Walk in Darkness 2:66-68, 70, 72
Who? 14:69, 76-77
Whole Hog 3:408
Whole Lives 8:311
"Why Do You Write about Russia?" 4:287
"Why I Write" 26:259
Why Is the House Dissolving 10:235, 253, 254-55
"Why Not" 26:35
Wichita University 11:280, 282-84
Wideman, John Edgar 7:34
Widower's Son, The 2:388
Wiebe, Dallas 9:83, 84
Wiener Library, London 19:219-20
Wieners, John 16:191-92
Wier and Pouce 14:172, 177, 178
Wier, Dara 7:18
Wiesel, Elie 4:353-62
    Elman 3:76
Wife of Winter, The 20:61, 63, 65
Wiggins, Evelina 4:58-59

Wiggins, Robert **23**:229
Wilbur, Richard
    Creeley **10**:66-67
    Davison **4**:134-35
    Hall **7**:62
    Wilson **5**:349
Wilcox, Donald **9**:149
Wild Dog **5**:350
Wild Duck, The **4**:75
*Wild Gardens of the Loup Garou,
    The* **21**:141
Wild Nights **9**:292-93
Wild With All Regret **12**:248
Wildcat **4**:215
Wilde, Oscar **14**:247, 269
Wilder, Charles **9**:198, 201
Wilder, Laura Ingalls **6**:121
Wilder, Thornton
    Boyle **1**:119
    Olson **12**:228, 229-30
    Rosenthal **6**:276
Wilentz, Ted **6**:185
Wiley, Grace **19**:291-92
Wiley, Wild Willie **5**:148
Wilhelm, Kate 5:297-310
    Knight **10**:221, 223, 224, 225,
        226-29
    Moorcock **5**:180
    Wolfe **9**:305, 306, 308
Wilhelm, Richard **5**:309
Wilkie, Wendell **24**:113
Wilkins, Roy **1**:40
Wilkinson, Maxwell Penrose **19**:128,
    129, 132
Willamette University **1**:369
William Allen White Award **2**:126
William and Mary, College of **7**:132,
    134
William Carlos Williams Award
    24:25
William Godwin **6**:320
William Saroyan **5**:217
William the Conqueror Prize **12**:199
Williams, Alan **25**:201
Williams, Bert **6**:258
Williams, C.K. 26:311-29
Williams College
    Clarke **16**:84
    Delbanco **2**:159
    Higgins **8**:91
Williams, Cora **1**:376
Williams, Cratis **15**:287, 288
Williams, Emmett **8**:89, 92
Williams, Flossie **8**:310
Williams, Glenn "Blossom" **2**:102,
    104, 106, 110, 112
Williams, Harrison **1**:291
Williams Institute, Berkeley, Calif.
    1:376, 377
Williams, John A. 3:413-33
    Major **6**:186
Williams, John Henry **3**:417, 418,
    422
Williams, Jonathan 12:339-58
    Broughton **12**:56
    Corman **2**:140

Gray **2**:194
Williams, Loring **22**:241-42, 245
Williams, Miller 20:319-44
    Aubert **20**:24
    Holden **22**:62
    Kumin **8**:215
Williams, Ola Mae Jones **3**:417, 418,
    420, 422, 423, 425, 428
Williams, Oscar **8**:113, 116
Williams, Paul **10**:287, 288, 293-94,
    295
Williams, Ralph **10**:219
Williams, Tennessee
    Bowles **1**:86, 88, 90, 91, 92
    Cassity **8**:43
    Forrest **7**:23-24
    Katz **14**:176-77
    Nims **17**:180
    Norse **18**:282-83
    Sinclair **5**:273
    Weiss **2**:443
Williams, Tom **1**:73, 74
Williams, Vanessa **6**:153-54
Williams, Virginia **10**:293-94, 295
Williams, William Carlos
    Armantrout **25**:17-18
    Bell **12**:35-36
    Corman **2**:136, 137, 139
    Cruz **17**:9, 10-11
    Enslin **3**:90, 94
    Eshleman **6**:131
    Ghiselin **10**:140
    Gregor **10**:149
    Kyger **16**:192
    Norse **18**:281-85
    Rimmer **10**:287
    Rosenblum **11**:342, 345
    Souster **14**:315
    Thayler **11**:359, 360, 363
    Turnbull **14**:336
    Weiss **2**:445, 446
    Whittemore **8**:306, 310
    Williams **12**:352
Williamson, Alan **4**:249
Williamson, Jack 8:313-27
    Gunn **2**:248, 250
    Wolfe **9**:305, 311
Willie Masters' Lonesome Wife **9**:112
Willis, Stan **24**:333
Willkie, Wendell **20**:303-04
Wilner, Herbert **3**:221
Wilson, Adrian **12**:52
Wilson, Angus
    Purdy **1**:303
    Settle **1**:315
    Wilson **5**:319, 320
Wilson, Colin 5:311-31
    Eshleman **6**:129
Wilson, Edmund
    Blais **4**:73, 74
    Kazin **7**:92, 93
    Tillinghast **23**:318
    Wesker **7**:236
Wilson, Edward O. 16:291-308
    Van Proyen **25**:394
Wilson, Francis **9**:98

Wilson, Gahan **20**:51
*Wilson Harris the Uncompromising
    Imagination* **16**:134
Wilson, James Southall **4**:58
Wilson, Keith 5:333-57
    Enslin **3**:98
    McCord **9**:187
Wilson, Richard **10**:203, 211
Wilson, Richard L. **3**:179
Wilson, Robin Scott
    Knight **10**:225
    Wolfe **9**:306
Wilson, Thomas J. **4**:134
Wilson, Woodrow **1**:108-09
Wiltwyck School for Boys **3**:423,
    424
Wimberley, L.C. **8**:274
Winchell, Walter **2**:104
"Wind and Two Young Barn
    Owls" **26**:153
Wind, Fragments for a Beginning
    5:166
Wind Heart, The **2**:329
Wind in the Willows, The
    Boyle **1**:100, 101
    Wolff **22**:300
Window on the Black Sea **26**:133
Windrose: Poems 1929–1979 **10**:135
Winesburg, Ohio
    Brown **6**:47-48
    Jones **11**:185
Wing, Elaine **24**:137-38, 145, 148
Wing Leader **9**:107, 108, 120
Wingo, Michael **25**:386-87
Winn, Dilys **3**:390
Winnicott, D.W. **24**:190
Winning Through **12**:2
Winnipeg, Manitoba, Canada **25**:149
Winstanley **4**:105
Winter, Ella **12**:49
Winter in the Hills, A **4**:330
Winter Kills **1**:196
Winter Talent, A **3**:38, 39
"Winter Warrior, The" **2**:58
Winters without Snow **21**:138
Winters, Yvor
    Broughton **12**:48-49
    Davie **3**:36, 37, 38
    Elman **3**:74, 75, 76
    Guerard **2**:222, 223, 228
    Hall **7**:64
    Pinsky **4**:245-47
    Shapiro **23**:294-95
Wirsen, Carl David af **1**:391
Wisconsin News **1**:376
Wise Child **3**:113-14
Wise, Matthew M. **7**:182
Wise, Stephen S. **4**:129
Wisniewski, Jim **24**:67, 72, 73, 74-
    75
Witching Hour, The **2**:249, 255, 258
With House Silence **26**:222
"With Ignorance" **26**:323-24
"With Loss of Eden" **7**:146
"With Malice Towards One and
    All" **9**:234

With Naked Foot **11**:112
Witheford, Hubert **23**:12
"Witness, The" **6**:253, 266
Witter Bynner Prize **7**:187
Wittgenstein, Ludwig
  Bernstein **24**:42-43
  Stevenson **9**:282
Wivenhoe Park Review, The **22**:14
Wizard of Loneliness, The **2**:330-31
WKY radio, Oklahoma City, Okla.
  2:169
WMEX radio, Boston, Mass. **3**:91
Wodehouse, P.G.
  Dennison **6**:110
  Glanville **9**:17
  Konwicki **9**:129
Wolf, Dan **6**:171
Wolf Willow **9**:260, 269
Wolfe, Bernie **2**:66
Wolfe, Gene 9:297-313
  Moorcock **5**:180
Wolfe, Thomas
  Cassity **8**:42
  Eastlake **1**:208
  Morgan **20**:275
  Vizenor **22**:273-74
  Wolfe **9**:298
Wolff, Tobias 22:279-306
Wolfsong **24**:295-96
Wollheim, Donald A.
  Bradley **10**:27
  Hoffman **10**:173
  Kennedy **9**:78
  Knight **10**:203, 205, 206, 207,
    208, 211, 214-15, 225
  Pohl **1**:294
  Silverberg **3**:271, 276
  Zebrowski **19**:368, 370
Woman Beware Woman **9**:293
Woman Hating **21**:10, 11, 15
Woman of Independent Means, A
  1:226, 232, 233
Woman on the Edge of Time **1**:277
Woman on the Shore, The **17**:213
Woman Who Escaped from Shame,
  The **11**:248
Woman's College of North Carolina
  9:84
Woman's Day **1**:314
Woman's Home Companion **1**:120
Women and Sex **11**:70
Women in the Wall **2**:352
Women of Wonder: Science Fiction
  Stories by Women about Women
  18:341
Women Writing and Writing about
  Women **9**:285
Women's movement
  Dworkin **21**:10-16
  El Saadawi **11**:68, 70-71
  Enslin **3**:94
  Owens **2**:361, 368
  Piercy **1**:273, 274, 275, 276
  Rule **18**:317, 323
  See also Sexism

Women's University, Kyoto, Japan
  2:140
Wonderful Focus of You, The **16**:201
Wonder's Child **9**:311
Wood, Grant **1**:164
Wood, Ira **1**:278-81
Wood, Nancy Lee **19**:335-38
Woodbridge, Conn. **6**:271, 272-73
Woodcock, George 6:311-29
  Symons **3**:390
Wooden Horse, The **15**:228, 230
Wooden Hunters **18**:83
Woodhull, Victoria **1**:383
Woodroffe, John **10**:291
Woodrow Wilson National Fellowship
  Aubert **20**:22
  Bromige **26**:28
  Busch **1**:131
  Corn **25**:137
  Delbanco **2**:158
  Dillard **7**:11
  Kammen **23**:140
  McCord **9**:181
Woolf, Virginia
  Blais **4**:79
  Brown **10**:37
  Fuller **10**:114, 115
  See **22**:213
Worcester College for the Blind
  21:64
Worcester Telegram **4**:227-28
Word Band, The **21**:231, 232-33
Word Prints **8**:192-93
Word, The (Irving Wallace) **1**:384,
  385, 397-98
WORD UP, Black Poetry of the '80s
  from the Deep South **21**:238-39
Wordplays 2 **2**:361
Words, The (Jean-Paul Sartre) **4**:49-
  50
Wordsand **8**:179, 196
Wordsworth, William
  Glazier **24**:221, 236
  Heyen **9**:37
  Jennings **5**:106
  O'Faolain **2**:344
Working class **6**:29, 30, 33, 36
Working Firewood for the Night
  15:382-83, 384-85
Works Progress Administration
  Cassill **1**:164, 165
  Corcoran **2**:116
  Honig **8**:109
World According to Garp, The **3**:15,
  29
World and Africa, The **2**:300
World and Its Streets, Places, The
  23:29, 35, 38
World and the Book, The **8**:157
World Anthology: Poems from the St.
  Mark's Poetry Project, The
  17:279
World Between, A **19**:331-32
World Between the Eyes, The **4**:122
World Church Service **4**:276, 277
World Federalist Movement **2**:192

World hunger **23**:46
World I Breathe, The **26**:69
World Inside, The **3**:281
World Journal Tribune **2**:401
World Literature **1**:343
World of Canadian Writing, The
  6:323
World of W.B. Yeats, The **5**:287
World Science Fiction Association
  Aldiss **2**:29
  Gunn **2**:248, 257
  Pohl **1**:295-96
World Science Fiction Convention
  3:274, 281
World Telegram **2**:400
World, The
  Hahn **11**:110-11
  Owens **2**:366
  Pinsky **4**:250
  Waldman **17**:279
World War I
  Aldiss **2**:16
  Boyle **1**:103
  Caldwell **1**:140
  Cartland **8**:20
  Cela **10**:53-55
  Corman **2**:129
  Duncan **2**:165
  Gilbert **15**:183-84
  Grumbach **2**:203
  Gunn **2**:237
  Hamburger **4**:161
  Hauser **11**:123, 125, 126
  Howes **3**:133
  Jacobsen **18**:208-09
  Katz **9**:53
  Lem **1**:255
  Lessing **14**:183, 192
  Murchie **19**:294-95
  Roditi **14**:240-41
  Rosenthal **6**:278
  Salisbury **15**:314, 315, 317-18,
    320, 321
  Salvadori **25**:344-45
  Settle **1**:307
  Shadbolt **3**:255
  Symons **3**:381
  Taylor **26**:249
  Thomas **4**:301
  Wagoner **3**:399
  Wain **4**:319
  Wellek **7**:208, 209-10
  West **7**:268, 269-70
  White **4**:339
  Wilson **5**:328
  Woodcock **6**:314, 315
  Wright **5**:360
World War II
  Abse **1**:19-20
  Adcock **23**:3, 4-5
  Aldiss **2**:19-21, 23
  Allen, Dick **11**:5-6
  Allen, Walter **6**:20-21
  Anderson **2**:38-39
  Andre **13**:21
  Appleman **18**:28-29

Arden **4**:42-43, 44
Ashby **6**:35, 40
Awoonor **13**:39-40
Barnstone **15**:73
Barrio **15**:113-15
Becker **1**:33, 34
Bell **12**:29, 30
Bennett **13**:79, 82-83
Blaise **3**:20
Booth **2**:48
Bourjaily **1**:67-68
Bowles **1**:86
Boyle **1**:117-20
Brée **15**:138-43
Brown, Dee **6**:54-55
Brown, Rosellen **10**:29
Brunner **8**:2-3
Busch **1**:127, 130
Caldwell **1**:148-49
Cartland **8**:24
Cassill **1**:165-67
Caute **4**:97-98, 101
Ciardi **2**:90-93, 95
Clement **16**:92-94
Cohen **18**:89-90
Condon **1**:193
Connell **2**:102-06
Coppel **9**:3
Corcoran **2**:118
Corman **2**:133
Davie **3**:32-34
Davison **4**:130-31
DeMarinis **24**:119
Dennison **6**:110
Dillard **7**:4, 7, 12
Dillon **3**:55-56
Duncan **2**:166-69
Eastlake **1**:202-08, 211
Easton **14**:143, 145, 146, 147,
    151-52, 153, 154
Epstein **12**:59-60, 61, 62-63
Fast **18**:179-83
Federman **8**:69-70
Fisher **10**:90, 92
Fitzgerald **10**:104-05
Freeling **12**:79-80
Fuchs **5**:53-54
Fuller **10**:111-12, 124-25
Geduld **21**:45-59
Ghiselin **10**:133-35
Gilbert **15**:189-91
Glanville **9**:15-16
Gray, Francine du Plessix **2**:183-
    84, 188-89, 197
Gray, Simon **3**:102
Green **11**:90-94
Gregor **10**:149, 161
Grumbach **2**:203, 207, 208-09
Guerard **2**:224-26
Gunn **2**:239, 243-45, 252
Gurik **23**:100, 107
Hahn **11**:114-15
Hall **12**:124, 126-28
Hamburger **4**:163-64
Harwood **19**:136-38
Hassan **12**:145-46

Heyen **9**:33-35
Holden **8**:100
Honig **8**:109-12
Hood **17**:82-83
Houston **16**:175-77
Hrabal **12**:189
Jennings **5**:107
Jolley **13**:113, 114, 117
Jones **5**:120, 121
Josipovici **8**:146, 148-49
Katz **14**:162
Kazin **7**:91-93
Kerrigan **11**:204, 216
Killens **2**:286, 287
Kirk **9**:95-96
Kirkup **4**:183
Knebel **3**:170, 177-78
Koller **5**:158-59
Konwicki **9**:126, 134
Kumin **8**:212-14
Lem **1**:256, 258
Lessing **14**:196, 197, 198-99, 200-
    01
Lind **4**:196, 201
Livesay **8**:234
Lottman **12**:202, 203, 204
Mahapatra **9**:139-42
Manuel **9**:159-62
Markfield **3**:208, 209, 210
Mathews **6**:230
Matthews **15**:259-61
McCord **9**:172
Megged **13**:142-43, 149, 150
Menashe **11**:226, 228
Meredith **14**:226-27
Moorcock **5**:173
Morgan, Ted **4**:224-25
Morgan, Theodore **3**:237
Morris **13**:171
Mott **7**:115-18, 122
Mrozek **10**:266, 268, 270
Murchie **19**:295-96, 299
Nichols, J.G. **2**:308, 310, 311-12,
    313-17
Nichols, John **2**:322
Olson **12**:232
Owens **2**:355
Peters **8**:239
Petesch **12**:242
Plymell **11**:277-78, 279
Pohl **1**:287-89
Rabassa **9**:198-201
Raworth **11**:297, 298
Rimmer **10**:288, 289-92
Roditi **14**:262, 263-65, 266-67
Rosenthal **6**:276, 277, 278-79
Rowse **8**:257, 260
St. Clair **8**:272
Salisbury **15**:314, 321-24
Salvadori **25**:364-65
Samarakis **16**:251-57
Sanders **21**:255-56
Schevill **12**:273
Settle **1**:312-313, 318
Shadbolt **3**:255
Shapiro **6**:291, 293, 294-300

Silkin **5**:247-48, 249, 250, 253
Sillitoe **2**:374-75
Silverberg **3**:270
Simic **4**:267-71
Simpson **4**:291
Sinclair **5**:267-68
Sisson **3**:299-300
Skelton **5**:280
Škvorecký **1**:330-32
Slade **9**:237
Solotaroff **2**:393
Sparshott **15**:349-50
Stafford **3**:327, 331, 332-33, 337
Stegner **9**:266
Stevenson **9**:277
Still **17**:242-44
Swanberg **13**:264-67
Sward **13**:286
Tarn **16**:272-74
Thayler **11**:357
Thomas, D.M. **11**:381-82
Thomas, R.S. **4**:305, 307
Tillinghast **23**:304
Van Brunt **15**:369
Van Itallie **2**:406-07, 409
Vivante **12**:287, 288-91, 295
Voinovich **12**:307-08, 311-12
Wain **4**:321, 325
Wakoski **1**:354
Wallace **1**:379
Weintraub **20**:297-316
Weiss **2**:435
Wellek **7**:224-25
West **7**:268
White **4**:337-39
Whittemore **8**:301-03
Wilhelm **5**:297, 301, 307
Williams **3**:419-20
Williamson **8**:322
Wilson **5**:340, 341
Wolfe **9**:300-01
Woodcock **6**:320-21
Wright, Charles **7**:290
Wright, David **5**:364-65
Zinoviev **10**:326-27
World within World **8**:194
World without End **2**:190, 200-01
World Zionist Federation **4**:196
Worlds **25**:201
Worlds Apart **25**:201
Worlds Beyond **10**:215-16
Worlds Enough and Time **25**:211
World's Fair, Chicago, 1936 **2**:216-
    17
World's Fair, New York **20**:303
"Worlds" trilogy **25**:210
Wounded Thammuz **21**:66
WOV radio, New York City **3**:424
W.P. Kinsella: Tall Tales in Various
    Voices **7**:107
Wrecking Crew **23**:191-92
Wrestling **19**:263-64
Wright, C.D. **22:307-17**
Wright, Charles **7:287-303**
   Ai **13**:9
Wright, Charles Stevenson **6**:187

Wright, David　5:359-75
　Ashby　**6**:44
　Heath-Stubbs　**21**:67, 68
　Sisson　**3**:301, 302, 304
Wright, Farnsworth　**8**:318
Wright, Frank Lloyd　**12**:256
Wright, James
　Heyen　**9**:44
　Ruark　**23**:271, 279-82
Wright, Lee　**13**:340-41
Wright, R. Glenn　**10**:229
Wright, Richard
　Emanuel　**18**:133, 140
　Kazin　**7**:90
　Major　**6**:184, 185, 186, 189
Wright, Sarah Elizabeth　**2**:288
Wright State University　**11**:14-16
Wright, Stuart　**5**:77
Write On! Notes from a Writers
　Workshop　**2**:306
"Write Success into Your Résumé"
　26:154-55
Writer and Politics, The　**6**:321
Writers Action Group　**4**:84, 86, 88
Writer's Center, The　**15**:379
Writer's Digest
　Block　**11**:36
　Grumman　**25**:187
　Jerome　**8**:134-35
Writers' Guild (Great Britain)
　Brophy　**4**:82, 86, 88
　Caute　**4**:109
"Writers Mind, The"　**2**:368
Writers' Revisions　**3**:203
Writers' Union of Canada
　Cohen　**18**:86-87
　Horwood　**15**:251
　Rule　**18**:318
　Skelton　**5**:291
Writing a Novel　**26**:59
Writing Crime Fiction　**8**:177
Writing Fiction　**6**:102
Writing Life of James M. Cain, The
　3:203
Writing Like a Woman　**24**:272
Writing of One Novel, The　**1**:390,
　392, 395
Writing the Australian Crawl　**3**:334
"Wrong Bed—Moira, The"　**22**:186
Wrong, Dennis H.　**8**:180
Wurlitzer, Rudolph　**14**:177
Wuthering Heights　**1**:313
Wyatt, Thomas　**10**:252
Wyler, William　**21**:39
Wylie, Craig　**12**:38
Wylie, Dirk　**1**:289
Wylie, Elinor　**8**:227
Wylie, Max　**2**:329
Wynand, Derk　**7**:101
Wynne-Tyson, Jon　**5**:261
Wynter, Bryan　**5**:369

X (magazine)
　Ashby　**6**:43-44
　Sisson　**3**:302
　Wright　**5**:371

X-Rated Videotape Guide, The　**10**:303-04
X-Rays　**7**:144

Yacoubi, Ahmed　**25**:246-47
Yaddo (artists' colony)
　Bell　**12**:19, 38
　Furman　**18**:198-99
　Jacobsen　**18**:213-14
　Lelchuk　**20**:247-48
　Nims　**17**:190-91
　Peters　**8**:247
　Stegner　**9**:265
　Turco　**22**:238-39, 244
　Wagoner　**3**:403, 405
Yale Daily News　**3**:315
Yale Literary Magazine　**3**:314
Yale Series of Younger Poets
　Competition　**4**:137
Yale University
　Barnstone　**15**:107
　Boyd　**11**:51-52, 54
　Bruce-Novoa　**18**:75-76
　Burroway　**6**:93
　Clarke　**16**:82-83, 85-86
　Epstein　**12**:67-68, 69, 72
　Higgins　**8**:85
　Morgan　**4**:227
　Raffel　**9**:211, 212
　Slavitt　**3**:311, 312, 314-16, 317,
　　321, 324
　Tarn　**16**:276
　Van Itallie　**2**:422
　Weiss, Paul　**12**:331-32
　Weiss, Theodore　**2**:435-36
　Whittemore　**8**:301, 302
　Wiesel　**4**:359
Yamamoto, Izuru　**26**:90
Yankee Clipper　**1**:84
Yankee Pine　**2**:118
Yashima, Taro　**2**:136
Yates, David　**8**:141
Yates, Richard　**9**:114, 116
Yawning Heights, The　**10**:333-35
Yazoo River　**24**:281-82
Year before Last　**1**:115
Year in San Fernando, The　**18**:1, 17-18, 21
Year of Our Birth, The　**23**:215, 218,
　219, 227, 228
Year of the Century: 1876, The　**6**:57
Yearbook of Jazz　**1**:344
Yeats Summer School　**21**:292, 293
Yeats, William Butler
　Becker　**1**:37
　Belitt　**4**:60
　Connell　**2**:97
　Dillon　**3**:53, 64
　Howes　**3**:142-43
　Kennedy　**9**:80, 81
　Nichols　**2**:318
　Pinsky　**4**:237
　Rosenblum　**11**:342
　Simmons　**21**:294
　Stevenson　**9**:281
　Van Itallie　**2**:412

Wain　**4**:328
White　**4**:333, 336
Yedioth Ahronoth　**4**:356, 357
Yellen, Samuel
　Eshleman　**6**:131, 132
　Wagoner　**3**:404
Yellow House on the Corner, The
　19:105, 106
"Yellow Pad, The"　**22**:192-94
Yellow Silk　**24**:24
Yellow Silk Award　**24**:24
Yellowhorse　**6**:57
Yenching University, Peking, China
　1:34
Yerma　**1**:89, 90, 91
Yesod　**26**:194
Yevtushenko, Yevgeny　**11**:149
Yglesias, Helen　20:345-59
Yiddish language
　Katz　**9**:55, 58, 63, 64-65
　Weiss　**2**:426-27
Yih Chia-Shun　**7**:66
YM-YWHA Poetry Center
　Burroway　**6**:90
　Wakoski　**1**:362
Ynyshir Nature Reserve　**4**:309
Yoga
　Rimmer　**10**:291
　Sward　**13**:295-96, 300
　Wilson　**5**:348
Yojana　**9**:232
York, England　**4**:39
York University
　Blaise　**3**:28
　Glover　**23**:88
　Kelly　**22**:115, 118
Yorke, Matthew　**9**:293
You and I . . . Searching for
　Tomorrow　**10**:305
You Could Live If They Let You　**3**:225
You Have Seen Their Faces　**1**:148
You See　**26**:31
You Won't Remember This　**20**:55-56,
　64, 71, 72
Young America Weekly　**1**:376
Young, Brigham　**1**:388, 389-90
Young Cherry Trees Secured against
　Hares　**8**:84
Young Communist League　**1**:286
Young, Geoffrey　**9**:179
"Young Goodman Brown"　**11**:181
Young in One Another's Arms, The
　18:320
Young, Izzy　**10**:172
Young, Karl　**11**:345, 348
Young, Lafayette　**9**:179
Young Lonigan　**7**:89
Young Lovers, The　**5**:79
Young Presidents Organization　**1**:40
Young, Stark　**7**:92
Young, Vernon　**9**:147
Young Wives' Tale, A　**1**:382
Youngblood　**2**:281, 282, 285, 287,
　288, 289, 290-91, 296, 305
Youngest Camel, The　**1**:123
Youngstein, Max　**1**:194

"Your Place or Mine?" **2**:70
Ysaÿe, Eugène **1**:112-13
Yugoslavia
    Aldiss **2**:26-28
    Dacey **17**:32-33
Yvain (Le Chevalier au lion) **9**:219

Z-D Generation, The **21**:270
Zagajewski, Adam **26**:328
Zakharchenko, Vasili **1**:286
Zalaznick, Sheldon **2**:400
Zalmen; or, The Madness of God
    4:358
Zangwill, Israel **7**:236
Zanuck, Darryl F. **1**:384, 385
Zanuck, Darryl F., Productions
    1:389
Zanuck, Richard D. **1**:384, 385
Zap **11**:293
Zatz, Asa **9**:200
Zavrian, Suzanne **8**:293
Zebrowski, George 19:361-82
    Dann **20**:84, 88, 89-90, 96-97
    Sargent **18**:337-45
Zeidner, Lisa 24:355-66

Zemach, Margot **6**:154-55
Zembla's Rocks **14**:136
Zen
    Delbanco **2**:156
    Hamill **15**:207-08, 214
    Kirkup **4**:191
    Kyger **16**:192-93, 194, 195
    Lowitz **26**:172, 173
Zen Contemplations **4**:191
Zen There Was Murder **8**:170
Zend, Robert
    Colombo **22**:54
    Sward **13**:297-99
Zeromski, Stefan **9**:129
Ziegler, Evarts **1**:384
Zimbabwe **14**:54
Zimbabwe Tapes, The **4**:109
Zimmer, Paul **12**:249, 250
Zinn, Howard **1**:51
Zinoviev, Alexander 10:323-39
Zinzin Road, The **3**:181
Zionism
    Elman **3**:72
    Lind **4**:196-97, 200, 201
    Wiesel **4**:355-56

Zoline, Pamela **4**:152
Zoline, Patsy **5**:164
Zolotov Affair, The **10**:299
Zolotow, Nina **26**:182
Zone Journals **7**:295
Zoo Story, The **5**:217-18
Zoritte, Eda **13**:150, 151, 152, 154,
    158
Zukofsky, Celia **3**:92
Zukofsky, Louis
    Bernstein **24**:34
    Corman **2**:138, 140, 142, 144,
        145-46
    Creeley **10**:73, 74
    Enslin **3**:92, 93, 94
    Eshleman **6**:140
    Grumman **25**:173, 174
    Kelly **19**:199
    Rakosi **5**:207
    Turnbull **14**:335
Zukofsky, Paul **12**:346
Zuntz, Günther **8**:278
Zürich **25**:109, 110
Zycie Nauki (The Life of Science)
    1:259